No More Gallant a Deed

First Sergeant James A. Wright, with his sergeant's stripes on his outer jacket and his Second Corps "white club" insignia on his inner blouse

No More Gallant a Deed

A CIVIL WAR MEMOIR
OF THE FIRST MINNESOTA VOLUNTEERS

James A. Wright

EDITED BY STEVEN J. KEILLOR

MINNESOTA HISTORICAL SOCIETY PRESS

www.mnhs.org/mhspress

Manufactured in the United States of America

10 9 8 7 6 5 4 3 2 1

International Standard Book Number
978-1-68134-052-4

⊗ The paper used in this publication meets the minimum requirements of the American National Standard for Information Sciences Permanence for Printed Library Materials, ANSI Z 39.48-1984.

Library of Congress Cataloging-in-Publication Data

Wright, James A., b. 1840
    No more gallant a deed : a Civil War memoir of the First Minnesota Volunteers / James A. Wright ; edited by Steven J. Keillor
      p. cm.
    Includes index
    ISBN 978-1-68134-052-4 (alk. paper)
    1. Wright, James A., b. 1840.
    2. United States Army. Minnesota Infantry Regiment, 1st (1861–1864).
    3. Minnesota—History—Civil War, 1861–1865—Personal Narratives.
    4. United States—History—Civil War, 1861–1865—Personal Narratives.
    5. Soldiers—Minnesota—Red Wing—Biography.
    6. Red Wing (Minn.)—Biography.
    I. Keillor, Steven J. (Steven James).
    II. Title
E515.5 1st . W75 2001
973.7'476'092—dc21
[B]   2001030393

To My Old Comrades of Company F

JAMES A. WRIGHT

* * *

To Stan Keillor, My Comrade in Many
Boyhood Civil War Battles

STEVEN J. KEILLOR

No More Gallant a Deed

Preface PAGE *xi*

Introduction PAGE *5*

1 The little band of would-be soldiers PAGE *9*
1855–APRIL 1861

2 The happy land of Canaan PAGE *19*
APRIL–JUNE 1861

3 Finest body of troops that has yet appeared upon our streets PAGE *35*
JUNE–JULY 1861

4 We lived an awful long time in three hours PAGE *45*
JULY 1861

5 All quiet along the Potomac PAGE *66*
JULY–OCTOBER 1861

6 Somebodies that blundered PAGE *81*
OCTOBER 1861–FEBRUARY 1862

7 Look back—there is a sight for you PAGE *97*
FEBRUARY–MARCH 1862

8 Knights of the knapsack PAGE *110*
APRIL–JUNE 1862

9 *Minnesota, stand firm! Don't run, Minnesota* PAGE 133
JUNE 1862

10 *Every mother's son of us preferred to live* PAGE 154
JUNE–JULY 1862

11 *There is a Divinity that shapes our ends, rough hew them as we may* PAGE 172
JULY–AUGUST 1862

12 *A realistic scene of war such as is but rarely witnessed* PAGE 193
SEPTEMBER 1862

13 *I am a pilgrim and I am a stranger* PAGE 207
SEPTEMBER–NOVEMBER 1862

14 *Come on, boys! Let's join a regiment that don't run* PAGE 226
NOVEMBER–DECEMBER 1862

15 *Only been singed a little* PAGE 249
DECEMBER 1862–MAY 1863

16 *Close the column, lengthen the step, quicken the time* PAGE 268
MAY–JUNE 1863

17 *It could not be quite so bad as that* PAGE 288
JUNE–JULY 2, 1863

18 *Expecting every minute to be blown to atoms* PAGE 301
JULY 3–5, 1863

19 *I took dinner at the home of Miss Redhead today* PAGE 319
JULY–SEPTEMBER 1863

20 *It looked like a fight or a foot-race* PAGE 345
SEPTEMBER–OCTOBER 1863

21 *Conscientious scruples about being shot* PAGE *368*
OCTOBER–NOVEMBER 1863

22 *Oh! Ain't you glad you got out of the Wilderness* PAGE *390*
DECEMBER 1863–FEBRUARY 1864

23 *Is it true, sergeant, we are to go home?* PAGE *404*
FEBRUARY–MAY 1864

Epilogue PAGE *421*
The thinned ranks answered

Appendix PAGE *431*

Index PAGE *437*

Preface

IT WAS MONDAY, AUGUST 13, 1906, and some 140,00 Union veterans and family members were streaming into Minneapolis for the week-long national encampment of the Grand Army of the Republic. Four hundred trains arrived in the city that day, and 75,000 visitors came through the Union Station alone. Individual regiments held their own reunions to coincide with this national gathering. A *Minneapolis Journal* reporter attended the annual reunion of the First Minnesota Regiment, held at the Soldiers' Home near Minnehaha Falls. William A. Brack, a veteran of that famous unit, "was accosted by a little, short man who wore the Massachusetts badge."

"Hello, Brack, you don't remember me, do you?"

"I know you, all right, but you've got me on the name."

"Don't you remember the little red-haired sergeant of F company? That's me. I'm 'Jimmy' Wright."

"Yes, I remember you now, but your hair isn't red."

"No, I've dyed it," said facetious Jimmy, whose hair was white like his comrade's.[1]

From Minneapolis James A. Wright traveled to his home town, Red Wing, where members of Company F held their own reunion at the home of their lieutenant, Hezekiah Bruce. Here, the veterans asked Wright to prepare "an outline history of the company" to be included in a "proposed history of the reg[imen]t" and also to "be published in the local paper at Red Wing." (Before the military bureaucracy identified it by one letter, Company F was the Goodhue County Volunteers, recruited from Red Wing and vicinity.)[2]

A reporter from the *Red Wing Republican* interviewed Wright and wrote a story about "the hearty old veteran, still well preserved" despite "terrible battles and marches of the Civil War." He may have talked to Editor Jens K. Grondahl about publishing his company history, although the publishing "arrangements" were left to Red Wing native and fellow veteran, Enos F. Grow.[3]

Using his wartime diary, letters he sent to his mother, and books and official records available to him in Beverly, Massachusetts, Wright worked for the next five years on his history of Company F. A sixty-six-year-old widower who worked for the public welfare board in Beverly and was active in the local GAR Post, he had time and resources for this project. Periodically, he sent installments to Grondahl, after cautioning him "that I am regularly employed and I must do this work out of hours." The last one he sent on May 20, 1911, apologizing to Grondahl "that I have been so long about it and that it has covered so much space." It covered 875 typewritten pages, with almost no left or right margins, no chapter divisions, and few paragraph divisions. He titled it, "The Story of Company F., First Regiment, By James A. Wright, One of its Orderly Sergeants." Sensing the editor's likely reaction, he added, "Now that it is completed I am in doubt what ought to be done with it, for there is so much to it that I fear it will be more difficult to use it. . . . I fear I have been giving you a 'white elephant.'" He urged Grondahl to edit it as he saw fit.[4]

Grondahl balked at editing such a lengthy account or printing it in serial installments in his paper. Shortly after receiving the final installment, Grondahl wrote to Martin Maginnis, a prominent veteran of the First Minnesota, to praise Wright's "great work" and to suggest that his comrades recognize his efforts and appoint a committee "to co-operate with the State Historical Society with regard to its preservation."[5] He also advised Wright either to publish it or send it to the Minnesota Historical Society for "preservation."[6] No action having been taken, Grondahl donated to the society in the summer of 1921 what was undoubtedly the original typescript Wright had finished mailing to him ten years earlier. The *Minnesota History Bulletin* reported Grondahl's gift of this "accession of importance." Despite the title, the *Bulletin* reported, Wright "recounts the experiences not only of his company but also to some extent of the entire regiment" for its entire term of service.[7]

In 1921, William Watts Folwell, president emeritus of the historical society and the University of Minnesota, was researching and writing the second of his four-volume history of Minnesota. A Civil War veteran himself, Folwell was intrigued by Wright's account: "The more I read the more interesting and valuable it seemed to me." To avoid arousing false hope of publication, however, he cautioned Wright, "Our society is too poor to print such and so large a work at present, but the day will come when it will be printed, and your merits as an author be recognized."[8]

Partly, this praise may have been gallantly designed to persuade Wright to donate to the society "the diaries and letters to which you refer as sources of your information." Folwell assured Wright that "[s]uch original documents are highly prized by historians as you no doubt are aware. Histories are like lawyers' arguments needing to be supported by evidence." He closed by citing his Civil War service—"and so [I] have the right to subscribe myself as your admiring comrade."[9]

Wright did not take the bait: as for the original documents, "I think all they contain are fairly covered in what I have written." He did describe to Folwell how he came to write his history of Company F and told about the 1906 encampment, the Red Wing newspaper, and Grow's proposed role. He described his sources, if he did not hand them over. "As to the diaries, they were chiefly a notation of events as things developed, written on slips of paper and sent to my mother, in the letters I wrote to her, and she endeavored to preserve both, and did, turning them over to me when I returned; but as letters from 'the boys' used to be passed around among friends in those days, there is an occasional break in both letters and notes."[10]

In a footnote to his second volume, Folwell criticized as well as praised the memoir. Wright "gives a very graphic account" of Bull Run; his "style is that of a practiced journalist"; the parts "relating to personal experiences and observations derived from the author's diary are often very interesting and valuable"; yet the bulk of the memoir, "drawn from well-known sources . . . is good reading but adds little to existing knowledge."[11]

Others who have written of the First Minnesota Regiment have also used Wright's memoir as a source—in *The Last Full Measure,* Richard Moe quoted it extensively in his account of the First at Gettysburg—but no one has taken Folwell's suggestion that it is worthy of publication.

I came across Wright's memoir while researching the history of Burnside Township, which included the Spring Creek neighborhood where Wright's family settled in 1855. Township 113 North, Range 15 West had no name when Amelia Wright brought her eight children there, to land that her late husband David had claimed the previous year. Later, it was called Milton, Union, and finally, in 1864, Burnside—presumably after the Union general who led the Army of the Potomac to defeat at Fredericksburg. The 1857 state census indicates that Amelia's mother, Nancy Crews (seventy-six years old), had joined the family, which included James (listed as nineteen—an error), William (age fifteen), Reuben (six), and Sarah (four). Next door lived the eldest son, George W. (twenty-six), with his wife, Mary S. Wright, and their one-year-old daughter, Florence.[12]

The family had come from Macon County, Illinois. They had followed a migration path common among Upland Southerners. Amelia Crews was the great-granddaughter of William Hooper, one of North Carolina's signers of the Declaration of Independence. Her parents had moved to Kentucky, where she met David Wright, a Methodist circuit rider in southern Kentucky and northern Tennessee. They married in 1828, and the following year David received permission to "locate"—to cease his itinerancy, to settle down, and to serve a congregation (or two). As with many frontier families, however, settling down was done in stages. They moved to Sangamon County, Illinois (Lincoln country) in 1836, and James was born there on November 27, 1840. In 1845, they moved about twenty or thirty miles east to Macon County. In all these places, David and Amelia had been latecomers, who paid high prices for land and had a limited selection to choose from. But when David traveled to Goodhue County in 1854 to find land, he was getting in on the beginnings of settlement there. The Treaty of Mendota in 1851 had opened the west bank of the Mississippi River to settlers; Goodhue

County was organized in 1853; and Township 113 North, Range 15 West had just been surveyed.[13]

They came to a Methodist beachhead in frontier Minnesota. The Methodists held their first camp meeting in Minnesota that August (1855) at the nearby Leman Bates farm. Undoubtedly, the Wrights were among the one hundred in attendance. That summer Methodists constructed the first building for Hamline University, which James Wright later entered—probably in the fall of 1859, as an eighteen-year-old freshman. The 1860 U.S. Census reported five Methodist clergymen living in the township. The Methodists were in transition from a system of itinerant preachers, many of them bachelors, to one of married, "located" clergy. (Population was too sparse in frontier Minnesota for itinerancy to be dispensed with totally.) Township 113 was a good transitional site—good farmland on which a pastor could raise a family, yet located on the Government (Military) Road from Mendota to Wabasha and on the Mississippi River, for easy access to distant camp meetings, Methodist classes, and clerical conferences. And it was near a Methodist preparatory school and college where a minister's children could get an education. Rev. David Wright probably planned to live just such a half-itinerant, half-settled life here, and likely heard about the area from Chauncy or Norris Hobart or another Methodist minister already in the Red Wing area.[14] Even James Wright's middle name—Asbury (after Methodist Bishop Francis Asbury)—indicated that his upbringing was as Methodist as one could be in Minnesota Territory.

The presence of Minnesota's first institution of higher education indicated Red Wing's ambition to become a major city in the new state. Wright often mentioned the Minnesota soldiers' pride in representing their young state well before easterners' eyes. Also present in a unit recruited in one locality was a local pride in bringing honor to Red Wing and Goodhue County. These were not men distributed randomly among numerous regiments or companies, becoming anonymous strangers whose glorious charges or cowardly retreats brought honor or shame only to themselves as individuals. Company F literally represented Red Wing and its surrounding area on the national stage during this intensely watched and well-publicized conflict. Wright was fighting for the glory of Red Wing, the state of Minnesota, and Methodism.

He was fighting for democracy and the Union, too. He was a descendant of a signer of the Declaration, and that fact would have swelled his pride in the Union. It cannot be emphasized too strongly that Wright and Company F (and First Minnesota companies from other towns) made a collective democratic, voluntary decision to enlist and to go to war. There was no draft in April 1861. In America's twentieth-century wars, men have typically volunteered or been drafted individually and then been incorporated into already-existing units or new units composed of strangers, not of men from one locality who knew each other. The Goodhue volunteers enlisted en masse, at a mass meeting featuring resolutions passed by majority vote, and into a new military company that originally consisted of Goodhue County men only.

The mass meeting on April 17, 1861, in the courtroom of the Goodhue County Courthouse was nothing if not a political event, complete with a resolutions committee deliberately balanced between Democrats and Republicans, patriotic speeches, and historical allusions. "Judge Welch was called to the chair, and as the venerable man spoke of the revolutionary incidents of his boyhood and the present state of our country, the tears of emotion ran down his aged cheeks." He passionately defended the Union created by the American Revolution: "Peace to all men of good will; but death to the traitor who would tear down the flag of our country." This commonly held sentiment underlay the participants' agreement to "bury forever the political hatchet," which had raged fiercely between the Democrat's *Red Wing Sentinel* and the aptly named *Goodhue County Republican.*[15]

When the company of volunteers met the next Thursday, "pursuant to adjournment," they functioned as any voluntary association might: a chairman presided, a secretary took the minutes, motions were made and voted on, officers were elected, and another adjournment approved. These were not perfunctory procedures. At the morning session, a motion to elect officers was defeated. In the afternoon, when more members were present, they chose officers—first, William Colvill, Jr., the *Sentinel* editor, as captain. "Mr. Colvill made a few remarks amid tumultuous cheering." A motion to delay voting on a first lieutenant went down to defeat, and A. E. Welch was narrowly elected: thirty-nine votes for Welch and thirty-two votes for Mark A. Hoyt. The election of a second lieutenant went to two ballots. Finally they decided their fate democratically: "*Resolved exc, That Captain Colvill is hereby authorized to tender the services of this company to the Governor.*"[16]

Wright described how these citizen-members in a voluntary association were transformed into soldiers who obeyed orders rather than voting on them. Yet they retained their strong faith in American democracy and their patriotic love of the Union.

It must be remembered that, although he used his wartime diaries and letters as sources, Wright wrote his memoir in 1906–11. He could not help but be affected by events since the Civil War, by national dialogue on the war, and by the emerging genre of the Civil War memoir. In subtle ways, the successes of the preserved Union in the forty years after Appomattox influenced his telling of the Civil War story—as did his own frequent "addresses before school assemblies on Patriotic day observance" in Massachusetts long after the war ended.[17] The details of his story are based on 1860s records, but he had repeated the moral of the story many times. In 1911 he noted to Grondahl, "Here in the east the papers are publishing a great deal about the beginning of the war—fifty years ago—and there seems to be a real interest in it."[18] When he sat down to write, he was an active member in the GAR's John H. Chipman Jr. Post 89 in Beverly. He had served as its commander, adjutant, chaplain, and "only patriotic instructor."[19] He attended at least one other GAR national encampment—in Atlantic City in 1910, while he was writing his memoir. His active reminiscing with other veterans and his reading of Civil War books that poured from the presses after 1880 also had an impact on his narrative.

In his book on the GAR, historian Stuart McConnell discussed how generals' memoirs, especially Ulysses S. Grant's best-selling *Personal Memoirs* (1885–86) with its above-the-clouds detached objectivity, influenced how privates wrote their own accounts. They "followed one of two paths . . . either they copied their officers in trying to connect" their small role in battle "to the broad tactics and campaigns or they dwelt on sentimental 'scenes of camp and battle' " and omitted "the confusion and bloodshed of combat, so apparent in the wartime letters and diaries of the men."[20] Wright followed both paths—and the path of simply copying the letters and diaries—which is why his typescript went to 875 pages. He felt obligated to add to his diaries and letters—to report on movements of the rest of the Union Army and the Confederates; to quote at length from official reports and from generals' memoirs; to comment on such matters as disputes regarding tactics, battle results, and casualty figures. For example, he attempted to defend the conduct of the Army of the Potomac against its critics. But a real virtue of his work is that he did not omit war's horrors.

He had available to him the first volume of *Minnesota in the Civil and Indian Wars,* which included William Lochren's chapter on the First Minnesota. He consulted other published sources as well. He sent the typescript to Enos F. Grow and possibly other veterans of Company F so that they could review it for minor errors of fact.[21]

Thus, his memoir reflects pride in the Army of the Potomac, democracy, and the Union, as well as in Red Wing, the state of Minnesota, and frontier Methodism. What it does not always reflect is "the style . . . of a practiced journalist." Wright's skill at narrating events, his command of the English language, his historical and literary allusions, all reflect his two-year college education, later reading, and subsequent jobs as schoolteacher and clerk. Yet his typescript needed editing, as Wright admitted.

My main goal as editor has been to separate out what Folwell called "personal experiences and observations" of 1861–64 from quotes and paraphrases of "well-known sources" that add "little to existing knowledge" and were written after the war—to cull out what McConnell identified as dutiful attempts to imitate the generals. Thus I have omitted numerous lengthy passages derived from (often quoted from) official reports or published works on the Civil War. I have also reduced the number of occasions where he informed us what happened "as we now know it." Where Wright expressed doubt about a certain statement but was actually correct, I have eliminated his words of doubt. Where he was wrong, I have kept his version but have added a footnote to present the differing, but widely accepted, version.

A memoir based on a diary risks frequent repetition—one rainy day after another and one wearying march after another. Where Wright seems uninterested in these details and only alludes to them in a perfunctory manner, I omit such repetitious passages—without sacrificing the strengths of a day-by-day account of the company and regiment.

The resulting memoir is more heavily edited than most other Civil War reminiscences, but the rationale for that is that Wright's typescript is too lengthy and too rough to be published in its unedited form. And it is justified by Wright's own appeals to Grondahl to edit his work: ". . . we make no pretense as a writer and shall have to depend on you to do a little editing." Later he instructed, "I . . . give you full permission to correct any apparent errors . . . and am perfectly willing to give you liberty to edit the wording to any reasonable extent, so long as the statements of fact are not changed." He realized, by May 1911 when he had finished the typescript, "that I have tried to tell too much."[22] Ultimately the publication of the memoir is warranted by the superior quality of Wright's "personal experiences and observations" that vividly portray the confusion, fatigue, terror, boredom, and courage of the Civil War. They deserve to be read.

I made more minor changes. I had to supply chapter divisions and, in places, paragraph divisions. I altered existing paragraph divisions where such changes seemed necessary to aid the reader's understanding of complicated battle maneuvers, tactics, and marches. In a few sections, Wright did not take the trouble to convert his diary entries, in present tense, to his narrative format, with its past tense and more unified flow of thought. I have done so, with as little change to the wording as possible, by eliminating quotation marks, changing tenses, and deleting the reference to the diary. I have altered the editorial "we" to "I" where it clearly refers to Wright alone, not to others. He often used single quotation marks around words or phrases that were idiomatic or colloquial expressions. Where they have become common usage, I omitted the marks. Double quotation marks are used for quotations; single marks, for idioms or colloquialisms. Where they are so long or so numerous as to annoy the reader, I altered his frequent use of run-on and compound sentences by starting a new sentence and omitting the "and." I retained his underlining of words for emphasis. Errors in spelling and punctuation are silently emended.

In a few cases of individual names, I have retained Wright's spelling because there is no consensus on the correct spelling. The name of Company F's original captain appears as Colville in some sources; however, his former newspaper, the *Sentinel,* presents him as Colvill in its reports of the April 1861 meetings—as does Wright in his memoir. The name of the devout sergeant in Company F is left as Phil Hamline (apparently no relation to Leonidas Hamline, the Methodist bishop after whom the university is named), although other sources give it as Hamlin.

Like any historical project, this one could not have been done alone. My thanks go to: Gregory M. Britton, Sarah P. Rubinstein, Hamp Smith, and Deborah Miller of the Minnesota Historical Society; to Heather Craig of the Goodhue County Historical Society; to David Heiller, editor of the *Askov American,* who rented an office to me while I worked on this project; and to my wife, Margaret, and daughter, Amanda, who accompanied me on a research trip to Beverly and patiently walked throughout Central Cemetery looking (in vain) for Wright's grave. Special thanks go to Christopher Herrick, Wright's great-grandson, for providing information, showing Wright's letters and photographs to me, and allowing reproduction of some of these in this book.

STEVEN J. KEILLOR

1. *Minneapolis Journal,* August 13, 1906, p. 1, 6.

2. James A. Wright to William W. Folwell, December 14, 1921, box 49, William Watts Folwell and Family Papers, Minnesota Historical Society (hereinafter MHS), St. Paul; *Red Wing Republican,* August 22, 1906, p. 7. It may have been in Minneapolis that Company F made its request of Wright, but its Red Wing reunion seems the more likely occasion. Note also Wright's statement in his preface that Company F veterans "forty years ago" (probably at the 1871 reunion in Red Wing) picked Wright for a committee "to gather material for a history of the regiment."

3. *Red Wing Republican,* August 22, 1906, p. 7; Wright to Folwell, December 14, 1921.

4. Wright to J[ens] K. Grondahl, August 13, 1907, Wright to Editor Republican [Grondahl], May 20, 1911, and Wright to L. A. Hancock, August 30, 1923, all in box 1, James A. Wright Papers, MHS; Wright to Folwell, December 14, 1921. The 875-page manuscript is in the Wright Papers.

5. Editor Republican [Grondahl] to Major Martin McGinnis, June 20, 1911, photocopy in box 1, Wright Papers.

6. Wright to Grondahl, February 4, 1914, box 1, Wright Papers.

7. Wright to Hancock, August 30, 1923, p. 3; Grondahl to Folwell, November 15, 1921, box 49, Folwell Papers; *Minnesota History Bulletin,* 4 (August–November 1921): 171.

8. Folwell to Wright, December 4, 1921, box 49, Folwell Papers. Possibly the costs of printing Folwell's four-volume work made publication of Wright's memoir financially impossible.

9. Folwell to Wright, December 4, 1921.

10. Wright to Folwell, December 14, 1921.

11. William Watts Folwell, *A History of Minnesota,* rev. ed. (St. Paul: Minnesota Historical Society, 1961), 2:86n4.

12. Minnesota State Census, 1857, Goodhue County, Township 112, range 15, microfilm roll 2, MHS.

13. *Red Wing Daily Republican,* March 9, 1889, p. 3, and August 22, 1906, p. 7; Rev. W. E. Arnold, *A History of Methodism in Kentucky* (Louisville: Herald Press, 1935), 2:78, 143. Amelia's brother Hooper Crews was also a circuit rider who moved to Illinois and "located" there as pastor of the Indiana Avenue Methodist Church in Chicago; Arnold, *Methodism in Kentucky,* 2:146–47. William Hooper (1742–90) was the son of a Scottish immigrant, a graduate of Harvard, a North Carolina lawyer and politician, and a signer of the Declaration of Independence. Benson J. Lossing, *Biographical Sketches of the Signers of the Declaration of Independence: The Declaration Historically Considered . . . and of the Federal Constitution* (New York: Derby and Jackson, 1848).

14. Merrill Earl Jarchow, "The Social and Cultural Aspects of the Methodist Church in Pioneer Minnesota," Master's thesis (University of Minnesota, 1933), 44–47, copy in MHS; James Peet, "North-Western Correspondence," *Northern Christian Advocate,* August 22, 1855, clipping in Methodist Episcopal Church Papers, MHS; Chauncy Hobart to James Peet, February 21, 1855, box 1, James Peet Papers, MHS; Chauncy Hobart, *History of Methodism in Minnesota* (Red Wing: Red Wing Printing Co., 1887), 74–78; Malcolm Chesney Shurtleff, "The Introduction of Methodism in Minnesota," Master's thesis (University of Minnesota, 1922), 38, 39, 42, copy in MHS; U.S. Census, 1860, Goodhue County, Milton Township, microfilm, MHS.

15. *Red Wing Sentinel,* April 24, 1861, p. 2; *Goodhue County Republican,* April 26, 1861, p.2.

16. *Red Wing Sentinel,* April 24, 1861, p. 2.

17. *Salem* (Massachusetts) *Evening News,* August 26, p.5, and August 29, p. 8, both 1936.

18. Wright to Editor Republican [Grondahl], May 20, 1911, Wright Papers.

19. "Man about Town" column, *Salem Evening News,* August 29, 1936, p. 8; *A Directory of the City of Beverly . . . for 1895 96* (Salem: Henry M. Meek, 1895), 152; *Directory of Salem and Beverly* (Salem: Henry M. Meek Pub. Co., 1926), 32:892. All cited works on Beverly are in the Beverly Public Library.

20. Stuart McConnell, *Glorious Contentment: The Grand Army of the Republic, 1865–1900* (Chapel Hill: University of North Carolina Press, 1992), 167–78 (quote, p. 169).

21. Wright to Grondahl, October 23, 1907, and May 27, 1911, both box 1, Wright Papers.

22. Wright to Grondahl, August 13, September 7, and December 14, all 1907, and May 20, 1911, all in Wright Papers.

No More Gallant a Deed

"I shall try to tell a simple story
of three years service, not far from
the storm center of the rebellion . . . "

JAMES A. WRIGHT

Introduction
"Story of Company F, First Minnesota Regiment"

BY JAMES A. WRIGHT,
ONE OF ITS ORDERLY SERGEANTS

SOMETHING LIKE FORTY YEARS AGO, at a reunion of the First Regiment of Minnesota Volunteer Infantry, the members of Company F, then present, chose me to represent them, as one of a committee of ten, to gather material for a history of the regiment. I am aware that it is now pretty late in the day to make a report but, at the time, the matter interested me and I made an effort to do something towards a general history of the regiment, which was all that was contemplated. The matter came to nothing and a few years later I left the state. Since then I have been separated from my company and regimental comrades, having made but one visit to the state—in 1906—and have given the matter but little further attention. Some years after I left the state there was a brief general history of all of the regiments published, by the state, and it does not now seem probable that there will be anything more.[1]

When I was in Red Wing in 1906, it was suggested that there should be something on record concerning Company F, as a matter of local history, and that I should take the responsibility of preparing it. I heartily concurred as to the desirability of having such a record but demurred as to the responsibility of preparing it. My mind being engrossed with other things, I did not give the matter serious attention at the time and allowed it to pass, but it has recently been called to my attention again, and I have concluded to make an effort in that direction.

I know that it has been a long time since Company F had a legal existence and almost as long since it chose me to represent it, in a historical way, so that all claims and obligations are outlawed. I trust, however, that the above explanation will be received in mitigation of all charges of 'breaking out' or 'butting in' that may be preferred against me on account of these sketches. I feel assured that my comrades of Company F, who always recognized my *innate modesty*, will exonerate me from any charges of egotism in trying to give a brief, connected account of the company in which we jointly shared the fortunes of a great war. It was an honorable service.

I desire to say at the beginning that for many things I shall be obliged to depend upon my memory, but that is reinforced by memoranda of the more important events, and I also have nearly all of the letters written home to my mother while in the service.

I cannot hope to avoid *all* errors, but will endeavor to the best of my ability and recollection to do so. If any member of the company, who may read any of these articles, observes any important misstatement, it is hoped that he will write to me at once and point it out that it may be corrected. It will be in this way that a complete and correct record may be made, if my memory is at fault. I hope that every living member of the company who may read any of these papers—I trust they will find their way to every one—will write to me. I earnestly desire to hear from them all. I believe that it is generally accepted as a fact that men who have offered themselves for any purpose, tending to the public good, and particularly those who have exposed themselves to the hazards of war, are worthy of mention to the generations that come after them and share the benefits of their labors and sacrifices.

I cannot assume otherwise than that the generations who have grown up in Red Wing, and in Goodhue County, since the War of the Rebellion will be pleased to learn of the part taken by those then living in the city and county in maintaining the integrity of the great nation of which we are all so proud today. As a member of Company F during all of its official life, and for about half of that time its First—or Orderly—Sergeant, I had an opportunity to know something of its services, and I assume the right to speak. I do this with an earnest desire to do simple justice to my old comrades of the company, whose many soldierly qualities of endurance and obedience I have seen tested to the utmost, and not found wanting. In common with other regiments sent out by the then young state of Minnesota, under the calls of President Lincoln, the First Minnesota Regiment tried to do what it could for the good of the country at large, and for the credit of the state it represented. Company F, as a part of that regiment, was faithful to do its part to the same end. We claim for Company F nothing more than this, and we ask nothing more in the way of consideration.

It was my first purpose to give only a roster of the company and indicate what the fates served out to them individually, but a recent letter from the editor of the *Red Wing Republican* has induced me to amplify somewhat my first intention. I do this with an earnest desire to present the personnel of the company along with its service; and thinking that its history, by one of its own members, though it may be but indifferently told, will be of some interest to old comrades, and to the families and children of those who 'have crossed the river.' I undertake this knowing very well that I have no special fitness for the work, after waiting for two score years for someone else to do it, and believing that if I do not do it that in all probability it will never be done. All labor in this work is a labor of love and is simply an expression of regard and appreciation for my old companions-in-arms.

With an old comrade's warmest greeting to each of my living comrades, I tender these articles. With a word of sympathy and a kind wish in remembrance of the days of our association together, I present them to the relatives and friends of all who have 'answered the last roll-call.' To my comrades of other companies, and of other regiments, if they should chance to read this, I send a cordial greeting. May I not also express the hope that the boys and girls of Red Wing and Goodhue County will try to get interested in what I write? I trust they will not consider it egotism if I suggest that they may find something that will help them to understand the history of the war period of our country better than they otherwise might.

I shall try to tell a simple story of three years' service, not far from the storm center of the rebellion, claiming only that Company F was a fair average of those who offered themselves in defense of the government and asking that my statements be received only for what they are really worth. As a tribute of affection for the companions of much of my military life, as a token of regard for all comrades of the war and lovers of the flag, I dedicate these papers to my old comrades of Company F, living and dead, and to their children and grandchildren.

JAMES A. WRIGHT
Beverly, Massachusetts

---

1. Wright refers to the brief regimental histories in Minnesota Board of Commissioners on Publication of History of Minnesota in Civil and Indian Wars, *Minnesota in Civil and Indian Wars, 1861–1865,* vol. 1 (St. Paul, 1890). William Lochren wrote the chapter on the First Minnesota.

The little band of would-be soldiers

1855-APRIL 1861

I WAS NOT BORN IN MINNESOTA and I have made but one brief visit to the state in more than thirty years, but I was struck by Minnesota lightning in my boyhood days and I served in Company F of the First Minnesota Regiment in the Civil War. I claim to have been regularly initiated and still consider myself a Minnesotian.

I was once a citizen of Red Wing, and I still have a fond and filial feeling for the old place nestling in the shadows of the everlasting hills beside the Father of Waters. I first set my boyish feet on the pebbly beach at the 'upper landing' when the *Lady Franklin* shoved up to the shore near the store and warehouses of Hoyt, Smith, and Gambia, on the afternoon of April 22, 1855.

It was to be our future home, as we then planned it, and we surveyed the surroundings with intense interest, and they have remained a memory ever since. Since then I have wandered far and looked upon many landscapes, but I have not forgotten. It is true that the hills have shrunk some in comparison with greater hills as experience has broadened, but they have lost nothing of their scenic attractions. An autumn evening sunset, looking up the Mississippi from the top of Barn Bluff, is hardly surpassed and never to be forgotten. Since that far-off day, more than a half century ago, the tide of time has surged onward and many changes have come—to the individual, to the little village of Red Wing, the territory of Minnesota, and the nation of which we are a part. The recollection of some of these makes a lump rise in the throat and the eyes grow dim, while others set the heart throbbing fast with state and national pride.

When I first set foot on Minnesota soil, I was a little, slender, red-headed, freckle-faced urchin of fourteen summers and fifteen winters, with but scant bodily strength, knowledge, or experience to fit me for the rough, hard life before me on the frontier. I was one of a broken family of nine, from whom death had but recently removed the head. A widowed mother and two sisters older than myself; one sister and four brothers all younger than I, completed the family roster. We were to make our home in a house out in Spring Creek Valley about five miles from Red Wing, for which our father had bargained before his death. We went

Red Wing's wood-frame businesses clung to the west
bank of the Mississippi River at the foot of Barn Bluff
at the lower landing. In 1855, the Wrights landed
near where the photographer stood.

that evening to the home of Samuel Spates on the bluff, not far from where the almshouse now stands, where we spent the night.[1]

When we went to our home-to-be the next morning, the first sight was discouraging, and a little closer investigation made it a distinct disappointment, which the copious tears of some of the company could not wash away. It was a log house roofed with boards; some of the windows were broken; one door was off of the hinges; and the mud and chinking was coming out from between the logs. And, worse yet, some emigrant with liberal ideas about the use of unoccupied property had apparently used one-half of the house to shelter himself and the other to stable his oxen. It had been purchased by our father the previous fall with the intention of going there in the spring, but he died on his way home, and we

1. Reverend Samuel Spates was a Methodist minister and former missionary to the Ojibwe; he had recently settled near Spring Creek. James Wright's father, David, was a Methodist preacher. In 1855, four Methodist clergymen lived near the Wright family. That guaranteed them neighborly assistance.

knew but little of what he had done or planned to do. Because there did not seem to be anything else that we could do, we went to work to clean up the house and make it temporarily habitable, for we must sleep there that night. Neighbors were not numerous, but they were very kind and generously assisted us to make ourselves comfortable. A family council decided to build a new house nearer the bluffs and to use the old one for a stable. As soon as practicable the necessary arrangements were made and the work begun.

Before it was completed, one of those violent thunderstorms, which were an occasional feature of Minnesota summers in those early days, came up in the night of June 15, 1855, after a hot day, and spent its fury along the Spring Creek Valley. In her efforts to equalize the electrical forces in the clouds and the earth, Nature passed a current through the house, tearing off the roof, shattering one end of it, and setting fire to the bedding and other material. The oldest of my sisters and the next to youngest brother were killed, and all the rest of the family more or less shocked or stunned.[2]

It was an awful calamity to the already-broken household. The fire was extinguished by the pouring rain and the efforts of those the least disabled. Kind and sympathetic neighbors came again and helped us to bury our dead and did all they could to make the future look less hopeless. The damaged furniture was moved to the unfinished house, where we camped until it was finished over our heads.

Interesting as it might be to follow my early experiences as a pioneer, such is not my purpose. I have only mentioned them that I might introduce myself and consistently show my connection with the events of which I propose to write. Circumstances over which I seemed to have no control had shifted me from my boyhood home to the sunset side of the Mississippi and, a few years later, circumstances again placed me in the midst of fraternal strife. In both cases I simply tried to do the best I could and make the best of circumstances. I will only add that after the storm, with a cheerfulness and hopefulness that now seems almost surprising, we—the mother and remaining children—worked hard to finish the home and provide for ourselves.

With added years and experience, matters improved, and I was investing all of my surplus in trying to get an education—opportunities having been exceedingly limited up to that time—at Hamline University, which was then located in Red Wing. There I met many others, from various parts of the state, animated by like desires. Life was opening interestingly and hopefully when the clouds of disunion, which had been gathering for years, broke in the storms of a great civil war.

The seeds of secession, which had been industriously sown to the winds by windy politicians North and South and nurtured to maturity by designing

2. According to his obituary, James Wright "was burned from shoulder to the finger tips on his right hand" by this lightning strike, and for the rest of his life "two crooked fingers served as a reminder of the incident"; *Salem Evening News,* August 26, 1936, p. 5.

demagogues or their ignorant dupes, were ripe for the whirlwind harvest. We hear much about the 'twentieth century activity' and the 'strenuous life of the present,' but prompt and intense action has not been limited to the last decade. There were stirring times half a century ago, and when the plans for secession were developed into action at Fort Sumter, there was 'something doing' right away, all over the country. Before that there was doubt and question as to the rights and powers of the government, uncertainty as to what its policy would be or should be, but Sumter's guns settled the whole question for the time being as certainly as the sunrise asserts the day. Wigfall's advice to Jefferson Davis to "sprinkle blood in the faces of the people" had its arousing and uniting effect far beyond what he anticipated or desired.[3]

The firing on Fort Sumter was an affront to national dignity as well as a declaration of what the seceding states had determined to do. All over the northern states, wherever the news was told, it was almost like a personal challenge to fight, emphasized by a slap in the face. It called for immediate and aggressive action, and brought a sudden and momentous crisis into hundreds of thousands of lives, and turned their thoughts from personal affairs to national honor and safety.

It was then the little band of would-be soldiers who called themselves the Goodhue Volunteers—and to whom these papers are dedicated—came into existence. They may not have been the first to respond under Lincoln's first call for 75,000 men, but they were far from the last. They were the first contribution of Goodhue County to defend the government, Red Wing's first sacrifice laid on the national altar. I regret my lack of power to portray the spirit in which that sacrifice was made. I certainly believe that it was as truly a sacrifice, and as sincerely offered, as men often make. It is true that there might have been degrees in the sincerity and motives almost as varied as the personality of the individuals, but they were prompted by a single fact—the attempt to overthrow the government—and dominated by a single purpose—to defend its integrity.

They were, with few exceptions, young men and unmarried. Nearly one-third of them were, or had been until recently, attending school at Hamline University, and they had their plans and cherished ambitions, but they put aside all inviting prospects and personal interests, and promptly offered themselves to their country. They placed their lives at the disposal of the government to restore its authority and recover its property. Others had done as much in other wars. It was being done at that time by others in other places. It was done by others in Red Wing and elsewhere—later, repeatedly. Nonetheless, it was a test that showed the quality and fiber of the men who composed Company F.

It was no trivial thing to offer to die that the nation might continue to live. It was probably true that every one that offered sincerely hoped that the "last full

3. Former U.S. Senator Louis T. Wigfall of Texas was in Charleston and played a prominent part in the taking of Fort Sumter; Mark W. Boatner III, *The Civil War Dictionary*, rev. ed. (New York: Vintage Books, 1991), 918.

measure of devotion" would not be required of *him*, but to go meant to take the chance, and when the chances were against them they were not found wanting.

It is difficult to portray the intense interest there was in Red Wing when the firing on Fort Sumter made it evident that the South was fully determined upon war, and had actually begun it. Up to that time many had not believed it possible, and a larger number had hoped for some other solution. There was but one line of telegraph along the river—a single wire—and it was often not in good working order, so there were frequently delays in the transmission of news or a lack of desired details. In common with other states, Minnesota was deeply interested in the national troubles and keenly alive to the critical condition of governmental affairs, but it was not planning or preparing for war. The people of the state deprecated war and hoped for peace.

Before the attack on Fort Sumter, Governor Alexander Ramsey had gone on to Washington for a consultation with other governors and government officials, hoping to find some way out of the troubled situation other than across battlefields. When Sumter yielded on Saturday, April 13, 1861, he was in Washington, and early Sunday morning, April 14, he went to the War Department and made a verbal tender of 1,000 men. Secretary of War Simon Cameron informed him that he was going to call at the White House and requested that the offer be put in writing to take with him. Governor Ramsey at once complied with the request and wrote, in part, as follows: "As the executive of the State of Minnesota, I hereby tender to the government of the United States, on the part of the state, 1,000 men to be ready for service as soon as the necessary information can be communicated to the people there." He also assured the President that the two senators had knowledge of—and approved of—his offer.

There was no doubt but the necessary number of men could be easily and quickly obtained, but the promise to have them ready at the time stated was a pretty rash statement under the then conditions. It is not likely that the governor, the two senators, or any of the state officials had any adequate conception of what it meant to enlist, organize, uniform, arm, drill, and equip a regiment of a thousand men. Like the rest of us, they had it all to learn.

This offer was made to—and accepted by—President Lincoln early in the day, Sunday, April 14, the day before the call was formally issued. It is

The first and only building of Hamline University in Red Wing. Built in 1856, it housed a chapel, several classrooms, a library, a laboratory, reading rooms, and dormitory rooms.

claimed that the First Minnesota Regiment was the first regiment of *volunteers* tendered in the Civil War. I know not if this is correct, but it is certain that they were officially tendered—and accepted—before they were formally requested, and I have heard of none of an earlier date. On Monday, April 15, the official call for 75,000 volunteers was issued by the government to the states, and on Tuesday, April 16, Lieutenant Governor Ignatius Donnelly—in the absence of the governor—issued the call for one regiment of ten companies to serve for three months. Companies were to organize at once and be ready to report at St. Paul when ordered.

At that time, Minnesota had no organized, active militia, as in some of the older states, only a few independent or skeleton companies, and but few of these had arms or uniforms.[4] In Red Wing there was no organized company or ever had been, the farthest point reached in that direction being a fire company armed with buckets and a Wide Awake company with torches.

Measures were taken at once to form a company in Red Wing, and a public meeting was held to further the matter. There was great excitement—and I believe a real satisfaction—when it was known that the government was to act, to try to do something to assert its authority and stop the forcible seizure of public property. There was a paper circulated, and at a public meeting held at the courthouse on the evening of the 17th, names enough were signed to make it assured that it was certain to be promptly filled. It was supposed to be desirable to organize as quickly as possible to make it certain of 'getting in,' and a meeting was held to choose officers. This was done in the usual way of selection—nomination and voting—and resulted in the choice of William Colvill, Jr., for captain; A. Edward Welch, first lieutenant; and Mark A. Hoyt, second lieutenant. The noncommissioned officers also were chosen in the same way. I do not recall that there was any special rivalry for the official positions, but I presume that there was—as there generally is.

William Colvill was a lawyer, a Democrat, and the editor of the *Red Wing Sentinel,* born in New York and about 30 years old. I do not know how it happened that he was the choice for captain, as I am sure that the majority of the company were Republicans, but I presume that the question of party politics did not enter into the case, and for the time being party lines were obliterated. He was much older than the majority, and that might have had its influence, or—as his height was six feet and four inches—the same influences that brought Saul to the

4. Under the state militia law of 1858, Minnesota did have an organized militia that at one time included thirteen companies; however, only three of them—Minnesota Pioneer Guards (St. Paul), St. Anthony Zouaves, and Stillwater Guard—accepted the state adjutant general's offer to enlist as units in the First Minnesota; Richard Moe, *The Last Full Measure: The Life and Death of the First Minnesota Volunteers* (New York: Henry Holt & Company, 1993; St. Paul: Minnesota Historical Society Press, 2001), 9–10; William Watts Folwell, *A History of Minnesota,* rev. ed. (St. Paul: Minnesota Historical Society, 1961), 2:27–28, 78.

kingship of Israel might have operated in his favor. Be that as it may, and whatever the influences, the choice proved a good one, and he rose to the command of the regiment and led it at Gettysburg with great credit to himself, the regiment, and the state.

The first lieutenant was a son of Judge Welch, a young law student of about 23, and a former student at Hamline University. The second lieutenant was the son of a Methodist minister, Rev. B. F. Hoyt, and himself preparing to preach. He also was a student at Hamline University.

I am not sure of the exact number of men at the time of the organization, but my recollection is 87. These came from all parts of the county, though the majority were from Red Wing and its immediate vicinity. They varied in height from five feet four to six feet four, and they varied in temperament, complexion, and color of the hair through as wide a range. As may be readily understood, they also varied in natural and acquired capabilities. Some of the boys who had been at the university for a couple of years had read Horace and the "Anabasis";[5] and there were others that had but a very slight acquaintance with any written language, and whose chirographic attainments were limited to signing the pay roll with the paymasters' assistance. They were no doubt fairly representative of the people of Goodhue County at that time, and that they were controlled by a single purpose is evident from the prompt way in which they responded to President Lincoln's call for assistance. A collection of their tintypes as they appeared when first assembling for drill would be interesting, and I would give a quarter's pension if I could get them. They would make fine illustrations for these papers.

Nearly one-third of the whole were — or had been — students at Hamline and were more or less acquainted, but many were entire strangers until they came together in the company. The military experience of the whole bunch did not count for much, and what little there was was scarcely available on account of the possessors' inability to speak intelligible 'United States.' There was but very little military training laying around loose in Red Wing at that time so far as I know. "Uncle Billy" Gordon, who went with us to the fort, had been — or claimed to have been — with Wellington at Waterloo. There were, of course, a few who had some little experience in militia companies in other states, but not enough to be important or of practical benefit. There were three in the company who had served in the military of foreign countries, but only one of these — Nicholas Hammer — had been in active service.

There was no formal enlistment as was the custom later. We just signed our names on a paper as men sign a petition, agreeing to go, and the next day after the choosing of the officers, we assembled for drill. The drill was limited to attempts to face to the right and left, in concert, and to trying to keep step in marching.

5. The *Anabasis* was an account written by the Greek historian and general Xenophon concerning the Persian Emperor Cyrus's expedition into central Asia in 401–400 B.C.

Taken all together, we were, I presume, about as verdant a lot of innocents—so far as military training was concerned—as could have been gathered up at random. From the captain down we had it all to learn, but we were all anxious to learn all we could as soon as we could and spent all of our spare time trying. There was a carpenter named Whitney, who had been an officer in a militia company in another state, who was interested enough to try to teach us, and we acquired a little knowledge in that way before we went to St. Paul. We used to drill on the sand on Broadway in front of Parker's Hotel, and usually had a curious crowd watching us. All told, we might have drilled half a dozen times before leaving for the state capital, and I am not certain but we began to put on military airs before we left Red Wing. Those were busy days, and, when not drilling or posting ourselves on 'news from the front,' we were arranging matters to go.

A large majority were young men, and many of them were away from home and had enlisted without previous notice to parents or others that had a claim to be consulted. This was particularly true of the young men at the university. In most cases, there were long and earnest protests against going—from the families at home—and in many cases it was a difficult matter to adjust the differences of opinion between those who had decided to go and those most interested at the home fireside. There were a few who could not stand the pressure and yielded to the entreaties or commands of the home council and canceled their agreement.

In my own case, I found it pretty hard to withstand the pleadings and tears of a widowed mother and others of the family. "Don't go, James! You are not strong, and never was! There will be plenty without *you*!" These and many other like arguments were used, which it was hard to meet, but in the end I held to my determination to go. It was but natural that the family and near friends should shrink from the exposure of those dear to them to the hazards of war and pass the duty of public defense along to someone else. Artemus Ward was not the only one who preferred to put down the rebellion by the sacrifice "of all of his first wife's relations," and this feeling was not so much a lack of patriotism as the pleadings of consanguinity.[6]

I had been taught to condemn war as a thing that civilized Christian people ought not to engage in. I deprecate war and always have, and for me to go was contrary to all previous intentions or expectations. Up to the actual firing on Fort Sumter, I had no idea or purpose to become a soldier; although I did have a pretty positive conviction that the government ought to be maintained, I had not come to the conclusion that I ought to help maintain it. The firing on the flag in Charleston harbor had brought the matter home to me in a personal way I had not dreamed of before, and I could see but one course for able-bodied, self-respecting men to pursue. The overt act seemed to put 'iron in the blood.' There

6. Charles Farrar Browne (pseudonym, Artemus Ward) was an American humorist whose Civil War–era writings were greatly enjoyed by Abraham Lincoln.

was no longer a question in my mind as to the right to coerce a state or do anything else necessary to restore the national authority. As the matter was presented, it was either submit or fight. Something within me rose in emphatic protest against the attempt to divide the nation. After the attack on Sumter, the only consistent attitude of a loyal man was with a rifle at his shoulder, and the only logical argument a bullet. I had that same feeling as long as armed men defied the government. "Get your gun and go, John," appeared to be about the only thing to do—and I did it. Looking at it today in the light of experience, I see no reason to repudiate my boyish conclusions.

The days passed quickly—and I am not sure just how many—before the order came to assemble at St. Paul, but I think it was April 23 that we left Red Wing. We had but two ways of public travel then in the state: the stagecoach and the steamboats. When one was running, the other was not, which really reduced it to one. The boats were just beginning to run, as the ice had but recently gone out of the river and their spring schedules were not yet established. Those who lived in other places had gone to their homes to bid the loved ones good-bye and came in the night before or the morning of departure.

I recall that I came in from my mother's the evening before, after quite a solemn parting with the folks at home and a farewell to some of the neighbors. There was to be a supper that evening at Robert Brown's, given by some of those who were not going, to some of their schoolmates who were. There were eighteen present, but it was not a real jolly feast. The boys did not eat with their usual appetites, and there was a shadow over us. The attempt at toasts and songs was not exactly a failure, for many good things were said—and well said—but feelings were too intense for smooth elocutionary effort. I know not if there is another, except myself, of that company living today.

Later that evening, there was a gathering at the university chapel, a sort of farewell reception to those who were going, by their remaining classmates and teachers. This was the last of several meetings held there since the call to arms. Hamline University, as it then was, under the patronage of the Methodist Church, was a radiating center of patriotism of the active, fighting kind. I remember with pride that about the first thing the students did after they heard of the firing on Fort Sumter was to call a meeting and take measures to procure a flag. The boys bought the bunting, and the girls made the flag. I do not think that there were any ready-made flags in those days. A standard was erected on the top of the building and the flag was hoisted with songs and speeches, the day the call was issued.

At the chapel that evening, many kind things were said to us who were going— much more than we really deserved. They tried to put a hopeful coloring over it all—pictured us returning at the end of three months, the war over and we again at our studies. They promised, too, if such was not the case, and the victory was not yet gained, and more men were needed, that they would follow in the same spirit we were going. Neither was this any idle promise made to cheer our departure. They meant it and kept their promise to the extent of draining the school of pupils and teachers until it was crippled and its future existence seriously threatened. The Methodists of Minnesota at that time were a loyal, fighting combination that meant business and backed the government right manfully. The meeting was a generous outpouring of good will and sympathy that followed us as a pleasant memory through years of war.

On the day we were to leave, we had an assembly at the landing, each one carrying a blanket, a quilt, or a robe. We had been advised to carry something to cover us while sleeping, it being uncertain when we should be supplied with these things. Leaving these at the warehouse, we marched uptown to the Episcopal Church, that being the place where our captain and first lieutenant attended service. Here a short service was held. We each were given a prayer book, and Rev. Mr. Wells made a farewell address.

After this, we were dismissed to meet at the landing in time for the boat. It was expected about noon but was some hours late—as usual. We were all there and an immense crowd had gathered long before the boat came. The Red Wing Band, which had volunteered to go with us to St. Paul, entertained with selections and patriotic airs. When the boat came, there were tender parting scenes and hurried farewells such as had not been witnessed beside the great river since the white man came. A warning whistle called for 'all aboard,' and we gathered up our rolls of bedding and filed up the gang-plank. The band went to the hurricane deck, and the volunteers gathered at the rail for a last look on shore.

The steamer backed away from the levee and headed up the river. There was a cheer from the crowd, a response from the boat, and the band played "Annie Laurie." The individuals on the shore blended into a sea of upturned faces and waving handkerchiefs, an occasional hat flew into the air, and the echoes of cheering mingled with the strains of the band. I am quite sure that the boys waved back a parting salute to those on shore—it were ungallant not to do it—but when I looked around at the others the most of them appeared to have a personal use for their handkerchiefs nearer their own faces. The boat forced her way against the swollen spring current but slowly, and we watched the troubled, discolored water as it passed, each one busy with his own thoughts.

The wind was raw and the afternoon waning, and the boys soon gathered in groups at the lee rail in the shelter of the smoke-stacks or went to the cabins to 'talk it over.' It was a pretty serious business we had embarked in. We all felt it and realized that it was unreasonable to suppose that *all* would return. Even boys think seriously, sometimes, and I have no doubt that each one made a mental calculation as to a safe return. It is a merciful Providence that veils the future and leaves hope to go with us until the angel of death puts aside the curtain.

The happy land of Canaan

APRIL–JUNE 1861

BESIDES OUR COMPANY there were quite a number of passengers on the boat to whom we seemed a matter of interest—or curiosity. After supper—a ticket included meals in those days—there was a patriotic meeting in the after cabin, started by some of the passengers, and all were invited to participate. Someone was escorted to the piano, and there were patriotic songs and speeches, and flattering and encouraging words were spoken to those "who were going out to fight the battles of their country, and right." When a response was called for, our second lieutenant, Mark A. Hoyt, was called out by the Hamline Boys, who knew him as one that was always ready with a speech or a song. He was a well-favored young fellow of 23 about to graduate from the university, and was preparing himself for the ministry. He was a born orator and came to the front splendidly in a short speech that received the hearty applause of all who heard it.

It was some time after dark before we made the landing at St. Paul, but we were expected, and the Pioneer Guards were on hand to receive us. We were much impressed with the appearance of the guards as they escorted us up the streets—they carried guns and looked like *real soldiers*. At the landing and on the march we were greeted with cheers and shouts, such as "Bully for you, boys," "Hurrah for Old Goodhue," and like expressions. Some of the irreverent or unsympathetic ones inquired if our "mothers knew we were out" and where we were "going to stay" that night. That last was a question about which we were not yet informed, but it was settled a little later when we halted at the Atheneum[1]—I think it was—and were told that we were to camp there.

Wherever it was we made our first bivouac, it was a rather uncomfortable night of it as we tried to sleep on the seats and floor, wrapped in the blankets and quilts we had brought with us. As is inevitable when a company of youngsters get together, there was considerable of amusement at the expense of someone else, but the victims took it good-naturedly and tried to get even in kind. I recall expressing a desire to sleep, and was awakened several times before morning to answer the inquiry if I had been asleep or not. If called on the next morning to express

1. Built by the German Reading Society in 1858, the Atheneum was a one-story, wood-frame building on the corner of Walnut and Exchange Streets in St. Paul.

an opinion, I dare say that we would have voted them to be poor accommodations, but after three years of army life we considered them great.

The next morning we picked up a breakfast wherever we could find it about the city and then got ready for our first march. We then started for Fort Snelling, the old government fort across the Mississippi and about five miles above the city. It was well along in the forenoon when we reached the river at the ferry, which was the only means of crossing, and waited for the ferryman to take us over. This ferry was what was then called a 'lazy man's ferry,' which meant that it was operated by an arrangement by which the current propelled the boat across the stream, the direction being changed by ropes and pulleys at either end of the boat. At the time we arrived, there was 'something out of gear' about the propelling force, and we were delayed for a time, but it was brought to a working condition, and we were safe across before noon.

We marched up the winding way at the south side of the fort, along a sandy road, up a ravine, and past the blockhouse to the main entrance. This fort had been built many years before as a government station, but had been in practical disuse for some years and occupied only by caretakers. It was splendidly situated on the bluffs at the junction of the Minnesota and Mississippi rivers, and was large enough for the accommodation of a regiment. When we arrived at the fort, we found that arrangements were being made for our reception, but that nothing was yet completed. When put in order, it made an excellent place for the rendezvous of the Minnesota volunteers. We were not yet inured to campaigning, and were tired and hungry when we marched into the fort.

The "lazy man's ferry" or "rope ferry" waiting to leave the Mississippi's east bank and head for Fort Snelling atop the west bank bluff, just above the mouth of the Minnesota River

A contract had been made by somebody with somebody to feed somebody, but the representative of the contractor who had bargained to do the feeding (who was at the fort) did not seem to understand who he was to feed, what he was to do, or how he was to do it.[2] There was considerable to try the patience of a hungry crowd before a shift was made to give us something to eat, but when it was secured we ate it and felt better.

The companies from Hastings, Wabasha, and Winona also came in that day—those towns being convenient for the boats. There was plenty of room in the old barracks; quarters were assigned to the company; and we all went to work to clean them up and make arrangements to occupy them. This preparation for camp-life was our first tour of 'fatigue duty,' but we did not know then that there was any name for it. Loads of straw came in, and a liberal allowance was given for each bunk. We paired off for sleeping according to the individual preferences, and made our arrangements for soldier housekeeping. The bunks were simply shallow board boxes; and these, filled with straw and covered with a blanket, made the beds; the overcoats of the two made the covering. A guard was detailed and posted, and, without any attempt at other military formalities, we spent our first night under guard. There was, I think, a cannon at the fort but no ammunition to fire it, and there was a flag staff but no flag or halyards. Some of the boys who had heard something about routine life in a garrison were anxious for a flag and the morning and evening guns—and later all of these were provided—but for that evening we had to retire without them.

It was not in the nature of things that we should go quietly to bed, for three or four hundred young men, gathered from a score of towns for any purpose but a funeral, are certain to make an attempt to have some fun; and this first night at the fort was not an exception. There was no attempt to do more in the way of discipline than to confine the crowd to the limits of the fort, and there was the usual amount of 'sky larking' and attempts at funny tricks.

It was not all boyish fun either, for each company had in it many fine singers, and after supper—as the night settled down—some of them began to sing, here and there, in front of the quarters or on the parade; and groups gathered to listen. It was not long before this was the chief attraction, and the singers were surrounded by crowds of interested and attentive listeners. There was a really fine rendition of patriotic and sentimental songs, which lasted until the singers grew hoarse, and the listeners began to grow homesick.

When the surplus energy had worked itself off to restful proportions, the embryo warriors went to their straw pallets in the old wooden barracks and slept, while the waters of the Mississippi and the Minnesota—the two great rivers of the

2. For some weeks, Governor Ramsey quarreled with the quartermaster general in Washington over whether the state of Minnesota or the national government ought to pay for clothing and equipment for the regiment. Apparently, the state paid Eustis and Lamb for furnishing food to the regiment while it was stationed at Fort Snelling; Moe, *Last Full Measure,* 22.

state—united and hurried southward to where traitors were plotting and planning to divide the nation.

The next day brought work and an earnest effort at drill. Our officers had procured some books of instruction, which they were studying diligently and teaching to the company at the same time. I am not sure but I should say that the officers and men studied the tactics together, for they brought their books to the drill grounds and prompted themselves or corrected their errors by referring to the books. These books were, I believe, the old Scott *Tactics* and were changed for the new *Light Infantry Tactics* a few weeks later, when we had to *unlearn* a part of it.[3]

We each received a tin cup, tin plate, knife, fork, and spoon, and went to the place where the food was cooked for our meals—receiving them at an open window and going to our quarters to eat them. It was not a very satisfactory arrangement from the first. The food was not very well cooked, and it was worse served, causing some complaint that the quantity was not equal to the appetites and the quality not what it should be; however, it was expected to be better when things were got in 'running order.'

We were very busy, and the days passed quickly. The papers were filled with exciting news, and when not drilling or eating, we read them and discussed the 'news from the seat of war' and talked about going to 'the front.' We began very early to use the military phrases then in vogue, and, when news was scarce, there was always someone ready with some exciting rumor. 'Camp rumors' made their appearance very soon after we began camping.

I think that the companies from Stillwater and Faribault joined us Saturday, April 27, and Sunday was properly observed. Morning and evening service was held in the little chapel near the western gate. My recollection is that Rev. Cyrus Brooks—a Methodist minister and the father of Cyrus A. Brooks, one of the Company F boys—preached.

Monday, April 29, was a day full of important events to the young volunteers. For the first time, what was to be the First Regiment of Minnesota Volunteers was brought together. It was also mustered into the U.S. service and organized into a regiment, thus making a binding contract with the government. Before noon the companies from St. Paul, St. Anthony, and Minneapolis came in with flags and bands. A garrison flag, rope for the halyards, and ammunition for the cannon also came; and at twelve o'clock the flag was hoisted while the bands played, and a national salute was fired—not omitting a shot for any of the states that declared that they had seceded.

3. Winfield Scott's three-volume *Infantry Tactics* (1835), which was based on the use of muskets, was the U.S. Army's manual for decades. William J. Hardee's two-volume *Rifle and Light Infantry Tactics* (1855) became the standard manual on drill and tactics for both sides in the Civil War. Scott was general-in-chief of the army in 1861; Hardee taught at West Point and became a Confederate general.

This was the first time that the regiment-that-was-to-be had ever seen itself; and its prospective field officers were present and looked it over carefully as the companies formed for the flag raising; and, in fact, the colonel-to-be took charge of the ceremonies. It was on this occasion—at the close of the cheering—that some of the boys gave the best imitation that they could of an Indian war-whoop, and it became thereafter a distinctive part of the regimental cheering. The mustering-in was reserved for the afternoon, and it was an occasion of tense—and intense—interest. I question if another regiment was so mustered.

The companies formed one at a time in the order of seniority of acceptance—in single rank—and were looked over by a trio of doctors walking in front and rear of the men. After that, they took position in front of the company and required each man to walk past them for a few paces, to face to the right or left, and to march a few paces farther, then face about, and return to his place in the line. If the doctors saw anything about the candidate or his movements that made them desirous of investigating further, he was directed to step aside and wait. If not, then his medical examination was completed. A few men—one in ten perhaps—were thus culled out and had a more personal examination. Some of these who were held up were finally passed, and others were rejected. Company F had six or seven that were not accepted. This may or may not have been a strict physical examination, and certainly was not the close individual examination practiced later, but I am of the impression that the First Regiment lost less than the average by death or disability by disease.

After the examination, we were ready to be sworn in, and this was done a company at a time. Taking off our hats, we each raised his right hand; Captain A. D. Nelson of the regular army pronounced the oath; and we repeated it after him in concert, pledging our lives and sacred honor to its fulfillment. I think that we fully realized that we had made a pretty large promise and assumed a very solemn obligation.

Many people had gathered—as they did every day—but there was a marked stillness during the administration of the oath. It was late in the afternoon before the muster was completed (and I am not sure that it was completed that day), but I recall that it was almost sundown when I observed a group of Sioux Indians, wrapped in their blankets near the western gate, solemnly watching the proceedings. Soon after, the sunset gun was fired, and the flag lowered; and after that it became a part of the daily routine.

With the muster came the appointment of the field officers of the regiment by Gov. Ramsey, as follows:

Colonel, Willis A. Gorman;
Lieutenant Colonel, Stephen Miller;
Major, William H. Dike;
Surgeon, Jacob H. Stewart;

Assistant Surgeon, Charles W. Le Boutillier;
Chaplain, Edward D. Neill.

Gorman was an ex-governor, a lawyer, and a Democratic politician. He had also been colonel of the Fourth Indiana in the Mexican War, and I presume that it was this experience that gave him the position. He was a medium-sized man, 46 years old, dark hair and mustache, getting gray. A fine, soldierly-looking fellow with a strong, clear, ringing voice that could be heard and *felt*, and, as we soon learned, he was an expert in the use of classical cuss words.

With the muster and appointment of staff officers came the assignment of letters as the company designation—made according to dates of acceptance of the companies—which made the Goodhue Volunteers Company F of the regiment.

Colonel Gorman certainly showed great energy and an appreciation of what we needed, and we made a business of drilling. He drilled us about ten hours a day in his earnest efforts to remedy our neglected education in the manner and methods of war. He tried to show us how little we knew, how much we ought to know, and the best and quickest way to acquire it. It was drill, drill, drill, and then drill some more, until arms and legs were weary and heads were dizzy. For nearly all of the hours of daylight—and once, at least, at night—we marched and countermarched, in single and in double ranks, quick and double-quick time; we filed, obliqued, and wheeled, to the right and to the left—in sections, platoons, and companies; passed obstacles, removed obstructions, and scaled walls. He kept us too busy to get homesick or feel the monotony of camp life so long as we were interested to learn.

As I look at it in the light of later experience, much of what he did and the way he did it was 'fuss and feathers,' but he certainly showed an understanding of the situation, a knowledge of what was required, and an energy in trying to get it done. That entitles him to credit. There were three things that presented themselves for immediate attention, and for which he was dependent upon others. These were the feeding, arming, and clothing of the regiment. These are easy, simple things when the commissary, ordinance, and quartermaster departments are in proper working order, and there are well-filled storehouses to draw from. When all of these departments have to be created—and there are neither storehouses nor supplies—it is another proposition. Regiments that came after us had the benefit of partially-organized departments, accumulating supplies, and experience, but there was not even a little *experience* for us to draw upon.

It was arranged to do the feeding by contract and to call on the national government for arms and clothing. All that could be obtained was promises—vague and indefinite ones at that. The traitor War Secretary, John B. Floyd, had left the department in a confused condition, depleted of all kinds of stores and left but little beside promises to give out.[4] When it was realized that the general government could not be depended upon for immediate supplies, efforts were made in other directions. All available arms were gathered up, but they were of three different kinds—and not enough to go around at that. It was determined to improvise a temporary uniform until the government could furnish some. Black hats, red shirts, dark blue pants and shoes, and a blanket were decided upon. Meantime, the drilling went on vigorously and great progress was made in doing things in concert with ease and rapidity. Order and routine were soon established, and we began to know what to expect and when to expect it, and governed ourselves accordingly. There was the reveille and other calls, the morning and evening ones, the hoisting and lowering the flag, guard mounting and roll calls, also sick call and three meals a day. The rest of the time we drilled.

To this routine—although we were without uniforms and some without guns—dress parades were soon added. The first attempt at a dress parade was Thursday evening, May 2nd, and there was a crowd present—as there was almost every day. If one of Edison's men had been around with a kinetoscope and secured a correct representation of all of the motions and maneuvers, it would be an interesting 'living picture,' but Edison himself had not been discovered then. The dress parade was a feature thereafter and improved with every performance.

Saturday, May 4th, orders came from Washington for six companies to go to the frontier forts as soon as armed and equipped, and the necessary transportation could be provided. Two companies each were to be sent to Forts Ridgely, Ripley, and Abercrombie to relieve the regulars then garrisoning them.[5] These three forts were the only protection to the frontiers from the Iowa line to the Red River against the numerous bands of Sioux and other Indians. It was as necessary that the frontiers should be guarded as that men should be sent south, but we had not thought of service on the frontiers when we enlisted, and now the very thought of being sent, *on foot*, hundreds of miles outside the confines of civilization, while a great war was being fought was extremely disheartening. However, 'orders were orders,' and we were beginning to comprehend that fact. Preparations were at once begun to collect food and means of transportation for the outgoing companies.

On May 7th, the governor received a telegram from Washington suggesting that the regiment change its term of enlistment from three months to three years,

4. John B. Floyd served as secretary of war under President James Buchanan from 1857 until December 29, 1860. He was suspected of transferring some federal arms to the South while secretary of war; he later became a Confederate general.
5. Fort Abercrombie was located just west of the Red River, near the mouth of the Whiskey River, and opposite the present-day town of Kent, Minnesota; Fort Ridgely was on the north side of the Minnesota River, halfway between New Ulm and Redwood Falls; Fort Ripley was on the west bank of the Mississippi River, several miles south of the mouth of the Crow Wing River.

allowing all who could not or did not wish to go for the longer period to be mustered out. This was another matter that came up for decision, and that had to be promptly decided, as there was no time for consultation with families and friends at home. I am surprised at the unanimity with which the boys decided to go. Under this proposition, there were, I believe, twenty-one who declined to go for the three years, and some of these would have stayed if a frontier garrison had not been one of the probabilities. Sixty-six of the original members of Company F decided to remain, and on Friday, May 10, 1861, the others were discharged. As soon as possible, others were secured to fill the places of those going home. The date of muster was not changed from April 29, 1861, and we were a three-year regiment from May 10, 1861.[6]

It was indeed a busy, active life at the fort, with much that was interesting, but to be surrounded by armed guards day and night and not allowed to go and come at will was irksome. It seemed humiliating to be thus placed under constant restraint. We objected on general principles, for we could not realize the necessity for these things until taught by experience. There were many attempts at evasion of the guards—successful ones, too, particularly by those whose homes were not far from the fort—but as a whole the boys yielded readily and good-naturedly to discipline.

There were other things besides being shut in that galled. The average man in the ranks felt himself the equal of his 'superior officer,' who may have been *superior* only in the official title he held. Any show of authority more than was thought to be necessary 'for the good of the service' was offensive and frequently was resented. These things gradually adjusted themselves, and, so far as Company F was concerned, matters went along smoothly.

The matter of rations concerned every one. We were being fed by contract, and temporary tables were provided from which the food was served. This seemed an improvement for a little time, but soon there was dissatisfaction. The meals were not served on time, and it was claimed that they were not equitably divided, and that the quality and the quantity were not what they should be.

The matter reached a climax one day when there was an unmistakably bad odor to the meat. By unanimous consent, it was declared unfit to eat. A start was made for the officers' quarters to make an exhibit. A promise was made that it should be better in the future, and we were directed to return to quarters.

The next question was what we were to have for dinner, and there was no satisfactory answer. Hungry men are not usually very amiable, and the boys retired—threatening a good many things—and found the men of other companies even more disturbed.

6. Wright noted, "it has been claimed that we were the senior three-years regiment." Military historian Mark Boatner III supports that claim, based on an unchanged mustering-in date of April 29; Boatner, *Civil War Dictionary,* 553.

Quite a crowd had assembled at the cook houses. Various individuals were 'saying things' to the chefs. By someone's suggestion or by a common impulse, words took the form of action, and the cooks and the cook houses were pelted with the plates and their contents. This was followed by a hurried return to quarters to keep out of the hands of the guards.

Of course, we went without dinner that day, but the result was a reconstruction of the ration department and a marked improvement, and meals were brought to the quarters at the call of the bugle. This was the only demonstration that I recall while at the fort, and it was known as the 'Bad Beef Riots.'

I saw but little of Minnesota's other regiments in the field, but, from what I saw from other states, I am sure that the First was always amenable to control.

There would not seem to be anything about spoilt beef to suggest poetry, but speaking of it reminds me of a rhythmic phase of the stay at the fort. There were several members of Company F whose thoughts appeared to assume the form of verse—the parody variety—and they began to work that way before they left Red Wing. When we arrived at the fort, they came in contact with others with like propensities and ambitions, and the result was an epidemic of doggerel that dealt with the current affairs at the fort in a free and easy way, and with a new version nearly every day. When the rations were a subject of anathema, there was a verse that ran something like this:

> Our lives would be merry
> But for our commissary,
> And in h—l we wish he was trainin'.
> For the rations are so poor
> The soldier boys are sure
> He'll never reach the Happy Land of Canaan.

After the reformation, it was changed to something like the following:

> Our lives have been merry
> Since our commissary
> We have been trainin'—
> To bring the grub around
> At the bugle sound
> To our quarters in the Happy Land of Canaan.

To these rhymsters, the fort was always "the Happy Land of Canaan."

After the order for six companies to go to the forts in the Indian Country, the outgoing companies were a prolific target of alleged poetry. It was not known what companies were to go, and the poets were thus left free to make their own selection. As Fort Abercrombie on the Red River was the farthest away—and therefore the least desirable—those going there were called Abercrombie Men. The poets all assumed that they were to remain at Fort Snelling, and the lives of those who went elsewhere were depicted in many and various ways, of which the following is a sample:

When at the frontier forts we stop,
We will plant our own potatoes then.
The rear rank cover and front rank drop,
Will be the drill of the Abercrombie Men.

Not only local matters, but the general news was twisted into shape to suit the fancies of our fun-loving rhymsters. Governor Wise of Virginia was making himself conspicuous by a free and intemperate use of his mouth; Governor Magoffin of Kentucky was offering to furnish a hundred thousand coffins in which to put the slain invaders of the South. They were referred to as follows:

Oh! The Wises and Magoffins
Have advertised for coffins,
To put us—when in battle we are slain—in.
But we'll build a big balloon
And we will ship them soon
To glory or—the Happy Land of Canaan.

Some of these screeds found their way to the printer, and some of them may be found in files of the local papers of that date, perhaps, but I am not sure that they were published for any intrinsic merit. I recall them as a phase of the early days at the fort and may not have quoted them accurately. There was much of this sort—and some of a higher rating—current for a time, but that kind of poetry could not stand the ordeal of actual war. It withered when exposed to the fumes of burning gunpowder. Production ceased as we neared the 'seat of war,' and I recall but few manifestations after we crossed the Potomac.

I did not intend to make so long a digression and will return to the story of organization. Soon after the order to scatter the regiment along the frontier, a wagonmaster was appointed and work began to improvise transportation. There was none, and that department, like all of the others, had to be organized. Colonel Gorman and the State authorities addressed themselves to the task before them with energy and to good purpose as soon as the enlistment matter was settled.

About this time, also, the matter of uniform was decided and arrangements were made to furnish each soldier two red flannel shirts, a pair of dark blue pants, a black slouch hat, and a blanket.[7] This made a good temporary outfit for the warm weather. The blanket, which was a first quality Mackinaw, could be used when needed to take the place of coat or overcoat. Dressed in this uniform, we resembled a lot of firemen out for muster. We were diligently practicing the new *Light Infantry Tactics*—just ordered by Act of Congress—and otherwise trying to fit ourselves for service as soldiers.

7. The adjutant general ordered $10,488 worth of clothing from the contractors, Culver and Farrington, who were expected to "look to the United States for payment"; Folwell, *Minnesota,* 2:80 (see note 38 on page 80).

Tuesday, May 21, we took our first practice march. That day, in response to an invitation from the people of Minneapolis and St. Anthony, we went to the Falls of St. Anthony, about 8 miles up the Mississippi, and had a picnic dinner on Nicollet Island. There were two towns—Minneapolis and St. Anthony—where the city of Minneapolis now is, and a company from each one of them in the regiment. The dinner was furnished by the citizens from these two places, prepared and served on the island by the ladies. Going and returning, we made a short halt at the Falls of Minnehaha for rest or observation, which relieved the march of severity and made the whole day an enjoyable affair. We had not all received our arms yet, but they were daily expected, and the regiment was practically filled for the three years.

Our next outing was Monday, May 27,[8] when the regiment went to St. Paul, a march of about the same distance. This was for a more definite purpose, and—as we were now more fully armed and uniformed and improved in drill, also—we made a more military appearance. Up to this time, Minnesota had never had an organized regiment, and, of course, it had never issued a state flag. One purpose of the trip was to receive a state flag, provided for the regiment by the ladies of St. Paul. It was therefore with more than ordinary interest that we prepared for this march, and, as there was no bridge then, it involved the crossing of the Mississippi River on the boat. It was no trifling matter to cross a thousand men on the old ferry, but it was done, and we were in the city by twelve o'clock. The march was made in good form, Colonel Gorman riding a fine horse that had recently been presented to him by some of his friends.

We massed on the easterly side of the Capitol for the presentation exercises. The flag was presented by Mrs. Anna I. Ramsey, the wife of Gov. Alexander Ramsey, who came out of the building carrying the flag in her hands. Her manner was dignified and earnest, and she spoke with a warmth of feeling and eloquence that touched our hearts and stirred our pride. A part of her remarks were as follows:

> To you is reserved a proud destiny. When the time comes that, from the source of the Father of Waters, you shall descend to where the fate of the nation is being decided, the solicitude and love of the entire state will follow you. From this Capitol to the most remote frontier cottage, no heart but shall send up a prayer for your safety and success; no eye but shall follow with affection the flutterings of your banner as you cover it with glory. In your hands we feel that the honor of our young state is safe. To you—with firm faith—we commit its virgin and unsullied fame. When the troubles that now agitate the nation are past, when the Rebellion is suppressed, and when once more peace folds her white wings among us, you will return to receive that praise and gratitude which you will have nobly earned; and, in after years, amid the avocations of your peaceful lives, men will point to you and

8. In his "Narrative of the First Regiment," Lieutenant William Lochren dated this trip to St. Paul on May 26; *Minnesota in the Civil and Indian Wars*, 1:4. Otherwise, Wright seems to have used Lochren's account as one of his main sources for the Fort Snelling period.

say: "There is one who, when his country's liberty was in danger, abandoned everything and rushed to her rescue. There is a soldier of the great army of freedom."

There was a response of enthusiastic cheers when she ceased speaking and handed the flag to Colonel Gorman, who was at home on the platform and made an eloquent reply, closing with these words:

We accept this flag as the emblem of the cause in which we have unsheathed our swords, and, with the help of the God of Battles, we will never allow them to return to their scabbards until treason shall be punished, and this flag, the Union, and the Constitution be vindicated and made perpetual. I now accept it in the name of the gallant officers and men of the First Minnesota Regiment, and most solemnly make the pledge to our noble young state, and to her people, and to our fathers, mothers, sisters, brothers, wives, and children—in this presence—never to surrender it to a foe until its folds have been baptized in our blood. We shall carry it wherever duty calls until it shall please a kind Providence to restore peace to our country and us to the bosom of our homes.

Then, handing the flag to Color Sergeant Howard Stansbury, he closed, saying, "Sir, To your hands I entrust this flag. It will remain in your keeping. Bear it aloft; and, should you fall in defense of it, let your last words be: 'Save the colors of the First Regiment.'"

The flag and the speech were received with cheers; the band played; and a national salute was fired. We then marched to the Winslow House, where a good dinner was served. When the dinner was over, the afternoon was already well gone, and we marched down to the levee and went aboard two steamboats—the *Hawk Eye State* and the *Northern Belle*—then at the landing, which carried us up the river and landed us on the Fort Snelling side of the river before it was fairly dark. We were thus saved a long march and the tedious ferrying process.

To us the day had been an eventful one. The presentation and reception of that flag—under the circumstances and in the manner it was presented—made a very strong impression on our minds that may have had its influence on our later history. I know that the men of Company F felt that a new and additional obligation had been placed upon them that faithful and heroic service alone could cancel.

Matters were now moving quickly, and affairs rapidly taking form for the future. Every day had its exciting news from the seat of war and was replete with hurried preparations for active service. There was a stream of visitors came to the fort every day to visit friends and relatives there and say good-bye, perhaps for the last time. I think it was the next day after the reception of the flag that Major William H. Dike with Companies B and G took a steamer at the fort landing and went up the Minnesota River to relieve Major Patten and two companies of the Second Infantry—Regulars—then at Fort Ridgely. And at a dress parade (which were now held regularly and attracted almost as big a crowd as a circus parade) about this time, Captain H. C. Lester of Company K presented a regimental flag—the Stars and Stripes—to the regiment, a gift from the ladies of Winona.

This, too, was made an impressive affair, and it was evident from the speeches on these occasions that much was expected of us. We were now well supplied with regimental and state flags, the gifts of loyal women of the state, and events were hastening us to the time when our loyalty to the flag and the state was to be put to the test of actual performance.

On Wednesday morning, May 29, Company A, Captain Alexander Wilkin commanding, started on the march for Fort Ripley, up the Mississippi River, to relieve Colonel Abercrombie and a portion of the Second Infantry then stationed there.

The rest of the regiment remained drilling diligently every day, and—as now nearly all were armed (some with Springfield rifles and some with Harpers Ferry muskets)—target practice was added to the drill. Most of the boys were accustomed to the use of firearms, but none had had experience with the government arms. Company F was armed with the Harpers Ferry musket. This was a long, heavy, smoothbore 69-caliber, carrying a round ball and three buckshot, with a single sight—an effective weapon at short range against those no better armed, but, deficient in accuracy and range, it was a poor arm against rifles. There was no regular range, and each company sought its own place for practice. On one occasion Company F used a little stone building some distance outside the fort, used for storing powder. A shirt arranged on sticks after the manner of a scarecrow and placed at the end of this building answered for the target. I cannot recall the firing distance or the record, but I know that there was disappointment as to results, which were all charged up to the guns. Company F had a good many fine marksmen, who were very handy with their rifles and who made good scores even with these 'shot guns,' as we called them, and perhaps the guns were not wholly to blame. In practice we used only the large ball, which I believe weighed an ounce.

On Thursday, June 6, Captain George N. Morgan with Company E started to join Company A, then eight days on the march towards Fort Ripley. We knew that efforts were being made to get the order sending our regiment to the frontier changed and hoped that this might be accomplished, as there was strong preference for Southern service rather than the border forts, but as additional companies were detached and sent away it seemed a failure. Monday, June 10, seemed to settle the whole matter, for on that day Lieutenant Colonel Stephen Miller—with Company C, Captain William H. Acker, and Company D, Captain Henry R. Putnam—started to march to Fort Abercrombie. Their departure left those remaining at Snelling depressed and dissatisfied. There seemed to be nothing for the regiment but service outside the lines of civilization. The real service for which we had enlisted—restoring the authority of the government and recovering its property—was apparently to be left in other hands than ours while we wasted our energies fighting buffalo flies and mosquitoes in the wilderness. The four companies remaining at the fort went the round of daily routine, performing increased guard and fatigue duties, expecting orders for some or all of them to follow those that had already gone.

Four days later all of this was changed, and the camp was wild with excitement. Friday, June 14, a call was issued for the Second Minnesota Regiment, in anticipation of which a number of companies had already been formed, and that same evening there came a dispatch from Washington ordering the First Regiment to Harrisburg. It was late in the evening when news of the order reached the fort, and we had already retired, when one of the guard came in with the story. We were already getting suspicious of 'camp rumors' and 'grapevine dispatches' and did not take much stock in it. A little later, it was confirmed from the officers' quarters, and there was great rejoicing.

As matters developed in 1862, there was a fine opportunity for great service on the frontiers, but, as they appeared then, to go to the forts seemed very like exile or imprisonment, and we wanted none of it. We had enlisted for active service; that seemed the only thing desirable; and we were really glad when the orders came to go South. Many times—later in our service—we would have been only too glad for the comfortable quarters at the forts and their immunity from danger, but I think that the only time that we really ever wished to be back there was when the Indians were ravaging the borders in 1862.

No time was lost in preparation to go. A mounted courier was sent away that night after Lieutenant Colonel Miller and his detachment—which had been now five days on the march—ordering its immediate return. Orders were also sent at once to Forts Ridgely and Ripley for the companies at those places to return immediately, leaving one officer and a few men in charge of the property until relieved. Some companies of the Second Regiment, it was understood, were to go at once to Ridgley and Ripley to organize and drill there, as we had at Snelling. The companies had gone out reluctantly and returned gladly, some of them marching all night to get in. By Friday morning, June 21, all but the details were in, Company E coming in that morning.

That last day and night at the fort were prolific with incidents and associated with partings that might be final. It was widely known that we were to go, and many came for a last look and a last word. It seemed to be a general impression that, of all that were going, but few or none were likely to return, and it certainly had a depressing effect. Many who could go to their homes and return at night were allowed leave of absence for the day. Many people came from a distance to the fort that last day. There was not much sleep that night, for we were late getting into our straw-furnished bunks, and the bugles called us out of them at the first suggestion of daylight—for one of the longest days of the year. Everything we proposed to carry with us was reduced to its smallest proportions and packed into the roll of blankets; a day's ration of meat and bread was put in our haversacks;

and our breakfasts were eaten. Ammunition was also issued to all who had cartridge boxes. There were some—about 150 — who had not yet been supplied with cartridge boxes, belts, etc.

At the call, we were ready to fall in with 'all our traps and calamities,' as one of the boys from the country expressed it (the Hamline University boys referred to them as *impediments*), and march to the parade ground, where we were massed to the colors. Reverend Edward D. Neill, who had been appointed chaplain, conducted a short service, consisting of a brief address, singing, prayer, and benediction. The steamers were already at the wharf below the fort as we took arms and blanket rolls and received the order to march.

A picture of the regiment as it appeared that morning would be a prize—at least, it would be highly prized by any of the old members now living. It was indeed a manly sight. A thousand men in red shirts and slouch hats gathered for war. It was not a beauty contest, and the men had not been selected altogether for their good looks—in fact, that had had nothing to do with it—but there were many men of fine features and physique. Of these, Company F had its share. Phil Hamline, Charley Harris, Len Squire, and Marcellus Millikin were a quartet to be proud of, and there were others that came in good seconds.

It was scarcely sixty days since the men of the regiment were about their usual business without inclination, purpose, or training for a military life; since then, they had devoted themselves to getting some idea and proficiency in the new undertaking. One thing was in their favor: most of them had spent some years on the frontier and were in a measure prepared to look out for themselves in an emergency. Nearly all were accustomed to the use of firearms, and many were excellent rifle shots. They faced the future hopefully, mindful of the great object and results they wished to obtain, and not unmindful of the hardships and personal risks that might be involved. Whatever the fortunes of war might bring them, they were resolved to acquit themselves creditably and give no cause for a blush of shame to those they left at their homes or the state they represented.

Colonel Gorman was looking fine that morning in a bright uniform, and his voice rang loud and distinct as he gave the orders that headed us for the western gate, then down past the blockhouse and through the winding ravine to the fort landing. Here the *War Eagle* and the *Northern Belle,* two fine steamboats, were tied to the bank, and a gang of 'roustabouts' were putting tents and other supplies on board. The regiment was here divided into two battalions, one going on board the *War Eagle* and the other, the *Northern Belle.* We were directed to retain our arms as we were to go ashore for a short parade in St. Paul.

Reaching the upper landing, the boats nosed up to the shore and swung with the current until the sides were along the bank, and gang-planks were shoved out. Going ashore, we formed and marched down through the city to the lower levee, where the boats were to meet us. It was still early in the morning, but thousands of people were on the street, and a large crowd followed us. Flags and handkerchiefs fluttered from windows and doors; greetings and good-byes were exchanged between those in the ranks and those on the street. A brief halt at the landing for a last word with any loved ones that might be there—and then we returned to the boats, which were to take us down the river to connect with the railroads. As soon as all were on board, the boats dropped away from the landing and headed down the stream, while the band played, and the cheers from the boat and shore echoed along the bluffs.

The War Eagle, *one of two steamboats that transported the First Minnesota Regiment down the Mississippi to the railheads at La Crosse and Prairie du Chien, about 1865*

Finest body of troops that has yet appeared upon our streets

JUNE-JULY 1861

COMPANY F WAS WITH THE RIGHT WING of the regiment on the *Northern Belle,* which was one of the popular steamboats of that day. Now that we were on the boat which was to carry us to the railroad at La Crosse, positions were assigned to the companies; arms were stacked; blankets and other property deposited near them; and a guard placed over them. Crowds greeted us at every landing and hailed us from the wood yards and other places where the boat did not touch. At Hastings, Red Wing, Wabasha, and Winona—where companies had been raised—short stops were made, and the company hailing from there was allowed a little time on shore.

At Red Wing the boat put in at the lower levee, and Company F went on shore, where all the town seemed to be gathered to greet it. It was a scene to be imagined rather than described, and no words of mine can now—or ever could—properly present it. It must be experienced, by parties at interest, to be understood and realized. Fathers, mothers, brothers, sisters, sweethearts, and friends (possibly a wife or two, but I recall none) were there to say good-bye. It was an aggregation of pathetic, heart-breaking partings, of flowing tears and clinging farewells, which the earnest prayers for "God bless and keep you" seemed to express but feebly. It is certain that in its few years of village life Red Wing had seen nothing like it, though it may have been repeated many times afterward in rapid succession as the war grew, and the demand for men increased.

In the midst of it all, a warning whistle called us to return. We marched on board through a lane of outstretched hands and such a shower of parting words, so kindly uttered, that we went with the fullest assurance that the hearts of the people were with us. The *Northern Belle* backed away from the bank, the crowd on shore cheered, and we answered; then the whistles on the saw mills were blown, and to these the steamer responded as she passed around Barn Bluff.

Well, I went to a quiet place and sat down to think about it. There were some others of Company F doing the same thing—for a short time—close by. It might perhaps have been for a longer time than it was had it not been that Jim Scurry appeared.

Jimmy Scurry was a young 'wild Irishman' who had *scurried* in from *somewhere*—and I think that none of us ever knew where he really did hail from (or cared, if he was ready to fight)—about the time the regiment was filling up for the three years. He was listed in Company F and made himself at home at once. Jimmy was about twenty-five years old, of medium size and build, and of ordinary appearance when quiet, but that was not his normal condition. When talking, he was excitable and, in manner and words, amusing—especially with his facial expressions. He had a way of screwing his mouth around from one side of his face to the other that was both comical and expressive without his saying a word.

He had no personal interest in the parting scenes at Red Wing, for—like the man who did not weep at the funeral—he 'belonged in another parish' and may not have been deeply impressed. Seeing our depressed countenances and being a really kind-hearted fellow, he set himself to the task of relieving the tension of feeling and producing a brighter atmosphere among us. After looking from one to another of the little group and indulging in a series of winks and grimaces, even taking off my hat and turning his head side-wise to look in my face, he said, "Well! Now byes ye do feels bad. Don't ye? Begorra, I thinks ye do. But ye are in for it now and ye might as well laugh as cry, and sure I had rather hear ye." He then indulged in a very hopeful view of the war: that it would not amount to much and would soon be over.

After considerable talk that took our thoughts away from ourselves and relieved us, he began to wonder what had brought *him* "into the war any way." Thought it must be because "there never was a war but there were Irishmen in it." Said he guessed that he had better "staid in the old country than to come over here and, maybe, get killed in a war for the niggers." Then, in a perfectly serious tone and expression, he said, "And, byes, when I think of the old mother over there, be jabbers, I cries, too." And then sure enough he was really crying. This was an unexpected climax—and perhaps as much to himself as to any of us—but it gave him a place in our hearts, and it certainly did not take away respect from either party.

We sailed down through Lake Pepin, and the boys began to assert themselves and observe the scenery. There was much to be seen and enjoyed in a trip on the river in June. At Wabasha, Company I went on shore, where an immense crowd was gathered to bid the boys of that company farewell. After their return, we again passed down the stream. It was almost sunset when we came in sight of Winona, and a prolonged whistle warned them of our coming. Here was another immense crowd of people awaiting our arrival. There was wild cheering, a brass band was playing, and a salute being fired, as Company K went on shore for the last adieux. When they had returned, it was getting dark, and, amid a tumult of cheering, the journey was resumed.

There were no more places at which the boat would stop, and it was some forty miles to the railroad. We were all tired after nearly eighteen hours that had been something of a strain—mentally and physically—and each one sought a place to rest. As we were without coats (and at night it was cool on the river), our blankets were made to serve—as they often did afterwards—and the most of us slept.

It was midnight or later when the scream of the whistle roused us to the fact that our journey by water was almost ended. When the boat touched the wharf, we were ready to go off and marched down the plank by the light of torches in iron 'jacks,' on which powdered rosin was sprinkled occasionally. Middle of the night as it was, we did not expect anyone to greet us, but there was a crowd of people present, who gave us a very hearty welcome. Only the *Northern Belle* stopped at La Crosse, as there were not cars sufficient at that place to transport all of the regiment. The *War Eagle* went on to Prairie du Chien, where there was another road connecting with the one from La Crosse before reaching Chicago. It took some time—dark as it was—to make the transfer to the cars, and meantime the people were gathering, and there were inquiries for this and that one who was supposed to be with us. Several found their friends in Company F, and there was hearty cheering when we drew out of the depot.

We were now in good passenger coaches, and two men occupied a seat. As each man had his gun, blankets, and all of his 'gear'—as some of the farmer boys called the equipment—it took some time to find a place for all of these (and ourselves). We managed, however, to get into positions comfortable enough for sleep, and the weary boys were soon sleeping soundly. After all the strain, it seemed really pleasant to relax into almost any position and forget all—our friends and enemies, the war and all the world—in oblivious, recreative slumber. I slept soundly for hours while the cars rushed onward. It was Sunday morning when we were again conscious of our surroundings and began to 'sit up and take notice' of things by the way.

At every station there were people waiting, who received us with hearty enthusiasm, cheered, and waved their handkerchiefs as we went on. The crowds increased as it grew later in the day. Of course, we understood the great interest of the people was not in the youthful, red-shirted strangers personally, but rather in the state they came from and the cause in which they were going.

Very soon after waking in the morning, we began to realize that we had stomachs, and they were rather empty stomachs. An investigation of the white cotton bags we carried—called haversacks—showed that they also were empty, or nearly so, but there was a partial relief from this condition. A good many of the people who came to the stations brought food with them, and many were supplied in this way. When we could see each other by daylight, the morning salutation was generally "How you look!" or "What a face!" Our faces were unmistakably dirty. At first, there did not seem to be any help for it, but before noon most of us managed to get a wash at the water tanks when there was a stop for wood and water. Railroad engines burned wood in those days, and the filling of the tanks with water was not so quickly done as now.

Somebody provided us a good dinner that day of boiled ham and bread. I am pretty sure that this was not a government ration, for I never knew the government to issue *ham*; and, as it was shipped on the cars, I do not suppose that it was a contribution from citizens on the way. I have been told that it was furnished by the railroad company, but that is as surprising as that the government should do it. From whatever source it came, we ate of it generously and remembered it gratefully.

The two parts of the regiment came together at Janesville, Wisconsin, and ran to Chicago in company. It was past five o'clock when we ran into the Chicago & Northwestern station at Chicago.

We knew that we were to march across the city, and we prepared to make the best appearance we could. Company, regimental, and state pride were always strong in the First Regiment. Every man tried to look and act his best as he got off of the cars and formed in line. It was to be our first appearance before strangers, and there was a vast company assembled. I presume that none of us had ever seen so large a crowd before, and it seemed to have been waiting for us. 'Long John' Wentworth gave us an official welcome. I believe that he was then mayor of the city.[1] He made a patriotic address in which he complimented our "stalwart appearance" and predicted wonderful results from our efforts to "save the nation from the devices of traitors." After his remarks, he marched with the colonel at the head of the regiment across the city.

That march was an ovation. I do not recall another like it in all our service. The sidewalks were blocked with a mass of people, who gazed intently as we passed—sympathy and approval in their looks—but scarcely a word was spoken; the only expression was a vigorous clapping of hands, which seemed to be universal. It was exceedingly appropriate for the day, and I do not know if it was pre-arranged, but it was very effective applause.

There were very complimentary notices in the papers the next morning. Among others, the *Tribune* said:

> Gallant Minnesota deserves high credit for her noble sons and their appearance yesterday. They have enjoyed in their make-up that rare and excellent process of selection and culling from the older states, which has thrown into the van of civilization the hardy lumbermen and first settlers of the wild. There are few regiments that we have seen that can compare to the brawn and muscle with these Minnesotians, used to the axe, the rifle, and the setting pole. There are unquestionably the finest body of troops that has yet appeared upon our streets.

It was dark before we were again in the cars at the Chicago and Fort Wayne station, and somewhat later before we were moving. As on the night before, we stowed ourselves as comfortably as we could and were not long in getting to sleep.

1. After leaving the Democratic Party, John Wentworth was one of Lincoln's allies in the late 1850s; he was mayor of Chicago in June 1861.

We waked occasionally. Some times we were running and sometimes not—as there were frequent stops for wood, water, or a hot box.[2] A 'hot box' was not slang in those days.

All day Monday, June 24, we hurried on our way, and everywhere we were received with a most loyal and encouraging welcome, expressed by cheers and waving flags and handkerchiefs. It was late in the night when we arrived at Pittsburgh, but there was more than the usual crowd present, and their greeting more of a material nature—a large supply of bread, meat, and hot coffee. It was indeed thoughtful and timely, for the supply of ham had been exhausted and a good many had been left to their own devices to get something to eat. We remained here for perhaps two hours. I think it was past midnight before we left, and when we did it was with a supply of coffee in our canteens and something in our haversacks. This was before places of refreshments were provided where hundreds of thousands of grateful soldiers were given a sandwich and a cup of coffee.

Leaving Pittsburgh, we climbed the Alleghenies in the darkness, and, soon after daylight, we were at Altoona and passed down the eastern slope during the early morning. There was a short stop at Huntingdon quite early in the day, and a committee of ladies brought in coffee, sandwiches, and other eatables, which made us a very acceptable breakfast, for which we were grateful. Huntingdon was the home of the 'Duke'—W. H. Wellington—of Company I. Running on to Harrisburg, we went into camp on the outskirts of the city near a canal, which afforded us an opportunity to bathe—and we were all in urgent need of a bath—and exercise a little, otherwise than by the jolting of the cars.

Our camp was near some other regiments that were drilling. We had expected to get clothing, knapsacks, etc., here. These things were not here, and we were told that they had been sent to us at Fort Snelling a few days before we left there. Tents were provided and pitched on the grass in an enclosure, and we tried to make ourselves comfortable. A day's rations were issued. After the tents were stretched, and a bath, and something to eat, we felt like different individuals. This was our introduction to the army tent, and we had a comfortable night's rest in them, so far as it went, but the morning nap had to be dispensed with.

About three o'clock in the morning, we were called out and, as soon as practicable, went on board a train of box and cattle cars and started for Baltimore. These cars were without seats and, withal, dirty. There was a general dislike for the poor accommodations; however, we were now nearing the 'seat of war'—of which we had heard much—and could not expect to go all of the way in first class coaches, and even these dirty cars were preferable to walking. Some of the boys were indignant at being "carried like cattle," but that was when we were new, and cattle cars would have been a luxury a year later.

2. A hot box is an overheated bearing on an axle or shaft.

After crossing the Susquehanna, it was evident that we were in a different country. There were fewer demonstrations of loyalty; the railroad was being guarded; and, as we journeyed towards Baltimore, they almost ceased. It was a close hot day long before we reached that city. It was necessary that we should march across the city. There was a large and undemonstrative crowd waiting when we got off the cars, and it seemed to increase rapidly. Remembering the 6th Massachusetts,[3] Colonel Gorman was determined to take no chances. We were ordered to load our muskets, which we did in the presence of the crowd, putting in a ball and three buckshot and then capping our guns.

There was no demonstration made then or during the march except an occasional cheer for Jefferson Davis from someone on the outer edge of the crowd. Many followed as we marched. I remember seeing one man in his shirtsleeves on a roof with a couple of bricks, but he did not throw them. There was a large gathering still attending us when we took the cars for Washington

At the Washington depot we found another train of box and cattle cars waiting for us, into which we managed to climb—boosting and pulling one another in at the side doors. These cars were less clean than the ones we had left on the other side of Baltimore, and we were more crowded. It was getting late in the afternoon—close and sultry—with standing room only. It did not take the boys of Company F long to decide that their car needed ventilation. This was accomplished in a short time by kicking the sheathing off of the sides. It was but forty miles to Washington, but we were nearly five hours on the way, and, meantime, there came up a violent thunderstorm, and the rain came in on the well-ventilated westerly side of the car. It was moist but it was cooling. It must have been near midnight before we found a resting place for the night

A part of the regiment went to the Capitol building, I believe, and a part found shelter in a church.[4] With the latter was Company F. Coffee and eatables were supplied us through the provision of our representatives in Congress, Colonel Cyrus Aldrich and William Windom. This was our first introduction to these worthy gentlemen, who, during the war, were always thoughtful and helpful to the solders from the state.

The next morning, June 27, we went into camp on Seventh Street—half a mile or so from the Capitol—where we remained until the morning of July 3rd. We had a fine place to camp and found plenty of water at the pumps on the street corners. Washington was then in a primitive state compared with the present: its

3. Union troops arriving by train in Baltimore had to get off at the Calvert Street Station and walk to the Camden Street ("Washington") Station to board cars for Washington. On April 19, a hostile mob killed four soldiers and wounded seventeen of the Sixth Massachusetts Regiment as it made this trek.
4. Four companies slept "in the Washington Assembly Rooms on Pennsylvania Avenue" while the other five stayed "in the old Plymouth Church near by"; Moe, *Last Full Measure*, 34.

streets unpaved; its public buildings in process of erection; and hogs running loose in the streets seemed to be doing most of the scavenger work.

The first thing after getting located in camp was to get a bath. The canal was not inviting, but there was a pump at nearly every street crossing, and at most of these there were large wooden troughs made from logs, which caught the waste water from the pumps. It was here that the boys gathered to scrub off the coatings of dirt they had gathered up in crossing half a dozen states. Stripped to the waist, by plentiful application of soap and water and vigorous scrubbing, they managed to relieve themselves of the accumulations of the long journey. Some of the boys declared that they were several pounds lighter after their ablutions, but that was probably an exaggeration.

It was a rare opportunity for the boys from the country to see the sights of Washington—of which they had often heard. I think as a rule we were disappointed. Aside from public buildings and grounds, there was nothing impressive except the streets, which were wide and very muddy whenever it rained. The dome of the Capitol was then in process of erection; Washington's monument was only a beginning; and the grounds around it were used as a cattle yard. Many of the dwelling houses seemed to be in a dilapidated condition, and a large portion of the population were Negroes.

As soon as camp was fixed, drill hours were announced, and we drilled every day and had a dress parade each evening. When not drilling, we were seeing what there was to be seen in our vicinity, or writing letters home. The few days in camp in Washington were busy days. It was here that letter writing may be said to have commenced, and it caused an immediate demand for paper, stamps, and envelopes. To tell the truth, a good many of us did not have the price of a postage stamp, in cash, and it was a conundrum as to how these things were to be provided. It was here that our two Congressmen came in quite handy. They provided us with paper and 'franked' envelopes. Being Congressmen, they could send letters by writing their names on the corner of the envelope. They did this and gave them to the boys. This no doubt was a use of the privilege not intended when the law was passed, and it may have been a species of 'graft,' but it was all right from the soldier's point of view. We were very grateful to these men who helped us to communicate with our people at home.

Many regiments from different states were then in Washington, and new ones were coming in every day, so that we had an opportunity to compare ourselves with others. As a rule, they were better dressed and better armed than we were, which caused some feelings of discontent in the regiment. Some of the boys wrote home about this, and their letters were published in the home papers; later, there was an official inquiry by the state. There were comparatively but a few of the regiment involved in this, and they were mostly of that class that is habitually 'looking for trouble.' I do not recall that any of Company F were mixed up in this affair, but there may have been a few sympathizers.

We were without coats, vests, or overcoats; many of the shirts had faded to almost any old color; and they had all shrunk very badly. Some of the pants were not of the best material and were soon torn or wore out. It was promised that clothing would be furnished at Harrisburg, but that plan had miscarried, and none came after we reached Washington. Some of the boys were really so ragged as not to be presentable on the streets, but this was true of but a few, and these cases may have been the result of accident or carelessness. Sometimes it was wet and chilly, and, being without coats, we could only protect ourselves by wearing our blankets. Men of other regiments occasionally poked fun at us by calling us 'braves' and 'Indians' and like terms. Some of these things were really humiliating to our boyish pride, when a comparison was made.

There was another thing—which was the real grievance to the most of us— and that was the guns that were given us. We wanted rifles. They were lighter, prettier, and we knew how to use them and were not satisfied with the 'shot guns' we had.

After all of the facts were known, even those who thought they were being 'monkeyed with' were satisfied. The first lot of clothes ordered for us failed to pass inspection, and the second lot was sent to us at the fort the 18th of June and, of course, had not arrived when we left on the morning of the 22nd. I understand that it did arrive at the fort all right and was issued to the Second Regiment. On the whole, it seems to me now that the uniform furnished us by the state— although a makeshift when it was found that nothing else was available—was a good serviceable one for the summer season. If an overcoat had been added, it would have been as good as the Fire Zouaves had.[5] Our black hats were certainly as good as any turban, fez, or 'military necessity' McClellan cap, and our dark blue pants certainly looked as well as any of the 'petticoat breeches' I have ever seen.

It is not so much the cut or color of the uniforms as the kind of men inside of them. The First Regiment was never without its percentage of 'kickers' and 'growlers,' but the dominant spirit was at all times soldierly, and the state and regimental pride all that they should have been; if anything, they might have been a little too prominent on some occasions. There were many interesting incidents connected with our brief camp in the city. We knew we were there but temporarily, and we wished to see the city, and the most of us found opportunity to see all places of public interest. The principal talk was of a 'forward movement.' Horace Greeley and others had raised the cry of "on to Richmond," and it was evident that matters were coming to a climax soon. Every day we expected orders that would send us in to Virginia to join the 'Army of Occupation' then on the south side of the Potomac. One incident of our stay here was a visit from President Lin-

5. Several Union regiments—most notably the Eleventh New York (Fire Zouaves)— adopted the gaudy uniform of France's Algerian infantry troops: bright red baggy trousers ("petticoat breeches") and turban or fez. New York City volunteer firemen predominated in the Eleventh New York, hence the name.

coln to the regiment. He came unheralded—and probably without knowing what
regiment it was—riding in a carriage and accompanied by Mrs. Lincoln. The carriage was soon surrounded by a crowd, where he sat for a time shaking hands and
talking with the boys as anyone might have done.

On the morning of the third of July orders came, tents were struck and loaded
in wagons, and we marched out of camp without knowing where we were going.
There was, of course, much guessing as to where we were going and what was expected of us, and some of us felt slighted that we were not informed. We soon
learned, however, that we were to have nothing to do with the planning of affairs.
The soldierly thing was to do as we were told and allow matters to develop in their
own way. Our march brought us to the Navy Yard, where we boarded a couple of
small steamers and dropped down the river. Some of the boys were suspicious
that they were going to make marines of us, and we were to serve with the gunboats, but all of these fancies ended when, about eight miles down the river, we
turned to the wharf of Alexandria.

We went on shore and formed on the wharf. After a little delay, we were
marched up into the city. We were detained for some time, probably waiting for
someone to decide what to do with us. Alexandria was an old city and was at the
tidewater end of the Chesapeake and Ohio Canal, which made it an ocean shipping point, but it had a decayed look. It was a place with a history, however—in
many ways connected with George Washington. It was from this point he set out
on his mission to the French commander at the mouth of the Allegheny; and it
was here that Braddock organized his expedition. It was here, too, that Colonel
Ellsworth had been killed but a few weeks before.[6]

We found in Alexandria the Fifth Massachusetts Militia doing guard duty.
They were camped outside of the city on the Fairfax road, near the reservoir. After a time, we marched out and pitched our camp near them. They were a neat,
soldierly-looking lot of men, quiet and well behaved in camp—making a favorable
contrast with some of the loosely-disciplined aggregations we had seen since coming to Washington. Our regiment fraternized at once with the Massachusetts men,
and I think there was mutual satisfaction when a little later we learned that we
were to be brigaded together. Just what a brigade was we did not quite understand
at that time, as we had never seen more than one regiment maneuvering under a
single commander.[7]

The sentiment of the people of Alexandria was decidedly 'secesh,' and they
were not averse to letting us know that they had no sympathy with us. While we
were in the city, we observed a number of posters—handbills—giving notice of a

6. A famous Zouave drillmaster, E. Elmer Ellsworth, raised the Fire Zouave regiment. He
was shot May 24 after taking down a Confederate flag flying from an Alexandria tavern.

7. A division consisted of two or more brigades; a brigade of two or more regiments; a
regiment of ten or twelve companies. Normally, a Union division had three brigades; and
a Union brigade, five regiments.

sale of Negroes to be held soon. The status of the Negro in the war was at that time not very well defined. The government had announced its purpose to "restore the Union as it was," and there was no disposition to interfere with the relations of the master and the slave. General Butler had recently declared that slaves were "contraband of war," which—while it settled the cases of those being used for military purposes—did not affect the mass of slave property.[8]

There was considerable talk about the proposed auction of slaves, and some of it was emphasized pretty strongly, too. It was the almost unanimous opinion that there ought not to be any auction of slaves within the Union lines. That auction was not held, but I do not know if the talk of the Minnesota and Massachusetts boys had anything to do with it. I am satisfied that a very large majority of the boys felt then that slavery was doomed. Though none of us had any inclination to pose as abolitionists, I think all were glad when a slave went free. Most certainly so if his owner was a secessionist.

8. General Benjamin Butler refused to return three slaves who came into his camp on May 23, 1861, claiming that citizens of seceded states were not protected by federal law. He called the slaves "contraband of war"—and that persisted as a general term.

We lived an awful long time in three hours

JULY 1861

WE WERE NOW WITH THE ADVANCED TROOPS and considered that we had reached the 'seat of war' and gone to 'the front.' The Fire Zouaves were camped not far away from us and were joined soon by the Eleventh Massachusetts and the Fourth Pennsylvania and some other regiments. Most of them, three-months men. The Fire Zouaves were the famous 'Ellsworth Zouaves.' They wore red shirts similar to ours but had a red fez cap with a blue tassel, instead of a hat.

A detail was sent out each night for picket duty, and we had no doubt but we should take a part in the 'forward movement' that all expected to commence any time. This was our initiation to real picket duty, and it is no exaggeration to say that we felt the importance of our duty and the responsibilities resting upon us. They were very carefully performed. Camp guard—to which we were getting accustomed—was a very tame affair compared with outside picket business—exposed at any time to a stealthy attack in the dark. The danger was not so great as our heated imaginations pictured it, but there was real danger possible, and it was a necessary precaution and the best of training. A week on picket at the front was better than a month of drill in the camp—and theory.

There were constant rumors of raids and attacks—to be made here and there—but nothing startling happened in our immediate front. Occasional parties of mounted men were seen by the outposts, but they were careful not to come in rifle range, and we simply watched.

On Monday, July 8, no trouble having come to us, we started out to look for it. Companies E, F, and K were sent out under command of Lieutenant Colonel Miller to scout the country towards Fairfax Court House. This was our first incursion into the 'enemy's country,' and it was a great day for the three companies, who had never attempted a like service before.

We went out expecting—and prepared for—a fight. If our luck had brought us in contact with any roving band of 'Seseshioners'—as Ed Cox used to call them—on a like expedition to ours, there would have been a tragedy of some sort without doubt. We went as far as Bailey's Cross Roads before we were recalled and saw nothing but a few solitary horsemen, who quickly disappeared when they saw us. This was the farthest advance made by infantry up to this time, and

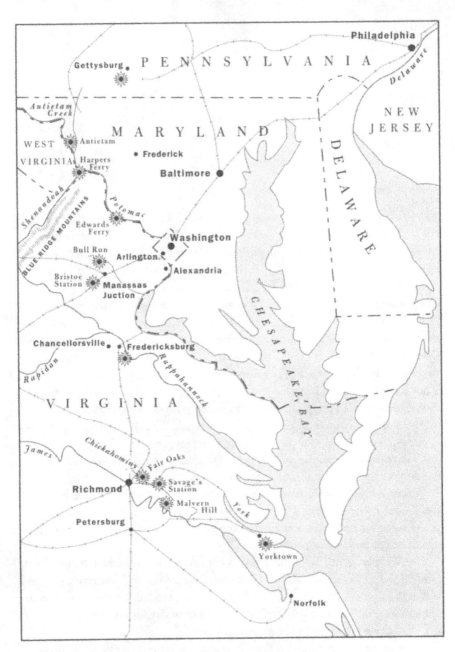

Battle sites of the First Minnesota

there was some fear that we might be cut off by mounted men coming in on roads—and all of these were picketed as we went out.

Lieutenant Colonel Miller had had no more experience in war than the rest of us, but he was a much older man—old enough to be our father. In fact, he had a son in the regiment older than most of us. While not a military man, he was a man of experience and mature judgment in ordinary affairs, and conducted the reconnaissance in good form and advanced until recalled. We returned late in the day, very tired and without prisoners or trophies of war, but it was an excellent day's drill of just the right sort. It would have been wise to send out parties every day and let them go until they came in contact with the enemy; we should have become acquainted in that way and have been much better prepared to deal with them.

When not on picket or other duty, we were drilling, and Colonel Gorman insisted on having a dress parade whenever it was possible. There was as yet not much sickness; there was a ready adaptability to our rude outdoor life by the most of the boys; and there was not even time to get homesick. Besides drill and camp dutes, we did our own washing and—for a few days—our cooking also, but about this time we picked up a couple of 'smoked Yankees'—mulattoes—whom we judged to be 'contraband of war,' and set them doing the cooking for the company under the direction of a non-commissioned officer. The regiment had brought out a good band with it, which gave nightly concerts before Taps and then the little bands of singers in each company were apparently always ready to sing.

The poetic fire seemed to be dying out, but there were occasional flashes of it yet. The sweaty days and the amateur washing—or the nature of the goods—or something else, had made our nice red shirts shrink, and the more they were washed the smaller and shorter they grew—and they were never very long. Some of them also turned almost black and were so short that they would scarcely connect with the waistband of the trousers. It was about this time that I heard one of the minstrels chanting to this effect:

> A man without a wife,
> A ship without a sail,
> But the meanest thing in life
> Is a shirt without a tail.

Soon after our location back to Alexandria, Oscar King, who had been appointed the regimental sutler—that is, had been given the privilege of selling goods to the regiment—came with a stock of goods which he offered for sale. As we were all practically 'strapped,' it seemed to be an absurdity to bring things to sell to us. He issued checks (on himself), sold them on credit to the boys—the same being a lien on the payroll and to be cashed by the paymaster—and then took the checks in pay for his goods. In this way he did a thriving business in the regiment, and besides he did a cash business with men of other regiments. If they had money. Some of the boys declared that a part of the sutler's business was an assumption of the duties of the chaplain, as it included 'spiritual' consolation. As this was for officers only, it was considered an unfair discrimination.

There is a legend to the effect that some of the boys planned to equalize matters by 'acquiring' some of the to-them-prohibited stuff without the knowledge of the sutler, chaplain, or other officers. And that their plans succeeded to the amount of a whole barrel, a part of which was 'issued for immediate consumption,' and the rest *cached* for some future occasion. The future occasion did not arrive until the spring of 1862. It is not reported that King ever got his pay, but as it was a *private* transaction, it is not necessary for us to inquire.

We were in camp here less than two weeks, but there was a great deal crowded into that time. One thing surprised me then—and I have wondered at it since—how some of the boys managed to get so much information as to what was being done and what it was planned to do. Every day had its story of what was to be done on the morrow, but when tomorrow came it failed to 'materialize.' Many fanciful stories were current in camp for the week preceding the march for Bull Run. Of course, they soon failed to pass current and were referred to as 'grapevine dispatches.' There was a fair crop of them at other places, but camp rumors never flourished so bountifully anywhere else as at that first camp near Alexandria. It is certain that someone had a brilliant and super-heated imagination.

On the evening of July 15—when we had about concluded that it was all talk—we were ordered to be prepared to move at a moment's notice. It did not take long to make all necessary preparations. The tents were to be left standing, and a detail of ten men from each company—with a complement of officers—was to remain in charge of the camp. The selection was to be made from the sick and those the least able to march. About every company had that number of sick and ailing. Each man going was to carry his canteen, haversack with three days' rations, and his blanket, besides gun and accouterments. The blanket was rolled lengthwise, and the ends tied together, and it was carried over the left shoulder with the tied ends at the right hip. In the blanket were soap, towel, etc., and also twenty rounds of extra cartridges, which with the forty in the box made a total of sixty rounds to each man. It was all arranged that night who of the company were to remain with 'the stuff.' I think we all found an opportunity to write a few lines to the folks at home, informing them of the contemplated movement and saying a word of farewell.

It is almost surprising—realizing the possibilities of death or wounds as we did—that we marched out so cheerfully the next morning to take our chances. I am quite sure that we all understood the personal risks—perhaps exaggerated them—but I think none of us thought seriously of being defeated. We seemed to feel assured of success.

There were two officers and—I feel quite sure—eighty-six enlisted men who left the camp at Alexandria for the Bull Run campaign on the morning of July 16,

1861. There were not more and might have been one less. The commissioned officers of Company F were: Captain William Colvill, First Lieutenant A. Edward Welch, and Second Lieutenant Mark A. Hoyt. Noncommissioned officers were: First Sergeant Martin Maginnis, Second Sergeant Hezekiah Bruce, Third Sergeant Calvin P. Clark, Fourth Sergeant Henry T. Bevans, and Fifth Sergeant Charles N. Harris. The corporals were: John Barrows, William D. Bennett, Fred E. Miller, Amos G. Schofield, Merritt G. Standish, John Williams, E. Oscar Williams, and James A. Wright. I recall that Lieutenant Mark A. Hoyt was one of the officers of the guard left behind us, and I feel quite certain that Corporal John Williams also was left, as his wife was then in the camp at Alexandria.

For the first time, our brigade — the First of the Third Division — was assembled as a brigade. It was composed of the Fourth Pennsylvania, the Fifth and Eleventh Massachusetts, and First Minnesota. The brigade was commanded by Colonel William B. Franklin; and the division, Colonel Samuel P. Heintzelman — both of the regular army.[1] It seems a little surprising that it had not been got together and drilled and maneuvered as a brigade and division before starting on the march, but that is not the only surprising thing about that campaign. If this had been done a few times, perhaps the brigade commanders might have been able to get more than one regiment in action at a time.

We started early, and it took some time to get fairly moving. The roads were dusty, and the day was very hot. The march was not hurried, and camp was made before night on a ridge covered with a second growth of scrub pines near Fairfax Court House.

Each man carried his rations as issued from the commissary, and they consisted of coffee, sugar, crackers, and salt pork. Each one did his own cooking while on the march. Although the cooks and wagons followed as far as Centreville, they were not with us. None of the boys were expert cooks, but all managed to make a shift at it and get something to eat. Many of the boys had provided themselves with coffee pots — or small pails — to make coffee in and small frying pans to cook meat in, and found them very convenient. A 'mess' with a coffee pot, a frying pan, and a hatchet were pretty well fixed, and with a little experience could always prepare a meal at short notice — provided they had the necessary materials.

There had been no conflict with the enemy during the day, and we rested quietly during the night, sleeping on the ground under the pines, which sheltered us from the dew.

The next morning, Wednesday, July 17, the march was continued. There were frequent halts and delays, considerable skirmishing and some artillery firing, but no real fighting. We took no active part in these affairs, though near enough to hear them and feel a little of the excitement. One of these episodes was an attempt to

1. Franklin and Heintzelman had both been promoted to the rank of brigadier general on May 17, 1861.

capture an outpost on the railroad, which failed, as they ran off as soon as our men came in sight, leaving their dinner cooking.

We bivouacked in the bushes again that night near Sangster's Station on the Orange and Alexandria Railroad. During these two days, we had occasionally passed a few houses near each other and, frequently, single houses in little cleared patches in the woods, but for the most of the way the country was rough and densely wooded, with pines and cedars predominating. Our division had apparently gone across the country and principally on the by-roads.

Thursday morning, the 18th, the march was continued near the railroad, and that morning our regiment led the brigade. As on the previous days, there were frequent halts as the advance felt its way. Finally, the regiment was halted in the woods at the edge of a field, while two companies—A and B, led by Lieutenant Colonel Miller—scouted some miles to the front and left. While waiting for the return of Lt. Col. Miller and his party, artillery firing began to our right and front. As the firing continued and increased, our interest became intense. We were sure a great battle was being fought, while we seemed to be forgotten or lost in the brush. We could hear the distant musketry, also, occasionally.

After an hour or more, the firing gradually ceased, and about the same time the two absent companies returned—they having gone until they had discovered the enemy and retired without attacking, as they were instructed. This was the fight at Blackburn's Ford, in which the advanced division under General Tyler was engaged. Of course, we were burning to know all about the affair, and there were many conjectures, but very little information obtainable. This was the third day out, and, although we had started with three days' rations, we were not accustomed to taking a three days' supply at a time, and the most of us were out of food and hungry.

There had been strict orders issued against foraging, before we marched. There were also some cattle and sheep in the edge of the wood across the clearing, and the sight of these was too much for the hungry stomachs of some of the boys, and a small party went after them. They succeeded in getting some of these, which they skinned and cut up in the bushes, but in coming out they accidentally met Colonel Franklin, who at once began an inquiry.

About the same time, Colonel Gorman rode up, and, when he sensed the situation, opened on the culprits with a lively fire of cuss words, asserting that they were a lot of "born thieves" and a "disgrace to their state and to their mothers." He brought matters to a head by requesting Colonel Franklin to let him make an example of them for the good of the regiment in the future. This was assented to by Col. Franklin, who was probably glad to have the matter taken off of his hands, and rode away. After he was gone, Col. Gorman—who looked very black and uncompromising—said, "Now, —— you, take up that meat and go to your companies, and don't ever disgrace the regiment by getting *caught* in any such scrape again."

It is perhaps needless to say that the boys were extra careful after that not to get *caught*. I do not think that Company F took a leading part in this affair, but there was a fair representation in the following. I saw 'Lengthy' wiping the blood off of his butcher knife with a bunch of leaves, and 'Barb' gave us a piece of sheep, which we broiled and ate with relish. I am not asserting that this was the right and proper thing to do—perhaps it was not—but we were in the enemy's country and hungry. Right or wrong, we were doing just what has been done under like conditions since the days of David.

For the third night we slept under the skies, but instead of twinkling stars there were threatening clouds, and it rained a little that night and in the early morning. Friday the 19th, we marched to Centreville, where all of Heintzelman's division was brought together; there were also many other troops there. What seemed to us a great army—probably 10,000 or 12,000 men—were gathered there, and more were coming. There was considerable skirmishing going on, but we took no part in it—that day or the next—and remained at the bivouac all day Saturday. It was a time of uncertainty and anxious waiting.

We could form but little opinion of how matters stood, when or where the next move would be made, but we felt assured that affairs had reached an acute stage, and that a crisis would come soon. When it did come we had no doubt that we would be 'in it' and share the fortunes of war with the rest, whatever they might be. After the repulse of General Tyler's command on the 18th, some of us may have begun to feel the possibility of a defeat, but I am sure that the feeling—as to results—was one of assured confidence, no matter what might be the fate of individuals. We went to our blankets that evening knowing that we were to be aroused to march before daylight, and having no doubt but that the morrow would bring a battle. These were not pleasant thoughts to retire with, nor calculated to bring soothing reflections inviting sleep, but we did manage to put aside the wicked war and all of its attendant troubles, and slept until awakened to fall in for the march.

I am not sure what time it was when we were called, but it could not have been very long after midnight.[2] My recollection is that the moon was shining when we formed for the march. Soon after forming, it was evident that there was some hindrance to the program of arrangements—whatever it was—and, after several attempts to move on, it was learned that some other troops (Hunter's division) were crossing our line of march—apparently from our right to our left. We—being the flanking column with nearly three times the distance to march—should have had the right of way, but we did not get it, and I have never learned why.

While waiting here, we 'rested at will' and there was a mingling of the boys of other companies, who were getting acquainted, and I think also some from other regiments in the brigade. I recall that there was a feeling of dissatisfaction that we

---

2. It was 2:00 A.M. Hunter's division was ahead of Heintzelman's in the line of march, which was badly delayed.

had been called so much earlier than was really necessary, but there was a general feeling of determination and hopefulness. I think none of us knew at that time that we were to make a long march to turn the enemy's right flank. If we had, ordinary common sense would have suggested that we should not have been wasting precious hours on that hillside. We were all so new to the war—and absolutely inexperienced in battle—that we had no basis for a judgment, and our opinions were only reflections of our wishes.

Just when the coming light of day began to make things distinctly visible, while talking with Charley Harris, he was accosted by William A. Croffut,[3] who was—or recently had been—connected with a Minneapolis paper, but who was there as a representative of some paper for the occasion. After an introduction, there was a short talk with Croffut, who questioned us as to the "state of our minds" at the near-approaching hour of battle. Neither of us could truthfully affirm that we were not somewhat disturbed as to our individual safety for the day—though we both tried to consider the matter hopefully and referred lightly to what might happen. We each left a message for our friends and, in case of "an accident," requested a complimentary obituary notice. After that we shook hands and parted.

Charley got his obituary and—as it was a little premature—lived to read it. A privilege granted to but few. The long, anxious delay had tired us. It was sometime after sunrise, possibly six o'clock, when the road was clear, and we were fairly moving, following after some other division.

We marched for some distance in the rear of other troops over a good road, the Warrenton Turnpike. Soon after crossing a small stream, Cub Run, we turned to the right on a woods road. We—the regiment—were now at the head of the column and were followed by Ricketts's Battery. Behind the battery were the 11th Massachusetts and 5th Massachusetts, completing the brigade. The 4th Pennsylvania, being a three months' regiment and its time being out that day, had remained at Centreville or returned to Washington. It was said of them that they "marched to the rear to the music of the enemy's guns," but their colonel, Hartranft,[4] remained—acting as aide on the staff of Colonel Franklin.

Soon after getting on this by-road, arrangements were made to deploy the first two companies—A and F—if desirable, but it was not found necessary. Our march was now much more rapid than it had been. The day was very hot and,

3. Croffut began the (St. Anthony) *Falls Evening News* in September 1857, with Edwin Clark; they acquired the *Minnesota Republican* the next month and renamed it the *Minnesota State News* in 1859. In May 1861, Croffut left for the *New York Tribune,* which he represented that night he interviewed Wright. George S. Hage, *Newspapers on the Minnesota Frontier, 1849–1860* (St. Paul: Minnesota Historical Society, 1967), 47, 74, 158; Folwell, *Minnesota,* 2:86n3.

4. John Frederick Hartranft received the Medal of Honor for volunteering to remain for the Battle of Bull Run. He ended the war a major general and later served as governor of Pennsylvania (1872–78).

in the woods, on the narrow roads, exceedingly close. From these conditions and our rapid marching, we were sweating profusely, and the march was taxing the men severely. About this time, we began to hear the report of a cannon occasionally, which continued for some time and increased in frequency. This firing seemed to be to our left and rear, and we appeared to be marching away from it.

When still some distance from the ford, near Sudley Springs Church, the artillery firing was heard again and increased to quite a rapid discharge. Musketry firing was also heard. About this time, our regiment was hurried forward at the double quick, and, when we reached the crossing, we were badly winded. As soon as we reached the ford, there was a rush to get water wading in to fill our canteens and pouring it onto our heads. Meantime there was a pretty lively artillery fire going on and intermittent musketry firing.

There was but a short halt at the ford, when we reformed and waded the stream, following the road up a little rise, and then leaving it by turning to the left into a small, open wood. The other regiments of the brigade remained—for a time—on the other side of the stream, but the battery followed us over. During this time, there was rapid firing going on, and we laid down for a few minutes in this wood.

Here we could smell the smoke and hear firing out in the field in front. Near us in this wood was the Second Rhode Island, which had been in the fight and for some reason retired into this wood. They had some of their wounded with them. While here, Frank Bachelor told some of us that he had always had a great curiosity to know how one would feel in battle, but that had all passed now. He expressed himself as "satisfied, now, that his curiosity had carried him too far." I do not recall any other attempt at 'jesting in the face of death' on that occasion— though it was not uncommon as we became more familiar with war. While here, Lieutenant Minor T. Thomas climbed a tree to take an observation, and when he came down reported the enemy retreating. We stopped in this wood but a few minutes, and while here the battery—Ricketts's—had passed to the right of the wood and began firing. When we left this wood we—Company F at least—left our blankets in a pile in the woods, but I do not know by whose order. They were hot and in the way.

Coming out of this wood, the regiment was formed in 'column of division' and marched almost directly to the front. The first division was composed of Companies A and F, and, being small, I was the corporal on the left of the first division. As we advanced to the front—far enough to see over the brow of the hill—I got a glimpse of what was in front of us. There was a valley, half a mile or more in width, through which ran a road and a crooked stream. There were some houses, fields, orchards or groves, clumps of bushes along the stream, and wooded hills beyond the valley. There were some troops down in the valley along the road, and I think some were across the stream. I did not observe that they were firing, and I presume that they were sheltered by the hill from the rebel batteries. There were some guns of the enemy on the hill across the valley—in the edge of the wood— which were throwing shell our way, but I think they were intended for the battery to our right, which was firing in that direction.

The ridge we were then on, I presume, was Buck Hill. There were several regiments along the ridge to our left which had been engaged and, I believe, had driven some of the enemy from that position.

We remained here but a very short time, and, when we moved, marched by the right flank—in fours—obliquely to the right—across the fields down the hill to a road, which we followed across the stream (Young's Branch) for a little distance, then turned to the left into a pasture or field, marching toward the hill on which the rebel battery was situated.[5] Coming up a little rise, we crossed the road and were ordered to form line of battle 'on right by file into line.' While coming across the fields and down the hill, we were subject to the fire of their artillery. But when we reached the low ground we were sheltered from it, and—at the point where we were forming—were not exposed, except to the shells bursting in the air above us.

The distance marched must have been a mile or more. A part of the time we moved at double quick, and there was considerable dodging as the shells screeched over our heads. It was a new and trying ordeal that strained the nerves and hurt our feelings, but I am not aware that any other hurt was done. The formation of the line of battle was at right angles to the direction we were marching and brought the first two companies in front of a wood and but a short distance from it. The advance was led by Company A—Captain Alexander Wilkin—and was followed immediately by Company F—Captain William Colvill—and was made without any deployment of skirmishers or advance guard.

A good many things happened in the 'thin space of time' we were getting into line, and I do not think that I can give them consecutively.

Just as we were beginning the movement, I heard a shouting, the thunder of hoofs, and 'chucking' of wheels behind us. Looking backwards, I saw the artillery coming towards us—apparently over nearly the same route we had come. The horses had their noses and tails extended, and the drivers were lying low over their necks, yelling and plying their whips. It was a splendid, thrilling sight. It was Ricketts's and Griffin's batteries racing into position—and to destruction. Judged by results, they had much better remained on the other side and fired from a safer distance, but 'all the same' the movement was splendidly made. Crossing the stream, they broke through the regiment before it was half formed and separated the first division from the rest of the regiment. I had only time for a glance as we hurried into line, when other things absorbed my attention, and I thought no

5. The road was the Sudley Road, which ran south to Henry House Hill, on which the Confederate battery was located.

more of the batteries until we were later taken to the left to try to recover them—then a wreck on the plateau[6] and covered by the enemy's guns.

Just as I came into line, a mounted officer came from somewhere to the right and halted in front of Company A and inquired if it belonged to an Alabama regiment. Being questioned as to where he belonged, he mentioned the Second Mississippi Regiment, and was invited to dismount—at once. He slid off of his horse on the opposite side—as if to shield himself—but came around his head and gave himself up. There was a young man with Company A, Javan B. Irvine,[7] who had not then enlisted, but had come along out of interest, curiosity, or some other motive, and had kept with the company up to this time. He was not armed, except a revolver, but to him Captain Wilkin gave the prisoner, instructing him to keep him safe. Irvine proved a resolute, trusty fellow, and the next day delivered his prisoner to the authorities in Washington. He proved to be Lieutenant Colonel Boone of the Second Mississippi and was the highest rank of any prisoner taken and delivered in Washington, and, so far as I know, the only commissioned officer brought in.

The most of the regiment—except the two companies, A and F—now followed in support of the batteries. At the same time (possibly a minute earlier or later) there was a commotion in front of the two companies—in the edge of the woods and scarce a stone's throw distant. Orders were given by Gen. Heintzelman, who had just ridden up, to "feel in the woods," and—at almost the same instant—shots began to come from the brush, and now and then a head was seen. As quickly as possible, we turned our old smooth-bores towards the woods and fired. Then 'things broke loose,' and we were immediately enveloped in a dense smoke that for a little time did not permit us to see anything clearly, but bullets were hissing above our heads, and we could see red flashes through the smoke in front of us—at which we directed our fire. Our fire seemed the most effective, and, after a few volleys, the enemy retired into the woods; our firing ceased; and by someone's order we were advanced into the woods.

It was not long after the firing began that I had a very narrow escape from serious wounds or possible death. I will first explain that our waist belts were made of ordinary harness leather and were a little less than two inches in width. They had a single hole in one end and a number of holes in the other, and were fastened with a brass plate with hooks on the under side—and could be adjusted to the size of the person.

A bullet—coming almost directly from the front—struck my belt plate with such force as to knock the breath out of me and tumble me over. At first I am not sure that I thought of anything, but, when I did think, imagined that I was 'done

6. Henry House Hill.
7. "Some months later, Irvine joined the regiment, and, in December 1861, his faithfulness when simply a citizen in sticking to his prisoner was recognized and rewarded by the government by a commission in the 13th regular infantry."

for' and thought of everything—all mixed up. Then I heard someone—I think that it was Oscar Williams—call my name. About that time, returning breath made me feel better and take a more hopeful view of the case, and I rolled over and got on to my feet. When I found that I was not killed, I was so glad that I felt first rate for a time and thought no more about it until the fighting was over.[8]

The force of the blow was sufficient to bend and dent the plate, and left a discolored spot on the flesh as large as the palm of the hand. I have always considered this one of my narrowest escapes. It was a heavy bullet, and had lost some of its initial force, but if it had struck anywhere except on that plate (with the leather underneath it), it would have mangled and bruised and might have gone half through me. An inch or so—to the right or left—up or down—would have missed the plate, and then I would have 'got it' in the 'bread basket,' and it might have proved entirely too much for my digestion.

Lively skirmishing followed, and we were for a time separated from the other companies of the regiment. Our advance was opposed by the enemy, firing from behind trees and other protection, but we advanced in the same manner, drove them back into the woods, and captured a few prisoners—Alabamians. In advancing, we had crossed a fence and went for some distance into the woods. Meantime, though we were making a pretty lively racket ourselves, we heard very heavy firing to our left where the batteries and the rest of the regiment had gone.

We were now brought out of the woods—I suppose for the purpose of connecting with the regiment, as that would have been the natural thing to do.

Several of the boys had been hit while in the woods or at the first firing, but I do not believe that our loss was severe. Henry R. Childs, of the company, while advancing into the woods, was wounded in the head and shoulder, and was left insensible in the bushes. He afterwards 'came to himself' and, finding the company gone, started to follow it. Coming out of the woods to the open ground, he saw an advancing line of the enemy's skirmishers, who ordered him to halt and fired on him, but he ran for it and managed to escape, believing—as he said—in the old adage that 'he that fights and runs away may live to fight another day.'

Coming out of the woods at a point near where we entered, we formed in a close skirmish line and—advancing among the young pines and bushes, which were scarcely as high as our heads—we moved towards the higher ground that was on our left when we first began firing. There was cannonading going on at this time, but only a weak and irregular fire of small arms.

When we reached the crest of the hill,[9] we were greeted with a sharp fire which came from the woods to the right oblique—as we could tell by the smoke, but we could see nothing but an occasional head. We answered this fire and laid down

8. This and the following paragraph are taken from an unnumbered page—"Extra Sheet No. 1—Belongs to the Bull Run Period." The editor placed them here as this seemed the most likely time and place where Wright received this wound.

9. Wright, apparently, refers to Henry House Hill.

there among the little pines along the crest of the hill—loading while lying down and rising to fire. While lying on my right side—ramming a cartridge, which was lodged part way down the barrel—I had my feet crossed to hold the butt of the musket and my left knee bent—when a bullet cut through my pants and across the inside of my left knee, but did no serious damage. It was a pretty close call for a leg. An increasingly hot fire came from the woods on the right front, and a number were hit. A body of the enemy came along the fence as if to get to our right, and we retired to the shelter of the hill.

About this time, Lieut. Col. Miller came—with some of the other companies of the right wing—to our assistance, and we were formed in the road. We then joined with some other troops in an attempt to recover the guns of the batteries. It was successful only so far as it drove the enemy from the immediate vicinity of the guns, and, after suffering severe loss, we retired again to the cut in the roadway.

The wreck of the batteries was at the crest of the hill to our left, surrounded by dead men and horses. It was a position that ought not to have been taken by a battery, exposed as it was to a close fire of artillery and infantry, and, I presume, it would not have been taken if the true condition of things had been understood. The guns were at a point between the two forces and covered by the guns of both sides from sheltered positions, but neither side could maintain a position, where they were, long enough to remove them.

After our retirement to the road, there was a considerable time when matters were comparatively quiet. Then we were advanced to meet a force of the enemy coming out of the woods to our right front, and there was more sharp fighting. We retired to the shelter of the road and soon drove them off—after which there was another period of quiet.

In all of these movements there was more or less of confusion and disorder. We had not reached a stage of discipline when anything else could be reasonably expected. Especially of men under fire for the first time and subjected to severe losses. We were human, and, therefore, we were all more or less excited, confused, and uncertain as to what had been accomplished and what more we were expected to attempt. A good many had left to care for the wounded, and others had gone to the stream to get water, for we were all suffering greatly from the heat, thirst, and exhaustion. When it is remembered that we had but little rest the night before; that the morning march of 12 miles had been a severe test to our powers of endurance; that our subsequent movements had been hurried—down hill and up—over fences and through woods; also, that we were under the severe mental strain of battle, which is more exhausting than physical action—then our condition can be partly comprehended.

We were really in a pitiable condition that under more favorable circumstances would have called for immediate relief. There did not seem to be a breath of air stirring; the early afternoon sun was shining directly into the roadway; we were sweating profusely and suffering from the heat—clothing torn and disordered—

and our faces smeared with powder and dirt. We cared nothing for *looks* just then, but the *feel* of the situation was very unsatisfactory as we waited to see what was next on the program.

Sherman had not then defined war in a single brief sentence, but I heard the one important word in it uttered several times that day—suggested, no doubt, by the day's experiences. We had read that 'to make war was to be hungry and thirsty'; that it 'was to suffer and to die'; that it was 'to obey.' We had been trying to do all of those things and assumed that we were getting 'about what was coming to us' and we naturally wondered if there was any more 'coming.' I think that all there realized that we had been hit pretty hard, but I do not think that any of us supposed that we were beaten. At least I recall no suggestion to that effect.

We remained for some time in this position, when we were disturbed by some cannon shots that came from the right and a little to our rear. At first we supposed that it was some of our batteries that did not realize that we were so far to the front—but a little observation showed a line of battle advancing on our right flank. There was great anxiety to know if they were friends or enemies. About this time, there was a dash of cavalry coming out of a crossroad to our right, but it was repulsed before it reached us.[10] The conviction now began to assert itself that those fellows coming in on our right were enemies and, if so, entirely too strong for us to contend with.

Lieutenant Colonel Miller was the highest officer present with that portion of the regiment, and he gave the order to retire and indicated the direction—directly to the rear. In leaving the position in the road, we observed that everybody seemed to be going, and, in crossing a little rise of ground, we were fired on by some of the advance skirmishers of this new force, but I do not think that there was a shot from those with whom we had been contending.

This new enemy—we then supposed—was the advance of Johnston's forces from the Shenandoah Valley, but we have since learned that it was the last of them, under command of Kirby Smith, and that we had been fighting Johnston's forces all day. And that this force had got off of the cars at Gainesville and marched towards the firing at an opportune time. Without them, the story of Bull Run might have been a very different one.

After passing this rise, we were sheltered from this musketry fire, but the battery off at the right was throwing shells almost directly down the little valley.

After crossing the stream, which was neither deep nor wide, we started to go up the hill to the point where we had come in, and were again exposed to the batteries which fired upon us going down. There was much haste and confusion going up the hill. It was a 'go as you please' until we reached the top, where we were out of the range. A hospital had been located at the Sudley Church; an effort had

10. Jeb Stuart's Confederate cavalry charged the Fire Zouaves and hurled them back but did not advance farther, which may be why Wright mistakenly thought they were repulsed.

been made to get the wounded there; and both of the surgeons—Stewart and Le Boutillier—were there. Some of the wounded were being assisted up the hill at the time, and I helped to carry Joe Garrison on a blanket a part of the way. At the same time, Corporal Schofield was being helped by some of the others of the company.

After we reached the top of the hill,[11] I think there was but very little more firing. There were portions of a number of regiments and some batteries there, with guns in position for firing, but there did not seem to be anyone that knew just what to do. As many as possible of the regiment were assembled here, and an attempt made to find the other companies. After a little delay, we were directed to the ford across Bull Run, where we found what remained of the left wing of the regiment.

It was the first time we had seen or been in close connection with them since forming in line at the beginning of our fighting, and we now learned something of their part in the fight. It had been a terrible experience. Following Ricketts's Battery—with the left very near the guns—they had come into line and faced the woods. At almost the same time, they saw a force coming out of the woods, and there was uncertainty as to their identity, which caused them to hold their fire—until fired upon. Almost the same time, they received the fire from the batteries which Colonel Franklin says were only about 1,000 feet away.

This was a very destructive fire—killed and wounded many men of the regiment and practically disabled the battery, as it was able to fire but a few rounds. The regiment returned this fire with such effect as to drive back this force, but their position was untenable on account of the enemy's artillery. They were obliged to retire to the shelter of the hill, which position they maintained until ordered to withdraw, but—in the meantime—they took part in one or two other attempts to recover the guns. These attempts were failures—but all attempts of the enemy were also failures. If we could not remove the guns, neither could they so long as our forces remained in the shelter of the hill to protect them.

It was after we had reached the top of the hill and were nearly ready to march away, when a large force came out of the woods and charged on the deserted guns, swinging their hats and cheering. Whether these were some of the troops that had been there during the fighting—or some of those who had just come up—of course, I do not know. This was just at the time that the battery near us—Arnold's, I think it was—limbered up to leave. I saw no other display of their infantry, except those that were coming across the fields on our right.

When we left the position of the hill, both of the surgeons remained with the wounded and fell into the hands of the enemy. This was voluntary on their part.

When we joined the regiment on the other side of the stream, we found several other regiments—or parts of regiments—there, but all were without orders. About this time, Governor William Sprague of Rhode Island joined his regiment

11. Wright apparently was referring to Buck Hill.

and brought the news that our forces were retreating. It was decided by him—or someone else—to return to the bivouac at Centreville.

I do not know the time, but I judge it to have been between four and five o'clock in the afternoon. It was not far from 12 o'clock when we first came under fire. If it was four o'clock when we recrossed Bull Run, then it was probably three or later when we left the cut in the road where we did the last fighting. This is the best estimate that I can make of the time, and, if correct, we were confronting the enemy—within musket range—three hours or more. If that was all, then we *lived an awful long time in three hours.*

When getting ready to march, Colonel Gorman offered the regiment for service as a rear guard, but Governor Sprague claimed this for his regiment. This brought on a little discussion as to which was the senior in rank—which involved the command of the troops present. They were unable to agree, but Sprague settled it—at least to his own satisfaction—by claiming his rank as governor.[12]

With this matter settled, we started for Centreville with the Rhode Island regiment in the rear and ours next in order. In this manner we marched until overtaken by a body of our cavalry—when we were considerably broken up by their hurriedly passing through us, obliging us to take to the sides of the road.

When we reached the main road, we found carriages, hacks, wagons, and artillery on the road, and all moving—or trying to move—in the same direction we were. Some were stalled and some were broken down. There were frequent collisions and several wrecks, and we saw one runaway—a pair of horses attached to a hack. Of course, it was not possible to march in regular formation under such conditions, and we were too tired to attempt more than was necessary and made our way the best we could and as fast as we could. At one point, the road passed over a hill that was in range of the enemy's artillery across Bull Run, and they were throwing shells in that direction. This added to the confusion and hurried matters, also, along that stretch of road.

It was getting dark when we reached Centreville and went to the place where we had spent Friday and Saturday nights and where some wagons had been left—with regimental and company property and some Negro cooks. I think that about one-half of those who had gone out of there that morning had returned. Not more. Where were the rest? At that time, we had no definite knowledge of the others and were anxious to learn the fate of absent ones. We sat or laid down on the ground, and for a little time there were inquiries about this and that one—when and where they had been seen last—but nature asserted herself, and it was but a few minutes before the majority were sleeping soundly.

12. Sprague was at Bull Run issuing orders and may have had an ex officio rank, but he is not listed as commanding either the First or Second Rhode Island. Frank J. Welcher, *The Union Army, 1861–1865: Organization and Operations,* Vol. 1, *The Eastern Theater* (Bloomington: Indiana University Press, 1989), 637; Robert Hunt Rhodes, ed., *All for the Union: The Civil War Diary of Elisha Hunt Rhodes* (New York: Orion Books, 1991), 26–41.

It seemed but a moment—though it might have been an hour—when we were awakened and found a supply of coffee and crackers awaiting us. I do not know as I had realized that I was hungry, but the smell of that coffee made it evident at once. We drank an unknown quantity of the coffee, but it was not a small quantity, and we felt greatly refreshed and strengthened. We also filled our canteens. It was now quite dark and threatening rain, but we again laid down to sleep.

It was not long after this that we were again called up and told that we were to march soon. This was a surprise to us, as we expected to spend the night there. No one knew where we were to go. It was now raining a little and very dark. We had had no opportunity to recover the blankets we had piled up in the woods, and the rain and night air were chilling. I do not know what became of the blankets we left, but I have been told by a Massachusetts comrade who was in the field hospital at Sudley Church that our surgeons sent and had many of them brought in to lay the wounded on.

When we fell in, we marched down to the Warrenton Turnpike and formed on the left-hand side of the road, and we began to consider the probability of our going back. Up to that time, I do not think there was any expectation of a general retreat. I do not know who organized the order of march, but it was a pretty complicated arrangement for a dark night. In the main roadway there was a line of wagons and a line of artillery, side by side, and a line of infantry marching in fours on either side. Our regiment with others was on the left, and on the right was the Jersey Brigade, a body of troops which had not been actively engaged. I knew that the New Jersey men were on the opposite side of the road, and that there were wagons between, but it was too dark to see.

Everyone who made that terrible march knows that 'confusion worse confounded' was *produced* in large quantities that were painfully evident to all of the senses but seeing. When we started on the march, it was raining hard and so dark that you could not recognize the comrade with whom you touched elbows. It was, I judge, ten o'clock or later.

Since leaving the bivouac 20 to 22 hours before, we had marched 25 to 30 miles, under the scorching heat of the mid-summer sun, much of the way through smothering clouds of pulverized clay, which covered our clothing and filled the eyes, ears, nose, and mouth, and was breathed into the lungs. Added to these were the excitement and mental strain of the battle and the bitter, humiliating results: defeat and disaster. To all of these was now to be added another march of 25 miles or more. None of us—of the ranks—really knew where we were going or what distance it was intended to march. All we actually knew was that we were headed back over the road we had come, and that it was dark as Egypt and raining diligently.

When this 'mixed multitude' of men, mules, horses, and wheels was set in motion, the situation was intensified. Wagons collided or got off the pike into the ditch; teams balked, and drivers swore and called for assistance; we of the infantry blundered along the sides of the road as best we could—bumping into each other and everything else bump-able—tired beyond all previous experience and in anything but an amiable frame of mind. After vain attempts to keep some kind of a formation by touch and by calling each other's names or the company letter, all efforts in that direction were given up, and we just plodded along in the pouring rain the best we could.

When the rain began to fall, it was cooling and refreshing, but—as it saturated our scant clothing and poured over us in a continuous shower-bath fresh from the clouds—it became the reverse of agreeable and added much to our discomfort. The accumulations of dust on the road became sloppy mud very quickly, and the gathering water ran in little streams across the road or along the sides and collected in the depressions. Unable to see where we should go, we waded through these—often over our shoes in water and mud. The day's operations had left a liberal deposit of dust, sand, and gravel in our shoes, and the addition of water increased the discomfort and added to the abrasions of our tired, blistered feet.

To start on such a march, under such conditions, after the efforts of the day, was a great undertaking. While the darkness lasted, it was each man for himself. When men felt that they had gone as far as they could, they turned aside in the woods and, finding a place where they could rest against a tree or stump, went to sleep. When awakened by the pitiless, drenching rain—as soon or later they were—they roused up by sheer will power and forced their stiffened, benumbed limbs to carry them onward.

Personally, that is the way I covered the distance between Centreville and Fairfax. I did not know where I was or what the hour of the night when—after a little debate with myself—I decided to rest awhile and think the situation over. With a comrade, I went a little ways into the bushes, curled up, and went to sleep without doing any thinking.

Daylight was coming, and the rain had almost ceased, when I awoke. We heard voices and knew that men were passing. Satisfying ourselves that they were not enemies, we went back into the road—though so stiff and sore that it was with difficulty we could walk. Groups of men, here and there, had made fires and were boiling coffee, and others were moving along. Going a little ways, we found two members of the company and several more of the regiment at a fire, making coffee in their tincups and little pails. Of course, we joined them at the same occupation, realizing that we were hungry.

After drinking a pint or so of strong, hot coffee and eating crackers and salt pork, we felt refreshed and continued our march. Many groups were marching, and others were halted—cooking—and we soon found others of the company and regiment and, naturally, we kept together. We soon came to Fairfax, where we found some of the wagons and artillery. From Fairfax, we took the road to Alexandria where our tents and the detail had remained. It was nearly twelve miles, but we made the distance before noon.

Here there was food and drink and a warm welcome from those who had kept the camp. Some had come in before us, and others arrived later. Some water to wash our begrimed faces and something to eat, and, meantime, there was a general inquiry for the missing ones. In my tent, I was so fortunate as to have left a blanket, and I had a shirt and some underclothes, but I did not stop to change then. In a very few minutes, I was sleeping. I had slept, seemingly, but a little time when I was 'stirred up' and told that an order had come to move.

It was now well along in the afternoon, and more of the company and regiment had come in. Tents were struck and—with all the other company material—were loaded into the wagons, and we fell in for the march—we knew not where. The rain had ceased during the day, but as night came on it was threatening again. As we passed through Alexandria, it seemed impossible that it had been but a fortnight since we first marched through the city. It seemed like months.

When we reached Fort Runyon, near the Virginia end of the Long Bridge, it was getting dark and raining hard. Here we found more of the company and regiment, and there were glad greetings for some that it was feared were dead or in the hands of the rebels. I do not mean by that that there was anything like rejoicing in the general sense of the word. We had marched out in confidence, expecting a victory, but we had suffered a defeat which had wilted our pride—very much as the great physical efforts had exhausted our strength. We were sincerely glad the price in blood was no greater.

After a short halt, we crossed the Long Bridge and marched to Pennsylvania Avenue. Here there was another halt. It rained furiously, and the only shelter we had was an iron picket fence. We got a splendid shower-bath, but we had had all we wanted of that kind.

After what seemed a long time, we were admitted to some churches for the night. Food and coffee—plenty of it—was soon brought in. It was now getting quite late, and we could take our choice of sleeping on a seat or on the floor between two seats; only, there were not seats enough for all, and some must take the floor anyway. I was too tired to be particular, and gratefully glad to find shelter from the storm anywhere, and turned in on the pulpit floor. Before retiring that night, I found an opportunity to write a few words to my mother, and I think that evening or the next morning most of the boys managed to let their people know that they were still alive.

The next morning, Tuesday, July 23, the storm had ceased, and we again occupied the camp on Seventh Street out of which we had marched on the morning of July 3. It did not seem possible that but twenty days had elapsed since we had left it. Neither did it seem possible that the 800 depressed, ragged, mud-stained, and foot-sore men who limped into camp and began the work of pitching their tents could be the same ones who had gone out from there less than three weeks before. We were a pretty hard-looking crowd. The blow had fallen with a heavy hand, and we felt its stunning effects. Mechanically, we went to work, but the interest grew as our work progressed.

Before noon, the tents were up, most of the boys had found another shirt in their knapsacks (or washed the one they wore), taken a bath, and presented a better appearance. Tents were stretched, rations were drawn, and the sun was shining and matters began to assume a brighter hue. Our clothing had been a subject of complaint before we marched, and it was much more so now, but it was the result of the battle that lay nearest our hearts.

The recent battle and the fate of our missing comrades, which we did not then definitely know, was the one subject of conversation. I recall an expression of one of my tentmates as we sat on the ground in the tent eating our dinners. "Well," he said, "anyhow, it does seem good to have a roof over our heads and a visible means of support." There was another thing connected with that, the second day after the battle, that has since caused me to feel a sincere pride in the company. Every man not killed, wounded, or captured was 'present or accounted for' at the evening roll call, with his gun and equipments.

The poet Walt Whitman, and others, have written profusely and, I think, unfairly and ignorantly, of the return of the army to Washington. A specimen of his statements is sufficient to indicate their absurdity. He says: "Where are the vaunts and proud boasts with which you went forth? Where are your banners and your bands of music, and your *ropes to bring back your prisoners*? Well, there is not a band playing, and there isn't a flag but clings ashamed and lank to its standard."

A grown man of very ordinary capabilities ought to have known better. We did go out with confidence, but I heard no boasting by the soldiers themselves—but I do not claim to know what noncombatants may have done or said. There were *no ropes*, and I do not suppose that any soldier ever had a *thought of providing one*. Our flag was not in any sense ashamed of us, nor we of it. The colors had been bravely borne. All of the color guard but one had been wounded, and the flag itself riddled with bullets, but it was dearer to us than ever, and its display brought neither censure nor discredit to us or it. Every man of the company—and, I believe, of the regiment—had clung to his musket as a man overboard would cling to a life preserver.

It is not my purpose to comment on the strategy or tactics at Bull Run or elsewhere, or the criticism that followed, but we know now that while the plan may have been good, it was most bunglingly executed, and later experience has shown the unwisdom of sending in a regiment at a time to be beaten in detail. It was really an absurd thing to do. I have often thought, too, what a glorious opportunity there was to have sent a brigade around our right flank at the time we were first engaged and taken their line and batteries in reverse. It seems now that it would have been entirely feasible and must have wrecked Beauregard's army. But it is useless to 'cry for spilled milk' and—as ours was badly spilled—I leave this part of the subject without further comment.

The official loss of the regiment as I find it is: killed 42, wounded 108, and missing 30.[13] Many of the wounded and the missing were prisoners. I do not know the exact number in the regiment on the Bull Run Campaign. If we set it at 900, then the total loss of 180 men was twenty percent of the whole number. The strength of Company F when it left the state was 3 officers and 96 enlisted men. When we started on the campaign, Lieut. Hoyt and ten enlisted men were left at the camp. There were 2 officers and 86 enlisted men went out in the company. The loss of the company was: 8 killed or died of their wounds; wounded, 12; and missing, 3—for a total of 23. The total casualties were 23—more than twenty-five percent.[14]

Sergeant Charles N. Harris was one of the wounded. A rebel bullet shattered his shoulder at Bull Run, and he was captured and taken to Richmond. He recovered, was paroled, sent home, and finally exchanged. It was supposed at the time that he was dead, and, under that belief, his obituary was printed and funeral services were held. It was thus that he had an opportunity to read of his own funeral.

Company F was not 'spoiling for a fight' when it started for Bull Run or on any other occasion, but it meant business, as it always did when confronting an enemy, and did its level best to make things interesting for its 'friends, the enemy.' It did not 'move as steadily as if on parade' or 'march undismayed in the face of batteries' or 'smile at bursting shells'; but it did try to march wherever it was ordered; we were all more or less *scared*—and in my case it was *more*; we *dodged* the shell on the hillside both going and returning; and all through the fight we fully realized that it was a serious business, and I have no doubt we 'looked it.' In a word, we fully understood that life and limb were in danger, and the fact impressed itself upon us—much as it would on anyone under like circumstances.

I desire only to add a few words from the official reports that have a bearing on the matter. Colonel W. B. Franklin of the regular army, who commanded the brigade, said:

> The First Minnesota Regiment moved from its position on the left of the field to the support of Ricketts' battery and gallantly engaged the enemy at that point. It was so near the enemy's lines that friend and foe were for a time confused. The regiment behaved exceedingly well and finally retired from the field in good order.

I may add, without injustice to any other command, that no other regiment in the brigade or division received such high commendation, and some were directly censured.

13. These casualty figures do not match those given in Moe, *Last Full Measure*, 63.
14. For Wright's descriptions of the members of Company F who were killed or wounded or captured at Bull Run and the Peninsula Campaign, see Appendix.

All quiet along the Potomac

JULY-OCTOBER 1861

WHEN COMPANY F, with the rest of the regiment, was again located in the camp on Seventh Street, it turned at once to the daily duties of the soldier in camp, but the shadow of the battle continued upon it. Notwithstanding our efforts to rise above it, there was a funereal depression over the camp; the names of the absent comrades were most frequently on our lips; and our thoughts would continue to dwell on the terrible tragedy of Sunday that had involved a fourth part of our number in the casualties of battle.

The papers were filled with exaggerated accounts of the battle and of what followed, and of possible attempts to capture the capital, and of dismal forebodings for the future. It was but natural the possibility of an attack on Washington should be a subject of speculation, and, for a day or two, it was reasonably supposed to be in some danger, but beyond that time such was not really the case. When the attack did not come promptly, the capital and our camps were considered reasonably safe, and all acute apprehensions ceased.

It was evident to us then that if we must fight them again—and we knew we must, sometime—we could not hope for more favorable conditions than would be offered with them as the attacking party. They had promised in their high-sounding style, if we attempted to 'invade the sacred soil' that we would be 'welcomed with bloody hands to hospitable graves'—and had given us a sample of that sanguinary sort of reception at Bull Run. Now we were at home again and ready to reciprocate in kind to the best of our ability.

I believe the plain truth to be that, when the fighting ceased Sunday afternoon, they were in no better condition to continue it than the Union troops were. It is certain that they made no attempt at pursuit worthy of the name nor any real effort to reap the legitimate results of the great victory they claimed later. It is true that they had the semblance of victory, but it was—in reality—a drawn battle which left neither party in a condition to immediately resume hostilities. It is true that the Union army abandoned the field, and that demoralization followed; but it is also true that its opponent was left paralyzed and too demoralized to follow. The result encouraged and inflated the South, as it made things look *easy*, but otherwise it did not help much. This result was indeed bitter medicine to the North, and humiliating to its pride, and we in the army felt it keenly, but it also revealed the magnitude of the contest, made the situation plain, and aroused it to put forth efforts commensurate to the work to be done.

With an opportunity to wash, rest, get something to eat—and with freedom from attack—we began gradually to think less of our recent bitter experience and more about ourselves—and here, unfortunately, there was a lack of encouraging conditions.

There was complaint before we went into Virginia about the lack of clothing. Our quartermaster, Lieutenant George H. Woods, had been sent back from Fairfax on July 17 by Colonel Gorman with instructions to procure a supply of clothing and told not to return without it. When we returned to Washington, we understood that he had received nothing but promises, and, as these had been coming since some time before we left the state, it was disappointing and unsatisfactory. Our clothing had been bad before we went to Alexandria and now after three weeks of active campaigning, ranging the forests and fields, in dust, rain, and mud, it was much worse. Originally, our outward clothing had consisted simply of a hat, shirt, pants, and shoes supplemented by an Indian blanket and was all we had ever had but a change of shirts. Now there were many who did not have the extra shirt or any means to get one, and whose pants would have been more appropriately placed on a scarecrow. We were told that Quartermaster General Montgomery C. Meigs—having made three attempts to supply the regiment (which had failed because they had been gobbled up by some other regiment)—had given orders that a new lot be boxed and billed direct to the regiment from the manufactory. I believe that something of that kind was done before we received anything, which shows the great pressure for supplies in those early days of the war.

There was some feeling also about the non-appearance of the paymaster and the quality of the rations. We were living on salt meats, crackers, and coffee, and perhaps we ought to have been glad to get even those, but, like the Israelites in the wilderness, we wanted fresh meat and vegetables. If we had had money, we would have willingly bought those things, but "of silver and of gold we had none." There were thousands of 'beef critters' herded in the suburbs and in the open grounds about the base of Washington's monument, and we could not understand why we should not have some of them to eat.

We did not know all of the "whys and wherefores," as one of the company phrased it, but we felt that we had not been properly and intelligently handled at Bull Run, which had shaken our confidence in our general officers, and now it seemed apparent that there was something lacking in the clothing and commissary departments. Conditions seemed adverse and discouraging, and perhaps we did not meet them at once in the proper spirit. A better day was near at hand and, I presume, it would have come just the same and just as soon if we had not worried and 'growled' about it. However that may be, in our inexperience we chose to exercise a soldier's privilege and 'grumbled some,' which seemed to relieve us whether it expedited matters or not.

The adjutant general of the state, General John B. Sanborn, came on to Washington to inquire into the condition of the regiment and use any influence the state might have to get the regiment properly clothed, and provide for the sick and wounded. It was about this time, too, that letters began to come from the homes of the boys, bringing messages of sympathy and commendation, which was just the kind of tonic fellows in our situation needed. It was about this time, too, that we received rations of fresh beef and fresh bread, and also changed the old Harpers Ferry muskets for new Springfield rifles, caliber 58. All of this was encouraging, and within a few days there came a supply of pants, shirts, shoes, and blouses.

The issuing and adjustment of these made interesting employment for a time, for all of our spare hours from drill and dress parades. (A good many had to be excused for lack of a shirt or a pair of shoes or pants.) Some of the boys asserted that these garments were all 'warranted to shrink to a small man and stretch to a large one,' but the guarantee was not considered good. After our experiences with the red shirts (the new ones were white), it was generally considered that the services of a tailor would prove more satisfactory. All of the tailors in the company found work for a few days, and, in many cases, it was 'every man his own tailor.'

Matters pertaining to the complete outfit of the regiment now progressed rapidly. Among other things, a wagon train was provided for it, consisting of thirty wagons, and the enlisted 'wagoners' and others who were detailed to assist them got busy organizing the transportation. With the strange and but half-trained mules, it was no small job to 'lick them into shape' and at once make them a reliable and efficient means of transportation. The regiment, however, was able to furnish plenty of men who had had experience with long-eared quadrupeds and who in reasonably short time had their mules in such a state of docility that four or six of them were easily steered by a single line attached to the bridle of the 'near leader.' At first this method was an experimental matter, and seemed unsafe and hazardous. In time it became a science and was performed by the professional mule skinner in a highly artistic manner with a great degree of certainty. Seated on the 'hurricane deck' of the 'nigh wheeler,' the 'professor' piloted his wagon through flooded streams, over muddy roads, and among trees, stumps, and rocks with surprising skill. It was all done by a pull and a haw, a jerk and a gee and, in emergencies, a vigorous application of the 'black snake' accompanied by explosive and strongly-emphasized seafaring language.

John Brown (not 'Old Osawatomie') was the enlisted wagoner of Company F, but he had gone out with the company to Bull Run and had been wounded and was not yet in condition to take an active part in the 'breaking in.' But he was on hand in good time and before his time was out had been promoted to a wagonmaster and frequently had charge of important trains. I believe that it was Alvah and Chris Eastman that were detailed to serve as teamsters from Company F.

It was Friday, August 2, that we pulled down our tents on Seventh Street and started out of Washington to the westward. Rumor had it that we were to go to some point up the river in Maryland. After a march of a few miles—getting well out of the city—we went into camp at Brightwood. This was a pretty place with plenty of shade and much more desirable for a military camp than the city, except the water supply was not so convenient as the pumps in the city, but the water may have been better.

I think that it was the next day that the paymaster came, and we received our first pay, for two months. This payment was in gold and we—the enlisted men—were paid at the rate of $11 a month, and it goes without saying that we were glad to get it, for I doubt if the boys had left the state with a dollar per capita in their possession.

The amount actually received was much less than $11 as—under the allotment system—before we had left the state, arrangements had been made by which such an amount as the soldier designated was reserved and paid directly to the parents or those dependent upon him. The sum of all of the money thus assigned was sent to the agent in the state, who made the distribution to the families of the soldier. In this way, a certain specified sum was insured to those at home and greater safety provided for its transmission. Many of the boys in the company in this way sent home from $6 to $8 a month and, thus, while serving their country in the army, were at the same time helping their families at home to pay the war prices for whatever they had to buy.

In my own case, I allotted all but $3 a month to my mother, who, as I well knew, needed it much more than I did, and whose prayers were following me day and night. Who can say but it was in answer to her prayers that I lived to see the end of the war? I have often felt a distinct impression that such was the case. It will thus be seen that I served through the first three years for less than ten cents a day and had all of the money that I really needed. A little cash was always convenient, but a large amount was not necessary.

In the army or out of it, a fairly decent suit of clothes and a few dollars in the 'inside pocket' make a man feel better satisfied with himself—and other people better satisfied with him—on general principles. It had something of this effect on the boys of the regiment generally. The improved rations, the change in camp, the cash, and the clothing certainly tended towards an improved feeling. Perhaps the most potent factor of all was that these things were evidence that we were not forgotten by the state that we represented, and that it had sent an official a thousand miles to look into the condition of things.

It was a matter of trivial importance, but I should not leave the camp at Brightwood without a reference to the scare we had there. Something happened that made us grab our guns and rush out with 'each particular hair on end like quills of the fretful porcupine.' In the dead stillness of the night, when all the sentries were quietly sleeping, there was 'something doing' very suddenly and very vigorously. It was too dark to see anything, but there was a wild commotion in the wagon camp—a ripping, tearing, rending sound, and galloping feet through the camp, and crashing through the bushes. It was an unintelligible combination of sounds—human, animal, and the destruction of things material, and noise enough for a hundred charging horsemen. I presume that the first thought of everyone was that the camp was attacked by the Black Horse Cavalry, Gilmore's Gang, or Harry White's Raiders, or all of them together.

At first there was confusion and calls of "What is it? What is it?" Then there was a call to "Fall in!," and about the time the boys 'came to' enough to sense things and were trying to find a place to form ranks, someone called out it was all right, "only them —— mules broke loose."

That is what it proved to be: a stampede of the mules. Some of the half-broken half-breeds, who were presumably disgusted with the restraints of harnesses and halters, had started a little secession movement of their own. Whatever may have been the incentive—freedom or fright—some of those mules, which were anchored to the wagons and trees, had 'parted their cables' and drifted off into the darkness and bushes.

It took a good portion of the next day to hunt up the vagrants and return them to duty. No great harm was done, and it was all over in about a minute, but it was a genuine scare while it lasted. It was also a prolific source of jokes and amusement for some days after, but there was nothing in the least amusing about it until the cause was understood. A good many unauthenticated and questionable stories were given currency in the camp the next day about the way some of the fellows conducted themselves, and the remarks they made. But we shall leave them to rest with other unrecorded incidents of our soldier life.

While at Brightwood, I think it was, Dr. John H. Murphy joined us, but I am not sure that he was ever credited to the regiment. I think that he came rather as a contract or volunteer surgeon to fill the place of one of our regular surgeons, Stewart or Le Boutillier, who remained and were captured at Bull Run. Dr. Murphy I had met in Red Wing before the war began, and I believe that he was a brother-in-law of Dr. William W. Sweeney.[1] Dr. Murphy was a jolly good-natured fellow who always had a good word and a funny story ready. It was about this time that I began to be sent occasionally with the sick at 'sick call,' and it was often amusing the way he jollied some of them. Withal, he was a good surgeon, and we were sorry when he was commissioned to the Fourth Regiment and left us.

Dr. Daniel W. Hand was commissioned as assistant surgeon, and he joined us a little while before Dr. Murphy came. He was with us but a short time before his quiet ability was recognized. He was made a brigade surgeon and placed in charge of a hospital camp. There were a number of the sick, besides the

1. Dr. William W. Sweeney was an early settler of Red Wing and quite prominent in its affairs.

wounded, then with the regiment, and, while at Brightwood, some hospital tents were erected there and our sick placed in them. My recollection is that Dr. Hand remained behind with the sick when we left there.

I think that it was Monday, August 5th, early in the morning, that we received marching orders, and it was rumored that we were to go somewhere on the Upper Potomac to relieve a Wisconsin regiment and do guard duty. In a short time we had everything packed and in the wagons, and the march began. The day was fair and not excessively warm so that we made a fairly good day's march, camping at night near Rockville, tired but in good condition.

Rockville was a pleasantly situated village whose inhabitants received us without any manifestation of feeling one way or the other, but that night and the next morning they did considerable trading with the regiment in milk, butter, and eggs—which, I have no doubt, pleased them. This was almost the first time that the boys had had any money or an opportunity to buy things of that kind. At that time we had not been weaned from these things and vegetables fresh from the farms, and it was a real hardship to do without them. As we were marching alone, and no other regiment was occupying the country, we had an excellent opportunity to get those things in abundance, and the natives were not averse to trading with us at a profit, whatever they may have thought of our purpose in coming there. Our first few weeks along the Potomac were the best chance the regiment ever had to obtain these things.

The next day we continued on by Darnestown, camping near that place at night. It was warmer and rained some in the afternoon and at night. This evening, as on the night before, there was a strong guard posted on all of the roads leading into the camp, and all precautions taken against a surprise. A portion of Company F was on outpost that night and passed a rather uncomfortable time of it—though some of the boys 'made connections' with some of the green corn in the adjoining field, and it was found to be pretty good when roasted before a fire of coals.

Wednesday was a close, muggy day, and it rained a little at times, but we continued the march and camped towards night near Seneca Mills, placing a picket along the river and on the roads, as on previous nights.

We were now, I think, in advance of all of the troops moving out of Washington to the westward, and the next troops on the river west of us were supposed to be at or near Williamsport, above Harpers Ferry. At this time we were acting under the orders of Gen. Charles P. Stone, but were practically an independent command, covering the Maryland side of the Potomac from Seneca Mills to the mouth of the Monocacy. At this time, Gen. Nathaniel P. Banks was organizing a force to occupy the country about Frederick City and to the west of the Monocacy. We were followed in our march by the 34th New York, the 42nd New York (Tammany), and the 82nd New York (Second Militia), but none of these connected with us or started before the 7th or 8th of the month. Our regiment was at this time the nucleus around which later was gathered eleven other regiments, which were very closely associated with it through all of its service. With some minor changes, and the necessary additions to cover their losses, this dozen regiments stood together 'for better and for worse' all through the long war.

We remained in the vicinity of Seneca Mills for about a week, picketing the river and patrolling the country above and to the west and northward. Wednesday, August 14, we marched up the river and the next day made camp near Poolesville, Maryland. The location of this camp was decided upon after considerable investigation. It was on the high ground about two miles from the river—as it was considered more healthy to be above the river fogs—and then it was out of range from the Virginia shore and screened from observation.

Poolesville was a small country hamlet surrounded by farms, and it apparently contained some well-to-do people with fine, comfortable houses. But, for the greater part, the farms were not large and the houses but the ordinary unpainted affairs common in that part of the country. We did not receive a hearty welcome from the people in this vicinity—neither was there any open evidence of dislike. It was soon apparent that they did not generally sympathize with the object of our coming, and that they would rejoice at our departure, but they made no demonstrations of secession sentiments. Harry White, who was already becoming noted as a raider, was a native of this section of the state, but if he made any visits to his home that winter they were quiet ones. It is probable, however, that he was kept well posted as to what was going on about his old home.

The same day that we located the camp near Poolesville, three companies were sent to picket the river. The country in the vicinity of the proposed camp was examined and some outlying guards stationed—to avoid a 'surprise party'— on the principal roads leading to the camp. It was our custom during this winter to send out the pickets by companies, three at a time, carrying three days' rations and remaining three days.

To make the situation clear, I should perhaps explain that the Chesapeake and Ohio Canal is located along the Potomac, on the Maryland side; and there were some locks near Edwards Ferry, where there was a road crossing the river[2] and leading to Leesburg a few miles away. This canal, being dug as nearly straight as a conveniently level bed could be found, did not conform strictly to the course of the river but was at variable distances from it. For the purposes of observation there was generally a better location in the bends of the river—between it and the canal—and it was here that the pickets were usually posted. There was a bridge over the canal at Edwards Ferry and at other points where roads crossed it.

Company F was one of the companies sent on picket. Its headquarters were located at the ferry house, but the company was divided into squads, placed in command of a non-commissioned officer, and stationed at various points above

2. The ferry was the crossing link between the roads on the Maryland and Virginia sides of the Potomac.

and below the crossing. The squad with which I was associated was on the river—between it and the canal—and above the locks a few hundred yards. Each squad made itself comfortable as circumstances would admit, kept one man on the watch during the day and two at night, and set the tour of duty usually at two hours. There was a day patrol and an inspection of the posts at night. In this way, there was a continuous and close observation of the Virginia side of the river.

Across the river on the Virginia side, there was a small stream, apparently coming out of a marsh, called Goose Creek, which ran into the Potomac a short distance below the ferry. The country on both sides of the river was hilly and densely wooded, except the cleared fields, and there was no wide range of vision but from the hilltops some distance back from the river. On the Maryland side, there were many farms, but on the Virginia side there were not so many near the river, and they were of less size. For the greater part, in this vicinity, there was thick woods and underbrush. There did not appear to be much going on over on that side. Occasionally a man—and sometimes two or three—would be seen on a by-road or at the edge of a clearing, but they were seldom long in sight or in large numbers. Sometimes a few horsemen would ride down the road and take a momentary observation, then gallop away. There was no show of hostility, but we knew we were being watched from a safe distance. On account of woods, this could easily be done without exposure.

Our instructions were not to fire on anyone unless fired upon, and they would not have run any great risk if they came to the water's edge. At first, we kept somewhat under cover, as we did not know what instructions those fellows had and neither did we care to expose ourselves to a chance shot, but, after a time, we made no attempt at concealment and frequently went to the water to wash.

The Potomac at this place was somewhat less in width than the Mississippi at Red Wing, but there was much less water in the ordinary stages. In many places it was fordable at low stages of the water, but at the time of our coming the recent rains had raised the water, and it was swimming at all points. As things were, we got along peaceably, and, so far as I now recall, there was not a shot fired from either side during our first tour of duty at the river.

I think that it was our last day that the Tammany Regiment came to the river at Conrad's Ferry about four miles above us, and, for some reason, the fellows on the other side seemed to resent their coming. There was some firing between them soon after, and continued nearly every day. On Saturday morning, August 24, the booming of a gun was heard and was repeated at short intervals for some time. This was an alarming sound, and we were all anxious to know the cause. At first, it was supposed to be a salute, but as it continued—and in irregular order—we were soon satisfied that it was something else. The apparent location of the firing was on the river above us.

The New York regiment was attacked from across the river, and they were using artillery and musketry. There was an order to send at once a detail of sharpshooters to try their rifles on them. Thirty men were sent off immediately, and three companies, including Company F, soon after followed them.

When we arrived, the detail was already at work, firing at the men serving the battery at the top of a hill, about a half of a mile away. The Tammany boys had made barricades at favorable places, but—as they had smooth-bore guns—they could not reach the men, not even enough to make them uncomfortable. When the rifles were used on them, these made a different impression. It was reported that some were seen to fall. It did not take long to convince them that it was not as safe as it had been. Company F was posted at a bend in the river, and, taking cover wherever we could find it, fired a few shots into the bushes on the other side— and got a few (in the bushes over our heads) in return. There were but a few shots from the battery after we came, and the musketry firing did not last much longer.

After waiting for some hours, we returned to camp, it being pretty evident that the 'incident was closed.' It was a little difficult to comprehend the object of that attack as made. There was no attempt at crossing nor any large display of infantry, who fired only from the cover of bushes.

The affair at Conrad's Ferry[3] had brought the regiment into comparison with some of the other troops and caused some comment on the characteristics of the men from the different states. Colonel Gorman, in his report to Governor Ramsey, referred to this: "The contrast between the New York and the Minnesota troops, as to discipline and coolness, was so clearly manifest as to elicit marked praise." Ours was never a noisy regiment in camp or elsewhere, though they could make considerable noise on an occasion, but orders were always obeyed quietly and without comment. There were other regiments that were noisy, irregular in all of their actions, and clamorous on all occasions. The two regiments certainly carried themselves in a different fashion, but, all the same, the New York boys proved to be splendid fighters when put to the test.

After a few days of expectancy, things again settled down quietly, and drill and picket went on as usual. Since leaving the state, we had never (up to this time) remained for two full weeks in one place, but now—as there seemed a probability of our remaining here for even a longer time than that—we began to plan things accordingly. Some temporary sheds of poles and brush were erected to cook under; a 'bean hole' was dug; and other arrangements made for cooking again by companies. A regimental bake-oven was built, bakers detailed, and fresh bread provided for the regiment.

Perhaps I ought to explain that a *'bean hole'* is a trench in the ground, dug deep enough and broad enough to take in several large-sized camp kettles. Wood is then burned in this hole until it is thoroughly heated and filled with live coals. The beans—which have been soaked for some hours or parboiled for a short time—are then placed in the kettles, which are of iron—with a liberal supply of

3. Conrad's Ferry was located about four miles upstream from Edwards Ferry.

salt pork. Water is added as may be thought necessary, and the kettles are covered with a tight-fitting cover. The live coals are then shoveled out of the trench; the kettles placed in it; the coals shoveled back until all the space around the kettles is filled and they are covered several inches deep; then the whole is covered with dirt, leaving only a small vent for ventilation.

Beans prepared in this way, put in the hole in the evening, and allowed to remain over night, are all ready for breakfast in the morning. If there were no mistakes or accidents, the results are as fine and wholesome baked beans as any one could desire—and there is no better way to cook the bean. At first, they did not always come out all right, but a little experimenting brought very satisfactory results as a rule. It was found that fresh beef—and even 'salt horse' when properly freshened—was very palatable when cooked in this way.[4]

Fresh bread, fresh meat regularly, and the baked beans were very acceptable additions to the field rations we had been living on most of the time since we had left the state. Having a little money now, we were able to procure fresh vegetables at our own expense. In those days the government did not include any fresh vegetables in the army ration—except potatoes 'when practicable.' During our first three years in the service, it was but seldom 'practicable'—except when the company furnished the cash and did their own purveying. The building of the ovens and the baking of the bread were all done by details from the regiment.

So far as temporal, physical comforts were concerned, we were better situated at Camp Stone than at any other period after we left Fort Snelling, but even at that it was a rough, hard experience, and there were other discomforts than physical ones.

There was a class of eloquent, earnest patriots who came prominently before the people early in the war and remained active until it closed, but so far as I know, none of them ever shouldered a musket or did any other kind of fighting, except with their mouths. Their intentions were the best, and they had great zeal, but it was not always "according to knowledge" and only tended to embarrass and discourage the government and its soldiers. They put themselves in evidence chiefly through the public press and first made themselves felt when they raised the cry of "On to Richmond." Then—apparently appalled by the results of that abortive effort by the way of Bull Run—for a little time they were still, but reappeared again under the veiled sarcasm of a headline in quotation marks declaring that it was "All quiet along the Potomac."

In fact, it was not 'all quiet' on that portion of the Potomac where the Corps of Observation was located.[5] Energy and effort may have been misdirected and

4. "Salt horse" was salted or pickled beef.
5. Formed August 17, 1861, the Corps of Observation on the upper Potomac was simply those troops under Charles P. Stone's command. In October they were named Stone's Division, but, confusingly, the term "Corps of Observation" was used for another two months. Welcher, *Union Army*, Vol. 1, *Eastern Theater*, 248.

unsuccessful; the mistakes of those days were undoubtedly many; but those days of organization and drill were very active, busy ones. There were ten companies in the regiment, and three of them were constantly on picket, which was almost as hard as continuous guard duty. For those not on the picket line, there was the usual routine of police, fatigue, and guard duty, and many hours of drill every day when the weather was not absolutely prohibitive. Besides, our forage was being collected from the surrounding country, and about every other day there was a detail and a guard to bring it in. In addition to these, there was the uncertainty ever attendant upon two hostile armies when confronting each other.

The country did not seem to understand then—or since then—what was really being done, not only on the Potomac but wherever our armies were being gathered, organized, and drilled. The great fighting machines, the armies, had to be built, tested, adjusted, and men trained to use them, before they could be used effectively. Save Generals Winfield Scott and John Wool, it is not probable that there was a man in the Union army that had ever actually commanded a brigade in action—and but few that had ever even directed a full regiment under fire. The armies were ready before the leaders were found. And this the press, and the people in their partisan spirit and impatient moods, seemed not to understand.

I speak of these things here because frequently the ill-advised action of some of the leaders at home touched the sensitive side of the soldier, made him feel that he was coming far short of what was expected of him, and consequently made him feel dissatisfied with his situation.

About the first of September, it was rumored we were to be formed into a brigade, and that other regiments were coming to join it, and a crossing might be made into Virginia. It was also talked that Colonel Gorman was to be made a general, and that we were to have a new colonel. This was a matter about which we—the men in the regiment—had a great interest but about which we had no voice in the choosing.

Except for an occasional spat between the pickets, there were no 'disturbances of the peace' in our vicinity. The paymaster came again and paid us in gold for the last time, but we were not then aware of it. More clothing also came, and this time we drew overcoats and dress coats, and new hats with a feather on one side and a brass spread eagle on the other. There were also 'shoulder scales' and some other redundant 'brass work,' which we transported for a time and then 'chucked it overboard' on the Peninsula.

It was about the middle of September when the Fifteenth Massachusetts Regiment camped near us and were joined soon after by the Nineteenth and Twentieth regiments from the same state. In the early part of the war there was considerable prejudice and rivalry between regiments from different states—and even between the city and country regiments from the same state—and the coming of new regiments was a matter of interest. The Seventh Michigan also camped in the neighborhood, and our little military community, camped here and there among

Camp Stone, the six-month home of the First Minnesota and its sister regiments, from mid-August 1861 to late February 1862

the woods and farms, made the Maryland hills re-echo with bugle calls and drum beats, and used every vacant pasture and stubble-field for drill grounds.

Brigadier General Charles P. Stone was in command of all of the troops in this vicinity. About the first of October, the formation was begun which later resulted in a division of three brigades.[6] So far as I can now recall it, the first of these brigades was formed with three regiments as follows: First Minnesota, Thirty-Fourth New York (Herkimer Regiment), and the Eighty-Second New York (Second Militia). Our colonel, Willis A. Gorman, became Brigadier General Gorman and assumed command of this brigade. It was not until after the affair at Ball's Bluff that the Fifteenth Massachusetts was added to the brigade.

After the promotion of Col. Gorman, the regiment was left in command of Lieutenant Colonel Stephen Miller, but it was rumored that someone else might be sent to command the regiment, and that the man was an ex-captain of the regular army. This was hardly to our liking, as we had some doubts about a regular fitting on to our regiment in good form, and there was some anxiety as to how we would get along together. I recall that this was a subject of conversation on several occasions after we had heard who he was and that he was coming. Level-headed Corporal Phil Hamline took a common sense view of it and declared that it would be the "best thing for us that could happen"—arguing that a man who had learned his trade ought to be a better workman than one who had simply taken it up without the training.

6. Before Ball's Bluff, Stone's Division consisted of three brigades: the First (Frederick W. Lander's), the Second (Gorman's), and the Third (led by Edward D. Baker); Welcher, *Union Army,* Vol. 1, *Eastern Theater,* 248. Wright correctly placed the First Minnesota in Gorman's Brigade, but it was the Second Brigade, not the First.

It was not long to wait before we knew the name of the man that was to command us and a brief history of his life. His full name was Napoleon Jackson Tecumseh Dana, which certainly was high-sounding and suggestive of France and Indians. His history—so far as we got it then—was comparatively more brief than the name. He had graduated from West Point and had been made a Second Lieutenant in 1842; had served with credit in the regular army in Mexico and afterwards until 1855, when he had resigned, being then a full captain; and had since been in the banking business in St. Paul, Minnesota.

Colonel Dana joined the regiment October 12, 1861. He at once assumed command in a way that indicated that he was a quiet, dignified gentleman and was going to act on the supposition that others were, until the contrary was in evidence. It did not take us long to learn that we had a man over us that knew his business as a soldier and could teach others in a way that was pleasing. He at once interested himself in all of the affairs of the regiment: its arms, its drill, its clothing, its food, its sanitary arrangements, and the care of its sick.

Being one of the latter, I have occasion to remember it. The First was a remarkably healthy regiment, losing but 27 men and 2 officers to disease during the first three years, which was something less than three percent. Without any definite knowledge about it, I consider it a safe assertion that this was not more than one-fifth or one-sixth of the average percentage of deaths from disease among the regiments with which we served. One cause for this may have been that the severe test of our first campaign had taken from us a large proportion of

Officers of the First Minnesota at Camp Stone,
apparently on the parade ground in front of their tents

the weaker ones. Be that as it may, there were quite a number of men in Company F who were practically used up by it and never really recovered from it. These were men whose physical abilities were not quite up to the requirements of the service and who, sooner or later, were discharged and sent home or transferred to the Invalid Corps.[7]

Our camp at Poolesville was considered to be in a healthy location, but there was considerable sickness in the camp there until the frosts came to kill the malaria. Most of it was of a malarial type and not really so dangerous as debilitating and disagreeable. Along the river and canal nearly every night, there was a fog, and, as the nights grew longer and cooler, these fogs increased in density and hung over the low lands later in the mornings. There was but little of this at the camp, but all on picket were exposed to its influence, and it was not long before it began to show its effects.

My own case is a sample of many others. It was towards the last of September, and for some days I had realized that the drilling each day had taken a little more out of me than the night had restored, and that the strenuous exercises we were going through were gradually using me up. This was not a pleasant conclusion to come to—especially under the circumstances—and I tried to 'brace up' against it, but it was not a success.

It was Company F's turn to go to the river for a three days' stay on picket. I went with it—though advised to stay in camp—hoping to feel better when I got there. The squad to which I belonged was sent across the canal, above the locks, and I was 'done up' and shivering with cold when we arrived there—though it was a fine comfortable day.

There was a little shelter of brush under a tree, where those not on duty slept, and I was at once put to bed, but all of the blankets of the squad were not sufficient to warm me. It was proposed to remove me to the camp, but to this I objected, hoping that I would feel better soon. After an hour or two under the blankets, I realized that I had reached the other extreme and that I was burning with fever and exceedingly thirsty. This was followed late in the day by a profuse sweat, which brought relief, and sleep followed.

When I awoke some time in the night, the fever had passed and I was hungry— or thought I was—but it was not army rations I wanted. I had in mind some corn bread and fried chicken, such as mother used to prepare, and a cup of coffee with cream in it. I was wakeful the rest of the night and, as soon as light came, I got up, went to the river, washed my hands and face, and concluded I felt better.

When the morning meal was ready, I tried to eat some of the crackers and a little of the meat, and drank some of the coffee. My stomach had not just approved

7. The Invalid Corps (later known as the Veteran Reserve Corps) consisted of those soldiers and officers unable to serve in the field but fit for garrison duty. Those from the Army of the Potomac were stationed in the Washington area. Welcher, *Union Army,* Vol. 1, *Eastern Theater,* 563.

of any of these things, and it was not long before it went on a strike and ejected the whole of them. The effort of doing this had started another sweat and taken away my strength, so that I went back to the blankets. It was not long before I discovered that I was getting 'cold feet' and fingers, and soon I was shaking again. This chill lasted for something more than an hour, then there was a throbbing headache and some hours of burning fever and intense thirst before the sweating process reduced matters to an approximately normal condition. As it was late in the day and I was considered as well off there as in camp—so long as there was no trouble—I remained with the squad at the picket post.

The next morning, I returned to the camp, and the doctor came, felt my pulse, asked to see my tongue, and furnished me with a liberal supply of quinine, which he advised me to take promptly. I did this and was made as comfortable as I could be in my own tent.

But it did not appear to make any difference. There came nausea, a chill, intense thirst, then a fever and a sweat, after which there was a more natural condition of things and a desire for something to eat—something that you knew you could not get. When not shivering with a chill or athirst with fever, I was dosing with quinine, and that was the routine for the next two weeks. I would wake in the morning hopeful that I might 'skip a day,' get up and about the camp for a little while, then the chill, the fever, and sweat.

It was not a pleasing program, and the few comparatively comfortable waking hours I had were all embittered by the doctor's drugs. I have still a vivid impression of those long days and nights when I lay in the tent, thirsty and feverish—thinking of the cool springs I had known in Minnesota and longing for a drink from their delicious waters—or dragged about the camp discouraged and homesick. I was not really dangerously sick, but very uncomfortably so, and the worst during my term of service. It was a matter of great satisfaction when I passed a day without the recurrence of the chill; better yet when they ceased altogether, and I began really to want something to eat, without any remonstrances on the part of my stomach as soon as I began to eat it.

Somebodies that blundered

OCTOBER 1861-FEBRUARY 1862

IT WAS BUT A FEW DAYS after the arrival of Col. Dana when the pickets coming from the river told of the building of some scows at the ferry house. That was taken as a suggestion that there might soon be an attempt to cross the river. It was also supposed at this time that a considerable force of the enemy was being gathered on the opposite side of the river, about Leesburg. It was on Saturday, October 19, that General George A. McCall, who commanded a force across the river about Chain Bridge, advanced up the river to Dranesville, on the road to Leesburg and 12 or 15 miles from it. When this movement was made, and McCall had occupied Dranesville, General McClellan sent notice of it to General Stone (commanding at Edwards Ferry), informing him of what had been done and directing him to "keep a good lookout upon Leesburg." He also said, "Perhaps a slight demonstration on your part would have the effect to move them."

It is not pleasant or satisfactory to contemplate or write about Ball's Bluff, and I should pass it if it did not leave the chronicle incomplete. Briefly, it was another of those unfortunate affairs that seemingly ought never to occur but—in war and in peace—are of frequent occurrence. It should be classed with railroad wrecks and steamship disasters that result from misapprehension, incompetence, negligence, or criminal carelessness when 'somebody has blundered.' There were several 'somebodies that blundered' in the production of that bloody contretemps.

The affairs at Ball's Bluff and at Edwards Ferry occurred at the same time, and, no doubt, they were intended to be cooperative, but there was no unity of action and apparently no attempt in that direction. I will first try to tell what happened at Edwards Ferry—as that was where the regiment was—and then give some idea of the more important matter farther up the river.[1] As I was still in the 'quinine brigade,' I remained in camp and must therefore tell of it as it came to me through others.

It was Sunday afternoon, October 20, 1861—soon after one o'clock—when the seven companies then in camp got orders to prepare to march at once with one day's rations and full cartridge boxes. It took but a short time to get ready,

---

1. Ball's Bluff was on the Virginia side of the river, opposite Harrison's Island, which was located a short distance downstream from Conrad's Ferry and about three and a half miles upstream from Edwards Ferry.

and they left the camp marching towards Edwards Ferry. It was known also that the other regiments of the brigade were also called out, and that all were going to the river.

Before reaching the river, there was a display of the brigade on the bluffs—in which the Seventh Michigan[2] joined—and a battery fired some shells into the woods over the river. After this, the whole force was marched to the ferry; the battery continued to fire; Companies E and K put the three scows into the river and poled to the Virginia side; while the rest of the regiment remained in position on the Maryland side, with their rifles ready to fire if they should be attacked. Reaching the other side, the two companies landed, deployed as skirmishers, and advanced for a short distance without meeting any opposition. It now being nearly dark, they were recalled, and soon after all returned to camp.

This was probably all that, at the time, was intended, and where the affair should have ended—but it did not. Sometime between midnight and morning, orders came to be at the ferry at daylight, fully equipped with one day's rations. Reaching the ferry before sunrise, the three scows (all there were) were manned. Companies C and D crossed under a fire of artillery—as on the evening before— and deployed and advanced to cover the crossing of the rest of the regiment. The three scows had to be 'poled'; they would carry only about 100 men at a time; and it took nine or ten minutes each way—which made crossing slow work. But the seven companies were all on the Virginia side by about 8:30 o'clock. (Three companies—A, B, and G—were still on picket.)

When the regiment was all over, it formed in line of battle with its left on Goose Creek and the right extending towards the river to protect the crossing of the rest of the brigade. A small force of cavalry (about 20) were brought over, and the rest of the brigade crossed as rapidly as possible, but it was slow, tedious work. This cavalry, a part of Van Alen's regiment[3]—supported by two companies of the First Minnesota Regiment—made a scout up the road towards Leesburg. General Stone said that it went "nearly if not quite two miles from the ferry," when the cavalry (which was in advance) "came suddenly upon a Mississippi regiment, received its fire, and returned it with their pistols." One of the party had his horse shot. It captured one of the 4th Virginia cavalrymen, horse, and equipments, and returned without further loss.

There was no more fighting that day nor any further attempt to advance. All efforts being devoted to the crossing of the men. The 34th New York came up from Seneca Mills in the afternoon and crossed over; and the three companies of our regiment that were on picket came that night and joined the regiment on the Virginia side. By night 2,250 men had crossed the river at Edwards Ferry.

2. The Seventh Michigan Regiment belonged to Lander's First Brigade, not to Gorman's Second, but it accompanied the Second Brigade on this expedition; Welcher, *Union Army*, Vol. 1, *Eastern Theater*, 621.

3. Colonel James H. Van Alen commanded the Third New York Cavalry at the time.

It was during this day that the fighting and disaster at Ball's Bluff occurred—something like four miles further up the stream—but nothing was known of this until it was all over. At the camp, nothing was heard but the occasional boom of a cannon, and we were told that nothing more could be heard at the river. Colonel Dana said in his report that it was at first planned to return to the Maryland side that (Monday) night, and that some of them did cross, but the order was countermanded, and they were returned. He also said that he was charged with the duty of covering the crossing and, for that purpose, formed the regiment and held it in readiness for action. When it was decided to remain longer on the Virginia side, the regiment continued on the outposts.

During the day of Monday, General Gorman was in command of the crossing and continued to gather in all of the boats that he could find—and by night had collected nine canal, flat, scow, and row boats. These were put in charge of Quartermaster Foote of the 82nd New York, who directed their movements. The crossing of men continued as rapidly as possible, and, before twelve o'clock Tuesday, about 4,500 men had been crossed over. This included two pieces of artillery and about 100 of the Van Allen Cavalry.

During the day Tuesday, there was no advance movement attempted in force, but skirmishers were kept well out to the front, and these were occasionally engaged, the most important affair being about four o'clock in the afternoon. At that time, General Frederick W. Lander, who had some sort of a command[4] with the troops on the river above us, came over at Edwards Ferry to take a look at the situation from that position. His investigations stirred up the enemy in the bushes at the front, and a sharp picket fight ensued in which the enemy displayed considerable force. In this affair, Gen. Lander was shot in the leg, Lewis Mitchell of Company I was killed, and one other of the company wounded.

It had rained much of the time since the movement began, and now it turned quite cold, and a high wind was blowing. Colonel Dana said that "the regiment furnished sixty-five men to man the boats for the purpose of crossing the other troops, horses, and guns. With great labor and in perfect silence, this trying task was fully and satisfactorily accomplished. As the first streak of dawn (Thursday October 24, 1861) made its appearance, the First Minnesota, again alone with General Stone, stood on the Virginia shore, and everything else living had been placed on board, the men were ordered to follow."

At the time that this move began, Colonel Dana had been less than ten days with the regiment, and he and his men had not yet got fully acquainted. After four days and nights in arduous effort—and under trying circumstances together—he gave his opinion of the regiment, in closing his report, as follows: "What can I say

---

4. Brigadier General Lander commanded the First Brigade of Stone's Division. Only one of his regiments was with Gorman, so he was just an observer with Gorman's attacking force. His leg wound contributed to his death from pneumonia in March 1862.

for the men of Minnesota more than that for these few days of hardship and toil they proved themselves worthy of their state and of the fame they have acquired for her! Patient, bold, obedient, orderly, and disciplined. I claim for them the title of veterans." This was strong praise for the regiment, and it came from an old regular officer, too. It should be said here that the boys returned to the camp full of confidence in the new colonel and with many complimentary words for the careful, considerate way he had directed affairs.

As in going over, the return crossing was under the direction of General Gorman. He spoke of the strong wind and said he was directed to make the necessary arrangements on the Maryland side and to "call to this work the boatmen and lumbermen of the First Regiment"; and that to these he added other details; and that the crossing was made between 9 o'clock at night and 5 o'clock the next morning. And he added: "The Minnesota lumbermen performed their part with such skill as to merit special notice."

Having outlined what happened at Edwards Ferry, I will now try to indicate something of the greater affair at Ball's Bluff—but more briefly.

On Sunday afternoon, October 20th—at the time that the demonstration was made at Edwards Ferry—a similar move was made at Harrison's Island (opposite Ball's Bluff). The 15th, 19th, and 20th Massachusetts regiments and the 42nd New York, with some artillery, were called out. Captain Chase Philbrick of the 15th Massachusetts was sent over the river with 20 men to make an examination of that side. He advanced for some distance along an obscure road, and did not return promptly, and meanwhile the troops remained in position awaiting his return. When he did return, he reported that he had gone within about a mile of Leesburg—unmolested; had discovered a small encampment in the woods, without pickets; and had withdrawn without discovery.

General Stone said that he got this report about ten o'clock Sunday night and that he sent orders for several companies of the 15th and 20th Massachusetts to cross the river. Colonel Devens of the 15th Massachusetts crossed about 300 men as directed, and Colonel Lee—with 100 men of the 20th—took a position to protect their return if they should be pursued. Colonel Devens reported that he found no enemy. This condition did not remain true for long and, after a skirmish with a small force, he retired to the position of Colonel Lee on the bluff. Then, with his supports, he again advanced into an open field, an unfortunate location, where he was joined by portions of the 42nd New York and the First California (71st Pennsylvania).[5] These troops—portions of four regiments—were in a clearing about a half of a mile in length and about 500 yards in width, lying parallel to the river.

5. The 71st Pennsylvania Regiment was commonly known as the First California, so named in honor of its commander, Colonel Edward D. Baker, a San Francisco lawyer and friend of President Lincoln.

Colonel Edward D. Baker came to see General Stone at Edwards Ferry and was given authority by Gen. Stone to go to Harrison's Island and take full command of all of the troops there—and left to his discretion to retire the troops from the Virginia side or cross others to support them.

It was afternoon—probably between one and two o'clock—when Colonel Baker joined Colonel Devens and assumed command. About that time or very soon after, an attack was begun from the woods on the right of his force and continued along the front to the left. The enemy had already gained positions in the woods on three sides of him and fired from concealment while his force was exposed in the open.

It was an unequal contest from the first. Colonel Baker was killed, and Colonel Devens and Colonel Cogswell[6] did the best they could to save their commands. The men fought bravely but were driven back to the river in confusion—where some succeeded in recrossing to Harrison's Island, but more than half of the force were shot, captured, or drowned. The disaster was complete before any information of the critical condition of affairs reached Gen. Stone, in command at Edwards Ferry, and any attempt to succor was hopeless and useless.

All of this occurred within four miles or so of Edwards Ferry, where the First Regiment had crossed (that is, seven companies of it) before nine o'clock that morning. There were no connecting roads except by Leesburg, and what would have happened if the First Regiment had pushed out on the Leesburg road until it was involved in serious fighting—before its supports had crossed—is guesswork. The responsibility of its not doing this rests with Gen. Stone, who was present and directed its movements. Separated by four miles of roadless woods and thickets, neither of the forces across the river could communicate with or directly aid the other. For either party to have communicated with the other involved the crossing of the river twice and a ride of four miles. To have aided after that involved a march of four miles through brush, in which two miles an hour would have been rapid progress—if no enemy had been encountered. In case of attack, all that either party could do was to fight it out. There were plenty of men almost in rifle range, but they were on the Maryland side of the river and had no sufficient means of getting to their aid.

That unfortunate affair caused much depression through the North; and there was much adverse criticism—in and out of the army; and the responsibility for the failure charged here and there. It is certain that there was no proper and sufficient means provided for crossing the river at either place, and it is not probable that it was intended to cross any large force or do any serious fighting.

Much might be said about this, but I return to the regiment.

The regiment—the seven companies that did not have to go on picket— returned to the camp early in the forenoon of Thursday the 24th—tired, cold,

---

6. Colonel Milton Cogswell commanded the 42nd New York (Tammany) Regiment.

hungry, and sleepy. The first thing after arrival in camp was the roll call, which showed all 'present and accounted for.' Then there was a demand for something to eat and a sleep in the tents. I remember that I was very glad to see them all back again and anxious to know all that had happened. After they had slept, I listened with interest to the incidents of the last four days. Some of these were amusing, and one of them I will try to relate here as it was told to me.

All of the boats used in the crossing had to be pushed back and forth with poles. They were only scow and canal boats, and never intended to be used in any such way, and the river was so swollen by the rains that this was both difficult and dangerous—without experience.

Company F had several men who had some knowledge of rafting, and naturally they were selected when the detail to man the boats was called for. Among these was Josiah Richardson, whose home was—if I mistake not—at Wacouta or somewhere about the head of Lake Pepin. 'Joe' was one of the older men in the company, well-developed physically but otherwise a somewhat peculiar combination of contradictory characteristics. He was a Virginian by birth, who had never made but a very limited acquaintance with the schoolmaster before he drifted down the Ohio and worked up the Mississippi, where he had found employment for the most part on the river. Joe had had a pretty large amount of rough and hard experience, and it had to a degree at least 'soured the milk of human kindness in his bosom.' Joe growled and found fault, generally and on general principles, with all in authority over him from the President down to the eighth corporal, but he did not always really mean it.

His pet aversion were the boyish young officers, which he called 'Basswood Lieutenants.' Joe also had an impediment in his speech which amounted to genuine stuttering when he got excited or angry—and either one of these conditions was liable to prevail upon comparatively slight provocation—and then he was ready to say and do almost anything. For all of his drawbacks, Joe was far from being a bad-hearted fellow. He proved a good soldier in his way and could be depended on in an emergency and would stand by to the finish.

On the return from the Virginia side, Joe—by virtue of his experience—was 'head poler' on one of the canal boats. The wind was blowing hard; the water was rough; the current swift and the river rising—all of which made the management of the boats increasingly difficult and hard work. It so happened that this boat was in charge of one of Joe's Basswood Lieutenants, who gave some directions which Joe thought unsuitable, and there was a difference of opinion developed right off.

When the Maryland shore was reached, Joe complained to General Gorman, who had charge of receiving the troops as fast as they came over, and declared that he could not work under a man that did not "know anything." Gorman asked Joe if he did not know how to pole the boat without anyone to tell him, and Joe stuttered out a strong and profane assertion to the effect that he did—and was told to go and do it then.

Joe immediately wanted to know what he should do if he was interfered with by someone that "d-d-d-d'nt know his b-b-biz." General Gorman, whose thoughts were busy about many things just then and no doubt was desirous of dismissing Joe, said to "knock him in the river." Joe went back to his boat muttering and stuttering to the effect that he'd "be d-d-d-d if he d-d-d-d'nt." Before a round trip had been accomplished, Joe had, as he claimed, 'obeyed orders' and landed the officer in the river. It should also be recorded that he was prompt to help fish him out, and that there the matter ended.

After the return to the camps, drilling was resumed industriously, and included brigade and division movements. Colonel Dana was careful and patient and gave us many hours of drill—in the manual and in marching—which gave the regiment a smoothness and unity in its movements and the handling of its arms which it had not previously had. This he continued as long as he was with us—including the use of the bayonet. We still kept this up after he had left us, and it is not claiming more than was accorded us to assert that we became one among the best-drilled regiments in the Army of the Potomac.

There are many memories connected with that fall and winter of waiting and preparation, but I shall note but a few.

While Gorman commanded the regiment—and after he commanded the brigade—he had trouble with illicit dealers of things that would intoxicate. That was a trouble that came to every man that commanded a regiment and tried to maintain discipline and good order—as it comes to every town and municipality that tries to control the trade.

The first difficulty was about some Negroes that were caught bringing some liquor into the camp, and the owner naturally 'mixed in' and advised that they be whipped by the soldiers to whom they had sold the liquor—as the best way to suppress it so far as the Negroes were concerned. This was done as privately as possible, and the punishment, as may be supposed, was very mild. In fact, the whole thing was considered as a joke rather than a serious punishment. This was taken up by some of the papers and came near stopping the star that was soon to adorn Gorman's shoulders—which would have been anything but a joke to him.

The other incident was 'on the general,' too, but it did not portend any such serious consequences. A sutler of the 34th New York, or his clerk, had been caught selling whiskey to enlisted men, and, after inquiry, was decorated with empty bottles and drummed out of the camp—to make the punishment ridiculous rather than severe.

A few days after (possibly the next one), when the brigade was out for review and things were progressing finely, a correspondent of some paper, with whom Gorman was not acquainted, came riding up to the general to pay his respects and take notes of the proceedings. Now this correspondent happened to resemble in appearance (or Gorman thought he did) the man he had sent out of the camp with the necklace of bottles.

Without waiting to verify his suppositions, he at once boiled over with wrath at what he supposed to be the 'crust' of the deposed sutler, and exploded with a variety of choice profanity at him—in his best style. The correspondent—and correspondents are supposed to have as much 'cheek' as sutlers—could not understand it and retired in disorder. A little later, matters were explained to both parties by one of the staff, and they shook hands and rode together during the rest of the afternoon.

At this time, sutlers were allowed to bring in whiskey for the officers but were not allowed to sell it to the men. Knowing that it was there and that it was being sold to the officers, the men wanting it generally managed to get it. As may be readily understood, whiskey in a military camp, as elsewhere, is a disturbing element, whether in the hands (mouths) of officers or men, and has to be dealt with. The temptation to the average sutler to increase his profits by selling to the enlisted men was generally too great for his integrity. When forbidden to keep or sell it, they resorted to smuggling it in under various false labels.

I recall that the sutler of the First tried it, got caught with the goods, and had to stand their confiscation. He then realized that it was not a safe experiment to try a second time with Col. Dana. I certainly am no advocate for selling liquor to soldiers. Neither would I refuse it to the enlisted men and furnish it to the officer. Both are much better without it except in emergencies—and my observation is that one is as likely to use it discreetly as the other—and that both generally use it indiscreetly. Among the enlisted men of Company F—as of every other company—there were some who, by an occasional indulgence in drink, hurt their standing in the company and spoiled their chances of promotion. Brave men, splendid soldiers, kind comrades, and good fellows with fine ideals—but forgetful of all else occasionally when there was an opportunity to get a drink.

Animals generally have better judgment than men as to what they eat and drink. I have no recollection of seeing a horse or a mule drunk during all of my army life, but I have seen men.

And that reminds me that not all of the labor of putting down the Great Rebellion was done by the soldiers, but that their faithful, long-suffering allies—the horse and the mule—did their part, and supplemented our efforts in a very substantial way. Like their human associates, they suffered hardships, disease, wounds, and death that the 'nation might live.' On every great march, the dead bodies of the mules were strewn by the roadside, and wounded and dead horses were on every battlefield.

And these reflections remind me of an incident one afternoon while we were at Poolesville. At the battle of Bull Run, where Ricketts's Battery was so roughly handled, many of the men and horses were killed and wounded, and only the fragments escaped. It was, however, reorganized and refitted, and—under the command of Lieutenant Kirby—joined us at Poolesville.

Among the killed was Lieutenant Ramsey. His horse, a fine intelligent animal, was wounded, but he came off with the wreck of the battery and kept with the other horses until the return to Washington, and then had been brought along to the camp up the river. Had it not been that he was the lieutenant's horse he would probably have been 'turned in' or shot, but someone looked out for him because he had been the lieutenant's favorite. With some other unserviceable horses, he was turned loose in a field near the battery. Quite a portion of his tail had been cut off by a cannon shot—or fragment of a shell—and he was cut across the rump on both legs, and was very thin in flesh.

One afternoon, the brigade formed in the field where these loose horses were and awaited the coming of the battery, which was to be included in the exercises. The horse lay stretched at full length, enjoying a sun-bath, and only raised his head, but made no attempt to get up, when we formed near him. When the battery came trotting up the road and the bugle sounded for them to file into the field, it had an entirely different effect. At the first blast of the bugle, he sprang to his feet and, gazing at it, he neighed sharply in recognition. Then, with his head up and his stub-tail vibrating, he trotted to his position and kept it until the guns were in battery and he was led away.

There were many days of waiting after the affair at Ball's Bluff. Naturally, when we returned to the camps, we did not expect to remain there long, but supposed that another move would soon be made and that better provision would be made for crossing. That we should remain there until spring did not then seem possible. Day after day—as we drilled and picketed the river—we expected some move would be made and we would start somewhere and attempt to do something. As the beautiful autumn days passed and no new move was made, I know that there grew up a feeling of anxiety and uneasiness as to what was to be done next. We had not learned to live simply in the present and let the future take care of itself.

With two large bodies of armed men confronting each other—and their pickets within rifle range—almost anything is likely to happen; and the most unlikely thing of all is that they should remain so for a hundred days without either party attacking. Yet that was what did happen, and I accept the fact without trying to account for it. We of the ranks had no responsibility in the matter, but we really felt much, for we were still in a transitory state—still citizens rather than soldiers in thought and feeling.

Perhaps the people at home will never give the soldier boys at the front full credit for all of the care and anxiety they had for those they had left at home. I doubt if there was a man in the company that did not have more or less violent attacks of homesickness. His hours of intense longing to see the faces of loved ones, hear again the familiar voices, and enjoy again the comfort and associations of his home, wherever or however humble it may have been. I know that many of the boys had left homes where they were greatly needed for the welfare and support of the family. That they had gone—most of them—against the protests of those left behind, blindly hoping that they would be at home again before the winter came, but the war had not prospered, and others had enlisted in the new regiments forming. The people were feeling the burden of the war very keenly, and the letters from home made this painfully evident.

My own case will fully represent many other families in Minnesota at that and later periods of the war. I, the oldest of the boys at home, had enlisted in April in 1861. My next younger brother, William H. Wright, had gone into Company I of the Second Regiment in July. And Beverly M. Wright, the last one of the boys old enough to get into the army, had joined Company A of the Fifth Regiment in December. The mother, with two children, was left at home—and neither of them old enough to help much towards a living. It will thus be seen that the first year of the war had completely exhausted the military resources of the family. It may seem contradictory—no doubt it is—but while I had gone into the war myself, I hoped that my brothers would not go and advised that they should not, but I have no doubt that they felt as I did—that they must.

I know that many others of the company were also deeply and genuinely troubled about these things. I recall the case of one of the recruits (which Dr. Murphy diagnosed as "nostalgia"), who really broke down and was discharged before we left the winter camp. Homesickness, at least in a military sense, is demoralizing, and the wanderer from home must not permit it to interfere with his usefulness. I know that many of the boys had to fight long and hard against it. Constant employment and something to interest and take up the mind are the best possible antidotes. There was plenty of the first ingredient furnished us at Camp Stone in the way of drill and picket duty, and for the latter we were left to ourselves.

Newspapers came to the camp quite regularly, and these were read with great interest. Aside from the letters we had from home and friends, they were about the only sources of information we had—except the camp rumors, and these we always had, but they had ceased to be considered important. The general news was a matter of continued interest, and all public affairs received an amount of thought and consideration that they never would have commanded if we had been at home.

Then those who could sing were generally ready to enliven the occasion with a song—and Company F had a number to whom it was always a pleasure to listen. Truth compels me to say that there were some who could not sing 'a little bit,' who were sometimes not averse to trying. This was sometimes amusing, but it was not always unalloyed satisfaction and sometimes brought a mild protest in the form of an inquiry about the tune and reference to the death of an ancient cow.

Amusement of some sort when not on duty was a positive necessity, and it was generally found in a proper and beneficial way, but there were exceptions, and cards and 'chuck-a-luck' had their manipulators and patrons. Writing letters was another thing that claimed some of the time of about all of the boys of Company F—and a number of them were quite devoted to it. Another thing was visiting among the regiments that were near us. Several of the boys found old friends or relatives in these regiments, and that led to forming many pleasant acquaintances among our companion regiments. (There was, of course, a much closer association with the other companies of our own regiment.)

When the regiments first came together, there was a pretty strong feeling of rivalry between them—somewhat similar to that between baseball teams today, only it was for the honor of their states rather than the division of the gate money that they were anxious about. There was a story about Colonel Gorman and the First Regiment when he commanded it. The chaplain of the 15th Massachusetts came to call on the chaplain of the First Minnesota, and together they went to pay their respects to Col. Gorman. After the introduction and a few commonplace remarks about other things, the conversation returned to religious matters, and the visiting chaplain informed the chaplain of the First that a "corporal and two men" had been baptized in his regiment recently. This attracted Gorman's attention, and he straightened up and called loudly for the adjutant. Upon the appearance of that official, he said in his most commanding, military voice: "*Adjutant, detail a sergeant and four men to be baptized at dress parade this evening,*" saying that he "would be d-d-d if he was going to be outdone by any Eastern regiment."

In going among other regiments as the holiday season approached, it was learned that they were getting many little things from their homes, but we—being so far away—did not expect anything. There were some things, however, that came—among others, some sheets, towels, and night shirts from the ladies of Red Wing and Lake City. The First Regiment, however, came in for a share of the things useful that were sent from Massachusetts. One of the officers of the regiment was born in Salem, Massachusetts, and lived there until married. His wife was also a Salem woman, and, when he left for the war, went to her people in Salem. When things were being gathered up to send to the soldiers, she suggested her husband's regiment to receive a part of these, and they were sent accordingly. I cannot tell now who or how many of the boys of Company F had a share in these things. I remember that I did—from what follows—and there were others.

I had received a pair of mittens—I suppose they should be called—with a thumb and finger. Pinned into one of the mittens was a neatly written note (as there were in some of the others), asking that whoever received them should answer it. At first, I was uncertain whether to consider mine as an invitation to correspond or an attempt to confuse—as it was written in three different languages, which were mixed in a very puzzling order. The note (which was but a few lines) began in Latin and was a mixture of that language, French, and English, and was signed with a girl's first name and the Latin for Deity. The rest of the address was plainly written, including the box number.

A desire to respond in kind—as far as I was able—prompted me to answer. Then, as one of the boys suggested, "it was hardly good manners to accept a gift and refuse to acknowledge its receipt, when requested"—and I proposed to wear the mittens.

I pretty nearly exhausted Company F's knowledge of all of the languages but the English (there were some members of the company had an inexhaustible supply of that) in my efforts to translate the mongrel manuscript, and then did not know whether it was right or not. I concluded to give the Latin for Deity an English construction, add it to the name, and send a letter to it, as addressed.

My next effort was to prepare a letter, and I gave it considerable care, mixing English and Latin, and adding a few words of the Sioux and Swedish languages. To this I signed my name and added a postscript, suggesting that, if any further correspondence was agreeable, I should prefer plain United States. I had a reply in good time, written in a readable language, and learned that my correspondent was attending the Young Ladies Seminary at Ipswich, Massachusetts. This correspondence lasted for more than a year, but it never reached an acute state and finally ceased.

As the weather grew cold and the nights were below freezing, there was an improvement in the health of those who were suffering from chills and fever. Before that time, I had returned to duty and recovered a good appetite for army rations, and all of the world looked brighter to me, because now I could eat whatever I could get and enjoy it.

With the increasing cold, we found the cloth tents but a slight protection; we had not learned how to hibernate then; and we began to think of other ways to be more comfortable. I think that it was about Christmas—when it began to seem likely that we should winter there—that permission was given to build log huts. As soon as it was settled that we could do this, the location was decided upon, and the work begun at once, each company putting up its own quarters. The weather happened to be favorable, and, with all at work, it did not take long to get some good-sized and respectable-looking log houses ready for occupancy.

By chinking with split pieces of wood and daubing with clay, they made a good protection against the storms and the cold. They were without floors; covered with boards; a place for a fire in the center; and a hole in the roof to let the smoke out. The bunks were along the walls on the sides and three tiers in height. Two of these houses did not quite shelter the whole company. So one 'mess'—in which I was included—built a shelter with logs about four feet high, the size of a wall tent; dug out some of the dirt; and banked it against the logs on the outside; and stretched a tent and flag over it. It was lighter than the houses, but not quite so good a protection from the storms or cold, but we contrived a small fireplace at the back end in which we could have a fire—when the wind did not blow too hard.

With this arrangement, the company was brought into closer personal relations than when divided into tents and messes—and the individuality of the boys became more conspicuous. Sometimes there was a little clashing between those of different dispositions, temperaments, and manner of looking at things (for we had all kinds in the company), but as a whole things went pleasantly. There is but little doubt that we were one of the best-housed regiments on the Potomac that winter. We had learned to consider it a 'big thing' to be sheltered from the storms.

We also managed to provide ourselves with the daily papers and some books that were read and talked of with a good deal of interest. Some of the companies collected small libraries. I recall that Company F had a copy of Shakespeare that contributed much to a pleasant passing of a stormy day when we were confined to quarters. It was the daily papers that were of the greatest interest and the most discussed as they brought us the news every day, and we were all intensely interested in public affairs, particularly of the war.

Then, too, after the building of the houses, Company F organized a lyceum in which all kinds of questions were considered. I had the honor to be the chairman or president of this organization and have now in my possession the constitution and bylaws and records of the meetings. Robert W. Leeson was secretary; Randolph C. Barnes, vice-president; James F. Bachelor and E. Oscar Williams, censors.

We discussed live questions, and there were some earnest, eloquent speeches made at every meeting. The first meeting was in "committee of the whole, on the condition of the country," and it was decided that it was "serious, in the extreme." Another was: "Do present indications point to a speedy close of the war?" This was decided in the negative by a vote of the meeting. The last question discussed—a few days before leaving Camp Stone—was: "Resolved that the overthrow of Secession and the downfall of Slavery, in America, will be simultaneous." The decision was in the affirmative and was by vote of the meeting.

The meetings were held in one of the large houses, lighted by candles stuck in the shanks of bayonets, which made very good candlesticks. The president sat on a half barrel, the secretary on a block of wood, and the audience on the bunks or such seats as they could provide. Not all of the discussion of these, and very many other, questions was confined to the meetings of the lyceum or its members. Any and all members of Company F felt at liberty to propose any question they thought advisable and challenge discussion by an expression of opinion, and usually there was someone to take an adverse view, which was generally followed by an argument.

Some of them got so in the habit of 'arguing the point' that their cases were considered 'chronic' before they left the service. I should not be surprised if some of them or their friends still suffer with occasional 'hemorrhages of words.' One of the characteristics of Company F was that it admitted and practiced the doctrine of free speech. It was thought sometimes that some of its members took advantage of this and were a little too *free* in that direction. A military camp (when not on duty) is an excellent place for the development of human nature *as it is*— and, on the whole, it developed along ordinary and well-defined lines, but, occasionally it was abnormal and eccentric. There were some specimens—good ones—in the company. They did much to break the monotony of camp life, but, strange to say, they were themselves sometimes monotonous. There was in the company—as among the same number anywhere else—a broad diversion of personality; but—as opposed to secession and armed rebellion—it was a unit, positive and emphatic.

In speaking of the diversity of characteristics in Company F, I ought not to forget one class of whom I have not yet spoken. Chaplain Edward D. Neill reported that the First was not a "religious regiment"—and no doubt correctly, as a large majority were not attracted to religious observances. Company F was not a 'religious' company, but Company F—like every other company—had its little circle of praying men who used to gather at convenient times in some tent or under the trees for prayer. The real leader of these was big, manly Sergeant Phillip Hamline. No man in the company but respected him and his sentiments, and he and his associates were always treated with all proper consideration by the other members of the company. There were many earnest, praying men in the regiment, and my guess is that about all of the men did some praying on special occasions.

It must not be supposed that, now that we had provided a more substantial shelter from the storm than our tents, that we occupied it all of the time. The constant recurrence of picket duty kept us at the river nearly one-third of the time—rain or shine—and there we had but little shelter. I recall that the company was sent in haste to support the pickets opposite Harrison's Island. That it was late in the day and that we found no shelter but some rail shed covered with cornstalks; and that it was snowing and blowing furiously. It continued to storm the whole time we were out, and efforts to make a fire sufficient to warm us—without smoking us out—were very unsatisfactory and finally resulted in burning the cornstalks and rails, which left us without any protection.

Inhabitants of Minnesota and the Northern states may sometimes think of that section as the 'sunny South,' but we who were there that winter remember much of it as anything but sunny. At times it was cold, reaching zero or lower, and there was a period of 16 days without a single pleasant one. I have a distinct recollection of visiting the picket posts in blinding storms of snow and sleet, when at the river; or sitting under some rude shelter with my overcoat cape pulled over my head, listening to the crushing and grinding of the masses of ice going down the stream. The soldier is an outdoor animal, and the weather conditions have much to do with his comfort or discomfort.

The cold was not so severe and snows not so deep as in Minnesota, but the *mud was deeper*. The mud was something that had to be experienced to be properly sensed. It was a revelation to us from the North. We did not know that just mud could be so *deep, so sticky, and so nasty*. Its color was something like a burnt brick. I am afraid to try to tell how bad it was lest I be accused of exaggeration, but it was a subject that scarcely admits of that. Going to and from the river, we used to tie strings about our trousers at the ankles, to keep the mud out of our shoes, and they were usually plastered with the reddish mud nearly to the knees. It took a mighty effort on the part of six mules to move even a small load, and, in many places, the axles of the wagons would smooth off the top of the mud. Under such conditions, any concerted movement was not likely to be successful, and was not attempted.

After the holidays, we began to look forward to the coming spring when we knew that there would be some movements of the great armies that had been gathered. Almost with the beginning of the year, preparation began, and it first touched the Corps of Observation when Brigadier General John Sedgwick was made a Major General and sent to command it—about the middle of January 1862. It got a little nearer to us about a fortnight later—February 3—when Col. Dana was made a brigadier and appointed to the Third Brigade.[7]

With his going, the regiment was left in command of Lieutenant Colonel Stephen Miller. The regiment had been used as a stepping stone to a higher position by one regular officer, and it was to be used by another. We perhaps did not just sense this at the time, and if we had would not have complained, for the regiment did not suffer anything by their coming and, in both cases, regretted their going. When Dana left us, it was not known to us of the ranks who was likely to succeed him, but there is always a lively interest among the men of a regiment or a company as to who will command them—especially if the look ahead indicates trouble.

At this time, preparations for an early movement were in progress and, in fact, it had already begun on the Ohio and Kentucky. I believe that the order for a general, concerted movement had already been issued—though not yet published—to begin on Washington's Birthday, February 22, 1862. It was decided that the Army of the Potomac should try to seize a point on the railroad southwest of Manassas Junction, and the move should begin Feb. 22. The general order and date was changed as the situation developed, to meet conditions.

As the winter wore away and the days lengthened, we were almost impatient to move. It seems a little surprising now that this should have been the case, for we knew that to move meant fighting, and that fighting meant death and wounds to some of us, but we were weary of waiting and wanted the war ended. None of us were so weary of life as to wish to throw it away. But we fully understood at this time that the only way to end the war successfully and save the nation undivided was to fight it to a conclusion. It was for this purpose that we had placed ourselves in the hands of the government. It was in this spirit that we contemplated the near future and prepared for the active campaign.

It is certain that the greatest possible fighting strength of Company F when it started on the trail in the spring of 1862 could not have exceeded 2 officers and

7. Sedgwick remained a brigade commander in Heintzelman's Division until February 19, 1862, when he was named to replace Stone as head of this division, which Gorman temporarily led until the nineteenth; Welcher, *Union Army*, Vol. 1, *Eastern Theater*, 247–48.

71 men, a total of 73, and it was probably one or two less than that number. Captain William Colvill commanded the company, and the second-in-command was Second Lieutenant Martin Maginnis, recently commissioned from first sergeant (or orderly sergeant as they were then called). The warrant—or noncommissioned—officers of the company were: First Sergeant Hezekiah Bruce, Second Sergeant Calvin P. Clark, Third Sergeant Henry T. Bevans, Fourth Sergeant Charles N. Harris (then held a prisoner), and Fifth Sergeant James A. Wright (recently appointed.)

Saturday, February 22nd, was Washington's Birthday, and we had been hearing the national salutes all the morning which had been fired in the different camps. This was the day for the army to move, and it was understood that a portion of it was moving, but our division was to hold that place for a few days.

Monday, February 24, was a raw, chilly day with a boisterous wind all day, and the night was freezing. We had orders that morning to pack our knapsacks and be ready to march at a moment's notice and immediately there was 'hurrying to and fro' in preparation. It did not take long to put our things in our knapsacks and get rations in our haversacks all ready to move.

It may seem a little singular, but we did not know where we were going. A year ago, if we had made all preparations to go somewhere—and had our hats on, ready to start—and did not have some idea of where we were going, we would have been thought hopelessly insane. But a year ago we were not in the army, and that is one of the differences between a citizen and a soldier. Then we had to think for ourselves; now there is someone to do that for us. This is not always pleasant or satisfactory, but it is military and we were trying to make the best of it.

At six o'clock that evening, we were told that we were to make a night march, and, an hour later, that we would remain in the camp until morning. Whoever was doing our thinking had evidently had a 'second thought.' With the riotous, freezing gale, it was more comfortable in the old camp, and we were glad to remain there.

Look back—there is a sight for you

FEBRUARY-MARCH 1862

I SHOULD AT THIS POINT in the story formally introduce the division to those who may read these papers. The division was first brought together in the autumn of 1861 on the upper Potomac and was first known as the Corps of Observation. It was then more of an aggregation of regiments than anything else and was commanded by General Charles P. Stone. Massachusetts, Michigan, Minnesota, New York, and Pennsylvania furnished the original contingents, and, later, Maine added a regiment to make up the losses of the service.

I speak of it now as it was organized under "Uncle John" Sedgwick, who first commanded it as an active, organized body: The First Brigade consisted of the Fifteenth Massachusetts, First Minnesota, Thirty-Fourth New York, and Eighty-Second New York (Second Militia), and it was commanded by our first colonel, Brigadier General W. A. Gorman; the Second Brigade was made up of the Sixty-Ninth Pennsylvania, Seventy-First Pennsylvania ("First California"), Seventy-Second Pennsylvania, and One Hundred and Sixth Pennsylvania, commanded by Brigadier General William W. Burns, of the regulars;[1] the Third Brigade was composed of the Nineteenth Massachusetts, Twentieth Massachusetts, Seventh Michigan, and the Forty-Second New York (Tammany Regiment), and it was commanded by our second colonel, N. J. T. Dana.

When the armies were organized into 'Corps de Armee' after the French plan, it became the Second Division of the Second Corps, Army of the Potomac, and wore a white 'club,' or trefoil, for a badge.[2] I make no claims for its superiority or its 'firstness,' but it was a good one, and it 'got there' occasionally.

The whole force numbered at this time in the vicinity of 10,000 men. All of these officers were newly-appointed to their positions, and none of the regiments except ours had had any other experience in actual fighting than what they had gained in the affairs along the river during the winter.

It was about 8 o'clock the morning of February 25, 1862, that it formed in line for the first time for any other purpose than drill. The cavalry led the march, and

1. This was the Philadelphia Brigade, so-called because all of its regiments were from Pennsylvania. Welcher, *Union Army*, Vol. 1, *Eastern Theater*, 248, has Dana's (First), Gorman's (Second), Burns's (Third).
2. On March 8, 1862, Lincoln's presidential order created the Second Corps (along with others). The Second Corps did not receive its trefoil badge until February 1863.

the trains followed the infantry and artillery. It was a cold morning, with a strong wind, and fleecy white clouds were scudding across the sky, giving alternate clouds and sunshine. It had frozen quite hard during the night, making ice almost hard enough to bear a man's weight, but this was soon broken up—where there was water or the mud was any depth—which made one of the unpleasant conditions of the march. As the sun rose higher and the temperature got above freezing, conditions grew worse. First—thin, spattery, reddish-yellow mud was everywhere and made the roads very slippery—and, later, they were deep with sticky mud and hard to get through. This made it especially hard on the artillery and trains, as they had to 'double up' frequently to get over—through—the worst places.

It was also pretty hard on the 'knights of the knapsack'—as the infantrymen were sometimes called. Most of us had put more in our 'bureaus' than later experience approved of, as we were just beginning then to deal with the problem of transportation in personal practice.

Our general direction was up the river but at some distance from it, and we made about 14 miles, camping towards night in a sheltered ravine near Greenfield (or Winfield) Mills. The First Brigade led the division, and our regiment the brigade, so we were the first into the bivouac, but it was long after night before the trains got in. Few if any of us had dry feet, and we were all well-splattered—with mud to our knees. Our first care was to make coffee and dry our feet, and it was not long before many little fires were burning, surrounded by interested groups, busy preparing their evening meal; each 'mess' doing their own cooking, of such as they had brought with them.

On the march, it was the custom of our regiment for each one to receive his rations as they came from the commissary, and we then formed into 'messes' according to inclination or convenience. When a halt was made for the night, one would gather wood and make a fire; another take the canteens and fill them with water; while others selected a place to sleep and prepared for the night. It was always desirable to do this before dark. Then leaves, twigs, 'pine feathers,' or anything soft and dry to intervene between the ground and the blanket, were gathered. As the ground was freezing again, as soon as we halted and stacked arms, there was a lively hunt for anything that would answer.

It was my part of the program to prepare the place for sleeping. By the time I had kicked the sticks and stones from a place on the lee side of some bushes, 'preempted' it by depositing our knapsacks on it, and gathered what I could find in the way of bedding—some of the others had a fire nearby, a supply of wood on hand, and the coffee was boiling.

It did not take a second call of "grub pile" to bring the mess together about the fire. We had brought our appetites along with us; and we made a hearty meal and enjoyed it; and the whole bill of fare was crackers, cold meat, and black coffee. We had wonderful appetites in those days after a day's march, and it was a heavy strain on the government to satisfy them.

The most of us had dry stockings to put on and managed to dry those we had worn—and our shoes—before 'turning in.' As soon as the necessary preparations were made, there was a disposition to get under the blankets. I slept with my overcoat on, and the cape wrapped about my head, and I think that was the rule. We got along pretty well for a winter night out of doors, but it was not comfortable, and we were glad when it was morning.

In fact, before it was light we were called up and got breakfast, and, soon after, we were on the march. We kept moving until we reached the railroad at Adamstown about noon, where we halted to await cars to take us to Harpers Ferry. While here, several men who had broken down on the march were sent away, one being Charley Adams of Company F. After some hours of waiting, several trains of cars of the box and flat varieties trundled into sight, and we gladly climbed into and onto these, thinking that almost anything was better than tramping through Maryland mud.

These cars soon brought us to Sandy Hook (the nearest station to Harpers Ferry), where we left them, and—as the bridge had been burned and no pontoons were yet ready—we marched to a point near where they were laying the bridge and prepared to spend the night in another nearby ravine. As we had no tents, and a storm was now threatening, the prospect of a 'bad night' was 'good'—but far from agreeable. The strong wind was giving the pontoon men lots of trouble, and it was not thought likely that they could complete the bridge before dark. But when it was almost dark and beginning to rain, we were informed that it was completed, troops were crossing, and we were to go over. Hastening to the river, we found a pontoon laid at a point a little above the government buldings—to the Virginia side. The wind was still blowing, and a mixture of snow and rain was falling.

This was our first experience on a bridge of boats; the high wind and rapid current made the pontoons unsteady; and the planks were slippery from the storm. But we made the passage in safety and found partial shelter from the storm in the half-ruined buildings of the U.S. gun works and out-buildings.

It was this point that John Brown—in his fanatical raid in October 1859—seized and held, for a time, defying the authorities of Virginia and the United States until overcome by force. A part of the regiment occupied the same buildings in which he and his followers tried to defend themselves. These buildings still bore the marks of the struggle, and the more recent attempt at destruction by the United States officials. The broken and partly-burned condition of the buildings made them but an imperfect protection from the storm—which increased hourly—but there were dry places that were very much better than being in the open without tents.

When the morning came and we could see, we were able—with a little work and our rubber blankets—to improve matters for our comfort, and we remained there during the day and night of the 27th. The storm continued all day with a very high wind, so that but little could be done in crossing men or materiel. Several mishaps had occurred, and one man was drowned. On the 28th, the storm having blown itself out, we went farther up town and found better quarters in some vacant buildings. I suppose that it was trespass, but those who had occupied them had left them, and we were not disposed to remain exposed to the storm with unoccupied houses at hand. Most of the people seemed to have left that portion of the town, and those houses might have been once occupied by those in government employ before the trouble came. During the day, the paymaster got over, and we received two months' pay.

Company F was detailed as a temporary provost guard and sent down to a house on a street near the Shenandoah River. Perhaps I should explain that the provost guards are the policemen of the army, and that all large encampments of soldiers need them just as towns and cities need policemen. Saturday evening we had an arrest to make—the only one of importance—for the State of Indiana, and the charge was murder. A state official had come on with the necessary papers, but they had to be served by the military. The man was found in his tent, arrested, and delivered to the state officers, who took him away, and we never heard more of it.

Sunday morning, we were relieved from our duties as provost guard, and directed to return to the regiment. We did not find it at the place where we had left it, and followed after it to Bolivar Heights, a range of high hills west of the town, where we overtook it. It was a sightly place, giving splendid views of the surroundings, but—as the promise of spring in the air of yesterday had vanished, and dull, grey clouds veiled the sun—a sheltered nook would have been preferable for the camp.

The tents arrived soon after noon, but a snowstorm got there first, and we had to make camp in a driving storm. It did not take long to pitch the tents, and dig a trench around them to keep out the melting snow, and shelter ourselves inside of them. There were no arrangements for warming the tents, and all we could do was to spread our rubber blankets and wrap up in the others to keep warm. Some of the boys tried making fires on the ground in their tents, as the Indians used to do in their tepees, but the tents were not built for that, and it was not a success—except for the smoking-out part.

Rations were still scarce in the camp, and, when the storm abated towards Monday night, some of the boys left the camp "to skirmish around a little for provender," as they told some of their chums. They did not return until after dark, and then very quietly—one at a time—but there was an odor of fresh mutton being cooked in the camp soon after. Of course, they could not go out or return by the guards—regularly—without a permit from an officer; so I judge their proceedings were irregular, but I never heard the details of the expedition. No one was *caught* this time, which showed that they had heeded Colonel Gorman's injunction, but I presume there were complaints, as there were stringent orders against foraging read at dress parade the next evening.

Tuesday, March 4th, was a nice, bright day, and much of the snow melted. A part of the division moved on towards Charlestown, the county seat or, as it was known in that section, the 'Court House.' But our brigade remained at Bolivar, cold and uncomfortable, until the morning of the 7th.

While waiting here, we had a fine opportunity to observe the splendid scenery of Harpers Ferry and its surroundings, and enjoyed it greatly. It is a grandly picturesque place, and, to one who knew only the prairies of Illinois and the bluffs along the Mississippi, it was magnificent in its grandeur. We were not out on a sightseeing expedition, but, so long as we were there, we did not shut our eyes to the beauties of nature.

Bolivar Heights are a range of high hills on the Virginia side, running at right angles to the Potomac and lying to the west of Harpers Ferry and the little village of Bolivar—and at a considerable elevation above them. Looking to the northward from Bolivar across the Potomac are the Maryland Heights. These are a magnificent range of hills running parallel with the river, quite close to it, and somewhat higher than Bolivar Heights. Looking to the eastward across the Shenandoah River is the Loudoun Heights, running parallel with that river—about the same height as Bolivar and extending southward to the Bull Run ranges. The Potomac runs at the base of the Maryland Heights; and the Shenandoah at the base of the Loudoun Heights; the two uniting in their passage through a gap between the two ranges.

The whole scene was one to impress itself on the mind and set one to thinking if it had always been thus. And, if not, how it had happened to assume its present form. At some long-past time, in some great convulsion of nature, did the pentup waters between the Loudoun and Blue Ridge ranges break their mountain barriers and make a channel to the sea? Or was that huge chasm, through which the united waters rush, worn away by the erosions of many centuries? Whether it was the result of nature's dynamics in a day or the abrasions of thousands of years, the effect is the same, and the scene one that clings to the memory.

In the angle made by the two rivers and enclosed on three sides by the great hills, the town of Harpers Ferry is situated. It must have been a beautiful place in its days of prosperity; but, in my mind, it is associated with decay and ruin. I saw it only after it had been marred by the ruthless hand of war, its factories desolated by fire, and its dwellings deserted. The splendid waterpower caused this place to be chosen by the government for the location of one of its principal factories for the production of small arms. The large supply of arms there caused John Brown to attempt its seizure, which, in turn, resulted in his being hung. There were about 80,000 muskets there at the time that Virginia decided to seize the factories and arsenal. Harpers Ferry—dominated as it is by the hills on three sides of it—is not an easily defensible place, except by a large force.[3]

Friday morning, we left the camp at Bolivar and marched for Charlestown. Being the rear guard, we did not arrive until some time after noon. It was my turn for guard duty, and I felt it was good fortune that it did not storm. (It was a rarity to go on guard without a storm.) We had a fine camping place near Charlestown, and the improved weather conditions made us all feel more comfortable and cheerful.

We spent Saturday and Sunday at Charlestown. The two days were pleasant, and we had an opportunity to see the place—but not much of the people. As a rule, they carefully avoided us. It was here that John Brown was tried and hung on the 2nd of December, 1859, and the spot where the gallows was erected was a place of interest to many. The county seat, Charlestown, had been a place of considerable importance. It had had a railroad and a telegraph line, but both of these had been damaged quite seriously by the rebels before they had left. Parties were at work rebuilding the bridges and restoring the wires. The *Virginia Free Press,* a weekly paper of some note, had been published there, but, like many other things blighted by the war, it had been discontinued. On Sunday, March 9th, Chaplain Neill preached in one of the churches,[4] and the regiment attended, marching in a body in full uniform. (I think that this was brought about by an arrangement between our chaplain and the minister of the church, but I cannot speak positively as to that.)

On Monday morning, March 10, we were awakened early and ordered to prepare to march. We hastened our breakfast and, soon after daylight, we left the camp. Our brigade led the division, and the First Regiment headed the brigade, but a company of Van Allen's cavalry preceded us. We were closely followed by the rest of the brigade and by John A. Tomkins's Battery A, First Rhode Island Light Artillery. There had been considerable skirmishing at the outposts, and the enemy was supposed to be in force at Winchester—perhaps nearer. It seemed almost certain that there would be trouble somewhere before night.

Our line of march was along the Winchester and Berryville turnpike, and we expected to strike them before reaching the latter place. The pike was a fairly good road, and we advanced rapidly. It was threatening a storm, and we were scarcely on the road before a mild rain set in and continued for some hours. This made the road slippery and added to the fatigue—in addition to the discomforts of a cold rain. With our rubber blankets, we were able to cover our shoulders and

3. Wanting to reopen the Baltimore and Ohio Railroad and realizing Harpers Ferry was not defensible nor an adequate defense of the railroad, General McClellan sent two brigades of Sedgwick's Division to help Nathaniel Banks capture the lower Shenandoah Valley.

4. Neill, a Presbyterian, preached at Charlestown's Presbyterian church; Moe, *Last Full Measure,* 114.

bodies, but our legs and feet were soon soaked. Towards noon, the storm ceased, and, soon after, the cavalry in advance began firing occasionally.

It was some time after noon, when about two miles out of Berryville, that they showed a disposition to dispute the further advance of the cavalry. We first sighted them posted along a ridge and around some stacks in a field, something like a mile in front. Preparations were at once made to attack them. Two companies of the regiment—B and K—were deployed forward to skirmish, and the rest of the regiment formed line of battle in support. The battery galloped up and swung into position on the rising ground to the left of the road, and the cavalry moved off across the fields to get on the enemy's flank. All of this was done very quickly and without confusion, showing the results of the constant training we had been having.

The skirmishers advanced; the regiment followed; and the battery began shelling. There was an immediate commotion among the people on the hill, and, as soon as our skirmishers opened fire, they commenced to leave.

It was at this time that the sun shone out brightly below the clouds, which were lifting before a strong westerly wind. Someone said, "Look back—there is a sight for you." Looking, we saw that the other regiments of the brigade had broken from the marching column and were coming into battle front; the smoke of the guns was blown quickly away over their heads in fleecy, white clouds; beyond them, the rest of the division was coming over a hill—apparently, out of a background of dark clouds. In the sunshine it made a magnificent picture—a splendid battle scene with its landscape and clouds, moving battalions, streaming flags, and smoking guns—which thrilled us with its beauty and its completeness.

It was realistic, too, to the highest degree, for we were hastening forward, and we did not then know if we were to meet 200 or 10,000 of the enemy over the ridge. As our skirmishers went forward, the enemy's disappeared back of the ridge, where they had horses in waiting, and the next seen of them they were mounted and scurrying away. Of course, we could not keep up with mounted men, but we followed as rapidly as possible into and through the town, and our cavalry pursued for some distance beyond. There were a few casualties and a few captures, but the cavalry suffered all of the loss and brought in all of the prisoners.

The infantry took possession of the town, hoisted the Stars and Stripes, posted troops and artillery, stationed pickets, and prepared to bivouac for the night, as it was now about sunset. Our regiment halted in a grove on the outer edge of the village, where we spent the night, and we were glad that it was not our turn for picket. It was now clear and freezing, and we had rather an uncomfortable night of it without tents. There was considerable firing between the pickets during the night but no serious alarms.

There was a paper published at this place called the *Berryville Conservator*, and a portion of the paper had been set up before our arrival, but the editor and his help had 'skedaddled' along with the soldiers. The printers in the regiment—and among them Company F's contingent was prominent—managed to get into the office of the 'secesh sheet,' changed the name of the paper to that of *The First Minnesota* and its policy to one of radical support of the Union cause. A paper was set up, struck off, and ready for distribution before morning, when it found ready sale around the camps.

Early in the morning, the cavalry—backed by a strong infantry force—was sent out after the fellows that had been making a disturbance during the night. They were found a couple of miles down the road, attacked, and pursued for some miles. In this running fight, several were killed and wounded, and a number of prisoners were taken. Our cavalry also suffered some loss. We remained in the bivouac during the day, and it was the talk of the camp that we had come into the valley as a support to the forces of General James Shields, and that we were waiting some 'bagging' movement on his part.[5] I do not think that I ever really understood the plan of our operations in the Valley at this time.

In the afternoon, wagons came up with rations and tents, and we started to pitch our tents, but at about the same time there was an alarm, and we at once prepared to march. Going to the front, we found it not to be a serious matter and we returned to the camp before night. Sleeping in our tents we found preferable to lying in the open—even if they were not heated.

Early Thursday morning, we left the camp and 'struck the pike' for Winchester, where it was thought the main force of the enemy in the Valley was located. A little before we were to leave the camp, a medium-sized man with grey hair, mustache, and goatee came to the regiment and announced himself as Alfred Sully, the newly-appointed colonel, and that he was there to assume command of the First Regiment. Having verified his assertions to the satisfaction of Lieutenant Colonel Miller he was presented as the Colonel, and without further words or ceremony he at once took command. We were getting somewhat used to having new colonels, but it would not be true to assert that we were indifferent, for we were properly anxious about—and keenly observant of—this new man. We were already in line and started almost immediately on the march.

He was, we understood, a regular and came direct from active service in the West. He did not attempt to 'put on any style'; there was no effort at display and self-assertion; he gave but few orders, and these were in as few words as possible and in but an ordinary, commonplace way. Of course, he was 'talked over' and judgment passed on him, and, long before night, I heard several assertions to the effect that "he would do," but I am inclined to think that most of the boys felt like reserving their opinions until better acquainted. All of the information that we had about him at that time was that he was the senior captain in the regular army; that he had graduated from West Point in 1841; that he had served in the Mexican and Indian wars; and that he had a good record back of him.

---

5. For less than one year (1857–58), James Shields had been U.S. Senator from Minnesota, but his association with the state was brief; Folwell, *Minnesota,* 2:6–9.

We marched steadily and rapidly until towards noon, when—near Winchester—we were halted. It was the talk that Jackson's forces had retreated from Winchester, and, as a supporting force, we were not needed any longer and were to return or go to some other place. The enemy in the Valley was to be left to others. There was talk, too, that we were ordered to some point down the coast, but at this time we had ceased to attach any importance to the stories of the camp.

After an hour or two of rest, we returned to Berryville, where we halted and spent the night—it being late when we arrived. Here, again, our new colonel made a further good impression (to that which had been gaining all day) by the brief, business-like way he gave the orders to halt, stack arms, and break ranks—directing that we make ourselves as comfortable as we could for the night.

Up to this time, it had been the custom to keep a guard around the camp and confine men to its limits, unless they had special permit to go outside. It was announced the next morning that, until further orders, there would be no more guards about the camp, but that the men were expected to meet all of the requirements for their presence in the camp without being forced to by a guard. This was—so far as their presence in the camp was concerned—placing the men and officers on an equality, and it worked well. There were no further orders for a camp guard as long as he commanded the regiment or any increase of complaints of men absent without leave. This arrangement was mutually satisfactory, made no sort of trouble, and it made the new colonel 'solid' with the boys, as they did not have to go on guard half so often. Of course, it was necessary to have a guard at headquarters and at the commissary tent, but it took comparatively few men for this to what it did to circle the camp.

Early Friday morning, we were moving on the return march from Berryville and halted for the night in the outskirts of Charlestown. Both going out and returning, we had frequently to wade streams, which wet our feet. The trains had cut up the surface of the road very badly; and the sharp, broken stone, of which it was made, cut our shoes and bruised our feet; while the water and sand caused them to chafe and blister. Many of us were getting sore feet. I had started with a good pair of shoes—almost new—and now my shoes were practically sole-less, and my feet in bad condition. Many were worse off than I was.

It was late Saturday afternoon before we reached Bolivar—wet, cold, hungry, tired, and foot-sore. By this time, about every one that had not carried an extra pair of shoes was practically barefoot. It may seem surprising that a pair of shoes should not last a week, but that 'pike road'—after its surface was broken by the heavy trains—was very destructive. Then, too, our shoes were not always of the best quality.

On Sunday, we spent the day in our tents resting and trying to repair our damaged feet, and during the day I managed to get a pair of shoes from the Quartermaster—as did several others of the company. I had learned something and tried after that to have an extra pair of shoes always ready for such an emergency. I recall that there were some cattle butchered that morning, and we got a supply of suet and gave our shoes a coating of tallow in the hope to make them more durable.

Monday morning, we were awakened by the bands of some of the regiments playing 'St. Patrick's Day in the Morning.' The most of the regiments had bands at the first of the war, and the First took out East an excellent band. W. H. Colling was the leader. He was a tall man and his pet name was 'Nail Rod.' M. S. Kellogg and Benjamin Hazen were band members from Red Wing. Pete Hoffman was the drummer celebrity of the band. He had served with Sherman's Battery in the regulars, and was an expert with the drum sticks. The drum major's name was Fletcher Rowell, and it was Ernest Myer, perhaps, that used to trill the bugle. The bands were sent home after the Peninsula campaign, if I remember correctly, as a matter of economy.

I think that it was Monday evening, March 17, that we were officially informed that the army had been organized into 'Corps de Armee' and that our division was to be the Second Division of the Second Corps. The division was to remain under its present commander, Brigadier General John Sedgwick, and the corps was to be commanded by Major General Edwin V. Sumner, one of the senior colonels of the regular army.

We remained at Bolivar for the next four days. The first of these was a fair spring day, and we had drill and dress parade, but the following three were a continuous storm of rain, sleet, and snow, with high winds. We had not expected any such weather in the sunny South at that season, and we had seen much better in March in Minnesota. The natives there said that it was unusual and charged the Yankees with "bringing their weather with them."

Some of the boys found a number of copies of the Virginia papers of the year before that made interesting reading for a rainy day. Having been published in the winter and spring of 1861, when the question of seceding was before the people, they dealt largely with that question. It was pretty evident that Virginia was forced into secession by a few of its leaders and the states farther south that had already seceded. In one of these papers, there was a dispatch from Governor Pickens of South Carolina to Governor Letcher of Virginia, immediately after the firing on Fort Sumter. It said: "The war has begun; what will Virginia do?" One of the papers spoke very highly of the patriotic action of Colonel Robert E. Lee in leaving the United States Army and joining with the Confederacy (and this was coupled with an order for the assembling of the Virginia Militia). Being then of immature judgment, and also in the employ of the United States, we young fellows could not see anything patriotic in his action.

On the afternoon of March 21, we had orders to be in readiness to march at six o'clock the next morning. On Saturday morning, the 22nd, the storm continued, and we marched, but not so early as ordered. I recall that as we went down the muddy, slippery street, the water was running a flood and the best use we could make of our rubber blankets was to protect our bodies. We were really a comical sight as we splashed through the mud and water—each man with his head through the opening in his blanket; his hat pulled tightly onto his head and the brim turned down; carrying his rifle in the crook of his right arm with the muzzle down, and the lock and breech under the blanket to keep them dry.

Thus equipped, we passed down from Bolivar Heights, through Bolivar and Harpers Ferry, across the Potomac, and down to Sandy Hook, where we halted to wait for the cars. It was afternoon before cars were available, and we were very glad that they were covered cars—though the storm had now ceased its severity—but we were very closely crowded, and it was anything but 'pleasant riding on the rail.' It was past midnight when we reached Washington. Getting out at the depot of the Baltimore and Ohio road, we went into the 'Soldier's Retreat' to pass the rest of the night.

I perhaps ought to explain that the Soldier's Retreat was a building erected to give temporary shelter and food to soldiers in transit—provided and maintained, wholly or in part, by patriotic people from private contributions. The one at Washington was called the Soldier's Retreat; the one in Philadelphia, The Union Volunteer Refreshment Saloon; and the one in Chicago, which the First Regiment helped to dedicate in February 1864, The Soldier's Rest. It does not matter what they were called or where they were located, they were a grand and good thing, and they touched a responsive chord in the better nature of all who shared in the benevolent provision.

Ours was a case in point. Since leaving the camp, there had been no opportunity to cook any food or make a cup of coffee. When we left the cars and entered the Retreat, we were met with an odor of cooking coffee that was positively exhilarating. We were expected; hot coffee was waiting for us; and there was no time lost in serving it. If the good people who had originated and promoted that plan of giving 'aid and comfort' to the soldiers while traveling had heard the many and grateful benedictions from the hungry partakers of their benefactions, I am sure it would have encouraged them in their good work. Giving one a cup of coffee and permitting one to sleep on a bare board may not seem like a very high grade of hospitality, but we judge of things by comparison, and compared with remaining out in the streets supperless or sleeping on the frozen ground (as we had done several times recently) it was almost luxurious.

After filling up with hot coffee and government crackers, we wrapped ourselves in our blankets and slept on the floor until morning, when we were all ready for more coffee. We got it, too, and a loaf of soft bread, the first we had had since leaving Camp Stone.

After breakfast, we marched to the Capitol grounds and found a place of shelter in some old buildings near there. The usual Sunday morning inspection was postponed until the afternoon—that we might get ourselves in a better appearing condition—and was followed by a dress parade, which attracted a large crowd. Colonel Sully appeared to put us on exhibition and to be pleased with the results.

Both Monday and Tuesday evenings we held dress parades on the Capitol grounds, which brought out immense crowds of people. They were really 'swell affairs,' and everything went off in a way that brought a storm of applause at the close. A review before President Lincoln was planned for the afternoon of Wednesday, previous to the dress parade, but both were indefinitely postponed by orders to march.

Just before night, we left our temporary encampment and marched by the way of Long Bridge into Virginia. This was our fourth invasion of the 'sacred soil,' and we went forward hopefully. We halted after passing Fort Runyon and waited by the roadside. After waiting for some time, a train of flat cars came up the track, and we ran slowly down to Alexandria. Protecting ourselves the best we could from the storm, we waited until it began to get light, when we were marched out to the camping place we had occupied before going to Bull Run in July 1861. Here we went into bivouac without tents, and, as the storm was now pretty well spent, we tried to make fires and get something for breakfast. A Soldier's Retreat would have been appreciated that night and morning, but we were in Virginia where they did not have such things for Union soldiers. The only thing that Virginia offered in the way of hospitality to Union soldiers was "hospitable graves." There were not many of our fellows looking for graves that morning—though most of them looked grave enough.

There were a few, however, that were out looking for a 'burial place'—the place where they had buried the remains of the barrel of whiskey they had 'acquired' from the sutler the night before we had started for Bull Run. They found it, too, all right; dug it up; and brought it into camp (the contents). It got there before the coffee was boiling—and, naturally, something a little stronger than coffee was acceptable to almost everyone. In our wet and chilled condition, there were but a few that refused a swallow of the 'resurrected' whiskey, no matter what they might have done with common 'corn juice' under ordinary circumstances. It could not have been found more opportunely or at a time when it would do less harm.

During the morning, the sky cleared, and it was learned that there were many regiments in and about Alexandria. Many ships—steamers and sailing vessels—were in the river; troops of all arms, provisions, and military stores of all kinds, were going on board; and we were told this loading process had been going on night and day for some time. We were there to take shipping for some point down the river.

Having learned that the Second Regiment of Berdan Sharpshooters[6] were encamped nearby—and knowing that there was a company from Minnesota in the regiment in which were some old friends—we obtained leave and hunted them

6. New Yorker Hiram Berdan, who was the best rifle marksman in the nation before the Civil War, initiated the recruiting of two regiments of sharpshooters. He led the First while the Second was commanded by Colonel Henry A. Post. Both regiments were used mainly as skirmishers.

up. We found them encamped not far off and, like ourselves, waiting orders. It was delightful to meet old friends and townspeople, and there were many things to talk about—though they had been away from home since the previous October. I recall meeting Jim Hawes, Dan Heald, Abe Howe, Albert and Frank Little, John T. Veeder, and Abe Wright. I am quite sure that there were some others, whose names I fail to remember, from Red Wing and vicinity. The next day we had a visit from the Red Wing boys in the Sharpshooters, and all found many friends in Company F. It was the first meeting of the kind since we left home. This was Company A of the Second Berdan, and our good friend Abraham Wright was then orderly sergeant of the company.

Saturday afternoon, we left the camp and marched to the wharf at Alexandria. We watched with interest the scene presented in the loading of troops and stores. The river was swarming with floating craft of various descriptions. Barrels, boxes, and bales; horses, mules, wagons, gun carriages, guns, and caissons; saddles, harnesses; hay, grain, and all kinds of supplies were being put on board as rapidly as possible. It was indeed a big job when it was decided to transfer the army with all of its materiel from Alexandria to Fortress Monroe.

We were obliged to wait for a time before going on board and were naturally interested in the *modus operandi* of a great army 'taking to the water.' We were seeing things on a different scale and in a different way from what we had ever seen them before. Apparently everything available that would float had been gathered into the Potomac, which has a depth here that will admit ocean steamers, and many of them were being pulled about by noisy little tugs that puffed and screeched up and down the stream, towing vessels to and from the landings. The *impedimenta* of the army was being hurried on board of these craft at every available point and as rapidly as possible. While waiting, we found amusement in watching the busy scene, especially the way the horses and mules were hoisted on board in 'slings' with a 'tackle'; the surprised animals being lifted into the air, swung over the vessel, and spun into the hold with great rapidity.

Our regiment was divided into two parts, and we were directed to go on board two small steamers, the *Jenny Lind* and the *Golden Gate.* It did not take long to transfer the regimental effects from the wharf to the boats and get ourselves on board. All company tents and surplus property was left behind, and (though we did not then know it), thereafter, while we remained in the 'tented field' we were to remain 'tentless.' Like the snail, we were to carry our habitations on our backs or use the 'blue canopy' for a covering.

Company F was on board the *Jenny Lind,* and we were in a closely-crowded condition. It was snowing when we were going on board, and snow squalls continued until night. After all were on board, we pulled out into the stream, took two transports in tow, and steamed down near Fort Washington, where we anchored for the night. There was a keen, raw wind, and we passed an uncomfortable night on the decks of the steamer.

Knights of the knapsack

APRIL-JUNE 1862

SWINGING TO THE TIDE on the Potomac in sight of Fort Washington and with Mount Vernon and Washington's tomb not far away, we naturally thought and talked of The Father of His Country, and wondered what view he would take of the then condition of affairs. The bare idea that he *could* have endorsed the course that Virginia had taken seemed revolting, but someone—I think that it was Frank Bachelor—asserted that he "had been a rebel once" and that he "might, if alive, do it again." This, of course, brought on an argument, and there were a variety of opinions, which, as usual, settled nothing.

It seemed to me that if Washington could in any way have been cognizant of what was transpiring in his old haunts, that he would have been mightily disturbed in 'his last slumber' and said worse things to his Lee relative—R. E.—than he did to that other Lee—R. H.—at the battle of Monmouth.[1]

Nothing occurred of particular note, but there was plenty to interest in the scenery along the shore, the old historic places along the river sharing our attention with the recently-vacated earthworks of the enemy. Washington, his predecessors, and his compeers had made the earlier history of Virginia. Perhaps we might have a place in some of the later editions? It was a pretty large thought for our youthful minds, but we entertained it and talked about it, and considered the possibilities of what might be before we journeyed again towards the North Star.

At this time, we had begun to understand quite distinctly that the common soldier had but one thing to do—obey orders to the best of his ability—and that therein lay his whole duty. He had nothing to do with the formulating of plans. It was a pretty hard lesson for the independent youngster to learn, and it had not been learned without considerable wear and tear to our feelings, which were still sensitive to the touch. But it was not particularly different in our American army from what it was in the Roman legions in the days of the old Centurion that we used to study about in Sunday school. In setting forth his own importance as a captain of a company, he incidentally showed how it was with the other fellows, when he said, "I say unto one, 'Go,' and he goeth; and to another, 'Come,' and he

1. Calling him a "damned poltroon," George Washington at Monmouth lost his temper at General Charles Lee—not at Richard Henry Lee, nor at Robert E. Lee's father, Henry ("Lighthorse Harry") Lee. Robert E. Lee was married to a descendant of Martha Washington.

cometh; and to my servant, 'Do,' and he doeth it." We were the *other fellows*, the 'under-me-soldiers,' and realized it. But if the great purpose for which we had placed ourselves "under authority" could be accomplished in that way, then we were ready to meet all the conditions to the best of our ability.

As we came down Chesapeake Bay, one of the sailors had pointed out the location of Cape Henry and Cape Charles, and told us that the Atlantic Ocean lay beyond them. This was our first view of the ocean, if what we were then able to see can be called a view. Here were historical associations running back to the very beginning of the English-speaking people on the American Continent. It was between those capes that Newport's ships first came in April 1607. It was near where we then were that Captain John Smith had dropped his anchor April 26, 1607; and found what he considered a safe harbor; and, as expressive of his feelings, called it Point Comfort. Over two hundred and fifty years had been transferred from time to eternity since then. Many things had changed and much had been wrought, touching the history of that section and of all of the world.

The latest event—then scarce three weeks old—was the fight between the *Merrimac* and the *Monitor,* an official notice to all the world that naval warfare had been revolutionized, and that they must remodel their navies to meet the new conditions. One of the parties to that contest, the original *Monitor,* was lying near where we anchored, and was a matter of intense interest. Lying low on the water and of insignificant appearance, there was nothing to indicate its great power as an engine of war. We had a good view of it in the morning as we were going to the shore, and observed some of the marks of the *Merrimac*'s shots which had left a few dents and scratches on the turret.

Tuesday morning, April 1, leaving its tow at anchor, the *Jenny Lind* steamed to shore and landed. After a little delay, we went into bivouac between the Fortress and the ruined village of Hampton. We enjoyed the air, the sunshine, and the pleasure of release from the crowded and cramped condition of the boat to the freedom of our feet on the land.

Some of the boys went fishing for oysters at low tide and found them plentiful. On one side of us was what had been the village of Hampton, now only burned and blackened ruins, without inhabitants as far as we could observe—the result of an effort of General John B. Magruder of the Confederate forces to annex Fortress Monroe to the Confederacy. On the other side of us was Fortress Monroe, then, as now, the largest and finest fortress owned by the United States. We managed to go all around it and view its walls from across the moats, but were not allowed inside. Some heavy guns were being mounted outside the walls as a water battery. A force of men were busy drilling an artesian well to insure a better water supply for the garrison. This was one of the first defensive places on the coast. It was first planned in 1614—for a palisaded fort for a defense to the first settlers—and a few years later was improved and enlarged. So far as I can learn, it has been practically a military post ever since.

A great army was here already, and more were arriving every hour, going into camp along the shore from Newport News to a point beyond the fort. At Big Bethel and beyond Hampton were the enemy's pickets, and it was expected that we would move against them soon, and, at the first movement, that there would be fighting. We remained at the bivouac awaiting orders until the afternoon of April fourth, when we were directed to draw three days' rations and to be prepared to march early the next morning.

Long before daylight, we were in line and drawn out on the road, but it was not until after daylight that we were fairly moving. The morning was beautiful and grew into an unusually warm day for the season, and this caused many of the boys to shed their dress coats and extra blankets—an act that they regretted before the next forty-eight hours were over. There was some firing at the front early in the day, and it was repeated at intervals during the afternoon. Just enough to remind us of the business we were on, but there was no serious fighting.

An incident of the day was our first sight of McClellan, the commander of our army. He rode by, followed by a numerous staff and a cavalry escort, all well-dressed and splendidly mounted. Of course, everybody cheered for 'Little Mac' with hearty, hopeful earnestness, for in those earlier days of the war we still had great confidence in our leaders and ourselves. Notwithstanding the result of previous efforts, we blindly hoped to capture Richmond and end the war in time to celebrate the Fourth of July at home. It was well for our peace of mind that spring morning that we failed to perceive that our troubles and misfortunes were—most of them—yet to come.

General McClellan and Colonel Sully were old comrades and friends, and it was reported from the head of the regiment that, in passing, Gen. McClellan, in acknowledging the formal salute, had called out pleasantly to Col. Sully, "How are you, Alf?" And Sully had promptly responded, "All O.K. How is George?"

We continued the march early the next morning. Meantime, the beautiful weather that had smiled upon us for three or four days was frowning now, with heavy clouds and a drizzling rain, and there was a chill in the air that convinced everyone that had parted with an extra coat or blanket that their action had been 'a little previous.'

At Big Bethel, where we had spent the night, the enemy had several small forts and barricades and had evidently been there in some force, but they had retired with only light skirmishing. After leaving the bivouac, we marched rapidly for a short time, and there was sharp firing of both artillery and musketry, which led us to anticipate that there would be severe fighting soon. For the rest of the day, there were long halts, sudden starts, and rapid marching, and that general expectation of troops who are following a force that is skirmishing its way. In many places, trees had been cut down to obstruct the road; they had to be removed.

We halted that night in what seemed to be a swamp in the woods. There was a mixture of rain and snow falling; the water was dripping from the trees; and everywhere underfoot was mud and water. In the morning, we found a little more satisfactory location nearby, but there was no escape from the mud. The whole peninsula was covered with mud and ooze. We called this place "Camp Misery" on account of its disagreeable location, utter lack of all physical comforts, and the long-continued storm of cold rain.

The amount of physical labor performed by the troops in front of Yorktown was great and severe. It would be tedious to follow the daily routine, but we were almost constantly on duty. One day we would be building roads at the rear[2] and assisting to get up guns and supplies; and the next, sharpshooting along the front. One night we would be building breastworks and digging ditches at the advanced positions; and the next, guarding others while they worked. Who of the comrades does not recall "those hours of toil and danger," as some of the boys used to sing, when we were making corduroy roads and trying to get up supplies?

Who does not remember the mules of the Peninsula campaign? How they used to struggle along over those miserable roads, tugging doggedly at their heavy loads, suffering and dying—literally and numerously—in the service of their country? How they mired in the treacherous swamps, broke their legs between the unsteady logs of the corduroy, and suffered other mishaps that brought death—until the margins of the roads, often covered with water, were outlined by the dead mules? Who does not remember the 'concerts' that the hungry mules used to give us in the early morning, about feeding time, when rations were scarce?

It was a dreary, cheerless, miserable existence for men and mules in front of Yorktown—made so to a great degree by the adverse weather conditions. We felt that we could fully sympathize with our Revolutionary ancestors and their French allies in their investment of the same place eighty-odd years before. It was encouraging and sustaining to feel during the discomforts and dangers of the siege that Washington and other illustrious men had been there before us.

Illustrative of life in front of Yorktown, I will relate an incident of one of the 'boys in blue' of Company F who was familiarly known as Dixie. The regiment had spent the night on picket; it had rained incessantly; and we were wet to the skin and chilled to the bone. When relieved in the morning, we had returned to our comfortless camp at the rear—presenting much of the appearance and about as animated as a lot of rained-on fowls. Like all perpetually-hungry soldiers, we at once made preparations for cooking and devouring our rations.

Dixie was observed sitting with his back against an old pine stump, his elbows on his knees, and his chin in his hands. He was gazing with a woebegone expression at his haversack, which lay open between his feet, disclosing its contents in anything but a desirable condition to a hungry man. The water had in some way

2. The army's best roadmaking unit was "the 1st Minnesota regiment, whose skilled woodsmen could clear a mile of road and corduroy a quarter of it in a day"; Stephen W. Sears, *To the Gates of Richmond: The Peninsula Campaign* (New York: Ticknor and Fields, 1992), 58.

gotten into his rations. The hardtack was softened by the moisture; the coffee, which had been in an envelope, was loose and adhering to the pork and wet crackers; while sugar and salt had experienced dissolution and vanished. Dixie's 'bonnie suit of blue' was the worse for wear, wet and stained with mud from the trenches, while his face bore evidence of fatigue and suffering.

"What is the matter, Dixie?" asked a sergeant.

"I - I wish I was in father's barn," said Dixie, with tears in his eyes and voice.

"Well, suppose you were, what then?"

"I'd go to the house *darned quick*," replied Dixie with a mournful smile and a quivering lip.

I relate this incident with no other emotions than those of deep respect for his genuine human feelings, so quaintly expressed. The writer was himself suffering too keenly from homesickness and the discomforts of the situation to do otherwise than sympathize with his discouraged mood. Many a man who was as brave as a lion in battle—as he sat or stood by a smoky campfire of wet, green pine wood that sizzled and sputtered in the falling rain; or wet, cold, tired, and hungry, as he spread his blanket on the damp ground—longed for the accommodations of his father's barn, whether he expressed his feelings in words or not. Let no one think of Dixie as a puerile specimen of a soldier boy. He was not. On the contrary, he was a tall, handsome fellow, and usually in excellent spirits. He proved his soldierly qualities on all of the Peninsula battlefields and met a gallant death at Antietam in Maryland.

Much of the land was now overflowed from the frequent heavy rains. The only means of observation other than the skirmish line were the balloons. These were still something of a novelty in war. Though occasional attempts had been made to show their practical utility, I am not sure that the experiments as a whole were satisfactory.

There was one attempt, at least, that came near having a disastrous termination. It was the morning of April 11th that a balloon was seen above the trees to our right and, naturally, attracted attention.[3] It was the custom to anchor these balloons when they had reached a height of a few hundred feet and pull them down at the close of observation. This morning, through some mishap, the balloon did not stop but kept rising until it was certain that its retaining ropes were broken. It seemed to be going directly over the Confederate works, and at a great height. It was now a matter of intense interest, and we all considered that the occupants had a fair chance of getting their breakfasts in Richmond.

In a very short time, it was seen to be descending and also coming back towards our lines on a returning current, which they had fortunately struck. It came

3. This mishap occurred to General Porter on April 11 when he took the balloon *Intrepid* up—apparently alone. A shift in wind and his reach for the gas valve rescued him. Sears, *To the Gates of Richmond*, 54; Henry S. Commager, *The Blue and the Gray* (New York: Fairfax Press, 1982), 310–12.

down in the camp of our division, and the occupants escaped with no more serious injury than a rolling in the mud (the basket upset when it struck the ground, and spilled them out) and, perhaps, some rents in their clothes. One of the occupants was General Fitz John Porter, but I do not recall the name of the aeronaut who was managing the balloon. Whoever he was, he was a brave fellow, as it was said that the vent valve of the balloon would not work quick enough, and he climbed the netting and cut a hole in the balloon that the gas might escape and let it descend.

April 11th was almost a memorable day for us. We not only had a better camping place, but tents were issued to us; there was a fragrance of spring in the air; and the birds were singing in the trees, unmindful of human strife. These tents were not 'Marquees' or even the wall tents we had had in Maryland, but a diminutive model of the old 'A tent' with the two ends cut out. They were called 'shelter tents' and the boys renamed them 'dog tents' on account of their likeness, when set up, to an ordinary dog kennel. In a little while, they became generally known as 'pup tents' and were so called to the close of the war.

They were sectional in their construction, and each soldier drew a section or piece, and it was charged to him, as was other property in his possession. It was simply a piece of cotton or coarse linen cloth, perhaps six feet long by five in width—not more than that. On one side and the two ends, there was a row of button holes at the edge; and one row of buttons about three inches back; and a cord loop at each corner on the side where there were no buttons or holes.

To use these, two soldiers 'pooled their issues' (issues of tent cloth), cut two forked stakes of a proper height, and a pole of the right length. The stakes were stuck in the ground about six feet apart; the 'ridge pole' was placed in the forks of the stakes; the sides of the two pieces of cloth were buttoned together; they were then stretched over the ridge pole, drawn tight, and spread as far apart as they would go and still touch the ground; and secured at the corners by driving a pin through the loop into the ground. The ends were left open or closed with the rubber blankets, as the weather made it desirable.

Two soldiers occupied one of these tents. There were no other tents than these furnished to the enlisted men or line officers while on active duty. The only difference was that company officers were allowed two pieces of tent each, and they were carried for them, while the enlisted man was allowed but one and had to carry it himself. This relieved the mules, but it added to the burdens of the men. They were not a very good shelter, but they were much better than none, and the last ten days' exposure to the inclement weather made us feel that they were a great addition to our means of comfort. They simply provided a sheltered place where two soldiers could spread their blankets and crawl into at night, and find a little protection from dew and rain.

Soon after we had been definitely settled as to location, Companies F and E were sent to the picket line. We were instructed to keep out of sight and not to fire unless it was necessary to repel an advance. I do not remember that we did any firing, but the enemy 'felt for us' several times. At such time, we laid low or took to the big trees. There was no one hit, though they 'barked' a number of trees over our heads.

There was the usual Sunday morning inspection, April 13, and notice was given of a general inspection for the next day. Our chaplain preached in the afternoon, for the first time since we were at Charlestown—and, incidentally, referred to the siege of Yorktown in 1781 when Cornwallis surrendered to the forces of Washington and Lafayette. He told us that the grandfather of our present colonel, Alfred Sully, had been killed during that siege.

There was scarcely a night without its alarms or a day without its tragedies, and frequently there was sharp firing at several places at the same time. Many incidents, some tragic and some amusing, occurred in connection with those awakenings to face an unseen foe in the darkness of the forest. I cannot refrain from recounting one of the latter in this connection.

Our regiment, not being in the trenches, was placed in reserve to be used in case of an attack and ordered to 'sleep on our arms,' which meant that we should have our guns ready for instant use. It was an extremely dark night, and early in the evening there had been a violent thunderstorm. The heavy masses of clouds floated so near the earth that they appeared to touch the tops of the pines, and the rain fell in streams as if the clouds had been ripped open by coming in contact with the trees. Many of the boys had provided temporary shelters with their blankets and rubbers, near where we were to form if necessary. The officers were grouped among the trees a little ways to the rear, trying to make the best of an unpleasant situation.

The night was wearing away with less than the usual amount of firing when suddenly the shots began to come 'in twos and threes'—the premonitory symptoms of an irruption. These were quickly followed by heavy volleys of musketry and the batteries joined in to help make the 'night hideous' and the shells were screeching and smashing among the trees. "Ah! then and there was hurrying to and fro."

With the first volley, Colonel Sully had sprung to his feet, and, with a sharp command of "Fall in, men!" he had started to the line where we were to form. In his haste and the darkness, he ran into one of these impromptu shelters, from which the occupants had not yet made their exit. The shelter went down a complete wreck, and the colonel sprawled over it into the mud just in the rear of the rapidly-forming line.

About this time, the first terrific outburst had spent itself, and there was a little lull in the firing. One of the occupants—having extricated himself from the wet blankets, and not knowing exactly whether he had been run over by someone or had a man fired at him from the batteries, and being considerably disturbed over matters as they were—sought to relieve his feelings by a vigorous use of expletives. Meantime, the Colonel—who had regained his feet, shook the water from him, and spit the mud out of his mouth—let loose a volley of the choicest cuss words that he had been able to pick up during his long service on the frontiers.

By this time, the soldier had recognized his Colonel by his swearing, and was more anxious to find his place in line than anything else just then. But he sought to explain matters by asserting that he had been run over and his shelter broken down. Col. Sully, no doubt impressed with the ridiculousness of the situation, made matters easy by saying, "There, there, keep cool, young man. I did not see your shack,"—adding parenthetically, "it was a d—n, little, black thing anyway." (There is a railway postal clerk, who has headquarters in Red Wing, that might be induced to give further particulars.)

Company F and the regiment were very fortunate during the siege as to casualties. Not a man of the company was seriously injured by a bullet or shell during the whole time, but many of us had close calls. I remember one morning just at daylight. I was passing along the outposts and stopped for a moment to speak with George Daucher, who was one of the older men of the company. He was a German by birth, spoke with a decided accent betokening his nativity, and appeared always to take everything as a matter of course. There had been a great deal of firing during the night, and I inquired how it had been with him. He replied, "All richt! all richt! But my nachbor over there" (jerking his thumb towards the enemy's pickets)—"he raise hell on his vatch, all nicht." Just then a bullet clipped a twig from a bush close to our heads and buried itself in a tree, a few feet to the rear, and caused us to lie down very quickly.

As the days went by, we crept closer up to their line of works, and the outposts were constantly in short range of each other. The morning of April 29th there were two of the Seventy-Second Pennsylvania shot as they came to relieve us. This was the dangerous part of it—in daylight. When we returned to the camp, we learned that a shell that had been thrown the day before had fallen into a wagon in the rear of the camp. It was supposed to come from some of the Confederate mortars near Yorktown. This was the anniversary of our muster into the service of the United States.

We remained in supporting distance to Dana's position until the morning of May 1, when we returned to our own brigade. I recall that, while returning, we gathered wild flowers and came into the camp with the muzzles of our rifles decorated with them. It was understood that preparations were nearly completed for a general bombardment and assault. In leaving the picket line the next morning, we were subject to a sharp fusillade of musketry, and some shells were also thrown into the woods as we came out. Someone said that they "acted as if they did not want us anywhere around there," and another answered that it "did appear *unfriendly*" but thought that they were "a little *sensitive* and we ought not to *notice it*." We did not. They shot very close, but no one was hit.

Sunday morning, May 4th, long before it was light, we were aroused and marched to the front so as to be in position at daylight. On reaching the line, we were ordered to return immediately to camp, pack all of our things, and report at the picket line. It was reported that the enemy had evacuated the intrenchments and was retreating towards Richmond. Hastening back to the camp, we hurriedly packed our 'kits,' and, in full marching order, returned to the picket line—reaching there about sunrise. Dana's Brigade occupied the line immediately to our right, and moved first to occupy the vacated works, and Gorman's Brigade followed.

It was one of the few really beautiful mornings in April and early May in 1862. It was Sunday, and there was a Sabbath-like stillness everywhere, except for the occasional boom of a gun off to the right. It was now recalled that the firing had ceased on our front about three o'clock that morning, which was probably the time that the pickets had been withdrawn. Many heavy guns were left in the works, and there was evidence that the final departure had been in haste. Many tents were left standing, and much materiel was left behind. Camp kettles and bake ovens were found in and about the tents. Thousands of huge knives, of rude workmanship, were found. Nearly all of our boys had them for a time and used them for cutting tent poles, wood, etc., as one would a hatchet.

Not long after entering the works, we were warned to keep away from these forts and out of the roads, and were told that torpedoes were buried in many places; that a number had been exploded; and several persons had been killed by them. It was the explosion of these that we had supposed was artillery firing in the morning. These 'torpedoes' were large shells prepared to explode upon being moved, and to be the innocent cause of their explosion was almost certain death. This plan of operations was devised by General Gabriel J. Rains, an old regular army officer, and it was then considered a very despicable method of warfare.[4]

It was said that a telegraph operator tried to open the door of an office and was blown to atoms—and the building also. A man entered a house and picked up some article from a table and was instantly killed. They were buried in the roads, embankments of the forts, and similar places. Some rebel prisoners were compelled to hunt out and dig up these 'infernal machines.' It was said that 30 of them were found in a space of ten rods square. We did not come in contact with that method of 'absent treatment' after that.

Early Monday afternoon, as the distant firing increased, we were ordered to be ready to march. Late in the afternoon, we started to join the other two corps, which had preceded us in the pursuit and were then fighting near Williamsburg.

The result of that night's march was much like the one described in the nursery rhymes where the "King and 20,000 men marched up the hill and marched

---

4. Rains developed these devices—buried shells with pressure-sensitive fuses or trip-wires—as early as 1840 during the Seminole War; Sears, *To the Gates of Richmond,* 66.

down again." Nevertheless, it was a memorable night's march and, like the meeting of the witches on the heath, was "in thunder, lightning and in rain."

The roads were execrable in the broadest sense of that comprehensive term, and already filled with artillery and wagons sunk to the axles in the tenacious ooze of the 'sacred soil.' The drivers were making vigorous and noisy efforts to gratify the popular cry of "On to Richmond," but with only a small degree of success. By whipping, spurring, and energetic swearing, the drivers would force their tired teams to founder along for a short distance; then the weary, discouraged horses and mules would relax their efforts; and the helpless drivers could laugh or swear—it was all the same to the mules. We were compelled to take to the sides of the roads on account of the wagons, which were literally 'in it,' and we waded and splashed along as best we could among the trees and stumps.

Meantime, it began to grow dark, and the booming of the cannon in front—to which we had been listening since the early afternoon—ceased or was outclassed or drowned by a thunderstorm. With the coming on of night, the trains ceased all efforts to advance. The teamsters sitting in their saddles or climbing on to the wagons stated their views of the situation in language more expressive than elegant. In the darkness, we still continued our efforts to go forward. Occasionally, a flash of lightning illuminated for an instant the scene of a narrow roadway and a rain-dripping forest, peopled with stalled mules and stumbling men—which quickly relapsed into darkness seemingly as black as that which covered chaos before the days of creation.

Now and then, a half-uttered exclamation ending in a grunt or a gurgle came out of the blackness, indicating that the head of some unlucky 'Knight of the Knapsack' had come in contact with the carelessly-carried gun of a comrade; or that he had collided with a tree; or tumbled over some obstacle into the water and the mud. These noises—with the tramp and splash of feet and the rattle of tin cups and canteens—told where the column was moving. This kind of effort to get to the front, which resulted in but little advancement compared with the tremendous outlay of energy it required, was continued for some hours, when we came to a standstill.

For a time we remained stationary. Then orders came to return to Yorktown. The march was resumed, but in the reverse direction, and we wearily remeasured our steps over and *through* those miry roads to Yorktown. I do not know how far we went or if the whole division or only the First Brigade were engaged in it, but I do know that we were wet, weary, muddy, and disgusted when we returned about daylight, the morning of the sixth, and went into bivouac on the open ground outside the old village.

We were roused in the early afternoon and told to get ready to go on board the transports. While waiting here, we had an opportunity to look about us a little and pass judgment upon the preparations the enemy had made to receive us. They were both great and extensive. Parapets, embankments, and ditches; high, broad, and deep; extending as far as we could see. There were some old embankments still recognizable, which had been built by the forces of Washington or Cornwallis (probably the former). Not far off was a partly-broken monument marking the spot where Cornwallis had surrendered his sword almost 81 years before— October 19, 1781.

It was the purpose of those in command to send Franklin's and Sedgwick's divisions up the river to establish a new base at West Point, near the mouth of the Pamunkey, that being much nearer than Shipping Point, which had been the base since the operations began against Yorktown. It was late in the afternoon before we had orders to move, and nearly dark before we were on board. Then a dense fog set in that kept us waiting until morning. The First Minnesota was on the steamer *Long Branch* and passed a much more comfortable night. The uncovered and crowded deck of an army transport lacks many of the comforts and conveniences of a first-class cabin passage; but, as compared with the previous night's experience, there were several things that made it preferable; and we appreciated them.

Wednesday morning, May 7, we steamed up the river to West Point. Before we arrived, we heard the sound of firing, which continued until some time after we had landed. As we passed up, a gunboat—which I believe was the *Marblehead*— was shelling the shore, and some Rebel batteries in the woods on shore were replying. The *Long Branch* anchored, and we went ashore in small boats, to the hair-raising music of shrieking shells, which occasionally knocked the splinters from some of the transports or made transient rainbows in the spray they threw up as they skipped along the water. The tide was running out, and, when the boats touched bottom, we stepped overboard and waded ashore.

On shore, we formed line under the bank and took a position on the right of a Zouave regiment that had also, seemingly, just come on shore. There was sharp musketry firing at this time, and a line of battle already formed had advanced into the woods as we had come from the transports. This was now hotly engaged, judging from the firing, and we were held in readiness to support them if necessary. The advance of the line soon drove off the enemy, and our gunboats continued for some time to throw shell after them. It had been a sharp fight but was soon over, and the resistance of the enemy was very brief after there was actual conflict of infantry.

We remained at that place until the morning of the 9th, when we first made a scout through the woods and later marched to Eltham's Landing three or four miles up the Pamunkey River. We made a temporary camp on the higher ground in a bend of the river, but that was only a few feet above the high tide level. We remained near this place until the morning of the 15th, and there were four days of beautiful spring weather, under whose influence the condition of the roads and the men improved rapidly.

It was the snows of Russia that ruined Napoleon's army, and thus far, we, too, had been fighting the elements and suffered vastly more from them than the enemy. Thus far, our company had not lost a man from bullets, but there were at this time a dozen or more off-duty on account of sickness. The excessive labor, the exposure, and the extreme weather conditions were having their effect, and many men were breaking down under them.

While we were lying at this point resting and unloading supplies, other portions of the army were moving. On the afternoon of May 14, we drew three days' rations and received orders to march in the morning. General McClellan had declared in his official dispatches that he would "push the enemy to the wall." Yorktown had been evacuated; the battle of Williamsburg had been fought; the affair at West Point was over; and the enemy was being slowly pressed back upon Richmond.

We marched in the early morning in a heavy rain. The little improvement in the roads was soon neutralized by the rain and the grinding of wheels; the tramping of feet of men and horses soon beat the roads into little rivers of mud and water. Most of the time we were half knee-deep in the mud and in places more than that, and it took all day to make about 8 miles. We bivouacked that night in a pine wood near New Kent Court House, where we remained until Sunday morning, the 18th, when we advanced about four miles and halted in a wheat field—seemingly to let other troops pass, but later we stretched our 'shelters' and remained until the morning of the 21st.

Wednesday morning, May 21, we left camp at an early hour. It was a beautiful morning and proved a very hot day for the season. The regiment led the division that morning. We marched beyond White House Landing (on the Pamunkey) and camped on the easterly side of the railroad from White House to Richmond. Also, we passed a small church by the way, which our scholarly Chaplain pointed out as the place where Washington was married.[5]

We remained here one day, the 22nd, during which there was a terrific storm of rain and hail with much thunder and lightning. On the 23rd, we left camp early in the morning, crossed the railroad, and marched four or five miles, which brought us to the right of the army and to a point near the Chickahominy River. It will be remembered that it was the treacherous mud of the Chickahominy swamps that held Captain John Smith fast when he was captured by the followers of Powhatan. He had some remuneration for his misfortunes—as his life was saved by Pocahontas—but we had to suffer all of the horrors of the Chickahominy swamps without any such palliating circumstances.

Some days before this, a crossing had been made at Bottom's Bridge by General Silas Casey's division, followed by others of the Third and Fourth Corps—and, at this time, the greater part of these two corps were across the

5. Also, White House plantation was where Washington courted the widow Martha Custis. Robert E. Lee's wife, Martha's granddaughter, was staying there just days before the First Minnesota arrived; Sears, *To the Gates of Richmond*, 104.

Chickahominy and within 12 or 14 miles of Richmond. And all day we had heard the sound of cannonading at intervals which indicated that they were 'feeling' for one another in the woods. Up to this time, we had been preceded by the other corps—or, at least, two of them. We had taken no part in the skirmishing or advance work. But we had expended a great deal of time and muscle on roads and supplies.

Tuesday, May 27th, we were again detailed as a 'pioneer corps' and sent out to build a bridge across the turbid waters of the Chickahominy. When not excited from 'excessive liquidation,' the Chickahominy was not a very formidable river. At the point we were directed to bridge it, the river proper was perhaps forty feet in width and three feet more or less in depth when in ordinary stage of water. But it seemed to gather water very quickly and in immense quantities. The banks were low and soon overflowed, when it became a fast river a fourth of a mile or more in width. The army was now divided by the river, and it was very desirable to establish connections as soon as possible, and, to that end, several bridges were ordered to be built.

There were three wagon bridges on the river within a distance of about 12 miles. In this interval of 12 miles between Bottom's Bridge and Meadow Bridge, it was intended to build several bridges and make roads across the swamps.[6]

We went to the river early in the morning (armed, of course), but a six-mule team brought out axes, spades, and augurs. I do not recall that there were any other tools. It was a warm May day, and the place abounded in moderate-sized trees. Nearby there was a small field. In this field we stacked arms, hung up our haversacks and canteens on our guns, and proceeded to cut down and cut into lengths, as directed, such of the trees as were selected. As the trees were cut, they were carried to the river by the men or 'snaked' there by the mules.

As soon as there was an accumulation of material at the bank, the construction of the bridge was begun, and the work went forward rapidly. There were no piles in the ordinary use of the term or any pile driver or other instrument for driving them. I think that there were a few temporary stakes driven with an axe to mark the location, and perhaps a few to act as a temporary stay to the logs as they were put into position.

The whole structure was a simple one, and just such a one as I had seen built across the Cannon River when the first stage road was made to St. Paul.[7] 'Cribs'— or pens—of logs were built at proper distances apart, to the desired height. On these cribs, log 'stringers' were laid; and on these, the flooring of the bridge. The

6. The three wagon bridges were Mechanicsville Turnpike Bridge, New Bridge, and possibly Bottom's or Meadow (unless Wright counts the railroad bridge). Future Minnesota historian William W. Folwell, in the 50th New York, helped build the four others needed; Sears, *To the Gates of Richmond,* 112, 213.

7. The Wright's home was only a mile and a half from where the Mendota to Wabasha Government (Military) Road crossed the Cannon River. The bridge was apparently built in 1855.

logs of these cribs were notched together at the corners and were fastened with pins and withes, until the increasing weight—as they were built up—forced them to the bottom. These cribs had to be held in position until they found a resting place in the mud.

When once grounded, further progress was easy; and the whole thing was a very simple affair; and it proved effective. (Of course, all of this first work of the construction had to be done in the water, which in some parts was up to the neck of a man of my size.) As soon as the first crib was raised to the desired level, 'stringers' were laid from the bank and pinned to the top logs of the crib, and on this a floor of halved (split) logs was laid. This flooring may have been spiked down, but I do not remember that it was. As soon as the floor was laid to the first crib, a detail was set to work carrying stones and dropping them into it. There were plenty of loose stones along the bank and in the little clearing where we had stacked arms. When these cribs (which were simply log pens) were filled with stones, they were pretty securely anchored and answered very well for piers.

I do not know who ordered the bridge built or who designed the construction, but the work was done by the First Minnesota Regiment under the immediate direction of the company officers. I do not recall that there was any engineer officer present or who had the general supervision of the work. The use of grapevines for withes, or 'binders,' I think was suggested by Captain Mark Downie of Company B; and it was this feature that gave it the name of the Grapevine Bridge.[8] It is also sometimes referred to as 'Sumner's Bridge.'

The bridge was important because it was the only bridge that was available, when the test came, to reinforce the troops on that side when attacked four days later. Without assistance, they would, in all human probability, have been overwhelmed and obliged to surrender. The bridge was available because of its strong construction, and the strong point of the construction was those stone-filled piers. This bridge—that portion of it crossing the main stream—was built by our regiment in one day, but some of the approaches and corduroy work was not completed that evening and was finished by others.[9] If the First Minnesota had performed no other service on the Peninsula but the building of this bridge, it would still be entitled to great praise for a good job well done, but it not only built the bridge, it led the way across it to the relief of the hard-pressed left wing.

It is worthy of note, too, that it was constructed of just such material as nature had provided nearby, and with but commonplace tools. The only thing that I

8. Sears claims the Grapevine Bridge was named "after an old bridge formerly on the site that took its name from the river's twisting channels"; *To the Gates of Richmond*, 113.

9. The Fifth New Hampshire also claimed to have built the Grapevine Bridge; apparently both regiments built sections of it. Sears, *To the Gates of Richmond*, 113; William J. Miller, "I Only Wait for the River: McClellan and His Engineers on the Chickahominy," in *The Richmond Campaign of 1862: The Peninsula and the Seven Days*, ed. Gary W. Gallagher (Chapel Hill: University of North Carolina Press, 2000), 52–53.

recall at variance with this general statement was a barrel on a stump. That was not indigenous to the spot where I saw it.

The sun had gone down behind the trees before we quit work, and, of course, we then expected to return in the morning and complete the approaches and corduroy the swampy places. But in the army one never can calculate that far ahead.

Towards morning, we were roused quietly; returned to camp; drew three days' rations; and, soon after daylight, were on the march up the river to support the Fifth Corps in its movements against the forces of the Confederate General Lawrence Branch around Hanover Court House. Here, we were told, there had been some pretty severe fighting while we were building the bridge. After marching five or six miles, we halted and rested by the road for a couple of hours, listening occasionally to lively cannonading some miles ahead. We were then told to make ourselves comfortable and be in readiness to respond to any call for assistance. We then changed our location into the pine woods, for it was a warm day, and the shade was very acceptable.

We remained here until the afternoon of the next day, listening at intervals to the distant booming of the cannon and seeing at times squads of prisoners and ambulances with the wounded pass. Our stay here would have been pleasant but for the mental strain of expectation and the physical irritation of an insect that was new to the most of us. We had not been long in the pine woods before it was discovered that woodticks were plentiful, and that they were just as likely to fasten on to a soldier as a sheep when opportunity offered. Most of the boys had company when they left that bivouac that they would have preferred to have left behind. There was another pest, whose classical name is *pediculus* (louse), that insisted on a familiar acquaintance with the soldiers.

Along in the afternoon of the 29th, matters seemed to have quieted down, and we had orders to return to the camp near the Chickahominy, which we reached about dark. From the time the army was divided, and a part of it was placed on the south side of the river, there was considerable talk of the danger of an attack on either wing—when we would be at a disadvantage, because the other wing could not go to their assistance promptly. Early Saturday morning, the 31st, the river was reported to be rising rapidly, and, coupled with this, was more than the usual amount of firing on the other side.

There are two things that impress this day on my memory with more than ordinary distinctness: the presentation of the "Sanford Battery"[10] and the first day of the battle of Fair Oaks.

It was early in the forenoon that the assembly was sounded and, when the regiment fell in, several letters of a congratulatory nature were read. The first of these was from Henry S. Sanford, minister resident at the court in Brussels, to Governor Alexander Ramsey of Minnesota. It said, among other things:

10. The complete story of this battery is told in Folwell, *Minnesota,* 2:87 (especially note 5).

I have directed a small battery, consisting of three steel rifled cannon of six pounds caliber, with suitable ammunition, to be shipped to New York by this week's steamer from England and to be held there subject to your order. I beg to present them, through you, to the state of which you are the honored head, for the First Minnesota Volunteers. The efficiency and discipline of that regiment, as detailed in the public prints, and the conspicuous valor displayed by it in the field at Bull Run and Ball's Bluff won my admiration, and my pride was heightened here in a foreign land by encomiums which its conduct elicited from strangers.

Governor Ramsey wrote to Sanford acknowledging the generous gift, and sent a letter to Colonel Alfred Sully "to request that at the earliest favorable opportunity, you will cause the letter of Gen. Sanford, in which he speaks in such flattering terms of our brave troops, and my letter of acceptance to him, to be read at the head of the regiment."

The battery was never in service with the regiment, that being impracticable under the formation of the army and the stress of affairs. The battery consisted of three rifled guns (and at that time rifled cannon were not so common), ammunition, and harnesses. On each of the guns was the following inscription: "To the First Minnesota Regiment Volunteers. Tribute to Patriotism and Valor. Brussels, 1861."

The reading of such an order could not be otherwise than gratifying. While these letters were being read to the regiment, the dull booming of hostile cannon came from the other side of the river, and their echoes mingled with the heavier thunder of a coming shower. When we were dismissed, we hastened to our little shelters to avoid the shower that again drenched us.

It was at this time known that the river was rising rapidly, and that the bridges were in danger of being carried away. We also knew that just such a condition as that was favorable to the enemy, and there was no doubt in our minds but the enemy would improve his opportunities to the utmost. About noon, volleys of musketry were added to the skirmish fire we had been hearing all of the morning, and there was increasing frequency in the artillery firing. There was intense anxiety in the camp for possible results.

We then received orders to hold ourselves in readiness to march, in light marching order, with three days' rations and sixty rounds of ammunition. Inspection of arms and ammunition was had, and we quietly filled our haversacks and canteens. The near approach of danger does not seem to have a tendency to make people talkative, but the contrary. It was my duty to distribute the cartridges, and—as the boys gathered about the ammunition boxes, and I dealt out an extra twenty rounds to each one—I observed that but few words were spoken. I have no doubt that their minds were busy calculating their personal chances in the desperate game of war then being played. I know that my own mental organization was active, and I was wondering whether I should see the end of the battle or the battle would see the end of me, and whether that end would be victory or defeat.

I was not able to come to any definite conclusion, but I was not one of those fellows that 'would rather fight than eat' and always went into battle with grave forebodings of the consequences, personally.

We waited for orders. The boys—with equipments on and their guns in their hands—gathered in groups, looking across the swollen river to the woods from which the smoke was rising, and listening to the rapidly-increasing fire, which seemed to be coming nearer all of the time. It was not long before the order came to fall in, and the Second Division was formed, with the right near the bridge.

The First Regiment led the brigade and was the first to test the bridge and go to the assistance of the troops on the south side. And it was Company F that led the regiment. After we had reached the river, there was a short halt and a consultation of our colonel and the brigade and division commanders. They were near the bridge, and, as they talked, they looked across the stream. But they did not call us into the council, and, as we were too far away to hear, I do not know whether they talked of the danger of crossing or what was likely to happen after we had crossed.

Whatever may have been the subject of their consultation, the matter of crossing took precedence in ours. As we stood there waiting orders to move, the attempt to cross seemed a dubious and dangerous experiment. The bridge—strong as it was—was not built in expectation of a second deluge, and was writhing and quivering in the turbid, rushing waters in a way that threatened immediate destruction. The river was overflowing its banks; the approach to the bridge was already under the water, which was almost level with the floor of the bridge; and the bottom lands beyond were overflowed for many rods.

There was not long to consider consequences (and we really had no responsibility in the matter) before Col. Sully said, "Forward men," and in obedience we literally 'waded in.' When fairly onto the bridge, our weight pressed down the flooring until the water ran over it in places, and it shook and trembled with the force of the current; but it gave us a safe passage over the main stream, and we waded the overflowed bottom land on the other side—where the water in some places came to our hips—and climbed the hill beyond.

At the top of the hill, we halted only long enough to close up and then crossed the field and entered the woods in the direction of the nearest firing, which was a muffled crackle of musketry and the occasional boom of a cannon. Farther away to the left, the battle was raging noisily. Soon after entering the woods, we halted, and loaded and capped our rifles in readiness for instant use. After loading, we kept on through the woods until reaching a farm road—moving as rapidly as possible and naturally in somewhat broken formation.

It was perhaps two miles from where we entered the woods to the point where we came to the contending line. Before reaching this line, we began meeting stragglers and wounded men going to the rear—also some squads of prisoners under guard. There is always a lot of drift and wreckage in the rear of a fighting line, and they tell fearful stories of 'all cut to pieces' and general disaster. As we drew nearer, the woods were blue with smoke and redolent with the fumes of burnt powder. It was also very warm and close in the woods, and we were sweating freely from the heat and hurried marching.

Coming out of the woods, we could see men moving to the rear across a field to our left and forming a line near a fence and the woods; and there was a battery floundering in the mud trying to change its position. This was a portion of General John Abercrombie's brigade forming a new line at the edge of the woods. Colonel Sully had kept the regiment well closed-up during the march through the woods, and at this time none of the other regiments of the brigade were in sight.

We had now reached a point not far from the railroad at Fair Oaks Station, and halted for a moment's rest. Colonel Sully was here met by General Darius N. Couch, a division commander, and they held a short consultation.

Of his own volition or by direction of General Couch, Col. Sully decided to take a position on the higher ground some distance to the right and near a white house. Just as we were fairly moving, General Sumner, the corps commander, rode up, his horse floundering in the mud and panting with the great exertion it required to get over the water-soaked ground. General Sumner's pet name was the 'Bull of the Woods.' We never know why he was so called or just how the name fitted him, but it seemed all right. He was a heroic, fighting general, and we believed in him. He called out, as we passed, "Step off with a will, boys. It is a race."

Our course lay across a field of young corn but recently plowed and partly under water. In places, the water was to our knees, and the mud was deep and sticky. We plowed our way through it and reached the higher ground. Then Company F, which was the right company, deployed to the front and advanced to the crest of the hill near the house. The distance we had come was between a fourth and a half of a mile, and we had covered it as quickly as we could, but there was no time to spare.

When we reached the top of the hill, the rebel skirmishers were just coming out of the woods five or six hundred yards to our right and front. Some of them had already crossed the fence and were coming through the green oats. Our arrival seemed very opportune. There were a number of small outbuildings around the house, and, by direction of Col. Sully, we took position along the garden and yard fences, a small stable, some rail pens filled with corn, some hog pens, etc.

We promptly opened fire on the fellows down in the oats and at the edge of the field, and soon drove them to the shelter of the woods. It was quite evident that they were surprised to find us there and ready for business. From behind the fence and the shelter of the woods, they kept up a desultory fire on us; and, from behind the fences and buildings, we returned the fire; but the range was too great for effective work.

The regiment was quickly formed on our left and extended along the yard and garden fences almost to the woods on its left, but the line held by the regiment was at an oblique angle to the line of the woods. Some other regiments were hurried into position on our left before any of the regiments of our brigade came up. It thus happened that we were entirely separated from our brigade, and we held the extreme right of the Union line, and, as it happened, it was as safe and comfortable a position as there was on the line. But it did not appear in that light for the first half hour that we held it.

The safe or unsafe place on the fighting line is about as difficult to pick out beforehand as it is to tell where and when the next bolt of lightning will strike. One of the incalculable and surprising things connected with battles is the irregular, uncertain, disproportionate, and eccentric way that losses occur in action. A division is sent in or is attacked, and when the fight is over it is found that one of the three brigades has suffered half or two-thirds of the loss. And it cannot be told beforehand what brigade, regiment, or company it is going to be—anymore than you can tell who of a dozen persons in good health will be the next to die or who will be the next victim of a railroad accident. It often happens, too, that those who are seemingly the most exposed escape with but slight losses. Fair Oaks was a good example of this.

From the position of Company F, there was a good view to the front and the right. Peeking around the corner of the corn pens, one could see for some distance along a road that ran into the woods. A column of the enemy could be seen crossing this road and going to our right. This was reported to Col. Sully and caused him some anxiety for a time. Several flags were carried across this road, and it seemed evident that our right was to be attacked in strong force. Then it was noticed that this line had reversed its direction and was marching towards the left; and this continued for some little time before it faced to the front and attacked. When it did attack, the left of their line only came under the oblique fire of the left of the First Regiment.

It was a tense and anxious few minutes as we waited for the attack which we felt sure was coming. General Gorman says that it came within ten minutes after he got his brigade in line—which is probably true, for everyone appeared to be hurrying to the limit—but it seemed a long time to wait before we heard the thunder of Kirby's guns as the enemy came out of the woods in a furious assault. This was followed by some splendid volleys of musketry that rolled along the line with deadly effect, and was succeeded by a rapid firing at will.

Our fire was heavier than the enemy could make headway against or endure, and they were compelled to retire. Their fire was heavy but not well-directed, as most of it was aimed too high, but it covered the greater portion of the regiment, and was delivered at short range. Everything being obscured by the smoke which seemed to cling to the ground, it was impossible to see any of the movements, but the noise of the fighting, and the yelling and cheering, was evidence that things were going our way. Northern men *cheered*, and Southern men *yelled*. I cannot, on paper, describe the difference, but there was as much difference as there is between the crowing of a rooster and the cackling of a hen.

Just previous to this, a couple of guns and a regiment of infantry came to take a position on our right, and I think that General Sedgwick came with them. This prolonged the line to our right and at an angle with it—the right flank being 'refused.'

It was growing dusk when the enemy advanced to this last attack; and they were apparently reinforced and more determined than ever; and the fighting continued longer; but it ended as before by a retreat to the cover of the woods. This time they were followed and severely punished. In fact, it was a bayonet charge of Gorman's Brigade that started them 'going'; and they lost heavily in killed and wounded; and many prisoners were gathered in. In this attack, the storm of bullets had been heavier than before and had extended farther, from which it was supposed that we were fighting a greater force. As the enemy yielded, the left of the regiment was swung into the woods, and a number of prisoners were taken. As it was now getting dark, the firing died away to the occasional crack of a rifle in the woods, where a skirmish line remained. It was evident that the fighting for the day was over.

Among the prisoners brought in to the Courtney House yard (where the regiment was stationed) were a number of officers, and with these was a Colonel Long[11] of a North Carolina regiment and a Lieutenant Colonel Lightfoot. Long had been an officer in the regular army and a lieutenant in Col. Sully's company when he was a Captain in the Regulars. The two greeted each other pleasantly, with a few words about their present situations and old times. One of these men— it was said at the time—was a son-in-law of General Edwin V. Sumner, the corps commander. It was the talk that night that Gen. Sumner refused to see his rebellious son-in-law, and ordered him sent away with the other prisoners.[12]

As soon as it was assured that there was not to be a renewal of the fighting, there was a relaxation from the battle tension and a general inquiry as to who had been killed or wounded. The firing had been very heavy and the smoke almost suffocating, and it was a relief to learn that the loss of the regiment had been exceedingly light—2 killed and 5 wounded. The only explanation I can give for this is that the lightnings of war had not happened to strike us that time.

Company F had but one man hit. That was Nicholas Hammer. He was shot through the head, and the brain seemed to be oozing from the wound, but, strange to say, he lived until towards daylight the next morning. He was not conscious nor paralyzed and did not seem to suffer much. He talked in his native tongue—seemingly to himself—moaning quietly, and at times it seemed as if he were trying to

11. Armistead L. Long, a Confederate staff officer, was Edwin Sumner's son-in-law and his aide-de-camp until June 10, 1861, when he headed south. Long was not captured; however, a North Carolina colonel was. Moe, *Last Full Measure*, 141.

12. Armistead Long had been a first lieutenant stationed in the West, where he could have served under Sully. The rest of the story was what Wright elsewhere calls a "grapevine dispatch," or "camp rumor," or a case of mistaken identity.

sing softly to himself as he sometimes did when sitting around the campfire. I am not sure that he spoke a word that was understood.

He was a German by birth, was 31 years old, and had served in a cavalry regiment in 'the old country.' He was a gentlemanly, well-educated man, and a fine musician—always considerate and obliging to us younger fellows. Personally, I recall many little favors at his hands. His home at one time had been at Manitowoc, Wisconsin, and I think that he had not been long in Minnesota when he enlisted. He joined us at the fort about the middle of May 1861, and, from memory, I cannot associate him with any place that I know in Goodhue County.

I was not far from Hammer when he was hit, but was not looking at him, when I heard a peculiar sound which caused me to look in that direction, and I saw him sinking, quivering and helpless, to the ground. His death made a deep impression upon some of us, as we were not then as familiar with scenes of blood as we became later.

After the pickets were posted for the night, and all was done that could be done for the wounded, the next thing was to get something to eat and spend the night as comfortably as we could. Fires were made in sheltered places to boil some coffee in our tin cups, and then we prepared to sleep in line of battle with our rifles at hand—ready to fight at the call—but there was no special alarm. It was not a comfortable night on the muddy, water-soaked ground, surrounded by the wreck of the battle, and the surgeons and their helpers caring for the wounded. But it was short. It was late when we laid down, and we were called early to be ready for any emergency.

It was not long after daylight Sunday morning when the fighting was renewed by the advance of the Union skirmishers. As on the previous day, the plan was to hold fast with the Union right (which was the most advanced of the Union troops on the south side of the river, and the nearest connecting point with the Fifth and Sixth Corps still on the northern side) and bring up the other troops to a line on that point.

The movement Sunday morning—so far as Sedgwick's Division was concerned—was a swinging of the left of the division, pivoting on the right, which was held by the First Regiment. This resulted in some sharp fighting, which was participated in by both Sedgwick's and Richardson's divisions of the Second Corps and the troops of the Third and Fourth Corps. There were some hours of sharp fighting, which was begun by the advance of our skirmishers, which the enemy resented by making a savage attack. That was met by our troops, who in turn assaulted and drove the enemy from the field.

Before noon, the enemy had all disappeared towards Richmond, having been fought to a standstill and driven to the cover of the entrenchments about Richmond. The other corps were brought up to a position in line with that held by our regiment, which maintained its position at the Courtney House, but I am not aware that there was an attempt made to follow the enemy and do him more damage while in a disorganized condition. It was unfortunate that the retiring enemy was not followed by every available man. The enemy had fought his full strength; his commander, Joseph E. Johnston, was badly wounded; and his forces were in a confused retreat. Yet the Union army was divided by an overflowing river; the portion on the south side was wearied by two days of fighting; supplies of food and ammunition were not abundant; and the condition of the roads was next to impossible to move the artillery. But the opportunity was worth the trial—though no man can say positively what the result would have been.

Having been detached in the hurried dispositions of Saturday from the rest of the brigade, we had not participated in its successful assault upon the enemy. But we had heard about it and were proud of them. When the 34th and 82nd New York and 15th Massachusetts—the other three regiments of the brigade—came to join us at the Courtney farm after the fighting, they got a splendid welcome from the Minnesotians, who shouted and cheered with royal good will when they returned. They had been 'tried in the furnace of war' and had not been 'found wanting.' There had been a little irritation and questioning before this, but ever afterward there was a strong fraternity and good will.

Another incident of the day was a greeting from Gen. McClellan as he was inspecting the lines—and a few complimentary words.

On Sunday evening, June 1, Companies C and F were sent out to the front on picket and spent the night in the woods, with our rifles within reach of our hands. It rained and was a dreary night. We could hear the whistling of engines and the rumble of trains as the cars ran in and out of Richmond, probably carrying off the wounded that did not fall into our hands and bringing out supplies and reinforcements.

On our return from picket, we found that details had been sent out to bury the dead, and those in camp were at work making a temporary breastwork of logs and dirt about the Courtney premises. At first it was a crude affair only intended for temporary defense, and we called it Fort Sully in honor of our colonel. We found also that Captain William F. Russell with the Second Company of Minnesota Sharpshooters had come on from Minnesota and had joined the regiment. They were attached to the regiment and borne on the rolls as Company L, but they were not made a part of the regiment or consolidated with it. Sharpshooters were frequently attached to regiments or brigades in this way.

Much might be written of this battlefield, but I refrain from anything more than a mild suggestion of its horrors, for it was horrible beyond the power of words to describe. All day Sunday and much of Monday, parties were out hunting for and burying the dead. These were buried in trenches (dug conveniently near) in the clothes they wore, wrapped in blankets or tent cloths, and usually buried without a prayer or other ceremony. Everywhere were scattered around guns, accouterments, knapsacks, haversacks, hats, caps, blankets, overcoats, and all kinds of clothing—frequently cut and blood-clotted. Much of this territory was then under water, and many bodies were not recovered for some days after. On Sunday the sun shone; the day was hot; and long before night there was a most unpleasant odor from the field which grew worse for some days and had not wholly departed when we did. I can almost smell it today when I talk or think of the Peninsula, and, by shutting my eyes, it is easy to imagine the flocks of buzzards wheeling in circles above the woods.

All of these things shocked and depressed us, for it was the first time that we had remained to occupy the field and to realize what it was like after the storm of battle had swept over it. On the other hand, the fact that we had met the enemy in open fight and forced him to retire, leaving his dead and wounded behind him, aroused our soldierly instincts and made us hopeful for the future.

9

Minnesota, stand firm! Don't run, Minnesota!

JUNE 1862

WE HAD LEFT THE CAMP on the other side of the Chickahominy on Saturday, May 31, carrying only our rubber blankets, rations, and cartridges. By Monday night, we had eaten up our rations and fired away many of our cartridges during the fighting. Though the rubbers were an excellent thing in their way, we found it uncomfortable trying to make them serve as waterproof, blanket, and overcoat. We comforted ourselves by remembering that we were a blouse and a rubber blanket better off than we were on the Bull Run campaign, but we suffered much before we connected with our knapsacks, blankets, and tent cloths.

We were on short rations for a week, and it was not until Saturday, June 7, that the trains came over from the north side of the Chickahominy bringing our things, which we had left in the care of the disabled men in the old camp. It was difficult, too, to get proper care and accommodations for the sick. I have no doubt that the delay in getting supplies grew out of the swollen river and the broken bridges. And, no doubt, the large number of wounded and exhausted men after the fighting—many of the enemy's wounded being in our hands—overtaxed our surgeons and their resources for the time being.

During all of the week, when not otherwise engaged, we had put in the time adding to and increasing our defenses about the Courtney House. In the field off to the right we had built a 'star fort' providing for ten guns and made connecting breastworks with traverses and other protections from enfilading fire. We had had several days of good weather, and the mud was drying up rapidly.

Sunday, June 8, was a fine day, and we were hoping for a day of rest and quiet, but it proved to be a day of alarms and noisy disturbances. It really began Saturday night; and one whole brigade (Burns's) was sent out in front as a reserve to the pickets; and there was a racket going on all night. It grew stronger early in the morning, and, about seven o'clock, some sharp volleys brought us into line ready for action. The enemy did not advance as we hoped they would, but began shelling pretty lively, most of their shells falling short. After a little time, there was a lull; and then they began again—this time from another battery or after changing position—and more lively than ever; and the shells passed over us. In anticipation of an advance on their part, several regiments were sent out to the support of Burns's troops, and our regiment was sent into the woods on the left to be in position for an attack on their flank in case they advanced and Burns's men were compelled to retire.

133

This movement of the enemy—if it was really intended for an advance—was checked; and the enemy's infantry retired; but they continued to throw shells at intervals. When this emergency was over, we went back to Fort Sully.

It was not long before another cannonade broke out, and this time we were hurried out to support a New York battery of 20 pounders that was brought up to throw some heavier shells at them. Shells flew lively for a time from both sides and dropped promiscuously in the woods and about the camps, then slackened off, and finally ceased. After the morning disturbances were over, we returned to the position at the Courtney House.

Soon after, there was an incident of another character, which some of the boys thought might as well have been omitted as it was not a matter of necessity; but, as it involved a matter of courtesy to representatives of some foreign governments, it was probably the wise thing to do—even if it did require us to stand for some time in the sun on a hot day. General Prim,[1] a noted Spanish officer, came to see the American army in the field. General Prim—with his staff and accompanied by several of McClellan's staff, including the foreign officers Comte de Paris, the Duke of Chartres, and Prince de Joinville, and a number of other general officers—came to pay his respects to General Sumner. It was quite a show of foreign military men, and our regiment was called out to extend the usual military reception. There was a great interchange of courtesies and compliments, and we were told afterwards that the regiment came in for its share.

It was right here that our quiet, grey-haired, accomplished, and versatile colonel came in handy and, as usual, was found ready for the occasion. Col. Sully spoke both Spanish and French, and was the medium of communication for Gen. Sumner. General Prim and others expressed a desire to see Sully's regiment, and we were accordingly paraded and gave a brief exhibit of our drill. He then rode uncovered along the front, followed by the cavalcade of officers, and we gave three cheers and a 'tiger' as he rode away.

At the close of these exercises, which were about mid-afternoon, we were dismissed and went to our little tents, and spent the rest of the day in comparative quiet—though now and then a shell would come shrieking over from the direction of Richmond and burst unpleasantly near. It was a wonder then, and still is, how so many shells could be thrown and so little real damage done. It was the next day, I think, about five o'clock in the afternoon, when the rebels (who had been shelling intermittently all day) began a furious cannonading of the woods in our front. Many of the shells flew close over our heads and burst a little to the rear. The objects of their spite were some working parties in the woods, but they entirely overshot these. There were some casualties, however, to the rear, but none in the regiment.

1. General Juan Prim y Prats was a military observer sent to the Union Army by the Spanish government; Sears, *To the Gates of Richmond,* 160.

That night, June 12, there was a night attack on the pickets; and some sharp fighting resulted; and there were a number of killed and wounded. We were at the front that night building some new fortifications, but not at the point of attack. We took our arms and formed line but did not mix in, as the rumpus was too far away to the left to reach us. While the racket was going on, we watched an eclipse of the moon which occurred that night.

Our method of building our defenses was to put up a log barricade supported by traverses, then dig from the inside and bank the dirt against the outside, which left a wooden wall on our side which was perpendicular and cleaner than the dirt.

About sunrise on June 13 a detail came out with coffee, and we ceased work to eat breakfast. As usual the enemy was firing, and their shells were coming in unusually low. Augustus Ellison of Company I took his plate and coffee and sat with his back to the barricade of logs, saying "What is the use to build breastworks if you do not use them?" That sounded reasonable, and others did the same. Before he had finished his coffee, a shot struck the log near which his head was—although some six feet away from him—displaced it, and drove it against the back of his head with such force as to crush his skull and cause almost instant death. 'Gus' will be remembered as an ante-war student at Hamline, and at first planned to go with Company F, but afterwards decided to go with the Wabasha company. He was a genial, whole-souled fellow, and, so far as I can now recall, was the first of the regiment to meet death by the random shelling that was practiced in front of Richmond.

There was no good water to drink, and most of it was polluted from the fields, swamps, or the camps. Malarial fevers and camp dysentery were very prevalent. Comparatively few men were exempt, and many were sick in the field hospitals or their tents, and many others were excused from duty and moping about the camps. We know now that there were nearly 30,000 men absent as sick about this time, which was about 20 percent of the whole force *nominally* under McClellan's command—and others were being sent off every day.[2] The sanitary situation was bad and getting worse every day. There was at least another 20 percent unfit for duty in the camps. This unfortunate unsanitary situation by its continuance threatened the military situation also, as the effective force at the front was being weakened every day.

At this time, plans were not working out as successfully as had been hoped, and conditions were growing daily more serious. After the battle of Fair Oaks, that portion of the army on the south side of the Chickahominy was located from 5 to 6 miles from Richmond and practically confronting the outer fortifications defending the city. The Confederates had retreated within these fortifications and were daily being reinforced, troops being brought from all points to defend the

2. Sears gives 11,000 as the number "sick enough to be declared unfit for duty" as of June 20; Sears, *To the Gates of Richmond,* 163.

rebel capital. McClellan's army was divided by an overflowing river with broken bridges—a most unfortunate position—and his first efforts were the restoration of communication between the two wings of the army. As soon as possible, the bridges were repaired, and others were built; and at this time there were seven or eight bridges between Bottom's Bridge and New Bridge that were safe for infantry and artillery in any ordinary stage of water.

Wednesday the 18th was a remarkably quiet day, as the previous night had been. About six or seven o'clock there was an attack on Burns's Brigade—or, rather, the pickets in its front—which continued until dark. The night passed quietly after that until about two o'clock, when there was a movement of the enemy which caused us to be quietly awakened and formed in line ready for any movement that might be required. But none was required, and we made none. As far as I can recall, we never knew why we were called out. I do not suppose that it was to observe the beauty of the night, which was splendid.

The moon did not seem to shine with the clear brilliancy in Virginia that it does in Minnesota. I do not know how it would have seemed if I had been sitting on somebody's doorstep in good company, for we never found (in Virginia) any doorstep where we were welcome. But there was certainly a softness and a smoothness about some of those moonlit nights that seemed to penetrate and infuse itself into one's very soul. This was one of the nights that I remember for the

After the battle of Fair Oaks, soldiers of the First Minnesota
were part of the force facing Richmond.

sharp contrast with human strife and war. We were not called on to move—only hold ourselves in readiness for action—and waited until the sun dimmed the glory of the night by its superior light. I do not remember that we heard a shot fired or a hostile sound or any sound but the plaintive cries of the whip-poor-wills in the woods behind us.

When the sun rose, we hastened to get our breakfast, and that was scarcely finished before large details were called for to go to the rear to work on the roads, which were getting in fair condition, except in the swamps. We of the ranks had no hint of it then, but McClellan was at that time preparing the roads for a change of base to the James River. And, as matters turned out, it was a wise forethought.

The remaining days spent in front of Richmond were long, anxious days. The nights were broken with frequent alarms. Every hour of the day and night we were ready for attack or defense. Our whole line was bombarded with artillery by day; and the pickets were firing all night; and the point held by our brigade seemed to be the objective. Sunday, June 22, there was almost constant skirmishing from morning until night, and both sides seemed reluctant to quit then. Monday morning there was an outbreak in front of Richardson's Division, said to have been provoked by an advance of his pickets during the storm. Tuesday, the 24th, after a lively little fight on our brigade front early in the morning, there was less than the usual amount of firing.

I was on duty as sergeant of the guard, and a rare thing happened in camp that day. It was the visit of two ladies: Mrs. Wilkinson of Minnesota and Mrs. Talmadge of Iowa.[3] These were the first women that we had seen since leaving Camp Stone in Maryland who did not scowl and turn away or 'look daggers' at us. Of course, we 'small fry' did not have an opportunity to speak to them, but it was refreshing just to look at them. They had come on some mission about the sick, I think, and their stay in camp was but brief—coming and going in the same ambulance from and to the Fair Oaks Station on the Richmond and York River Railroad.

The whole medical establishment of the Army of the Potomac was burdened to a point that threatened a breakdown. They were doing all that men could do to meet the emergency forced upon them by a three-fold excess of typhoid, malaria, and dysentery, which was almost an epidemic. So far as I know there was nothing to eat in the camps but the field rations, which were all right for well men but revolting to the sick. The months of hard work and exposure in the swamps; the drinking of impure water, additionally polluted by the drainage from the camps and the battlefield, where thousands of dead were buried (not to mention dead horses and mules everywhere)—had done their work, a more deadly work than the enemy's bullets.

3. Probably these were the wife of Senator Morton S. Wilkinson of Minnesota and the wife of an Iowa politician.

More than one-half of the company were suffering from malaria or dysentery to a degree that greatly impaired their strength or wholly unfitted them for duty, and but few who were not suffering in some way. Several were sick in their little tents, lying on the ground, and eating such food as their comrades could prepare for them out of their rations. One of these was Hiram A. Skinner, who died a few days later in an ambulance as he was being removed to the general hospital. A night on guard—as I was the night of the 24th—was a revelation of the situation that could not be questioned. The coming and going of the men to and from the 'sinks' all night long, their expressions of pain, and the words they uttered as they feebly went and came are not soon or easily forgotten.

Skinner was the first man of the company to die from disease since its organization. He was not so observant of sanitary rules as most of us tried to be, and he was one of a very few in the company who had occasionally to be prompted in that direction. Wasted and stricken by disease, discouraged and homesick, he seemed to give up the struggle and died.

His case was a type of many another who, when no longer able to perform their daily duties, were excused, went to their little tents, and laid down to think of themselves, home, and its associations. Then the weakened vitality would seem to react upon and paralyze all of the other faculties until volition and hope were changed to submission and despair—and the end came soon. It was the prevalent belief in the camp that there was nothing gave so sure a hold on life as the determination to hold on to it to the last. Of course, we realized that there was a limit to the power of the will, as in other things, but what was called 'having grit' and 'keeping a stiff upper lip' under adverse conditions did seem to help out wonderfully sometimes.

I presume that almost everyone who had any extended experience in the service can recall some comrade who grew discouraged and seemed to 'give it up' and died—and some other one apparently in as bad or worse condition who pulled through because they had more 'sand.'

It was evident to us who 'kept the camp' through the night of June 24th that something more than ordinary was being planned for the morning. This was apparent from the frequent and hurried coming and going of aides and orderlies between the division and brigade headquarters. Such things as these are always interesting to soldiers and seldom escape the notice of those who are likely to participate in whatever is planned. The conduct of the campaign, like the diseases of the camp, was rapidly approaching the acute stages. General McClellan had received positive information during the day of the 24th that Stonewall Jackson's forces were moving on his right flank and would certainly strike it in two or three days.

With the approach of dawn, June 25, there came activity as well as vigilance. All of the regiments were under arms before it was light, as usual, but when dismissed for breakfast had orders to be ready to fall in at a moment's notice. It was not until about eight o'clock, however, that any open movement began. The movement then attempted was a swinging forward of the left of the troops on the south side of the river so as to bring them up on a line with the right. This involved a movement of the Third and Fourth Corps and the First Division of the Second Corps. The purpose of all this was to attack the Confederates about Old Tavern, advance all of the troops on the south side, and seize the higher ground, thus uncovering Mechanicsville and uniting all of the army on the south side.

The movement began in earnest about 8 o'clock by the advance of Hooker's Division of Heintzelman's Corps (the Third), and was supported in its movements by Kearney's Division of the same corps. Richardson's Division of the Second Corps made a demonstration, and Sedgwick's Division was held in readiness for action. The point held by our brigade, being already on the most advanced portion of the line, was the pivot on which the movement was made, and the brigade was not advanced but held in readiness for action.

After being relieved from guard the morning of the 25th, I had joined the company on the picket line and spent the day at the front. As we were not called upon to attempt anything aggressive, we kept well under cover, watched for any movement on the part of the enemy opposite us, and listened to the firing. The musketry firing all seemed to be on our left, and we could tell from the noise that our men were gradually advancing. The artillery firing was along the whole front, and many of the shells from both sides passed over us. When there was a lull, as frequently happened, we could hear the guns across the river to the right, showing that the Fifth Corps also was included in the general disturbance.

Being on the picket line, we were obliged to keep well-sheltered and in our places, and could see very little. We had to get all of our information of the important happenings about us through our ears—and remain stationary while we did it. The day was hot, and the hours dragged slowly until the sun sank behind the trees to the westward and the summer twilight resolved itself into the 'shades of night.' Even then the angry boom of the cannon and the spiteful crack of the rifles did not wholly cease. It was long after dark before it settled down to the ordinary contentions of the pickets. Twice during the night the firing grew to volleys, with artillery accompaniments, but the night passed without any material change in the situation. At night our men occupied all—or nearly all—of the disputed territory and held a line within four miles of Richmond.

When the efforts of our troops to gain ground towards Richmond ceased with the close of the day, it was the general impression that they would be renewed with increased forces and greater efforts when the new day came. As the boys of the company talked over the situation that night—as we understood it from the reports that had come to us of the successful operations of the day—we planned vigorous and important work for the next day. It was the talk that the Sixth Corps, which had recently established itself on our right, would join with us in a general attack in the morning.

We now know that something of that kind was planned. But our camp strategists and the 'general commanding' had both failed to include Jackson in their calculations, and the results were the failure of all plans. General T. J. Jackson had been again sent to the Valley, and, while McClellan's army was threatening Richmond, he was menacing Washington. Now again, though watched and threatened by the forces under Banks, Frémont, and McDowell, he had evaded them all, and, unopposed and without being followed, he had come to the aid of Lee against McClellan. The coming of Jackson undoubtedly brought a superior force against McClellan, and it seemed to stay all other proceedings until the result of Jackson's movements should be determined.[4]

Early on the morning of the 26th, artillery firing was resumed, but it was little more than the ordinary daily shelling. When relieved from picket, we returned to our shelter tents and tried to get a little much-needed rest with but unsatisfactory results. There was a stir and activity about the camp that indicated that important movements were at hand. Rations and ammunition were to be drawn and distributed and sick men taken to the surgeons to have their cases considered. Some of these were hurried away and others told that they were to remain with the regiment.

We had orders to be in readiness to form at call, and sought some shady place to lie down and sleep. As no advance was begun, it was evident that something had gone wrong. Many rumors were current, and it was known that large herds of cattle and trains of wagons were crossing from the opposite side of the river, but there was nothing in all of that that seemed out of harmony with a concentration of the whole army against Richmond. One of the rumors of the camp was that a large force was moving to turn our right, and this was soon confirmed by the booming of guns some miles away—across and up the river. There was frequent cannonading and demonstrations along our own front, which kept us in a state of constant readiness and expectation.

It was some time after noon when the nearer and increased firing across the Chickahominy made it certain that serious fighting was going on.[5] From our position, we could hear the firing, see something of the rising drifts of white smoke and the bursting shells—but it was all too far away to see more than that or to form any definite idea of the movements that were being made or their results.

Soon after dark the firing ceased, and, a little later, a succession of cheers came from the lines of the enemy opposite us. It was wild, jubilant yelling and made us fear the worst. It seemed to be a challenge, and we answered them with cheers and shouts. This set them to yelling more vigorously than before. For 'a thin space of

4. Misled by Allen Pinkerton's estimates, McClellan thought the Confederates had 180,000 to 200,000 men opposite his 104,000. In actuality, his army outnumbered Lee's 92,000-man army; Sears, *To the Gates of Richmond*, 190, 195.
5. This was the Battle of Mechanicsville, the second of the Seven Days' Battles (Oak Grove on June 25 was the first).

time' there was a fierce rivalry at cheering, and lungs were exercised to the limit. We did not know just what the 'Johnnies' were cheering about, but we did know that our cheers were based on about the same feelings that prompt a boy to whistle when he is passing a lonely graveyard. We knew very well that the cheering was intended to convey to us the impression of a victory for our foes, and we knew of nothing to disprove such an assumption. Our cheering was simply a boyish defiance, which may have been amusing, but it was harmless. That night there was a wild din and racket on the picket line all night long, and there was little rest or sleep for anyone.

There was a good many things to think about during the night. If beaten on the right, then our communications a single line of railroad—were at the mercy of the enemy, and all of our energies must be directed towards self-preservation. We began then to understand that the movement of the trains to the south side was to get them out of the reach of the enemy before he arrived, but we did not know then that since the 18th of June supplies had been loading at White House to be sent around by water to a new base on the James—and that some of these had already gone up the river.

With the first grey light of the 27th, there was a violent demonstration along our front; and for some hours we waited for an attack, which was constantly threatened; and these demonstrations continued at intervals during the day. It seems to have been a matter of uncertainty with those in high command just where the real attack would be made—until after noon, when it became evident that Fitz John Porter was to be attacked in his new position. (From Beaver Dam Creek, where the fighting had occurred the day before, Porter had withdrawn four to five miles and formed his new line with his left resting on the river.)

This fight is generally called Gaines' Mills, but it was really fought about New and Old Cold Harbor. It was soon after noon when the fighting began in earnest; and it was much nearer to us than that of the previous day; but from our position in the breastworks we could only judge of affairs over the river by the sound of the guns and the smoke. The volleys of musketry could be plainly heard; and great masses of smoke that formed in white clouds in the sunlight were constantly rising from the lines engaged; and the booming of cannon was, at times, almost continuous. Occasionally someone would go a safe distance to the rear and climb a tree for observations, but these reports were far from satisfactory or reassuring.

The tension of uncertainty and waiting made the day a long anxious one, but our attention was chiefly devoted to the enemy in our own front, who were very active—apparently in strong force—and frequently threatening an attack with artillery and infantry.

Somewhere about four o'clock, we (our brigade) were withdrawn from the front and sent to the river, where we found that Meagher's and French's Brigades of Richardson's Division were waiting. These two brigades crossed over soon after our arrival and were engaged in repelling the last assaults of the enemy. Our brigade was held at the river until after dark. Then we were placed in position to support Smith's Division of Franklin's Corps.

Later in the night, we returned to our old position and spent the remainder of the night in the breastworks. There were other changes of troops during the night, much firing along the front, and but little rest for anyone. In fact, we were under arms most of the night, ready to defend our own position or go to the defense of any threatened point. There had been savage fighting along Porter's front all the afternoon; he had made a splendid fight and held the enemy in check until about dark, when a portion of his line was compelled to fall back; and later, the whole line was retired towards the bridges.

The morning of the 28th gave promise of a hot day, which was more than fulfilled as the day grew. As may well be imagined, it was a busy day for the Army of the Potomac. A long, sweltering day, full of anxiety and suspense. With the crossing of the right wing to the south side of the river, the bridges were broken up, and troops put into position to cover the river and protect the trains. Beyond this, we of the ranks knew nothing more than we could see or guess. We held our front and seemed to be waiting, but we now know that a movement to the James River was then in progress and had been since the night. After its months of labor and effort, skirmishing and fighting, the Army of the Potomac found itself massed in an unfavorable position and encumbered with its trains and supplies—threatened and harassed on three sides by an increasing force of the enemy.

The army could not move to attack in force without endangering the loss of the trains. If its trains were lost, it would soon be helpless for any movement until again supplied. It seemed the part of common sense to hold on to the trains and supplies then in hand. These consisted of about 4,100 wagons (4- to 6-mule teams), 450 ambulances (1 and 2 horses)—containing 8 days' rations, sick, wounded, and ammunition. Fifty siege guns (6 to 10 horses) and about 330 field guns—with their accompaniments, caissons, and battery wagons (drawn by 6 or 8 horses) and the pontoons—constituted the rest of the materiel of the army that was movable on wheels.[6] This vast accumulation of 'rolling stock' had to be taken across a swamp and then across the country for about 20 miles to the James River. After getting across the swamps, the right flank would be exposed to Lee's immense army defending the capital. They also could be followed in force—and the left attacked also—if the Confederates succeeded in crossing the Chickahominy below the swamp. The only outlet—without exposing the trains at once to certain shelling and possible stampede and loss—was through the swamp.

Gen. McClellan had already planned to change his base to the James, and it was but natural that he should now move at once to execute his plans, holding other things in abeyance until that was accomplished.

6. Sears gives lower figures: 281 field guns, 26 siege guns, and "something over 3,800 wagons and ambulances"; Sears, *To the Gates of Richmond*, 256.

The Second and Third Corps, and Smith's Division of the Sixth Corps, were left to cover the original front towards Richmond and guard the rear along the Chickahominy and prevent the enemy from crossing or rebuilding the bridges. It was absolutely necessary to hold the enemy in check until the trains could be got through the swamp. The passage of these, with the troops to protect them on that side, took from the beginning of the movement the night of the 27th until late in the afternoon of the 29th—nearly two days.

Strong demonstrations were made at times during the 28th along the entire front and the river, where they were trying to rebuild the bridges. The latter work was effectually interfered with by our artillerists and sharpshooters. In one of their demonstrations against Smith's position, the First Minnesota was sent out and held for a time in reserve in case of need. We were subject to a severe shelling but returned to our position without any loss and without firing a shot.

In the readjustment of the line, one of Smith's brigades had abandoned a partly-finished redoubt, but had retired only a short distance and had left two regiments—the 23rd New York and the 49th Pennsylvania—lying down in easy rifle range. The enemy observed the earthwork apparently without defenders and seemed not to know of the situation of the troops nearby. The enemy threw out a force to investigate the movements they had seen; and a couple of regiments advanced in good form and charged the abandoned redoubt with a rush and a yell, and raised a shout of triumph as they reached it. Just at the height of their triumphal shouting, the New Yorkers and the Pennsylvanians sprang to their feet and gave them a volley that fairly riddled them and sent them hurrying back to their own side more rapidly than they had come out, leaving many killed and wounded behind them. Among the latter was a Colonel Lamar, who was seriously and probably fatally wounded, and made a prisoner. He was said to have been one of the men connected with the *Wanderer,* one of the last slave-ship enterprises.

As the afternoon waned and there were no more attempts against the new position of the right, we returned about dark to our old position for the night. At this time it was understood that the army was to "change its base," and we all knew that this meant a retreat from in front of Richmond, but the significance of the movement was not comprehended by the most of us. We felt the depression and gloom of the probable failure of a great enterprise to which we had given our best efforts, but the determination was to continue those efforts to the end no matter what the results might be.

Before going out to the support of Smith's troops, we had packed our knapsacks, leaving only our shelter tents standing, and these had been left that they might continue to be observed by the enemy. On our return after dark, we took down our shelter tents. Each one took a piece as a part of his personal belongings and placed it in or strapped it upon his knapsack. Then, with all of our personal property in our knapsacks, with three days' rations in our haversacks (less what we had eaten that day) and with 100 rounds of ammunition in our cartridge boxes and about our persons—we were ready, as some of the boys said, "for a fight or a foot-race." When these preliminaries were all attended to and our canteens filled and suppers eaten, companies were formed. We were told that we were to be ready to march at any time—quietly, at command.

It must have been towards midnight when all of these preparations were completed, and we stretched ourselves upon the ground as animals do when weary. It was not many minutes before we slept, for we were well nigh exhausted by the almost constant duty of the last four days and nights. When we laid down, we expected to be called up soon and march.

It was no part of the plan of the enemy that we should have a quiet night's rest. There was an almost constant fusillade going on all night; naps were brief and often interrupted; and we got but little refreshing rest or sleep. Before the first gray token of the morning could be seen, we were quietly called into line and stood ready to move. While we waited, a few men managed to make coffee; and a hasty breakfast of coffee, crackers, and raw pork was eaten as we stood in ranks. Though the night had been warm, the fog and the morning air seemed really chilly, and a pint of hot coffee—strong and black, without milk or sugar—which we hastily swallowed—certainly did cheer and strengthen us.

As the light of the morning increased, line of battle was formed, and, slowly and cautiously, we withdrew from the position we had held against all contestants since the 31st of May. We must now seek a new position to protect the trains now crossing the White Oak Swamp and connect with the rest of the army on the other side. There was a dense fog covering everything and concealing the movement from our enemies. I think that they were wholly unaware of the fact that we had "like the Arab folded our tents and stolen away" until some little time after we had left.

We moved slowly to the rear and had gone less than two miles when a halt was made. The fog was burning off, and the morning was very warm now that the sun was making its power felt. The lifting fog showed, too, that there were acres of wagons that had not yet started. This was a surprise to us of the ranks, but, of course, it must have been known to those directing the movement. There was a brief halt; and then a line of battle was formed, facing the direction from which we had come; and a skirmish line was sent back to locate the enemy. In this formation, the First Brigade was placed in the second line in support of a Rhode Island Battery, and there were only three regiments present. Gen. Gorman being sick, the brigade was commanded by Col. Alfred Sully, and the First was under the command of Lieutenant Col. Stephen Miller.

The investigations of the skirmishers showed that the enemy had discovered our departure and was already sending out a skirmish line to locate us. With both parties active, a collision could not be long delayed, and there was a lively exchange of shots between the skirmishers. The enemy's skirmishers were followed by a line of battle; our skirmishers retired to our line; and some sharp fighting ensued, which resulted in the withdrawal of the enemy after they discovered that we were disposed to stay there. This was followed by a season of artillery firing, in which several batteries on both sides took an active part, and during which we laid down in the edge of a wood. There were plenty of shells flying about, and a number of them spent their force among the trees close by, but we suffered no damage from them except the unpleasant sensation one has when he thinks he is 'going to get it.'

Not satisfied with results, the enemy again sent forward an increased force of infantry and made quite a determined attack, but were again quickly driven back and retired out of sight. For a little while, it was comparatively still except an occasional shell, when there was an outburst of artillery, and they again broke cover with an increased force and advanced more rapidly and farther than before. But the rifle fire of our infantry—as soon as they came in effective range—was too much for them, and they quickly retired.

This seemed to satisfy them that it was safer to keep a respectful distance, and they made us no further trouble except a desultory shelling as long as we remained there. There was considerable loss on both sides, but, as our men kept covered as much as possible until the moment of firing, it seems certain that their loss must have been greatly in excess of ours. The position where this fighting occurred in the morning is known as Allen's Farm. It is also sometimes called 'the Peach Orchard,' and was two miles, more or less, from Savage's Station on the Richmond and York River Railroad.

Soon after this, Smith's Division and the rest of the Sixth Corps on this side of the swamp retired to the right and rear. General Sumner, being informed of the new position taken by General Franklin's Sixth Corps, at once retired towards Savage's Station to place the Second Corps in proper relation to Smith's Division and thus shorten and concentrate the line.

It was noon or a little later when we began to retire to the station. There was a bright sunshine, but little air stirring, and it was suffocatingly hot. The last week of hot sun had dried the ground very rapidly. The passing artillery, wagons, animals, and men had pulverized the surface of the roads and wherever they marched to an impalpable powder. This rose like a fog wherever a battery, a line of wagons, or a column of men moved. As there was no wind to carry it away, it settled back upon those who had stirred it up or the ones immediately following them. I might, with considerable truth, have said *into* instead of "*upon*", for we breathed it into our throats and nostrils; it settled into our eyes and ears; it stuck to our sweating skin wherever exposed—on hands, necks, and faces; and our uniforms looked as if we had been rolled in the ashes.

As there was no enemy threatening when we were ready to go, the line of battle broke to the rear by brigades and retired by columns. The march was at a quick step, and the dust and the scorching mid-day heat made the movement a trying one—particularly to those enfeebled by sickness; and all of us reached the station very tired. We halted for a little time on the northerly side of the railroad—resting at will with our arms in our hands—then crossed to the southerly side of the road, where there was more room and some shade. Here, Sedgwick's Division was massed and stacked arms, Richardson's Division remaining on the other side of the railroad and covering the approaches to the station in that direction.

It was somewhere about two o'clock when we arrived at the station, and perhaps a half hour later when we stacked arms. When arms were stacked, some laid down immediately and were sleeping soundly in a minute or two. But, as the breakfast had been hastily eaten before daylight, there was a general movement to make a cup of coffee. Canteens that contained any water were emptied into tin cups, and, while some made fires, others hunted for water to replenish the canteens. In a few minutes, we were sitting on the ground eating crackers and pork and drinking hot coffee.

At the same time, we were looking around on a scene of war, desolation, and wholesale destruction which under any ordinary conditions would have claimed our undivided attention. It was indeed a wild, weird, and wonderful picture that presented itself to us as we approached the station and observed the smoke and flames of the burning stores. The Fifteenth Massachusetts of our brigade had been sent to the station the night before, and they had been the principal actors in destroying whatever could not be carried away.

About the time we arrived, a train consisting of an engine, tender, and four or five cars loaded chiefly with ammunition was destroyed in a novel manner. The train was fired, and the engine—with a full head of steam on and the throttle wide open—was started down the track towards the bridge across the Chickahominy, which had been partly destroyed and was then held by the enemy. It shot down the grade, enveloped in flames, and the cars were being rapidly shattered to pieces by the bursting shells as it disappeared around the curve into the woods. A moment or two later, a terrific explosion was heard and a dense, cone-shaped cloud rose above the woods and, gradually expanding, floated away. A trembling mass of white vapor that soon vanished.

The 'special artists on the spot' as usual gave the illustrated papers exaggerated sketches of the burning train with its freight of explosives sweeping with fearful havoc through a column of the enemy just crossing the bridge (from which the rails had been removed) and plunging into the river. I saw the flying train with its meteoric tail of fire, heard the bursting shells and the thunderous explosion, and beheld the rising cloud, but am of the opinion that the wholesale destruction of the 'Johnnies' was a fancy of the specials.

For perhaps the first time, the Second Division of the Second Corps was gathered in a compact body, with its artillery with it, and the First Division nearby. Our division occupied the open ground between the railroad and the Williamsburg Road, while Richardson's Division lay to the right and rear. There were three batteries in position with guns pointed up the railroad towards the Williamsburg

The Union Army field hospital at Savage's Station, Virginia, shortly after the battle. A "street" between two rows of hospital tents can be seen beyond the fence in the center.

Road and the intervening woods and fields. Looking westward from the clearing we occupied, the ground fell off into a ravine and along the edges of this ravine there were some small trees, and in it was brush and undergrowth. Beyond this, on the higher ground, was another clearing, which may have been about half a mile square, and beyond this clearing were woods and bushes. In this timber, and to the left of it, the Third Corps (Gen. Heintzelman) was supposed to be located.

There was another cleared field on the north side of the railroad of considerable size, which was nearly filled with hospital tents. There were, I should say, some hundreds of these large tents, nicely laid out in streets, with cots, beds, attendants, and surgeons. As many of the sick and wounded as were able to walk had started on with the trains; as many as the ambulances could carry had gone on in them; and there still remained some 2,500 of the helpless sick and wounded in the tents. These with the surgeons and attendants were to be left behind when we retired, and many more were to be added to them before we went—as events proved.

With this general outline of the place, one can better understand what followed. I should also add that Smith's Division of the Sixth Corps[7] had taken a position in the wood off to our left, beyond the Williamsburg Road. These three divisions with their artillery probably numbered 18,000 or 20,000 men—at rest,

7. Only "Smith's Vermont brigade, under command of William T. H. Brooks," was stationed on the left; Sears, *To the Gates of Richmond,* 272.

guns stacked, and the men who were not cooking or eating were lying on the ground asleep.

Sleeping or waking, every face was marked with lines of weariness and anxiety—many with sunken cheeks and hollow eyes that told of their weakened physical condition. This would have been more apparent if there had been less grime on their faces, accumulated during recent operations. It did not take long after arms were stacked, and water procured, for the coffee to boil in our tin cups, and sleeping comrades were awakened to eat.

There was not much said, for the boys were too tired to be talkative, but as a little group of Company F sat under the shade of some small trees eating crackers and drinking coffee someone remarked, "What would the folks say if they could see us now?" It was evident where the comrade's thoughts were wandering. There was no immediate response, but it was certain everyone's mind had reverted to the faraway home and its tender associations. Then someone said, "Did you know that this was Sunday?" Another added, "They have all been to church today and have been praying for us"; while another looked around and asserted that "it was evident that we needed it."

Not much more was said, and within five minutes after the last swallow of coffee nearly everyone was sleeping, but it is probable that the last thoughts of each one before unconsciousness in sleep was of his home. It seemed to us then as if ages had passed since we had left our homes. Some of the boys used to refer to things that had happened before their enlistment as *"when they were on earth the first time."* I cannot understand why the time seemed so long then, as it does not now. It was only fourteen months almost to an hour since we had been mustered in, and but a little more than twelve months since we were steaming down the Mississippi; but somehow it seemed like many years.

We had not slept long before we were wakened by a stir in the camp, and it was reported that the 'Railroad Monitor' was coming down the track and was going to shell us. The 'Railroad Monitor' was a heavy gun which the enemy had mounted on a flat car and protected by an armor of iron rails. This had been used before, but as we were then north of the road we had had no experience with it. But we had heard of it. It was not at all soothing to feel that there was the possibility of a hundred pound shell dropping in our midst at any moment. There was no call to fall in; they did not shell us; nothing was visible up the road; and it was considered a needless alarm and given little further attention. This, I think, was before four o'clock (not later), and many of the boys slept on and knew nothing of it.

There is no doubt but the enemy was at this time moving to attack both along the railroad and the Williamsburg Road; suspicious movements were observed by our outposts and reported and doubtless would have been investigated had it not been understood that the front south of the railroad was covered by the Third Corps. These men coming out of the brush had been seen by men of our regiment and others. And it was the second time that men had appeared at the edge of this wood. After there was talk of the 'ironclad' coming down the railroad, we were in rather an expectant mood, and eyes were often turned towards the woods and the railroad; and when those men first appeared, they were seen and the question raised as to who they were. That was a question which, at that distance, we could not decide; and it was the impression that our men should be in that direction. Events proved that the Third Corps was not there or anywhere in that vicinity.

It was hazardous in the extreme for Heintzelman to have gone without notice and left his fellow campaigners, who had withdrawn behind his right, exposed to a front and flank attack. But for a fortunate happening, it might have proved a costly bit of blundering. Gen. Franklin and Gen. Sedgwick rode over the field, saw the group of men come out of the wood, and Sedgwick exclaimed, "Why, those men are rebels!" They sought General Sumner for instructions and awoke him.

When once it became evident that a fight was on, there was no time lost in preparing for it. As the first shell shrieked over our heads, there was a multitudinous cry of "Fall in!" from the orderly sergeants, and the companies were promptly in line. Company, regimental, and general officers came quickly. General Burns of the Second Brigade of our division was the first to move, sending out the 72nd Pennsylvania and following it with the 106th Pennsylvania.

The 72nd was a Zouave regiment and well-drilled, and it made a fine showing as the men deployed to the front at the double quick and spread out in a strong skirmish line in the open field, after crossing the ravine. I rarely ever saw a skirmish line go into action more promptly or in better form. Meantime, the shells were coming more rapidly as the regiments were forming—officers and orderlies galloping here and there—while our batteries were shifting the position of guns and teams and preparing to reply.

Burns's regiments had scarcely reached the field across the ravine before an order came for our regiment to follow them. We wondered then how it happened that we were detached from our own brigade and sent to assist another brigade, which had not yet got into action and had two spare regiments of its own close by. This was not the only time in its history that the regiment was used in an emergency because it happened to be the 'most handy' and in readiness for action.

When the order to advance came to the regiment, we were in line and moved at once, directly towards the field across which Burns's two regiments were moving. By this time our artillery was coming into action, and our direction would bring us directly in the line of their fire. It was said that they were to withhold their fire. As we neared the ravine, we had orders to lie down, *flat*; and we dropped to the ground.

Almost instantly, the discharge from a full battery swept over us at an elevation calculated to just clear us. Their fire seemed almost hot enough to scorch us, and two or three men were slightly injured by sabots (pieces of wood on which the shells rested to give them the full force of the explosive). The most serious of these was Harrison Lyons of Company A, but none of F had been touched.

As soon as the cyclone of shells had passed, we sprang to our feet and hurried down across the ravine into the field beyond. We were pelted all the way down by the enemy's shells, and, as we crossed the ravine and after we had come out into the field, the fire from both sides was crossing over our heads. It was an interesting position and not at the moment fraught with immediate danger.

When the field was reached, Gen. Burns directed Lieutenant Col. Miller to place the regiment on the left of his line, which at that time was close to the woods, and we hastened in that direction. A moment or two later, we heard the shrill voice of Lt. Col. Miller saying, "They are flanking us, General Burns; they are doing it now!" This was not exactly the formal military way of doing it, but it conveyed important information in a way that got the instant attention of Gen. Burns. It was at this time that rifle firing began on the right—probably by the 72nd Pennsylvania.

The regiment as it was placed for action formed an obtuse angle with the apex at or near the Williamsburg Road. Seven companies formed the line on the left of the angle and three on the right. Company F was on the right—the right-flank company of the regiment. All of our movements had been made as quickly as possible, for there seemed urgent need of haste. The distance we had gone was a mile or more, and, as the heat was intense, we reached the edge of the wood out of breath and sweating profusely.

As we halted at the edge of the woods—into which the skirmishers sent out from Burns's Brigade had already entered—there was an almost continuous roll of musketry from the line on our right—which was being answered by the enemy—and the artillery on both sides was active. As we came up to the woods, noises were heard; someone shouted and there was an answering shout; then we cheered and there was a response of yells. From this we knew that the enemy was not far off, and we prepared for their coming.

Our skirmishers began to work their way into the tangled undergrowth, and they did not have to go far before they came in contact with the enemy—when they came out more quickly than they had gone in and were followed by a fusillade of bullets. The brush completely hid the enemy from our sight, but, as the bullets came with vicious, spiteful force, it was evidence that they were in effective range, and the order was given to commence firing.

We immediately leveled our rifles at the woods and 'blazed away.' The enemy came on yelling and firing, and we replied to the best of our ability. It was a red-hot fight in short meter, and both sides meant apparently to settle the future of the Nation and the Confederacy then and there. In the advance to our last position, we had kept touch with the regiment, and that had drawn us away from the regiment on our right. There was now an interval of perhaps a hundred feet or more—and Company F opened its right a little to partly cover this ground. (I do not think that the enemy could see to detect the weak spot.) That weakened the line by its having a less number of defenders than a well-closed line would have had. As there was but little air stirring, the smoke from our rifles seemed to bank up against the woods. As it was now beginning to grow dusk, one could see but imperfectly more than twenty feet and scarcely at all to twice that distance.

The enemy was pushing the attack savagely, and our line was holding its own and replying with a rapid and continuous fire. Very little could be seen in the semi-darkness, but the spurts of flame and sparks dripping from the guns as they were fired showed where the men stood and the determined fight they were making. We were suffering seriously from the fire that was poured into us. The regiment on our right was yielding to it and was being gradually forced back. They did not break, but backed down the slope, firing as they retired, and the enemy followed them. This widened the interval and exposed us to a flank fire, which made the situation critical and not long to be endured.

It was at this moment we heard the sharp, penetrating voice of Lieut. Col. Miller close behind us saying, "Minnesota, stand firm! Don't run, Minnesota!" It was more of an entreaty than a command, but it answered just as well. We had lots of State pride, and I certainly believe that "Minnesota" was the magic word that encouraged us to stand and face that terrible storm of bullets that swept our line.

We felt sure, too, that others would be sent to our relief. Once or twice, a cheer that sounded faint and far-off in the confusion of the fighting had been heard behind us, but in a hasty glance in that direction nothing could be seen through the smoke and gathering darkness save the lurid flash of our batteries on the hill, which were still throwing shells over our heads (and over the heads of the rebels, too). The enemy came through the opening on our right, and we were enveloped—front and flank—in a scorching fire that seemed impossible to stand for another minute. Retreat, surrender, or annihilation seemed to be the alternatives.

Then we heard the cheering once more—close behind us, too—a good, open-mouthed, ringing hurrah. No music ever sounded sweeter or more melodious than that welcome, defiant cheering to our battle-stunned ears. It was the ever-reliable Fifteenth Massachusetts and Eighty-Second New York of our own brigade, led by Kimball and Hudson. "We are with you, Minnesota!" they shouted as—crowding to the front and extending to the right—they emptied their rifles into the faces of the enemy that had been punishing us so severely.

The crisis was safely passed. The enemy who had passed us on the right now turned back, and their whole line retreated into the woods. There on the smoking field, with the wild refrain of the battle still ringing in their ears, the boys from Minnesota, Massachusetts, and New York—mingling together—united in a good old Union hurrah. There had been pleasant comradeship between the Massachusetts and Minnesota men before, and thenceforth they were brothers. The enemy left us in undisturbed possession of the field, and it was now quite dark with some gathering clouds.

Naturally, as soon as the fighting was over, there was an effort to determine the extent of our losses and make the best disposition for the care of the wounded. There was but little that could be done. The most hopeful thing for every sick and wounded man that had the strength left was to try to make his way with the army. As there was no transportation, those who could not get away by their own efforts must be left at the hospital back at the station, where there were surgeons and attendants. If left there, of course, they would fall into the hands of the enemy. This was one of the cruel fortunes of war which in emergencies cannot be escaped. And the emergency was upon us then.

Two were dead; 14 were wounded. One-third of the company present. Martin Willman and Ferris Johnson—two corporals that stood together in the center of the company like the brave fellows they were—had fallen where they fought, facing the enemy. Edward E. Davis was shot through the body and died later in the hospital. Calvin P. Clark, who had at one time been the orderly sergeant of the company, was also shot through the body, and Ransom Mott had a shattered arm. Martin Maginnis, our second lieutenant, had a shot in the left shoulder. Others were more or less seriously wounded.

More than any other action, perhaps, this was Company F's fight, and looking back to it today, it was one to remember and be proud of. I am not claiming that Company F did more or better than the other companies. Nothing of the kind. All obeyed orders and took the consequences; and that is the limit of soldierly good conduct. This time we were sent where the battle-lightning happened to strike—and it struck us hard.

The regiment had gone into the fight as a unit and kept together, but three companies faced to the west and seven to the south, and the two wings of the regiment were fighting different bodies of men. Both wings were badly exposed and had to fight persistently and against odds to hold the position until assistance could get there. In this fighting, 4 were killed and 44 wounded—a total of 48. Of these, Company F had 2 killed and 14 wounded—a total of 16. Exactly one-third of the loss, which included one-half of the dead. The loss in Company C was nearly as large as in Company F.

Lieutenant Colonel Miller writes, "General Burns said to me the next day, '*Your regiment did nobly, sir,*' and I heartily concur in the sentiment."

For some little time after the enemy was driven off on our front, there was now and then a rifle shot from the bushes, and generally someone responded to it, but after a while these ceased on both sides. Before the wind rose, we could hear the cries and calls of the wounded—and voices occasionally—out in the woods. Aside from that, there was almost an oppressive stillness, compared with the uproar of the fighting. As we lay there waiting, we began to notice the glimmer of lightning and hear the distant rolling of thunder. Soon there came a murmur of wind among the trees, and a breeze brought a little relief from the sweltering heat.

It was about this time that the company drew back a little from the woods, formed company, counted off, and laid down again to await orders. Whether Captain Colvill did this under orders or of his own volition that he might be in readiness, I do not know.

Captain Colvill, who had been feeling poorly for some days, had taken his place at the head of the company that morning and kept it during the day; and had said but little more than was necessary to give the required orders. He had kept close to the company while it was in action, and, when the gap was opened between our regiment and the 106th Pennsylvania, he had said, "Spread out a little," and pointed in that direction. When the enemy came out of the woods on the right, he had called attention to them and said, "Give it to them fellows!" When the fight was over, he had laid down with the rest of us. He was a man of iron nerve and will, but he was not a man without feelings and sensibility. I have thought sometimes that the thermometer of his real feelings might not have registered greatly different from the rest of us if the record had been made public. But he certainly could face danger with the *greatest show of indifference* of any man I ever knew. And he was there in an emergency and ready to meet it without fuss or flourish.

Every mother's son of us preferred to live

JUNE-JULY 1862

AFTER WE HAD LAIN ON THE GROUND for a little time, the companies were called up quietly, and the regiment formed in line, was led out, and joined the brigade. While we were doing this, a mass of whirling clouds—heralded by a display of lightning and thunder and driven by a strong wind—passed over us. There was a dash of summer rain—big, splashing drops and just enough of it to thoroughly wet us—and then the clouds rolled by, and in a little while the stars were seen overhead. Meantime, we had gained the road and were marching back towards the station. The dash of rain and the breeze were refreshing while they lasted, but when the breeze ceased the heat was as great as before.

The marching was a series of starts and halts, and was wearisome and aggravating—as most night marches are—particularly after we had started over the rough and imperfect road across the swamp. Not far ahead of the regiment was a battery, and it met with difficulties in its progress. Hour after hour we tramped on, listening to the thump and thud of the horses' feet, the grind and chuck of the wheels of the carriages—varied by occasional halts, *damns*, and stronger expletives—and we followed blindly after.

For the most part we went in silence, for we had reached a condition where mere words did not amount to much. Occasionally there was heard a word of sympathy or regret for one or another of the poor fellows we had left behind; and occasionally there was a word of speculation as to how much farther we must go before we could lie down and rest. Now and then someone would say how thirsty he was, and that he could not possibly keep on much longer. These were stimulated to continue their efforts by conundrums like this: "What will you do? Lay down here and die in the swamp? Or be captured? Better keep on." I do not think a man of the company fell out during that night's march.

It was fairly daylight of the 30th of June when we emerged from White Oak Swamp and passed to the rear of Smith's Division, which had preceded us and formed its lines to defend the crossing. They had made the passage about three o'clock in the morning. It was an hour or so later when we passed them. Batteries were in position and infantry in support of them. Most of the men were lying on the ground asleep, but a few were cooking their breakfasts about little fires.

We looked with satisfaction upon the troops at rest, and, as we turned to the side of the road in the rear of them, we too expected to halt there with them. Arms were stacked, and some dropped on the ground and slept while others started fires to make coffee. For some hours, I had been tormented by a feverish thirst and a violent headache. The last part of the way I had known that my strength was failing and was oppressed with the feeling that I might have to 'give it up' and lay down by the roadside. Personally, I was very glad at the prospect of a halt. I found water (such as it was), tried to quench my thirst by drinking lots of it, then filled my canteen and went back to the gun stacks and laid down, thinking to make some coffee a little later.

Before the coffee was boiling, orders came to "move on," and Sergeant Bruce was calling, "Fall in, Company F." The company formed—some of the boys with their cups of half-boiled coffee in their hands and 'saying things.'

After a little delay—apparently awaiting orders—we moved in a southerly direction. The halt had probably been made only to close up the division and to report (for the necessary orders) as to our position. The sun was now climbing towards the zenith, and the heat was very trying to the tired men. The little rain of the night before had apparently had no effect on the dust, which rose in suffocating clouds wherever it was stirred up by wheels or feet. It was plain that we were up with the trains again. The roads were filled with wagons moving out, and there were acres and acres of them massed in the fields—feeding the mules.

While we had been holding back the forces of Magruder and Jackson north of the swamp, during the day of the 29th all of the trains and Slocum's and McCall's divisions had crossed to the south side of White Oak Swamp, and the Third Corps also had preceded us to that side. During the day of the 30th, these trains were to be pushed on in the rear of the troops to Malvern Hill, and this movement was now in progress.

When we had crossed the swamp, all of the army was on the south side with its trains and materiel, and one of the critical stages of the movement was passed, but it would take another day for them to reach the river. To accomplish this in safety and make the movement a success, the forces which crossed the swamp in the night must get in supporting distance of those who had preceded them, cover all of the roads from Richmond and the rear, and 'stand off' the enemy until another night. There was every reason to expect that all of the forces at the command of Lee and Jeff Davis would be upon us before mid-day. Every effort possible would be made to break our long line and to capture, stampede, or burn the trains. There was sure to be lively times, and troops were hurried into position as they were most available and without much regard to corps organizations.

It will be seen from this that we had a 'far-flung battle line,' behind which the trains must pass and which must be held to insure their safety. The only division not assigned to this line was the Second of the Second Corps (Sedgwick's), which was held out for a general reserve and—after the brief halt already mentioned—was moving to a point at Glendale crossroads near Nelson's farm.

Then we halted again; some of the boys dropped to the ground without ceremony and went to sleep very quickly; while others improved the time to get something to eat. My head was still throbbing with pain, and I had no desire to eat, and at once found a shady place and tried to sleep.

Ever since we halted, we had heard at irregular intervals a few shots back at the rear, and now they were coming more rapidly and from other points. We were sleepy and, if permitted, could have slept on undisturbed 'despite the roar of great guns,' but there seemed no rest for us. There was a call for the reserve, and our brigade was hurriedly returned to the right.

There was a furious cannonading going on from both sides when we arrived, but no infantry firing except some skirmishing off in the swamp to the left. Jackson had been trying to force a passage through the swamp, had massed his artillery for this purpose, had knocked to pieces a couple of our regular batteries (Mott's and Hazzard's) and killed Captain Hazzard.[1] Some of our rifled guns a little farther back and on higher ground got the range on the Confederate guns and punished them so severely that they were compelled to retire. Jackson did not succeed in pushing his infantry across, and, as our presence was not needed here longer, we returned to the center.

When we had reached a point near our former position, we halted and laid down to rest, which we greatly needed. Weak as many were from disease before the movement began, the intense activity of the last six days had seriously impaired everyone physically, and many were greatly affected by the heat.

While waiting here, someone brought me some coffee and urged that I drink it to keep up my strength. Though my head was still throbbing with pain, and I really did not want it, I considered it best to drink it, as I was so weak that I scarcely felt able to stand. I drank the coffee and ate some crackers and pork, and for a little time felt better—but not for long. I had not eaten very much; I had not really relished it; and it did not take long to discover that I had added nausea to my aching head. It was at this time that our brigade was again called for, and for the first time in my soldier life, I found myself unable to go when the regiment advanced.

Dr. Hand gave me something which he said ought to quiet my stomach and relieve my head. I sat down in a fence corner with my rifle across my knees and my head in my hands. Instead of having a quieting effect, the dose seemed to seriously disturb my 'interior department.' So much so that I stood up and leaned against the fence. Notwithstanding the heat of the day, I felt chilly; a deathly sensation came over me; and, after a violent effort, there was an expulsion of all that I had eaten recently—accompanied by a liberal amount of a greenish and ex-

1. Rufus D. Pettit's battery, not Mott's, joined Hazzard's in opposing Jackson's advance, which was only a weak effort to cross the White Oak Bridge, but Sully's brigade was one of those sent to stop him; Welcher, *Union Army*, Vol. 1, *Eastern Theater*, 825, 826; Sears, *To the Gates of Richmond*, 285–89.

ceedingly bitter liquid substance, which may have been a concentration of the quinine I had been taking for the malaria. Then a cold dew gathered on my skin. This was followed a little later by an ooze of natural sweat which brought relief to my head, and I would have slept if I had not resisted the inclination.

After a little while, I followed after the regiment and found it lying down to protect itself from shells and stray bullets. There was a 'hurry up call' for the reserves, from some point off to the left, and our brigade was sent forward at the double quick. The boys were suffering intensely from heat, thirst, and fatigue, but did their best to meet the demands made upon them. But some were compelled to drop out. The sounds of strife increased moment by moment as we hurried on.

Firing by batteries and sections, the artillery vomited forth their murderous missiles with fire, smoke, and stunning explosions. The very earth seemed to shake and the air to shudder with the thunder of the discharges. The flying shells shrieked wildly over our heads; tore through the trees; plowed along the ground or burst in the air, scattering their severed fragments with sharp, incisive explosions. Heavy volleys of musketry rolled and crashed along the contending lines like the beating waves of an incoming tide. Dust, smoke, and noise—and in the midst of it all—but dimly outlined in the smoke—regiments and batteries were hastening to join in the wild melee. It was a wild, awe-inspiring scene and well calculated to make a small man like myself feel his insignificance. I felt it, too, and at the same time realized that I occupied a much larger space than I wished I did.

Sherman had not then defined war as hell, but, since he has, I recognize the entire appropriateness of the definition. The day was hot enough to suggest it, and the sun, seen through the smoke, seemed bathed in blood. The dense, sulphurous smoke spread along the ground and rose among the trees, while the volleys of musketry rolled and crashed like the growling and gnashing of a mighty chorus of demons. Everything looked weird and unnatural, more like the exhibition of some supernatural power than the result of any human agency. It took no great stretch of imagination to almost believe that by some mysterious chance we had crossed into the confines of Hades. That in the previous night's darkness, instead of making the passage of the White Oak Swamp as we supposed, we had forded the fabled Styx at ebb-tide and were then wandering in the land that Bob Ingersoll did not believe in.[2] That Old King Pluto had taken to the field in person, set into active operation all of his infernal engines of destruction, and was marshalling all of the 'imps of darkness' to dispute possession with us.

It was in truth a memorable scene as we hurried up to aid the shattered and hard-pressed fighting line. Sweating and panting for breath, we reached the desired point and found the troops of McCall's Division being forced out of the woods. His Pennsylvania Reserves had been attacked by a greatly superior force

2. Robert Ingersoll was a well-known, late nineteenth-century atheist.

under Longstreet and A. P. Hill, who were trying to break our line by a flank attack. The fighting had involved Slocum's, Kearney's, McCall's, and Hooker's divisions on the front, and Sedgwick's Division, on reserve, had been called to help check them.

When we arrived, the regiment was at first held in reserve in support of a battery, and we laid down to avoid needless exposure and to rest until our turn should come. The Third Brigade (Dana's) of our division had preceded us and was then making a lively and successful fight. Battery A, 1st Rhode Island Light Artillery was making an earnest effort to check the enemy's advance by raining case and shrapnel on the advancing line.

The regiment was called up and ordered to advance and attack. One moment we halted to allow any who chose to throw aside their knapsacks and to adjust the line. Just then General Dana rode up and—saying, "I will place my old regiment"—directed our movements towards the desired point.

The colors moved to the front, and the line of battle followed. It was a tense, critical moment as we advanced and must, seemingly, be fraught with most serious consequences, as the enemy was still pouring out of the woods. Their assault, however, had already spent its force; or they were not ready to engage a new enemy; and they did not wait to try conclusions with the bayonet, but with a parting volley retired into the woods. We had been exposed to a rattling fire as we advanced; and this was continued in an irregular way for a time; and we had suffered considerable loss, but not in the wholesale manner that appeared probable.

Halting at the edge of the woods after firing a few rounds, we laid down in line—very glad for an opportunity to rest, though still exposed to a random fire. The contest for the day was closing. The sun sank, red and fiery, behind the great curtain of smoke that hung like a pall over the battle-scourged woods and fields. The day was merging into night, and the sounds of strife had died away to the occasional booming of a cannon or the spasmodic cracking of rifles. These were heard off to the left, then far away to the right, and again near us, and once more on our left—the death rattle of the expiring conflict.

The most serious loss of the day to Company F came in one of those temporary outbreaks that marked the close of the fighting, just as it was getting too dark to see anything with distinctness or certainty.

When we halted at the woods, we had been cautioned not to fire, as it was believed that our own men were coming in front of us, and though shots came frequently from the front it was still thought that they were only stray bullets. (But it was now almost certain that there was a gap between the left of Meade's brigade and the right of the next in line, and that we were more advanced and almost exactly covered it.) One of these stray shots struck Captain Colvill in the left shoulder, and he was obliged to go to the rear, being seriously wounded. This left the company in command of Second Lieutenant Martin Maginnis, who had also been wounded in the left shoulder the night before at Savage's Station but was still with the company. In the next few minutes, he proved himself to be the right man in the right place.

It was now getting so dark that objects could only be distinguished by their outlines. We were at the edge of a field fronting a wood of scattered trees and low bushes, and from these woods shots kept coming at irregular intervals. This plainly indicated that there were none of our own troops immediately in our front—as, if there had been, there would have been a return fire. But—as we had been told that there were and ordered not to fire—our boys resisted the natural inclination to strike back and exposed themselves as little as possible. But for that order and the fear of firing into our own men, we would have given them a volley when the captain was shot.

When we first halted at the edge of the wood, I think that the order was to kneel down, but it was not many minutes before the most of the boys had modified that order to suit their exhausted condition and had lain down. I know that I had adapted it to my 'played out' feelings and was lying on the 'front side of my back' with my hands on my rifle in front of me. Some of the company may have already fallen asleep, as our physical condition was such that it was almost impossible to remain at rest for five consecutive minutes without sleeping, regardless of danger, unless it was known to be positive and imminent.

It was very soon after the wounding of Capt. Colvill when some men's heads and the top of a standard appeared in the brush almost directly in front of the right of the company. Lieutenant Maginnis (and perhaps some others) was standing, and the stir attracted attention. Something had aroused Lieut. Maginnis's suspicions that the flag he had caught a glimpse of was not the Stars and Stripes. They were no doubt aware of our presence. They seemed to be uncertain whether to regard us as friends or enemies.

One of them came a little ways towards us and said quietly, "Who are you?" To this informal challenge, Lieut. Maginnis answered evasively—as is usual in cases of doubt—saying, "Well! Who are you?"—or something to that effect. The response to this came in decisive tones and a little louder than before, "Are you *Confederate* or *Yankee*?"

This left no doubt in the mind of Lieut. Maginnis or anyone else that heard it that they were rebels, and he ordered the company to fire—repeating the command "Fire" once or twice. The boys of the company sprang up and fired into the woods in front. Other companies took it up, and the fire ran down the regiment towards the left, and we continued to load and fire until ordered to cease. We got a scattering fire in return, and the people in our front ran back into the bushes, and were almost instantly out of sight in the woods and darkness.

Until the moment of discovery, they were not aware that they were so near us; and that they were moving diagonally across our front instead of directly towards us—and, consequently, got our fire on the flank or nearly so, and were not faced in the right direction to return it. For this reason, we got only a light return fire, and they withdrew promptly from their unfavorable position rather than try to rectify it in the dark after being fired on.

There was doubt on the part of Lieut. Col. Miller as to whether we had not made a mistake, as he had been informed that some of our own troops were in his front. He was out of humor with the company and angry at Lieutenant Maginnis for giving the order. He was not convinced to the contrary until some of the men wounded by our fire were brought in from the bushes, and it was made certain that the Sixteenth North Carolina had been in our front. (They would soon have reached the flank of Dana's Brigade if they had been allowed to go on unchecked. They might also have 'got the drop' on the regiment and fired first.) When satisfied, he gave us credit for having done the right thing and complimented Lieutenant Maginnis, who took great risk in ordering us to fire. If it had been one of our own regiments, he would have been subject to a court martial and possible cashiering, or worse. To him belongs the credit.

The only loss to the company was Robert W. Leeson, who was shot through the lower part of the body and died soon after. Bob was always on good terms with his comrades, and there were but few men in the company that would have been more generally missed. He was a Hamline Boy and will be kindly and pleasantly remembered by the antebellum students at the university and by many of the older residents of Red Wing and Goodhue County.

His father, John Leeson, was one of the earlier settlers and was identified with the first settlement on Spring Creek, now in the town of Burnside. The family was there when we arrived in April 1855, and I think they had come the year before. They were our nearest neighbors, and we were indebted to them for many acts of neighborly kindness, rendered with a hearty earnestness that made them easily accepted and gratefully remembered. There was quite a family of the boys, and all that were old enough got into the army before the war was over.

Robert, who was the oldest of the boys, was the first of the boy friends I made in the territory, and I have reason to remember him kindly. He was a little older than I, and had a way of saying and doing things that was peculiarly his own—but it was soon evident that he was 'on the level' and to be relied upon. We both had a fondness for dogs and guns, and, as there was an abundance of game in those days, we enjoyed a day off now and then, hunting and fishing. We were both also interested in trying to get a little more education than was afforded by the public schools of that day and started in a course of study at Hamline University, which was interrupted by the cannonading at Sumter.

He was somewhat careless of dress and personal appearance; his hair was but seldom smoothly combed; he never 'put on airs' or assumed any undue importance. But he mastered his lessons, was physically a match for any one of his size in the rough sports on the school grounds, and could generally hold his own and a little more in the debates in the lyceum. Together we shared the vicissitudes of soldier life until the closing hours of that terrible, trying day on the Peninsula when he was called to give "the last full measure of devotion" in the cause for which we had volunteered. I am glad of this opportunity to pay a feeble tribute of respect to a boyhood friend, classmate, and comrade.

As a rule it is a figure of speech, a poetical license, a bit of fiction, when it is said of anyone that 'he was *glad to die* for his country.' So far as I know, 'every mother's son' of us preferred to *live*. The 'frozen facts' are that not one of us was really anxious to die for his country or any other cause, and we did not mean to do it if we could honorably avoid it. We preferred, intended, planned, and made every possible effort to *live just as long as we could*. But we knew that some must die. When the time and the occasion called for the risks, we were all ready to take them—and the consequences—as a matter of *duty*, but hardly of *preference*.

Leeson was young; life was pregnant with hope; and he had plans and ambitions for the future, as we all had. In common with all who enlisted, he had placed these and life itself a hazard to the fortunes of war, and quietly and faithfully met all of the requirements of a soldier's life 'even unto death.' It is not in the power of mortal man to do more. Bob was not a 'pink of perfection,' but he was kind-hearted and sympathetic, a pleasant and ready-witted companion, an excellent soldier and a reliable comrade. And he died as every real soldier should be ready to accept death, if duty requires it—on the firing line facing the foe. One of his favorite commendations of others was: "He did his level best." It is a brief and appropriate eulogy when applied to himself. He sleeps today in an unmarked grave, but those who knew him best remember him most kindly.

From the wounding of Capt. Colvill and the killing of Leeson to the end of the affair with the Carolinians was but a few minutes—as day changes to night—and after it came comparative silence, as far as firing was concerned. Kind nature had thrown a veil of shadows and darkness over all of the field of battle with its ghastly appalling scenes,

> Where the death-dew of war
> Stained the daisy's bright star,
> And God's broken images cumbered the plain.

When all firing had ceased and there seemed no reason to expect any further fighting, the company laid down, resting at will, and in a very few minutes the most of the boys were sleeping. But a few were required to be on guard against a surprise.

With the going down of the sun, the sharp headache had partially left me, but I was suffering intensely from thirst, and my canteen was empty—as were most others—and I was very anxious to get some water. Remembering a ditch we had crossed in advancing, I took a few canteens and went back to try to find some water. Reaching the little stream, which seemed but a ditch across some low ground—and the water was the draining of the fields—"liquid mud and wigglers," someone asserted after they drank it. But it was much better than none.

After drinking and filling the canteens, I sat for a few minutes, leaning against the cool, moist bank of the ditch and tried to think, but every sense and feeling seemed numbed and confused, and every fiber of my body ached.

Realizing that to rest there longer would be to sleep, I started to return to the regiment. I never knew just how it happened, but in returning somehow I passed it without knowing it. Probably, I went between the right of our regiment and Dana's Brigade, as there was an interval of some rods.

Thinking that I had gone too far, I inquired of some of the wounded and found that I was on the ground over which Dana's Brigade had moved. I was still uncertain as to where I ought to go and went farther into the woods. In a little ways, I came to the edge of the woods, a road, and a broken fence—and beyond this a field or open ground. Through this wood and the field beyond, the tide of battle had swept, and the dead and dying from both sides were scattered.

Across this open ground, at the edge of another wood, fires were burning, and I could see men moving about them. Apparently the rebels were there in bivouac. In the open ground and nearer to me, squads of men were moving about with torches and stretchers, calling out the names of individuals, letters of companies, and numbers and states of regiments. Apparently each regiment was collecting its own wounded, and I frequently heard the number of Alabama regiments called. Nothing could be seen distinctly, not even the outlines of a man at any distance, except about the fires or where they carried torches. Watching and listening for a moment, I was satisfied that I had no desire to go farther in that direction and retired promptly through the woods.

When I had nearly reached the edge of the woods (returning), I was halted and recognized the voice of Capt. Nathan Messick of Company G, to whom I made myself known. He was stationing a few men a little ways to the front as a precaution against surprise, and said that he was about to give instructions to 'shoot first and challenge afterwards.' Having told him what I had seen and heard, I went to the company, where I found most of the boys sleeping, and laid down to sleep.

I was scarcely asleep before someone came from Lt. Col. Miller for me to go to where he was lying on the ground, a little ways to the rear. He questioned me as to what I had seen and heard. He still appeared to feel that there was, or should be, some of our own troops in the front. He told me to go out again and observe them for a time and come in and report to him what I saw or heard. For the first and only time, I protested against being put on further duty and pleaded my used-up condition. He was very kind and fatherly about it, said that he knew that we were all about played-out, and that he was sorry for me. But he desired someone to go; that perhaps I was as able as anyone; and it would be remembered to my advantage.

I went of course—twice, before the time came to march. There was nothing else to do. But I never went to duty more reluctantly in my life. I was very, very tired, and would almost have given a quit claim to the balance of my existence for the privilege of lying down and sleeping and thus becoming unconscious of all of the misery and suffering about me.

When I had gone out to the front again—from both sides of me and before me—I could hear the cries and groans of the wounded. Calling for water, calling for someone to help them, and calling to Heaven for relief, but there seemed to be none. There were suppressed moans, anguish-wrung groans, pain-extorted exclamations and prayers—even prayers for death. Here and there I came upon the dead forms of friends and enemies of the morning, but neither friends nor enemies now—only their inanimate bodies, no longer capable of emotions, the shattered, devastated works from which their gallant spirits like beaten garrisons had been forced to flee.

At one time, for a few minutes, I thought I was a promising candidate for Libby or some other rebel prison, but escaped all right, standing still in a fence corner as a regiment marched by on the road. Possibly I was not in as great danger as I supposed, but I was greatly relieved when the tramp of receding feet and the rattle of tin cups and canteens against the bayonet shanks died away in the distance. I promptly vacated that vicinity.

When I came in and reported to Lt. Col. Miller, he expressed his satisfaction with what I had done and again promised to remember me.[3] He said that I could go to the company. I very gladly did this and found them sleeping. I stretched my weary body on the ground, and, holding my hands on my again-aching head, I also slept.

I do not know how long I slept. It seemed but a moment and could not have been half an hour, when I was awakened by someone pulling at me and talking to me—telling me in a low voice to "get up"—that we were to march. I felt out of humor at being disturbed, rubbed my eyes, and tried to think where I was and what was wanted, but failed to realize anything in particular and lapsed into forgetfulness. Then I felt the strong hand of Corporal Hamline shaking me and assisting to 'stand me on end.' With returning consciousness, I assisted in hunting for and awakening others as quietly as I could. It was quite dark; the boys were very sleepy; and it took a little time to get them all awake and into line; and even then some of them seemed dazed and confused.

After a little delay, the regiment formed and marched quietly back to a road, where it joined the rest of the brigade and started on another wearing night march. It was an ordinarily dark night, and the stars were shining. The darkness of the night and the extreme fatigue of the men made progress as slow and silent as a funeral procession—but little being said as we toiled on over the dusty roads. It was too dark to *see* the dust, but we could *taste* it. Several of the company found

3. "Lieut. Col. Miller did not forget. He afterwards became Colonel of the Seventh Minnesota Regiment and, later, governor of the state. Among the souvenirs of the war, I have three commissions signed by him while governor."

themselves unable to keep along at the slow pace we were moving and had to fall out of the ranks. At this time, five of the company were absent.

When there was light enough to look in each other's faces again, it was plain we were all getting rapidly worse—in appearance at least—in the last few days. Seemingly, everyone had aged perceptibly in the last 24 hours and showed it in appearance and action. Ablutions had been suspended for two or three days. Clothing was disordered, torn, and covered with accumulations from the road, the swamp, and the field during the last week's operations. Enameled with grime and dirt; hair uncombed; eyes red, inflamed, and swollen; faces and lips, hands and necks, were discolored with powder stains and the dust, through which the perspiration had washed little channels, making our cheeks look like outline maps.

We were in truth a sorry and *seedy-looking* lot, and Minnesota would not have recognized us as her 'first offering on the altar of her country.' Our own mothers could scarcely have identified us as the little tots they had spanked and coddled, as occasion required, and later sent away to be soldier boys and fight for Uncle Sam. If they could have observed us that July morning, they would doubtless have judged us to be a lot of disreputable vagabonds upon whom the teachings of their mothers that 'cleanliness was next to godliness' had been barren of results. A few rough jokes were passed upon the personal appearance of this or that one, but for the most part the march was without attempts at mirth or jollity.

We were passing among fields and farmhouses, apparently forsaken, but with growing crops and on higher ground than any on which we had yet been on the Peninsula. In some of the fields the wheat had been cut and was standing in the shocks, but generally it was not yet harvested, though it was fully ripe.

The sun was shining in all the glory of a mid-summer morning when we came in sight of our lines at Malvern Hill. Passing over some low ground and a small stream—where Couch's Division of the Third Corps was lying down in line of battle, facing in the direction from which we had come—we were within the lines and began slowly to ascend the hill, passing diagonally to our left along the slope of the hill. By this movement, we were being placed on the hillside in the second line (and not far from the center) as it faced in the direction from which the enemy might be expected. It was a grand position at Malvern Hill to fight a defensive battle—as we instinctively recognized. The sight of it unloosed some of the silent tongues and made us feel somewhat as Paul did when he met the brethren at the Three Taverns and "thanked God and took courage." Only it was the *enemy* and not the *brethren* we were expecting to meet.

Malvern Hill is a crest or range of high land near Turkey Bend on the James River—the top of which is practically level and about 200 feet above the water. It is a mile and a half (perhaps more) in length and about half that in width on an average. For the greater part, its sides were of easy access and had been cultivated. Western Run, a considerable stream that drains quite a large extent of swampy and low land, partially circuits the high land on three sides and empties into the

James. Along this stream, on both sides of it, were heavy forests and brush wood, covering the low ground and swamps. There appeared to be but two good roads that came to the hill. One of these, coming directly down the river from Richmond, passed between the river and the hill, to Haxall Landing. And the other, the Quaker Road, passed over the hill. We had come in on the Quaker Road. Where these roads crossed the stream, the low land had been cleared, and this was crossed by ditches that were a serious hindrance to the enemy in handling his artillery.

On this elevated plateau, along its sloping sides and on the low ground at the edge of the woods, the several corps of the Army of the Potomac were now assembled and were being assigned to positions to defend it.

Under the cover of the gunboats, at Haxall's plantation, our immense trains had found a place of safety at last. Those not already there were hurrying in that direction.

As soon as we were permitted to halt, we spread ourselves out on the grass and went to sleep, because we could not keep awake more than sixty seconds if at rest. I presume some of the boys made coffee as soon as we halted, as we heard some of them assert that they were *starving*, but sleep was the easiest thing for me to do. But our rest—like most enjoyable things—was but brief.

We were returned to consciousness by the booming of guns and shrieking of shells, showing that our enemies had taken the road early and followed us closely. They had located us and placed a battery on the (their) left of the road and were calling on us to 'move on.' For a time, they tossed the shells over rapidly and these screamed shrilly as they cut the air above our heads or struck and pounded along the ground. One of these 'daisy cutters' struck a loaded wagon that was going up the hill, smashing a wheel and tearing to pieces the hind portion of the box. Our boys took the opportunity to replenish their haversacks with crackers.

On the march in—after it became light—we had found many exhausted men along the road. Under orders, we had brought in as many of these as we could induce to make another effort, requiring them to form on the rear of the company. These men also were glad to get some of this 'extra issue of hard bread' at the instance of the Confederate Ordnance Department. Some of these men remained with us until the afternoon, but the most of them soon left to try to find their own organizations.

Soon after the firing began, we formed in line and waited for orders. The rebel artillery practice was uncommonly good that morning, and several men were hit by scraps of the bursting shells, but I do not recall that anyone was killed. We thought that our experiences of the last week should have been enough to have deadened every sense and schooled every nerve so that we could meet the shock of an earthquake without a quiver—but that lively morning bombardment showed that we were mistaken. I noticed this particularly as the regiment stood for a few minutes at shoulder arms, previous to a change of position. As the shells from our own and the enemy's guns passed over us, I noticed a wiggling vibration of the line of muskets—as if the motion had been imparted by the passing projectiles.

I apprehend that there are but few men with self-control sufficient and nerves so strong that they are undisturbed by the close flight of those fiendish, howling, screeching missiles. I cannot now recall that I ever saw one, and I agree with the author of the California ballad when he says,

> "Music," says Halleck, "is everywhere";
> And harmony guides the whole creation.
> Yet, when a bullet sings in the air
> So close to your hat it stirs your hair,
> To enjoy it then requires a taste quite rare,
> With a certain amount of cultivation.

Personally, I failed to acquire that 'amount of cultivation' in all of my experience, even when under fire daily for weeks.

We had many guns in position on the hill, and it did not take many minutes to shift some of them to bear on the battery that was using us for a target in their morning practice. Then there was trouble for the 'other fellows.' After a few shots from another position, they withdrew out of range.

Before the first shelling ceased, we were under arms and moved to the right and formed in line of battle in support of some batteries. It was here that we received the second shelling. It was a savage, spiteful fusillade, and the shells burst in the air above us and plowed the hillside behind us, but all passed over us without serious damage.

Shortly after this, some of the enemy's skirmishers came through the woods along the stream in front. There was scattering rifle fire for a short time, but they were driven back by the skirmishers of the first line. It was probably about eight o'clock when they first shelled us and ten or eleven when their skirmishers came into the woods on our front.

Shortly after the skirmish in front of us, we were again moved to the right, connecting with Smith's Division of the Sixth Corps, and were put in the first line. The movement to get into position was by the right flank until we had reached Smith's left, and then by the front down the slope of a hill through a field of growing oats. This led us to expect an immediate attack, but none of the enemy attempted to come through the woods in our front while here. Similar movements were being enacted at other points along our line of defense. The enemy was trying to find a place favorable for an attack, and our officers were placing regiments and batteries to make the whole line as strong as possible.

It was noon or later when we took our last position. Being now in the front line, we were cautioned to expect an attack at any moment. It would have been a relief to have been assured that we were not to be further molested. It was certainly after noon when McClellan and his staff inspected the lines, and some hours later when the first serious attack was made. This was the last of the rapid series of battles known as the "Seven Days." During the quieter portions of the afternoon and the early evening, most of the boys—a few at a time—had managed to make a cup of coffee and had eaten most of their rations. By this time, I was ravenously hungry, and coffee and crackers tasted good.

The most of us were dozing as we sat or lay on the ground, when there was a burst of artillery and a roll of musketry that startled the echoes and aroused us all. It was an attack on the right of Couch's Division and the left of Kearney's a quarter of a mile or so to our left. There was sharp fighting, but the Union forces had a decided advantage for artillery, and it was soon repulsed. But similar attacks were made to the left along Morell's front and to Kearney's right, and in each case they were compelled to retire.

After this, there was a season of comparative quiet, broken about five o'clock by another attempt to advance, which brought on fierce and continuous fighting until long after dark. The Union position was such that the artillery could be massed and used with crushing effect without the enemy being able to make any adequate response in kind. To overcome this, an attempt was made to storm the hill at a point near the Crew house, and several times repeated, but it was impossible and hopeless of achievement.

Our regiment took no more active part than as attentive listeners. Until night came, we were constantly expecting an attack, as there was a force of the enemy in the woods across the run, but there seems not to have been any available road for artillery. The noise of the artillery on our left was beyond anything we had heard at that time, while there was a well-sustained roar of musketry, and for a time the gunboats also added the thunderous explosions and wild shrieking of their heavy shells. As night came on, the noise and flash of guns and shells made a scene not often witnessed, even in connection with great battles. When all of this had ceased, there was an ominous and oppressive silence.

We did not know of it then, but during the day the trains had been moving down the river about 8 miles to Harrison's Landing, and thither it was planned that the army should go after defending this point during the day. General Porter says he protested against going until positive orders came, which was about ten o'clock at the night of Tuesday, July 1. Couch followed Porter, and then the Third and Second Corps in order. Keyes' Fourth Corps was left to cover the rear with Averill's cavalry as the rear guard. We knew nothing then of plans or orders, and simply waited, changing position several times, taking the place of retiring troops, and acting as outposts on that part of the line.

While fighting continued, men were kept aroused and ready for action, but when the noise of strife ceased and danger seemed less imminent, the feeling of fatigue and exhaustion reasserted itself. Whenever we were halted—even for a few minutes—the boys would lie down and be asleep very quickly, and it took a deal of calling and shaking and a longer time to wake them than it did to get to sleep. Sometimes even rougher measures had to be used, and then they 'came out of it' dazed and confused. I really think some slept while standing in the ranks, and others, when 'shaken up,' stood on their feet and marched off without becoming sufficiently awake to sense things and know what they were doing.

One of the younger members of Company F—who was perhaps in as good or better condition on the morning of June 25 than the average man of the company—had come pretty close to the limit of his physical resources. He had been wounded at Savage's Station—though not disabled—and had still kept his gun and place in the company. On the 30th, he had been overcome by the hot sun and hurried march, and had fallen unconscious. At the last place where we halted before we left Malvern Hill, many of the company had curled up on the ground. When the order came to march, they were 'stirred up' and told to get into line, and did as ordered. He was *fast asleep*.

We had gone some distance—too far to return—before it was noticed that he was not carrying a gun. He was asked when it had been left behind. It was not until the question had been repeated and emphasized by a shake that he 'waked up' to the fact that he had left his rifle and haversack where he had laid down the last time. Of course, he was very much chagrined when he realized that he was minus a gun, and he resolved to have another one as soon as he could get it. This was not so difficult a matter as might be supposed, as there were a great many sleepy men carrying guns that morning—and some of them might have been carried off bodily without knowing it. It is sufficient to say that he acquired another rifle and, without explaining *how*, I will say that it was *not* on a regular requisition.

It was in the early dawn of Wednesday, July 2, when we were ready to leave the hill and continue the march down the river. Since the sun had gone down the night before, there had been a great change in the weather conditions. As the night passed, the wind blew in from another quarter; clouds overcast the sky; and a chilly mist came up from the river and the swamp. During the day, we had been sweating and thirsting under a hot summer sun. In the dawn of the next morning we were almost shivering from the cold and the moisture. At the time we marched, a fine rain was falling, and we were soon wet to the skin.

By the time we came to the River Road, it was raining hard, we were water-soaked and chilled, and the road was slippery and muddy. It was some hours before we were fairly moving and in order on the road. In our worn-out condition, the movement to Harrison's Bar proved a severe trial. It was a sort of 'last straw' affair and came very near breaking our soldier backs—and, above all, did not seem necessary. The rain continued—a driving, pelting storm—and the water was running in every little gully and depression. The active operation of wheels and feet cut and trod the porous soil into a deep, sticky mortar, which increased the difficulty of marching to the soldiers and made the passage of artillery and trains doubly laborious.

The men kept in their places well and toiled on through the mud, but every step required a special effort of will and muscle. I was perhaps in as good condition as the average man in the company at that time, but I doubt if I was ever nearer completely played out.

We reached a halting place and—without formality—were told to make ourselves as comfortable as we could. It was a most welcome order, and there was no time lost in obeying it.

Before halting, we had turned from the road into a field of standing wheat—a large field ripe for harvesting—and it is one of the minor incidents of war that it was quickly and totally destroyed. In an hour's time that promising field was only a trampled muddy bivouac covered with soldiers—wet, weary, and hungry to a degree unknown in ordinary life.

It was a highly esteemed privilege and an absolute positive enjoyment to be allowed to lie down undisturbed in the mud, and I lost no time in making a personal use of the opportunity. My possessions consisted of: a dirty rifle, a cartridge box and belt with a few rounds of ammunition, a collapsed knapsack, a piece of tent cloth (I had lost my rubber blanket), a battered canteen, and an empty haversack. Fixing the bayonet, I inverted the rifle and thrust the bayonet into the ground. I then pulled together some of the wheat stalks, spread my piece of tent upon them, and deposited the other things upon it, taking off the belt and cartridge box for the first time in about a week. I then laid down—as I was in the habit of doing—on my right side with my head on my arm, and covered myself as well as I could with the part of the tent cloth that was not under me—and my head with my hat.

It was my thought to rest for awhile, 'skirmish' for something to eat, and then fix some place for the night. It was somewhere between three and four in the afternoon when we got stationary in the field. I recall a pleasurable feeling at the thought of rest—undisturbed rest—and then I was 'lost to sight and sound' for the next 15 or 16 hours.

I was restored to consciousness by someone shaking me and saying, "The rebels are coming." I heard an occasional cannon shot in the distance. We got ready to form, but it proved only a scouting party feeling for our outposts, and, after finding them, they retired.

I was still tired and sleepy; my feet were sore and swollen; my whole body ached; and neck and arm were stiff from lying so long in one position. It is said to have rained hard during the night, but I was not conscious of it.

Finding a piece of soap in my knapsack, I went to the river which was nearby for a bath (as soon as there seemed no danger of an attack). Being already wet, I washed not only myself but all of my clothing, wringing it out and putting it on again. As the sun was now shining through the clouds, there was a prospect of its drying. It took some time and lots of soap to remove the several layers of dirt, but perseverance accomplished it. After drawing rations and drinking a quart of strong coffee, I felt 'like somebody' again.

So far as the Army of the Potomac was concerned, it was an exhausted but not a defeated army, and its morale was good. It promptly put itself in fighting condition on the morning of the 3rd of July by drawing three days' rations and a fresh supply of ammunition. Even when 'lying around loose' in the mud in the wheatfield the night of the 2nd, I am sure that the Second Division would have got into line at the command and attempted the execution of any order given. Before the evening roll call of the 3rd, all of the men not sick or disabled had cleaned their rifles and washed their clothes. Though it was weeks before they recovered their ordinary elasticity of spirits and movement, there was nothing of the disappointment and depression that followed Fredericksburg. We knew that we had failed in the movement against Richmond, but we then had no doubt of another attempt just as soon as in condition to make it.

During the 3rd, we tried to renovate our clothing and personal appearance a little, and the most of us found an opportunity to write a few words to our friends at home. The greater portion of the day and the night following was devoted to trying to make up for lost sleep, and everywhere men lay on the ground asleep regardless of anything else.

Early Friday morning, July Fourth, somewhat improved by the rest but still lame and tired, we marched about two miles and took up a new position, halting in line of battle and stacking arms. Our new location was on higher and drier ground than where we had spent the two preceding nights, but that does not mean that we camped on a hill or that it was particularly dry—only that we did not camp in a swamp as we had been doing most of the time for months. At the ends of our company streets and almost anywhere in the camp, by digging three or four feet you would get a foot or more of water. Most of the water used while we remained there was obtained by digging these miniature wells in the sand and using a barrel, with both heads knocked out, for curbing. That was not ideal from a sanitary point of view, but better than any other camp on the Peninsula except at the Courtney House.

The place where we were camped was a portion of higher ground of considerable extent lying between two marshy creeks and enclosed on three sides by them and the river. Included in this was the old Harrison plantation. The house where President William Henry Harrison was born was still standing, a substantial structure of two stories and an attic. It was near this house that headquarters were located, but the house itself was, I think, used for a hospital and the roof for a signal station. My recollection is that there were two towers built on the roof— one near either end—with scaffolds for the 'wig-waggers' to stand on. It was from there that they watched with their telescopes and waved their messages to other stations. I recall but one other large house farther out, the Westover Mansion, a larger house and with a more modern appearance. On these plantations, and between the two creeks and their borders of swamps, there was plenty of room for all of the army and its immense trains.

For a low-lying section, it was a place of great natural strength and capable of an easy defense. There were no dominating higher lands near, and no bluffs to interfere with the fire from the gunboats if they should be needed. The two streams referred to—with their attendant marshes—were a strong, natural protection to the flanks. The space between the streams was easily defensible by forts and breastworks that made the camp a perfectly safe one so long as the gunboats controlled the river below.

The enemy fully recognized this, and never at any time tried to do more than annoy us from the opposite side of the river, under cover of the night.

It being the national anniversary of the Declaration of Independence, salutes were fired and the usual military observance. About noon time we formed in line, and General McClellan rode by followed by a numerous staff, and the batteries fired the national salute. He bared his head as he passed the regimental flags and was greeted by cheers and swinging hats. His management of the retreat from the Chickahominy to the James had not lessened the confidence or enthusiasm of his army. They still trusted him as a capable and patriotic leader.

On that day, General McClellan issued an address to his army:

> Soldiers of the Army of the Potomac:
> Your achievements of the last ten days have illustrated the valor and endurance of the American soldier. Attacked by vastly superior forces, and without hope of reinforcements, you have succeeded in changing your base of operations by a flank movement, always regarded as the most hazardous of military expedients.... Your conduct ranks you with the celebrated armies of history.... On this our Nation's birthday, we declare to our foes, who are rebels against the best interests of mankind, that this army shall enter the Capital of their so-called Confederacy, that our National Constitution shall prevail, and that the Union, which alone can insure internal peace and external security to each State, must and shall be preserved, cost what it may in time, treasure, and blood.
> George B. McClellan, Major-General, Commanding

Lee also issued an address to his army congratulating them that "the siege of Richmond was raised" and the object of McClellan's campaign "completely frustrated." Jefferson Davis proclaimed a day of thanksgiving for the people of Richmond on the same grounds, and as events proved both were timely and appropriate.

Each day of the Seven Days added a full year to our ages, and the whole campaign left us ten years older than we began it. I am sure that every man of the company *felt* that, practically, that was true. They '*looked it*' anyway, and not one of them was the rollicking noisy boy he was before. And he *never was afterwards.*

There is a Divinity that shapes our ends, rough hew them as we may

JULY-AUGUST 1862

I GO BACK TO HARRISON'S LANDING and matters as they were on July Fourth, 1862, after McClellan had passed and his congratulatory order had been read. There was a little uncertainty whether we were there to go into camp or temporarily placed in a position to occupy it until further orders.

Saturday morning, July 5th, orders were more definite. And—judging that we were likely to remain there for a few days—a parade ground and the locations for company streets and tents were marked off—a formality we had not indulged in for some time. We then stretched our little shelter tents. The most of us tried to protect our tents from the direct rays of the sun by providing some sort of an arbor of bushes. A few days later, this was done more systematically by planting forked poles and making a scaffolding covering the tent and a few feet in front of it, and covering this with green bushes. This plan made the little tents under them much more comfortable, it only being necessary to remove the old branches once in three or four days and to gather new ones. Without doing something of this kind, the heat seemed unbearable.

On Wednesday, July 9th, President Lincoln visited the camp, and the army was called out in review. Our corps formed near its camp, and President Lincoln and Gen. McClellan, with a numerous staff, rode by. The officers were in their best uniforms, but the President was only plainly dressed. He rode a fine-looking horse but wore a venerable-looking 'plug' hat. The President did not appear to the best advantage on horseback. I saw him on several occasions; and he did not appear at ease; and his hat, when not in his hand, was usually well pulled down or tipped back.

I do not know if one of the results of the President's visit was that we lost our chaplain, Rev. Edward D. Neill, but he left us soon after and went to be a chaplain of some of the great hospitals in Philadelphia. It was not long before he was appointed one of Lincoln's private secretaries.

Monday, July 21, was the anniversary of our first battle—Bull Run. After the sun had gone down and the diminished heat made life more endurable, some of us talked of it and tried to figure out how much had been accomplished in the year. Results were not what we had hoped for, but we looked for better fortunes in the future. Perhaps it was all due to 'first impressions,' but there was at that time a general agreement that on no occasion since had the bullets seemed to fly so thick as at Bull Run.

A series of reviews had been ordered for the several corps. The Second Corps, the senior corps present, was to be reviewed the next day. The First Minnesota, being the senior volunteer regiment, was to have the right of the line at the head of the division. It is needless to say we made the best appearance possible, and did our best when marching, and the result was a mention in general orders and a high compliment from our corps commander. The following was read at dress parade in all of the regiments the next evening:

> The General commanding would hereby announce to this Corps de Armee the fine appearance on review today of the First Minnesota and Nineteenth Massachusetts regiments. The condition of these regiments is an honor to their States and reflects great credit on their commanders.
>
> By command of Major General Sumner.

It was no small thing to be complimented by the 'Bull-of-the-Woods' (popular Indian name for Gen. Sumner), for the occasions were rare when he did anything of the kind. Then to have come from a new state on the frontier and have placed ourselves where we were rated with the best from the older and wealthier states was a worthy distinction.

The night following July 31, the 60,000 or 70,000 soldiers camped at the landing were sleeping—or trying to—when something happened. I am not sure that it can properly be called a 'surprise party,' but it was a tremendous *surprise* to the *party* on our side of the river. This great camp of sleeping men was suddenly aroused by bursting shells, thrown among them at the rate of about 60 a minute. This midnight assault by half a dozen batteries created a momentary panic and more. It was pandemonium on a large scale with military accompaniments. But the real damage was nothing like what might have been expected. I think the actual loss was about 30 men killed and wounded, some horses and mules killed, and some wagons, tents, and other property damaged.

At the first alarm, of course, we crawled out of our little tents, but no one knew what it meant. Probably few of us remember just what we said or did, but we were long enough in the service now to think quickly of our rifles and be ready promptly to use them. It did not take long to understand that the shells were coming from the other side of the river, and that our camp was the target.

For a little while it was the old case of the 'boys stoning the frogs.' We were the frogs, and they were the boys, and they were having all the fun. It was not long, however, before some of the Union batteries got into action, quickly followed by others. Then they were getting back more than they sent, and, as soon as this was the case, they limbered up and left. Some of the gunboats also added their heavier guns to the field batteries, and no doubt they had their influence in deciding them to go at once. A brigade of Union troops crossed over and occupied Coggin's Point, and there was no further attempt at molestation.

As a huge practical joke with tragical results, from the boys' standpoint it may have been a success, but, as one of the frogs, I have formed a different opinion. Being unaccompanied by any means of crossing the river or any sufficient force to take any advantage of the bombardment, it seems to me a wanton and barbarous act. In the mildest judgment possible, it may be classed with 'shooting up' a town for the fun of the excitement, regardless of consequences.

There was a tragi-comic incident in the brigade camp one afternoon. Some of the mounted men, when they would come down to the river to water or wash their horses, had attacks of the 'speed mania.' Horseflesh was considered valuable, and it was also considered dangerous and detrimental to race the horses in hot weather. An order was issued against it, but, like any other order without a penalty attached, it was not much regarded. As a further corrective, guards were stationed with orders to stop and arrest those who failed to observe the order. A man on horseback generally feels a little superior to an ordinary man on foot, and there was a decided aversion to taking orders from them. Instead of prompt obedience, they generally rode away at full speed and sometimes they faced to the rear with their thumbs to their noses.

General Gorman observed one of these performances, and it made him very angry. There being no one else at hand, he found relief by giving the guard a volcanic reprimand for not stopping the men who were disobeying orders.

In self-defense, the sentry asserted that he had halted them, but they had not heeded his challenge.

Gorman wanted to know of the guard if he did not "understand his duties and the dignity and authority of a sentry on duty? What was his gun for? If it was not loaded? If he did not know how to shoot?" And several other similar conundrums—ending by ordering the sentry to arrest *every person riding at a gallop along the road*—and threatening him with the guardhouse if he failed to enforce his orders. Raising his hand, the general turned towards his tent.

The sentry saluted and walked away, throwing his rifle across his left arm and examining the cap on it as he did so, apparently satisfied to 'let it go at that.'

The sequel came quickly, heralded by the sound of hoofbeats and a cloud of dust up the road. Then an officer came at a lively gallop, followed by an orderly at the regulation distance.

The sentry faced to the road, close beside it, and called on them to halt.

The officer looked surprised, saluted, but did not slacken his gait—and the sentry promptly brought his rifle to his shoulder. There was a flash, a bang, and the horse and his rider rolled in the road. The sentry's bullet had gone through the horse, passing within a few inches of the officer's leg, killing the horse and tumbling his rider in the road in front of him.

General Gorman's tent was but a few rods away, and he lost no time in getting to the scene of disturbance. The officer was scratched, bruised, and covered with dirt, but not seriously injured, and was soon on his feet and very angry. He indulged in some very strong language, got his revolver, and threatened to shoot the guard, who had quickly reloaded his rifle and was standing at attention.

Gen. Gorman was not the man to 'go back' on a soldier under such circumstances, and he promptly took him under his protection, declaring that he had obeyed his orders—though he had not intended that they should apply to officers—and he should not be harmed or threatened. The officer was not easily pacified, and demanded the immediate arrest and punishment of the sentry. But Gorman was persistent that he was not to be troubled, and offered to see that the officer was provided with another horse.

In the end, the general seemed to have his way, and the officer went to Gorman's tent to have his clothes brushed, and perhaps they took something liquid to give the incident a more cheerful appearance. I never heard the sentry was punished or put to any trouble or inconvenience. Later instructions relieved mounted officers from subjection to this order, and there was no more racing through the camps during the few days more we remained there.

Monday morning, August 4, we had a short battalion drill and were excused from further duty until late in the afternoon—about six o'clock—when we formed and left the camp in light marching order and carrying two days' rations. The entire division was on the march, accompanied by its artillery and preceded by Colonel William W. Averill's cavalry. Passing by country roads in the rear of Malvern Hill, we proceeded in a somewhat roundabout way to a point near Glendale, reaching there early in the morning of August 5th. Here we halted for a time, and the cavalry—with infantry supports—scouted towards White Oak Swamp and up the roads towards Richmond. There was considerable firing for a time, but all Confederate forces in that vicinity soon retired, and matters continued quiet after that. The cavalry brought in 30 or 40 prisoners and a number of extra horses that they had picked up.

Later in the day, we moved to Malvern Hill and made connection with Hooker's Division on and near the battlefield, coming in over the Quaker Road, the same as on the morning of the battle. There was some sharp skirmishing attending these movements, but the enemy showed a disposition to retire promptly when pressed towards Richmond. Remaining in position until late in the afternoon of the 6th, offering opportunity for attack if the enemy wished it, we retired to Malvern Hill.

During the night we returned to Harrison's Landing, reaching the camp about daylight the next morning, having been out three nights and two days. The weather was hot, and we had done considerable marching, but the results were rather beneficial than otherwise, as it had given us a change.

While out on this tramp, we had found an abundance of blackberries, large and deliciously ripe. As opportunity offered, we had gathered and eaten them in untold quantities, because we were ravenously hungry for anything outside of the field rations we had been living on for the last five months. We were eating the berries because they tasted good, and did not realize at the time that we were taking medicine. They proved a splendid corrective for the diarrhea, from which the majority of us were suffering—much better than the opium and tannin we had been taking.

After getting into camp from the night march, naturally the first thoughts were to eat and sleep. When we awoke we heard many rumors as to what we were going to do. There were so many of them that it was certain that they were not all correct, but it seemed very probable that we were on the eve of a general movement. One of the plans of the camp strategists was to "move directly upon Richmond"—and that did not seem probable as our own and Hooker's divisions had just returned from a point nearly halfway there. Another story was that we would "cross the river and cut off Richmond." And another still that we were to go overland and join the new army under Pope. The latter proved the nearer correct, but we did not attempt to go overland, which might have been better.

When McClellan's army went to the Peninsula, a stipulated force had been left for the defense of Washington. Lately this force was given the name of the Army of Virginia, and General John Pope had been placed in command. It was then on the Rappahannock, or between that river and the Rapidan. By intent or misfortune, Gen. Pope's first order on assuming command was in no sense calculated to improve the situation. There was not really much to this order but a bombastic laudation of himself and his previous exploits, intermixed with a liberal expression of contempt for the ordinary rules of warfare and mention of the brilliant results that would follow. Naturally, it was offensive to everyone in authority that felt aggrieved or was looking for a grievance.

Saturday morning, August 16th, we left the camp early in the morning. Going about three miles, we halted, formed in line of battle, threw out a skirmish line and pickets, and remained in that position until the next morning.

When we went to Harrison's Landing, it was very much as ships run into a port in time of a storm, to sail out again when the stress is over and the damages repaired. We had not found the place an agreeable one—though it had given us safe shelter for more than forty days—and we were now glad to leave it to go on the 'war path' again.

The monotony of a military camp soon begins to assert itself, and it does not take very long for the average soldier to feel that he prefers to take *some chances* rather than endure it any longer than necessary. There was also the strong public reason that had called us into the service—still urgent. The rebellion was not yet put down.

It was naturally expected that the enemy would know of our departure at once and that we would be followed—and liable to attack—and we were held in readiness for anything that might come. When no enemy appeared, we were permitted to 'rest at will,' which in this case meant that we could go anywhere in call. We spent the rest of the day picking blackberries and sleeping in the shade.

Sunday, August 17 was clear and fairly comfortable in the early morning hours, but as the sun rose higher it shone with increased heat, and the day proved a 'scorcher.' During the forenoon, we reached and passed through Charles City Court House, an historical place of considerable note in the earlier days of Virginia. We halted at the crossroad leading to Cole's Ferry across the Chickahominy, about two o'clock, and all were glad to rest, as the heat and the dust had made the march exhausting and disagreeable. After two or three hours' rest, the march was resumed, and we reached Barrett's Ferry across the Chickhominy, and went into bivouac about midnight. This was the point on the Chickahominy selected for a crossing, and, as it was not far from the James, there was considerable tidewater and the river was quite wide.

Early Monday morning, there was an attack on the pickets, but it lasted only a few minutes before they were driven off, and there was but a slight loss on either side. It was some time after sunrise when it came our turn to cross. As it was our first crossing on a pontoon bridge of any great length, we had been viewing the frail-looking structure at a distance and trying to calculate its strength and safety. From where we were, it looked something like walking on a tight rope, but as others were crossing safely we saw no reason why we could not and we moved onto it with confidence. The wind was blowing a little, and the tide was running up— which made the bridge a little unsteady—and it also had a rising and falling motion, but there was no difficulty about getting over all right. The only precautions taken were to look straight ahead and *not* to keep step.

Tuesday morning, August 19th, we were on the road early and marched continuously until we reached the city of Williamsburg. This was a somewhat noted place in the earlier history of Virginia and had been the capital in the old colonial days.

Wednesday morning, August 20th, the march was continued over the roads, now deep with dust that rose in choking, smothering clouds that completely covered the marching column and almost obscured the sun. We reached Yorktown early in the afternoon and halted there until the next morning. We were in the midst of another 'heated term,' and the march under the blazing August sun had been particularly trying—and was made more so by the dust and lack of water. As soon as opportunity offered, we were glad to take off our clothes, beat the dust out of them, and hang them on the bushes to air while we treated ourselves to a bath in the York River.

Soon after daylight, Thursday morning, August 21, the column was moving towards Big Bethel on a road we had helped to make and over which we had passed several times. Then the whole country was flooded, and you were compelled to wade in water and mud wherever you went and build corduroy roads wherever you wished to move wagons. Now it all seemed as dry as a desert, and we waded in dust, which rose in suffocating clouds whenever it was stirred by men or animals.

Many mules had perished in drawing up supplies, and they were disposed of in the easiest and simplest manner, which was to draw them to the side of the road and let the buzzards do the rest. There were plenty of 'Turkey Buzzards' in that country in those days. They were always circling in the blue above us with an eye cast earthward, 'looking for a job,' and they reported promptly whenever they sighted one. The carcass of one day was a skeleton the next, a pile of bare bones lying on a piece of raw hide. Many of these had marked the road sides. All that could be seen of them now were bits of sun-shriveled hide and scattered, dust-covered bones, and the most prominent among these was the one made famous by Samson at Ramath Lehi some 3,000 years ago.[1] A regiment of Samsons could have been armed by collecting the jawbones between Yorktown and Fortress Monroe.

Friday morning, August 22, we moved on to Newport News. A cold, drizzling rain was falling. The change overnight from heat and dust to rain and mud was not exactly agreeable, but the lower temperature and moisture was preferable. We arrived at Newport News soon after noon and went into bivouac on the higher ground near the water—wet, tired, and hungry, but by this time the storm was abating.

Newport News was then but an insignificant, straggling village—even if it might be called a village. In plain sight, almost in musket shot, of this place the great naval battle between the *Monitor* and *Merrimac* was fought. Nearly in front of it, the wrecks of the *Congress* and of the *Cumberland,* which were sunk before the *Monitor* arrived, could then be seen. On one of them a flag was still flying. A little farther down was the bar on which the old frigate *Minnesota* ran aground during the fight, but fortunately escaped their fate.

The history of this section of Virginia was not only notable during the War of the Rebellion, but it was associated with other wars—also, with the earliest history of the English people in America. That we, from the latest state admitted to the Union, should be there using 'forcible persuasion' to prevent one of the 'original thirteen' from going out of it was certainly a surprising turn in the affairs of our nation.

A look around on the morning of the 23rd showed a busy scene along the waterfront. Vessels loading and departing, and others coming in, also to load and hasten away. Day and night the work went on, and there was no question but the army was leaving the Peninsula.

Sunday, August 24th, there was a parade, an inspection of arms and clothing, and an attempt to supply some of the deficiencies from the failure to connect with our knapsacks. Just before night, the bugles sounded the assembly, and we marched to the landing only to find that there was no vessel ready for us. It was

1. According to Judges 15:14-17, Samson slew one thousand Philistines with a donkey's jawbone at Ramath Lehi, which means "jawbone hill" in Hebrew.

thought one would come soon, so we waited on the wharf, and finally lay down there and slept until morning.

The next day we got aboard the ocean steamer *Mississippi,* one of the old Aspinwall liners, and dropped down to Fortress Monroe. It was a large steamer for those days, and all four regiments of Gorman's brigade were on board besides Gen. Gorman and staff and a section of the signal corps. Every bit of available space was utilized, and there was very scant room for sleeping. There was a little incident connected with the boarding of the ship that gave a little amusement for the time being, and I will try to relate it here.

While waiting for the steamer, some men of the brigade had managed to obtain some whiskey, and one of the 82nd New York was in an exhilarated condition when he came on the ship. At the time he arrived on the upper deck, General Gorman was there talking to the sailing master of the vessel and was telling him of his wish that he move down to Fortress Monroe.

The New York man, who was of the Bowery Boy[2] type and belligerently drunk, 'butted in' promptly, saying, "Captain of the *Mississippi,* run your own boat. You know your 'biz'."

General Gorman was evidently surprised, looked savagely at the man for a moment, and called out, "Guard, arrest that man!"

The man was disposed to be aggressive. There was no guard near enough to immediately obey the order. And he responded, "Yes! Call the guard, will you! You can't do it yourself."

This was just a little too much for the general's bellicose nature, and he looked inquiringly at the fellow, who was making defiant motions with his fists. Waiving all rank and dignity, without taking time to say so, he blurted out, "I can, sir! By G-d, I will, sir! I'll show you, sir!"

Someone cried out, "Form a ring, form a ring."

But before that or any other formality could be arranged, the general had sprung upon the man; they had clinched; and the man had found himself on his back on the deck, and Gorman standing over him. The fellow still had judgment enough to take in the situation and called out, "I give it up."

By this time, a corporal with a file of men had arrived, and the matter ended by Gorman telling the guard to take the man away until he was sober enough to know the proper conduct of a soldier. The guard took the man. Gorman made a salute to the crowd, who cheered him, and turned to talk again with the captain of the boat. So far as I know that ended the matter.

Early Wednesday morning, we anchored off Aquia Creek, and, as the tide was out, the troops began going ashore in the lighters. When a part of the men were

2. New York City's Bowery Boys (named after a downtown district) were young males—journeymen or apprentices—with distinctive clothing and a love for the drinking and sporting life of the metropolis's rougher neighborhoods.

already on shore, there was a change in the program; and they were recalled; and the steamer continued on up the river.

Thursday forenoon, August 28, we steamed up to the wharf at Alexandria and at once began landing—at the same landing where we had gone on shore on the 3rd of July 1861, and from which we had embarked for the Peninsula on March 29, 1862.

We had seen no newspapers since leaving Newport News; neither had we heard any definite news; but those who had gone ashore at Aquia Creek had heard many ugly rumors of fighting on the upper Rappahannock. The fact that we were recalled and were going farther north to land indicated that matters were not progressing favorably. There had been much speculation during the day as we had steamed up the river, and some of the more imaginative ones believed that they could see smoke and hear cannonading off among the Virginia hills. Perhaps they did, for we now know that there was considerable of it going on that day.

After getting on shore, the brigade was formed in the streets to await orders. We were without rations, without wagons, and without artillery. We did get some New York papers, but they were full of conflicting rumors about what it was believed had happened or was about to happen. There was but little that was definite or positive.

There was one item of news that especially attracted the attention of our regiment. There were references to an Indian outbreak on the Minnesota frontiers. There were but few details, but enough to make it certain that the matter was serious and to awaken anxious thoughts among those whose homes were in the western part of the state. Several members of Company F, who had joined the company at the fort, had come from the western counties—and we all had friends that way. Naturally, anything that pertained to the safety of our own state greatly interested us, and we would all gladly have hurried to the defense of the state we represented.

After waiting for some time in the streets, the brigade marched to the outskirts of the city and again waited for orders and rations. The orders came first, and they were to the effect that we were to march at once on the road leading to Fairfax, and that teams with rations would follow us. In compliance with these instructions, the march was begun soon after noon over the main road to Fairfax Court House.

When three or four miles out, we were overtaken by a mounted orderly with orders to halt. Soon after, a quartermaster came over the hill to our rear with a small train of wagons and down into the little valley where we had halted, with the mules at a gallop. When they had halted, bags of sugar and coffee, barrels of pork, and boxes of crackers were dumped on to the ground; receipted for; and distributed to the regimental commissaries. It took but a little more time to apportion them out to the companies and the men. We were all ravenously hungry, as we had had but little to eat that day, and fires were at once started to boil the coffee, and fry or broil some slices of fat pork.

The sun was getting low when we had finished our suppers. While we were eating, a staff officer with a few orderlies had galloped up and spent a few minutes with the brigade commander, and then mounted and hurried back towards Alexandria. In a few minutes, it was understood that we were to wait there for further orders.

While waiting there, some stragglers and wounded men came by from the front. They brought news that Lee's army was at Manassas, in the rear of Gen. Pope's forces, which were retiring down the Rappahannock. We had learned that that kind of talk in the rear of a fighting force was common and not generally correct. That the worst possible place from which to consider a fighting force, as a rule, was a few miles in its rear. We did not place much confidence in these sinister stories, and when they had gone and a comparison of their reports showed a wide disagreement we disbelieved them.

(We know now that there was more than the usual amount of fact in their statements. That there were fourteen brigades of infantry and three of cavalry under Jackson and Stuart at Bull Run and Centreville. That day Gen. Fitz Lee, with a brigade of cavalry, had been raiding about half way between Centreville and Alexandria.)

When it grew dark and no orders came, we laid down to sleep without stretching tents or making other preparations. Just found a soft place near the gun stacks and lay down as any tired animal might. Some time in the night, orders came to return to Alexandria, and we were called up and began the return march.

At daylight of Friday, August 29th, we were again in the streets of the old city, where Washington had first assembled his Virginia militiamen more than a century before to go with Braddock's ill-fated expedition. After a short halt here, we continued on up the river about eight miles to the Virginia end of the Long Bridge. Here there was another halt of an hour or two, during which time unfamiliar aides and officers were coming and going, and it was evident to us—now that we had grown familiar with real war—that there was anxiety and uncertainty among those who had the responsibility of directing operations.

From Fort Runyon we marched up the Potomac on the Virginia side. Our route led us past the forts, then garrisoned by some regiments of heavy artillery, and the men serving in those forts lined the roadside and plied us with questions as to who we were, where we came from, and where we were going. Intelligent answers might have been given to all but the last of these—but they were not always. The boys seemed to feel that they were being 'guyed' by the 'Heavies' and gave irrelevant and frequently incorrect answers. It did seem at first as if we were being made a show of for the amusement of the 'Soft Breads,' but something occurred a little later that made things appear different.

As we halted for a brief rest near one of these forts, we were greeted with cheers and were met by details of men with kettles of coffee and hand-barrows loaded with bread. Every man received a loaf of bread, and our tin cups and canteens were filled with coffee. A cup of coffee and a loaf of bread may not appear to be much, but, accompanied by good will and expressed sympathy, they sometimes count for a great deal. This kindly act may have been forgotten by the givers, but it is still held in kind remembrance by those who received. That loaf of fresh bread was a *real luxury*. If anyone wishes to know just how good real bread can be, let him eat only crackers as the 'staff of life' for six months and then try a loaf.

From the Aqueduct Bridge we moved on up the river, and it was after midnight when we bivouacked a short distance beyond Chain Bridge. During the next day we reconnoitered the country towards Fairfax and Alexandria. The heat was excessive; the dust was deep; and we all suffered severely from thirst. That dust covered us until we were the same color as the soil, and it appealed unpleasantly to at least four of the five senses: we could see it, feel it, smell it, taste it, and *almost hear it grit* between our teeth.

During these two days, the second battle of Bull Run was fought, partly on the same grounds as the first. All that we knew of it at the time was the occasional sound of the artillery. It was a close and very hot day, and all that we could hear was the dull thud of the guns when we happened to be at rest, as it was more than thirty miles away. If we had continued the march direct to Centreville on the afternoon of the 28th, we should have reached the front in time to have participated in the fighting on the 30th. Whether that would have made a difference in the results is problematical—as we had neither artillery nor trains—but it seems as if the effort should have been in that direction.

Sunday morning, August 31, we were up early and drew two days' rations of crackers and pork from some wagons that had come in during the night. We prepared our breakfasts as best we could over smoky fires that burned but indifferently on account of the wet wood and falling rain.

While eating these by the side of the road, we were joined by a number of the men of the regiment that had been absent, sick, or wounded. The most of these were the men that had left us at Harrison's Landing before the march down the Peninsula, but a few were of those who had left us earlier on account of wounds or sickness. I think that there were five for Company F, and one of these was Capt. Colvill. He had been out of the hospital at Baltimore but a few days and not yet fully recovered from his wound. When he left the hospital, he had gone for a few days' visit to his old home in New York, but, hearing that the Army of the Potomac had come back to Washington, he had hastened to join the regiment. We were all glad to welcome back the absent ones and to see the tall form of the captain at the head of the company again.

We also learned that our knapsacks had come up the river to Alexandria. All of the division was together at this time, including the batteries, but we were still without wagons or other supplies. There was a little delay in starting, but it was not long before the bugles called us into line. We took arms and moved off in obedience to Col. Sully's brief order, "Forward." At Fairfax, and before we arrived there, we met many stragglers and wounded men, and passed them in groups lying beside the road, and continued to meet them all day.

I have several times referred to the wounded and stragglers, and perhaps I ought to give some explanation concerning them. Perhaps it is hardly fair that they should be classed together, but they usually are, and are generally found together after a battle.

It must be remembered that production and destruction both make waste material, and that some of it is valuable and some is not. When grain is threshed, there is also both straw and chaff. When trees are felled for lumber, there are logs, stumps, chips, and limbs scattered around where they have fallen. When a horse runs away, there is usually a broken vehicle, and bruises and fractures for men and horses. In a railway wreck, there are broken engines and cars, and injured people. When a stream overflows—by a spring freshet or a burst dam—there is much material floating on the water, whirling in the eddies, and lodging along the shore as the water recedes. When a cyclone passes, there is a displacement of things material, and damages to life and property along its course. These things, we know, are natural, accidental, or climatic, and we learn to expect them.

Something similar happens in warfare when armies meet in conflict. When large bodies of men—provided with approved weapons and engines of warfare— meet on a battlefield, there is a culmination of destructive forces that is appalling in degree and extent. Think of 25,000; 50,000; or 100,000 men—going out to meet a similar force for the purpose of destroying each other. Think of them spread over many miles of country, as they must be; passing on every available road and by-road—over fences, farms, and hills—through thickets, forests, and cornfields—across ravines, streams, and swamps; placing artillery on every hilltop, covering every roadway and open space; putting infantry behind every stone wall, fence, hedge, wood, or other place of shelter.

Then from every vantage point and place of concealment they push every means of assault and ply every device and effort—usually for days and always until one party or the other yields or both withdraw from exhaustion.

In the advance and the attack, squads, companies, regiments, and brigades have been detached and sent here and there as sudden emergencies required. And, thus separated from their usual associates, they cannot rejoin them until the 'ruction' is over, possibly not for days after. Crossing streams, moving through woods, in the dense smoke of the firing, and in the darkness of night—individuals, companies, and regiments may easily go astray and frequently do get lost (for the time being). Some regiments may be obliged to defend themselves from two directions at the same time. One portion may have been able to advance while the other has not, or has been driven back. Or both may have advanced in the direction of their enemies, but they are divided.

Commands are given but are not heard or understood on account of the noise. Someone who should act under orders for the moment must act on his own judgment. Orders are sent by messengers, but the messenger is killed or captured before he can give them. Or the one to whom they are sent is dead or captured or driven away before he gets them.

There is a constant succession of adverse happenings from the beginning to the end of a conflict that tend toward dispersion and disorganization.

There was one traitor among the chosen twelve. There are deserters from every cause and delinquents found whenever the test is applied. There is a certain percentage in every marching column and battle line that are looking for an opportunity to get away from it before matters get too serious—and opportunity is seldom lacking in the complicated movements of a great army. Besides the dead and those too seriously wounded to get away, there is an equal or greater number of those less severely injured, who very properly try to leave the field and thus avoid the danger of additional wounds or capture. While it is always understood that men must not stop fighting to assist the wounded, it is frequently done—and those who assist in removing a wounded comrade cannot always get back even if they try very hard—and some do not always try hard.

From these suggestions of movements, conditions, causes, and opportunities—legitimate and otherwise—it can be seen that it is inevitable that there should be a large drift to the rear from every great battle—just as naturally as everything that floats goes down with the flood. It is this drift that is spoken of in a general way as 'the wounded and stragglers.' The great majority of these are good men and good soldiers, under good conditions, but they are misplaced for the time being by the exigencies or accidents of battle or march. There are also many of the other class who have *voluntarily* misplaced themselves, and in the expressive language of the camp they were variously referred to as shirks, bums, sneaks, skulkers, etc. The difference between a straggler and one of the above-named is simple, but not always evident. The straggler gets back to his command as *soon* as he can, and the shirk stays away as *long* as he can—a very material difference.

As a result of the fighting on the 29th and 30th of August, there were thousands of wounded men and 'stragglers' in the rear of the army, making their way towards Washington or lying beside the road. Just as common and natural as to find straw and chaff after thrashing grain; limbs, chips, and stumps after felling trees; debris and wreckage after a collision or a cyclone; or driftwood after a freshet.

It was after dark when we reached Centreville. We did not know or care where we were. All we cared for, just then, was to lie down, lie down and rest. And that was what we did. It was good to rest even on the bare earth—exposed to the dripping clouds over us and saturated from the collecting water beneath us. When morning came, we were up as soon as there was light enough to see and managed to make coffee between showers.

As soon as we had eaten our crackers and pork, and drunk our coffee, we formed line and marched up Centreville Heights. We had marched up the same hill on Sunday morning, July 21, 1861. As that Sunday morning, we had been obliged to halt until a column of troops had crossed the road in our front, so this September morning in 1862, we were delayed for a short time by King's Division of McDowell's Corps crossing our line of march. While we waited, a thunderstorm passed over, and the rain fell copiously.

Knowing that the Second Berdan Regiment, in which the First Company of Minnesota Sharpshooters was serving, belonged to this division, we made inquiries and were on the watch for them. We were rewarded by an opportunity to shake hands with Captain Abraham Wright and several other Red Wing boys in Company A of that regiment. It was raining, and we were all wet and soiled from the storm and the road. And there was only time for a word of greeting, a handshake, a query as to how they had fared in the recent fighting, and a word of goodbye. But it was a pleasure to see the faces of some of those we had known in Minnesota, even though it was under the stormy clouds of nature and the disheartening clouds of defeat.

Both sides had lost heavily, and the Union forces had withdrawn across Bull Run and gathered near Centreville. During the day of the 31st, there had been no aggressive movements by either side, and about all the consolation there was left to the Union troops was that they had left their antagonists too crippled and disorganized to immediately follow or further trouble them.

As soon as the way was open, we resumed the march to the front, and on the opposite side of the road a column of those recently in action was passing to the rear. Their worn and haggard appearance reminded us of our own experiences on similar occasions, which made us appreciative and sympathetic. We were hailed as "fresh troops" and frequently greeted with cheers as we passed, but we were only 'fresh' in the sense that we had not recently been engaged in battle.

Passing the troops that had been in bivouac, we relieved the pickets a half a mile or so beyond them, and were told that there were no other of our troops between us and the enemy. It was not definitely known where the enemy was located, but it was supposed that the 'woods were full of them' and a shot liable to come at any moment. The first move was to get a little information as to our position and definitely locate the enemy, as, when one is liable to an attack, it is always safer to be so nearly in touch with your foe that you may be aware of any move he may be making.

With this object in view, our regiment was ordered out, and, deploying to the front, we began cautiously to feel our way through a skirt of woods beyond which there was a field. Our orders were not to fire unless fired upon, as it was not desired to bring on an engagement at that time. Passing through the woods, we observed the pickets of the enemy on the opposite side of the field at the edge of the next wood. Without any demonstration to make our presence known, we lay down among the bushes and briars along a broken fence to watch for the enemy.

It was soon apparent that the enemy was moving along a road, portions of which we could see scarcely a half of a mile away, and were going in the same direction that our troops were marching. The two roads were not more than three miles apart. We could not avoid the conclusion that there was a first-rate chance for trouble at some place in our rear before the day was over. Infantry, artillery, wagons, and pack-mules passed over the little rises of ground, visible through the openings among the trees, in an almost constant procession—and seemingly not aware of our presence. Of course we were interested and anxious, but we had learned to live in the present, and, while a few watched, the rest of the boys laid down in the fence corners and slept.

Monday, September 1, 1862, was a succession of sunshine and showers, and it closed with a violent thunderstorm that swept down from the Bull Run Mountains a few miles to the westward just before nightfall. At that time, the other troops were all gone or on the road, and we were waiting by the side of the road for the return of a squadron of cavalry that had been scouting towards the battlefield.

The thunder of the passing storm was still echoing back from the mountains; the rain was still falling; and the daylight fading when the cavalrymen came in. Men and horses were wet from the storm, splattered with mud, and evidently very tired. There was a short halt and some conversation between the commander of the cavalry and Col. Sully, which did not appear to be satisfactory to either— when the cavalry passed on and we followed in the wake of the retreating army.

The road was—or had been—a good 'pike,' but grinding wheels and trampling feet, aided by copious moisture, had worked it into an adhesive mortar or pools of liquid mud. The rain ceased, but the clouds were still over us. A darkness blacker than a traitor's heart settled over the woods and field, rendering everything invisible. No words of mine can fittingly describe that stumbling, floundering, wearying midnight march over and *through* those execrable roads.

It was an all-night march, and daylight was coming as we passed near Chantilly, a little hamlet on the road to Fairfax Court House. Here we found evidences of a recent 'raid': the sight of some dead horses and mules; and broken and overturned wagons; also wounded men that were being brought out of the woods. Here we came inside the pickets and halted for a time, and during the halt we learned something of what had been going on in our rear the night before during the thunderstorm. Having knowledge of the movement of the enemy on the Little River Pike, a road that would intersect the one on which the Union troops were marching, at Fairfax Court House—the divisions of Hooker, Stevens, Kearney, and Reno were posted on that road between Chantilly and Germantown to meet them. The fighting began about five o'clock and continued until dark, and the storm broke upon them in the midst of the battle. The fighting had not been long continued, but it had involved a considerable force and been sharply contested on both sides—and the losses quite serious. Our army had lost two general officers, both of whom had won distinction as 'fighting men': Major General Phil

Kearney and General Isaac I. Stevens. The Confederates called this battle Ox Hill, but it is generally known as Chantilly.

Coming inside the lines at that early morning hour—hungry, splattered with mud, and weary from marching all night—to be met at the picket line with the news of another drawn battle and the death of two of our hopeful leaders did not cheer the present or brighten the future. It is almost certain that the troops which we had observed on the move when we made the reconnaissance were of Longstreet's Corps. We must have marched very close to the right of the enemy's line during the night.

Halting near the picket line until after sunrise, we then moved on to the outskirts of Fairfax. The army was retreating—"retiring on Washington," we called it. All of the open ground about Fairfax was filled with troops and trains. Tired, dirty (often ragged), and hungry men were pressing about the commissary wagons, getting rations of crackers, sugar, and coffee. The last two articles were generally received on blankets spread on the ground, and carried away by the corners to be distributed to hungry comrades who were anxiously waiting for them. Thousands of little fires were burning, and around these were groups of *unsoldierly-looking* soldiers, cooking and eating. Tired, hungry, mud-splattered mules—all in harness and many of them still hitched to the heavy wagons they had dragged through the mud the day before—alternately gnawed at anything and everything in sight or brayed loudly in protest at their forage-less condition.

It did not take the boys long to prepare their breakfasts—their appetites prompting haste as it had been nearly 15 hours since we had eaten. As soon as we had eaten, we prepared to sleep near the guns, as it was thought an attack might begin at any time.

It was after noon when we were called up and had an inspection of arms and the condition of the men generally. The regiment was to be the rear guard when all other troops had retired. All whom the doctor considered unfit for another night march were to be sent off with the brigade.

Troops were already beginning to leave. As those near me moved out, I lay on the ground and watched them. Regiment after regiment filed out of the field into the road, the dark line of blue relieved occasionally by the brighter colors of a Zouave regiment. Ordinarily quite susceptible to inspiring influences of martial array and moving battalions, I must confess that what I saw did not stir my patriotic blood to a quicker flow. On the contrary. Despondent thoughts filled my mind as I looked on the moving regiments with their soiled and torn banners and thinned ranks; the men in mud-stained clothing with rusty rifles and faces that told of weariness of mind and body, and of battles and marches recently past. Marches and battles still lay between us and victory, and the outlook was not cheerful.

I was called from dwelling upon it by orders to send away all who had been decided unfit. When this had been done, the regiment was reduced to about 300 men. With a section of Battery A, First Rhode Island Light Artillery, it was to remain on the outskirts of the town until after dark, and then follow—covering the road during the night.

A portion of the regiment was placed in a position to defend the road, and the rest of it posted as pickets at the edge of the woods, beyond which some of our cavalry still remained on outpost duty.

The sun was dropping near the horizon when the cavalry on picket came in, mounted their horses, and rode away. All of the other troops had been gone for some time, and we were now left alone—with a part of the regiment in line, and the rest deployed as skirmishers.

Matters did not remain quiet very long. The enemy began an immediate investigation to find out where the cavalry had gone, and soon came in contact with our skirmishers. Not satisfied with that, they began to crowd them a little, and these retired before them as Col. Sully had directed, for it was not the purpose to fight if it could be avoided.

As the skirmishers came in, the regiment retired to the edge of the woods covering the road on which we intended to march—followed by the enemy's skirmish line, and their bullets singing about our heads. Taking shelter behind the remains of a fence (there were no whole fences where the army passed the second time) and the trees and bushes that grew where it had been, we returned their fire, and they prudently halted just out of effective range. A large force of cavalry came out of the woods and formed in line in front of us, as if preparing to charge us.

Col. Sully, who was an old Indian fighter, took in the situation and formed his plans accordingly. We were instructed that the order might be given to 'disperse.' And if it was we were to hasten to the rear, through the woods, and form at the guns, whose location would be made known by the bugles. Meantime, both sides were indulging in a lively skirmish fire with apparently but little effect, but it was a situation that was not likely to continue very long. Col. Sully ordered the section of artillery to retire, and the battery boys promptly 'limbered up' and trotted off down the road.

At almost the same time, there was a movement on the part of the enemy. Gaps opened in their line; a battery galloped to the front, swung into position, and opened fire, their first shots going well above our heads.

It was clear that our position was untenable against such odds and that we must vacate—'go at once and stand not on the order of our going.' Then for the first—and so far as I now recall the only—time when in action, we had the order to "disperse" and rally on the guns down the road. The order was obeyed by facing to the rear and running into the woods, with the canister from the enemy rattling among the trees behind us. Our mounted officers galloped off down the road and joined the battery, which had halted a half of a mile or so to the rear at a point known as Flint Hill. It was too dark when we got into the woods to see clearly, but we were able to move rapidly and keep together—though not in order—and we soon heard the bugle calling us to the guns. In less than ten minutes, we had reached them and formed on either side of the road with the guns in the center.

We were pretty well 'winded' when we got there, but no time was lost in getting into position, and the orders were to observe perfect silence and not to fire until ordered.

Of course, we did not know what the enemy would do when they discovered that we were gone, but it was expected that they would follow at once, and that was just what they did. We had scarcely got back to regular breathing after our run, when we heard them coming and prepared to receive them. The clatter of hoofs on the rocky road told plainly of their coming and we stood at the 'ready' waiting the order to fire, but it was too dark to see anything. It was a tense moment. They were approaching rapidly. We grasped our rifles with a firmer grip and listened anxiously for the expected order.

When their advance had reached a point almost on a line with the extremities of the two wings of the regiment, Col. Sully, who stood beside the guns, broke the silence with the formal challenge, "Who comes there?"

After an instant of pause, someone answered with surprise expressed in their voice, "Who the *devil* are you?"

There was another brief pause, when Col. Sully said, "I challenged first."

Then came a flash and the report of a pistol. A bullet 'zipped' near the colonel's head. His mounted orderly, Johnny Leach, who stood near him, raised his gun and fired. At almost the same instant, Col. Sully in a full, strong voice gave the command to fire.

Our rifles were at our shoulders in anticipation of the order, and a crashing volley was the immediate response. At the same moment, the two guns of Battery A—double-shotted with canister—added their thunder to the riot of noise that had broken the previous stillness. The light from the guns gave a view of the road for an instant—as one may see things by a flash of lightning—and it was a picture of confusion, a mass of struggling men and horses.

It was certain that our fire had been well-directed and effective. At the instant of our firing, there had come a scattering fire, followed by a few later shots, and we loaded again and fired at will. It was quickly evident that the chief effort of the enemy was to get out of the way as soon as possible, and the firing ceased. There was a mixture of cries, curses, commands—and the crashing of horses among the trees—and galloping away up the road—and that troop of 'Rebel Rough Riders' was gone. But not all, for some were unable to go, and cries, groans, and prayers could be heard.

We had suffered a loss of one officer and four men wounded. Two of these—Corporal Andrew Bayer and William Shadinger—belonged to Company F. In recoiling, one of the guns had run the trail against some obstruction and overturned it. As soon as this was righted, and the wounded placed on the guns, the march was resumed. No attempt was made to look after the wounded of the enemy or carry them with us. We were now a long distance in the rear, open to renewed attacks and liable to be intercepted by this mounted force passing us on some by-road and getting between us and the column we were guarding.

The march was resumed as soon as it could be done and still bring off the guns and our wounded. It was an ordinarily dark night, and the stars were shining, so that we were able to make our way fairly well, except when the road was through the woods, when it was more difficult.

When about to pass through the little village of Vienna, we were met by an aide who came to ascertain the situation, as the firing had been plainly heard at the rear of the column, and they were getting anxious for our safety. He also reported that the Nineteenth Massachusetts Regiment had been detached and was coming back to assist us. Col. Sully reported himself and regiment all right, without need of assistance, and coming on as rapidly as the condition of things permitted. The aide left with a caution to hasten the march as there was danger of being cut off in the present position.

We did not dream of it then, but another tragedy was to be added to the already too long list of accidents connected with military movements at night—and that, too, at a moment when the greatest danger seemed to be over.

The moon had risen and was now getting above the trees and dispersing the darker shades of the night. Suddenly, there was a flash like 'heat lightning' from a hill on our right. A shell shrieked across the sky and exploded in the woods in front of us. Just at that time, we were passing a slight curve in the road, and the 19th Massachusetts was but a few hundred yards in front of us, having reversed its march to the rear, and was again moving towards Washington (but of this we did not know at the time). There was noise and a commotion on the road in front of us; fitful flashes of light were seen; and the sound of firing heard.

Of course, we did not *know* what it meant, but there was only one interpretation to be put upon it by men in our situation, and that was that we were attacked. There was but one thing to do, and that was to defend ourselves. The sound of rifles and the crack of pistols could be distinguished, and the outlines of men and horses in the road could be seen. The men, apparently, were getting out of the road, the horsemen coming towards us, and the firing increasing.

We hastily vacated the road as they approached, and a body of mounted men swept by us—yelling, swearing, and firing. At this instant, a scattering volley came from the same direction as the horsemen, and the 'minnies' came spitting and spattering among us.

Our training as soldiers and the instinct of self-preservation all prompted us to resistance, and—without waiting for orders—we fired—some at the passing horsemen and some up the road, from which direction most of the bullets were coming. The horsemen disappeared down the road, and the firing ceased.

The whole affair had scarcely exceeded a minute in duration. But in that brief interval, brave men who had periled their lives together in defense of their country suffered death and wounds at the hands of each other. A number of men had been hit. There were calls for help, suppressed cries, and calls for comrades. In too many instances those called for could answer but feebly or not at all. The loss of the regiment had been two killed and nine wounded. One belonged to Company F: Private Almeron Davis, shot in the shoulder, I think.

There were some dead horses and wounded cavalrymen found in the road, and it was then learned that a squadron of New York cavalry had charged the Nineteenth Mass.—supposing they were the enemy—and had ridden through them and continued on through our regiment, firing as they passed. Later we knew that the Nineteenth had got out of the road rather than be ridden down, fired at them as they passed, and sent a volley after them. It was an unfortunate, pitiable affair, but none of the participants are really to blame for their part in it.[3] It was simply a mistake, when everyone was trying to do the best they could and really did the proper and common-sense thing as they understood the situation. The loss of the Nineteenth and of the cavalry was about the same as our regiment.

We gathered up our dead and wounded, and—having no ambulances—a party was sent back to Vienna to secure some sort of transportation for them. It was here that that grim old regular, Colonel Sully, showed that he had a kind heart beneath his rough exterior and, by his action on this occasion, formed a new tie of attachment between himself and the men of the First Regiment whom he had so ably commanded on several trying occasions.

There was delay in finding transportation, and orders came to move on, but he delayed the movement and asked for transportation. None could be furnished, and the order was repeated to continue the march as the moon was now up and there was increased danger of an attack. He again declined to go without his wounded and again demanded transportation for them. He declared that he never had abandoned dead or helpless comrades except when actually forced to do so, and that he would not do it now. When the order was repeated, he grew wrathy, used a few of his strongest cuss words, and declared that there would be more dead and wounded to keep them company before he left them behind. Soon after, the detail returned with some conveyances in which the wounded were quickly placed, and the march was resumed.

The moon was now high in the sky and shining as brightly and peacefully as if there was no such thing as war or strife in the world. However it may have *appeared* to the 'man in the moon,' we weary mundane mortals marching on through the night *knew differently* and reflected bitterly on recent experiences. The quiet moonlit evening seemed like a mockery as we passed on as rapidly as we could to close up with the brigade.

3. One of the Minnesotans heard this story of how the incident began: "One of the cavalry men going to one of the caissons, dropped a cap which exploded, this created a panic among the teams and scared the horses, which in turn alarmed the cavalry and [they] dashed off down the road through our ranks"; Moe, *Last Full Measure,* 176.

For a little time the boys talked volubly of what had happened—as people might talk of a wreck on the shore or a boiler explosion—and then moved on in depressed silence. I recall but few expressions after the first half hour. One of the Hamline Boys, who usually took a hopeful view of things and sometimes tried to repeat appropriate passages from Shakespeare or some other poet, made an attempt at a quotation. He believed in an overruling Providence and frequently quoted, "There is a Divinity *shapes our ends*, rough hew them as we may."[4] As he made the quotation that night, in the middle of a period of silent marching, it indicated that his customary faith had been materially weakened, for it was to this effect: "There is a Divinity that shapes our ends, *rough* hew them as we may."

It was long after midnight—perhaps two or three o'clock in the morning— when we reached the bivouac of the division near Chain Bridge, filed off the road, stacked arms, and laid down to sleep—tentless and supperless—until morning.

We did not spend much time looking for a soft spot to lie down on. I presume that it was not more than ten minutes before nearly everyone was sleeping—forgetful of the early evening's accidents, personal troubles, and public calamities.

4. *Hamlet,* act 5, scene 2, lines 10-11. The couplet is: "There's a divinity that shapes our ends, / Rough-hew them how we will." Sergeant Phil Hamline is likely the one citing this passage.

A realistic scene of war such as is but rarely witnessed

SEPTEMBER 1862

AS WE LAID DOWN, we heard cheering not far off, and we were wondering what anyone could find to cheer about, when someone came by and told us that McClellan had been placed in command of the defenses of Washington and was at that time visiting the camps of the troops which had come in during the day. We were altogether too tired to enthuse over the matter at that time, but it was good news, as it made it certain that there would be some sort of orderly direction of affairs to take the place of the disorder and confusion that we had observed everywhere since we had landed at Alexandria nearly a week before.

When we were called up, the sun was shining, and we were wet with dew and chilled from the night air. Troops were already moving when we awakened, and, not long after we drank our coffee, we were called into line and followed them. Going to the river, we crossed the Potomac on the Chain Bridge and marched to Tennallytown, Maryland, near which place we bivouacked late in the afternoon. We drew two days' rations (one of fresh meat) and, after a hearty supper just before dark, we spread our rubber and tentcloth and put in the first full night's sleep we had had an opportunity to take in ten days. It was luxurious and freshened us up wonderfully.

Our brief campaign in Virginia in front of Washington under 'Old Brains' (as General Henry W. Halleck was popularly called) had ended. Theoretically, enlisted men have no right to express opinions of their superior officers, but they *always have them* and sometimes they do assert them. During the ten days we had been 'pestling around' under his orders, we had begun to doubt if he had a full supply of the article his 'pet name' suggested. We were glad to be again under the orders of our old commander.

Thursday morning, September 4, the reveille bugles called us at daylight, and we expected to march, but we did not. Our night of slumber was followed by a day of comparative rest. We got a mail and the newspapers that day and were in touch with the world again. It was very agreeable to have letters once more and read the news. We improved the opportunity to write letters home, and inquiry was made by our quartermaster for our knapsacks, but they were not found. One of the letters I received was from my mother and brought the pleasing news that my younger brother, Beverly M. Wright—who had enlisted in Company A of the Fifth Minnesota Regiment and who had been injured at Farmington, Mississippi, in the early part of May 1862 and since then had been in the hospital—was improving and was soon to be sent home to recruit.

During the day there joined us quite a number of men of the regiment who had been absent, sick, or wounded—several of them belonging to Company F— looking in good condition after their sojourn in the hospitals.

Another event of the day gave me much personal pleasure. Sergeant Charles N. Harris, who had been wounded and left at Bull Run, came out to see us. He had recovered (except for one arm which he never regained the use of), had been paroled, and sent home. He was now in Washington but had recently come from his home in Minnesota and brought us lots of home news. We had been class-mates at school and very good friends since the first time we had met.

We sat on my rubber blanket in the shade of the tree, and he told me his expe-riences after he was wounded, his captivity, and release; and I recounted some of the experiences of the company since he had left it. We talked of the war that was desolating the land—speculated as to when and how it might end and what might be the future of our country and ourselves afterwards. It was not a cheerful out-look—any view we could take of it—but we were hopeful for brighter days.

Charley almost cried that he could no longer take an active part, and told me that it made him feel mean and selfish to think of trying to do anything for him-self while the war continued and his old comrades were in it. He was still a mem-ber of the company, a prisoner on parole, and hoping that when exchanged he might get some appointment where he could be of service despite his useless arm—for it was certain that he could never again handle a rifle.

We talked of our homes, of the old days at school (which, somehow, seemed so far back in our life), of schoolmates and mutual friends, until our feelings got pretty close to the surface. Then we clasped hands for a farewell that we felt might be final, as I knew we were to march in the morning. When the war was over, he had gone to Nevada, and he died in California about four years ago, but it never was our privilege to meet again.

Friday morning, September 5th, there was an inspection of arms and cloth-ing; towards noon we marched in the direction of Rockville, bivouacking that night about three miles from that place and throwing out a strong picket, for there was a report that the enemy was crossing into Maryland. Saturday morning, we were moving early; we were the advance of the movement and were still without our trains or supplies of any kind. Sunday, the division did not move but re-mained in bivouac in line of battle, the First Minnesota and the Fifteenth Massa-chusetts being posted on the Gaithersburg Road with pickets well out to the front. Monday, a portion of our trains arrived; three days' rations were issued and distributed; and we were joined by the First Division that had been with us on the Peninsula and by a portion of a new division being formed under General William H. French.

Tuesday, we advanced to Seneca Creek. As we rested on the sides of the road, a country dog—one of the yellow cur variety—came trotting down the dusty road, casting inquiring glances to either side as if looking for his master. Someone met his advances with a fierce "Get out, you whelp!" and the frightened canine immediately bolted down the road between the lines of men. Now and then someone would jump up and yell at the flying yellow streak as it passed, until it disappeared in a cloud of dust. "Dusted out of sight," someone said.

Thursday the 11th, about noon, we came in sight of Hyattstown. Here there was a show of force that stopped the cavalry. Kirby's and Tompkin's batteries were put in position and threw a few shells among them, which induced them to retire. The First Minnesota and 'First California' (71st Pennsylvania) advanced and occupied the town.

It was then found that there was a body of the enemy on a range of hills across a valley outside of town, with a battery in position. Under cover of our artillery, these two regiments continued to advance down a hill, through some fields of corn in the valley, and then up the bluffs on which the enemy was posted. The enemy's battery gave its full attention to ours, and their skirmishers, who were at the edge of a cornfield on the hillside, kept well-hidden, fired at long range, and retired as we advanced. As soon as we had possession of the hills, which was a range running northeast from Sugar Loaf Mountain, they ceased resistance and left us in peaceable possession.

There was a small stream in the valley, a spring, and a 'spring house,' where the farmer's wife kept her milk and butter. This happened to lie in the section over which a portion of Company F advanced. There was a short halt at the stream for the boys to fill their canteens, and it was not all water that went into them either. I am afraid that the farmer's wife had to 'pail the cows' and do some churning before the farmer had any buttermilk to drink or butter for his biscuits. Company F did not have any biscuits, but some of the boys had butter—and milk in their coffee that night. The temptation was simply too much to resist. The boys justified themselves with reasonings: "If these people were 'Union,' they should be willing to contribute a few quarts of milk and a little butter; and if they were 'Secesh,' *they ought to be made to do it and it served them right.*"

Saturday morning, September 13th, our division moved as soon as it was light, reached the Monocacy River in the afternoon, and crossed into Frederick, the capital of Maryland. The place had been occupied by the Confederate forces under Jackson and Longstreet for three days, and their main body had left there the afternoon of the 10th, but the rear guard did not leave until driven out by the advance of our cavalry. The railroad bridge had been burned, but the wagon bridge was not destroyed, and it was on this that we crossed. We passed through the city and bivouacked on the westerly side. Many Union flags were flying, and we received a hearty welcome.

We got a mail that night, and a letter from home brought me the sad news of my brother Beverly's death. He had left the hospital at Jefferson Barracks, about the time I had left the camp at Harrison's Landing, to go home but had died on the boat when near Keokuk, Iowa. I lay on the ground some hours that night, watching the stars and thinking of those at home, and longing to be with them. It was a troubled heart that I carried with me over the mountains in the succeeding days. Think of a widowed mother at home with her minor children, with her older sons in Maryland and Kentucky exposed to the hazards of battle, and you have a picture of many thousands of homes at that time, both in the North and in the South.

The advance over the Catoctin Mountains began at daylight of Sunday morning, September 14th. It was a most beautiful morning, and the fresh mountain air of Maryland was something we had been dreaming about when we were festering in the swamps of tidewater Virginia. The march 'over the mountain wall' was wearisome, and we were pretty well 'blowed' when we reached the crest about noon or a little earlier. We rested on the mountain for near two hours, ate our noonday lunch, and watched affairs in front of us.

There was an extensive view, and skirmishing was in progress when we arrived at the top. Behind us, in the valley of the Monocacy, lay the capital of Maryland, 'green-walled by the hills' and 'fair as the garden of the Lord.' In front of us was the Middleton Valley, almost equally beautiful, dotted with groves and orchards, fields and farm buildings, and radiant in afternoon sunlight. But the Sabbath stillness was broken by booming cannon, and banks of smoke marked the battle lines. With the South Mountain range for a background—its wooded sides rising a thousand feet or more—there was spread out before us a realistic scene of war such as is but rarely witnessed. Columns of troops were crossing the valley on converging lines to support those already engaged. This was at Turner's Gap, and a similar action was going on at Crampton Pass about six miles farther down the range, where the forces under Franklin were fighting.

We had not climbed the mountain to observe the scenery; neither had we waited there to enjoy it, splendid as it was; and as soon as the road was clear we resumed the march. Our place in line that day was well towards the rear, and we had to time our movements to those in front of us. As we passed down, we got a general idea of what was being done in front of us—though it was all too far away to be seen in detail or clearly understood.

The main road through Turner's Gap was a winding one and not so difficult to get over when there was no opposition, but the sides were covered with timber, rocks, ledges, and ravines—which afforded excellent cover for the infantry— and there was plenty of artillery posted at the crest and near to it. The Union forces were making a front attack and also trying to get to the top of the range on either flank. A part of the Union force led by General Jacob D. Cox succeeded in reaching the crest a mile or more to the left, early in the afternoon, but a force under General Hooker on the right was not so fortunate and it did not gain it until nearly sundown. Meantime, a fierce cannonade and infantry attack was being made at the pass and on both sides of the road.

Coming down Catoctin Mountain, we crossed the valley diagonally, passed through the old hamlet of Middletown, and continued on for some miles, when we halted near a small stream. The sun had dropped behind the range, and the shadow of South Mountain was thrown far out across the valley, as we rested for a few minutes. We had marched about sixteen miles since morning and, since leaving the crest of the Catoctin range, had been moving rapidly.

As we had come on, the noise of the cannon and the volleys of musketry had been plainly heard, but down by the stream there was only an indistinct murmur, not unlike the sound of a strong wind in a leafless forest. We knew that the firing still continued from the flash of the guns on the mountain, but the sound seemed to be passing above our heads. A few minutes later, when we had crossed the stream and come onto higher ground, we again heard it and not more than a mile away.

Passing many troops halted beside the road, our brigade went to the front, filed to the left up the hill, and relieved John Gibbon's Brigade of the First Corps,[1] then in the front line. Just as we were filing off the road some men came down from the right carrying a man on a stretcher, who it was said was General Jesse L. Reno of the Ninth Corps, fatally wounded a few minutes before. At this time, the heavy firing had practically ceased, but now and then a shell was thrown from their batteries near the top of the range, and there was a spitting, spattering fire coming from behind a stone wall and the rocks and bushes on the side of the mountain.

As it was not the purpose to do any further fighting that night, we ignored their fire and laid down to be as little exposed as possible. In a short time the firing ceased entirely. Some of us slept that night while others watched, taking turns until morning. It was cold without a woolen blanket.

As soon as it was light in the morning, it was discovered that the enemy was gone, and immediately plans were made to follow them. The advance was taken by Pleasonton's cavalry. The Eighth Illinois, I think, and the First and Second Corps followed them. Crossing South Mountain, we came down the westerly side, turning to the left and passing through the village of Boonsboro. We bivouacked on the Sharpsburg road until morning. The cavalry had had a lively little fight at Boonsboro and captured a few prisoners, and there was some skirmishing and artillery firing between the advance parties, but we were not called on to take any part in it.

The morning of the 16th, we moved forward a couple of miles or so and went into bivouac by brigades on the easterly side of a rise of ground running parallel

---

1. Gibbon's famous Iron Brigade—or Black Hat Brigade, so called because of their black slouch hats—consisted of the Second, Sixth, and Seventh Wisconsin Regiments, the Nineteenth Indiana, and (by the Battle of South Mountain), the Twenty-fourth Michigan.

with the Antietam Creek and not far from it. Here we spent the day sheltered from sight and from the batteries of the enemy on the other side of the stream about Sharpsburg, where the tops of the houses could be seen from our ridge. From the crest of that little rise of ground, there was considerable to be seen of what was supposed to be the location of the enemy, but one needed a stronger motive than simple curiosity to keep him there very long. They seemed to have plenty of artillery over there, and they were very prompt to fire whenever they observed watchers on the hill.

There were some internal changes going on in the regiment that were of interest to Company F. Lieutenant Colonel Miller had been commissioned Colonel of the Minnesota Seventh Regiment, then organizing, and was to leave at once for the state. His resignation and a number of new commissions made several changes. Captain Colvill was promoted to be Major. Second Lieutenant Martin Maginnis was made a First Lieutenant and transferred to Company H. It was about this time that the new method was adopted to recognize seniority among officers by transfer instead of changing the position of companies in the line. This brought John J. McCallum of Company G to Company F as its Captain, and John Ball of Company K, as its First Lieutenant. Second Lieut. Josias King, promoted from Sergeant in Company A, was temporarily detailed to the company. It was not the choice of the company to go into battle under officers with whom they had had no experience, but they had no choice in the matter, and the officers proved to be good ones.

It is the theory of war that there are *no vacancies in actual service*. That when a superior falls or leaves for any cause, the next in seniority or rank takes his place and performs his duties until such time as the matter is covered by general or special orders. For this reason, both rank and *seniority* are important. This rule applies to all grades from major general to corporal.

This brings our story up to the battle of Antietam, or Sharpsburg, as the Confederates call it. I do not know what time we were called up in the morning, but it was before two o'clock and very dark. I think that the sky was clouded in the early morning. After we had made some coffee, and while it was yet dark, I was sent with a detail to get extra ammunition. This ammunition was at or near the location of the Philadelphia Brigade; and General Oliver O. Howard, who then commanded it, was having morning prayers with his staff in a tent; and we had to wait a few minutes.[2] The skirmishing had already begun, and some one irreverently suggested that he had better hurry up and give us the bullets.

2. Made up of the 69th, 71st, 72nd, and 106th Pennsylvania Regiments, the Philadelphia Brigade at Antietam was the Second Brigade in Sedgwick's Division. The First Minnesota was in Gorman's First Brigade. Their former colonel, Dana, led the Third Brigade. Tompkins's and Woodruff's batteries were assigned to the division. Welcher, *Union Army,* Vol. 1, *Eastern Theater,* 786–87.

After getting and distributing the extra cartridges, there was some time to wait, and we listened to the fighting across the creek above us. The 'fires of battle' flashed up against gray, overhanging clouds and reflected back to waiting watchers do not start the same thoughts or stir the same feelings as a moonlit scene beside a quiet river. The angry roar of cannon, echoed back from the hills, and the snarls and growls of an intermittent rifle fire rolling through the valley at the break of day—is not so cheerful a greeting as the pleasant "good morning" of a friend. Picture the scene, add to it the fact that you are under orders to '*go in*,' and remember that we were still human, and you may fairly judge of our feelings that historical September morning that ushered in the bloodiest single day's fighting that was ever done on the American Continent. It was not a favorable time for quiet meditation.

When the order came to march soon after 7 o'clock, the three brigades moved in concert, by the right flank, in column of fours—each at a separate crossing and without its artillery. It was the talk that the artillery had gone—or was to go—higher up the stream to cross on some bridge or at some regular ford, and would join us on the other side. (I do not recall that it did join us to give us its usual helpful backing.)

The banks of the Antietam were not so very high but steep and covered with small trees, bushes, and briars. Each brigade made its way out of its bivouac, made its way down the bank, waded across, and scrambled up the other side. The Antietam is not a large stream—not so large as the Cannon River in its ordinary summer stages—and there was no real difficulty in an individual getting across if he was willing to wade. We were wet to the hips and the water was streaming from our trousers as we hurried on to close up into our places.

When the whole division had crossed and closed up, it was in three parallel lines—eight or ten rods apart—in column of fours and faced by the right flank. Gorman's First Brigade was in the first line, and the First Minnesota Regiment was leading the brigade, with Company F as the right flank company; and it thus happened that Company F led Sedgwick's Division onto the field. Dana's Third Brigade was next in line with the Nineteenth Massachusetts on the right, with Howard's Second Brigade in the third line.

As soon as closed up, we moved on by the right flank for some time, then changed directions by the left flank—which brought the division into three lines about 40 to 50 yards apart, with a brigade front. I am not sure as to direction, but I have an impression that at first our general course was north or northerly, and the change of direction faced us west or westerly.

Our movement must have been observed by the enemy from the time we started, for as soon as we came onto the higher ground they began throwing shell in our direction and continued their attentions as long as we were in sight all day. The Confederates seemed to have plenty of artillery and used it freely, while our guns did not appear to me to be replying in kind and quantity, except at intervals.

Our batteries at other points were 'getting back at them' the best they could, but there did not seem to be any artillery *with us*, and we saw no batteries following after us or in action near us.

After changing direction, we were more exposed, and their fire increased as we advanced. The movement was made rapidly and in good order, although crossing fields and fences and passing through woods and cornfields. In passing, we crossed the ground where the First and Twelfth Corps had been fighting in the early morning hours, and there were dead, wounded, and other evidences of the struggle which we had heard—but we saw no bodies of troops, neither did we hear any heavy musketry.

While advancing, we came to a fence which we were directed to climb, and just as we were getting over it, a man came out of the brush to the right and rear. He wore an officer's hat and a rubber coat. He warned us that the enemy was not far off. In answer to a question from our captain, he said that he was General Marsena Patrick, and a moment later he turned back and disappeared in the bushes. It was not long before 'things broke loose' on the left.

I will not try to tell in detail what happened after we reached the fence and the firing began. I am confident that the right of the regiment, at least, was thrown out into the field, and that Company F was on the plowed ground when David Abbott was shot. I am sure we were out in the open when the move was made to flank us on the right. We could plainly see the line of 'Butternuts' at the foot of the hill, across the field, running to our right at a 'trail arms.' Our fire was directed upon them, and it drove them to cover, checking the movement.

Most of the line to the left was out of sight in the bushes before the firing began. And what of it was not was quickly invisible from the smoke, which alone showed its position. At this time, and just previous, the firing on the left was something almost unprecedented. It told with fearful effect on account of the massed condition of the division—and only one brigade, ours, was in a position to resent this fire. By the crash and noise we knew that the fire was passing around our left. Glancing to the rear, it was evident from the movement of Howard's Brigade that things were not going the way we had hoped they would—but at that time we had no realization of the fearful blow that had been dealt to the left and rear of the division.[3]

At this moment, the division was the center of a concentrated infantry fire, poured into it from three sides—with Stuart's and Pelham's batteries firing canister and tossing shell at it from a hill on the right. It is surprising that it escaped as well as it did. Nothing but its fine discipline and splendid *esprit de corps* saved it from a stampede or a worse disaster. No troops on the right penetrated farther

3. The fearful blow was enfilade fire from Lafayette McLaws's Division, newly arrived on the field. The Minnesotans were farther away from McLaws's men and not as severely hit as Dana's or Howard's Brigades. Moe, *Last Full Measure*, 184.

into the enemy's line than did the Second Division of the Second Corps, and none suffered greater losses. If its flank had been properly protected, it is not unreasonable to believe that it would have forced its way through and taken the enemy's line in reverse. But it was not, and speculation as to results is idle.

The First Minnesota Regiment was the last of the division to retire, and it withdrew slowly, facing about and firing at command. Colonel Sully had the regiment well in hand, and he was not particular to keep the regulation distance to the rear—being sometimes almost in line with the file closers. When we made the stand—where the Eighty-Second New York and the Nineteenth Massachusetts formed on our right and left—the gravity of the situation was forced upon us, and only our hot return fire saved us from capture. The right and the left were thrown back, and the radiating fire of the three regiments covered nearly a half circle.

Falling back from this point (as the enemy was again moving to our right as well as to our left), our regiment—or at least the right of it—passed a house and other buildings, and some stacks of grain or hay.[4] There were some cattle there who had been kept in the yard or had run there from fright. Some of these had been shot and the others—angry or crazed at the smell of their blood—were running here and there bellowing.

Until reaching this point, the regiment had kept its alignment. A temporary stand was made there, and some passed on about 100 yards farther to a stone wall. A portion of Company F remained there, as there was good cover at that point, and, being busy, did not hear the order to form farther back. Leaving this place, we went to our left and rear, retiring up a slight rise 75 to 100 yards, and took position behind the stone wall.

The enemy was advancing in force, and we immediately knelt beside the wall and began firing. The wall was not very high, but it made a good cover when kneeling and was a safe protection from bullets. We need not be exposed except at the moment of firing.

The enemy were elated with their success and made a determined effort to drive us out, but—failing to induce us to go and suffering seriously from the fire we were able to pour upon them from our sheltered position—they retired out of range.

They were undoubtedly hastened in their conclusion to leave by the rapid fire of a section of artillery[5] a little higher up the hill—to our right and rear—which came into position very soon after we were settled behind the wall. I do not know what battery it was, but we were glad at their opportune arrival and cheered when they began firing. I have no recollection of any other guns near us or taking part in any of the fighting previous to this time. If Kirby had been with us with his

4. This was apparently the Nicodemus farm; Moe, *Last Full Measure*, 187.
5. The "section of artillery" was Cowan's, Frank's, and Cothran's batteries; Welcher, *Union Army*, Vol. 1, *Eastern Theater*, 782.

Napoleons, and Tomkins and Hazard with their steel rifles, to cover us with their fire and pound the Confederate batteries, it would certainly have been cheering.

Later the enemy placed artillery to rake our line and were likely to knock the stones of the wall about our heads. We drew a little farther to the left to avoid this fire and to connect more closely with the rest of the brigade. This position we held until the close of the action, though it was modified and slightly changed during the afternoon after the arrival of Franklin's Corps.

The aggressive fighting of Sedgwick's Division was over (I judge) about ten o'clock.[6] After our repulse, we knew that there was heavy fighting a half a mile or more to our left. We later knew that this was done by French's Third Division and Richardson's First Division of our Second Corps—about Roulette's farm and Bloody Lane (the Sunken Road)—but it did not reach us or connect with us at any time. These two divisions were more fortunate than Sedgwick's in that they did not have to advance so far, were not subject to flank or rear attacks, and were able to deploy so that the whole force could inflict as well as receive damage. They were also supported by artillery, which by this time had arrived.

The Sixth Corps came in that morning from Pleasant Valley, and its First Division under Smith was sent to the support of French's and Richardson's divisions. Later, when the Sixth Corps' other divisions arrived, they formed in order as if for an attack, but no attack was made. It was certainly the purpose to renew the attack with the Sixth Corps, for we were held in readiness to support such a movement, but none was made, not even a demonstration.

The real fighting on the right was over by one o'clock or about that time. After that both sides were on the defensive. There were some movements of detachments in which some sharp fighting occurred, and generally the aggressors—from whichever side they came—were severely punished.

The aggressive event of the afternoon on the part of the Union army was the attack on Lee's right by McClellan's left under Ambrose Burnside with the Ninth Corps and Jacob Cox's Division temporarily with it. This force stormed the bridge and gained the heights overlooking the village of Sharpsburg, but had hardly got possession before his left flank was attacked by a force under General A. P. Hill, just arriving from Harpers Ferry. To meet this attack, Burnside moved his left to face it—opening an interval in his line, into which the enemy advanced and compelled the withdrawal of his right from the heights.

This was the situation when the fighting practically ceased, and night came. Of course, there was a contending fire of more or less volume here and there until after dark, but it is hardly correct to say that 'darkness ended the fighting,' which had almost ceased before dark. The fighting at Antietam was over—though we then expected to renew it in the morning. It had been a desperate struggle

6. Wright is correct in his assessment of the time; Welcher, *Union Army*, Vol. 1, *Eastern Theater*, 782.

through a long, bloody day—the bloodiest in American history. Everywhere the Union forces had pushed up against the Confederate lines, there had been savage fighting, but they had held their position, and both sides rested at night just out of range of each other's guns.

The fighting had been over a stretch of country of from three to four miles in length and one (more or less) in width. This territory included woods, waste lands, pastures, fields, farm houses, barns, storehouses, cow yards, pigpens, etc.— and the outskirts of a country village, Sharpsburg. The wheat, oats, and hay had been harvested and gathered into the barns or in stacks, but the corn—apparently the principal crop—was still green and standing in the fields. There was a 'pike' from Sharpsburg to Hagerstown, and another coming down from Keedysville and crossing the Antietam into Sharpsburg. Besides these, there were country roads, farm roads, wood roads, and lanes crossing in various directions. Besides the Antietam, there were some other small streams entering it—and hills, valleys, ravines, rocks, ledges, and all of the inequalities usually found in a broken country along a river.

All of these things are of advantage to those fighting on the defensive as the Confederates were—screening them from sight and in some cases making the strongest natural defenses. Some of these were the scenes of the most desperate conflicts, as Bloody Lane (the Sunken Road) and the ledges about the Dunker Church.

Over all of this section, in the morning the spoiler's hand had not touched the farm buildings or the fences; the corn stood unbroken and green in the fields; and the leaves on the trees were beginning to blush with the tints of early autumn. At night, that peaceful country landscape had been sadly marred by the day of strife. Houses (some of them) had been shattered by shot from both sides, and the gathered crops had been burned by exploding shells. Fences had been broken down and the fields trampled by hurrying battalions until they looked as if they had been swept by a tornado. Fields of standing corn had been torn to shreds and cut away by volleys of musketry and blasts of canister until there were but few stalks left standing. The shrubs and bushes where the batteries stood when in action were leafless, scorched, blackened, and burned; fences had been demolished; the ground furrowed and the trees split, splintered, and torn by the missiles they had started on missions of destruction.

This widespread and wasteful destruction of inanimate things—great as it was—was greatly exceeded by the awful destruction of human life. The green sward had been stained with a brighter crimson than nature gives to the dying leaves—by the blood of the day's sacrifice from more than twenty-two thousand victims (counting both sides). About 4,000 of these were dead or dying.

When the fighting had subsided to a degree that further serious movements were not expected, preparations for the night and any emergency of the morning were made. For the dead, whose 'bodies were out of pain and souls out of prison,' there was nothing but burial. On a battlefield, there are more pitiful sights than the dead and more urgent matters than disposal of their remains—even when the bullets cease to fly and the shells to burst. The wounded have a right to the first care and always receive it. Hospital attendants, surgeons, and ambulance men had been busy all day and continued all night, aided by volunteer assistants.

When all has been done that it is possible under existing conditions to do, the amount of unrelieved suffering is still something to touch the most callous nature.

It is not to the dead and wounded alone that all of the suffering of the day has come. Is there not something to be said for those who have escaped the casualty list but have shared in all of the movements and dangers of the day and have had a 'fighting edge' on for the last 18 or 20 hours? Coffee, crackers, and pork before two o'clock that morning is all they have eaten in 24 hours—except a cracker perhaps while lying in line. Corps, divisions, brigades, regiments, and companies have been shattered in the struggles—as a tree may be riven by lightning—and suffered a loss of from a fifth to one-half of their numbers. Broken in organization, despoiled of their leaders, and diminished in numbers.

Now that the crisis for the day was over and darkness veiled our movements, there was reaction from the tremendous mental strain, and defrauded physical nature demanded relief. The rolls were called and inquiries made about the missing ones—as to time, place, and by whom they were last seen—and what their condition was. It is in this way the losses of a day's fighting are estimated and reports are made. Then—unless it is certain they are already cared for or are in the hands of the enemy—interested comrades try to find and relieve them.

In preparation for tomorrow, we must rest, refill our cartridge boxes and stomachs. We had gone into action with 60 rounds—40 in our boxes and 20 in our pockets—and used from 40 to 50 each. Dispositions were made for the night, and ammunition was brought up and distributed. Fires were lit in sheltered places a little to the rear, and coffee made in our tin cups. Then—sitting on the ground where we intended to sleep, talking briefly of the events of the day, and trying to understand them—we ate crackers and pork from our haversacks and drank our coffee—hot, strong, and lots of it. The day had seemed warm, but now that night had come, it felt chilly and there was a threat of rain. But for the hot coffee we would have felt the cold as we wrapped ourselves in such coverings as we had with us and slept in line of battle with our equipments on and our rifles beside us.

For some hours we slept undisturbed, then were awakened, told that it was morning (though it was yet dark), and formed in line ready for action. We awoke chilled, for the morning was cool; everything was wet with the heavy dew; and it was the reverse of pleasant to await the coming of daylight and—we knew not what—but expected fighting.

When daylight came, no demonstrations were made by either side, and neither attempted to advance. Had either party pushed out its skirmishers a hundred yards, there would have been contact, and fighting must have ensued. It was a day of waiting, uncertainty, and expectation, but without aggressive action. It is true that there were some 'spats' between the outposts, where they were already in rifle range, but these were spasomdic, brief, and without general results. So far as I know there was no attempt by either party to even 'feel' of the position of the other.

Many of the wounded were brought in and some of the dead were buried, but it was by mutual consent and a forebearance to fire, rather than an agreement. Confederate General Roger A. Pryor showed himself in front of our First Division (then commanded by General Hancock on account of the wounding of General Richardson) with a flag of truce. Learning the rank of the bearer, Gen. Hancock sent out Gen. Meagher to see what was wanted. It was then learned that he had not been sent out by any higher authority than himself and that the substance of what he had to communicate was to the effect that "if a flag of truce was sent over, he thought that it would be acceptable to their side." General Hancock did not know of any reason for sending one and said so. I think that, officially, the matter ended there.

The long, anxious day ended as all days—pleasant or otherwise—must, and again we slept in line with our rifles at hand, without disturbance.

Before lying down, we were notified that we were to be ready to move at daylight. Very soon after, it was reported that the enemy had 'quit without warning,' and a few minutes later this was confirmed. It was evident that they had gone in the night to avoid unpleasant 'parting scenes' and any further trouble. Those fellows had not proved pleasant neighbors, and we were not sorry—even at their unceremonious departure.

A portion of the Fifth Corps under Gen. Charles Griffin started out to locate their position before a general movement. It was found that they had retired across the river, and a couple of brigades crossed over and overhauled their rear guard—when a fight ensued in which five guns and some hundreds of prisoners were captured. After this affair, the two brigades (Griffin's and Barnes's) recrossed to the north side of the river.

Our corps remained on the field for three days—the 19th, 20th, and 21st—with large details engaged in burying the dead and burning the dead horses. This naturally gave us an opportunity to see some of the revolting things that follow a great battle. I have no disposition to try to give them in detail and refrain from any general description. It was a gruesome, unpleasant task that shocked one's better nature and offended the sight—and sense of smell. Bishop Whipple[7] visited the regiment and preached on Sunday, September 21, and it was fortunate that the wind was from the east to carry the stench away from us.

7. Henry B. Whipple was the Protestant Episcopal bishop of Minnesota. He was a relative of General Halleck and was then on a trip to Washington to discuss the recent Dakota War with President Lincoln; Folwell, *Minnesota*, 2:206, 208.

Occasionally, I have seen statements descriptive of battlefields speaking of the dead as lying in 'windrows,' but I judge them to be more figures of speech than matters of fact. Personally, I cannot recall that I ever did actually see them in windrows, but I think that I came nearer to it at Antietam than even at the 'High water mark of the Rebellion' where Pickett's Charge ended.

Corporal Horatio N. Barber was one of the older men of the company—30—and a model for steady nerves and cool, calculating action—whether he was going into a fight or sitting in a game of poker. Crossing the field on the 19th, he called to me to come to a point where it was said that Hood's Texans had fought, and I went with him.

On one side of the road was a cornfield (or had been) and on the other a stubble field with its aftergrowth of weeds. On one side of the road was a board fence and on the other a 'post and rail' fence. The fighting had been apparently across the road. The fences were perforated and splintered in a way that showed that they could not have been of any protection to those back of them, and comparatively few stalks of corn were left standing. On the side of the fence where the corn was not, we counted 19 dead men in a distance of 11 sections of the fence—and none of them were more than a rod away from it. There were others lying farther out in the weeds and stubble. The whole distance could hardly have been more than 150 feet. I recall no other place in the open where there were so many dead in so small a space, and Barber declared that it was a sight that never could be forgotten.

At daylight, Monday morning, the Second Corps marched for Harpers Ferry. We were glad to leave behind us the little village of Sharpsburg to recover as best it could from the destruction and havoc of the battle. We had first seen it from the slopes of the mountain, surrounded by patches of field and forest, and almost perfect in its autumnal beauty. At our coming we had found an old-fashioned country neighborhood—almost ideal for the times, the people living in peace and enjoying all of the comforts of long-settled, undisturbed life on the farms where the most of them were born. But we left it with homes, fields, and forests marred, shattered, devastated, and ruined.

I doubt not but the inhabitants were as glad that we were going as we were to go. They had our sympathy, and we had not intentionally harmed one of them.

To be driven from these homes by the clash of armies and to return to find their houses battered and shattered with shell—some of them burned; fences, crops, and stock ruined and gone—was to them a great personal calamity. The only gain to the town was its 4,000 or more new-made graves, and people are not generally desirous of gain in that direction.

Some of those people who had returned before we left were very bitter and resentful at their losses and talked to the soldiers of their misfortunes. About the only comfort we could give them was that 'it was the fortunes of war,' and they ought to be thankful as long as they had whole bodies with breath in them.

I am a pilgrim and I am a stranger

SEPTEMBER-NOVEMBER 1862

SUNDAY, SEPTEMBER 21, had been a warm day, and Monday proved to be an-other, which made our rapid march down the river exhausting. When we reached a point a little above the old factory buildings at Harpers Ferry, it was found that the pontoons a mile or so farther down were filled with troops and trains of the Twelfth Corps, and that there would be some hours waiting before our turn came.

Finding that it was possible, Gen. Sumner determined to ford the river, as it would save a couple of miles marching and several hours of tedious delay. He gave the order, and, dressed as we were, we marched in and waded to the opposite bank. The water, I judge, was about four feet deep—at least it was full breast-high to one of my stature—and very swift. But we crossed without any serious accidents, though some of the boys slipped on the stones in the bottom, got a complete immersion, and had to be helped out.

Coming out of the water without stopping to let it drain from our clothes, we climbed the steep bank and marched to a plateau on the easterly side of Bolivar Heights and were told that we were to camp there for the time being. It was very near where we had camped in the latter part of March previous. In fact, we had marched down those same heights in the early forenoon of March 22, and now we were returning in the early afternoon of September 22—six months almost to the hour. Like birds of passage, we seemed to be moving north or south semi-annually. Perhaps 'hunted animals' doubling on their tracks would be a more appropriate figure.

We were very agreeably surprised to find that some of the wagons had already arrived, and, as soon as arms were stacked, rations were drawn and coffee was made. Very soon after, more of the brigade train came in, and we were able to get some camp kettles and soap for the first time (when we had time to use them) since leaving Harrison's Landing.

This was an opportunity not to be lost, and we hastened to the bank of the Shenandoah to wash our over-soiled clothing and indulge in a bath in the clear-running water of that beautiful mountain river. It was something we had been longing for ever since we had left the Peninsula. Fires were made; water heated; clothes washed and boiled and hung on the bushes to dry; and then our efforts were made more personal. However much they may have needed it, the individuals could not be boiled, but they were subjected to a series of applications of soap, water, and scrubbing until the natural color of the skin was developed—to a degree that satisfied us of our own identity. Then we rinsed off with a plunge in the river, rubbed down, and wrapped a blanket around us, and lay on the bank to wait for our clothes to dry, for we had no 'changes of raiment.' Thousands of soldiers were engaged as we were as far as we could see up or down the river, but I do not recall that I ever saw a picture of it in the papers.

It was an interesting sight as well as a sanitary measure. I think that it was the 14th of August that we had sent away our knapsacks on the barges down the James. At some date not long before that, I had changed my shirts, but since then I had worn the same clothing, and there had been no opportunity to draw, buy, borrow, beg, or steal any others or to properly wash the ones we wore. The best we had been able to do was to take them off and dust them two or three times and air them for a few minutes. There were plenty of knapsacks and clothing scattered all over the battlefield without claimants—and to be had for the picking up. I might have overcome all scruples and prejudices if they had been clean, but I saw none but were soiled and I let them remain there. I did, however, appropriate a knapsack and a couple of blankets, as the increasing coolness of the nights admonished me that they were a coming necessity.

When the sun dropped behind the heights, our clothes were not yet wholly dry, but we put them on just the same. As soon as the clammy feeling of the still-damp garments was overcome, we felt better, and there was quite an improvement in the appearance, individually and collectively. Some of the boys used to refer to the movements from Harrison's Landing to Harpers Ferry as "the forty days without change of shirts."

After dressing, we returned to the bivouac realizing that we were hungry, a sensation that the most of us had not really felt for several days. The seventy-odd hours' contact with the loathsome sight of discolored and swollen corpses, misery, wreck, ruin, and general destruction of life and property was depressing in the extreme and took away desire for both food and drink. To get where we could breathe untainted air and find water to drink that we could feel was not contaminated by the dead was a relief that was in itself almost exhilarating. We returned to the camping place—with a satisfaction with ourselves and surroundings that we had not felt for many days—cooked our suppers, ate them with relish, and prepared to lie down for the night.

The day of our arrival at Harpers Ferry—September 22, 1862—is historical, because it was on this day that President Lincoln issued the first Emancipation Proclamation. But of that fact we were not then aware, and, besides, our minds were turned to more personal matters.

The next day we rested quietly in bivouac, were treated to a ration of fresh beef, wrote letters home, viewed the magnificent scenery with which we were surrounded, and tried to feel that we belonged to the human race and were back again in a peaceful world. We received a mail with letters from home, and Washington and New York papers were brought into the camp and sold readily for 15 cents each. The *New York Tribune,* I remember, had full accounts of the battle of Antietam—the first we had seen except the brief dispatches—and we were all greatly interested in reading the story. One may participate in a great battle and not know much about it except that portion limited to his personal observation—and personal observation is generally quite limited to a man in the ranks.

Such a clash of arms as occurred at Antietam is but feebly represented as a big train wreck, followed by an explosion and fire, and supplemented by a cyclone with a cloud-burst and a wash-out. From the division commanders down to the 'high privates on the left flank of the company,' many had been killed and disabled, and their places had to be filled temporarily or permanently, and the depleted ranks recruited.

Our division was perhaps a fair sample. Sedgwick, its commander, was wounded and never was with it again—going to the Sixth Corps when recovered. There was a change in every brigade commander following Antietam: Gen. Gorman was sent to Gen. Samuel Curtis in Arkansas; Gen. Howard of the Second Brigade took Sedgwick's place as division commander; and Gen. Dana was absent wounded. The places of these officers were filled by Colonels Sully, Joshua T. Owen, and Norman J. Hall—of the 1st Minnesota, 69th Pennsylvania, and 7th Michigan. A little later—Sept. 25—Col. Sully was made a brigadier; the newly-appointed Lieutenant Colonel George N. Morgan was made colonel of the regiment; our former captain, Major Colvill, became lieutenant colonel; and Captain Charles P. Adams, major.

Among the line officers there were also changes. When Gen. Sully chose his official family, Captain John J. McCallum—in command of Company F less than two weeks—went with him as his Assistant Adjutant General. Lieutenant Josias King, who was with the company temporarily, went as an aide.[1] This left Company F with but one commissioned officer, First Lieutenant John Ball, who had to look to his noncoms for any needed assistants.

The 24th, 25th, and 26th, we rested quietly in camp and made ourselves as comfortable as we could, doing only the necessary duties. Personally, I was very glad of this opportunity to rest and doctor my injured foot, which was still sore and swollen.

There was some discussion of the Emancipation Proclamation, about which there was a diversity of personal views and some talk about the rights of private property. But as a 'war measure' it was very generally approved, and I think that there were none at that time but believed that a successful ending of the war—from our standpoint—meant the end of slavery. But up to this time the most of the

---

1. Josias King claimed to be the first to volunteer for the Union army; a statue of him is in St. Paul; Moe, *Last Full Measure,* 312.

efforts of the government had been to 'restore the Union as it was.' It was about this time, too, that the papers began to publish adverse criticisms on the conduct of the war, and to misstate conditions and misconstrue actions.

On Tuesday, September 30th, our regiment was ordered for picket and left the camp about four o'clock, going out three or four miles on the Charlestown road. Company F was divided into four sections, and three of these were stationed as lookouts at some distance apart, and the fourth was held in reserve. I was sent with one of the squads to a crossroad on a hill, not far from the railroad, with instructions to keep a careful watch and report all that was unusual or of importance. It was almost sundown when we relieved the squad posted there and made our preparations for the night.

Looking around, all we could see that looked suspicious were three cows in the corner of a pasture a few rods down the hill. Corporal Jefferson Benner suggested that they ought to be investigated and went down the hill for that purpose. A little later I saw he was drawing rations of milk from one of the cows, and when he returned he had his coffee pail full of milk, which satisfied me that he found 'supplies' ready to issue.

This was unusual, and it was important to our squad, but I did not feel that it was necessary to make an immediate report. Later, when I found that all of the squad had milk for their coffee, I considered the 'incident closed'—without a report.

When it was dark, a sentry was posted about 100 yards on the road to the front; and two others at about the same distance to the right and left on the crossroad; and a fourth at the point where the relief was to remain. When this was done, those not on duty wrapped themselves in their blankets—for the night was chilly, and but few had overcoats—and crept into a convenient thicket to sleep until called to relieve those on guard. The night was without particular events, and we slept pretty comfortably in the bushes, though it was quite cold with a white frost.

In the morning, the cows were not in sight, and there was no milk for the coffee. Twice during the day a squad of mounted men appeared on a hill about three-fourths of a mile away and remained for a few minutes, then turned, and disappeared behind the hill. There was but little else to break the monotony of watching and waiting, and not a shot was fired from either side. No doubt we were more frequently and carefully observed from the cover of some clump of bushes or neighboring cornfield where the cornstalks were still standing.

When we were relieved there was a cold rain falling. It was after dark when we reached our camp; it was raining hard, and most of us found our tents flooded, but we made the best of it and waited until morning to put them in better shape to protect us from the next storm. We learned that President Lincoln had visited the camp, and that there had been a short review of Gen. Sumner's command, which was all that was on the south side of the river. The coming of the president, and the review, seemed to indicate an early movement, but we thought best to protect ourselves from the next flood by making little ditches and embankments to turn away the water, something we had not done before because we had felt that each day there was likely to be the last.

It was about this time that our brigade was strengthened by a new regiment— the Nineteenth Maine. It was direct from home, with full ranks and fresh-looking uniforms, and made a longer line when formed for parade or drill than the four old regiments combined. They were a fine-looking body of men, served with us continually thereafter, and proved a splendid fighting regiment, but at this time they knew but very little about drill and were generally ignorant of soldiers' ways and camp life. Of course, they did and said many things that gave us—who had been in the service nearly as many months as they had days—an opportunity to plume ourselves on our superior knowledge. Soldiers, like students, never neglect such opportunities. On October 4, they made themselves *heard* in the camp in a way that caused consternation for the moment and was the cause of considerable 'guying' afterwards.

There were a good many shells 'lying about loose' (said to have been thrown out of the caissons of the artillery when Miles surrendered on September 15), and among them were some percussion shells 8 or 10 inches long and 3 or 4 inches in diameter.[2] These attracted the attention of some of the Nineteenth Maine, who were interested in the cooking; and these seemed to them to be about what they wanted to rest their kettles on when cooking their rations. They accordingly gathered up a few of them, set them in triangular formation, and placed some kettles on them. They appeared to make excellent legs for the camp kettles and remedied a defect the government had overlooked when it accepted legless kettles. They accordingly built a fire and started the supper cooking.

This was about the time the call for dress parade sounded, and all not otherwise engaged fell in for the last regimental duty of the day. The fire was burning nicely, and the water was already boiling when there was a hiss, a flash, a crash, and a roar—several times repeated; a dense cloud of smoke and steam went up; and a shower of fire, ashes, hot water, and fragments of iron and wood came down.

At first the cause was not understood, and it was supposed that a shell had been thrown from some long-range gun the enemy had succeeded in getting through the blockade from England, and that they were trying it on us from some distant point on the mountains up the Shenandoah. There was an immediate suspension of the dress parade formalities, and an investigation made.

When the wind had blown away the smoke and ashes, and the iron ceased to fall, the true cause was evident. By rare good luck or that benevolent fate that is said to look after inebriates and innocents, no one was killed or seriously injured—though several had narrow escapes. Had it not been for the dress parade

2. On September 15, 1862, Colonel D. S. Miles surrendered the post at Harpers Ferry and its 12,000-man Union garrison, along with 73 cannon, 13,000 firearms, and other supplies.

call, there might have been serious loss of life, for soldiers gather around cooking fires at mealtime as flies do about spilled sugar.

Of course, all sorts of fun was poked at the boys of the 19th for "trying to cook with loaded shells." And various suggestions were made regarding less violent methods as being "slower but more reliable." The only defense they made was of the "didn't know it was loaded" kind, and was generally coupled with the assertion that they would "know better next time"—but of course there was no next time. They soon became accustomed to soldier life and proved the best of comrades in the camp, on the march, and in battle line.

Sunday, October 5, was a beautiful autumn day, but there was a strong wind swept the heights, and the freshly fallen leaves were scurrying along the ground and collecting in the sheltered nooks and crannies. Gen. Howard sent out an invitation for all that desired to come to his headquarters for religious services, to assemble at 11 o'clock. Many of the boys went up, and Gen. Howard himself officiated as chaplain—reading the Scriptures, singing, and talking on the portion of Scripture read. In the afternoon, some of us went to a point on the heights overlooking the Potomac, where we sat for a time, gazing at the swift-flowing river and the distant mountains, and talking of Minnesota until we were heartsick and homesick.

On Sunday, October 12, we were ordered out for picket duty again. It was a dark, dull day, and the river and the valleys were marked by banks of fog. Special watchfulness was enjoined upon the pickets, and we were particularly observant, and saw but little. Several times, squads of the enemy were seen watching from the hill, but they made no hostile demonstrations, and we had been long enough in the service not to make any except when attacking. During the day we heard occasional artillery shots across the river in Maryland, but could not understand them. Later we learned that it was Stuart, the Confederate cavalry leader, returning from his raid, and that he had crossed the river at White's Ford, between Harpers Ferry and Washington, and made good his escape into Virginia.[3]

About ten o'clock Monday morning, we were relieved and returned to camp in a storm of cold rain that was driven in our faces by a fierce wind. The next day there was sunshine in place of the clouds. In the afternoon we had a brigade drill, the first one since coming to the camp. After the morning drill, there was a special inspection of arms, ammunition, and rations—and in the afternoon a regimental drill of about a half hour. All of these indicated an early move, and we were not surprised about 8 o'clock in the evening to receive orders to be ready to march at daylight in the morning.

When up, it did not take long to prepare our breakfasts and roll our blankets in light marching order. When we were out on the road, we learned that we were

3. This was Stuart's second "Ride Around McClellan." Annoyed, Lincoln observed, "If he goes around him once more, gentlemen, McClellan will be out."

detached from the brigade—loaned for the occasion—and made a part of a temporary brigade of 7 regiments for special duty, to be commanded by Col. Raymond Lee of the 20th Massachusetts. There was a similar brigade made up of regiments from the First Division and commanded by Col. Samuel K. Zook. The whole force was commanded by Gen. Winfield S. Hancock, then commanding the First Division.

We took the road towards Charlestown, where John Brown was hung. We had passed through Charlestown twice the previous March during the Valley campaign, and it is generally more satisfactory to know the lay of the land—even if we could not know what we were to find there. Our regiment was ordered to the front and deployed as skirmishers for the brigade.

There was a small cavalry force with us, and this kept in front until the enemy was first discovered when near Halltown. It was a mounted force, which promptly retired as we advanced, not even waiting for an admonitory shot, and our cavalry followed them. Infantry attacking cavalry, which can mount and ride away from them, is generally unsatisfactory and without results.

On a rise of ground approaching Charlestown, the enemy at last made a definite stand by displaying a considerable force, apparently of infantry and artillery as well as cavalry. Matters began to look like business, and our artillery was hurried up and into position, while the skirmishers laid down to await the results of their firing. Their first shot brought a prompt reply from a Confederate gun in a position among some trees. That made its exact location uncertain, but it received the attention of our artillerists at once. A little later, other guns made known their position by firing, and ours replied.

A lively cannonade followed, but it was long range and not especially effective—or, at least, the enemy's was not. A good many of the shells came too close for comfort, but I do not recall that a man of the regiment was hit. The only loss that I recall was that of Major Sproat's horse. Sproat was with the regiment in some volunteer capacity but never belonged to it. As I recall it, he was near a fence in some open woods—dismounted and holding his horse by the bridle—when the shot struck the horse in the breast, tearing away one shoulder. The cry of pain uttered by the stricken animal was almost human in expression and intense in its agony.

When our artillerists were certain that they had compelled all of the enemy's guns to make their location known by firing, the advance was ordered. The First Regiment was on the skirmish line. It advanced rapidly and was followed by the other regiments, but the enemy was equally prompt in retiring and were evidently not desirous to decrease the distance between their rear and our advance. Nothing more than a long-range skirmish fire was obtainable.

When we came to Charlestown, we found the fences laid down, and three bodies of cavalry drawn up just outside of the town preparatory to a charge, and the men on foot and the artillery passed to their rear. After a short halt for the regiments in the rear to close up, we again advanced, expecting them to charge, but if such was their plan they modified it by a change of direction and galloped away through the town. We advanced and occupied it, this being the second time we had assisted in the bloodless capture of the place.

After an hour or two of rest, we again prepared to advance, it being about the middle of the afternoon. It was overcast, and a light rain was falling. Advancing a couple of miles or so, we again uncovered the enemy, and some skirmishing ensued, but they retired as before when we advanced.

A little before night, after passing through a wood, we found them in considerable force on the hills less than a mile away. Here the lines were ordered to halt and wait for orders. It was now raining hard; it soon grew dark; and orders were issued against making fires. From the edge of the wood, the fires of the enemy could be seen—who seemed to make fires when they pleased.

We expected to spend the night there, but some time after dark orders came to return to Charlestown, and a guide was sent out to conduct us in. It was as dark as it could be—a moonless, starless night in thick woods and overhung with dense clouds. It is not very surprising that the guide became confused and lost his bearings; and this caused others to lose their tempers; and altogether it became an aggravated case of the 'blind leading the blind'—for we all might about as well have been temporarily blind as submerged in the intense blackness of such a night as that. The boys always claimed that we could have made the exit from the woods quicker without the guide.

During all of this time, it rained industriously, and we were wet, cold, and cross. Matters were not greatly improved when we got in, except that we were allowed to make fires. This was done; we made coffee and did the best we could until morning; and the best was not anything very satisfactory.

Towards noon, the storm ceased and preparations were made to return to our camp on Bolivar—or to repel an attack if the enemy felt inclined that way. The march was made without interference, though we learned at Halltown that a body of the enemy's cavalry had been through that place in the morning. We remained at Halltown over night. Saturday morning, October 18th, we returned to our camp on Bolivar.

On Wednesday, the 22nd, we were sent on picket again. Thursday we returned to camp and found letters and papers waiting for us. The arrival of a mail was always a matter of interest, and all whose duties did not require them to be in some other place were present awaiting its distribution. This was generally done by the orderly sergeant or someone acting for him. The letters were received from the regimental mail carrier and given out by calling off the names to whom addressed. There was always a look of expectancy on the faces of the crowd that came quickly together at the cry of "Mail!"—and an expression of disappointment where nothing was received.

Recruiting officers from the regular cavalry and artillery were allowed to seek recruits among the infantry regiments—thus getting men that had 'seen service.'

It was a rob-Peter-to-pay-Paul method of doing business, and its only justification was that it strengthened the cavalry at once, with experienced men. This order was not popular with company and regimental officers, whose men were taken away. But our Western boys, who were used to horses, were easily interested by the representatives from the First Regular Cavalry, who had been through our camp more than once 'talking the matter up.' There had been much talk about transferring or detaching, and it looked at one time as if there might be a stampede to the mounted service.

At this time, Company F was particularly open to these influences. The standing of a company or a regiment depends very much on its commander, and at this time the company was in a state of transition in that regard and scarcely knew 'where it was at.' It had lost all of its old officers by promotion the day before Antietam, and the new ones had come from other companies under a new method of regulating seniority, which we did not then fully understand. Now these were all gone but one lieutenant, and he was still comparatively a stranger. (Lieut. John Ball, afterwards Captain, remained with us until the close of our enlistment and proved a most excellent officer, but at this time we scarcely knew him.) It was things like these that weakened the strength of company and regimental ties and prompted a number in Company F to change their arm of service.

I admit my own inclination towards the light artillery. No doubt it was my loyalty to the old company, coupled with feelings that I was in the line of promotion, that decided me to stay where I was.

Six were 'absent, detached,' and ten others transferred to the cavalry while we lay at Harpers Ferry. These ten were: Sergeant E. Oscar Williams, Corporal Merritt G. Standish, and Privates William H. Burritt, George W. Grinnell, Butler Olsen, Eli F. Pitcher, James Scurry, Michael Shay, Amos Severson, and Lester A. Webb. These were all good soldiers, but their services may have been of as much or more value to the government in their changed position. Their going made a big hole in the company, and we who remained regretted their going.

A brief reference to those who left us would seem to be in place here. Of these, Williams and Standish were Hamline Boys and both well known in Red Wing by those conversant with school affairs. Burritt was made a bugler and was killed in one of the cavalry fights in 1863. Scurry reenlisted in Company F, was transferred to the First Battalion, and was mortally wounded at Deep Bottom, August 14, 1864.

Pitcher I remember very well, but I did not know his family and cannot now say from where he enlisted. He was a solid, well-built young fellow of medium size, light curly hair, and blue eyes. Good-natured and given to a species of dry humor that exhibited itself in acts rather than words. He had been hit in the left hand at Bull Run, and in 'trimming' it the doctor had cut off all but a part of one joint of the little finger. In fact, there was left only the skin and bone of that, but it healed up nicely. When among strangers, Pitcher would use that stub of a finger to remove some imaginary substance from his nose, and it would appear to observers as if he was pushing the whole of his finger up his nose trying to reach his brain. His hearty laugh at the amazed expression on the faces of those who saw him do this for the first time was contagious and joined in by all present.

On Friday, October 24, the boys left us who were mustered into the cavalry. It was something like the first evening after a funeral that evening in the camp after they were gone.

On Monday, October 27, we were on picket again, and the weather was fine but cold. It was believed that some of the enemy were in the habit of visiting a house at night that stood not far outside of the lines, to get such information as the inmates (mostly women) had been able to gather during the day. It was decided to try to catch some of them, if such was the case. Companies F and H were assigned the job under command of Major Adams and after dark went quietly to a point beyond the house and secreted themselves in the bushes and along a fence to await developments.

It was a long, tiresome wait. No one was stirring or saying a word above a suppressed whisper. The temperature was down to freezing, and the frost collected on everything not animate and was glistening in the moonlight.

At last we heard the welcome sound of a galloping horseman on the road to the front, and matters began to grow more interesting. He was coming at an easy gallop, singing softly to himself the refrain of a song, utterly unconscious of the fate that was impending.

He had already passed an outlying squad when a file of men stepped into the road, covered him with their rifles, and ordered him to halt.

With an oath, he wheeled as if to escape, but the road was barred by more rifles. He promptly signified his acceptance of the situation, and dismounted, and gave us his arms. He was in uniform, and—disclaiming any attempt to play the spy—declared that he was coming to see a lady friend. There was no proof to the contrary, and he was held simply as a prisoner of war.

We lingered for a long time, hoping to get others, but none came, and we returned inside the lines before midnight with our single prisoner, his horse, and equipment as the visible results of a night's watching by about 50 men. I do not know what final disposition was made of the prisoner, but the horse and saddle furnished the new major with a convenient mount.

In camp again, we learned that the corps on the Maryland side of the river were crossing into Virginia. It was evident the long expected advance of the army was about to begin, and we had the usual orders for rations and ammunition in anticipation of the order to march.[4] Wednesday afternoon the First Division of

4. Exasperated by McClellan's inactivity since Antietam, President Lincoln finally prodded him into moving south but waited to see how fast he moved and what results the November 4 election brought before deciding whether to remove him from command again.

our corps broke camp and, crossing the Shenandoah on a pontoon, went into bivouac on Loudoun Heights and farther south. The rest of the corps was to join it the next day.

Thursday morning, Oct. 30, after a breakfast at the usual time, we 'packed our kits' and prepared for the march. We were to await the movements of the other brigades and the removal of all trains and materiel and the taking up of the bridge across the Potomac; so that, after our crossing, the bridge across the Shenandoah might also be taken up.

It was about noon when the bugles sounded the assembly, and we slung our knapsacks, shouldered our rifles, formed company, and marched to the regimental parade ground. In taking down our tents, we had left the poles still standing, and the little collections of hay, straw, leaves, and twigs that had served for our beds lying where we had slept. It generally happened that someone set fire to the remains of a camp when it was left, not expecting to return, but this was forbidden, presumably because it was not thought best to thus advertise the hour of our departure. We left this miniature skeleton of a village behind us and took our place with the brigade, which soon joined the division.

It was a lovely October day, warm for the season, and in marked contrast to that stormy day in March when we had marched from Bolivar down through Harpers Ferry. It was not exactly like leaving home, far from it, but there are a good many thoughts skipping through one's mind on such occasions, and generally involving the future and the past, rather than the present. On that March morning we had been some 11 months in the service and thought that we knew considerable about soldier life. We had now been 18 months and had learned a lot during the last seven, but there was much more to learn, as the sequel proved—in experience if not in theory.

After crossing on the pontoons and passing around the northerly end of the Loudoun Heights, we moved up a valley on the easterly side of the hills. The afternoon was hot, and most of the marching was on an up-grade; and the march told upon us all before many miles had been covered. This was particularly true of the new regiment, the Nineteenth Maine, which took the road with us for the first time. They were mostly large men, but their knapsacks were even larger in proportion; and they were overloaded. They had made the same mistake that all new men make until they learn better by experience—trying to carry too much. It so happened that our regiment followed directly after the 19th and were in a position to profit by anything 'thrown overboard' that would 'come in handy in our business.' (We had only been able to get a partial supply of clothing.)

The afternoon was scarcely half gone before the men of the 19th Maine realized they had undertaken entirely too large a transportation contract, and some of them began to 'lighten ship.' Having had experience of our own carrying plethoric knapsacks, our boys were expecting something of that kind and had been debating in their own minds whether they needed an overcoat or a woolen blanket the most. As the march continued more of the men in front of us got disgusted with their heavy loads, and our boys coming after them had 'first pick.' The march continued until dark, and by that time about all of the boys in the regiment that were without had supplied themselves with either an overcoat or a blanket.

It was after dark before we went into bivouac on the easterly slope of the hills overlooking the Loudoun valley, and posted pickets towards the Shenandoah River. The whole valley was aglow with campfires for miles—in front of us and to our right and left—and it did not take long for us to illuminate the mountain side with additional fires and cook our suppers.

Friday, Oct. 31, we were astir early and prepared for the march, but later we learned that we were again to await the movements of other portions of the army, and pickets were placed on the crest of the ridge looking into the Shenandoah valley. Other troops were moving; large trains of supplies and an immense drove of cattle brought over from Maryland passed up the valley in sight of us; and we expected to follow later, as on the day before.

As it was the last of the month, the time was improved for the usual muster. This was our ninth bi-monthly muster and marked the expiration of just one-half of our term of service. Its beginning seemed far back in the past, and its ending— if we did not end first—was in the distant future.

I recall that a little squad of us sat in the moonlight late that night talking over our experiences and trying to forecast the future, as we frequently did, and wondering how and when the fratricidal war that had called us from our homes would end, and where we were likely to be at its ending. Sergeant Phil Hamline, that splendid example of moral and physical manhood who was ever a credit to Company F and the First Regiment, was cheerful and hopeful, and declared his confidence in an overruling Providence and his hope to live to see a successful ending of the war.

For sixteen months we had been wandering and fighting, from the Potomac to the James, and from the seacoast to the mountains, and apparently all we had to show for it was the long list of casualties. There certainly was not anything very encouraging in that, for, of all who had started, scarcely a third part were then present with the colors. However, we had learned to look at and talk of those things quite calmly—or pretend to—and each one that expressed himself seemed to think that as he had escaped so far there was an equally good chance for the future. I could see the logic of the reasoning, but I was compelled to admit that I could not see any promise of immunity in it for the future, and felt pretty sure that 'my turn' would come later.

Hamline was the most hopeful one of us all—as he always was—and after the talk had ceased he joined with others in singing 'camp meeting songs' for a time before we rolled up in our blankets for the night. Some of these still cling to my memory, and I hear the echoes of "I would not live always, I ask not to stay" and "Oh, we stand on Jordan's strand." The chorus was: "I am a pilgrim and I'm a stranger and I can tarry but for a night." When the war did end—with an undivided country, as his strong faith in the future had made him believe—he was not spared to see it but had been for a long time 'sleeping that sleep that knows no earthly waking' in the 'bivouac of the dead' at Gettysburg.

We waited all day without moving, though other troops and trains were moving all day. The day was beautiful out there, but there was a sharp contrast in the temperature, and a still, cold air seemed to settle down on us in the afternoon.

Saturday morning, Nov. 1, everything was covered with frost when the bugles called us from our blankets in the early gray of the morning, and we hastened to start fires and make coffee in readiness for marching. There was little delay in moving. The First Division led the corps; we, the Second Division, followed it; and the Third Division followed us. The most of the army seemed in advance of us and to our left.

The march during the day was up the westerly side of the valley, up the easterly slope of the Blue Ridge, with the Loudoun valley on our left, bordered on its further edge by the Bull Run range. It was nearly an hour after dark when we halted near Woodsville, and bivouacked in line of battle. The Army of the Potomac was in position to be deployed into line, if necessary, and in that event the Second Corps would be on the right of the line.

Sunday morning, Nov. 2, we were moving soon after sunrise in the same order as the day before, but after a short march our division was turned off on a road to the right leading over the mountains and halted for some hours, until skirmishers had gone through the gap and returned. We took no active part in this but laid by the side of the road.

On the return of the regiments that had been scouting, the march was continued. There was more or less artillery firing all day at intervals, but, as on the day before, we could only hear the distant thud of the guns and could not even judge how far away it might be. We knew in a general way that our cavalry, supported by infantry, was forcing theirs back, and that they were retiring just fast enough to avoid fighting our infantry.

It was again after dark before we halted in line, as the night before, and made coffee. We were still on the higher land with the valley on our left. In this valley were 65,000 to 75,000 men, with trains and herds of cattle. As seen from our position, the campfires in the valley that evening were a rare sight, extending for miles, front and rear and across the valley, and the glare of the thousands of fires reflected back from the overhanging clouds.

Monday morning, November 3, we were ready at daylight. We followed the cavalry, which had moved out early, and there was firing before we were fairly on the road, but it was soon over. We followed on until near noon when we again heard the boom of the light guns of the horse artillery, and we could see the smoke a mile or so away. A couple of hours later there seemed to be a prospect for a fight, and our regiment was detached and hastened to the front.

We deployed as skirmishers and advanced, followed by the brigade—ready to deploy into line—but before we were in firing distance the enemy retired, pursued by our cavalry—only to halt at the next advantageous cover and repeat the maneuver. During the rest of the day, they were continually making a show of resistance from sheltered positions but always retired when the infantry advanced, and we did not at any time get in fair range of them. We seemed to have only a small force of cavalry until about night, when it was reinforced; and the next time the enemy was forced from cover, these followed them in a charge, and we saw no more of them.

This was just before night, and soon after we were called in and joined the brigade, which went into bivouac in line. We camped that night to the right of Upperville, between that place and Ashby's Gap, and again the campfires were a splendid sight and covered a large portion of the valley.

Tuesday morning, reveille was sounded at daylight, and preparations were made for the march. We marched with empty haversacks, for in most instances there had not been much left in them after the morning meal. Our movement was to the right, towards Ashby's Gap, and seemed to include only our brigade, as there were no others in sight.

We were preceded by a small squad of cavalry, and some of the enemy were discovered before reaching the crest. The same order of movement was observed as on the day before. Our regiment was again advanced as skirmishers, but we had nothing more to do than support the mounted men, as there was nothing but cavalry in front of us, and they were prompt to get out of the way of our rifles. The cavalry followed them through the gap and picked up a dozen or so of prisoners, who reported that the greater portion of Lee's army was still in the valley.[5]

From the top of the mountain there was a fine view of both valleys—Loudoun and Shenandoah—with the Bull Run Range at the farther edge of the one, and the Little North Mountains across the other. It was a sight worth tramping miles to see, but the object of our coming was not so much to observe the scenery as it was to judge what movements the enemy might be making. There was a hazy cloud over the valley in the early part of the day, but this disappeared later so that much could be seen in detail. We lay down—waiting in position near the crest—and Gen. McClellan and his staff came up and spent some time in inspecting the country through their glasses and examining maps.

With the natural curiosity of a youngster to see the army commander and get a sight from the top of the ridge, I managed to get near enough so that I could see him quite plainly; and it was the best, the last, and about the only opportunity that I ever had to see him except when riding by. He was neatly but plainly dressed and did not appear so tall a man when standing on the ground as he did sitting on

5. Stonewall Jackson's Corps remained in the Shenandoah Valley, to the west of McClellan's forces.

a horse, but to us he was 'every inch a soldier.' He scanned the country very carefully, turning his glass in all directions, and talking to those about him, but of course we did not hear what he said. At the end of his observations he motioned for his horse, mounted easily and gracefully, and rode slowly down the road.

We knew then that there was a strong sentiment against him in the War Office, in the Cabinet, in Congress, in that auxiliary cabinet—the Committee on the Conduct of the War—and among the people, but it had not then publicly reached that degree of bitterness that it later attained. We little thought then that the order for his removal was already determined upon, and that within the next twenty-four hours it would be issued by the Secretary of War.

It was evident from the smoke of campfires and other indications, that there was still a large force in the valley, though there was information that a part of their army under Longstreet was about Culpepper. From the long lines of dust rising to the southward, it was certain that their army was on the move as well as ours. It was a fine section of the country, and there were many small farms and inviting-looking places in the country we had passed through the day before and around the little town of Paris, which lay in the valley behind us. Furthermore, that was a section over which no large bodies of either army had passed—at least we judged so from the fact that the fences were still standing when we came, but I am afraid that they were not all there when we left. Some of the 'top rails' were missing—probably *cremated*.

While waiting about the gap, and later in the day, a good many of the boys *granted themselves short leaves of absence from the ranks* and went to look for something to take the place of the government rations that they had not drawn that morning. There was plenty of the so-called Confederate scrip to be had from various sources, and our boys usually were provided with a supply of it. With liberal offers of this scrip, the boys managed generally to fill their haversacks with things they preferred to hard tack and pork, before they went into camp that night. I am not sure that all that the boys acquired that day was paid for—even with the worthless scrip. I recall that there was some talk among the boys that they were going to "*suspend*" the orders against foraging, which were quite strict, until such time as they could draw rations in the regular way; and, from the fact that some of them had fresh mutton and pork that night, I am inclined to think that, in individual cases, they did.

Soon after four o'clock the Second Brigade came up and relieved us, and we joined the division in bivouac not long after dark near Paris, where we found rations waiting for us. It had been a fine day, but cool as soon as the sun was down; and we were really enjoying the campaign thus far. There certainly was a wild sort of pleasure in the outdoor life we were leading and the splendid scenery about us.

We found that a mail had come that evening, and we had letters from home. There was quiet in the camp as the boys read their letters by the light of the campfires, and their thoughts, no doubt, were with the writers in their far-off homes, and of a character not to be joked over at the evening cantonment. Letters from home at about this period of the war were often discouraging in tone, as there was a continued rise in prices of everything needed and no apparent ending of the war; the cold season coming on and no adequate provision for the winter. What were they to do? How could they manage? These were questions that delayed sleep to the eyelids, and our meager pay offered no solution. The soldier in the camp was no more unmindful of those he had left at home than those at home were of him.

Thursday morning, Nov. 6, troops were moving early but instead of turning westward through Ashby's and Manassas Gaps into the Shenandoah Valley—as was thought to be the purpose—the direction was east and south in the direction of Warrenton and the Orange and Alexandria Railroad (O&ARR). Gen. Darius N. Couch, who then commanded the Second Corps, is authority for the statement that it was Gen. McClellan's plan to get into the open country about Culpepper or Gordonsville and use the O&ARR as a base of supplies and operate against the enemy wherever he might give him an opportunity. Whatever his plans were, they were ended prematurely by a change of commanders while in process of execution.

We had been two days in the front—which was twice as long as usual—and now the order of the march brought our division to the rear of the corps and our brigade to the rear of the division. Gen. Sully, with his brigade and Kirby's battery of regulars, was detailed to follow the movements of the other troops and trains, and march in the rear for their protection when all were on the road. This was not a new duty, or a desirable one, as it frequently meant lots of extra work and late arrival in camp, but it was all in a soldier's life, and we prepared to make the best of it.

From our position it was indeed a fine sight to see the long lines of infantry—separated here and there by a battery or a group of mounted officers—passing over the uneven, winding roads. These were followed later by the trains. Huge wagons, drawn by six mules, covered with canvas, and heavily loaded with supplies. Coming out of the fields where they were parked, they strung out on the road, following its tortuous course, creeping over the rises, and disappearing in the little valleys and depressions and behind the clumps of bushes. I do not know how many there were, but there were miles of them, and it seemed as if they would never, all of them, get onto the road and moving in order.

It was after noon before the road was open for us to march, and we bivouacked that night within 4 miles from where we were in the morning—though we marched farther than that to get there. There was a raw wind blowing in the morning; this increased in the afternoon to a lively gale; and, as night came on, the temperature went below freezing, and there were occasional flurries of snow. Our regiment prepared to spend the night on the sheltered side of a convenient stone wall, but some of the others were not quite so fortunate. By laying rails with one end on the wall and the other on the ground, and fastening our tent cloths onto them, we had a pretty good shelter; and we managed to collect some leaves and grass on which to spread our blankets before it got too dark to see. Then we cooked our suppers, ate them, and prepared to sleep, which meant simply the untying of our shoe strings, taking off of our belts, and getting under our blankets with our overcoat capes over our heads. In this way, all not required to be on guard managed to pass a fairly comfortable night.

Friday morning, November 7, there was the same pitiless, searching wind blowing; the ground was frozen hard enough to bear one's weight; and intermittent dashes of snow were decidedly suggestive of winter—and more of it than we had expected to see so early in the season. By the middle of the forenoon it was snowing quite hard; the ground was already white; and Gen. Sully changed the position of the brigade to a thick wood nearby, which made the position of all sheltered from the wind and more comfortable.

Some cattle were also brought in and butchered so that we had an extra ration of fresh beef, and the tallow came in handy to 'dope' our shoes with. The storm continued the rest of the day, and by night there were three or four inches of snow in the woods, and outside it was drifting like a mid-winter storm.

Saturday morning, everything was covered with snow, but we prepared our breakfasts, ate them, and came out of the woods ready to march. The trains were already moving out, and as soon as they were on the road we followed them. The storm had ceased, and as the morning passed the clouds broke up and the sun shone (at intervals), softening the snow, though it was still cold. But it made the going bad. The soft snow mixed with dirt collected in hard lumps— sometimes under the heel and sometimes under the bottom of the foot—which made walking very tiresome and caused some of the boys to use 'unrefined language.'

It packed in the shoes of the mules; and they—having four feet to the soldier's two—had twice as hard a time to get along. To add to their labors, the dirt and snow 'balled' on the wheels of the wagons, making them much harder to draw. The mules slipped on the hillsides when their strength was most needed to get the loads to the top; the wagons slowed on the sideling places; and some of them were overturned; and there were accidents to wagons and mules—not to mention a great deal of profanity on the part of the drivers.

Altogether, it was a pretty hard day for man and beast, for our feet were wet and cold, and our legs and shoulders were weary from the march and the weight of the knapsack and the rifle.

When we reached Rectortown, we found the wagons massed there awaiting orders—it was said—and we also halted to conform to their movements. It was almost dark and freezing again before the wagons were out of the way and we were again moving. If the day's march had been tiresome and tedious, the night march that followed was all of that and much more. It was nearly two o'clock in the morning when we closed up on the massed wagon trains, 8 or 10 miles from Warrenton.

During the night—it was said—we passed near army headquarters at Salem, and it was during this night march that we first heard that "McClellan had been superseded," though some of us did not understand just what that meant. It took a little discussion to make it clear, but few believed it. One of the current stories credited to President Lincoln, in whose sound common sense we all believed, represented him as advising "not to swap horses when swimming a river"; and changing generals when executing movement against the enemy seemed so much like a mid-river horse trade that we could not credit it and concluded that it was a 'grapevine dispatch.'

Usually the boys of Company F 'took things as they came' and met all sorts of privations and hardships good-naturedly—as a matter of course and to be expected—but that night they seemed to be in a super-sensitive condition; and there was considerable 'growling' and 'back talk' among them. Perhaps it was the cold—the trials and tribulations of the day continued into an aggravating night march for which there did not seem to be any sufficient reason—that made the boys less amiable than usual. Perhaps it was some occult electrical influence connected with the unseasonable storm that had got 'on to their nerves' as the other things had gotten onto their muscles and made them more 'touchy' than usual.

Early in the evening, before we had heard the rumors, there was an attempt at some of the pleasantries usually indulged in when occasion offered, when the object of them 'flared up' and gave a general warning that he would not be responsible for the "early decease" of any one that interfered with him. A little later, there was an argument over some trivial matter that under ordinary conditions would have passed unnoticed. When, under these conditions, we first heard the rumor of removal, it did not produce a feeling of cheerfulness and confidence, for most of us were in a state of feeling that would have prompted us to dispute the army regulations or the Ten Commandments if any one had quoted them.

I recall but one other occasion in the history of the company when there was a like state of feeling. That was a little more than a year later, when we returned from Mine Run and found our huts burned—there was a snowstorm, too—but that story can wait.

When we halted we had been for more than twenty hours on our feet—for it was stand up or lie down in the snow—and when we did halt it was still a question of lying down in the snow or standing up in it. We compromised matters by kicking and scraping it away from places large enough to lie down on and spread our blankets. It seemed good to lie down, and we soon forgot all of our troubles in sleep.

It was rather 'cold comfort,' however, as when we were waked at daylight we were pretty thoroughly chilled, and glad to get up and make fires and boil coffee.

Warmed outwardly by generous rail fires, and inwardly by strong, hot coffee, the boys were in their normal mental temperature.

As the wagons no longer needed guarding—being now in the midst of the army—Gen. Sully received orders to report to the division without following the movements of the trains further; and we were soon on the road. Feet and ankles were somewhat stiff from the wrenchings and missteps of the day and night before, but that soon passed and we made good progress over the frozen roads. As the sun got higher the snow softened, and the roads were deep with mud and slush, through which we were obliged to wade and which splashed us to the knees.

During the day we learned that it was true that McClellan was to be relieved by Gen. Ambrose E. Burnside. There was a positive, strong, and very general feeling that this was not for the best, but there never was, I am confident, any thought among the enlisted men of anything but prompt and loyal obedience to the order in full accord with the letter and spirit of the oath they took when they enlisted.

About the middle of the afternoon of Sunday, Nov. 9, we joined the division near Warrenton and went into bivouac, making ourselves as comfortable as we could for the night. The next day we did not march, but instead a general inspection was ordered, and later we were called into line to pay respect to the retiring commander, Gen. McClellan, and his successor, Gen. Burnside. Some sensational writers of that time indulged in assertions about the feeling in the Army of the Potomac and suggested danger of mutiny, etc., but there never was any danger in that direction. The Army of the Potomac was an intensely loyal army and proved its devotion too often to have it questioned because a few intense partisans allowed themselves to get over-excited, and a few sensational newspapers indulged in big headlines for political purposes.

It has been said that a majority of the commissioned officers of the First Minnesota sent in their resignations, but I have no knowledge that this is correct.[6] If they did, it was not generally known among the men. If it was true and they were withdrawn at the suggestion of that level-headed old soldier, Gen. Alfred Sully, this prompt reconsideration of their impulsive action was a commendation of their good common sense and better selves; and continued good service atones for their hasty attempt to unwisely express their loyalty to their chief.

6. This story is told by Lieutenant William Lochren in his history of the regiment; *Minnesota in the Civil and Indian Wars*, 1:28–29. Lochren stated that the regiment and the rest of the army was "stunned and exasperated almost to the point of mutiny."

Come on, boys! Let's join a regiment that don't run

NOVEMBER-DECEMBER 1862

IT WAS THURSDAY, NOV. 27, Thanksgiving Day, and it was also my birthday, but there was no special observance of either. We did the best we could with army rations, and were thankful that we were still alive and able to eat them. Thanksgiving was not the widespread homecoming day it has since become, and I believe President Lincoln was the first of the presidents to request its general observance. There were orders in camp to be prepared to march, and we went to our blankets expecting orders to move in the morning. But we did not go, and two days later we were still in our temporary camps, across from Fredericksburg.

Sunday, Nov. 30, was a fine comfortable day as the day before had been, and after inspection the chaplain preached to us in the open air. In the afternoon some of us got permission to leave the camp for a few hours and went down the river as far as army headquarters, at the Phillips House, to see the boys of the company that had joined the cavalry. We found them all right, had a pleasant visit, and got back to camp just too late for roll call. I was sent to Lieut. Ball's tent to receive a reprimand for it. Being a noncom, all of the blame was placed on my shoulders. However, there was no penalty, and we were only advised to be on time thereafter.

Going and coming, we passed on different roads and saw some fine places fronting the city on our side of the river. We also got our first good view of Fredericksburg and the country on the other side. The location of the enemy's camps could be easily told from the smoke, and some new-looking embankments were seen on the point of a hill, which we were told had but recently been thrown up. We did not then suppose that the attack we expected to make would be through the city.

Monday, December 1st, we again changed the location of our camp and occupied a piece of open wood, which was considered a more favorable location. We worked diligently; cut and split logs, and built pens, over which we stretched our tent cloths; then dug out some of the dirt from the inside and banked it up on the outside. We managed also to save the boards and other material we had gathered since coming there and used them, as before, to sleep on. After working all day, except an occasional pause to comment on the foolishness of expending so much labor upon something we might have to abandon before it was finished—at night we had the most complete shelter we had had since giving up our wall tents the previous March.

On Monday, the 8th, it was still cold, but the snow was disappearing. I was sent with a detail to bring up a supply of rations and heard the current news of the camp, which was that a move was to be made down the river to Port Royal and across the country towards Richmond. Of course, we had been too long in the service to place much reliance on the gossip about the various department head-quarters, but there was generally a foreshadowing of movements from those places—and it was something interesting to tell the boys.

Early in the afternoon orders came to prepare three days' cooked rations and keep that amount on hand, with the usual extra sixty rounds. The next day all not considered able to march were sent to the surgeon for examination, and it was understood they were to remain and keep the camp in case we were ordered out. It now began to look as if some plan of movement was agreed upon and was about to be tried.

On Wednesday afternoon, December 10th, we had orders to be ready to move at dark that night. An hour or two later it was changed to daylight the next morning. We had the afternoon to make preparations; and a good many letters were written; and numerous little things were left with those that were to remain in camp—to be returned to the owners if they got back safe and otherwise to be disposed of as directed. The most of us also wrote our names and address on slips of paper and pinned them inside of our blouses, that we might be the most easily identified 'in case of accident.'

Preparing to take the chances of a battle is not quite so bad as being ordered out for execution, but I imagine that in both cases the thoughts may run, in part at least, along kindred lines. In one case the question of who is to die is definitely stated, and in the other it is not yet decided who is to be the victim, but it is pretty certain there is to be one.

At the last roll call that night, there was a strong wind roaring through the tops of the trees; the sky was overcast; it was beginning to freeze; and scattered snow-flakes were falling. We were told that we were to be called in time to get our breakfasts and were advised to fill our canteens with coffee and to wear our overcoats and carry only the woolen and rubber blankets.

Then we went to our tents to get what rest and sleep we could in anticipation of the demands that were to be made upon us. I do not know how soon the others slept, but I do know that it was some time before my thoughts were running in channels that invited slumber.

At two o'clock in the morning, we were called up and at once began our preparations for breakfast and the march. Several inches of snow had fallen, and the temperature was below freezing, but the wind was not blowing so strong as on the night before. It was rather discouraging work, at first, starting fires in the snow to cook breakfast in the dark, but it was soon done, and we went to our tents to eat it.

When our stomachs were filled, we also filled our canteens and then turned our attention to other things. Putting on two pairs of stockings, we folded the bottom of the trousers about the ankle and pulled the top of the second pair up outside of them, and tied them with a bit of string. Then with a blouse and over-coat on, a haversack with four days' rations, a canteen of coffee, sixty rounds, and blanket roll, gun and equipments, we were ready to move when the order came.

Thus prepared to feed ourselves, meet the elements and the enemy, we left our tents at Sergeant Bruce's call of "Fall in Company F"—formed on the company parade—answered to our names—and waited for the order to march. It was not yet light and was still snowing a little, though the storm had practically ceased. There had been two or three cannon shots before this, and now volleys of mus-ketry were heard down the river.

Some one quoted a line or two from "Hohenlinden,"[1] but it was too early in the morning to be in a sentimental mood, and neither the hour nor the situation presented themselves in a poetical aspect. As a rule poetry, like other verdant things, does not thrive well below the freezing point.

A little later the regiment formed and joined the other four regiments, then coming out of their camps. The brigade was formed in the following order: 34th New York, 82nd New York, 16th Massachusetts, 19th Maine, and 1st Minnesota regiments—and marched down the river. It was now light, but there was a thick mist hanging over the town and the river—into which one could see but a few feet. This seemed to be the case in the early mornings on the swamps and rivers much the greater part of the time. It was a march of two miles or so to the point oppo-site the central part of the town, where it was proposed to lay one of the bridges.

The firing that we had heard had driven the engineers from their work. When we arrived, there was a brisk skirmish firing going on across the river in the dense fog, and also some long-range artillery firing between some of our batteries on the bank and some of the enemies on the bluffs back of the town. But it was all ran-dom shooting and a waste of ammunition. The engineers were again attempting to lay the bridge. Though it was impossible to see, the men on the other side seemed to know pretty nearly where to aim, and killed and wounded many of the workers.[2]

As there was nothing for us to do until the bridge was laid, Gen. Sully placed us in the rear of the hill where we were reasonably safe until it was necessary to expose ourselves. He was a careful commander in this respect and always found cover for his men when he could while he was waiting for orders. Back of the hill, we stacked arms and rested at will.

It was a crisp winter morning, and the breaking clouds were drifting across the sky before a westerly wind—after the easterly storm.

1. A poem by Scottish poet Thomas Campbell, "Hohenlinden," had lines fitting the cir-cumstances: "On Linden, when the sun was low / All bloodless lay the untrodden snow / And dark as winter was the flow / Of Iser, rolling rapidly." (Quote courtesy of Hamp Smith.)
2. The Confederate skirmishers whose rifle fire so effectively delayed the placement of pontoons were part of General William Barksdale's Brigade of four Mississippi regiments.

There was a pretty strong desire among us to take a personal view of the situation, as the fog began to lighten a little. One after another went to the top of the hill, near the batteries, and tried to see something, but there was not yet much visible. The river and the town were still shrouded in fog—though we could see the tops of the steeples in the town and the outlines of hills beyond it from which their artillery was firing. The river was between 300 yards and 400 yards wide, and from our position the other shore was not visible. Down by the river were detachments of the engineers (50th New York as we afterwards learned) trying to place the bridge.[3] There were also several regiments of infantry from our 3rd Brigade and from the 3rd Brigade of the First Division. A brisk fire was kept up, aimed at the opposite shore.

It was not considered a very safe place on the hill, as bullets and shells were being thrown about recklessly, and one did not care to remain long. There was so hot a fire coming from the other side that every attempt to lay the bridge cost numerous lives and ended in failure. There were 3 officers and 13 men lost in the first attempt. In another attempt, the 8th Connecticut lost about 80 men killed and wounded, trying to protect the engineers. Then the 57th and 66th New York tried to suppress the fire from the other shore by regular volleys and for some time kept up a continuous and well-sustained fire—in which they lost about 150 men—but it also failed to quiet the enemy.

Hours were consumed in these efforts and, as all of them were failures, it was determined to try to shell them out. Fredericksburg was a town of about 6,000 inhabitants at the head of tidewater on the Rappahannock. It had been a prominent shipping point before the days of railroads. The railroad from Aquia Creek to Richmond came in along the valley of Clayburn Run; crossed the river at this place; and passed through the lower part of the town, turning easterly along the lower ground until a favorable point was reached to gain the higher land. On the left or northerly side of the river (where we were) were the Stafford Hills, 75 to 100 feet high, with steep banks close to the river. On this side of the river, nearly opposite the upper part of the town, was Falmouth, an inconsiderable village, near which our camp was situated.

On the Fredericksburg side, the bluffs were a mile or more back from the river, and the town was built on the plain, from the river towards the hills. This plain, in a general way, might be called level, but of course it was broken by ridges, cut by hollows, and varied by irregular formations. There were portions of the land back of the town that were considerably lower than the main part of the town. Through this lower land back of the town—running from a dam at the falls above it—was a canal bringing water to run some mills, and this proved a very serious hindrance to the advance of the Union troops in the attack. The

3. Folwell served in the 50th New York Regiment of Engineers.

more thickly built part of the town was nearer the river, with scattered houses beyond the canal.[4]

The hills back of the town were about the same height as those on the opposite side of the river but of more irregular distance from it. Back of the town on both sides of the canal were scattered houses with gardens and orchards, small fields, trees, bushes, etc. Across these were streets, roads, fences, stone walls, and what is generally found on the outskirts of a town. There were some small streams coming from the hills above the town: Hazel Run, which came through the hills near the base of Marye's Hill and ran past the lower end of the town into the river; Deep Run, which came from the hills across the plain into the river a couple of miles below the town; and the Massaponax, which also came from the hills and entered the Rappahannock five or six miles below the town.

The Rappahannock, the Massaponax, and the hills formed an irregular triangle with sides six or seven miles in length, with the base on the Massaponax, and Fredericksburg near the apex. The operations and fighting in December 1862 were within this triangle—with the Confederates on the hills and the Federals attacking—and the two points of severest contact were on the ridge between Deep Run and the Massaponax, and at Marye's Hill opposite the town.

The plan of operations, so far as it developed, was to lay five bridges across the river. Two were laid at a point between the mouth of the Massaponax and Deep Run, since known as Franklin's Crossing. One of the other bridges was laid below the ruins of the railroad bridge and the other two above it; the first entering the lower part of the town, and the others, the center. The lower bridge was placed without any effective protests, but at the others there was very strenuous resistance.

The chief of artillery, Gen. Henry J. Hunt, had placed numerous batteries the night before with the idea of covering the crossing, and to these others were added as the efforts to place the bridges failed. It was finally decided to try to drive out the enemy's sharpshooters with artillery, and the order was reluctantly given to train the guns on the town. The artillery was assembled in four principal groups and covered more than that many miles along the heights along the northerly side of the river. Altogether, there were 147 guns, of all calibers, and they would throw a combined weight of about a ton of iron at a discharge. About two-thirds of these guns could concentrate their fire on the town, but, as events proved, none could get a direct fire upon the point occupied by those who were the most effective in resisting the laying of the bridges.

Everything was still veiled in fog when the firing on the town began, and for a time the dense clouds of smoke completely hid everything. Anything really de-

---

4. The canal itself reentered the Rappahannock north of town, but the mill's spillway became a drainage ditch that ran along the entire west side of town to Hazel Run. This ditch did interfere with the Union attack on the west side of town. Welcher, *Union Army*, Vol. 1, *Eastern Theater*, 708.

scriptive of that bombardment would be difficult to put into words, and I shall not try, as I wish to save some adjectives for a later occasion. It was undoubtedly the grandest exhibit of artificial thunder that ever started the echoes along the Rappahannock. Spectacular and terrible—but it failed of the purpose intended, and the results were insignificant when compared with the noise. There had been a straggling artillery fire all the morning—with the enemy returning a random fire over the town—and it was to avoid this that we had taken cover back of the ridge. When the shots began to quicken and merged into a roar that seemed to get louder as it continued, we were intensely interested.

One and another crept to the crest of the hill to look. There was a whirl of strangling smoke all around where the batteries were, and over the town were masses of smoke and mist—varied here and there by rising clouds, the underside of which were the color of red-hot iron, which indicated that the town was burning. I went to the top of the hill and looked over at the town. I was reminded of a Sunday school picture I had once seen of the burning of Sodom.

Under this bombardment, the pontoniers again tried to lay the bridge, and were met again by the same deadly rifle fire, and were obliged to retire again to the shore for shelter. Several fires were burning, but the results of the artillery firing, which had been terrific and well-sustained, were nothing like what we expected. *It was not destroyed.* Many of the houses were badly damaged by shells; and quite a number were burned; but many escaped any serious injury. Artillery is an ideal instrument of war—in my judgment—and it has its part and place in warfare, but it cannot meet the requirements of all occasions, and this was one where it did not work.

Most of the day and much ammunition had been consumed (perhaps I should say, wasted) in unavailing efforts from our side of the river. It was determined to send over men to the other side to get under the bank and try in that way to drive them off. Colonel Norman J. Hall of the Seventh Michigan (then commanding the Third Brigade) offered his brigade to make the attempt. The 7th Michigan and 19th Massachusetts volunteered to go first and made their preparations to get into the boats and try to row to the other side. The men of these two regiments had been frequently tried and never found lacking, and it was believed that if any two regiments could make it they could.

Riflemen were posted to fire on the rifle pits on the other shore; some light guns were brought to the front; and all opened fire. Under cover of this, the 7th Michigan rushed for the boats and pulled for the other side, followed by the 19th Massachusetts. It looked like a row to death, and the only hope of reaching the shore alive seemed to be in the rapidity of the movement, and that kindness of chance sometimes allows bullets to come exceedingly close to a man without serious harm.

The pontoons were not racing shells, but self-preservation, regimental pride, and state pride prompted strong arms to do their best, and the unwieldy pontoons—carrying 25 or 30 men—were driven across the water at a surprising rate. Those not engaged in rowing crouched low in the boats, ready to spring out and use their rifles as soon as over.

It was a tense moment of waiting while the crash of cannon and the crack of rifles mingled in a confusing roar, and the smoke hid everything.

Then the wind blew the smoke aside, and the boats were seen at the water's edge—and the men on shore forming under a bank and trying to get in a position for a flank fire. Many were shot in the boats while crossing and others after reaching the shore, but not more than might have been expected. There were a few minutes of savage fighting at close quarters, and the obstinate fellows who had clung to their trenches all day were killed, captured, or forced to run for it.

After being driven out of their holes, they retired to the houses on the first street and continued their resistance. The bridge-makers quickly completed the bridge, and the rest of the brigade hastened over and were followed in turn by the other two brigades. When the 20th Massachusetts of the 3rd Brigade got over, it was formed to clear the street. Some desperate fighting followed in which the enemy were forced back to the next street, but in doing this 97 officers and men were killed or wounded (most of them belonging to the 20th Massachusetts) in advancing about 150 feet.

Fighting was still lively as we crossed. We were first formed under the bank and expected to be called on for a flank movement to clear another street, but, as it was already getting dark and they had ceased to be aggressive, it was decided to wait. It had been a matter of great surprise that a brigade had been able to delay matters so long, but a couple of regiments of concealed riflemen protected from bullets and direct artillery fire on a river bank or in a mountain pass are a pretty formidable proposition. I for one am willing to give Barksdale and his brigade full credit for making the most of their opportunities on this occasion.

When it was decided to await daylight before attempting any further advance, we marched up to the first street and stacked arms. There was still a pretty lively exchange of shots on the next street and to our left, but it was slackening, and it was thought to be a good time to get our suppers. We were dismissed for that purpose with a warning to keep within call and be ready to form at the gun-stacks at the word of command.

We had been under arms, practically, for about 19 hours—walking or standing in the snow and slush (for it had thawed during the middle of the day). Most of us had wet feet, and some of us probably had 'cold feet,' too—literally and in the modern slang sense. Now that night had come, it was freezing again, and there was an 'eager and nipping air' coming down the river.

Many of the houses had been used for defense, and the most of them were open. We naturally went into the houses to make our coffee and find shelter; and, when inside, I do not think that anyone hesitated to use what they found there, whether it was food or cooking utensils. There were fireplaces in most of the rooms; and fires were soon burning; suppers cooked and eaten; and then the natural inquisitiveness of most of the men prompted them to prowl around a little to see what they could find; and some of them found 'liquids'; and those who had a hankering for something stronger than coffee 'got outside' of more or less of it. Whether it was a result of the day's operations or a natural result of an occasion like that, the line of *meum et tuum*[5] was not carefully drawn that night. A disposition to plunder was more strongly manifested than on any other occasion.

Plans were under way for a dance—at which James F. Bachelor of Company F was to be the chief fiddler—when we were called into line and moved to the front, where we passed the remainder of the night in discomfort. A part of the company was stationed near the street, and the remainder rested at will in a vacant lot a little to the rear. Naturally, we tried to get what sleep we could. The ground was covered with snow and ice; a keen wind was blowing; and the temperature was several degrees below freezing; and altogether it was not an inviting prospect for a night out of doors.

It was now the order not to go into the houses, but Lieutenant Ball was considerate and gave us all the liberty he could—only asking that we should be within call and get into line promptly if there should be an alarm, and men were not to take off their accouterments or their shoes. There was an immediate hunt in the dark for anything that would keep one off the snow and ice.

At first, I thought I was not going to find anything, but a little farther—beside a fence—I found a hogshead lying on its side, full of straw or hay. I was going to take the hay to sleep on, but finding that I could move the hogshead, I rolled it near where the rest were; turned the end that had a head in it towards the wind; made a bed of the hay and crept into it; and 'curled up' like a dog in a kennel, wrapping my blanket over my feet and pulling my overcoat cape over my head. I was called but once during the night and had several hours of sleep. I doubt if anyone on the front line had better quarters than I did that night. I felt rather selfish in its seclusion, but it was not made for two, and I did not lose any sleep thinking about it.

Once or twice there was an alarming rattle of musketry that made me listen for more. And now and again a shell shrieked over, but it was not long before I was all unmindful of war and strife, in peaceful, dream-less slumber. Returning consciousness—after my last nap—came towards morning when someone rocked the hogshead about a quarter turn, back and forward, and invited me to "come out of my hole."

I was told that it was morning—though it was still dark—and that the orders were to get our breakfasts and be ready to fall in. I was still sleepy, numb, and torpid from the cold and the cramped position in which I had slept, and had to move about a little to get my blood in circulation before I had perfect control of my feet.

---

5. This is a Latin phrase, meaning "mine and thine," thus the lines drawn by property ownership.

It was a sharp, cold morning. A fine mist was everywhere and so thick that one could scarcely see across the street after it was light.

Fires were kindled; coffee made; breakfast eaten; and canteens filled—as on the day before. By that time, there were evidences of daylight, and orders came for the regiment to form. As soon as it was light, we moved to the point held by the pickets and waited for the order to move, which came a little later. The movement was in concert with others, and our regiment was to cover the right front— with Company F deployed as skirmishers on the right. There had not been much firing since midnight, and it was believed that the enemy had retired from the town, but the real situation could only be determined by investigation.

Mindful of the severe losses of the 20th Massachusetts the night before when in close order in the street, we were cautioned to keep well-deployed, use the houses and fences for cover, and move as quietly as we could, guiding on the left. With these instructions, carrying our rifles at a trail, we started to clear the streets and houses of any enemy left in them. Knowing the spiteful tenacity with which they had contested the crossing and every foot of advance, we expected to find them and looked for flashes of fire and whistling bullets from behind houses and fences. Crossing the streets hastily, going cautiously across backyards, peering carefully over fences and around corners, we made our way to the outskirts of the town, where it was mostly vacant lots and small fields. No one had fired at us, and we had seen no one.

Now and then, there was a dog appeared suddenly, barked in earnest protest at our intrusion, and then ran snarling around the house, where he was generally met by someone coming from an opposite direction who made a demonstration that sent the bewildered canine yelping across the street or under some outbuilding.

Meantime, the fog was less dense as we got away from the river, and the light grew stronger as the sun rose higher, but still it was very foggy, and we could not see plainly very far. The line was halted on one of the outer streets, and a few of us were sent forward to a rise of ground to make observations.

The ground was lower, with a stream running through it, and beyond the hills. This stream proved to be a canal, and it bore an important part in the defense of the hills. On top of the hills were fortifications and on the hillsides—where not covered with trees and bushes—were rifle pits. The distance to the top of the hills was less than half a mile. Men were seen on the top of the hill and at the rifle pits, but not many in either place, and nothing was seen very distinctly.

As we watched, three men came along a road at the foot of the hills on the opposite side of the canal, passing from our left to the right, and, a little farther, turned to their left along a path up the hill. They did not appear to be armed, and they carried large bundles of clothing or bed clothes in their arms or over their shoulders. They were in fair rifle range, but there was no reason why we should shoot at them, and they passed undisturbed.

When the situation was reported, the instructions were to remain where we were until further orders. Only our division of the Second Corps and one division of Ninth Corps had come into the town that night, as there was no more room then. We had spread out that morning to get more room, and the business of the day[6] was to mass the other troops in the town, and it proved a tiresome business.

Our brigade had the right front of the troops that spread out into the city; the regiment covered the right of the brigade; and our company was deployed covering the right front and flank. In this position we remained all that day and the following night. There were two houses on the line we held, and these we occupied, using them as places of general rendezvous and shelter for those not on duty as pickets.

The day was not far advanced before the fellows on the hills began to object to any more people crossing the river—by firing at the bridges—and hindered matters considerably. As long as the fog shrouded us, we were not disturbed, but when that had dried up or blown away and they were aware of our location on the outer edge of the town, they did not wholly neglect us. They threw shells in our direction occasionally—one striking a chimney and another a corner of one of the houses we had taken possession of—but hurt no one. The pickets on the hillsides also had spells of firing at us that gave us an uncomfortable half hour or so occasionally. At such times we took to cover wherever we could find it, and, if they persisted, we watched for their smoke and tried to make them understand 'it was a game at which two could play.'

At the first of these disturbances, I found shelter behind a small enclosure of brickwork three or four feet high, and I think that it was Charley Berdan that was with me. We fired several times from behind this, and a number of bullets struck it. We did not know at the time that the protecting shelter marked the resting place of Mary Washington.[7] And if we had, I have no doubt but we would have crouched down there just the same. It might have *seemed* a little lacking in respect for the dead to be 'scrapping' with the descendants of her old neighbors over her grave, but, if she had been conscious that we were trying to preserve what her son had fought to establish, I doubt not that she would have willingly offered the protection we found there.

It is an immense work to cross an army over a river the size of the Rappahannock in the face of an enemy and in range of his artillery, and supply it with food and ammunition to fight a battle. It took practically all of that short winter day and the following night to get ready.

6. That is, the business of Friday, December 12.
7. Mary Washington was the mother of George Washington, and her "grave and unfinished monument" were on the west side of Fredericksburg, where the First Minnesota was stationed; Moe, *Last Full Measure,* 211.

When night approached, it was freezing again, and the fog spread out from the river and settled in the streets. We were to remain in position overnight and arranged to keep one-third of the company on duty two hours at a time and allow the others to rest four hours. Those not on duty went into the houses, cooked their suppers, and remained there until called. Shells were thrown at intervals during the night, but we suffered no harm from them, and we were not otherwise seriously disturbed. We were less exposed and no doubt passed the night more comfortably than the troops massed in the town (or than we did the night before).

Saturday morning, December 13, 1862, we were all up, had answered the roll call, prepared and eaten our breakfasts, filled our canteens, rolled our blankets, and were waiting for orders before it was fairly daylight. There was no doubt but the climax of the movement would come before the day was over. Who would move first or where the fight would be the hardest was at best a guess, but we expected to get into it somewhere, and we were learning to wait patiently and hopefully and then take it as it came.

As on previous mornings, everything was enveloped in fog. One could scarcely see twenty feet. It was a freezing winter morning. We had been now more than 24 hours on the picket line and under ordinary circumstances would have been relieved. As we were not, we were certain that a movement was intended. The night before there was a rumor of a movement down the river and an attempt to surprise the enemy, but we knew there could be no surprise then. There followed a seemingly long time of waiting—due largely to the fog but there may have been other causes—and I presume it was near ten o'clock before the sun dissipated it sufficiently to allow anything but a very limited range of vision.

There was 'something doing' before that at several points along the line, and preparations and getting into position for the attack had begun as soon as it was light enough to see. These involved considerable sharp skirmishing and some pretty lively artillery fire. None of it had extended to the right as far as our brigade except for a few shots from a battery on the hill. The brigade was just to the right of the Plank Road, and we were in position some time before any serious fighting began near us.[8]

The first attack on the part of the Union troops was made by Meade's Division of the First Corps and was supported by the remainder of his corps and the Third Corps. This fighting was several miles to our left, and we could hear nothing but the artillery, and not long after that more serious fighting began nearer to us.

It was not long before a battery was observed passing along a street back of us and, after a time, was seen to be in position on a little ridge to our right and rear. After it began firing, there was some movement of the enemy that was supposed

8. The Orange Plank Road was the northernmost of two major (and roughly parallel) roads from Marye's Heights to the town. The southern one was the Telegraph Road.

to endanger it, and our regiment was detached from the brigade and sent to a position in front of it for its better protection. This battery proved to be Battery I, 1st U.S. Artillery (regulars)—better known as Kirby's Battery but formerly as Ricketts's. This battery had been with us at Bull Run and on nearly every movement since, and there were cheers from the battery boys when they recognized us—to which we responded. Lieutenant Kirby warmly expressed his satisfaction that we had been sent to his front to keep in check the sharpshooters who had already wounded some of his men.

The regiment promptly adjusted itself to its new position and found good cover from the enemy's artillery on the hill and laid down to watch for the men who had been annoying the battery.

During all of this time there was a lively artillery fire going on over our heads—not only between Kirby's battery and one on the hill, but between several of our batteries on the Stafford Hills and about Falmouth, and those of the enemy on their range of hills. This firing from the opposing ranges was—the most of it—too long-range for effective service, but it undoubtedly took up some of the enemy's attention from us and added to the noise, if nothing more.

About this time, there was another move by the enemy on the hill that seemed to require some changes on our side to oppose it. Company F was detached and moved some distance to the right and deployed to be ready to check any aggressive action of the enemy.

This then was the situation that afternoon so far as our company, regiment, and brigade were concerned: the brigade held the right of the line, on the right of the Plank Road; and the regiment was on the right of the brigade, detached; with Company F on the right of the regiment, detached and deployed. It had been our fortune to be on the right of the line on several occasions, but we had never been quite so much 'in the air' as then. On account of the canal, it was doubtful if the enemy could get nearer than the other side of it, but that was deadly rifle range from which they could shoot the cannoniers. Our position was one that must be held for the safety of the battery, but it was not a point from which an advance could be made on account of the canal.

Neither the company nor the regiment had anything more to do with the selection of their position that day than on others. And, if left to them, it is not likely they would have made so good a choice. But it was undoubtedly the position we happened to hold that day that saved us from another 'killing.' General Howard and General Alfred Sully were the men that had the responsibility of placing us that day and to them, if to anybody, we owe thanks for fortunate location.

When we deployed, we made ourselves as inconspicuous as possible and literally 'laid low' behind the little hillocks and bushes, watching for a sight of the other fellows who were among the trees and in pits on the hillside. It was now thawing considerable; and the snow in the weeds and grass was getting soft; and in the open places it was melting and running down in little streams; and where there was no snow there was soft spattery mud. Under those conditions, it was not so pleasant lying on the ground that winter day as it would have been under other conditions of a June afternoon. But circumstances control our preferences sometimes, and we really *preferred* to lie down, get our clothing soaked with ice-cold water and our overcoats plastered with mud—to taking the chances of a bullet, standing.

The enemy was not satisfied even to let us do that in peace, for they kept the shells flying pretty close to our heads, and bullets struck the ground about us here and there, altogether too frequently according to our ideas.

It was at this time that one of those tragi-comic incidents, which are frequently associated with very serious affairs, occurred. Joe Richardson (of whom I have already made mention), lying near where I was, came over, pointed out a rise of ground a hundred yards or so to the right as a point behind which the enemy might approach unobserved, and expressed the opinion that someone should be sent there to watch. Joe was a good soldier but at times seemed to have rather an exaggerated idea of his own importance and was pretty free with suggestions and advice.

It certainly was a good point for observation, so far as that alone was concerned, but the exposure was (I thought) unnecessary, and I asked Joe if he would like to go out there. He shook his head but asserted that from that point they could "p-pe-pep-pepper us." There was little doubt of that if they got there (which I did not think they could), but I told him to go to Lieut. Ball and explain to him.

I did not hear Joe's conversation with the lieutenant but learned afterwards that he listened to his statement, said that his suggestions were good; that he had been thinking of it; and told him to post himself there.

In a few minutes he returned, saying briefly, "I-I-I g-g-got t-t-to g-g-go," and began adjusting himself to start. We were in light marching order with the rubber blanket outside the rolled woolen one, slung over the left shoulder, and the tied ends at the right side. It was evident that Joe did not relish going, but after pulling his blanket roll, haversack, canteen, and cartridge box into position, he started off in good form.

He had not gone many yards before he dodged at a passing shell, glanced back to see if anyone was looking, moved on a little farther, and dropped quickly to the ground as another screamed over his head. Sticking his head up and glancing about, he sprang to his feet and hurried on, 'ducking' as he went.

Reaching the top of the rise, he stood for an instant, crouched down, and then dropped—where he lay for a minute or two, poking his head up occasionally, then rolled a little to one side, and later crept backwards a few feet.

All the time the shells were shrieking above him. One struck some rods in front, passed over him, and went bounding into the town. And another burst in the air. Still another struck the ground a little in front, slid by—plowing a furrow in the frozen ground beside him—and exploded. For an instant, he was hidden in the blue smoke and a shower of mud and frozen clods. Then he was seen struggling to his feet and coming in at a lively trot.

He arrived out of breath, spitting and stuttering, covered with mud, and the blood oozing from the side of his face and chin. He told the lieutenant that he could not 'hold that position any longer' and had come in. Sitting down and wiping the mud and blood from his face, he said he felt weak and he "g-g-gu-guessed th-th-tha-that d-d-d'n sh-sh-shell ha-ha-had ma-m-made a c-c-cow-coward o-of m-m-me."

Joe was sent to the rear and was found not to be seriously wounded. After the surgeon had sponged and repaired the broken places in the cuticle with adhesive plaster, he came back to the company.

As he could now talk a little more coherently, he explained things, from his view of them, a little more in detail. He said that he saw some men across the canal who fired at him and made him feel as if he was ten or twelve feet high. Then he lay down, when the artillery men saw his rubber blanket, thought he was a piece of artillery, and had fired at him. Lieutenant Ball asked him if they had *dismounted* him, and Joe said, "p-pr-pret-pretty d-d-d'n n-near it, b-b-but I-I b-b-bro-brought off m-m-my g-g-gu-gun."

He seemed to think that they were really firing with him as the individual target and that the shell actually grazed him, but such was probably not literally true. At about that time the Confederates were firing on the general principle of hitting anything that happened to be in range, and his injuries were all from the gravel and dirt—but few men get in closer contact with a 'live shell' and live.

While these and other things were transpiring, matters were gradually shaping themselves for what the writers of that day called the "supreme tragedy" of the battle, the noise of which was increasing moment by moment. Many shells from both sides passed over us—smoking, shrieking, and some (from our own guns) bursting in the air above us; the roar of the cannon increasing until it was like continuous rolling thunder; and every interval of lesser sound was filled with the minor crash of rifles. The fog, which had mostly disappeared, was now replaced by smoke, and very little could be seen of our lines to the left or what progress was being made. As the fight increased, the most of the guns which had been throwing shells in our direction turned their muzzles towards other points, giving us only an occasional shot and leaving us to the care of the sharpshooters, who continued attentive.

Two others of the company were hit, and others had very narrow escapes, and all we could do was to watch and take an occasional shot when we saw a head for an instant or a puff of smoke.

The real fighting was all to our left, and, judging by the sound, it was in terrible, deadly earnest, and had not yet been successful.

It was getting late in the afternoon. There was a sensible slackening of the Confederate artillery fire. We saw the flank of a Confederate line coming down the hill.

It was some distance to our left front out of rifle range and was apparently marching obliquely to its right. We saw more of this line than any others at the point of
attack. We saw this but for a moment as it passed rapidly down the hill, but it was
long enough to see several men stagger and fall or run to the rear. This was probably one of Robert Ransom's brigades going to reinforce General Thomas Cobb
at the Stone Wall or in the Sunken Road.

It was an awful strain on even seasoned nerves to listen to these repeated attacks, which it was certain were not accomplishing their object.

It was almost night when we were ordered to the regiment, and it took its place
on the right of the brigade. The Second and Third Brigades had already advanced, and the 15th Massachusetts (of ours) had gone to their support, when we
came. The rest of the brigade joined it and awaited orders. About the time we
came to the brigade, we heard cheering to the front and left, and it suggested
something hopeful, as we recognized it as a Union cheer. Then came crashing volleys, followed shortly after by the 'ky-yi' of the 'rebel yell.' It was Humphreys' Division of the Fifth Corps making a last attempt to bring the results of the day's
fighting to something more than a phenomenal slaughter, but it only resulted in
increasing the number of the dead and wounded.

It was a terribly depressing hour as we heard from those who had been in the
assaults. The conviction forced itself upon us that the day's sacrifice had been for
nothing.

Before this time, night had come—dark and cold and cheerless; and the ever-
present, marrow-chilling mist spread out from the river; and a freezing temperature added itself to the usual horrors of a night after a great battle. Seven divisions
of an average strength of about 5,000 men had advanced successively and been
forced to retire, losing an average of 1,000 men each, killed and wounded. Thousands of helpless wounded, depleted of blood, were chilling to death in the frigid
night air. Words cannot picture it, and it is useless for me to attempt it.

Every effort was made to promptly care for the wounded, and, as soon as
darkness afforded cover, every part of the field not actually held by the enemy
was searched for the victims of the day—to find and bring them in. Almost every
house in the town inside the lines was used for hospital purposes. By candle-
light, by lantern light, and by torch light, the surgeons and their assistants were
busy all night.

About ten o'clock, General George Sykes's Division of the Fifth Corps came
to relieve us, but General Couch declined to be relieved—so it was said—and
would not give the order to withdraw his men until he had it in writing from General Sumner. When this order came, near midnight, the regulars took the front,
and our corps retired towards the town, being placed in a secondary line for the
rest of the night. Here, for the first time in nearly twenty-four hours, we had an
opportunity to make coffee over little fires kindled under an embankment, and af-

ter that spent the hours until morning sitting or lying in the street, as we were held in readiness to support Sykes's Division in case of need.

After the excitements of the day, its disastrous results, the awful surroundings, and the uncertainty of the future, there was but little sleep or rest that night. If there had been nothing to disturb us mentally and no threat in our surroundings, the weather conditions were enough to prevent sleep—but these were the least of our troubles.

As the morning approached, we retired to Princess Street and awaited daylight. Our feelings that dreary Sunday morning may be more easily imagined than described. We were expecting to renew the attack at some point and faced the situation determined to do all that it was possible to do. But it is useless to deny that the unavailing slaughter impressed us with all of its hopeless horror, and confidence in the ability of the commanding general was badly shaken.

Almost as soon as it was light, firing began between the advanced portions of the two armies, for our troops were lying as near to the enemy as it was possible to find shelter from their artillery on the heights and their sharpshooters in the trenches, behind the stone walls, and in houses. We held ourselves in readiness to fall in and march. As we were not immediately called, we improved the time to make coffee and eat our breakfasts, disturbed now and then by a shell or two that were evidently intended for our locality and came uncomfortably near. All of the morning, the fog hung over us, and while this lasted there could be nothing but random firing.

Towards noon, as this began to lighten and we could see things more distinctly, we were cautioned to keep under cover and do nothing to unnecessarily attract attention. With that thought in view, we were disposed along the street (running parallel to the heights), which offered convenient protection. On bits of boards, fencing, or anything we could find to interpose between our bodies and the cold and moisture from the ground, we laid down and during the day managed to get a few hours of disturbed and broken sleep, which was a great relief. Sometimes it was the cold that chilled us to the point of waking, and we had to get up and walk around to start the blood to a faster flow. And sometimes it was the explosion of a shell nearer than usual that brought us to a consciousness of our relations to the troublous times then prevailing on the Rappahannock.

As the sun dropped towards the horizon, it shone dimly again through haze and smoke; all of the warmth vanished out of the air; and there was again a freezing temperature.

When it was dark again, and the cold vapor was creeping out from the river and the canal, our regiment and the 15th Massachusetts had orders to form quietly and were instructed to dispose of our canteens and accouterments in such a way as to make no noise in marching. Then we marched to the front, slowly and quietly, halting a few minutes when we reached the line held by the regulars of Sykes's

Division, while Colonel Morgan of our regiment consulted with the officer in charge. Then we deployed and crept out to the front, and their pickets crept backwards and were lost in the darkness. It was in this way the front line was relieved.

They were no doubt glad to go, and we began a memorable twenty-four hours of tiresome and dangerous duty.

Colonel Morgan had orders to establish a new line as close to the enemy as it was possible to get. (Morgan was in command of the two regiments, as he was of the whole brigade for a time—General Sully being partly disabled from a wound on the 13th.) The posting of this line was a rather delicate operation, took considerable time, and one or two men were captured while doing it, but it proved to be well-located. Lieutenant Chris Heffelfinger and Corporal William Irvine of Company D crept out to make observations and got very close to the enemy. The lieutenant managed to get away, but Irvine was captured. Later, a detail was sent in for picks and shovels, and some trenches dug, and banks thrown up that also were found to be of great value.

Soon after getting located sufficiently to begin to look about at things in general, the northern sky was seen to be illuminated. At first sight, it suggested a large fire, but a little later the shifting lights showed that it was a splendid display of Northern Lights. It spread over the whole northern sky at times, coming apparently out of the northwest, and spread eastward and upward until it was in the northeast and almost overhead. The lights were very brilliant, shifted quickly, and presented nearly all of the colors of the rainbow. Such things were said to be very rare in that latitude, but I have not often seen so brilliant an auroral display.

There was still a little superstition among the people of that day about comets, eclipses, the aurora borealis, shooting stars, etc., and the scene was watched with more than ordinary interest on account of our surroundings. No doubt it was a matter of equal interest to 'our friends the enemy' only a few rods away—and they neglected to shoot at us almost entirely for some hours, but it is not certain that was the reason. Some were inclined to consider it an omen of evil import and were asking what it meant. No one was ready to interpret it, but someone ventured the opinion that whatever might follow it could not very well be any worse than what had already come and he "guessed we could stand it." Frank Bachelor, who did not often let an opportunity pass without attempting one of his 'transposition jokes,' declared he did not know what it was a 'sign of,' but he was sure it was "the fore-end of some runner."

Watching the magnificent kaleidoscope of the northern sky, listening for any sound of movement by the enemy, and thinking such thoughts as must come to anyone under such conditions—we passed the hours of that long cold winter night. I do not think any of us expected to stay there for twenty-four hours. We could see no reason for putting us in that position unless it was intended to try to go farther. We expected to be out of there and perhaps out of the world before the sun reached the meridian.

At last the dull gray of dawn dimmed the aurora with its increasing light, and objects grew more distinct as the morning advanced. There was fog everywhere but not so thick as usual, and we were soon able to locate the positions of the enemy near us, and it was necessary to change some of our positions in order to be reasonably safe.

It was scarcely light enough to be called day before the enemy gave us his attention. Here and there about us, a bullet would cut the frozen earth and pass on with a peculiar whining sound. Now and then a shell would cut the air with a devilish, laughing shriek that made our flesh creep and explode somewhere over or behind us, making us lie a little closer to the ground.

At first we appeared to be greatly exposed, and it did not seem as if we could last long in such a position, but we soon adjusted ourselves to the situation. We were warned to protect ourselves and allowed considerable liberty in doing it—not being required to keep in close order or exact line. There had been no digging at the point where our company was stationed, the natural formation being deemed sufficient. Each one soon found a little depression in which he could lie or a little rise behind which he could find shelter. To these natural provisions, he added his blanket roll or anything else he could find to interpose between his precious anatomy and possible danger.

When I had time to take in my surroundings, I saw that I was in a slight hollow or depression of irregular form and depth and curving to the rear on my right. There was no place where one could stand up and few where one could sit with safety.

At first the enemy fired at everything that moved, and we were cautioned not to fire or expose ourselves and only to fire when we were certain of someone to shoot at. We refrained from firing. After we got adjusted to our places, they kept the bullets whistling about us so frequently that we laid (literally) for them and did what we could to annoy them.

At first we were expecting an order to attempt something more heroic than lying on the ground—as we assumed that was the object of holding a position so close to them. After a time, they seemed to tire of the constant firing, and it gradually ceased. Then we were told that there was a short truce to remove some of the wounded still between the lines, but the men of both sides were to remain lying down, and for a time there was no firing. Then somehow 'it got to going again,' and by spells both the sharpshooters and the artillerymen did what they could to make it uncomfortable for us.

It was no joke to lie on the ground and watch the sun as it alternately shone or hid itself behind drifting clouds and did not seem to move. Several times I heard it asserted that the miracle wrought when Joshua was fighting the allied kings at Gibeon was being repeated. But that was a figure of speech by which someone voiced his dissatisfaction with the situation in which he was placed, rather than a statement of fact. I do not think that I can actually prove that the sun did stand still on the 15th day of December, 1862. But I do believe that there are men now living who will swear that, to the best of their knowledge and belief, it "hasted not to go down" that day if it ever did. (Except the time mentioned in Joshua, 10th chapter, and 13th verse.)

Occasionally, our rifled batteries on Stafford Hills and those of the enemy on the heights passed shells at each other over our heads, but the distance was too great, and it was little more than a noisy pastime. Once in a while, some of our batteries on the plain below the town threw shells at Marye's Hill in front of us, but they were not very effective.

Along in the early afternoon, one of our batteries in the town quietly got some of its guns into position and fired a dozen or so shells at the houses occupied by the sharpshooters. It was more fun for us to see them come out of the houses and scatter for cover than it was for them, no doubt. Of course, our battery could not stay there and quickly withdrew, but it relieved us for the time.

The enemy, however, appeared to be angry over it and soon got back at us 'right smart.' They managed to get a battery or two in position off to their left (our right) and opened on us suddenly—a hot, enfilading fire that raked our line. A rapid succession of shells came hissing, howling, and screeching over our heads, or struck the ground and bounded past with a vicious spitefulness. Their artillery and infantry all along the front joined in with this cyclonic bombardment, and there was a cloud of smoke covering the hills, and a riot of noise back of it.

This brought the crisis of the day. This was a little too much for some unseasoned regiments on our right, including the 127th Pennsylvania, and they sought the shelter of the houses in their rear. Against the scorching artillery fire that roared around us, we were powerless (with nothing but our rifles) and lay close to the ground as the only safe thing to do—waiting for their infantry to come out—as it was supposed it would after the big guns were through pounding us. For a few minutes, the situation presented a decidedly dubious appearance. When it was seen that the line was broken, and the men on our right were running to the rear, the climax came.

Company F was the right of the regiment and would be the first to be struck in flank by the enemy coming through the gap. And it was for us to decide first whether to stay or go with the stampeded line. It took 'sand,' but, to the credit of Goodhue, her representatives on the spot had plenty of it on hand and used it.

"Stay where you are, men," was the command from Lieutenant Ball.

Encouraging words were spoken to one another, and not a man offered to go, but on the contrary, called to the departing men of the 127th to come back. In response to these calls, a part of their left company did return after they had got some distance away.

One of the first of these to come to us was a sergeant who came trotting towards us, looking back, and calling to his comrades, "Come on, boys! Let's join a regiment that don't run." He dropped on the ground beside me and turned towards me an appealing face, full of conflicting emotions, while he made some uncomplimentary remarks about his departing comrades. He was a well-favored young fellow of about twenty—light hair and blue eyes—and unquestionably a brave man, but at the moment laboring under intense excitement, which he was controlling most manfully.

One of the last to come to us was a man of a little different makeup, but he, too, had the right kind of material in him (or he would not have come back). But at the moment he was, to use a military term, '*badly demoralized.*' He came in with a rush, as if he had been fired from one of the guns—yelling unintelligibly—and dropped down and squirmed around as if he would like to burrow into the ground like a mole. Someone asked him "what was the matter with him," and he replied in a shaky voice, "my regiment is *broke!*" And the last word he screamed out at the top of his voice.

When it was evident they were not coming, we began using our rifles wherever a head showed itself and contributed our share to the noise of the occasion, if nothing more. In this, those of the 127th who had joined us assisted.

Our batteries about Falmouth, which were nearest those guns of the enemy which had begun the trouble, opened on them from across the river. Other guns of ours were concentrated upon them and soon silenced them, but by that time other guns of theirs were in action, sending a hot fire at every exposed point. Of course, our batteries in position did not remain quiet, and some of them below the town shelled the hillside in our front with such good effect that it drove their infantry to cover and materially relieved us.

Meantime, the Nineteenth Maine and the Eighty-Second New York of our own brigade were hurried to our assistance. They came on the double quick with a gallant cheer and occupied some houses and an old road a few rods to the rear of the broken line, as it seemed a better defensive position. A detachment of the 82nd occupied a house between its left and the right of our company, and began a rattling fire.

For a time, the rapid firing continued, then slackened, and was soon reduced to ordinary skirmishing. When the noise had subsided to comparative quietness, and we had time to think, we were of the opinion that they had not really intended to advance and were only 'demonstrating against us.'

We were surprised to learn that not a man of the company had been hit. Shells were exploding in front of us, over us, on both sides of us, and behind us; their broken fragments and contents were cutting the air and tearing the ground around us; and we were seemingly in as great danger as at Savage's Station, where 16 men were hit. A possibility is that then we were standing or kneeling, and now we lay flat on the ground, which was a saving factor in the case.

This lively 'diversion' certainly did help to make the afternoon pass less monotonously, but we were not hankering for *amusement* of that kind, having already had more than we wanted.

The remaining hours of daylight passed in comparative peace. With the coming on of night, the firing ceased. They seemingly were tired of shooting at us or, like ourselves, were weary and wanted to rest. By night the temperature was about freezing again; a strong wind was blowing; and a fine mixture of rain and snow was falling. We were glad it was night, and glad the night was dark, for we could now stand up and walk about a little to start the circulation (we were stiff and sore from lying so long on the cold ground).

We waited, expecting to be relieved, until it began to look as if we were forgotten. Then, about nine o'clock, orders came for us to withdraw from the advanced position. When he received the order, Lieutenant Ball directed the sergeants to inform the men and caution them against making noise of any kind and to make sure that no one was left asleep. We were all well-nigh exhausted by the five days and nights we had been out, and very few had slept any for more than twenty-four hours.

When the company had been assembled—sitting on the ground—we got up and marched to the rear. It had been quiet for nearly two hours, and there was no evidence from the enemy that they knew of our going, and I am sure that they did not. The darkness, the rain, and the wind were all favorable to us. When we had gone some distance to the rear, we waited until the rest of the companies had joined us, and, a little later, the 15th Massachusetts. Crossing the canal, we passed through a line resting at will. A little farther on, we found the other regiments of the brigade resting in line on a side street, and we took our place with them.

Fires were burning in the street, and we were all hungry and *starving* for coffee. It was uncertain if we would remain there long enough for water to boil, but no time was lost in getting some and beginning that part of coffee-making. As it proved, we had not only time to make coffee but to drink it and to eat about all we had left in our haversacks. There was comfort and hope in the quart or so of coffee I drank, as well as warmth.

When we had joined the brigade, we were told that the army was recrossing the river. I know that there was a sense of relief at the thought that we could now stand on our feet without risking our lives, and that there would be more comfort in *living* with the river between us and those fellows back on the hills. But there was bitterness and depression in the thought of the conditions under which we were going. The remark of a comrade that it was the "fortune of war" did not lessen the feeling of rebellion I felt at the cruel fortune war had just dealt us.

After an hour or so, we marched to the bridge and crossed to the left, or northerly, side, where there was another short halt, when we were ordered to return to our camps. It was between one and two o'clock, Tuesday morning, December 16th, 1862, when we arrived, having been absent since the Thursday morning previous. It was still storming and freezing with a keen wind blowing. The sick men left behind had cared for the tents, and we were gratified to find them as we had left them.

We were soon inside and preparing to enjoy the protection and comfort they afforded. It seemed really good to remove my shoes and outer clothing and go to sleep under cover, between blankets, in a more human way than just lying down somewhere outside like a homeless brute. Thankful that I was still living and had an opportunity to indulge my desire for sleep, with so good a protection from the cold and the storm, it did not take long to forget everything in solid, dreamless, refreshing slumber. The last thing I remembered was someone singing softly, "Home, Sweet Home."

When I was awakened in the morning, I was ravenously hungry. I was told that a detail had already gone for rations, and I hastened to make a little fire, where we cooked and got water in preparation for breakfast.

When the detail returned from the commissary with rations, they brought word that our troops had all been withdrawn from the town and that the bridges had been swung to our side of the river. If the enemy had known of our going, they had made no demonstration to prevent it. That intangible thing called *discipline, esprit de corps, experience*—or what you choose to name it—never showed to better advantage than on this occasion in the movement of troops onto or off of a battlefield. We (2nd and 9th Corps) retired from within pistol range of a strong entrenched line of the enemy and crossed a river in shell range of their artillery without hindrance—and this seemingly without their knowledge.

Our breakfast was quickly prepared after the material arrived, and was eaten with keen relish and thankfulness. As individuals and as a regiment, we had full reason to feel grateful, for our loss—all things considered—had been unaccountably light. On this expedition we had been the 'luckiest regiment' in the Second Corps. The regiment had asked no favors, taken its place in line, performed every duty assigned it in a way to win the strongest commendations from regimental, brigade, and division commanders. It was claimed by some that the very light loss suffered in the regiment and the brigade was due to the coolness, forethought, and eminent common sense of Gen. Sully.[9] For this immunity, we felt grateful— whether it was all properly to be credited to our level-headed old colonel or whether a part of it was due to the usually erratic apportionment of losses.

There had not been a man killed. Two officers and 10 men were wounded, and two men captured the night of the 14th—a total of 14. Of this loss, 1 officer and 4 men fell to the share of Company F.

The loss of the brigade had been 104; and of the division, 914; and of the Corps, 3,833—the greatest of any corps engaged. It was an awful expenditure of blood for so unpromising an adventure. What fatuous reasoning or supposed knowledge caused the principal attack to be made through the town, against the hills back of it, guarded as they were by the intervening canal—I cannot guess. It

9. This claim was made by William Lochren in his "Narrative of the First Regiment," in *Minnesota in the Civil and Indian Wars,* 1:30.

can only be accounted for on the supposition of mental paralysis or absolute lack of knowledge of conditions. If it had been left to the Confederates to have chosen how they desired the Federal commander to proceed in his operations against them, it is not likely that anything more satisfactory to them could have been done—unless, indeed, the Union army had laid down its arms or marched into the river and drowned itself.

The men in the ranks knew when they were intelligently led, and they also knew when there was a lack of discretion in the direction of their movements. Of all of the men in the world, there were no better qualified or more competent judges of the character and capacity of a commander than the soldiers of his command, after going through a campaign under his leadership. They recognized this as an occasion where there had been indiscretion and incapacity to a degree of which they had hitherto had no experience—and forever afterwards wanted no more.

Only been singed a little

DECEMBER 1862-MAY 1863

THERE WAS ANOTHER SNOW STORM Saturday, and Sunday, December 21, was quite cold with a strong northerly wind blowing. We spent the day in our tents and, long before night, were satisfied that a shelter tent without fire on a raw winter day could be decidedly uncomfortable, and planned certain improvements to give more room and a fire inside—which my 'bunkie' and I proposed to make as soon as we could get the material together and do the work.

This work we began the next morning with a hunt for boards, sticks, and stones, and digging a place for a fire at the back of the tent. Over this we built a chimney of sticks. We dug more dirt from the inside of our tent and banked it up on the outside. We found some flat stones and a few bricks for the inside of the fireplace; made a stiff mortar of the clay we dug out; and plastered the inside of the sticks—several inches thick; and finished the outside by filling in between them. By this time it was night, but we were able to have a fire and planned to finish the next day.

The next morning the regiment was ordered out on picket, and we spent the next 24 hours a few miles out on the Warrenton road without any special incident, returning to camp Wednesday about noon.

Returning to camp, we brought with us a bundle of pine knots for kindling and two bricks for "andirons." We knew there was no certainty that we would remain there, even long enough to complete our work, but we were all trying to make ourselves as comfortable as we could. There was considerable ingenuity and skill shown in this, and every bit of board, stick, and flat stone to be found was gathered up and used. Previously a 'bean hole' had been provided; and now a shed was built over it of poles and brush; and three sides were enclosed with the same material.

Thursday, Dec. 25, was not a 'merry Christmas' to the Boys in Blue on the banks of the Rappahannock—but recently returned from their ill-starred expedition across the river—as it lacked home associations and all other usual accompaniments. And this was more particularly true of that little band of them sent there by the North Star State to represent her in the struggle with the advocates of secession, as they were so far away from the 'home base.' It was our second Christmas away from home and the gloomiest of them all, for we were not yet recovered from the depression of the late battles. Still, as always, there was a disposition to be cheerful and hopeful and lots of talk about the folks at home and the good Christmas dinner they would like to have—if they could only get it.

We spent the day, as did most others, working to make our tents more comfortable. Those boards came in handy to stake up around the sides where we had dug deeper. Poles resting on a couple of short logs took their place to sleep on. The dirt answered for a floor, and, since we could have a little fire, it was getting dry, and we could be comparatively comfortable. At our fireplace we could make coffee and do all of our cooking except the baking of beans or 'smothering' beef. We were constantly learning from experience, and it was surprising how little we could get along with—or, perhaps I should say, how much we could get along without.

The very severe weather and violent storms of the early winter was followed about this time by a 'mild spell' the last of December and the first of January following, which gave us a fine time for preparation. About this time, an order was issued allowing ovens to be built, and thus fresh bread was provided. These were very simple affairs—a row of brick arches where they would not be flooded when it rained—but they answered all purposes and the fresh bread was very acceptable. Though it may not have been any more nutritious, it was something our appetites craved.

On Thursday, January 8th, we had a battalion drill and a dress parade at night. Saturday, the 10th, we were to have a battalion drill, but a severe rainstorm postponed it, and on Sunday it was too unpleasant for any service. On Monday, I procured a pass for three, and we visited Lieut. Abraham Wright and our Red Wing friends in the First Sharpshooters, and spent a very pleasant day. On Tuesday the 13th, we went out on the Warrenton road a few miles and spent 24 hours on picket. It did not storm but was a cold and disagreeable tour of duty. Returning, I had a letter informing me of the very serious illness of my mother, holding out very little hope of her recovery, which left me a prey to anxiety.

On Friday we had orders to hold ourselves in readiness to move with the usual rations and ammunition. The next day the Second Corps had a review, but we did not march. On Sunday, the 18th, it was clear but quite cold, and the order to be in readiness to move was repeated: men not able to march were to remain where they were, but those going were to take everything with them. (As we now know it was planned to move up the river about six miles, cross over, and attack Lee's left and try in that way to get at his rear or oblige him to come out of his defenses.) The Second Corps, being mostly in sight of the enemy on the other side, was to remain in its camps as long as possible to screen the movement. This, as matters turned out, was a fortunate thing for our division, as it saved us considerable expense and hardship—and our camps.

Matters were previously planned, and lines of march and point of crossing selected, but the troops did not begin moving until the 19th. During the 20th, they were passing in our rear, going to our right, all day and all night. That night a general order was read at dress parade, simply stating that a movement was in progress that would take us against the enemy, asking every man to do his utmost, and promising victory as the result.

As results proved, it was the elements and not the enemy that the Army of the Potomac had to fight, and it was 'beaten to a stand-still.' Soon after night, a cold, copious rain began, which soon developed into a furious storm; and a howling gale with pouring rain swept the valley of the Rappahannock, as snow and a blizzard sometimes does on the upper Mississippi. It was a winter storm and flood, we were told, such as is but rarely seen in that region. It was not quite cold enough to freeze, but sufficiently cold to chill the marrow in the bones of the luckless men who—drenched to the skin—were marching all night in the pitiless storm. The clayey roads soon grew soft and went rapidly from bad to worse until they became impassable for wheels. A more uncomfortable night for men or beasts could scarcely be imagined.

When morning came, but little of the artillery and only a few of the pontoons had reached a point where they were available. The rest were stalled at various points along the roads. And the men were halted—or trying to march—all the way from Fredericksburg to Banks's Ford. The success of the expedition depended upon its secrecy and the rapidity of its execution, and both of these conditions were now lacking. The troops could not advance; the river was rising rapidly; and it became certain that the enemy knew of the move.

Orders were given to return to the camp, but this was more easily directed than accomplished. Some of the troops had already been out three days, and it took more than that time for all to get back with the artillery and pontoons. During the day of the 25th, they were dragging them by; and it took 14 horses to a pontoon boat and 12 to a field gun; and they were frequently stalled at that. Our division had remained in camp, with knapsacks packed ready for the word to take down our tents and march, but we were not ordered to move and thus escaped much hardship.

This movement was generally known at the time as the Mud March, and its results were not encouraging. General Burnside made complaints against some of his generals and asked that they be removed. President Lincoln did not see fit to comply with this request, and he then asked to be relieved of the command of the Army of the Potomac. This request was granted, the same order naming General Joseph Hooker as his successor.

The same order relieved Generals Franklin and Sumner; the latter at his own request, on account of age and broken health. He went to his home at Syracuse, New York, where he died about two months later. He issued a touching farewell address to his old command, the Second Corps, which he had commanded since its organization, recalling its services and urging a continuance of its efforts until a successful ending was reached. He reminded it of its great losses—greater than any other corps—and that it had never yet lost a gun or a color, and charged it to keep the record good. It might be said of the old corps that it did lose both guns and colors in 1864, but it kept its mortality list higher than all others trying to prevent it.

There was no such feeling of regret at the passing of Burnside as at the going of McClellan and Sumner, but still there was sincere regret at the want of success that had attended his brief tenure of command. He failed to inspire the highest confidence in his ability, but there was never a question as to his patriotism and sincere purpose to do his best for his country. His successor, 'Fighting Joe' Hooker, was aggressive almost to rashness, had been fairly successful as a division and corps commander, but he had done some things to impair confidence in his better judgment and was frequently at variance with his superiors, being inclined to 'talk too much with his mouth.' President Lincoln, when he appointed him, wrote him a fatherly letter, it was understood, containing much good advice and assured him of his full support.

Upon assuming command, Gen. Hooker started many changes, several of which appealed to the soldierly pride or patriotism of the men and were in other ways beneficial. He made a great effort to increase and improve the cavalry arm of the service, as McClellan had the artillery, and in the end greatly increased its efficiency. The adoption of distinctive badges to show the corps and divisions was one of the things that 'took' with the soldiers, and it was adopted by other armies. There did not seem to be much in these little flannel devices, but they gave an impulse to a good soldier's pride in his own that helped to create a spirit of emulation in the right direction.

An army that meets reverses is usually depressed, and for the time being loses something of its aggressiveness, but the depression resulting from Fredericksburg was greater and lasted longer than any other of which I have personal knowledge. This depression was not all the result of operations at the front. Much of it came from the 'fire in the rear,' which began to make itself seriously felt about this time. When the men then at the front had left their homes there appeared to be but one sentiment, and that was to preserve the Union at all hazards, but now, judging from letters and newspapers, there was a wide division of the people and many 'secesh sympathizers' who rejoiced at the reverses of our armies. Between the Copperheads, whose sympathies, talk, and action were with the South, and the extremists on the other hand, who were at variance with the President, his Cabinet, Congress, and military leaders—there was much done and said that added to the length and cost of the war and increased the number of the slain. At no time was this malign influence felt more keenly than during that winter on the Rappahannock, after the unsuccessful battle of Fredericksburg.

Under the influence of the new commander there was a return of spirits and confidence, and the army was soon in a fit condition for another struggle with the enemy.

Following March 19th, we had three days of rain and snow and a high wind. On the 19th, I was directed to report the number of bibles in the company and I was surprised to find so many. I still have in my possession the one given me by my sister-in-law, Mrs. Mary S. Wright, and which I carried with me in all my service.

On Monday, March 23, we were delighted to see the sun and feel its warmth. That day there was an order to store all extra clothing and material, and get it ready at once to send away. This set us to speculating about the next move—as to where we would go and how soon.

On the last day of the month, it was pleasant again, and we had a battalion drill and a dress parade. The next day was "All Fool's Day," and the usual jokes were perpetrated or attempted. The story was circulated that Governor Ramsey was coming, and when he did not come it was considered one of the jokes of the day. The next day, he did come, made us a short speech at dress parade, and later came around and shook hands and talked with the boys.

On Friday, April 3, at the close of the review, the brigade was massed, and Gov. Ramsey made a short speech presenting us a new flag. Owing to the high wind, I could hear but very little of what he said, or the reply of Lieutenant Colonel Colvill, who was then in command of the regiment. It was a beautiful silk flag, with the names of the battles inscribed upon it, "from the women of Minnesota to the regiment."

Before leaving for Washington that night, the Governor gave a short reception to the First Sergeants of the regiment, Capt. Nathan S. Messick having placed his tent at his disposal for that purpose. The Governor was a pleasant man to meet, said agreeable and flattering things to us all, and promised us his influence in the near future along the line of promotions, for which we were all looking. In my own case it was forgotten, or he was unable to accomplish it, and I believe that was the result in most other cases.

On Sunday, April 5th, there was a high wind and rain or snow all day, and Monday was of about the same kind—less the snow. I spent the most of these two days in my tent, wrapped in a blanket, reading "The Revelations of a Slave Smuggler," which Bill Smith of the 34th New York had loaned me. It was written by Phillip Drake and gave an account of the slave trade as carried on between the years 1816 and 1853. It presented the business of illicit importation of Negroes and selling them as slaves, as a system of deliberate robbery and murder at war with everything good and fair.

On Tuesday the weather was so much improved that we had dress parade at night, and there was an order for a big review to be given before the President the next day. The papers had reports of the investigations on the 'conduct of the War' by a congressional committee.[1] It was depressing to read, because it showed such a lack of harmony between the civil and the military leaders. Almost invariably

1. In December 1861, the Senate and House set up a seven-man Joint Committee on the Conduct of the War. Dominated by Radical Republicans critical of Lincoln, the committee's investigation of Fredericksburg was leaked to the press in January 1863; Stephen W. Sears, *Chancellorsville* (Boston: Houghton Mifflin, 1996), 11, 12.

one or the other failed to make connections in carrying out plans as agreed upon. Our chaplain told us not long ago that we "must do all we could, and then trust in God for a right result, which would be sure to come." Unless there was more united action than appeared to be in the prosecution of the war, only God's almighty power could bring the results we desired.

On April 8, 1863, the troops were stirring early and marched to the vicinity of the reviewing grounds in the rear of the Lacy and the Phillips houses, but it was noon before all had arrived, and formed for the march. We wore our best clothes, and had everything in the best shape we could because we wanted to look well and march well before the President, and it is not saying too much to assert that we did both.

The President, Gen. Hooker, the corps and division commanders with their numerous staffs and orderlies, rode by us; all richly dressed and finely mounted. The President rode a large bay, with a military saddle and ornamented blanket—but he was in plain citizen's dress and wore a tall hat. With him were his two sons: Robert in cadet uniform[2] and Tad in some fancy dress, riding a pony. Gen. Hooker rode his white horse. He was a splendid-looking man, on a horse or on his feet, clean-shaven (except some little places under his ears), but he had a very red face. We passed in review, closed en masse in column of division—as it would have taken many hours to have passed in fours. At the reviewing stand, Mrs. Lincoln sat in an ambulance and looked smiling and happy; but of course she was not (as her husband seemed) so care-worn; and it was said that Major Todd of the Confederate army, of whom we hear occasionally, was her brother.

It was almost dark when we got back to camp—and most of them had much farther to march than we did. It had been the greatest parade we ever took part in or saw, and the marching and the music were very good, but all movements were necessarily in close order to get through before night.

Sunday, April 12, was beautiful. We had inspection, and the chaplain (F. A. Conwell) preached twice, and we sat on the ground around him like a lot of Sioux. His subject was about loving one another and, as he explained it, it included those fellows across the river that butchered so many of our comrades last winter. I did not really hate them but I was of the opinion that I did not love them very much, though I did not know them. I certainly had a pretty strong aversion to the system of slavery which they represented, and an emphatic objection to the division of the country which they were trying to bring about. I did not desire to hurt them for any personal reason, but if they persisted in trying to divide the country, if opportunity offered I should certainly try to kill them. Of course, I did not wish to do this, but there did not seem to be any other way.

2. Wright appears to be in error. Other accounts note that Tad Lincoln was present but fail to mention Robert. Robert Lincoln was a student at Harvard from 1860 to 1864, which sparked some public criticism. Robert joined General Grant's staff in January 1865.

On Monday morning, much of our cavalry and the horse artillery was moving to our right, followed by a train of pack-mules. That afternoon we had an inspection of arms and ammunition, and it was understood that the army was soon to move. As we later knew, such was the plan; and the cavalry under Stoneman was to cut the railroads in Lee's rear, after passing his left; and the infantry to follow it with an attack on the left flank and rear. This was undoubtedly a good plan if promptly executed, but it was delayed by heavy rains and floods.

On the 14th, thinking that the army would soon be on the move, I procured a pass, and some of us went to see the Red Wing boys in the First Company of Sharpshooters. We found them well and in good spirits, expecting orders to move very soon. Besides our old friends in this company, we met another Red Wing boy, Otis Smith, a brother of C. J. F. and Ed, who was an officer in a company of New Hampshire sharpshooters in the Second Berdan.

When we returned that night, we learned that preliminary orders had been received looking to an early movement. We were to pack all clothing not worn—except a shirt, drawers, and stockings; and in place of clothing we were to carry five days' field rations in addition to the usual three. This part of the order was to be complied with at once, awaiting the order to move. This made us understand that the beginning of the campaign was near, and that we were only waiting for the roads to get hard enough to be reliable. The cavalry had been out two days; and considerable firing had been heard, which indicated that they had already found the enemy; and we were expecting to be started to their support at any hour of the day or night.

It was a beautiful spring evening when we answered the last roll call for the day and went to our little tents. Before morning we were waked by a roaring wind and a pouring rain, which continued for more than 24 hours, flooding all of the low country. It was three days before the weather settled. Meantime, the cavalry crossed the river, found and fought a portion of the enemy, driving them back on Brandy Station—when, on account of the roads and overflowed streams, they retired to the northerly side of the Rappahannock to await better conditions.

On Sunday, April 19th, the weather was fair again, and we had the usual inspection and services. We hear it frequently said that "the army did not observe the Sabbath," but this is only measurably true. An effort was certainly made to observe it, as far as might be, and still meet the conditions the service and the enemy imposed upon us. Gen. McClellan issued an order, and not long after he was relieved President Lincoln issued another; and the purport of both was to dispense with all unnecessary work. Of course, there were violations of these orders just as there are violations of the laws in civil life. There are times in sickness, fires, floods, and other emergencies when people believe it right to do what seems to be required regardless of the day. So it is when a battle is on. There does not seem to be a resting place until it is decided. Whenever the situation permitted there was always an opportunity for religious services, and many men improved and enjoyed those privileges.

On the 20th, another violent storm swept that section of the state, and it was five days more before the weather was fair again. On Wednesday Lieut. Ball returned, and on the same day Col. Morgan left the camp, sick. On Saturday, Apr. 25, we received four months' pay, and there lacked but a few days of being two more due us. We were paid in "greenbacks," as the government promises to pay were called—which, as compared with gold, were worth at that time less than fifty cents on the dollar. There was always rejoicing when the paymaster visited us. The majority of the boys sent their money home, under the "allotment system"; some spent it at the sutlers; and some risked it at poker and chuck-a-luck, and the majority were broke within a fortnight after the paymaster was gone.

Sunday morning, our camp was aroused by an indescribable confusion of noises in the camp of the Seventh New York Infantry, not far from our camp. Some of us went nearer to learn what it was and were told it was ordered home for discharge. It was a two years' regiment, principally Germans, and they were giving expression to their satisfaction by talking, shouting, and singing in their native tongue. These usually stolid Teutons were voluble as Frenchmen. We could not understand their words but we comprehended their feelings. There were 35 of these two years' regiments—all but two from New York—in the Army of the Potomac, whose time expired before June, and their going took 16,000 or 17,000 seasoned and trained men out of the Army of the Potomac. The Thirty-fourth New York Infantry of our brigade was one of these two years' regiments, but it did not leave us until later.[3]

As all of the seriously sick had been sent away to Aquia Creek, our chaplain preached morning and evening in one of the empty hospital tents, as the weather was still unfavorable. George L. Lewis, one of the men of the company who had been detailed with the Signal Corps since its organization, visited the company and talked about transferring to the Signal Corps now that it was made a separate organization.[4] He regretted to leave the company but was barred from promotion where he was if he did not transfer. He was a splendid fellow, and we were sorry to have him go but could not blame him for going and making the most of his opportunities.

3. On May 1, feeling their two years was up, six companies of the 34th New York Regiment refused to obey orders. When division commander John Gibbon confronted them, they changed their minds, but Gibbon relieved Alfred Sully of command because Sully had not been able to discipline them; Sears, *Chancellorsville*, 216–17.

4. Headed by Colonel Albert James Myer, the Signal Corps's telegraph operators were sorely needed in the upcoming campaign in the Wilderness, where flag signaling was very difficult. Their system did not meet the test, and civilian U.S. Military Telegraph operators took over; Sears, *Chancellorsville*, 194–96.

On Monday, the 27th, troops were passing the camp all day, moving up the river; and at night the First and Third Divisions of our corps had orders to march at daylight the next morning; while our division was directed to hold itself in readiness, waiting the order to move. The next morning was dark and rainy but we packed our knapsacks, with rations and ammunition as directed, but left our tents standing while the other two divisions moved off in the storm. Troops were passing all day in the rain, and the deserted camps about us looked lonesome. But there was plenty of wood now from the wreckage of the camps, although the need of it was not great since the weather was warmer.

The cavalry had begun a movement around the enemy's left, and were later followed by the Fifth, Eleventh and Twelfth Corps, and the First and Third divisions of our corps, the Second. At the same time the First, Third and Sixth Corps demonstrated against the enemy's right while our division (Second of the Second Corps) held its position on the Stafford Hills as far as possible—to screen the movement and confuse the enemy. It was a matter of uncertainty to us whether the main attack was to be made above or below us, and it was not until the night of the 30th of April when the Third Corps passed to our right that it became apparent that the principal attack was likely to be on that side of us. This opinion was confirmed when the First Corps followed it on the 1st of May, leaving the Sixth Corps across the river below the town, and our division still in its camp on the northerly side of the river.

It was now certain the campaign was on and fighting imminent. The camp of our division being the most conspicuously located was supposed to be the reason we remained in position; and we endeavored to have things go on as usual at the front; but as we covered the front of the whole corps now, we had to send out about three times the number of men. In the afternoon we sent a detail to the railroad station, unloading supplies. There was also considerable artillery firing on the river, below us as well as above us. Some of it had been directed at the station but without damage, as we learned from the detail.

It was also reported that the First and Sixth Corps were at the river below with batteries in position, and that it was their batteries that were replying to those of the enemy. Early Wednesday morning there was a lively bombardment below us, while the usual fog was too thick to see through. As we learned later, under cover of this a bridge was laid, and a part of the Sixth Corps crossed over and took position to defend the crossing.

This was the second anniversary of our muster into the U.S. service, and a detail spent the day on picket, in a drizzling rain, listening to the distant booming of cannon far away on the right and the nearer thunder of the Sixth Corps's guns below us—accompanied, as the latter was at intervals, by lively skirmish firing. Those of us not detailed passed the day in the camp, listening also, and speculating, as men will on what was being attempted, and its probable outcome.

Somehow there was a strong feeling of confidence in Gen. Hooker, and good results were hopefully looked for. We knew that the cavalry, which had gone out a fortnight before, had remained somewhere up the river; and we were told that three brigades were in the vicinity of Warrenton. It was the theory that this cavalry, with other forces, was to get between Lee and Richmond, cut off supplies by destroying roads and bridges, and thus compel him to weaken his front or withdraw from the river. This was the theory, and it appeared attractive, but we had learned that it was one thing to plan and another to execute.

Thursday morning, April 30th, before the picket details went out, we had our bi-monthly muster, and then those not on duty waited and listened as on the day before.

The fog lifted early that morning, and there was a better view of things than we had had for some days. We saw that there was a considerable force of our troops across the river about the mouth of Deep Run. There was artillery firing both above and below us, and just before night there was an interchange of musketry below the town. Our position on the heights overlooking the town (Fredericksburg) was favorable for observation and an interesting one, and we were greatly interested in all that we could see or hear—and were busy guessing at the rest of it. Our strategists—and we had them in Company F—were divided in opinion as to whether the main attack was to be made from above or below us, with the majority in favor of the former because the greater portion of the army had gone in that direction.

At night we had our orders to be ready to move at daylight and were ready at the time with everything packed but our tents, which were to stand until the order came to move. The fog was thick that morning, and it was 9 o'clock before we could see into the valley. Meantime, we were told that there was severe but successful fighting up the river, but we had no details. Our tents remained standing; the pickets were relieved with fresh details; and the day of May first passed like the one before it—watching and waiting. We seemed to be held in reserve or for some special purpose, but we did not doubt but we would be used somewhere before the movement was over.

The day was followed by a beautiful moonlit evening, and some of us went to a favorable point to look over the river and into the town, and sat for a time and talked of what might happen before another night—for we felt certain that we should be somewhere else. There had been heavy cannonading on both sides of us, and we supposed a severe battle had been fought above us but we were without positive information—but the movement was said to be a success.

We passed another night in our tents and were out of them before daylight, with everything ready for the march but stripping the covers from our tents. Matters went on much as on the two previous days, with cannonading on both sides of us, and an occasional shell directed at our camp. Just before night there was a lively artillery fire and some brisk skirmishing between the Sixth Corps, across the river below the town, and the enemy confronting it. This lasted until it was so dark that the firing made interesting fireworks, which absorbed our attention until it ceased. When it had ceased we were conscious of distant and rapid firing somewhere on our right, but there were no distinct explosions—only the smothered roar and jar of far-away firing, which we could *feel* after we had laid down in our tents.

Reports during the afternoon had represented the movement on the right as a splendid success, and we were hopeful of the best results. We did not know then that that dull roar of the battle which came so mildly to our ears spelled disaster to an army corps and a serious misfortune to the right wing of the army.[5] We had no suspicion then that the new commander—after such a fine display of field tactics, which deceived his enemy and placed more than half of his army on his left flank ready to attack him—had lost the initiative; been placed on the defensive; allowed his own right flank to be turned, attacked, crushed, and forced back on the remaining portions in a way that came critically near wrecking the whole line.

All unconscious of this stunning blow, we slept the sleep of youth and weariness—for we were really tired. It is true ours had been the easy part so far as personal danger and great effort were concerned, but they were not hours of pleasure or restfulness. One-half of the men had been on duty all of the time since our other two divisions had left; and four days of waiting, *for anything*, usually bring tiresome hours and willingness to end them in action—even though action might bring something of hazard with it. Aside from all personal considerations, we were deeply anxious, for we fully realized that the fate of our country was involved in the movement, and that present failure might mean permanent misfortune.

When we laid down in our tents we were told not to remove our clothing. It was scarcely midnight, and we seemed to have just fallen asleep when we were called and directed to wake the boys and form the company. In a very brief interval the men were up; had taken down and folded their tent cloths; placed them and their blankets in their knapsacks; put on their war harness; and answered to their names; and were ready to march.

After reporting the company, there was a brief wait before forming the regiment, and the men, resting at will, talked quietly in little groups or stood apart in silence. There was no attempt at hilarity or levity. I do not know just what thoughts were traversing the minds of my comrades as they stood there in the mist and the moonlight, at midnight, waiting for orders that might open—for them— the portals of eternity before sunrise. These thoughts certainly were not humorous but ranged from the Rappahannock to the northern border and probably included themselves and the loved ones they had left some two years since.

5. That evening of May 2, Stonewall Jackson's daring flank attack had surprised and almost destroyed Oliver O. Howard's Eleventh Corps, which held the Union right flank. This placed Hooker's position at Chancellorsville in extreme danger.

Wherever their thoughts may have been turning or whatever may have been their tenor, there was no time wasted upon them. Attention was called. We marched out of the little company street, joined the regiment, which took its place with the brigade, and marched to a point near the Lacy House where the division was assembling. Here we halted, with orders to rest at will, make no noise, and light no fires.

Instead of our division going either up or down the river to join either the right or the left—as we had supposed we might—preparations were being made to lay a bridge near where we had crossed on the 11th of December, 1862. It was evident we were to try to cross there again. It seemed an absurdity that our division alone should enter the city and try to do, now, what nearly half of the army had failed to accomplish a few months before—even though their force was weakened, as was supposed.

It was quickly learned that this time it was our brigade that was to lead, and we were to move as soon the preliminaries were all arranged. It was not a matter about which we had a choice, but we accepted the situation and went cheerfully and hopefully about what seemed a forlorn and almost hopeless undertaking. The Nineteenth Maine—having been detached two days before to guard the telegraph lines—was not with us, and the remaining four regiments were directed to send one officer and 25 men each to act as sharpshooters and, if necessary, to cross in the pontoons and drive away the enemy from the other shore.

A call for volunteers was made and quickly filled—Lieutenant Hezekiah Bruce, Corporal Charles W. Merritt, and Private James W. Imeson going from Company F.

Before we reached the Lacy House, we had heard firing on the front of the Sixth Corps, below the town; and it had continued at short intervals since, with increased force at each new outburst. It was known that the Sixth Corps had met with determined opposition when they had laid their bridge a few days before, and that it was only accomplished after a loss of about 60 men. Almost at this same point, on the 11th of December, it had cost some hundreds. Nothing less was expected now. That they did not have to cross the river in open boats in the face of a lively rifle fire from concealed men and engage in a deadly struggle with them (if they succeeded in getting there) was their good fortune.

As it seemed to us when the incident was closed—and ever since—the Fates of War, who had dealt very harshly with us on previous occasions and did again later, were very kind to the Old First both times at Fredericksburg. Each time there the situation seemed fraught with great risk, but the outcome was with but slight loss. We never could account for it except on the theory that it just happened that way, but we have always felt grateful.

Soon after the volunteers from our regiment went to join the others from the brigade, we marched off of the heights and took a position near the water, in readiness to support and cover them with the best fire possible. There was a mist on the hills, but down by the river there was a thick fog through which we could see but a few feet. (When on the heights, it had looked like snow in the moonlight, but down below the moon could not be seen through it.)

When in place we could see nothing, and, listening intently, we could hear nothing near us but the gurgling of the fast-flowing water and the barking of some dogs over in the town. Farther away, below the town, the intermittent skirmishing was continued, and the roar of a cannon was occasionally added. Then we heard the engineers coming and placing their boats into the river, and we waited— momentarily expecting to see the glimmer of fire through the fog and hear the zip of bullets. Not a flash was seen through the fog, nor a shot from the other shore.

The work progressed quietly and rapidly, without hindrance. It was not yet believed that it would be completed without opposition, but it was.

Meantime, a balmy spring morning had dawned. It was rapidly growing light, and the firing below the town was increasing to the proportions of serious fighting—judging by the noise. As soon as the bridge was passable, the 100 volunteers deployed into the town and were followed by the rest of the brigade and the division. As we marched out through the town, the sun was just rising and its warming rays beginning to dissipate the mists so we could see more plainly. We gained the outer edge of the town without being challenged by a single shot.

Our division crossed into the town and took a position on the right of the Sixth Corps, in front of the heights back of the city. The Sixth Corps was at the same time advancing through the lower part of the town and forcing itself into a position near enough to attempt to assault the heights. This was the situation when we had passed through the town.

It was known that a large portion of the enemy had been withdrawn, but it was not definitely known then what portion was then before us. (As we now know, it was Early's Division and Barksdale's Brigade of McLaws's Division, with Wilcox in support; the whole force numbering 12,000 to 15,000 men, holding the lines held by Longstreet and Jackson in December 1862.) The movement of our brigade to the right was intended to—and no doubt did—further weaken the force of the enemy at the point of attack.

It was between 10 and 11 o'clock; the fog was all gone; the sun was shining hotly with scarce a breeze stirring. The Sixth Corps had at last fought itself into favorable positions on the Telegraph and Plank roads and the valley of Hazel Run, and had two storming columns ready to test the strength of the enemy's lines on Marye's Hill. We had been lying for some time in the deserted Confederate entrenchments at the river, a target for their artillery, waiting and expectant.

The enemy had almost ceased to fire on us, and we were considering our whole movement a feint, when orders came to return into the town. We started at once by the left flank at the double-quick. We were scarcely moving before we heard a crashing roar of artillery and roaring crashes of musketry, followed by continuous discharges. These might have continued for ten minutes, possibly more, when we heard the cheering, and recognized it as a Union cheer and knew that it meant that matters were going favorable to our side.

At the time we were passing through the town and had just turned to the right on the street crossing the canal. Here we halted for a few minutes and unslung knapsacks, placing a guard over them, and then crossed the canal, passed up the heights and joined the Sixth Corps, which had dislodged the enemy, capturing artillery and prisoners. The enemy was getting away as fast as possible, returning a scattering fire, and detachments were pursuing them and picking up prisoners. It was a fine opportunity for cavalry but unfortunately there was none there. We took no more important part in this than to follow in support.

This break through their lines had divided their forces. Early, holding their right—not being directly attacked—had retired on the Bowling Green Road, going southeasterly; while Barksdale and Wilcox had retreated along the Plank Road to join Lee's forces in front of Hooker. Sedgwick's orders were to proceed through Fredericksburg and connect with Hooker's left—apparently assuming that the town and heights had been evacuated or that the opposition would not be strong enough to hinder him.

After moving out some miles and picking up many prisoners, there was a halt for a brief rest and to close up the lines. At this time Gen. Sedgwick directed Gen. Gibbon to return at once with his division to the north side of the river and use it to cover the bridges (which he had left spanning the river), his trains (then below the town), and trains and property generally on that side (which included the telegraph lines, railroad, trains, and stores at Aquia Creek). In obedience to this order, our brigade started at once and marched at quick time back into the town.

The day had been very warm for the season, and we were pretty tired when we got back into the town, where we halted for a few minutes rest and resumed our knapsacks. Slinging our knapsacks, we passed through the town, crossed the river, and went onto the heights near the Lacy House.

While still in the town we heard continued and rapid discharges of artillery, and when we halted on the hills we could see the smoke and hear both artillery and musketry. We did not remain long here, but it was long enough for us to see that the Sixth Corps had found the enemy in force before it could unite with the rest of the army under Hooker, and that it was then engaged in a savage fight on the hills about Salem Church.

Our regiment was detached from the brigade and, with Capt. George W. Adams's battery, was sent to guard the lower bridges. This was the point at which the Sixth Corps had crossed and, if not able to follow the corps, its trains must recross here. Over these bridges the wounded and dead in the morning's fight—and there was more than 1,000 of them—were then being brought to the railroad station. Just as we started for the lower ridges some clouds which had been gathering passed over and gave us a shower bath which, as the day had been warm, was not particularly disagreeable.

It was almost dark when we arrived at our destination, and we at once selected positions and made preparations to defend ourselves and the bridges if attacked. As it grew dark, we could still hear the sound of fighting on hills five or six miles away where the Sixth Corps was. Beside the natural interest for their success and welfare, we were particularly anxious for the 25 volunteers from our own regiment we now supposed were with them.

As soon as the regiment was stationed, and details made for picketing the bridge and river, we hastened to make coffee and then to prepare for the night, which from necessity was to be shelterless. We had been on our feet more than 20 hours and marched fully 20 miles since the previous midnight and were tired enough to sleep anywhere. There were but a few men left in the company after the details were made, and we were posted on the hill near one of the guns—Lieut. Ball and myself occupying the same blanket.

It was midnight or later, and we had been wakened and moistened by one or two showers, when we were aware that someone was coming and inquiring for the regiment. It proved to be Lieut. Bruce and his party returning, and we were delighted to find all were able to return. They told briefly of the day's experiences and their being sent back with prisoners gathered up in the pursuit, and their search for us after disposing of them. They had left the Sixth Corps before its fighting in the late afternoon had begun and knew nothing of the results.

It was not long before I slept again, and when I next awoke it was just coming light, and Lieut. Ball was sitting up on the blankets with his field glass in his hands. It was foggy as usual—but not quite so thick—and the hills across the river and the valley were dimly visible. The lieutenant said that he could see some men on the hills and requested me to look at them through the glass. I did so and could see a number of men sitting on their horses in a road nearly opposite us. They were faced towards us, and it was certain that our side of the river was a matter of interest to them, as they seemed to be watching it.

It was not yet fairly daylight, and that and the fog prevented seeing anything plainly, but we had no good reason to expect any of our own troops to be coming from that direction. Still, it might be a party of our cavalry who had been scouting, but if so why should they not come on without so much caution? These and other questions were asked as we observed them and tried to decide whether they were friends or enemies. If friends they could easily come nearer if they desired; and if enemies they must advance before they could harm us.

For the present, they were watched by a few and the others turned their attention to getting their breakfasts. When in the field, the intelligent soldier learns to adapt himself to conditions. He cooks and *eats* as soon after getting up in the morning or during a halt after a march, as opportunity offers. If he neglects this, some emergency or unexpected duty may indefinitely postpone his meal. I recall several occasions where we had to eat half-cooked rations hurriedly when forming and one when a soldier tried to save his coffee by drinking it as he started to march; and *I* not only scalded *my* mouth but spilled some of it *outside* of my neck and blistered my breast.

As we busied ourselves about the fires cooking, we looked and listened. We could hear firing up the river and a great cloud of smoke was hanging over the range of hills where Sedgwick's troops were seen the night before. In that distance, as yet, we could see nothing but the slowly rising smoke, but we felt certain this came from fighting as well as campfires.

Before our coffee was boiling, another squad of horsemen was reported, by those with glasses, to be watching us from the hills opposite. But with the naked eye at that distance we could see very little—and nothing plainly.

We had not finished the morning meal (and we were not long about it either) before a larger body of horsemen came down from the hills on the road from Hamilton's Crossing and rode towards Fredericksburg near the line of the railroad.[6] The sun was now shining and the fog disappearing. This body of mounted men was but dimly seen through the fog when it got on lower ground, but its direction could be seen as it moved towards the town until it was lost in the valley of Hazel Run.

A little later we saw a few men riding along the heights and another party on the Telegraph Road.

Very soon after, all doubts were dissipated by seeing the head of a column of infantry on the Bowling Green Road coming from the direction in which Early's Division had retreated. Those with glasses declared they carried Confederate flags and wore gray uniforms. The head of the column disappeared in the Hazel Run Valley and a little later reappeared on the heights and halted in the rear of the fortifications from which the enemy had been driven less than twenty-four hours before. They soon had artillery in position and, by way of a greeting, threw a few shells to our side of the river, but they were aimed at a point above Falmouth.

As we now know, these were Early's troops which had retreated 6 or 7 miles and—finding that they were not pursued—had halted and finally returned, reoccupied the heights, and taken up a position to threaten the town, to cut Sedgwick's communications, and to place him between the attacking forces.

It was mortifying to us to see the position that it had cost more than a thousand men to get Sunday morning go back to the enemy on Monday morning without a struggle. And when we recall that nearly 7,000 men had been sacrificed in December in a fruitless endeavor to gain it, it seems as if someone who should have directed had failed to understand the situation, been negligent—or the situation was already more critical on that part of the field than we then supposed.

6. The Richmond, Fredericksburg and Potomac Railroad entered Fredericksburg from the south, crossed the Rappahannock, and then became the Union supply line as it ran back to Aquia Creek.

When our division commander, General John Gibbon, understood the situation, he took prompt measures to protect the bridges, defend the line of the river, and remove trains and materiel from the town and from the other side below it—including the captured property and the wounded.

It was not long after Early got possession of the heights again before he had posted pickets facing the town and then started a part of his men to harass the rear of the Sixth Corps and make what trouble he could in that direction.

That portion of the brigade still in the town prepared to defend it—four companies of our regiment being sent back to assist—until the wounded stragglers, trains, and materiel could be gotten out. When not engaged in other duties, we rested on the bluffs.

There was fighting on the front and flanks of the Sixth Corps, and towards night it was apparent that it was being forced back or was withdrawn. Nothing could be plainly seen or positively known. It was, perhaps, about 5 o'clock when the increased firing indicated that one side or the other was forcing things to a crisis. As we now know, Sedgwick had made good use of the time when there was only slack fighting—partly changing front, contracting his line, and getting his flanks to rest on the river—so that he was prepared for the final attack and gave his enemies a costly repulse. A bridge had been laid at Banks's Ford and artillery posted, which did good service protecting Sedgwick's flanks. Over this bridge the Sixth Corps retired that night and took position on the northerly side of the river. During the day the trains and materiel left behind by the Sixth Corps were transferred to the north side of the river over the bridge we were guarding or the one above it through the town.

At dark that night this lower bridge was taken up and loaded on the wagons, and two companies were sent to picket the river below. About ten o'clock the remaining companies, including Company F, were ordered to the upper ridge. It was near 12 o'clock when we arrived, and two companies were posted in the rifle-pits near the water and the other two held in reserve by the battery on the hill. This position we held until about noon the next day.

When we arrived, wagons and wounded men were coming over from the town, and this continued until near morning, by which time all materiel and all of the men and the skirmishers had crossed. It was fairly daylight, with the usual mist over the water and the low land, when the skirmishers withdrew from the town; the anchors were taken up; and the farther end of the bridge loosened; and it was allowed to swing with the current.

It was but a little later when some of the enemy appeared on the other side—but dimly seen through the fog—and inquired when we were coming again. They were promptly assured that we would 'return to fight some other day,' and they said they would be there to welcome us.

Both sides kept well under cover, but not a shot was fired by either, although in fair range. There was some artillery firing about this time—and later—by batteries on both sides, over the town, but neither party fired into it.

Camp Vt. Min.
Near Station
May. 6th 1863

Dear Mother,

You have probably heard of the hard fighting along the line of the Rappahannock, and will be anxious to hear from me; so I improve the earliest opportunity to assure you that all is well with me, individually, and would to God I could say the same of our army, and our cause. After a weeks hard labor and fighting, in a series of fierce battles, the army is returning to its old camps. What has been our loss, as a whole, I do not know, or how near we have

First page and letterhead, showing the Union shield uniting all sections of the country; James A. Wright to his mother, Amelia Wright, May 6, 1863

When the boats were all on the wagons, we were relieved from further duty at this point and sent back down the river below the old railroad bridge.

That night and the next day we were posted on the river, not far from the station, and saw considerable of the transfer of the wounded to the trains which took them to the boats at Aquia Creek. The troops were returning to their former camps. Many wounded able to make their own way came in with them, as they had been coming for days, and long trains of ambulances brought many more of the helpless. The picture of these poor, blood-stained sufferers from the fierce encounters in the woods and ravines over the river is not one to be recalled without feelings of revulsion. We remained on the river for the next two days, and they kept coming in a seemingly endless stream and were sent away by trains to the boats on the Potomac.

It rained nearly all of the time and sometimes poured in floods. On the last of these two days, the storm had ceased. On Saturday, May 9th, the weather came off fine and warm: the grass was growing, leaves expanding, birds singing, and all nature reviving and rejoicing. By this time the weary and decimated regiments were back in or near their old camps, recuperating, but it cannot be said that they were rejoicing. However, the troops from the Chancellorsville campaign—disastrous as it had been—were less discouraged than after the Fredericksburg fighting in December (with the possible exception of the Eleventh Corps), because they had had a better chance to strike back at the enemy.

The loss of the First Regiment was very light, being but 9 men wounded—none fatally. Company F had but one man wounded, Almeron Davis. He had been wounded at Flint Hill on September 2, 1862, and now that he was hit again, the boys said he was forming the *habit* of being wounded and he was cautioned that it was a "*dangerous* habit," but he did not quit it until after Gettysburg, where he was again hit.

We considered ourselves very fortunate that we had got off with such slight loss on the last two occasions, and our good luck was frequently a subject of conversation. I recall one occasion when Sergeant Phil Hamline, who had an infinite trust in the guiding and protecting care of Deity, expressed his belief that we had been "providentially" shielded from losses and hardships in the last two movements.

Corporal 'Len' Squire, whose philosophy of life ran on different lines (akin to those of the man that asserted his belief that "what was to be would be and what *was not to be was to come yet*"), dissented from this opinion, and declared it was all "just luck." He said we had "skirted the edge of hell twice and only been *singed a little* but, next time, we might be *burned*."

On May 6 General Hooker issued a pompous congratulatory order to the army in which he put the best face possible on affairs, which, perhaps, was wise.

Close the column, lengthen the step, quicken the time

MAY-JUNE 1863

BESIDES THE LOSSES OF MEN in battle, sickness, disorganization, and the breaking down of men from the hardships, which are always attendant upon great campaigns—there were other causes to weaken the strength of the Army of the Potomac. The time of some 30,000 two years' men and nine months' men expired in May and early June, and the going of these—added to the losses of Fredericksburg and Chancellorsville—was taking away fully one-half of the fighting strength of the old Army of the Potomac. Every dictate of reason and common sense demanded that the Army of the Potomac, and every other army fronting an enemy, should be kept up to its full strength, and all losses should be replaced as soon as possible. This was not done. An effort to recruit for our badly depleted regiment failed. So far as I know no recruits came to the regiment in the spring of 1863; at least there was not one joined Company F.

Sunday, May 17th, was another beautiful and balmy day, and we had the usual morning inspection and after it religious services. These were held in front of brigade headquarters at 10:30, and all of the brigade was assembled there. That afternoon and evening there were services at the Lacy House, and interest in the occasion was materially increased as it was understood that ladies were to be present and take part in the exercises.

It was quite a rarity for the boys in blue to see a woman in that section that did not scowl at them, or otherwise give expression to unamiable feelings, and their presence no doubt attracted many. The women present were Mrs. Lee, Mrs. Harris, and Dr. Mary Walker, and each of them talked briefly about the work they were trying to do for the sick and suffering.[1] They had come there, from Philadelphia perhaps, to aid in the care of the wounded in the recent fighting, and Dr. Walker, who later gained much unenviable notoriety from her eccentric action, had established a temporary hospital on the grounds of the Lacy House. With the assistance of Mrs. Harris, Mrs. Lee, and some other merciful and self-sacrificing

1. Mary W. Lee founded the Union Refreshment Saloon in Philadelphia and was a nurse for the U.S. Sanitary Commission. Eliza Harris worked as a nurse, cook, and fundraiser, also for the Sanitary Commission. Dr. Mary Walker served as an army nurse until 1864 when she became the U.S. Army's first female assistant surgeon. A noted feminist, she became famous for wearing bloomers and, later, men's clothing.

women, much had been done to relieve the suffering of the wounded brought over from Fredericksburg.

Mrs. Lee, Mrs. Harris, and their assistants were a part of that numerous and noble association of women that are held in tender and grateful remembrance by all who come under their merciful ministrations. It was not often that they got so near to the fighting line, or remained so long at the front.

There was a story in circulation, I recall, that indicated that at least one of these women had fighting blood in her veins when roused to action. When the wounded were brought over from the Sunday morning fight at Fredericksburg, there were quite a number of the Confederate wounded brought with them, and they were all cared for together. Later when the women came to the hospital about the Lacy House, some Confederate women from Fredericksburg came over to help in caring for the wounded, and it was said they did good work, too, caring for Union and Confederate alike, but there was one exception.

One of the number was filled with such strong sentiments in favor of the Confederates that they dominated all other feelings. She lavished all her ministrations upon those with gray uniforms, which would have been permissible had she not taken pains to show her aversion for the wearers of the blue.

This was too much for the motherly Mrs. Lee (or Mrs. Harris, whichever it was) and she delivered a lecture on what she considered proper and improper conduct for a woman of Confederate sentiments in a Union hospital. This, of course, was disagreed with and resented by the southern woman, and a war of words followed. It was ended by the irate Union woman taking a piece of board from a cracker box and driving the undesirable attendant out of the tent, for which the wounded boys cheered her. A soldier escorted the offending woman across the river, which closed the incident.

On the 20th, Capt. Abraham Wright of the First Minnesota Sharpshooters and some of the men from his company came to visit their friends in Company F. It was a pleasure to meet them, and we dined together at Uncle Sam's expense, and spent some hours talking over old times, school friends, home affairs, and the possibilities of the future. We all had a tender spot in connection with our homes, and we could not talk of them without recognizing the cause of our separation from them, and the shadow of the war was over it all. We could not recall the names of old schoolmates without remembering those who had already been the victims of the war; and others who, like ourselves, had forfeited their future prospects in the cause of their country, and might at any time be called to give the last, full measure of devotion in its defense.

A little group of the Red Wing Boys sat on the terrace near the Lacy House, overlooking the battered town across the river, and talked of the war, thus far, and the prospects of coming campaigns, so far as we could guess them. Somehow—regardless of the hard blows, mishaps, and failures of the past—we managed to look hopefully to the future, and were ready and waiting to put it to the test of action whenever an order should come to move. Feeling that we were on the eve of important movements, we separated—not expecting to meet again before they developed in action. We had talked lightly of the possibilities of battle-wounds, capture, and death—with an assumed confidence we scarcely felt—and shook hands at parting, well knowing that there were many chances that we might never meet again.

Since the return from the last movement, the old status along the river had been resumed, with the Confederate pickets on one side and ours on the other, and only about 600 feet of fordable water between them. By mutual consent—without any formal agreement—there was no firing, and matters ran on as smoothly as the river.

Talking was prohibited and could not be indulged in openly, but there were frequent communications by means of little boats made of a bit of a board or a shingle, which, with a rudder and sail set at the right angles, would cross the stream with a favorable wind. In this way newspapers, coffee, tobacco, etc., were exchanged almost daily. In spite of orders, there was occasionally a bit of cheap talk going on between opposing pickets when there were no officers of either side present to stop it—just as youngsters will whisper in school when an opportunity presents itself and there is no one to prevent it.

This was very different from the early part of the war when the pickets shot at each other on sight, and killed one another whenever they could. Now that the men had had experience, and become seasoned soldiers, they had come to look upon this promiscuous shooting as useless killing, so far as results were concerned, and, except when a move was on warranting it, but little less than murder. The drawbacks to this more amicable practice, which we had come into without any prearrangement, were more opportunities for desertion, and there seem to be men always ready to desert any cause.

The Confederates had been taking a little advantage of this laxity to draw nets for fish, which seemed to be very plentiful in the river at that time. This was objected to by the Union commanders, on the ground that they were drawing supplies from the river under our guns; but they hesitated to forbid it as it was not considered important enough to hazard the lives of the pickets over. In drawing these nets, they waded into the water and usually removed their clothes.

This morning one of their men, when they were well out into the river, let go of the net and came to our side and said that he was not going back again. His hat was all of the clothing that he wore, but the pickets soon improvised a suit for him when it was apparent that he meant to stay. He said that he belonged to the 5th Mississippi and had been planning for some time to get away, and if permitted would take the oath of allegiance. He had in his hat some Richmond papers and about $150 in Confederate scrip. His companions had not tried to hinder his coming but called for him to return. As the man might be a spy—taking that method of getting into camp—he was turned over to the provost marshal and that was the last we heard of him.

A couple of days later one of the 52nd North Carolina came over—ostensibly to trade some tobacco for coffee—wading through the water to his neck. When safely on shore he waved his hand to his comrades on the other shore and told them that he was going to stay with the 'Yanks' awhile. They seemed very angry with him and threatened to shoot, but were warned by the pickets on our side not to begin it—and they did not. He also went into the hands of the 'provo'—as there was always a suspicion of insincerity attached to a desertion.

Just about this time, demands were made for men to fill the quotas of the artillery sufficiently to man their guns properly, and, as usual, details were made from the infantry for this purpose. This took two more men—Henry Burgtorf and Artemus L. M. Decker—from the company.

It is not possible that Company F started on the Gettysburg campaign with more than 2 officers and 32 men. The fighting strength of Company F could not have exceeded 32 rifles and 2 swords and was probably four or five rifles less than that number. Company F was only a fair sample of the other companies of the regiment, and of the other older regiments in the corps and army.

This shows very plainly the weakened condition of the army at that time, and it does not need an argument to show what a monumental blunder it was not to have kept the ranks of the old regiments filled. How much more crushing the blows given the Confederacy at Gettysburg might have been if there had been maximum numbers in the regiments which fought there, instead of the emaciated skeletons which the Union commanders were obliged to put into action?

Friday morning, June 5th, we had orders to hold ourselves in readiness to move promptly at command. Matters now assumed the added interest of an early movement. It was reported before night that the First Corps had left its camp, bag and baggage, and gone no one knew where—and other troops were getting ready to follow. The next day the Sixth Corps broke its camp, laid pontoons at Franklin's Crossing, whence they had crossed previous to the Chancellorsville campaign, and passed a part of the corps to the south side.

This, it was understood, was to ascertain definitely what forces were still in position on that side. This resulted in a lively cannonading, and some sharp skirmishing—enough to make it certain that there was a strong force in front of that part of the line. (We now know that Hill's Corps was there and that Ewell, who was moving towards Culpepper, was returned to supporting distance.)

Also, Gen. Hooker submitted a plan for crossing the army at this point and trying to turn Lee's right with his left, but it was not acceptable. The plan was turned down, wisely we presume, by President Lincoln—with a homely suggestion of what might happen. He said: "I would not take any risk of being entangled on the river, like an ox jumped half over a fence, and liable to be torn by dogs front and rear, without a chance to gore one way or kick the other."

Gen. Hooker was left to do other planning. As a prerequisite, he was attempting to keep tabs on Lee's movements and trying to fathom his purposes. While we of the ranks knew absolutely nothing of what the plans were, we all felt assured that something would *break loose*, somewhere, soon. We were expecting to get orders to change bases at any time.

Sunday, June 7, Capt. Ball complimented Company F on its appearance at the morning inspection and gave each one a pair of white gloves to be worn at dress parade that evening. So far as I can now recall, this was the first time that the company ever appeared with white gloves. There being no drill after the inspection and morning service, we were at liberty to follow our own inclinations. A number of us went to the terraces along the bluff in front of the Lacy House, where we could look over into the town and over the plain below it, where one division of the Sixth Corps was fronting a force of the enemy on their side of the river. There was some skirmishing and artillery firing at intervals all day. The rest of the day I spent in writing letters, as did many others.

One of the events was the going of the Thirty-fourth New York, which had served with us since the organization of the brigade at Camp Stone in the fall of 1861. It had not had our highest regard at its first coming and while we remained in camp. But when we had gone to the sterner work of actual fighting, it conducted itself with a gallantry that had promptly won our esteem, and they had maintained a reputation as steady and reliable fighters on many fields. They were mostly farmer boys, from Herkimer County, I think, and did not at first take kindly to the restraints and formalities of military and camp life, but they were the right kind of material and had made a record that entitled them to a vacation, now that their time had expired—being a two-year regiment.

We paraded to give them a formal farewell, marched with them to the depot, where we parted with mutual cheers and good wishes. As friends and comrades we regretted to part with them and would miss them. Their going left the old brigade weaker, instead of stronger, by the diminished number of their rifles in the next battle.

Saturday the 13th, it was apparent that our time of inaction was nearly at an end. Government stores were all sent off to the Potomac; the blacksmith and other shops were removed and all of the workmen with them; the stockades were emptied of the mules and the intelligent contrabands had gone with them, and everything pointed to an early 'change of base.'

Sunday, June 14th, dawned hot and close, and the morning light showed that the night had not been wholly a season of rest for many of the troops near us. The Sixth Corps had withdrawn from the south side of the river and taken up the bridges; and it and the other corps were moving or preparing to move. Our orders were to pack everything and hold ourselves in readiness to move—which we construed to be an assignment as rear guard, as had been the position of our division when McClellan changed his base on the Peninsula and when Pope retired from Manassas. Before 12 o'clock the others were gone, including our First and Third Divisions, and the last train had left for Aquia Creek.

No papers had reached us later than Friday morning's, and we were entirely ignorant then of the general situation. But we now know that all of the corps—or at least some portions of them—were on the move.

When the Sixth Corps left the river, men from our division covered the positions they had vacated. There were still some of the enemy to be seen on the other side, though there was little doubt the bulk of their force was gone.

As was usual under such conditions, those not required to be on duty gathered in little squads to discuss the situation as they understood it and guess at what they did not understand—which was a great deal. I remember well that for a long time that afternoon a little party of us lay on the bluff overlooking the town, and talked, as you might expect men to talk under such circumstances on the verge of important movements in which they felt their lives were involved.

I do not believe there was a single regret at going or any feeling like leaving home, though it was all of the home we had known for more than six months. There was a feeling of sadness—not to say horror—at the recollection of what we had seen and suffered since our coming and an anxious thought of what might be before us in the coming venture, which was tense with adverse possibilities.

From where we were, we could look over into the dirty and deserted streets of the war-wasted town of Fredericksburg. Behind us were the Stafford Hills, which at our coming had been crowned with woods, fields, and farmhouses; but now were bare and bald, denuded of fences and forests, and ornamented only by lonesome-looking houses and the wreckage of deserted camps. Before us ran the historic river with its burned bridges and bloody record. Beyond it the shattered town with its tenantless, shell-torn, half-burned houses. Then the plain where the loyal blood of so many Union soldiers had stained the December snow, and the hills from whose base, sides, and crests the 'lightnings of war' had shattered our lines and dotted the slope with stricken boys in blue.

The scene made an impressive picture of the cruel destructiveness of war. Surely secession had borne deceptive, bitter, and abundant fruit. Veritable 'Apples of Sodom' which had burst in blinding smoke or broke in ashes upon all who handled them, whether from choice or necessity. The citizens of Fredericksburg suffered much from the war, as did all living in the sections where great armies operated, and the northern soldiers sincerely sympathized with them.

We would have been very glad indeed if the noncombatants could all have been separated from the location and results of strife. People very naturally clung to their homes; commanders chose strategic, commanding, or available positions as their training, experience, judgment, or necessities dictated; and the property or life of an individual was as nothing compared to the results of a great battle. There was plenty of inspiration for moralizing in connection with army life, but dwelling upon them was generally (in a military sense) demoralizing or so considered.

It was getting late in the afternoon and the boys had started fires and were making coffee when an aide rode to the brigade headquarters nearby. A little later an order was sent to the commanders of regiments to hold their commands in readiness to form; company commanders were informed of it; and orderly sergeants communicated it to the men. We were only waiting for the order to fall in, and the men hastened their cooking and ate their suppers. Before this was finished, the other brigades were formed and ready to move.

Just at dusk the bugles broke the evening quiet along the river with the notes of the assembly. Companies formed, took their places in the regimental line, and marched to their positions in the brigade, which in turn followed the other two brigades, already gone. It was dark by the time we were fairly on the road—a warm, clear, starlit, summer evening.

We marched steadily and made fairly good time for four or five miles, when we overtook the rest of the division. It was halted, apparently waiting for us, and the men were lying beside the road—as it is the custom of soldiers when on a march to lie down whenever an opportunity offers. We, too, laid down to rest, though not yet very tired.

There were nearly 4,000 men, including the batteries, resting beside the road in the distance of a mile or less, but there was very little talking, and it seemed very quiet. Almost the only sounds we heard were the hooting of owls and the plaintive cries of whippoorwills and other night birds, with now and then the croaking of a frog or the barking of a dog. These were familiar sounds in Virginia at this season of the year when outside the radius of smoke and noise of the camps, and they were soothing us to sleep when the command, "Attention!" brought us to our feet and into line, waiting the command to move on.

We were surprised to learn that the leading regiment of the brigade was countermarching past us to the rear. In turn we followed after it, and the whole brigade tramped back to the river. Of course, we knew in a general way that we were sent back that we might have full knowledge of the situation—as there was no cavalry in the rear to give information—but we did not know then and do not yet know for what particular reason we made that ten-mile night march.

As soon as it was light, Monday morning, June 15th, we were called in and soon after started again on the road to Stafford Court House. The morning was hot and the march hurried, and we did not halt until we joined the division at Stafford Court House about 9 o'clock in the forenoon. Weary as we were, our first effort was to get our breakfasts, which were also our dinners. Then we sought the shade to sleep. We slept for some hours, until awakened, and again formed in line and the march was resumed. The mid-June sun was shining with intense rays from a clear sky and from about as near directly overhead as it gets in that latitude—making a sultry, summer afternoon. The calorific rays seemed to scorch and blister and burn, as if trying to rival a 'fiery furnace.'

It was one of the most heart-breaking marches of our experience, and many men wilted in the scorching heat and dust like mown grass. There were many prostrations—men staggering from the ranks and falling as if shot. There were a number of cases of fatal sunstroke, and some dying almost as quickly as if struck by a bullet in a vital part. All of the ambulances were filled with helpless men, and those left behind were coming in all of the first part of the night. The column halted late in the afternoon, and our division camped along a small stream an hour's march or so after crossing Aquia Creek.

This march was particularly trying to our brigade, as it had had an extra ten miles to march (going back to the river and returning) and but little rest or sleep for 24 hours. We were glad when the halt was ordered and lost no time making coffee and finding a place to spend the night. As the night was so warm we simply stretched out on the ground and slept. At three o'clock the reveille sounded; the regiments formed; and the march began. By eight o'clock we had passed Dumfries and halted at Quantico Creek. Here we got our breakfasts, drew two days' rations from some stores there, and rested about two hours.

The afternoon march was trying—though the heat was not quite so bad as the day before, as there was a breeze—but it was very severe and many prostrations. It was between 6 and 7 when we crossed the Occoquan at Wolf Run Shoals, below the mouth of the Bull Run, and went into bivouac. There was plenty of running water here and it was not long after the guns were stacked before the men were enjoying a bath, which was a real luxury after the march, the heat, and the dust.

Wednesday morning, June 17, we breakfasted before we marched. After marching 6 or 7 miles, our division turned to the left, going to the railroad at Sangster's Station, the first station south of Fairfax. Here we halted about three o'clock in three brigade lines. We remained in that position over night and the next day. One of the jokes of this bivouac was the catching of a tortoise, or land terrapin, and marking it "First Minnesota Regiment, July 17, 1861."

Friday morning, June 19, we were gladdened by the arrival of a mail and newspapers, the first for a week. The papers were filled with stories of raids of the Confederate cavalry into Maryland and Pennsylvania, but there was no positive knowledge of the actual location of the bulk of the Confederate infantry.

It was noon or after when the command was given to form and soon after we were moving. There was a delightful change in the temperature, and marching was only good exercise, compared with the laborious efforts in the extreme heat of the previous days. Between five and six we climbed the heights at Centreville and halted there, preparing to spend the night. We had made good time over the road and halted with every man in his place. This was our third time to camp here, and the boys cheered when they saw we were to camp on practically the same ground again.

Saturday morning, our division was waiting in bivouac, listening to the distant sound of artillery to the west and northwest until towards noon, when we got the order to prepare for the march and took down our shelters. A sutler of a battery was doing business there when we came and had promptly doubled his prices on our arrival. This had put a further strain on the usually tense relations between the army merchant and his transient customers. The delay in the march had added to the irritation, and left the men with nothing to do; while a 'diligent devil,' who is said to always find 'work for idle hands,' had been busy providing something.

Suddenly there was a disturbance in the crowd around the sutler's tent, and the guard there was promptly disarmed and dismissed by irate infantrymen. When this was observed by the men waiting near the gun stacks, there was a cry of "rally on the sutler" and a quick response. In an incredibly short time a rushing mob was focused on that sutler's tent. It had no more than gathered before it broke into fragments and dispersed. There was not much left for the sutler when it had gone; but a careful observer might have noticed that all who came away were not empty handed. I cannot now name any of Company F who were 'mixed up' in this affair, but I feel quite sure that it was represented.

Very soon after that, the bugles trilled attention, and the corps took up its march towards Thoroughfare Gap. Of course, I am not approving acts of that kind, as they were morally wrong, but no one need waste any sympathy on sutlers as a class, or this one in particular. He laid his case before the authorities, and an assessment was made on the division and taken out of the next payroll. That sutler made a 'quick sale' at a large profit.

We were marching over the same road on which we had left Centreville on the morning of July 21, 1861, but, instead of turning off to the right, we kept on the main road towards Gainesville and Warrenton. It was getting dark when we reached the crossing of Bull Run, and it was too dark to see anything before we had reached the scene of our first fight.

This was a disappointment to us as we had hoped to see it again—under less exciting conditions.

As we tramped along in the darkness and drizzle, we thought we could recognize the point where we had crossed the road 'going in,' but of this we could not be certain, as one could scarcely distinguish a man from a mule six feet away. It was after 12 o'clock that night when we reached Gainesville, where we halted by the roadside and slept as best we could until it was coming daylight. About ten o'clock on the morning of June 22, we reached the vicinity of Thoroughfare Gap.

Tuesday morning, June 23, Col. Colvill, then commanding the regiment, sent for me and informed me that he understood we were not likely to move that day (as there was an order for drawing rations that evening); and that he was planning to go to look over the Bull Run battlefield if he could get a pass; and invited me to go with him, as he did not wish to go unattended. This was an unexpected pleasure, and I at once asked and received permission to go. Others were planning to go also, but there was difficulty about getting horses and saddles, and only two besides the Colonel's were at the moment obtainable.

Mounted on these, Col. Colvill, Milton Bevans, and myself left the camp and rode through our Third Division. I had carried a rifle so long that it seemed like starting off bare-headed to go without it; and, though I was accustomed to the saddle, it had been so long since I had been astride of a horse that I felt really awkward.

At the pickets in the rear of the division, there was a question about allowing us to pass out, and we were obliged to ride to Gen. French's headquarters to settle it. There the officer on duty said that it was not safe to go without an escort; there was no cavalry at hand to go; and that the object was not worth sending one. We were about to give it up when it was suggested that "as the colonel had a pass he might go at his own discretion," but if he was "not back before sunset he would be considered as absent without leave."

Col. Colvill expressed himself as ready to assume all risks of that kind, and we were allowed to pass the pickets, but were cautioned to "keep an eye out for bushwhackers." When leaving camp, we had not considered there was much danger of these and had carried nothing more for weapons than cavalry pistols, and no one of the three had much skill or experience in their use.

Col. Colvill was mounted on his own horse, a splendid animal, and rode off at a gallop. Bevans and myself were not so well mounted, but we were able to follow and not get left. The warning at the picket line served to make us watchful, particularly in passing through Haymarket where, we were told, parties had frequently been fired on from the houses.

Between Haymarket and Gainesville we met a squadron of our cavalry, which had come through from Centreville that morning, and they reported that they had seen no enemy. This gave us a feeling of reasonable security, and we rode on through Gainesville and Groveton to the battlefield, which was about two miles beyond the latter place.

When the Sudley Spring Road was reached, we rode slowly and noted such points as we could remember. Some of the places were easily recognized, and about others there were some doubts as fences were gone and fields overgrown with weeds and briar. The bushes, too, had grown some in two years, and many of the trees had been cut.

After passing across the field and going to the place where Ricketts's and Griffin's batteries were posted, we went on farther towards the Stone Bridge and stopped at a house to try to get some dinner. There were only women and children there—some white and some black, and I cannot now say how many—but there was a promise of something to eat other than army rations if we would pay for it. We decided to wait the hour or so it would take to prepare it.

Col. Colvill went inside and chatted with the women while 'Mit' and I stayed outside, watching and allowing the horses to eat grass, of which there was an abundance about the house.

The dinner provided was hot biscuit, ham and eggs, fried, and there was plenty of it—which was unexpected and satisfactory. The colonel had his dinner in the house, *at a table*, but Bevans and I ate ours out in the yard, as it was thought best to be on the lookout, and we did not think it safe to let our borrowed horses get out of our sight. We had not seen anything to make us distrust the people in the house, but on general principles we were a bit suspicious of everybody.

After dinner, we rode down to Young's Branch to let the horses drink, and then onto the hill where the enemy had been located.[2] The house where Mrs. Henry was killed had been burned—so a Negro who lived a little farther to the left told us. He claimed that he was a free Negro and lived there "befoah the wah." He was talkative and appeared intelligent; but he was not very definite in his statements and indulged in large words; we doubted if he knew their real meaning.

From this point we followed what we supposed was the enemy's line until we reached the Sudley Spring Road. Then we rode again to the place where we were forming in line when Col. Boone of a Mississippi regiment had ridden out in front of us and was captured, and where we were first fired on from the woods. We had planned to go from this point to Sudley Church, which had been used as a hospital by the Union surgeons at the first battle, but now decided to ride in the other direction.

Almost everywhere there were evidences of one or the other of the battles. Pieces of clothing, hat, belts, knapsacks, etc., were silent witnesses of deadly strife—and many other things not so pleasant to remember or mention. I refrain from further description—more than to say that this locality had been the scene of two important battles (McDowell's in 1861 and Pope's in 1862) in which the positions had been partly reversed and lines crossing. The latter had been the greater as well as the more recent, and the evidences of it were more numerous and more conspicuous.

Many of the dead had not been buried for some days the Negro told us, and then covered where they lay. And even this had not been done with overmuch care, and we frequently saw partly exposed skeletons, where the washing of the rain or rooting of the hogs had uncovered them.

On a recently-cut stump, some grim jester had set a skull, as if in mockery of a real sentry. Much of the skin was still on it—dried and shrunken—and a bullet had passed through it from the right temple to a point above the left ear. There was nothing to indicate the color of the uniform he had worn or the flag he had followed. I rode away from this grinning, ghastly exhibit of a mutilated, dissevered head with the unpleasant reflection that my own might be transferred to a stump before the war ended.

Taking the road[3] to Manassas for a mile or so, we turned to the right to Groveton. We had not reached that point when we heard musketry firing—a score or more of shots—and so far away that we could scarcely be sure that it was the re-

2. Henry House Hill. The man they talked to was probably James Robinson, a free black whose house was just northeast of the Henry House.
3. Probably, they took the Manassas-Sudley Road.

port of firearms or the direction from which it came. But it was sufficient to make us uneasy. As we rode on we discussed the best thing to do if attacked and decided to run if we could and fight if we could not.

About this time, a couple of dogs came over the brow of a little hill in front of us, and we thought we heard a noise on the other side. At the top of the hill we met a boy driving a yoke of oxen hitched to a cart, on which was a rude rack made of poles, and a man carrying a pitchfork over his shoulder was following after it. He was a full-grown white man and apparently able-bodied. The only one we saw in that vicinity that day.

We stopped a moment to talk with him, and in answer to our inquiries, he said he had heard "some shootin'" and "reck'ed" that it was "over the branch," by which we judged he meant Catharpin Creek. He claimed to have neither seen nor heard anything from either party that day, but said that some of "Munford's men were at Sudley Springs the night before."[4]

We rode on at a lively gait through Groveton and to Gainesville, keeping an eye to the front and looking back from each hill, but no one attempted to interfere with us. Here we stopped to get a drink of water, and then passed on through Haymarket to the picket line of our Third Division.

The day had been pleasant, without dust or oppressive heat, and no Johnny Reb had fired buckshot at us or tried in any way to molest us. Just the same, the day had not gone without some anxiety, and we were glad to get inside the circle of protecting rifles. Going on to our own division we passed a wagon train, guarded by a detail from the regiment, taking rations to the troops at the gap.

Before daylight, Thursday, the 25th, it was certain that some portions of the enemy had made their way across the mountains—both above and below the position we held—and there was sharp skirmishing at the gap and on both of our flanks as soon as it began to grow light. The corps began moving as soon as it was light enough to see, but it was near 8 o'clock before our division (the Second), which was to be the rear guard, was ready to abandon its hold on the gap and take to the road (following the trains).

For a time, we were allowed to proceed in peace. Then a series of desultory, nagging attacks began on the flanks and rear, first at one point, then another. These were made by mounted men who attacked suddenly, galloping out of the enshrouding fog and mist; firing a volley or two; and riding away again into the blending clouds of smoke and vapor, or behind a sheltering hill or grove, as soon as they met a return fire. Several times it was considered prudent to strengthen the line of skirmishers that covered the rear and flanks; and twice our regiment shifted its formation from a marching column to a line of battle and hurried to the support of the skirmishers, but it never got near enough to Stuart's nimble horsemen

---

4. Colonel Thomas T. Munford was commanding one of Jeb Stuart's Confederate cavalry brigades in June 1863; Welcher, *Union Army*, Vol. 1, *Eastern Theater*, 722.

to fire a shot. It would have been in accord with our idea of what was due them for their annoying attentions, if we could have given them a volley at about thirty paces—or less.

We had reached Haymarket and were headed on a road that diverged to the left, running nearer the hills, when they used artillery for the first time that morning. From a hill on our right, as we marched, they fired in rapid succession obliquely across the line of march. The column was halted, and some regiments detached to go after them, and meantime their fire continued.

Several of their shells were sufficiently depressed to do damage, and one of them struck the hind legs of Col. Colvill's horse, tumbling man and horse into the muddy road. Fortunately, the colonel was able to clear his feet from the stirrups and quick-witted enough to roll out of the way of the struggling animal. He got to his feet without suffering any serious injury, but he was well-plastered with a coating of dull red Virginia mud. The colonel gave a fine exhibition of the cool nerve with which he was accustomed to accept good or ill fortune. He had hardly regained his feet before he ordered the horse shot, to end its suffering. Then he directed Milton Bevans, his orderly, to save the saddle and bridle and *find* him another horse.

Meantime, an attack was made on the troublesome battery and cavalry from another quarter, and they quickly departed. The whole affair had occupied but a few minutes, and as soon as it was over the march was resumed, as it would have been only a waste of time for infantry to pursue mounted men. This ended the serious attacks on the rear guard, though we were followed for some miles by small parties who improved every opportunity to take a shot and run.

With some of his personal effects across his arm, Colonel Colvill was in his place at the head of the regiment and continued the march on foot. It might be said here that it was not long before 'Mit' had *found* another horse, and he was in the saddle again. It was about an hour after dark when we reached the bivouac about Gum Spring, and a drenching rain was falling. We were directed to sleep with our guns beside us and near together.

Our division headed the corps next morning, June 26; and our regiment led the division; and thus we were the first to start. We had marched about 20 miles the previous day; and 10 or 12 more, as we understood it, would bring us to the Potomac if we continued on our present course.

Our general appearance that morning as we left the bivouac was about as animated and cheerful as a lot of rained-on fowls leaving their roost on a back fence to hunt for their morning meal in the wet grass. It was still raining a little. Our clothing was wet and spattered and smeared with mahogany-colored mud. The moisture, the sand, and the sharp stones of the road, which the wheels of the artillery and the trains had broken up badly, had been very destructive to shoe leather. Men who had left the Rappahannock twelve days before with new shoes on their feet were now practically bare-footed; and there were quite a number with feet so badly bruised or blistered that they walked like foundered horses.

It was not long after noon when we came onto the heights (on the Virginia side) overlooking the Potomac, and were able to recognize the country on the other side. We had reached the river at a point just below the mouth of Goose Creek, and we had spent the winter of 1861-2 in Maryland and picketed the opposite side of the river for about six months. There were two bridges laid across the river—one above and one below the mouth of Goose Creek—and one across the creek. Troops and trains were massed down by the river crossing, and climbing the hills on the other shore.

The trains massed on the lower ground, nearer the bridges, and the men fed and watered the mules. The artillery parked on the opposite side of the road. The artillerists watered and fed the horses. We had never seen the Second Corps with artillery and trains in so close a formation before. As night approached the mass of troops and trains down by the river diminished, as portions of it passed to the other side, until the trains were all over, and the lines of men moving. By this time the mules were again hitched to the wagons and the horses to the gun carriages—and moving nearer to the crossing.

Just before dark our division took arms, passed down the hill, and massed again near the river. Here, Companies F and I were detached to 'expedite' the crossing of our division teams. They were to cross in regular order at a walk and observe intervals of about the space occupied by the team, and our duty was to hurry up the tardy ones and retard those inclined to go too fast—similar to policemen at a crowded crossing. By deploying along the road and keeping a double line in the 'waiting list' ready to drive onto the bridge, we soon had a steady stream of wagons going in good order—and then kept the procession moving.

As it grew dark the pontoon men lighted torches—similar to those used at the boat landings on the Mississippi in the old steamboat days—at the ends of the bridges. The sun went down behind banks of clouds; and it was scarcely dark before a thunderstorm broke over us; and we were drenched with what felt like ice-cold water. This was repeated two or three times the first half of the night.

They were of brief duration, but in one or two of them were brilliant displays of nature's pyrotechnics. Driven by a furious wind, whirling masses of clouds surged across the sky; the rain came down at a horizontal slant of about 45 degrees; successive flashes of lightning alternatively illuminated the scene or left it in total darkness; and peals of thunder shook the hills. In the intervals of light the marching column could be seen with heads bowed to the wind, moving slowly over the heaving pontoons across the storm-swept river.

It was a scene to challenge a poet or a painter, but I have never read a poem or seen a picture of it. But that midnight passage of the Potomac by the Second Army Corps while the storm was on was a sight worth seeing and remembering. If some 'special artist' had been on the spot to have sketched it, it would have made as inspiring a picture as Washington Crossing the Delaware—a Civil War companion piece—but I imagine they were all asleep at that hour in some village hotel or farmhouse and never heard of it.

As soon as the last of our division was on the bridge, we were relieved, and our two companies followed it. Keeping at the rear of the column we were able to find the brigade and regiment without much trouble. It was lying in a field to the right of the road from Edwards Ferry, part way up the hill. Bedaubed with mud, hungry, sleepy, wet and weary; too tired, in fact, to try to do anything else at that hour—we wrapped our blankets around us, used our knapsack for a head rest, and soon slept. It must have been midnight or later; the storms had ceased; and stars were twinkling in the rifts of the passing clouds as we 'bunked down.'

It seemed only a few minutes later when Capt. Ball waked me, gave me a requisition on the regimental quartermaster for shoes, and directed me to find him, and, if he had any shoes of the required sizes, to get them. It was coming daylight, and I had slept some hours, brief as the time seemed. I went in search of the wagons, which I found with the division train.

The morning was fair, and the scene is still in memory. Lines of stacked rifles and rows of sleeping men—fields full of them. Batteries in park, here and there, and acres of wagons. Then more wagons, batteries, lines of rifles, and sleeping soldiers—with now and then one getting up. At the wagons I met others on like errands. I was able to get 7 pairs of shoes of approximate sizes and returned to the bivouac just as the first notes of the reveille were sounding.

This changed the appearance of things very materially in a few minutes. Recalled from 'slumberland,' the men sleepily 'sat up and began to take notice,' and a little later got in line and answered to roll call. The sound of the bugles stirred up the animals as well as the men. Horses at the picket ropes began pawing and whinnying. A few thousands of mules down near the river began to bray sonorously. Fires were started, and breakfasts cooked and eaten, and preparations made to march. The morning was fair, and we improved it to spread our blankets and allow some of the moisture to evaporate.

It was sometime after noon before the road was clear and we were moving. The rest and sleep had freshened us up, and, except those with sore feet, the boys took the road in good spirits. The afternoon sun was shining with about the usual summer heat, but it was not seriously oppressive. We kept on through Barnesville towards Sugar Loaf Mountain, and it was after 12 o'clock that night when we bivouacked near the latter place. As it was so late and the boys were so tired, the most of them at once laid down to sleep.

Just as they had located themselves for the night, an order came for the regiment to send out 160 men for picket. This was unexpected, as we had come in so late. There was considerable protest and some profanity when I called the detail, and it took half of the company or more to fill it. I explained that it "was orders," which settled the matter, and expressed my sympathy for those who must spend the remaining hours of the night watching. I could not find it in my heart to condemn very strongly either the protests or the profanity. After men had marched 20 miles in about half that many hours, it certainly was making a pretty heavy demand to send them a mile or so farther to stand in fence corners or clumps of bushes until daylight and then supplement that by another 25 mile march before they could sleep—but that was what was required.

(It was not then clearly understood just why we should post a strong picket facing towards Washington, but we now know that Stuart with his cavalry crossed that night from Virginia into Maryland, at Edwards Ferry, a little below where we had crossed the night before, and started on a raid between our army and Washington.)

Early Sunday morning, June 28th, we were in line and again bore banners northward. The day was fair, and the heat increased as the sun rose higher, until it was oppressively hot. The road was hilly, and we marched rapidly with only brief halts until near night when, after passing Monocacy Junction, we bivouacked on the banks of the Monocacy River two or three miles below Frederick City, the capital of Maryland. Much of the march had been over the same roads we had traveled in 1862 on the Antietam Campaign.

It was a hard day's work, particularly for those who had spent the previous night on picket, and the boys came in pretty well used up. About the time we halted, we heard the startling news that General Hooker had been relieved, and General George G. Meade appointed his successor in command of the Army of the Potomac ("that football of political intrigue and popular clamor," as it was sometimes called). It did not create so intense a feeling as the removal of McClellan had—for we were getting used to those things—but it was a matter of surprise that any change should have been made at that time. It appeared to us that Hooker was handling his army with energy and skill under the conditions imposed upon him.

Indications of daylight, Monday morning, June 29, came altogether too soon to suit our inclinations, but none too soon to begin the task assigned our corps for that day—the march to Uniontown, Maryland.

The beginning of the day was marked by a little *contretemps* that put us at a disadvantage all day and did not add to the amiability of anybody so far as I ever heard. Gen. Francis Amasa Walker, who was the Assigned Assistant Adjutant General of the Second Corps, says that the order of march was lost before he saw it.

It must be remembered that each soldier carried a rifle which—with bayonet, etc.—weighed about 11 pounds. Also, 100 rounds of ammunition, knapsack, haversack, canteen, coffee pot, and whatever cooking utensils he had; his blanket, tent cloth, rubber, all extra clothing, and whatever else he might have—writing paper, envelopes, keepsakes, or a book. These *impediments,* which must have weighed full 40 pounds, were useful and necessary, but often a real impediment to rapid transit, and could not be thrown away and replaced at will. The soldier must carry all of these things for himself and make his rations last him or suffer for the want of them.

The difference between a soldier on the march with all of his 'traps and calamities,' and a man out for a walking record, is about the same as that between a loaded pack-mule and a loose race-horse.

It was a misty, murky morning with a sultry air and cloud-covered skies. We had hurried the morning meal and were ready to fall in for the march—soldiers sitting on their knapsacks, line officers with their swords on, and orderlies holding the horses of the mounted officers. This had been the condition for an hour or so when the order came to move and was promptly obeyed. It was the turn of our division to lead the corps again, and our brigade the division, but the regiment was second in line.

The day proved a hot one. This day's march was marked by a bit of friction that but rarely occurred. Col. Charles H. Morgan was the Inspector General of the corps, and there is no doubt but he was an able and efficient officer, but because of his egoism he was not popular with the men. Inspectors are not generally. I suppose he was the officer most directly responsible for the lost order that morning and was anxious to make up for it as far as he could.

We had not been moving long before he put himself in evidence and directed a more rapid movement. After that he appeared frequently—galloping to the head of the column, or sitting on his horse by the road, joining each regimental commander as they passed, and giving them some injunction or command. And each time, after one of these brief conferences, the order passed down the line to "close the column," "lengthen the step," or "quicken the time." More than once, in his hurried rushes to the front, he had ridden so close to the marching column as to spatter men with dirt or mud—giving the impression that he would about as soon ride over an ordinary man as not. All old soldiers have seen that kind of a man on a horse. These things had a tendency to irritate.

There were streams to cross where there were no bridges; and men disliked to wet their feet, especially those already suffering from sores and bruises; and they would leave the ranks to get across without it if they could—and there was generally a foot bridge or log available—but of course it delayed them. Along midforenoon or later, we came to a stream which was a rod or more in width and about knee deep. The order was: go through it in close order, and Col. Morgan was there to enforce it, but for all that it was not literally or wholly obeyed.

On either side of the road was a log with the top side flattened, inviting one to pass over dry shod. Some of the officers and a number of the men darted from the ranks and ran over the logs, and those going through rushed in to the water in a spirit of reckless fun, yelling and splashing the water. The 15th Massachusetts, our 'chum' regiment, was following after us and got the same order. They were rather more open in their disobedience than we were—making more kinds of noises and making them louder than we did.

In fact, before the regiment was more than half across, there was a pretty strong 'barn-yard chorus' behind us; and we all knew that it was a 'benefit' for the

Inspector General—and he knew it, too. Some of the boys had been saying before this that he was "making himself altogether too *numerous*, for a cheap hand," and they were perfectly willing to join in the chorus. These things were not proper soldierly conduct, but they were very natural under the circumstances, and it might have been better for him to have ignored them.

However, he was very angry and did not try to conceal it, either. A little farther on, there was a brief halt to close up the column and rest a few minutes, and while we were here Col. Morgan rode by, going to the front. Some of the boys of the 15th repeated things he had said at the crossing—loud enough for him to hear—and there seemed to have been an accession of dogs and cats to the ranks, judging from the noise. Of course, as he passed on, our fellows were not as careful as they should have been to 'observe silence.'

In fact, there was not enough *silence* there to be *observed* at that particular moment—but there was plenty of it later.

These things were not a bit soothing to the irritated feelings of the Inspector General. They were more than the dignity of his position could stand. He caused Col. George H. Ward of the 15th Massachusetts and Col. William Colvill of our regiment to be placed under arrest for the "insubordination" of their commands. Under military law it was right to hold a commander responsible for the conduct of his command; also I admit that the conduct of the commands was unsoldierly and discreditable; but it looked to us like rank injustice. The colonels had had nothing more to do with it than they had in causing the order to be lost (which had delayed our start and put everyone 'out of sorts') or bringing on the morning showers that had made the roads slippery or the withering sunshine that had followed them.

The men were now positively angry. There were expressed desires to "mar his visage" with a boot heel or the butt of a musket, and some even suggested the use of the other end of the gun in the usual way. However, strong as was our resentment, it was clearly understood that our colonel was in disgrace wholly on our account, and any further demonstrations on our part would only make a bad matter worse, and there was a prompt compliance with his wish to "drop it for his sake."

The colonels turned over their commands to the next in rank and took their places at the rear of their regiments, under nominal arrest. The Inspector General had grace enough to discontinue his frequent passing of the marching column. There were mutterings in the ranks for a time, and then we moved on in dogged silence over the hilly roads under the scorching summer heat.

Perhaps it should be stated here that Cols. Colvill and Ward were released from arrest at their own request when it became probable that we should soon be engaged—that they might lead their regiments in action. Ward was killed, and Colvill was crippled for life, which ended all proceedings against them. Had the bullets reached Col. Morgan instead, there would have been much less regret in both regiments. He was no doubt a brave, loyal man and a capable officer, but he was not the only one with all of those good qualities who frequently forgot that a soldier in the ranks was still a *man*.

As we got farther away from the banks of the Potomac, it was observed that there was a different expression of feeling towards us. Instead of it being exceptional to get a friendly greeting, it became quite general. Flags, handkerchiefs, aprons, and sunbonnets were waved from windows, door-steps, and front-yard fences as we tramped hurriedly on. These things had a soothing effect on our disturbed feelings, and a little later, when we made a short halt, women and children came with baskets of buttered bread and *real* doughnuts, pails of water, and jugs of buttermilk. The boys cheered them with hearty good will.

This was not long after noon, and the halt was but brief. Then we trudged on again through the long, hot afternoon. The weight on our weary shoulders felt as if it was increasing with each rod we traveled, and it was in vain that we 'hunched up' the right shoulder or the left, or shifted the rifle more frequently from one to the other. It was there just the same and bore down incessantly.

We passed through Mt. Pleasant, Johnsville, and Libertytown, Maryland. The sun was getting low, and we were hoping to camp soon, but no order was given. Chafed shoulders and blistered feet were the rule, for we had wetted the latter frequently and had been sweating freely. The most of us had been marching with our blouses and shirts open, and when the sun ceased to shine we took off our hats, but still the heat was oppressive, and the sweat oozed from our bodies, and the *ache* increased in our weary shoulders and over-strained muscles as the march continued.

Daylight changed to twilight, and twilight to moonlight, and still we kept on.

Passing through a small village called Uniontown about nine o'clock that night, we went on a mile or so when the welcome command to halt was heard. This was near the line between Maryland and Pennsylvania, and I do not now recall which state the town was in.[5] As soon as the guns were stacked, the men threw off their knapsacks and belts and stretched themselves on the ground—too tired for anything but to rest. It had been a hard, grinding day's march, and we had covered 33 miles over hilly roads, but the day's work was not done.

Many of the men had fallen asleep, and a few were making coffee, when Adjutant John Peller brought an order for a detail to go on picket. This did seem to be "rubbing it in," as one of the boys expressed it, but it had to be—and, after a deal of protesting, about a third of the regiment, with Capt. Tom Sinclair in command of them, marched a couple of miles farther and watched at some crossroads until morning.

Tuesday, June 30th, was another hot day, and we remained in bivouac all day and the following night. This was the day for the bi-monthly muster, and I was glad that the captain's forethought had left but little work to be done on the rolls.

5. Uniontown is in Maryland, as is Union Mills, a short distance north.

These papers and the company books were transported in the regimental wagon, and when we left the Rappahannock I had folded them in an extra blanket I had. When the work on the rolls and books was finished, I kept the blanket and wrapped the books in a 'gunny bag' so that I was again provided for.

This work was done in the early morning, as it was understood we might march at any time. The picket detail had come in the morning also, and we had not been called on for another. Then arms and ammunition were inspected, and we made other preparations for the grand tragedy we felt would be enacted soon, somewhere in that vicinity. After that, we bathed our chafed and blistered feet, wrote letters home, and slept in the shade—pleased with the opportunity to rest and making the most of it.

At that time all kinds of rumors were in circulation but we of the ranks really knew very little of the real situation. At daylight the morning of July 1, 1863, it is highly improbable that either Meade or Lee was then planning to fight at Gettysburg or, seriously, anywhere else that day. While both commanders knew in a general way the location and strength of the other, neither had definite information on those points, and they were entirely ignorant of many other things it would have been to their advantage to have known.

17

It could not be quite so bad as that

JUNE-JULY 2, 1863

IN ITS WAY, Gettysburg was quite an important little center. Coming into it, from nearly every point of the compass, were ten or a dozen fairly good roads. When Lee turned south to collect his scattered troops and cover his communications, he followed the roads, and these concentrated his forces north and west of the town. When the Army of the Potomac had been deployed so that its right covered Baltimore and its left the passes in the mountains to Harpers Ferry—and the enemy's position was better understood—then the next move was to get its corps into supporting distances. The easiest and quickest way to do this was to follow the roads leading towards that portion of its front most endangered by the enemy. These converging roads brought both armies toward a common center and made a collision inevitable.

Without pre-arrangement on the part of either, the movements of both were so timed that the first actual contact was out west and northwest of the town, and after that most matters were governed by the exigencies of the moment.

From a self-centered and little-known town, the fighting there gave it a national prominence and almost world-wide fame. To one who shared its experiences, the word Gettysburg stirs conflicting memories. Memories of bloodshed, suffering, and wholesale death as pitiful and pathetic as ever overwhelmed grief-burdened hearts. Memories as grand and heroic as ever thrilled the soul of a soldier-patriot.

Gettysburg was a great battle—not only on account of the numbers engaged and the deadly intensity and determined pertinacity with which it was fought—but also on account of the tremendous issues involved, military and political, at home and abroad. The future of the Nation (I might almost say, the hopes of all the world regarding self-government) was the wager of battle. Greater issues but seldom, if ever, centered around a battlefield, and the very essence of them were as old as governments among men. Gettysburg was only another stirring chapter in the world-old contest between the rights of the individual and the use of arbitrary power.

More than thirty-three centuries before, the soldiers of Republican Greece had fought those of Despotic Persia over this same question on the plains of Marathon. American soldiers of the Union army met American soldiers of the Confederate army at Gettysburg, and the question at issue was the division of the states, and the source of disagreement was African slavery. At Marathon, Greek freedom repelled Asiatic despotism. At Gettysburg, the Slave-holder's Rebellion, conceived and prosecuted for the perpetuation and spread of slavery, was halted and turned back to final defeat at Appomattox.

On this evening of June 30, 1863, this same old Army of the Potomac—way-worn and foot-sore from nearly a month of marching; weather-beaten, soil-stained, dirty, and ragged from its weeks of tramping and camping in heat and in dust, in rain and in mud, by day and by night—was stretched along the border of Pennsylvania and Maryland for 45 or 50 miles. Before daylight of July 1, rifles in hand, it was hastening over converging roads—once again to flutter its battle-rent banners in the face of its country's foes and strike again for the integrity of the nation.

Our own corps, the Second, was in bivouac near Uniontown, Maryland. We were called early and were ordered to move forward to Taneytown, but there was another 'mix' or 'miss' about it, and we waited. Clouds covered the sky, a light rain was falling, and as the dawn grew to daylight it did not bring anything particularly cheering with it—or discouraging either, for that matter.

Soon after starting in the afternoon, we were ordered to move at quick time and to keep well closed up, and we felt the rapid marching. We thought we heard firing before getting to Taneytown (about 13 miles from Gettysburg), but when we were halted there we could not hear it; and we of the ranks then had no positive knowledge that the fighting had begun—though, as usual, there were plenty of grapevine dispatches.[1]

We had been on the road for two hours or more when it became certain that there was cannonading. This was when we were halted at a small stream filling our canteens and must have been somewhere about half way between Taneytown and Gettysburg.

Moving on from here inside of another half hour, we crossed a higher ridge, which gave us a more extended view than we had had for some time, and we could see and hear enough to satisfy us that there was real fighting going on. A heavy and well-sustained artillery fire was generating great masses of smoke which were rising and expanding into white clouds as the wind carried it away. On this, the late afternoon sun was shining, making the hills appear as if covered with snow. But none of us imagined there was a snowstorm there.

We were marching nearly north, and these clouds of smoke were almost in front of us and were passing to the right, from which I presume there was a westerly wind that day. We did not halt to view the scenery but pushed on at quick step.

Within another mile or so, we began to meet citizen and soldier refugees occasionally, and later we met many of them. We were naturally anxious to know

1. Since June 10, the Second Corps had been led by Winfield S. Hancock, but on July 1, Meade temporarily placed Hancock in command at Gettysburg, and Second Division commander John Gibbon was put in charge of the Second Corps. Some time at Taneytown was spent making these changes. Welcher, *Union Army,* Vol. 1, *Eastern Theater,* 721, 733.

how affairs were going at the front, but one does not often get encouraging news from men under such conditions. Generally, they tell a story consistent with their own actions in retiring as they have, and we heard only stories of defeat and disaster. (As we now know, their stories came much nearer the truth than is usual, but more about that later.)

It was now getting near night. Most of those skedaddlers wore the crescent badge of the Eleventh Corps, and were cooks and camp-followers rather than fighting men. But there were many who, we thought, should have remained at the front. The reputation of the Eleventh Corps (which originally was Sigel's command) had not been improved by what had happened at Chancellorsville, when struck by Jackson's turning force. Men of the other corps—even though they might not have done any better under the same conditions—were disposed to 'say things' about the Eleventh.

There was a song or poem referring to these men and their former commander, in which the chorus or last line closed with the words "I fights mit Sigel." When it became the Eleventh Corps, Gen. Oliver O. Howard succeeded Gen. Franz Sigel and the corps lost caste for its reported conduct at Chancellorsville. This song was parodied by fun-loving critics of other corps, and to the closing words "I fights mit Sigel" were added "but runs mit Howard." Several versions (mal-versions) of this song were rendered by the men for the benefit of those going to the rear, and severe criticisms indulged in, which perhaps were not altogether fair or just, but they seemed about the proper thing at the time.

At last it grew too dark to recognize badges or persons but the march continued, though more slowly and with frequent halts. The sound of the artillery died away and ceased before it was fairly dark, and we had heard no other sound of the fighting. We had met no broken or disordered regiments or companies, and argued that our lines still held, and those we had met were only the fragments which had been knocked off and were now drifting away.

After several halts, we at last formed in line of battle and stacked arms, and a strong picket force was placed to cover the front and flanks. This I think was between nine and ten o'clock. The pickets had special instructions to use the utmost care against surprises and mistakes, as either friends or enemies might appear from any direction. Those not required to watch hastened to make coffee and, this done, to bestow themselves for the night as best they could near the stacked guns. This was a brief matter, as they simply looked for a smooth spot as any animal might, spread their blankets, and laid down with their heads on their knapsacks. Then, covering their bodies with the unoccupied portions of the blanket and their faces with their old slouch hats, they slept.

Pregnant as the situation was with possibilities for the morrow (and they were not forgotten or ignored), I do not think much time was spent in their consideration by those not obliged to keep awake. We had been on our feet since soon after three o'clock that morning and had marched 20 or 22 miles, and it felt good to stretch ourselves on the ground and be at rest.

I had drunk not less than a pint of strong coffee, and it seems a bit surprising to me now, under all of the circumstances, that I slept so quickly and so soundly. (For years, less than half that quantity of only moderately-strong coffee at any hour except the morning meal means a sleepless night.) I do not know just where that night's bivouac was, but it was to the right of the road going from Taneytown to Gettysburg and from three to four miles from the latter place.

It was about one o'clock in the morning of July 2 when I was shaken into consciousness by Captain Ball and told to wake the men and form the company at once. It took a little time to rouse the boys from their sound slumbers and make them understand that we were to march at once, and with as little noise as possible.

There seemed to be a bit of mist or fog resting on the ground, but the moon was shining. The grass was wet, and the leaves on the trees and bushes were loaded with drops of moisture that glistened innocently in the moonlight if viewed at the right angle, but, if jarred accidentally, resented it by showering you with water.

The company was soon in line; the roll was called; the regiment formed and joined the brigade in the road. There was a little longer wait, during which we were charged to make no noise or speak except in an undertone. Then—without the formality of reveille, a bugle's notes, or a command that could have been heard forty feet away—we were moving. The Second Corps appeared to have roused up and started off automatically. There was an oppressive silence, broken only by the dull thump of marching feet. The march was not hurried, and there were several brief halts.

Though there was but little talking, and that in undertones, I presume our imaginations were active. We had a deep interest in results and a great curiosity to know what had really happened the day before. And we could not have been without some anxiety as to what might happen to the army, the regiment, or ourselves during the day that was soon to dawn, but I do not suppose that any one had a realizing expectation of what did happen. I do remember that some of us thought we ought to have been allowed to make coffee before marching and 'growled' about it.

(If any one had a premonition that we had reached the culminating battlefield of the war and that that day was to be the saddest, bloodiest, grandest, and most glorious day in the history of the regiment, I do not recall that I heard it suggested.)

Day dawned, and with the coming light we began to hear an occasional shot far away, and more to our right than in the direction we were marching. The day grew, and the sun rose with all of the early splendor of a mid-summer morning out among the hills and woods. The moving column tramped steadily on—the rhythmic contact of marching feet with the dirt roads irregularly punctuated by the distant rifle shots.

When the head of the division had passed the house of Mrs. Lydia Leister—
on the left of the road, where it begins to pass diagonally over Cemetery Ridge—
it turned from the road to the left, going up the easterly side of the ridge. It was at
this house General Meade had his headquarters. His flag was flying there; aides
were coming and going; and orderlies were holding horses in the yard. But we did
not see him.

This was about 6 o'clock in the morning—possibly a little earlier or later.
Our division first massed by brigades in columns of regiments, and stacked
arms. There was an opportunity to make coffee, which we were not slow to
improve.

While doing this, some men came over from the First Corps who had been in
the battle the day before, and we had the first intelligible account of what had occurred. As usual, statements were contradictory, and there was but little encour-
agement in any of the versions given. It was certain, however, that there had been
very severe fighting and that our forces had been driven back with heavy losses.
But, judging from what we had heard, it had been made a costly affair to the enemy as well.

While eating our breakfasts, Col. Colvill rejoined the regiment, having been
released from arrest, and he was received with a spontaneous outburst of cheering and clapping of hands. The welcome he received ought to have pleased any
man and no doubt did please him immensely, but he only said, "Keep still, boys.
D—n it; can't you keep quiet?" All the same, we all knew very well that he appreciated the reception we had given him and was much gratified with it. At the same
time there was another scene of a similar nature going on in the Fifteenth Massachusetts. The men of both regiments regretted their boyish actions—so far as
they had brought discredit to their commanders—and were heartily glad to have
them restored for the coming fight, but they were not yet in an amiable mood toward the Inspector General.

While these things were transpiring, the corps was being deployed into position on the ridge. The Third Division, under its new commander Gen. Alexander Hays, joined its right with the left of Robinson's Division of First Corps at
Ziegler's Grove, and extended to the left along the ridge. The Second Division
came next, Gen. John Gibbon commanding, and occupied the section including
the stone walls, the Bloody Angle, and the Clump of Trees. Only two brigades,
Webb's and Hall's, went into line; and Harrow's, to which we belonged, was apparently held in reserve.[2] Caldwell's First Division was some distance to the left
with Doubleday's Division, opposite the interval.

2. Brigadier General William Harrow led the First Brigade—formerly Sully's brigade—
succeeding Col. Byron Laflin. Harrow was ill, and Colonel George Ward apparently shared
the command on July 2; Harry W. Pfanz, *Gettysburg: The Second Day* (Chapel Hill: University of North Carolina Press, 1987), 71. By now, Hancock and Gibbon had returned to their
original commands, since Meade was on the field.

The Second Company of Minnesota Sharpshooters, which was attached to the regiment and known as Company L, was at this time detached and sent out with Kirby's Battery, to use the persuasive influence of their Sharps rifles if the enemy became too demonstrative. It was not long after this that Company C was detailed as a provost guard and posted near division headquarters to take charge of some prisoners and for general provost duty. Of course, before this time little squads of the boys had gone to the highest points near to take observations, but nothing of startling importance was to be seen.

There was not much firing, and the most of that seemed down below Ziegler's Grove in the edge of the town. Some men were visible on Seminary Ridge a mile or so to the front, which we supposed then were the enemy, but we have since questioned if they were not some of Sickles's Third Corps.

It is certain that Colonel Hiram Berdan reported the advance of the enemy before 2 o'clock.[3] The conduct of Gen. Sickles has been variously commented upon, criticized, complimented, and condemned, but in my humble judgment it was consistent and soldierly. He did not get orders to advance or retire; he knew he was about to be attacked; and put himself in position of defense, in what seemed to him the most defensible position.[4]

The two divisions of the Third Corps were formed on two sides of a square, practically, with the angle at or near Sherfy's house on the Emmitsburg Road. The right of Birney's Division was at the road and running to the left by the Peach Orchard and Wheat Field to a point near the Devil's Den. The left of Humphrey's Division connected with the right of Birney's and was extended near the Emmitsburg Road with its right between Rogers's and Codori's houses. The artillery was posted on the high ground in the angle. Along the sides and within the angle the principal fighting of the afternoon of July 2 occurred.

Going back to our little brigade on the easterly slope of Cemetery Ridge, I will endeavor very briefly to tell of some of the things that happened later. Though one might about as well attempt to follow the gyrations of a cyclone through a forest as to try to give them in detail. As I now recall it, the First Minnesota was the first regiment of the brigade to be sent off—and this was a short time before the cannonading began in serious earnest upon the Third Corps. Going to the crest of the ridge, we were placed in support of Battery C, 4th U.S. Artillery, which was on the ridge a little distance to the left of our division, but not then in action. Passing in the rear of the battery we took position a little ways to its left and laid down.

3. Around noon, Colonel Hiram Berdan, with four companies of sharpshooters and one regiment, found Rebels in Pitzer's Woods—but not Longstreet's main attack column, which did not arrive for three hours; Pfanz, *Second Day*, 98–102.
4. Major General Daniel Sickles advanced his line beyond Cemetery Ridge to the Peach Orchard (but not as far as Seminary Ridge), thus creating a dangerously exposed salient, whose right flank the First Minnesota later helped to defend.

Gen. Harrow, our brigade commander, said he sent us there by direction of Gen. Gibbon.

As we now know, the Nineteenth Maine, another regiment of our brigade, was sent out in front of the division, and the Eighty-second New York was sent out to the Emmitsburg Road, near the Codori House, to the right of the division. A little later the Fifteenth Massachusetts, the other regiment of the brigade, was sent to the support of the 82nd New York, and took its place on the right of the regiment. Thus, for some reason (we never knew why) our brigade was scattered and posted in front and on the flanks of the division. We were placed, and I think the others were, before the real fighting—as if in anticipation of some such result as came later.[5]

From our position we could see much of the movements of the 3rd Corps as it prepared to resist the enemy. It was not often that one was able to see so much of the maneuvering. At the time we were placed in this position there was not much artillery firing and very little of it was directed upon the ridge, but a little later a battery of the enemy on Seminary Ridge—looking to the right by the Codori House—began tossing shells in our vicinity, which were probably intended for Battery C or Brown's battery to its right. One of these shells fell in Company I, killing Sergeant Oscar Woodard and wounding Sergeant Oliver M. Knight.

Believing the regiment to be unnecessarily exposed where it was, it was ordered part way down the slope, on the left of the battery, and there we laid down again—as we did not desire to be more conspicuous than necessary. It was at about this time the Confederate batteries began a furious fire on the Third Corps, and from that time until night the battle was on in deadly earnest. (Gen. Edward Porter Alexander, Lee's chief of artillery, said that he had 46 guns in position to fire on the two lines of the Third Corps at and near the angle, and that they opened fire at 3:45.) It certainly was a furious storm of shells that was rained on the Union lines.

The batteries of the Third Corps, and others posted on the ridge, made a prompt response, and clouds of smoke obscured the movements of the troops. The infantry fire seemed to break out heavily—and at first on the left or left center of Birney's line—continuing there and extending quickly towards its right. In seemingly a very little time it extended along Humphreys's front, also, and other batteries on Seminary Ridge opened upon it.

It was an unequal contest. The divisions of Birney and Humphreys, formed at nearly a right angle, were being attacked by the Confederate divisions of

5. Gibbon and Harrow advanced these regiments to the Emmitsburg Road "in order to support the Third Corps's right flank, which was in the air south of the Codori barn"; the First Minnesota remained on Cemetery Ridge in support of Battery C; Pfanz, *Second Day*, 374–75, 385 (map).

Hood, McLaws, and Anderson, on both fronts. Any one of the three Confederate divisions was stronger than either of the Union divisions, and they must inevitably yield to their superior strength. The formation of Sickles's line was, in a degree at least, to the advantage of the enemy if they had force enough to make use of it—which they certainly had. The angle at which his lines were formed, projecting to the front, without a supporting force to strike at the flanks of his enemy, permitted an attack from two sides; and the batteries firing on the angle were able to get a concentrating and enfilading fire on both the artillery and the lines of infantry.

It was a wonderful scene we were witnessing. And it left no desire to have it repeated, for it is a fearful thing to see an army corps crushed in the collision of battle. It was a scene not easily effaced from the memory and exceedingly difficult to describe.

Matters developed rapidly, and infantry and artillery were hurried to assist the struggling lines at the front. The First Division of the Fifth Corps (then about two miles in the rear of the Round Tops as a support to the right flank) was ordered to Little Round Top to the support of the left. The First Division of the Second Corps, commanded by Gen. Caldwell, was hurried to the support of Birney's shattered lines, and the batteries on the ridge in our rear began firing.

Crashing, crushing, stunning discharges of artillery made the earth vibrate beneath us. Rolling, tearing, crackling volleys of musketry—Union cheers and Confederate yells, mingling with other noises of the strife—burst out from the concealing clouds of smoke in that indescribable mixture of sounds commonly called the 'roar of battle.' Along the lines of the contending forces, there was a whirling tempest of fire and smoke, and about them gathered clouds of sulphurous vapor—into which the reinforcements plunged and were lost sight of and out of which came streams of wounded and the fragments of broken regiments.

It was with feelings of anxiety beyond words to express that we watched the awful scene before us, listened to the tumultuous sounds, and wondered how it would end. We were only a single, little regiment—at most but 290 officers and men—posted alone on a hillside and apparently forgotten in the surge of greater events around us. Back of us on the crest, there were roaring cannon, bursts of flame, and billows of smoke; over our heads, from one side or the other, there was an almost incessant flight of screaming, screeching shells; before us was the deadly contest I have been trying to describe; and it was already apparent that our forces were yielding and that at some points the enemy had broken through and were advancing.

Occasionally a bullet knocked up the dirt in front of us, and it was soon observed that they were coming from some point on our left front, and that they were increasing in frequency. It was believed that a line of skirmishers or a body of sharpshooters had reached the cover of bushes and fences across the hollow and should be looked after. Company F (Capt. Ball) was detached and ordered to skirmish in that direction. I do not know if this was done in obedience to orders or if Col. Colvill acted upon his own judgment.

When Capt. Ball received the order, he advanced the company a few paces, faced by the left flank until beyond the left of the regiment, deployed, and moved to the left oblique. This direction was continued for two hundred yards or so, when it brought the right of the line to the edge of some marshy ground, and the left near a fence. Along the edge of this field next to the marsh, stones had been dumped as they were cleared from the land, and — about the piles of stones — weeds, briars, and bushes had grown up. These served as a partial screen, and the stone piles were a good protection against bullets.

Going over, we were subject to a sharp fire and I think James F. Bachelor was wounded. For some time before we went out, wounded men and others had been passing to the rear, and they were still coming back. They would come hurriedly out of the smoke over on the hill and about some houses — as if pursued — then gather in little groups, fire a shot or two, and continue to retire. It was not a flight, nor a panic, but a general yielding of a position they considered no longer tenable. As we then were, many were drifting back over the ground we had just crossed, and a few were trying to get over the low ground in front of us and were being fired on from the field on the opposite hillside.

As soon as we were thus satisfied that the fellows we could now see coming down the opposite slope were enemies, we proceeded to treat them as such and 'got busy' at once. Like ourselves, the enemy kept well covered for a time, but they were using their rifles quite freely.

Their bullets were hissing over us, cutting the weeds and bushes, plumping into the ground and spatting against the stones. It was *more* satisfactory to be trying to do something than it was to lie on the ground under the howling shrieking shells, or wait inactive, but we do not wish to be understood that there was anything *very satisfactory in being shot at.* It was now nearly night. The fire from the other side was increasing, and the smoke covered the field, but we were able to get glimpses of a line of battle coming down the hill. It was not coming directly towards us but apparently directing its course to our right, and the right of the skirmishers directed their fire upon it but the range was too great to be effective. (It was at this time that Capt. Ball sent Jonas Davis to Col. Colvill to report his situation and ask instructions.) This advancing line, I think, must have been the right of Wilcox's brigade, after it had turned the left of Carr's, about the Rogers House.[6] If so it was charged, a little later by the regiment.

Almost immediately after this came another force of the enemy, advancing on Wilcox's right and coming more directly towards us. Not much could be seen of

6.   The right wing of Joseph Carr's Brigade was at the Rogers House and was hit by Cadmus Wilcox's Brigade's left wing (Ninth and Fourteenth Alabama Regiments). The rest of the First Minnesota charged three-fourths of Wilcox's Brigade (Tenth, Eleventh, and Fourteenth Alabama). Pfanz, *Second Day,* 364, 410–11.

this, as it was obscured by smoke, trees, and bushes, but it was enough to make it certain the strong force of the enemy was coming our way. As they came on it was seen that they might pass to our left, as the others had to the right, but would come nearer to us across the marsh.[7]

We turned our rifles on them as soon as in range and got a fire in return. Capt. Ball shifted the company to the left which brought a part of it on higher ground and along a fence, and we continued the fire on their flank and rear as they were passing. They were moving hurriedly and in some disorder, probably caused by our fire. This force, we think, was the left of Barksdale's Brigade moving to attack the ridge.

Wilcox and Barksdale were acting independently of each other and moving on slightly diverging lines, so the interval widened as they advanced, and it so happened that Co. F was almost directly between these two forces, and near enough to fire on both. After these came another smaller force, moving rapidly towards us, whose fire we received and returned.

Up to this time we had kept out of sight and as much sheltered as possible. There was now sharp fighting on both sides of us. That on our left was at or near Little Round Top and that on the right was, we feel certain, the regiment. It was useless for our little company to remain longer and Capt. Ball gave the order to retire. We fell back a short distance, faced about, and began firing again. The captain was very anxious to find the regiment and uncertain as to where it was. Davis had not returned. After a little further hesitation, he gave the order to go directly back to the ridge.

This we did hurriedly but in fairly good order, continuing deployed until near the top of the hill, when we closed on the right to avoid a line of battle coming over the crest. I have no doubt some of the company will recall one of the officers of this line, who was short and fat and 'game as a rooster' but very much excited. He was swinging his hat in one hand and his sword in the other, shouting in a hoarse voice, "Forward! boys, forward!"

As soon as we reached the top of the ridge we were placed in line, with the fragments of other organizations that had been in action, as a reserve to this line.[8]

The regiment on the right of the line, going down as we came up, we recognized as the 111th N.Y. of Alexander Hays's Third Division of our corps and Col. George L. Willard's brigade. This brigade was made up of the 39th, 111th, 125th,

7. Barksdale's Brigade charged north while Wilcox's charged east—both towards the Rogers House. Both successful, in order "to avoid a collision, . . . Wilcox's brigade veered slightly left [northeast]" while "Barksdale's swung right to the east and Cemetery Ridge." That made it look as though both would miss Company F, but in fact, they closed up on Plum Run. Pfanz, *Second Day,* 349 (quote), 364, 405.

8. Company F was evidently part of a group that included battered Third Corps regiments that General Humphreys, partly by Hancock's command, had rallied on Cemetery Ridge; Pfanz, *Second Day,* 371–72, 409–10.

and 126th N.Y.; had never been with the corps in battle; and, excepting the 39th (Garibaldi Guards), had not had the fighting experience of the rest of the corps. They proved themselves of the right sort, remained with us, and were never found wanting.

In this attack on Barksdale's Mississippians, Col. Willard was killed and the brigade lost 714 (all but 33 of those killed or wounded), but the enemy was driven back, and Barksdale also was mortally wounded. It has been claimed that the fire of Company F wounded Barksdale. It is reasonably certain that Company F fired on the right flank and down the rear of his brigade, but I know of no positive data on which to base an assertion that he fell by its fire.

There were other troops assaulting the ridge at this time besides Barksdale's and Wilcox's brigades. The brigades of Perry and Wright—having turned the left of the last of the Third Corps still holding on at and about the Rogers House—forced them back and joined in the attempt to gain the hill, at the point held by our division. Naturally they came in contact with the outlying regiments of our brigade first.[9] The Nineteenth Maine was withdrawn in time to save it from exceptional losses, but the Eighty-second N.Y. and the Fifteenth Mass. held their position on the Emmitsburg Road, near the Codori House, until Cols. Ward and Huston were killed and nearly half of their men were dead or disabled.

As these retired up the hill, they were followed by a fierce assault, striking our third brigade and reaching Brown's Battery—and for a little time they had possession of it—when they were charged by the 19th Maine of our brigade and the 71st, 72nd, and 106th Pennsylvania of Webb's brigade and driven back across the Emmitsburg Road. Not only was the battery recaptured but two flags and many prisoners were taken. This practically ended the attack on this part of the line.

The fighting of Willard's Brigade was nearly in front of our position, while that of the rest of the regiment was to our right. None of it reached or came very near the point where we had been put in line with men from broken regiments of our own and the 3rd Corps.

Naturally there was great anxiety in the company to know what had been the fate of the regiment; as it seemed certain that it had been caught in the on-rush of the enemy, and there was little probability that it had escaped severe loss.

As soon as the crisis on our front appeared to be over, Capt. Ball directed me to call the roll of the company, and every man was present or accounted for. All things considered the loss had been surprisingly small, as we already knew. Corp. Marion Abbott had had his right arm shattered; James F. Bachelor had been shot

9. To support the Third Corps right, Gibbon had sent the 15th Massachusetts and 82nd New York north of the Codori House and the 19th Maine to support Weir's Battery south of the Codori House. They were all driven back to Cemetery Ridge. Pfanz, *Second Day*, 374–75, 384–85.

in the foot; and Levi King through the face. All had been seriously wounded and had already been cared for. Only Bachelor was ever able to return to duty. Davis, who had been sent away by Capt. Ball, had not returned.

Numerically not a large loss, but it was a sixth part of the muskets in line in the morning. Capt. Ball was very anxious to take the company and go to find the regiment, which we knew very well must be somewhere to our right, and asked permission to leave the line for that purpose. This was denied, with a promise that he could go in the morning and a suggestion that it could be done then more easily and quickly.

This was by no means satisfactory to the captain or the company; and there was a suggestion to go anyway; but our lessons of obedience had been pretty strongly impressed; and we remained where we were. Capt. Ball sent Sergeant Hamline down the line to the right to find the regiment, report the condition of the company, and ask for orders.

It had been a terrible day and, seemingly, a long, long time since we had come up the opposite side of that ridge that morning. We had not been called upon to make great physical exertion, but the nervous strain had been excessive. All were weary and hungry, for very little had been eaten since early morning, and it was about 10 o'clock at night.

Men had already made little fires and were making coffee and we joined them in preparation of our suppers. The menu was not very elaborate. Coffee, brown sugar, crackers and fat, salt pork, with every man his own cook. Simple and uninviting it may have been, as we prepared it, but the most of us had appetites that made it very relishable.

Then we laid down in line, with our rifles beside us, for we must get some rest for the morrow. At this time there was still some firing off to the right and in the rear of us, but none in our front. Wounded men were coming in all the time, and men were going out frequently to search for others.

About this time, Sergeant Hamline returned and told Capt. Ball that he had found only a few men of the regiment, and it was believed the rest were all killed or captured. This was indeed depressing news, and at first almost stunned us, though we were expecting bad news. Then there was a general expression of belief that "it could not be quite so bad as that."

Someone said: "These things are always reported worse than they are—at the first."

"They have been separated by the fighting and are scattered in the darkness; they will turn up all right in the morning—the most of them."

Many of the company wanted to go at once to where they were—about a quarter of a mile to the right or maybe a little more. At first Capt. Ball seemed disposed to do this. Then he said that he had been ordered to remain where he was until morning; that his name and regiment had been taken; and he thought it best to stay there.

Then we lay down again. It was a beautiful summer night. The moon was shining serenely, obscured occasionally by fleecy clouds, that drifted across the sky. Looking skyward there was nothing to suggest the terrible struggle of the day, but out in that blood-sodden field where the helpless and the dead lay in the moonlight, there was no lack of evidence of the intensity of the strife.

Expecting every minute to be blown to atoms

JULY 3-5, 1863

LYING ON THE GROUND with my head on my knapsack, I got two or three hours of sleep, when firing back of the Round Tops awoke me. It was just coming daylight.

A little in the rear of where the boys lay on the ground, Captain Ball was walking back and forth. I went to him, and he said that he had been there for some time, as he had been unable to sleep for thinking. Said that he had heard twice from the regiment during the night, and the loss was very great—he could not tell how great—and he was waiting permission to go to it.

As soon as it was fairly light, he ordered me to call up the men and get them ready to march. I did this, and as soon as ready we went down the rear of the line to the right. As we were going, a lively firing broke out on the right of the line about Culp's Hill, heavy volleys of musketry and an increasing artillery fire. We did not then quite comprehend the situation, and it seemed to us that those fellows were getting at it pretty early, but—as we now know—it was the 12th Corps making an attempt to dislodge that portion of the enemy which had invaded their weakened line the night before.

Going down the line past the weary, sleepy men, we found Capt. Nathan Messick with the colors and what was left of the regiment—47 men who had not been hit and a few that had. We had not been separated far or long, but the greetings were as sincere and earnest as if oceans had divided us and years had elapsed. There was a flood of inquiries about the missing ones. The answers left no doubts in our minds of the awful calamity that had befallen the regiment and gave us in substance the brief, bloody story of what had happened after we were detached and sent off in the direction of the Devil's Den.

The regiment had waited where we left it until Gen. Hancock, the corps commander, came in person to it and ordered it to charge a body of the enemy then advancing. Col. Colvill gave the order, and the men promptly obeyed it and started on one of the most desperate and bloody, forlorn movements that any organized body of soldiers was ever ordered to attempt. In the execution of this order it suffered a hitherto unheard of loss in open field fighting. Of the 262 in the 8 companies present who advanced in the charge, 215 had been killed or wounded. It was a fearful record and it stands today without a parallel in the history of open warfare since the invention of gunpowder.

There have been massacres: Capt. Lothrop and the 'Flower of Essex' at 'Bloody Brook' in western Massachusetts; Major Dade and his command in the Florida Everglades; and Gen. Custer and the Seventh Cavalry out on the Little Big Horn. But nowhere in history do we find an ordinary organization, without previous notice or preparation, delivering an attack in the open against greatly superior numbers, striking, disorganizing, and checking them, and then retiring with its colors after such a loss as the First Minnesota suffered at Gettysburg.

There were 63 instances in our own Civil War where the loss in killed and wounded (not missing or captured) in a single action exceeded 50 per cent of those engaged. The records, tabulated by Col. William F. Fox and called "Regimental losses in the Civil War," give that number—and the First Minnesota as the greatest sufferer. Fifteen of these instances, nearly one-fourth of them, occurred at Gettysburg.

It is difficult to say what would have happened in any given case if conditions and acts had been different. If Wilcox's brigade had not been interfered with as it was by the charge of our regiment, and Willard's brigade had not advanced to meet Barksdale as it did, then what? Wilcox and Barksdale would surely have advanced in conjunction with Perry and Wright, and that evening's 'shooting match' would have been transferred to the top of the ridge. We who went on to that ridge at just about the time they would have reached it, unhindered, know very well that our friends there were not prepared to give a proper reception to so large a number of uninvited callers.

It was not much more than fairly daylight when we joined the regiment—what was left of it—and listened to the pathetic story of its losses. Colonel Colvill, Lieutenant Colonel Charles P. Adams, Major Mark W. Downie, and Adjutant John Peller had all been wounded. Captain Louis Muller and Lieutenant Waldo Farrer were dead. Captain Joseph Periam and Lieutenants Charles H. Mason and David B. Demarest were mortally wounded. Captains Thomas Sinclair and William Harmon and Lieutenants Chris Heffelfinger and James DeGray were wounded.[1]

Capt. Nathan S. Messick of Company G, as senior captain, took command. All present numbered less than a full company—but a little more than two-thirds of one. There were 47 from the 8 companies, and Company F had not added more than 20—for a total of 67. To these a few detailed men might have been added later, but none came to our company.

Under ordinary circumstances, an organization that had suffered one-half the loss that we had would have been sent to the rear instead of the firing line. But this was no ordinary occasion. It was believed that every available man and gun would be needed for the defense of the ridge if another assault were made—and they

1. The official roster does not show William Harmon rising to the rank of captain, but only first lieutenant of Company C; *Minnesota in Civil and Indian Wars,*1:53.

were. Saving the fact of greater losses, we were a fair sample of other organizations of both armies.

What a pitiable picture we would have made that morning. The stains of powder and dirt, gathered in the marching and the fighting of the two previous days, still covered our hands and faces and clothing, and physical weariness and mental depression and suffering were written on every countenance.

In sharp contrast to this aggregation of mortals concentrated for mutual destruction, nature was in a smiling mood. The sun rose in a cloudless sky, its morning brightness partly veiled by the smoke from the myriads of fires soldiers had lighted to cook their breakfasts and from the rifle fire where the skirmishers of the 12th Corps were contending with Ewell's. The summer heat was tempered by a morning breeze.

The sun was not long above the horizon when we moved to join the brigade, and troops everywhere were getting into position. Some of the Confederate batteries over on Seminary Ridge and up about the Peach Orchard began shelling about this time. It may have been intended for a morning greeting or in sympathy with the firing on the right or a bit of "natural cussedness"—as some one asserted at the time—but I presume it was because they had observed our movements of preparation. Their action provoked our artillery to reply, and shells flew lively for a little time, and some of them unpleasantly near.

When we had reached the place which we were intended to occupy, the firing had impressed us that we were likely to be attacked at any time, and we began immediately to improvise the best protection we could out of anything we could find. We were told that we were to stay there, and we planned to stay as safely and as comfortably as we could.

We were on the slope of the hill[2] facing the enemy and had learned the value of protection until the moment of action came. We gathered rails, stones, sticks, brush, etc., which we piled in front of us; loosened the dirt with our bayonets; and scooped it onto these with our tin plates; and onto this we placed our knapsacks and blankets. Altogether, it made a barricade from 18 inches to 2 feet high that would protect against rifle bullets. This did not take long, as it was only a matter of three or four feet per man, and by the time it was completed the shelling had slackened to an occasional shot.

About this time the discovery was made that we had had no breakfast, that canteens were empty, and that we were hungry. Details were sent with canteens to get water, and when these returned coffee was made. No man can fully and rightly appreciate the value of a cup of coffee until he has partaken of one under some similar circumstances.

2. Cemetery Ridge—the First Minnesota was stationed about four hundred yards south of the Copse of Trees, the object of the Confederates' attack that day; Moe, *Last Full Measure,* 287.

After an examination of our rifles and ammunition, which each man was told to make and refill his box from the extra ones we carried—we laid down behind the little shelters we had made and went to sleep. It seems strange now that we could have done this, for at irregular intervals shells shrieked over us, or we heard the thud of a bullet in the ground, and the fighting on the right was still heard. But we did get an hour or two of needed and refreshing sleep. Now while we are sleeping in the morning sunlight in the open field on the westerly slope of Cemetery Ridge, I ask the reader to consider the situation as it was that morning.

Two great armies had 'sparred' from the Rappahannock to the Susquehanna and met with deadly blows for two days; both had suffered great losses, and neither had gained enough to make the other admit its advantage; and now each appeared to be waiting the action of the other before engaging in another round; and both were busy in preparation for a final struggle. The tinsel and shine of gold cords, brass buttons, and bright uniforms was dimmed by the dust and mud of three states. The 'pomp and circumstance' of martial fields had lost all of their allurements in the surfeiting harvest of death we were gathering. But the purpose for which we had gathered in the 'tented field' was as strong and controlling as at the beginning. Revolting as the scenes already enacted had been to our better natures, the conditions were imperative, and the contest must go on to the end. And that end must inevitably be success or failure, and the latter alternative was not to be considered—so long as we could fight.

It might have been ten o'clock—or earlier or later—when a more violent outbreak on the right (where there had been more or less fighting all the morning) wakened us from the sleep the most of us had been indulging in, and we sat up to listen. The roar of artillery and the rolling volleys of musketry were sufficient evidence of the serious work being done. In an hour or so, it ceased to be prominent, and news came round the line that the enemy had been driven back across Rock Creek with a loss of 2,000—killed, wounded, and prisoners—and 3 battle flags. This was encouraging news, and it proved to be true. It was in itself an important battle and a brilliant affair.

The forenoon of July 3 is generally referred to as having been quiet along the western slope of Cemetery Ridge, and so it was compared with the noise on the right, but it was only a relative term. There was spasmodic skirmishing and sharpshooting at intervals and a hectoring fire along the front much of the time—enough at least to keep us mindful of the situation. Down in front of our Third Division and to its right, it grew lively two or three times.

There was a house between the lines which the Confederates persistently used as a cover for sharpshooters, and they were dislodged from it two or three times only to return. At last Gen. Smythe ordered it burned and sent out a party which quickly accomplished it, but it drew the fire of some Confederate batteries.

Before noon it grew quite warm—or so it seemed to us lying there in the sun—and the hours moved slowly. It was while lying there at about this time that

Romulus E. Jacobs of Company F was hit by a sharpshooter, the ball passing through his shoulders and making a remarkably loud noise so that some thought at first it was an explosive bullet. But an examination showed that the ball had passed through numerous folds of his rubber blanket. Very little could be seen of the enemy on our front, though it was certain they were there yet, and, that being the case, if they did not attack we probably would.

All the morning, as we now know, Lee had been concentrating for a last, mighty effort to dislodge Meade's forces by a drive at their left center. Out about the Peach Orchard and in that vicinity he had massed 83 guns, and on Seminary Ridge 80 more—a total of 172. I suppose our general officers knew of this at the time, as they were adding to the batteries in our rear all the forenoon, and had 80 guns in battery covering the distance of about a mile on Cemetery Ridge before the enemy disclosed his purpose by beginning firing. But they could not have known its full extent.

It was about 1 o'clock when a shell came screeching over us and dropped with a dull explosion somewhere in the rear. This was followed by two more with pauses of a few seconds between. It was the signal for an artillery prelude to Pickett's charge and was followed by a veritable cyclone of shells. Never before or since, on this continent, has it been equaled.

Whatever the exact number of artillery may have been on either side or combined, we who had to lie on that bare hillside with the shots from both sides screaming over us were fully convinced that there were plenty of them. We were not particularly surprised when the firing began, for we were expecting almost anything. But we were astonished at its volume, extent, and duration. We were not unfamiliar with artillery fire, but this proved to be something far beyond all previous experience or conception, and the scene was terrific beyond description. It began fiercely, increased rapidly, and continued persistently.

The enemy's line of artillery was soon marked by banks of white vapor, from beneath which tongues of fire were incessantly darting. The position of the Union line from the Evergreen Cemetery to the Round Tops was wreathed in flame and smoke, with the latter drifting over us in whirling clouds. The enemy's guns formed an arc of nearly a quarter of a circle; the distance was from 1,500 to 2,000 yards. It quickly converged its fire on the ridge and principally on that portion of it held by the Second Corps and Doubleday's division of the First.

There was an incessant, discordant flight of shells—seemingly in and from all directions—howling, shrieking, striking, exploding, tearing, smashing, and destroying—producing a scene that words cannot present and was well nigh unbearable. The ground was torn up; fences and trees knocked to splinters; rocks and small stones were flying in the air; ammunition boxes and caissons were exploded with a frequency we had never known before; guns were dismounted; and men and horses were torn in pieces, as the enemy's massed artillery pounded and ploughed the crest of the ridge where our batteries were.

Fortunately for us, their fire was directed at our batteries, and I am not aware that a single shell dropped in the regiment, though many of them struck in front of us and bounded over us. This ordeal lasted, we are told, about two hours, but it seemed to me that it was running on into *years*. I had been badly scared many times before this but never quite so badly as then. I commended my soul to God, shut my teeth *hard*, and lay flat on the ground—expecting every minute to be blown to atoms.

At last it was noticed that the fire of our batteries was weakening and it slackened to irregular firing. This was surprising and alarming to us, who did not understand that it was ordered to mislead the enemy into thinking that they had silenced them.

Then the Confederate fire ceased on the center of their line, and we got onto our feet and 'pulled ourselves together' for what we felt certain was coming. We knew perfectly well that there would never have been any such expenditure of ammunition by any general in Lee's situation unless he meant to follow it up by an assault. Thus far it had been an artilleryman's fight, but now it was to be a more serious matter—to us at least.

Artillery firing is hard on the nerves and occasionally very destructive when conditions are favorable, but usually the effect is not nearly as great as the noise. A half hour's cannonading—as a rule—is not so destructive to life as a half a minute's 'blizzard' of musketry from a line of infantry at close range.

Soon it was said, "they are coming," and we stood and, eagerly watching, saw a long line of men coming out of the woods on Seminary Ridge. It was followed by others, on either flank. From where we were—looking over the Codori House—we could see near the center of the advancing line as they came down towards the Emmitsburg Road. It was a magnificent spectacle. A rising tide of armed men rolling towards us in steel-crested billows. It was an intensely interesting sight—especially to us who must face it, breast it, break it, or be broken by it.

The tense inaction of hours was ended, and we hastily made preparations to meet this avalanche of bayonets that was being projected against us. The line was adjusted, advancing it a few paces for better position. Then, front rank kneeling, we awaited their coming and the order to fire. Command was given not to fire until ordered—and then to fire at their feet. This was to correct, as far as possible, the tendency to overshoot.

As soon as their lines were fairly developed, they became a target for our artillery, which reopened with terrific discharge. Freeman McGilvery's guns on the ridge to our left, the batteries in our rear, and those to our right joined in the same kind of a converging fire that Longstreets' guns had rained on the Third Corps's lines the day before. From the Cemetery near the town to Little Round Top, there was a mighty thunder of guns and shrieking chorus of flying shells; the whole ridge was wreathed in smoke and flame; and the sulphurous vapor whirled in clouds around us.

It was a deadly, and effective fire, too, but not enough to stop or turn them back. But the right of their line did seem to shrink to its left, and its supports appeared to separate from it, as they got the full force of the fire.[3] When they crossed the Emmitsburg Road—passing on both sides of the Codori House—they were still 500 to 600 yards from the right of our division, where the Philadelphia Brigade held the line at the angle in the stone wall.

At this time, the right of Pickett's Division appeared to change its direction to the left by a partial wheel or oblique movement, exposing it to a flank fire. Gen. Hancock was quick to see this and prompt to take advantage of it by ordering the advance of Stannard's Brigade. By this movement, they were able to get an effective enfilading fire on Kemper's Confederate brigade, which was the right of Pickett's Division. By this movement Stannard's men were thrust into the opening between the right of Pickett's Division and its supports, Wilcox's and Perry's Brigades.

As the attacking line came on, it was seen that its change of direction would bring the point of first contact to our right. With its direction corrected to strike our line squarely, this immense flying wedge—which Lee hoped to drive through the center of the Union army and the heart of the Union—forged rapidly towards us. It was hammered and battered by shells and case shot and, as it came nearer, torn with canister from the batteries. It was being terribly punished, and there was a trail of dead and dying behind it, but its ranks were closed to the left, and it came determinedly on and began firing.

It was not until after that we got the order and sent a rolling fire to the right oblique, directed at their feet, which was about all we could see of them at the time—as all above their knees was covered with the smoke from their own guns. Then every man fired as rapidly as he could handle cartridges and adjust caps. At this time Pickett's three brigades were getting pretty well jammed together and were pushing directly for the angle of the low stone wall held by the Second Brigade of our division.

The two brigades on the right of Pettigrew's Division were now nearly on a line with Pickett's and were closing to their right. The head of Pickett's line struck the Seventy-First Pennsylvania (generally known as the First California), and matters were at a tension which could not last. Men were firing into each other at so short a distance, and with such deadly effect, that neither side could endure it long.

The crisis came when this point was reached, and the hold of the 71st Pennsylvania on the wall was broken, and the fire of two of Cushing's guns at this point was stopped. Through this opening General Lewis Armistead—with his hat on

3. Wright refers to Pickett's Division as the right wing—it marched by the left oblique before the Emmitsburg Road to close up with Pettigrew's and Trimble's Divisions on its left—and to Lang's (Perry's) and Wilcox's Brigades as the "supports"—they separated off to their right.

his sword, it is said—led all who would follow him directly against Cushing's remaining guns, a little to the rear and not far from the Clump of Trees.

Before they had reached the wall, the Third Brigade, commanded by Colonel Norman J. Hall of the 7th Michigan, began a wheel to the rear, on its right, and was directly on the flank of the force coming through the line. As the Third Brigade swung to the rear like a gate on its hinges, our brigade, the First, faced to the right and ran in the rear of the swinging line, past its flank. These movements were made at a run, and the men were cheering. In this way our whole division was thrown onto the flank and head of the column that had broken through the line and was attempting to capture Cushing's remaining guns.

It was a grand rush to get there in the quickest time, without much regard to the manner of it—and we knew very well what we were there for and proceeded to business without ceremony. Closing in on them with a rush and a cheer, there was shooting, stabbing, and clubbing—for there was no time to reload—and then the bloody work was over.

There was a cry of "we surrender." Rifles were thrown down, and hands were thrown up, and those who had borne them so defiantly ran a little to the rear and dropped down to shield themselves from the bullets of their comrades, who had not advanced so far. Ignoring these for the moment, we rushed for the low wall where the break had been made, and very quickly all who had passed it were killed, captured, or had fled. Many outside of the wall came in and surrendered.

As soon as the smoke lifted sufficiently to permit us to see, all that could be seen of the mighty force that had been driven so furiously against us was scattered and running to the rear. That is—all that were able to run. The bodies of many unfortunate victims marked the course of the assault. Some of these lay still where they had fallen, and others were trying to find some safer place.

It is very encouraging at a time like that, when you have done your best and know it, to see the backs of your enemies, and the space between you and them widening. It was so satisfactory that our fellows could not refrain from cheering, as we ceased firing and realized the situation. It was an occasion worthy of cheers—if ever—despite the fact that many were dead and dying. The 'high-water mark' of the rebellion had been reached, and the tidal wave of treason—which had drenched the land with fraternal blood—was running back toward final peace.

What a multitude of wrecks marked the place of its greatest culmination! What a scene it was! What a wild fury of excitement ruled the moment! Our whole division had been rushed to the point of attack at a full run and was a mixed and disordered mass, but it was an aggressive, fighting quantity of tremendous energy, and expended its force on the enemy like an explosion. In a very brief interval it was over.

Others of our force had hastened to our aid as fast as they could come, and all of the enemy able to escape had hurried to their own lines—their batteries throwing shells to cover their retreat. Those not able to get away and those not caring to take the risk of a run to the rear hastened into our lines, with uplifted hands, that they might escape danger from their own artillery.

As they began throwing shells, it was uncertain what might follow, and, to be prepared and present a proper front to the enemy, our line was quickly reformed. This was not really necessary, as was soon evident, and then we had an opportunity to note more considerately the situation about us. It had been a desperate, savage, determined assault by from 15,000 to 18,000; and it had been met by a force sufficiently strong and persistent to wreck it and send it back in fragments. But this had not been done without a great sacrifice. About one-third of the 'White Clubs' engaged had been killed or wounded. (The 2nd Corps badge was a trefoil similar to the ace of clubs used on playing cards, and the color of the 2nd Division was white.) Our depleted little regiment had lost 32 more men.

Now that the critical part of the struggle was apparently over, the intense feelings that had carried us through it subsided rapidly, and the usual relaxation following such high-pressure emotions followed. For about 65 hours we had been under almost constant physical or mental strain or both and had pretty nearly reached the limit of both. As soon as the need for further exercise of muscles or will ceased to be imperative, most of the men realized that they were bordering upon a condition of collapse.

Those who have not had the experience cannot easily understand how the intense energies necessary to carry men through days of action and excitement—and worked to their utmost in such struggle—use up the vital forces. But those who have 'been there' do not need to be shown.

I have frequently been asked why our army did not make immediate pursuit of their broken lines and destroy them? It was not then certain that their lines were 'broken,' and we know now they were not. Only their assault had failed. Gen. Meade decided that in his judgment it was best not to take the risk. So far as our division or corps was concerned (and we presume it was a fair sample of the others except the Sixth), it is much like asking why an engine does not continue on its way when it has exhausted its supply of fuel or water and the track ahead is obstructed.

The prisoners were collected and sent to the rear; the wounded were cared for, as well as they could be where there were so many; and each company tried to ascertain just what had happened to it. As the movements of the company had not been far or complicated, and were over open ground, this was an easier task than usual.

In this last movement Company F had had 2 men killed and 7 wounded. Sergeant Phil Hamline had been killed and Corporal Leonard Squire mortally wounded. The others wounded were: Cyrus Bondurant, Henry Burgtorf, Almeron Davis, Artemus L. M. Decker, Charles L. Hubbs, Corp. Horatio N. Barber, and James A. Wright, First Sergeant of the Company. Burgtorf, Decker, and

Hubbs were at the time on a detail with Cushing's Battery. Romulus E. Jacobs had been shot by a sharpshooter earlier in the day; and Marion F. Abbott, James F. Bachelor, and Levi King had been wounded the evening before—making the total loss of Company F at Gettysburg 13 (2 killed and 11 wounded.) This was just half of the men who started to march from the Rappahannock on the 14th of June.

It was a splendid record to have put every man into action after 17 days of such strenuous campaigning; and then, after two more days of fighting, to have every man accounted for at the close—one-half of them on the casualty list and the other half answering to their names in the ranks.

At Savage's Station one-third of the loss of the regiment had fallen on Company F, but at Gettysburg it was the most fortunate company in the regiment. Two captains, Nathan S. Messick of Company G and Wilson B. Farrell of Company C, were killed that afternoon. According to the best information I can find, the regiment took 330 officers and men into action at Gettysburg, and of these 247 were either killed or wounded. Six were reported missing in the first report, but later they were found dead. Seven officers and 71 enlisted men were killed or died of their wounds, and 139 others wounded.[4]

My own injuries were not of a serious nature, and I did not include my name in the list that I prepared for the acting adjutant the next morning, but it appeared in a later one. As the case was a little out of the ordinary, and it will indicate the measure of excitement under which men are sometimes acting, I will give it briefly.

When we were running to the right to close the break in the lines, it was a case of 'get there,' and each one was trying to make it as quickly as possible. There was not much regard to formation. I could only recall afterwards that Joe Richardson was just to my right and trying to talk as we ran. But his impediment of speech, the excitement, and the effort of running—to say nothing of the noise—were pretty effective hindrances.

Just then I was conscious of coming in contact with something. I was partly turned aside, staggered, confused, and half-blinded—but it was only for an instant. Then my vision cleared, and I 'braced up' and ran on again. And my mind was so wholly taken up with what was before me that I thought no more about it.

When the affair was nearly over, I again saw Joe, and he was still trying to talk, and with not much better success. He was evidently trying to combine some of his unique 'swear-words' with quotations from the Bible and ancient literature, and in that way do justice to the occasion, but it did not run together very smoothly. This is a specimen of what he was saying and a suggestion of the way he said it: "By the l-l-lovely l-l-little angels a-and th-the g-gr-great h-ho-horn s-sp-

---

4. Wright's subtotals of killed and wounded do not add up to his total of 247 casualties— and they differ from other lists of the First Minnesota's casualties at Gettysburg. The explanation likely lies in different definitions of "wounded." His 79 killed is close to Moe's "at least 80 Minnesotans killed or mortally wounded"; *Last Full Measure,* 296.

spoon, we-we'll sh-sh-show 'em th-th-there is a God in Is-Is-Israel. We-we are g-get-getting s-s-some s-s-sa-satisfaction now, ain't we, sa-sargent?"

All the time he was loading and capping his rifle. Then he said, "I-I se-see a-a m-m-man se-set-setting th-the t-tra-trail. Sh-sh-shall I sh-sh-shoot him?" And without waiting for an answer, he brought his gun to his shoulder and fired.

At the same time I saw one of the enemy—who was apparently trying to shelter himself behind a broken artillery carriage a little way in front of us—fall. Joe always insisted that the man was trying to shift the trail of the gun so as to aim it in our direction—and perhaps he was.

But it was of myself and not of Joe that I was going to write. It was not until after the excitement of the moment had subsided, and we began to get together, that I observed that my neck and face were bleeding. I then found that the left shoulder, breast, and sleeve of my blouse were ornamented with shreds of lead and splinters of wood, and several of the latter were driven into the side of my face and neck.

Some of the larger pieces of lead had gone through my clothes, and one had lodged in the left shoulder, and another just below the collar bone. A more careful inspection showed that the splinters were of seasoned walnut. They must have come from a gunstock and the lead from a bullet that struck something harder at the same time. But I never knew whose gun or more about it. The splinters and lead were easily removed and, though sore and painful for a time, were not disabling or serious. But the whole affair shows the absorbing degree of excitement under which we were acting.

After the care of the wounded (which was first to get them to the surgeons and sheltered from bullets, if firing should be resumed), our next care was something to eat, for we now began to realize that we were getting hungry. In the gathering darkness we built little fires and made coffee.

None of us knew where we were likely to be or what the morrow would bring for us to do, and as we drank our coffee we decided to bury Hamline that night. Search was made for a spade, and after some time a shovel was found. With this a shallow trench was dug beside a walnut tree, near which he had been killed, struck by four bullets. His blanket and tent cloth were spread in it. He was then laid upon them and covered with the remaining portions. Then those present knelt in silence about him with uncovered, bowed heads. I do not now recall that a word was spoken, but it was a sincere and reverential service fitting the time and the situation. Then we covered him over with the dirt and stones we had thrown out of the trench and placed at his head a board, on which his name, company, and regiment had been marked.

Then we went back to where *three* stacks of guns marked the position of Company F in the line—one of the largest companies in the regiment. It was now sometime after dark—ten o'clock or later—and we laid down to sleep and in a few minutes were oblivious to all of the suffering and sorrow about us.

Sancho Panza invoked a blessing on "the man that *invented* sleep," and it is a blessing, not only to the exhausted body but to the disturbed mind. It is true we were no longer the sensitive, sentimental youngsters we were when we left our northern homes. Mere sentiment had been knocked out of us by the actual experiences of years of active war. Military training and every-day surroundings had tended to repress expressions of feeling and had changed us to seasoned soldiers. But no one—though but moderately endowed with common sense and no more than the ordinary amount of compassion in his makeup—could fail to sympathize deeply with the overwhelming amount of suffering that existed and which they were powerless to relieve. Tens of thousands were suffering from wounds. Many were dying every hour. And many still living considered those already dead more fortunate than themselves. It was indeed a blessing, a gracious blessing, that our exhausted bodies and over-wrought minds could find respite and renewal in sleep.

I feel that I ought not to pass on without a word about the two members of Company F who gave that "last full measure of devotion" to their country of which Lincoln spoke at Gettysburg. I do not think it would have been possible to have taken two from the company who would have been so generally missed and so sincerely mourned. Big-chested, broad-shouldered young fellows, almost if not quite six feet tall, they were a couple of splendid specimens of physical development. Neither had had much in the way of educational advantages, but both were well-endowed mentally. Their standing in the company as soldiers was first class. Men of proved courage and 'plenty of sand'—to be depended upon anywhere and all of the time. As 'non coms' they were a credit to themselves and the company—and a commission to either of them would have been worthily bestowed with no discredit to the State of Minnesota.

I had no acquaintance with either until I met them as members of the company, but I judge their early life had been under very different environments. Squire was the older, 26 years, and he was not exactly a saint—as he sometimes asserted. He did not always refuse a drink. He would sometimes 'set into a game' and use profanity, but these things were not of a degree to in any way interfere with his duties as a soldier. I knew nothing of his family or where he enlisted from.

Hamline, in these things, was a strong contrast. He was in his 23rd year, was of a religious temperament, trained up in a good old-fashioned Methodist home, where the day begun and ended with reading the Bible and prayers. He was always and everywhere an honest, earnest, consistent, Christian man, whose open, unostentatious, frank, manly, and unobtrusive observance of what he considered his religious duties was well-known and respected by all who knew him. It did take moral courage of a high order to live the life he did, situated as he was.

I say without hesitation that I never knew a man who had a more absolute trust in God or one that made his religion more completely and beautifully a part of his daily life. No man in the company was more universally respected, and no one better deserved respect. Deprecating war, loving and praying for peace, he was fighting for his government as the performance of a sacred duty he owed to it and his God. He had the most implicit faith in an "overruling Providence" and seemed to feel that—no matter what happened to him personally—all that he was fighting for was certain to be accomplished. The results were splendid vindication of his sublime faith. His memory is a sweet perfume from the days of my association with him and is a halo over the service.

Squire died from his wounds and was buried with others of the regiment. Hamline and Squire were removed to the National Cemetery and reburied, with the rest of the dead from Minnesota who were not taken to their former homes for final burial.

There are a few things that I desire to say of the regiment as a whole. The fighting of July 2 had left it only a battered and shattered remnant—its field officers all disabled, and the average strength of its companies much less than a 'corporal's guard.'

Captain Messick was in command, and Corporal John Dehn carried the flag—he being the only one of the color guard of the day before able to be on his feet at the close of the fighting the evening of the 2nd—a new detail being necessary. In the 'mix-up' with Pickett's men he was shot through the hand, and the same shot splintered the flagstaff so that it broke in two pieces. Corporal Henry D. O'Brien then took the piece with the flag on and kept it until twice wounded, when it passed into the hands of Corporal William N. Irvine, who carried it through the fighting. The flag of the 28th Virginia was captured by Marshall Sherman. A portion of this staff was used to replace the broken portion of ours. The splice was made on the field by a little rough whittling and bound with a knapsack strap and was carried afterwards until the regiment went to the state the next February.

In spite of all efforts to equalize them, I still believe there is a difference between the measure of credit due those who were sacrificing to save—and those who were exerting themselves to destroy—the government, just as there is a difference between the incendiary who would burn and the fireman who would save buildings. This may be a bit of obsolete sentiment, or wartime prejudice, but I have never been able to entirely divest myself of it.

Whatever the exact losses on either side, it is certain that both armies suffered terribly during the three days of murderous fighting, and were in a shattered and exhausted condition at its close. Truly, Gettysburg was a scene of suffering and sacrifice to an eminent degree—and not equaled elsewhere during the war. After the lapse of 48 years, I cannot recall them without greater feelings of revulsion than those associated with any other battlefield where I shared a part. "God's broken images cumbered the plain, and wrecks of humanity were everywhere." The character of the fighting necessarily made the losses heavy and many organizations suffered to a marked degree. It was simply the fate of war and not the purpose or planning of anyone that placed the First Minnesota Regiment most prominently in the list of notable sacrifices.

When we had lain down to sleep, the moon was shining brightly and big in the sky. When we were awakened in the early morning of July 4th to 'get under arms,' it was covered with dull gray clouds, the heat was oppressive, and darkness gave way to daylight but slowly as we waited for sunrise.

When I roused up I found my neck was stiff and my face and shoulder were swollen, but I had already determined to stay with the company, and so informed Capt. Ball, and called the roll as usual. There was nothing in the lack of brightness and warm, oppressive air to relieve the depressed feelings that follow a battle when the excitement is gone. It is true that the four or five hours that we had slept, lying on the ground in line, had been more refreshing than one might suppose, but still it was an aggregation of forlorn, weary-looking individuals that gathered about the fires to make coffee when we were dismissed.

Unwashed and uncombed since we had left Uniontown, we had gathered the usual defilements of the road and the bivouac. To these ordinary accumulations of grime—which come to those who labor and sweat over dusty or muddy roads and sleep by the wayside where night or necessity dictates—had been added the uncompromising black of gunpowder. As it was our custom to tear the paper cartridges with our teeth, many loose grains of powder had adhered to our sweating faces and hands and been smeared over them, until a question as to the original Caucasian color might consistently have been raised. Also, the color of our uniforms might have been questioned, for the 'army blue' was less prominent than the chocolate and mahogany mud stains they had gathered crossing Maryland and Virginia. We were generally as soiled as pigs that had been rooting in the fields and sleeping in the fence corners. Every man's face showed anxiety and physical suffering, and the eyes were swollen or inflamed.

However, these things were of little consideration, in view of our situation and surroundings, and we sat on the ground and drank coffee and ate 'hard tack,' expecting all of the time to be called on to move or perform some duty—but we were not. It was not an inspiring morning, and I do not now recall anything that was said.

After we had eaten, we prepared to move and rested at will waiting orders, and it was not long before the most of the boys were lying about promiscuously, sleeping with their heads on their knapsacks, or sprawled on the ground. Before noon the sun was wholly obscured; distant thunder was heard; and a light rain was falling. A rainstorm to shelterless mortals usually brings a train of discomforts, but at first it was rather refreshing than otherwise, and as I sat on my knapsack I bared my head to the cooling moisture. It was really a blessing to the thirsty, fevered wounded, of whom there were still many on the field uncared for.

It is generally said that our army 'rested on the field' that day, which is true, but it must not be construed to mean that nothing was done by any of the troops.

Early in the morning a strong skirmish line was pushed out until it came in contact with the enemy, and skirmishing continued until the lines of both were located. It was talked that a council of war was being held and that there was an exchange of flags of truce. I presume that there were flags of truce concerning the wounded and dead. While it was evident that Lee was prepared with a strong force along the line of Seminary Ridge, it was known that he had withdrawn from the town and had drawn back both of his flanks.

As the hours passed and the storm increased, and we were not called on for any duty, I placed some flat stones beside a little bunch of bushes, put my knapsack on them to keep it out of the water, and sat on it with my rubber over me. I sat—as others were sitting—with my gun across my knees and the lock protected by my rubber to keep it dry. I turned down the brim of my old slouch hat to make the water run off at the front as I bent forward with my elbows resting on my knees.

It was not my intention to sleep, but the position seemed comfortable. The soothing rain or some other soporific influence closed my eyes and sealed my senses in dreamless slumber. When I awoke some hours later, I found myself lying on my side across my knapsack and gun with the right side of my face resting on my right arm and knees resting in the mud and water. My hat had fallen off and was partly filled with water, while the rubber blanket covered my head and shoulders—and not much else. With the exception of my head and shoulders, I was as wet as water could make me.

Long continuance in the same position with impeded circulation made my arms numb, and my whole body was stiff and sore. For the moment I was in doubt as to who I was or where I was, and could not seem to connect myself with any previous person or experience any more than if I had never existed. Then I gradually 'came to,' and things assumed a consistent relationship in my mind. It was with some difficulty that I could get on to my feet and pick up my rifle, and sometime before I had a normal use of my arms and legs.

When I was able to make an intelligent observation around me, I saw some of the boys busy putting up their tents, and others were lying on the ground, sleeping serenely—the rain falling on them and the muddy water running around and under them. I found that Sergeant Childs, who was my 'blanket companion' and buttoned his tent cloth to mine when we went through the formality of putting up our tents, had already procured the necessary sticks and said he was ready to put up the tent, as there were no orders to move yet and might not be any.

This met my approval, and it did not take long to select a place and put up the tent and find something to spread on the ground to keep our blankets out of the mud. As it was now near night and was not raining so hard, it was thought to be a good time to get our supper. Sergeant Childs went to find some water fit to make coffee while I tried to coax wet wood to burn. The water was all muddy from the rains, but such as we could get we used and tried not to think of the very impurities that might be held in solution.

I also found some soap in our haversack and washed my hands and bruised face and shoulder, after which I went to the surgeon, who washed it again with a sponge and applied adhesive plaster. By the time these things were done the coffee was ready to drink, and we went to the shelter of our tent to drink it. It should be remembered that the center of the tent was scarcely 4 feet high at the highest point and only broad enough for two to sleep beside each other, while one must be under the ridge to sit up. It was not very commodious quarters, and our clothing and all we had was more or less wet—as was the ground where we had pitched it—but it was some protection, and we were grateful for it.

By the time we had finished our coffee and crackers, which was practically all we had left to eat, it was time for the evening roll call.

It now seemed likely that we would remain where we were until morning, though of this we could not be certain. Capt. Ball directed us to make ourselves as comfortable as we could—each man caring for his own gun—and to be ready to fall in if called. At this time there was a generous display of lightning and jarring thunder to the west of us, and another heavy shower was imminent.

Before it grew too dark to see I wrote briefly in my diary, the first since we had reached the field. I said, "It is raining. The regiment has been waiting on the hill, near where it did the last fighting, all day. The loss of the regiment has been very severe. There are about 100 left, but many of them are wounded; myself among them, but not seriously. The battlefield is a fearfully horrid sight. There has been only skirmishing today."

The night was a series of lively thunderstorms with only brief intervals between them. The sound of one storm, passing away, had not ceased before the vivid lightning of another was seen, and the rolling thunder of its coming heard—and was followed by a downpour of rain that fairly flooded the surface of the ground. Nature was washing away the blood-stains of the battle. Of course our rude shelter did not wholly protect us from such a storm as it fell, and overflowing water ran along the ground under us.

In spite of these storms and frequent unpleasant awakenings—from additional moisture from above or below—we slept much of the time. At that time sleep seemed to be the most urgent demand of nature, and it was almost impossible to resist the inclination to sleep, when opportunity offered.

When morning came, it was still raining—a mild summer rain—but the lightning, the thunder, and the boisterous wind had ceased. The first news when we were called at daylight was that the enemy had gone. This was Sunday morning, July 5th. I do not recall that there was much rejoicing at the news, which was anticipated, but I am sure we were glad to be relieved of their presence, for they had proved themselves 'undesirable' neighbors.

Our first care was to get our breakfasts and put ourselves in readiness for whatever might be ordered. We should have drawn rations the day before and there had not been much left in our haversacks but cracker crumbs and coffee when we finished our suppers and these were all we had for breakfast that morning.

Soon after the morning report, July 5th, it was reported that we were not likely to march until afternoon, and Capt. Ball allowed Sergeant Benner and a couple of men to go out to try to find something to eat, as nature was reasserting herself and we were getting hungry, and it was uncertain when the wagons would arrive.

For my own part, I bathed my bruised face and laid down to sleep some more, after writing a short letter to my mother. I slept for an hour or two, and when I waked it was still raining, but I got up to walk around a little and try to find some way to mail the letter. Seeing some citizens not far off who had come into the camp, I requested one of them to take and mail my letter, which he agreed to do.

Speaking of the citizens reminds me of another one of the natives, a rather queer-looking specimen who made his appearance a little later. He wore a home-made straw hat with a broken brim and was coatless. He had an army blanket across his arm and carried a soldier's hat in his hand, which I presume he had picked up. He talked loudly and rapidly as if greatly excited and was lamenting the losses he had suffered.

The greatest of these appeared to be a colt, which he asserted was very valu-able and about which he seemed inconsolable. Said he was hunting for it and in-quired if it had been seen about there. His earnestness soon attracted a group about him, and the boys were amused that he should come to such a place at a time like that on an errand of that nature—and laughed at him.

As he continued to dwell so self-pityingly upon his personal losses, the ab-surdity of such deep feeling over the loss of an animal and the callous disregard for all the loss of life and human suffering about him impressed itself quite forcibly upon those who heard him. Someone invited him to "shut up," and he was told to "make himself scarce" as quickly as he could. As an incentive to prompt action, he was informed that he would be "killed in about a minute" if he remained there talking that way.

The man seemed surprised and hurt at the view of his case taken by the sol-diers, and hurried away. As he was going someone called after him to "drop that hat and blanket," which he did and disappeared.

About noon Sergeant Benner and the boys who had been out after 'grub' re-turned with three loaves of bread, some biscuits, and a part of a homemade cheese. Enough for our dinners and something more.

Soon after this, orders came to get ready to march, which raised a question as to what was to be done with the wounded men then with the regiment. As there were no sufficient accommodations or shelter, even for the more seriously wounded, it was thought that almost any place was better than to remain there. It was determined that all who were able to walk would do better if they should keep with their companies. This I had already decided to do, as I had a strong disin-clination to be in any way separated from the company.

About two o'clock, some wagons arrived, and we drew two-days' rations of coffee, sugar, crackers, and salt pork. I also arranged with one of the drivers to take charge of my knapsack and woolen blanket, retaining only the rubber blanket and piece of tent-cloth. A little later, there was an informal inspection of arms and ammunition, and an issue of extra cartridges.

It was about three o'clock by this time, and we formed for the march. It was only the skeleton of the old regiment—and a shrunken, diminutive one at that—that stood in line when the order came to move. We headed back on the Taneytown Road, over which we had marched coming on to the field.

I took dinner at the home of Miss Redhead today
JULY-SEPTEMBER 1863

VERY LITTLE WAS THEN KNOWN of where our enemies were—though there was little doubt but they were safe on the other side of the mountains. We had heard some firing late in the afternoon the day before, but it was pretty certain that the Sixth Corps, which had followed, had not overtaken them in time to prevent their getting through the pass or we should have heard more.

We had expected to march early that morning of July 6 but did not and finally remained where we were during the day, sleeping most of the time.

Tuesday morning, July 7, the camp was astir before it was light; breakfast was eaten; and we were in line before five o'clock. The day's rest had been beneficial to all, and it was evident there was a recovery of physical strength and elasticity of spirits among the boys. I do not mean that anyone was really dancing around from an excess of bodily energy or singing from the joy of simple existence. Far from that. Only that the boys were rallying from the tremendous physical and mental strain and the depression of the battle.

Between two and three o'clock, our division went into bivouac about a mile beyond Taneytown after a continuous march of ten miles. Though the march had not been long, we were both tired and hungry. Practically, we had been living on coffee, crackers, and salt pork for nearly a month, frequently enduring the extremes of exercise and exposure and other hardships incidental to active campaigning, and were in no condition for hard marching.

During the day, occasionally we had heard the sound of a distant gun but nothing to indicate any serious fighting. Many stories were in circulation, but we had very little real knowledge of the situation generally, more than that Lee had retreated west of the mountains. As our movement was down the easterly side, it was apparent that we were maneuvering to keep between his army and Washington.

We did not go into Taneytown but were told that many of the wounded were being cared for there by a corps of volunteer nurses from Philadelphia—and that they had brought a band with them to cheer them with music. Some of them visited the bivouac late in the afternoon. We were all intensely interested to see them, for it was a great rarity to see a peacefully-disposed woman those days, but we were so ragged and dirty we were ashamed to be seen. They looked at us, however, very much (we thought) as people look at wild animals in a menagerie. We heard the band playing, too, until we slept. "When This Cruel War Is Over" was new and popular, and its words and music stirred a longing response in our hearts.

Wednesday morning, July 8th, we were waked by a noisy thunderstorm before daylight and soon after had orders to get ready for the march. The storm did not last long, but the road was made so bad that marching was altogether disagreeable until we struck the Frederick City Pike near Middleburg, where the storm did not appear to have reached with such severity. A little before dark we bivouacked about five miles out of Frederick City, having marched about 20 miles.

All were tired, and we recalled the 29th of June when we had hurried northward over the same road. Was it possible that barely ten days had passed since that long-drawn-out march and the unpleasant episode with the Inspector General? Many—very many—of those whose feelings had been deeply stirred by his arbitrary action had ceased to be responsive to human influences—gracefully at rest in soldier's graves. The incident itself was seemingly far back in our lives, if not connected with another period of existence.

I was so completely used up by the day's tramp that I at once laid down, too tired to make an effort to prepare my supper. I soon slept. An hour or so later a comrade waked me with a cup of coffee and a slice of fried pork. I was also told that a mail had arrived at division headquarters and had been sent for.

This was decidedly interesting, as the arrival of a mail always was, and the last regular one had been the 18th of June. In a little while the regimental mail was brought in and distributed, and almost every one had one or more letters—many being for those who could never read them now. We were always glad to get letters, and they turned the thoughts towards home through the channels of tenderest feeling. Glad as we were to get letters, they frequently brought sad news. One of the letters I received that night brought its message of sorrow. What a tragedy life was in those dismal days of the war!

Thursday morning, July 9th, we were called before it was light. I realized that I was in no condition for a long tramp, but I could not bring myself to the point of dropping out, and got ready for the march. It could not have been much after five o'clock when we took to the road leading to Frederick City, marching at quick time.

The morning was fair and warm, and it was somewhere between 7 and 8 o'clock when we began passing through the city. Early as the hour was, there were many people on the street, and they showed a real interest and gave us a hearty welcome, waving hats and handkerchiefs. The city seemed full of soldiers off duty, and the Seventh New York Militia—a swell organization that was said to be composed entirely of wealthy men—was doing guard duty on the streets. We had met them before at Washington in 1861, when we first arrived there. It was not very polite, but the boys 'guyed' them pretty freely on their good clothes and ability to 'hold themselves aloof from mortal strife' and get all of the 'soft snaps' guarding cities.

Meantime, more firing was heard at intervals, and we pushed on as rapidly as possible over the muddy roads. It was near noon when we halted on the hills opposite Falling Waters and learned that the affair was over before any of the infantry arrived. The rear guard of one column of the Confederates, who were crossing on a pontoon at that point, had been caught by the cavalry under Kilpatrick and Buford and promptly attacked. After some hours of intermittent fighting the Confederates had cut loose the Maryland end of their bridge and allowed it to swing to the Virginia shore, leaving the rear guard on the Maryland side.

Lee's army was now all south of the Potomac in Virginia, and he hastened to reunite the two separated columns about Winchester, where he was met with supplies and reinforcements. It does not need to be said that it was a distinct and great disappointment to the Army of the Potomac that the Confederate Army of Northern Virginia should have succeeded in getting away without another hammering, but experience had taught us the uncertainty of results in war.

Going near the Antietam battlefield where we had fought the previous September, we passed through the old town of Sharpsburg and crossed the Antietam on the bridge where Burnside made his tardy assault late in the afternoon of Sept. 17, 1862. When near the top of the ridge which ends in Maryland Heights, near Harpers Ferry, we were left at a crossroad to await the coming of the division while the ambulances went back. Here we made ourselves as comfortable as we could; sleeping beside the road and between naps picking blackberries, which grew abundantly along the walls and fences and were now getting ripe.

Thursday morning, July 16, we took to the road over the mountain soon after sunrise. Passing Maryland Heights on our right, we went down into the valley and bivouacked near Sandy Hook. The river was still high and the water dirty, but it was an opportunity we had been waiting for, and the boys promptly improved it to take a long-deferred and much-needed bath and wash their shirts.

I was fortunate here in getting my knapsack again, which I had put in one of the wagons when we started from Gettysburg. This gave me a woolen blanket and a change of shirts and my self-respect rose to a degree that would have prompted me to have blacked my army brogans if I had possessed a pair worth shining. As it was I did not waste any energy in that direction and, after writing a brief letter to my mother, spent the remainder of the day with as little effort as possible.

Friday morning, July 17, I was called before it was fairly light and directed to make out requisitions for such shoes and clothing as was urgently needed—and three days' extra rations. We were obliged to wait some time, and then got three days' field rations, a partial supply of shoes, but no clothing.

Papers of the day before came in on a train while we were waiting, and, as we had seen them but rarely for more than a month, some of us made up a 'pot' of 15 cents and bought one. Besides the war news, there were big headlines and some surprising news about what were termed the Draft Riots in New York City, which had broken out there on the 13th.[1]

When we moved again, it was across the Potomac on a pontoon bridge into Harpers Ferry. Keeping through the lower portion of the town, we turned to the left and crossed the Shenandoah on another pontoon. Continuing the march around the northerly end of Loudoun Heights, we turned south into the Loudoun Valley. Meade's movement was through the Loudoun Valley on the easterly side of the Blue Ridge mountains, while Lee's was through the Shenandoah Valley on the westerly side—with the mountain range and the Shenandoah River between them.

Wednesday morning, July 22, we were on the road toward Ashby's Gap, near which place we bivouacked after the sun had gone down behind the range. Thursday, as soon as we were on the road, we moved rapidly. It was the general expectation that our army would push through Manassas Gap, and that there would be fighting somewhere on the other side, toward Front Royal or the river[2]—unless Lee had already slipped by. Friday morning, we advanced in support of the other two corps, who pushed into the Shenandoah Valley as far as Front Royal—only to find the enemy gone. Some sheep, and cattle, and a few stragglers were picked up, but Lee's army had made a safe retreat. We turned back through the Gap to the easterly end, where we halted for the night, tired and hungry.

Saturday morning, July 25, we were moving at 4:30. It was the middle of the afternoon when we reached a point on the railroad near White Plains—tired, sweaty, dirty, and ravenously hungry.

Sunday proved a very warm one. It was late in the afternoon when we finally halted not far from Warrenton, having marched about 20 miles. We did not know it then, but when the army reached the vicinity of Warrenton, the campaign was ended. The firing we heard every day was only skirmishing to locate the enemy's lines, and our delay there was to distribute the army along the upper Rappahannock to countervail any movement of the enemy.

By August 4, we made camp in the open field near the rest of the division and not far from a stream of fairly good water. This camp was five or six miles from the Rappahannock and the nearest place on it of note was Kelley's Ford. Here we located a formal camp and had orders from the brigade commander to put up our shelter tents, which left the impression that we were likely to remain there for a time. This was very welcome news, as several of the boys were lame from bruised feet and others suffering from camp diseases.

1. After the drawing of names of drafted men on July 12, a mob of fifty thousand rioted in New York City. They attacked policemen, Union soldiers, and blacks. On July 14, Meade sent two regiments and one battery to the city to help restore order. Numerous regiments followed.
2. Lee was retreating along the Shenandoah River and being resupplied from the fertile valley farms.

Thursday, August 6, was set apart for prayer and thankfulness for the recent successes of our armies at Gettysburg and Vicksburg. Its observance here was very much like Sunday, with religious services which were well-attended. Besides these, there was a lecture by a man from Delaware. He was a fine speaker and talked with much feeling. But after we had gone to our tents, we talked the matter over, and some of the boys expressed the opinion that talk is cheap, and that it would be a better evidence of 'all-wool-and-a-yard-wide' patriotism if he would enlist and shoulder a musket.

On Saturday, the guards picked up some men of the regiment for gambling. This was one of the vices of the camp, and it was surprising what a passion some men developed for it, while it did not seem to be in the least attractive to others. Personally, this manner of passing dull hours in the camp did not appeal to me, and there were pretty strict orders against it. It could only be indulged in 'on the sly,' but there were some who would take the risks of losing their money (and a night in the guardhouse) whenever they had money to lose. To an observer it was in a way amusing, somewhat surprising, and really an absurdity when men would sit on a blanket, lose all their money, declare they were 'dead broke,' and get up cursing their 'ill luck,' and never seem to blame themselves for doing it. Neither did they seem to profit by experience, but were ready to 'take a hand' the next time they had a dollar.

On Friday, August 14, the chaplain invited the boys to meet in the open space between our regiment and the 19th Maine. A large company gathered, and he made a short address. Many songs were sung; several prayers were offered; and the men remained to sing and talk after the meeting was dismissed. It began to seem like a restoration of the old spirit of the regiment, which had been badly depressed by its losses at Gettysburg.

I have never been able to sing, but I have always listened to singing with real satisfaction, and it suggested agreeable entertainment when I heard it planned to meet again the next evening to sing. However, all plans are subject to disarrangement, and this is especially true of soldiers in the field. We had no thought of it then, but before the next evening we had left the camp—on what proved to be the most pleasant expedition during our service.

Saturday morning, August 15, began with the usual duties of the camp and without thoughts of anything more until after the regular details had been sent out. Soon after this, the orderly's call summoned me to headquarters, and there the order was given to get the companies ready to march—taking all of our materiel with us—and await further orders.

These instructions created a stir in the camp, and, as the men packed their knapsacks, they indulged in guessing as to their final destination. There had been talk for some days that troops were being sent to New York City, and also that a part of the 11th Corps had gone to Charleston to assist in the operations against Ft. Sumter. Speculation was divided between those two places. It was also learned that the Seventh Michigan of our division and the Eighth Ohio of the 3rd Division had orders similar to those we had and were making like preparations.[3]

Our comrades of the other regiments in the brigade and division gathered around and plied us with questions and suggestions and frankly expressed their regrets that the good comradeship that had grown up between us was to be severed. For nearly two years we had been closely associated and shared the fortunes of war together. If further fighting was to be done, we could not hope for better companions—and it was gratifying to us that the 7th Michigan and 8th Ohio were to go with us, wherever we might be going.

It was afternoon when marching orders came, and when formed we found the whole division getting into line. Headed by the bands, the division escorted us out of the camp and paid us parting honors. We marched off with the men of the other regiments cheering and the bands playing "Bully for You." We had no band, only drummers and buglers detailed, but the band of the 72nd Pennsylvania Regiment had been sent to 'play us out of camp.'

We were joined by the 7th Michigan as we passed out of the camp and by the 8th Ohio on the road—whose colonel, Samuel S. Carroll (familiarly known as "Brick Top" because his hair was inclined to be red), took command of the detachment, being the senior officer present.

It was nearly sundown when we reached the railroad at Bealeton Station; and it was getting dark before a train was backed up on to a switch; and we were ordered to "pile on to it," which we did—literally. It was composed of ordinary flat cars without any more accommodations for passengers than a barn floor. We bestowed ourselves on these as compactly as we could, the floor being covered with men sitting on their knapsacks and rows along the sides with their feet hanging over the edges. It was not ideal as to position or comfort for a long journey, but for a short emergency trip of 60 miles or so, of a dark night, it was a whole lot better than walking and carrying a heavy knapsack.

We accepted the situation as better than we expected and, as we jolted over the uneven rails of the often-raided and poorly-repaired Orange & Alexandria Railroad, the boys talked about their probable destination and possible service required of them. At that time it was only certain that we were headed for Alexandria, which was a frequent starting point for our campaigns.

It was after midnight when the cars rattled into the suburbs of Alexandria, and we transferred ourselves to the ground. We had been well 'peppered' with dust and cinders, and at times almost strangled with smoke. The six hours of jolting had given us all of the 'exercise without effort' that we felt in need of, and we spread ourselves on the ground without waiting for orders—satisfied to remain where we were for the remainder of the night. Then, being familiar with the place,

---

3. The Seventh Michigan had suffered severe losses at Gettysburg, and the Eighth Ohio had fought well, launching a flank assault on Pettigrew's attackers on July 3.

having camped there three times before this, we located ourselves to wait for orders and prepared our breakfasts.

As the hours passed and no order came, we shifted our position to a more convenient location, hunted up sticks to put up our shelters, and tried to make ourselves comfortable.

At the evening roll call, the regiment was paraded, and an order was read forming a 'provisional brigade' of the three regiments from the Second Corps and formally placing Colonel Samuel Spriggs Carroll of the Eighth Ohio in command. The order also informed us that we had been selected for special service because of our discipline and good conduct in the past and expressed confidence that we would "add to the enviable record we had already made."

Sunday evening, I spent the night quietly in the bivouac and had Warren Ingersoll, an old-time student at Hamline—then a sergeant in the 8th Ohio—for company. We planned to try to get a pass the next day and look for some of the sick and wounded in the hospitals in Washington, if the brigade commander would grant it. Monday morning, after the details for the day were made, I obtained a leave of absence from Captain Ball. Ingersoll put in an appearance, provided with the necessary papers from Col. Carroll to allow us to cross the Long Bridge into Washington. Then we both hesitated about going on account of our worn and soiled uniforms. After all of our brushing and blacking, we were still very far from feeling any pride in the appearances of our clothing or the polish of our shoes.

There was almost a procession of teams on the road, and we had no difficulty in getting a ride into Washington. Reaching there, we went first to the Sanitary Commission, hoping there to find lists of the sick and wounded in the hospitals about the city, but were disappointed in finding only a partial list. However, Ingersoll learned that some people he knew in Ohio were employed about the commission work, and we looked for them and fortunately found them. After a little time in conversation and making proper excuses for our rough appearance to some ladies we were introduced to, it was arranged to go to some of the nearby hospitals and make inquiries—three of the ladies having errands there and we going with them.

We went into two large hospitals, all of them crowded with sick soldiers suffering from many diseases and in all conditions, from the dangerously acute to the hopefully convalescing stages. We found none of the wounded and only one sick soldier that belonged to the regiment. None of the company. It was our first visit to anything more than a field hospital. We had heard considerable of the treatment and mistreatment of soldiers in the hospitals, as returning patients told conflicting stories, but what we saw that day convinced us that all that could be done was being done for the relief of the sick. There were so many of them that it was a stupendous job.

There may have been (no doubt there were) cases of neglect and mistreatment, but they were chargeable to the individual nurse or attendant rather than the government or hospital management. We were told by a nurse, who said he had been about the hospitals for two years, that the wounded were usually cheerful and hopeful, even though they died; while men with fevers and sick men generally were the reverse and often very exacting. Many in the hospitals were not responsible for their acts, being delirious, and it was necessary to restrain them—even using force. 'Home Sickness,' we were told, was really causing the death of many men whose minds so continually dwelt upon themselves and their homes as to counteract all of the good effects of medicine and nursing.

It was mid-afternoon when we left the hospitals, thankful that thus far we had not been forced to become an inmate and sincerely hoping that we might not in the future.

At the suggestion of our friends of the Sanitary Commission, we went to the Navy Yard and were allowed to go down on a boat which was taking some stores to Alexandria.

It had been an interesting day, and we had been seeing things not often seen by us of the ranks. Though we had failed to find those we had been looking for, we had been treated very nicely by those we had met. When we had come in the presence of ladies (which we had not expected when we left the camp), we were very much disturbed about the appearance of our clothes. They very generously told us that they had drawn no uncomplimentary inferences, and excuses were not necessary, as they regarded our service-worn uniforms as 'badges of honor.'

We parted with our friends at the wharf (where they came on some errand), and went on board of a boat which was already to start, and soon arrived at Alexandria. We had eaten nothing since morning excepting some bread and cheese and were now getting hungry. We made friends with the steward of the boat and asked for something to eat. He said it was against orders and he was not allowed to *sell* anything to soldiers; however, he *gave* us some coffee, bread, and cold meat.

It was almost night when we got back to camp, and we felt that it had been quite a remarkable day in our soldier lives. We had spent very little time anywhere except about the hospitals, but wherever we went we saw officers and soldiers on the streets. The city seemed *full* of them, and provost guards were also in evidence wherever we went. Most of them were 'spick and span' as to their clothing and gave no evidence of the kind of service we had been doing. We decided they were 'soft breads' and wondered why they had not been sent to the front during the great campaign that had but recently ended. This pet Reserve Corps, that was *always* '*reserved*,' was one of the grievances of those whose duties brought them in frequent contact with the enemy.

Tuesday, it was learned that other regiments were coming in, and that apparently all of the corps were represented. It was now pretty well settled in our opinions that we were to go to New York, but, of course, we did not *know* anything about it.

It may be well (while waiting for a ship) to say something about the necessity of withdrawing troops from in front of a recognized enemy and sending them to the chief home city. If the war was continued, the armies must be kept up. Fire will not continue to burn unless the necessary fuel is supplied. If recruits did not come voluntarily, then they must be compelled to come—or we give up the fight. If the government could not enforce its authority at home, it were useless to attempt to do it anywhere else. The government decided to enforce the drafting in the city of New York, where it had been stopped by mob violence. It was hoped that the presence of 30 or 40 regiments, whose steadiness had been tested by actual service, might be sufficient. Had it been necessary there is no question but an order to fire would have been obeyed without hesitation, and we would have tried to make every shot tell. (Happily, this *dernier* resort was not required.)

Our regiment, with others that had 'seen service,' was detached from their commands and became a part of a force that was approximately estimated at 10,000 men, and which was quietly concentrated in and about New York City before attempting to continue the drafting.[4]

Wednesday, August 19, a transport was expected at any time, but it did not get in that day, and we spent another night in the bivouac. Thursday morning, it was after noon before the *Atlantic,* an ocean steamer, came up and anchored out in the stream to await the coming of the tide to get in to the wharf.

It was late in the afternoon before it could do this, and by that time the brigade was at the landing and hastened to bestow itself on board. Company F was detailed to remain on the shore and look after the supplies, baggage, etc. The officers' horses, tents, and supplies generally were there—and all put on board from the wharf before the turn of the tide. Then the vessel was taken out into the stream and anchored, and our company remained on the shore to receive the delayed rations.

While waiting there, a small steamer in the service of the Sanitary and Christian Commissions came down from Washington. On board were employees of both organizations—several of whom were ladies. These came on shore and among them was Miss Munsell, whom I had met in Washington the previous Monday. To meet her again was wholly unexpected, but none the less a pleasure, and I hastened to present myself and, after being recognized, piloted her and the others over to the gun stacks, near which the boys were passing the time. It goes without saying—where the opportunities were so rare—that the boys were all pleased to see the ladies. They were very soon the center of an interested little company asking questions and being answered.

In the midst of it, the wagons we were waiting for came, and we had to turn our attention to transferring their contents to the deck of the *Vulcan,* a lighter that lay

4. By August 23, at least twenty thousand troops had been sent to New York City and divided into two brigades under the command of General Edward Canby; the draft was resumed on August 19; Welcher, *Union Army,* Vol. 1, *Eastern Theater,* 14.

at the wharf with the crew impatiently waiting. This called for an early closing of the little sociable on the wharf, and hasty leaves were taken. But before going the ladies from the Christian Commission distributed paper, stamps, and envelopes, and I believe some other little things. This, I think, was all the company ever received from it. As I recall it, I was given a handkerchief, something I had not possessed for a long time.

As soon as the things from the wagons were on the transfer boat, we took our guns and followed them. By this time it was after sunset. The *Vulcan* steamed out to the *Atlantic,* and its load was soon aboard the steamer.

For a time the boys gathered at the rail and watched the lights on other vessels (and there were several nearby), on passing tugs and dispatch boats, and on the shore. For the third time we were afloat on the tide of the 'lordly Potomac,' which is indeed a great river, but is hardly 'in it' with the mighty Mississippi. We speculated a little as to where the steamer was likely to land us and the sort of reception we were liable to get. That there was 'trouble ahead' of us we had no doubt, for in the light of recent experiences any other conclusion seemed absurd. We judged that nothing but a matter of vital import warranted the withdrawal of so many of the old regiments. At that time we did not really know where we were going, and thought it was just as likely that it was a flank movement on Lee or Richmond or 'down the coast.'

It was August, and the day had been warm but now that the sun was down and we were out on the river the evening was pleasantly cool. After all conversation had ceased, I lay for a time listening to the gurgle of the water as it coursed along the side of the ship and looking at the stars glimmering overhead. It is at an hour like that that the thoughts of the wanderer fly homeward as naturally as chickens come home to roost. Mine winged a hasty flight in the direction of the North Star—but much nearer the earth. There swept over me a more intense longing for home and its associations than I had felt in many a day; and, somehow, there came with it a pretty strong conviction that I was never to see my home again or look into the faces of those I had left there. For a time I was completely unmanned, and I felt so badly for myself I cried—but I was careful not to let anyone know it—and it was all so unexpected and unaccountable that it surprised me.

If I ever felt a positive presentiment of impending evil when comfortably situated and no immediate danger threatening, I feel sure that was the time. It all came so forcibly and suddenly—without apparent cause—and impressed itself so deeply that it was some time before I reasoned myself into a more hopeful state of mind (I was acting more like a silly, sentimental boy than the sensible soldier I ought to be)—and slept. If I had told my forebodings to a comrade and then fallen overboard or suffered some other fatality before the expedition ended, it would have been considered a 'remarkable case of premonition.'

In such a case perhaps it would have been, but there was no such a tragic sequel to myself, but there was a fatal accident that night to a comrade in the regiment, with whom I had but a passing acquaintance. I have never felt that there was any connection whatever between my acute attack of *nostalgia* and that accident. At most it was only a coincidence of events.

When I awoke, it was with a realizing sense that the planks of the deck were harder than Virginia turf or mud. The usual mist was over the water, and our blankets were saturated with what had accumulated during the night.

As the light increased so that I could see through the fog to the shore, I was a little confused to find that I was looking at the opposite shore than the one that faced me when I had spread my blanket. I had changed to the opposite side of the ship or the staid old city of Alexandria had crossed to the other side of the river. I felt confident that neither of these changes had taken place, and the only other solution was that the water in the river was *running up stream*. And this was just what had happened; the turn of the tide had swung the ship to its anchor and the stern was now up the stream. I was not then familiar with the action of tides that reverse the currents of rivers within their limits once in 13 hours.

As soon as the boys began to stir about the ship, there was a rumor that Lieutenant August Kruger of Company A was missing and was believed to have been lost overboard. This proved to be true, and I cannot now recall that it was ever known just how it happened or when. But he was supposed to have fallen by a misstep getting on board or leaving the vessel during the night. It was not until after the steamer had started down the river that it was certain that he was missing, and nothing could be done then.

The *Atlantic* was a fine steamer of fair size built for the Liverpool trade and made rapid progress down the river as soon as the tide turned. We lay about the decks and watched the scenery, wrote letters, or slept as inclination prompted, and had not been so care free for many a day. About 1 o'clock we passed Point Lookout, Maryland, and steamed out in the Chesapeake in the face of a strong wind, which stirred the water into lively motion, and made some of us suspicious we were going to be seasick.

The conveniences for cooking were insufficient for the number on board, and there was some friction as to who should use them first; however there was no serious trouble, and we all managed to make coffee. The engineer bored a hole in each end of some barrels of 'salt horse' (corned beef) and inserted a pipe—allowing steam to exhaust through it for a few hours. This cooked it nicely and—as the steam condensed, it was allowed to run off—it was also nicely freshened.

Some time during the night we ran out between the 'Virginia Capes' (Charles and Henry), and when I waked Saturday morning, August 22, I was told that we were out on the Atlantic. There was fog all around us and clouds overhead, but it was not storming, and the wind was not blowing as it had been the previous afternoon. But we discovered there was something wrong as soon as we attempted to walk about.

I had slept well and felt all right when I waked, but that comfortable feeling did not last long after I began to think about getting some breakfast. I soon decided to postpone the morning meal. We were all 'land lubbers,' except possibly a few that may have had some experience with salt water. I was not really sick, not at first, only uncomfortable at the double motion of the vessel. There were long, swelling waves which the ship crossed diagonally, rolling to the right and to the left, and the bow and stern alternately rose and fell.

I tried to walk about a little, but could not make my feet keep time with the eccentric motion of the deck, and concluded to find a place where I could sit down and enjoy it. I found a place and sat down, and I think that I experienced some satisfaction when I observed there were a good many others who appeared to feel about as I did—and some who evidently felt worse—but I did not enjoy the situation or myself. My stomach or some other internal organ was protesting about something, and indulging in spasmodic threats of evicting its contents. These spasms were of such frequency and intensity that I was impelled to go to the rail and prepare for emergencies. In the next hour or so it made a contribution of all it had to Neptune.

Many were seasick, and many others were not at all affected. And those who were *not* appeared to enjoy the situation and got what amusement they could out of it. Even some of the victims at the rail tried to be funny, and make loose remarks as to their feelings, but the most of them did not attempt any such hypocrisy. Some made use of such profane expletives as they considered appropriate. As the sea grew quieter, and there was less rolling of the steamer, I learned that by lying down and closing my eyes I could rest more comfortably, and later I slept.

I was glad when increasing light indicated that the morning was at hand, and got up. We were not able to see much but were told that we were then near Sandy Hook. As the light increased and the fog lifted, we could see the shore and soon after passed near a fort and entered the 'Narrows' leading up to the city.[5] Here there was a strong current, and our progress was slower than it had been. I felt quite empty, but my stomach was not yet in a receptive mood, and a cracker and some coffee satisfied it. This was Sunday, August 23, a beautiful day and quite comfortable on the water.

As we steamed up between the New Jersey shore and Long Island, we began to think about getting ashore and what might follow, and packed our knapsacks. We had not seen any papers or heard any news since the morning of the 20th and were naturally anxious to hear about matters in New York and elsewhere. It was about 10 o'clock when we anchored off an island, on which there were two forts, and we were told that it was Governor's Island. Here we lay for some hours wait-

5. Sandy Hook, a peninsula on the New Jersey shore, points north to the Narrows, the strait between Staten Island and Long Island. Governor's Island is just south of the tip of Manhattan.

ing for orders. About 2 o'clock we were taken off on lighters and landed on the island, and we were glad to get our feet on the ground again.

Our regiment was assigned to the parade ground in the rear of Fort Columbus; and the companies took their positions, stacked arms, and prepared to bivouac there as they did in Virginia. As there was no growth of young trees to cut for tent poles—or anything else to use for that purpose—we decided to dispense with the formality of stretching tents and simply deposited our knapsacks where we intended to spread our blankets to sleep when night came. We were all pretty well satisfied to be where we could feel the ground under our feet and away from the offensive smell of the ship.

There were two forts, Columbus and Castle William, and a temporary battery down by the water at the lower end of the island. It was said that there were about 2,000 soldiers on the island before we came. Some of these were in the forts, and some were in tents outside. Some wood was furnished us towards night, and we were instructed to make our fires for cooking in the gutters at the side of a walk. By this time my recent disrelish for army rations had been replaced by an inclination to eat almost anything I could get. We were not called on for any special duty, and soon after the evening roll call we spread our blankets and prepared to sleep.

The process of getting ready to sleep in our soldier days was short and simple, and, when confronting an enemy, usually meant to unbutton the blouse and untie the shoes. But here, feeling safe from sudden attack, we dared to remove both and felt a sense of relief that we could do this without serious risk.

Monday we remained on the island. I was directed to send in estimates for all needed clothing and supplies, and tents sufficient for all of the company present. Practically this meant a complete new outfit for the company. Aside from this, and the routine of daily duties inseparable from military life, it was a day of leisure and more care-free than any we had experienced for years.

The day was not far advanced before papers were brought over from the city, and there was a rush to get them. All were anxious to know how affairs were with the army at the front, and what there was going on in the city of New York that we had been brought there. There was no very startling news from the armies. Matters were said to be 'quiet' in New York; and arrangements completed for the enforcement of the draft; and a sufficient force in and about the city to meet any resistance offered. Some of the papers cordially approved the course of the administration; and some bitterly opposed it and broadly condemned the government for the draft and the conduct of the war generally. We watched with keen interest the course of events which were to determine whether we would have to use our rifles or not in their final adjustment. We certainly were averse to any conflict in any of the northern cities where the lives of innocent people would be endangered, but we also recognized the absolute necessity of the government asserting its authority at home.

The day passed without any exciting incident, but there was much of interest to us men from the western frontiers, now sojourning on an island off the eastern coast. The number and variety of the ships at anchor, and the coming and going of all kinds of water craft, with a multiplicity of flags and pennants, made a constantly-changing panorama, and the screaming of tugs and whistling of steamers covered the whole scale of ear-piercing sounds.

That night we again spread our blankets on the parade near Fort Columbus. Toward morning some rain fell, enough to wet our blankets and make us think of the tents we were hoping to get soon.

Tuesday morning, we were up early—as soon as it was light. We saw a small boat coming out of the mist toward one of the landings. We naturally went in that direction, as we had nothing else to do. A detachment of the Fifth Wisconsin landed, having in charge a bunch of prisoners which they marched over to Castle William.

Our first thought was that these were conscripts (men who have been drafted) and were coming there to be kept until sent to the front. Inquiring of one of the guards, we learned they were not conscripts but men implicated in the July riots and later disturbances, and were to be kept as prisoners. There was another lot every morning while we remained on the island, and I inquired of one of the Wisconsin boys what they did with them. He said they were "cached in the castle," and added that they "had the casemates full of them."

Tuesday night the wind blew fiercely, and it rained hard, making it decidedly unpleasant for shelterless men. The water poured upon us from the skies, was driven at us latterly by the wind, and ran under us along the ground. We protected ourselves the best we could with our blankets and rubbers, but very few were able to preserve a dry spot on their bodies until morning. There had been some complaining before this that we were landed where there was nothing available to stretch our tents with and that the promised tents had not come.

I think that if it had been left to a vote of the boys that morning, there would have been a large majority in favor of going at once to the Rappahannock. For among the cedar and scrub pine of Virginia we could have found material and improvised some sort of shelter, but on this island the only growth was ornamental shrubbery—and not much of it at that. With only a scant amount of wood with which to do our cooking, wet to the skin, and buffeted by a chilly wind—the boys ate their rations Wednesday morning, and seasoned them with uncomplimentary remarks about the dilatory quartermaster, whoever he might be, who had failed to send the tents.

Before noon the weather was fair again, and we were comfortable. The papers reported that the draft was proceeding without any serious attempt to hinder it by demonstration or violence, and we judged that our stay in that vicinity was likely to be brief. A number applied for passes to go into the city but were denied leaves of absence, and this made them feel like prisoners. There is no doubt but it was wise under the prevailing conditions to keep men in uniforms off of the streets except when on duty.

Thursday was not far advanced before notice was received of the arrival of the tents and clothing, and we were soon busy receiving and distributing them. This was the first time the regiment had been housed in wall tents since the fall of 1861, before we built the huts we wintered in that winter. After leaving Camp Stone—excepting a few days in March 1862 when crowded into some Sibley tents during a snowstorm on Bolivar Heights—we had had only our shelter tents to house us.

Following the putting up of the tents came the giving out of clothing, which was not so easily accomplished, as the size and form of the wearer and the garments both had to be considered—and both were fixed quantities. The men accepted the nearest fit they could get, then exchanged among themselves until the best obtainable results by that means were reached. Then any further adjustment to the person had to be by the use of the scissors and a needle. This was the usual process when in camp, but when on the move they were generally worn as they came from the quartermaster. Several of the boys became quite expert in the use of the needle and could do good work in making over the government contractor's 'mis-fits,' and among these was Sergeant Henry R. Childs of Company F, my tentmate—after the war well known in Red Wing as a 'horse tailor.'

In the midst of their work putting up tents and getting new uniforms, Company F very unexpectedly had visitors from home. Harry Hoffman, one-time sheriff of Goodhue County, and Abe Thomas, a Red Wing merchant, being in New York, had heard that the regiment was somewhere about the city and had hunted it up. It was a genuine surprise when they marched up from the wharf after a dispatch boat had come in. If they felt half as glad to see us as we did to see them, they felt pretty good. They were recognized on sight and quickly surrounded and subjected to volleys of questions.

As they had had no thought of meeting the company in New York, they had brought no special messages, but they were given many to carry back and numerous little gifts of remembrance. They looked natural and familiar to us who had known them well. They declared we were all greatly changed, and they expressed surprise at our bronzed and weather-beaten appearance, and the very few men there were left for duty. Until seeing the little skeletons of companies, they had not realized how greatly they were diminished. It was the first time anyone directly from our home town had visited the regiment since it had left the state in June 1861. Their coming had turned our thoughts homeward, and not much else was talked of for the rest of the day.

At dress parade that evening (which was held for the first time since landing on the island), almost every one was in a new uniform, which caused some one to declare that we looked like 'soft breads'—new recruits. We felt quite grand sleeping in the tents that night, which were variously referred to as tepees, marquees, parlors, and bedrooms. They sheltered us from the dew, and we slept soundly, but probably no better than ordinarily when undisturbed by storm or cold.

Friday morning, August 28, soon after breakfast, there was an inspection of arms ordered, and at its conclusion we were cautioned to put ourselves in the best presentable condition as we were likely to be ordered into the city. This made us think that we were to go on duty in New York, and there were conjectures as to where we were to be stationed, what special duties we might be called on to perform, and whether we were to be a provost guard and patrol the streets or a reserve for the police. I do not think that anyone understood then that we were going to one of the city parks to hold a reception for a week or so.

The order came to pack our knapsacks and be ready to move, but the tents were to be left standing, which caused some to declare that they should have been labeled "for one night only." Later orders were to strike tents, roll them around the poles, and send a detail to carry them to the landing. Then a ferry boat came to the landing and the Eighth Ohio, carrying all of its baggage, was taken away to the Brooklyn side. On its return, our tents and all regimental property was transferred to its deck, and the regiment went aboard and was steamed over to the Brooklyn shore. Here our things were taken off, and a guard placed over them until teams should come for them.

We shouldered our knapsacks and marched to Washington Park, which was formerly the site of Fort Greene of Revolutionary time. It was a beautiful place overlooking the river, the harbor, and the cities of Brooklyn and New York. We had scarcely formed companies on the wharf before we were surrounded by a crowd of people, who watched us with apparently the same interest as the crowds that gather to witness the unloading of a circus. We at first judged it was from the same motive but soon learned that it was a sympathetic curiosity.

When we marched for the park the crowd followed. More joined them on the way and after we arrived, so that by the time the tents had come there was a great company assembled to witness putting them up. We had really never had much experience with tents, except the small shelters we carried with us, and none for more than a year. But we found little difficulty in getting them up in proper order and promptly, while the crowd around us asked us many questions and in various ways showed their interest and sympathy. Here, as at the wharf, the boys considered the curiosity of the crowd an intrusion and were disposed to treat it as such at first. But the expressions of interest and sympathy soon dissipated all our wishes to be left to ourselves and warmed our hearts towards the mixed multitude about us until we were appreciative and grateful.

Almost before our tents were up, practically every member of the company had established friendly relations with some one (or more) of the throng about them and in their awkward way were trying to respond to the rapid fire of questions from the boys and girls—and be nice and polite to the older ones. I say *awkward* advisedly, for the most of us had never had more than scant social advantages, and for years all branches of politeness had been out of practice from lack of opportunity. If the Southern sun had not bronzed our faces to about the shade of a half-worn russet shoe, I am sure they would have been crimson with blushes as we tried to talk with some of the ladies in a way creditable to the manners our mothers had taught us. At first we stopped to talk to those who questioned us, but—as that began to appear like waiting on the bank for the river to run by—we later resumed our work and before night had our tents in good order.

They were nice large tents, in which we could stand up—something we had not had since we started for the Peninsula in the spring of 1862. Straw, too, was brought to sleep on—a luxury not enjoyed since our first winters in the service. Then a mule team came with a load of cord wood and scattered it along the driveway through the park. We were instructed that the fires for cooking were to be made in the roadway.

As the day drew to a close, fires were started and coffee made and slices of pork were broiled or fried as we did in the field, each soldier his own cook. Some of the boys retired to their tents to eat, but the most of us sat on the grass at the edge of the walk and masticated our pork and crackers and drank our black coffee— surrounded by a company that observed us with apparently the same interest that youngsters watch the animals feeding when the circus comes.

At the first, it was rather trying to be exposed to the scrutiny of so many people, but it was soon apparent that the people were constantly coming and going and that, with a few exceptions, it was only the children that remained long.

We did not realize it then, but this was the beginning of a splendid picnic, which lasted until we started for the front again, and that still is a subject of pleasant memories. I am constrained to believe that it has rarely happened that a body of men coming unannounced among strangers has been so kindly received and heartily welcomed. To say that we enjoyed it immensely is expressing it moderately. After years among a people who shunned you, many of whom would have felt more satisfaction in looking at your mangled remains than in contributing to your comfort, it was indeed pleasant to feel that you were among friends again and hear expressions of sympathy.

At dark a guard was posted about the camp, and the men were notified that absence without leave would be severely punished, but citizens were allowed to pass at will until the evening roll call. When the visitors had ceased to come, and we had answered the final roll call for the day, we went into our tents, spread out the straw, covered it with a blanket and went to bed 'like white men' (removed all of our outer clothing). But it was some time before we slept, as the events of the afternoon were talked over and individual experiences compared—at least that is the way it was in the tent I occupied.

As I was eating my supper, an observing little boy had noticed that I drank the coffee straight and asked why I did not have milk in it. He expressed both surprise and sympathy when told that Uncle Sam did not include milk and butter in the soldier's menu. He seemed to think this a great hardship and in the generosity of his youthful heart promptly promised that he would bring me some for my break-fast, and mine was by no means the only promise of additions to the army rations for the next day. The quality of our food seemed to suggest to many of the inex-perienced an idea of semi-starvation. The manner of its preparation was, no doubt, interesting to the children, who came near and questioned, and to the grownups, who formed the outer circle of spectators and did not put their in-quisitiveness into words so promptly.

How easily, quickly, and naturally the boys from the western frontiers came into communication with the loyal people of one of the refined eastern cities. The bond of sympathy between the soldiers in the service and the patriotic people at home was that one was striving to accomplish something in which the other was intensely interested. The uniform was a sufficient endorsement for the people, and words of sympathy and kindly ministrations were all of the credentials the soldiers asked. Under those conditions it did not require a long time to establish agreeable relations.

Saturday morning the bugles called us from our blankets at sunrise, and we began a routine of camp life after the manner of soldiers in garrison. But our brigade commander kindly pruned it of many nonessential requirements, de-manding only that every man be at roll call and on hand for camp duties and de-tails. Between sunrise and sunset we could come and go without hindrance but required a pass to go into New York. In the company, Capt. Ball was considerate and lenient, practically putting the boys on parole for good behavior, and I do not now recall that there was a single instance in the company where this confidence was abused. We enjoyed all of the personal liberty consistent with our duties and military requirements.

Our little friends of the night before did not forget us or their promises—or oversleep. In the morning they were there with the goods. I had *cream* for my coffee that morning, brought to me in a *silver pitcher*; also generous slices of boiled ham and buttered bread, on a china plate wrapped in a *white napkin* and a few lumps of white sugar in a paper cone.

I had not really expected to see the boy again, and such a return was wholly outside the limits of my imagination. I really questioned the propriety of accept-ing. However, I did not refuse them and offered to pay for them.

But the little fellow (who was about 12 years old and said his name was Eddie Schemmerhorn, and he "lived on the avenue") looked me straight in the face with laughing eyes, put his hands behind him, and shook his head.

They were too tempting to refuse. They were as good as they looked when it came to eating them. I was careful to return the plate and the pitcher and napkin—with the nicest words of thanks I could put together. I wish to record here that my little friend was not the only one to make his promises good, for I think about all of the boys had something extra that morning from some source. And this I believe was true during our stay there. At least, my loyal little friend brought me something every day we remained in the park.

After breakfast, the tents and their surroundings were put in the best order possible, and each soldier was careful to see that his buttons were burnished and his boots blacked. This was wise, for long before noon the park was swarming with visitors, most of them women and children. At noon time there were many people in the park who had brought baskets of eatables and were ready to share with any of the 'boys in blue' who would accept their invitations. The boys saw their opportunity, were not averse to its enjoyment, and were soon on friendly terms with young and old.

It was now evident that it was not necessary to leave the camp to find something interesting. Thousands of people visited the camps that day to see, as some of them said, "the men who had been at the front." And they certainly accorded us all of the honors we asked and far more than we deserved. They were not the formal courtesies of the city, or the state, but the personal tributes of individuals, spontaneously offered.

That evening we had dress parade, and every man tried to appear at his best. Though it did seem something approaching burlesque for little squads of ten or twelve men, calling themselves companies, to go through the evolutions of a regimental dress parade. We had not practiced much in parades lately, but we had not forgotten the formula and made a fairly creditable performance. However, it was a small affair to those of us who recalled the long lines on the parade at Fort Snelling, in Washington, and at Camp Stone. So far as I recall, there had been no previous announcement, but many people were in the park and manifested their interest by clapping their hands at the close of the parade.

Sunday, August 30, was a day to be remembered. The first event after breakfast and guard mount was the regular Sunday inspection, and for this full preparations had been made. The quarters were in order, and the boys were all out in their new clothes (paper collars and white gloves), hair cut, faces shaved, boots blacked, buttons and rifle barrels properly polished. But nothing could remove the Virginia tan from our faces, which were about the color of ordinary sole-leather.

The day was fine. We were located in a beautiful park and surrounded by a great throng of people, more than half of them ladies. It would have been a pretty poor sort of a soldier that would not have been at his best, and I have no doubt but we were. After the inspection there were a few minutes of exercise in manual of arms, and the companies marched to their tents as the people applauded them.

With the inspection over, there were no more pressing duties to be performed until the evening parade, and each soldier spent the intervening time as his inclination and opportunities prompted and permitted.

A few of us thought to see how it would seem to be in a church again, and we went to the nearest one, down on Carleton Avenue. We were a little late, and the minister had already begun his sermon, but we were shown seats and tried to listen carefully to what he was saying—though I am afraid that the novelty of our situation distracted our attention. At the close, he prayed very earnestly that God would save our afflicted nation and bless the soldiers then in their city. The minister's name, if I am not mistaken, was Hill, and at the close of the service he hastened to meet and shake hands with the soldiers present. There was quite a number from our own and other regiments. Many of the people, too, came to shake our hands and say a word to us, expressing their pleasure (surprise it may have been) at seeing us in church.

Returning to the camp, we found it swarming with people dressed in their best clothes. We were a bit surprised at the amplitude of the women's skirts—expanded over the hoops then in fashion. We knew, of course, that the ladies were wearing hoops and had understood that they were large, but we had not realized they were quite so expansive.

When we returned to our tents it was after noon and our appetites were demanding attention. Besides government rations, I found bread, meat, and *cake* which my little friend who "lived on the avenue" had brought me in the morning.

There were many visitors in the camp. Coming and going, here and there, and groups of them talking at every tent. The boys seemed to be holding a sort of promiscuous reception—without the formality of introductions—which continued until the bugles sounded for the evening parade.

This was a signal to the visitors as well as to the soldiers. By the time we were ready to take position, we were surrounded so closely that it was difficult to move. The ground selected was a little ways from and somewhat lower than that on which the tents were pitched. Thither the companies marched through the crowds to form the line, and were immediately encompassed by a great multitude. It was a very quiet and attentive crowd during the ceremonies and the chaplain's prayer, but there was a great outburst of clapping hands at the dismissal.

The companies made their way back to quarters through the crowds—an undulating sea of smiling faces, clapping hands, and waving handkerchiefs. When I dismissed the company, nearly every soldier was held up by inquisitive individuals who wished to examine his rifle and equipments and know "how far it would shoot" and "how many rebels he had killed with it." I will not attempt to record the answers given, but I am suspicious there may have been some exaggeration on both points. All the evening the camp was a point of interest to visitors, and every soldier off duty seemed to have found a congenial companion and was sitting on the grass or walking about.

When the crowds were gone and the day's duties done, the boys gathered in their tents to talk it over—somewhat as they were accustomed to do after days of interest and excitement. I do not remember that any serious casualties were reported, but I am pretty sure that there were some 'missing' from nearly every tent. As they were supposed to be 'talking it over' somewhere else, there was no particular anxiety on account of these missing ones. There was no doubt but there was an opportunity for a rarely good time from the soldier's view point, and the boys were evidently disposed to make use of it.

The reveille bugles aroused us to the opening of another almost perfect summer day. This was Monday, August 31, and it was also the monthly muster. The regiment was not called on for any special duties beyond small details, and it now began to be apparent that there might be none. We had been brought there only as a reserve or emergency force, and the draft was said to be going on satisfactorily and without violence.

That evening Warren Ingersoll came over from the camp of the 8th Ohio and informed me that he had learned that the family of T. J. Smith, formerly of Red Wing, was then living in New York. He proposed going over to look them up the next day. Mollie Smith, a daughter in the family, had been a mutual classmate and, I think, was a distant relative of his. As I knew them well, I was not averse to going, and the necessary arrangements for a pass to cross the river were made that evening. Tuesday morning, after the morning duties were disposed of, I made my first visit into New York City, crossing over from Brooklyn on the Jackson Street Ferry.

After some inquiries we found their residence, 52 4th Avenue, and fortunately they were at home. Our visit was a complete surprise, as they had not seen any notice of either regiment being about the city and supposed both were in Virginia.

As it was early in the day, Mollie hunted up a lady friend, and the four of us went out to see some of the interesting places about the city. All of this was entirely agreeable to us, and we suspect the girls felt a little elated going on the street with their escorts in uniform.

On our return we found a good dinner awaiting us. For the first time in more than two years, I sat down at a family dinner, and I felt a bit of constraint and awkwardness. But not enough to prevent my eating a square meal and enjoying it. Mollie had told of many things about the school and old schoolmates and teachers, and, at dinner, her father told us more of affairs at home. From what we heard, we were impressed that the absence of so many men in the service was a serious drawback to the university and the city.

After dinner, we invited the girls to return with us to Brooklyn, which they did, visiting the camps of the three regiments in the park—First Minnesota, Eighth Ohio, and Seventh Michigan. Leaving them at the ferry slip, feeling that we had had an agreeable day off, we hastened back to camp, getting there just in time for the evening parade.

Wednesday brought many visitors to the camps, and there was a very general intermingling of soldiers and citizens. It was all very unconventional, and may not have been in accord with Mrs. Grundy's ideas of propriety,[6] but it was just about

6. Mrs. Grundy was the narrow-minded neighbor in the play *Speed the Plough* (1798). She was not seen, but the characters kept asking, "What will Mrs. Grundy say?"

what the situation called for. The soldiers in the camp had 'seen service' and in that respect were different from the most of those previously about the city, and the papers were publishing something of their experiences in the field, which attracted attention to them.

Many came, looked at us, and went away, apparently satisfied to have 'seen the animals.' Many others showed a deeper interest by asking questions and expressing sympathy. While camped in the park, we talked with many people about the war. All regretted its existence. There was no doubt but its long continuance and the increased prices of everything were as disheartening to those at home as in the field, perhaps more so, but they were no more ready to give up the struggle—though Horace Greeley and some of the old leaders were. The recent rioting over in New York was a prolific source of talk. If the stories told were true, there had been a bit of the worst kind of war right at their doors. We heard no expressions of sympathy with the mob or even excuses. Nothing but condemnation.

By this time the men of the company, and regiment as well, were making individual friends and getting invitations to dine out, and there were frequent requests for leaves of absence. As far as he could, our captain granted these, but it was always a condition that they should return in time for the evening parade.

A young lady, whom I had met at church Sunday and twice since then, had invited me to take dinner at her home, and I promised to go—if a pass was available. Thursday, September 3, I took dinner at the home of 'Miss Redhead.' Her mother said she considered that more appropriate than for her to go to the park, and, of course, I did not argue the matter.

I found the young lady and her mother both good company, and they gave me a nice dinner, but there was something lacking in being there without a comrade. They were Methodist people as to religion, and I presume it was owing to that fact, as much as anything else, that I had been invited there. I also learned that arrangements were then being made to have our regiment attend a supper at the church the next evening, and it was an inference that this also was coming about because our chaplain was an ardent Methodist.[7]

There was the usual throng in the park and at dress parade that evening. The invitation to attend the supper at the Carleton Avenue Methodist Episcopal Church was read, and the regiment was notified that it had been accepted.

At 7 o'clock Friday evening, the regiment was formed and marched to the Carleton Avenue M.E. Church, which was decorated with flags and flowers for our reception. The formal part of the exercises were a song, prayer, an address of welcome by the pastor, and a response by our chaplain. This was followed by other short speeches, music, and patriotic songs. Later a bountiful supper was served on temporary tables in the lower part of the church by the ladies of the church.

7. F. A. Conwell was the regiment's chaplain at this time; *History of Minnesota in the Civil and Indian Wars*, 1:49.

There appeared to be about as many of the committee as there were soldiers, and, while part of them served us with food, others talked and pinned bouquets on our blouses. It was a well furnished table, and to those of us accustomed to field rations only it was a royal feast, sufficient in quantity for even our soldier appetites. At the tables there were toasts, impromptu speeches, and singing. At ten o'clock the order was given to return to camp, and we left, giving 'three times three' and an 'injun' (First Regiment's war-whoop) for our entertainers.

Back in the camp—though the hour was getting late—it did not seem as if any one wanted to sleep. Every one appeared anxious to talk and tell how nicely some young lady had served him at the tables or complimented him when she ornamented him with a bouquet. I presume some of us may have been a little vain or boastful—as the rarity and enthusiasm of the occasion was really stimulating. If I remember correctly, there were plans talked over for future meetings between some of those in uniforms and the young ladies who had particularly pleased them. When tongues had grown weary and ears dull, we slept.

Saturday, September 5, many people who were at the church last evening were in the park to renew the acquaintance of those they met there, and we were all invited there to the services tomorrow evening. We heard that more troops were leaving, and no doubt our turn would soon come. Of course, if we were needed more at the front than there, we ought to go back at once, and will, willingly, but we would not relish the order, just yet. The three regiments had a review instead of dress parade that evening.

After the parade, we ate our suppers; matters were proceeding as usual; and there were many visitors in the camp when I received orders from Capt. Ball that all leaves were revoked, and the men must not be allowed to leave the camp. This disarranged some nice little plans for the evening, as I distinctly recall, but it was looked upon as a military necessity and submitted to with the best grace possible.

The camp was soon alive with rumors, but there was not much credence given them until near 8 o'clock when the order was given to pack our knapsacks and await orders, leaving the tents standing. This was scarcely completed before the bugles blew to 'strike tents.' This was unexpected, but it was promptly obeyed, and in a few minutes the little canvas city we had spread in the park nine days before disappeared more quickly than it had risen. The tents, it was explained, were borrowed from some accommodating quartermaster, and his wagons were coming there to take them away.

It was my duty to look after the tents of the company. The 'white walls' were taken down, rolled up, and piled where my tent had stood, and I was obliged to stay by them until the wagons came for them—which was an hour or so. But I was not obliged to wait alone, as 'my girl' was in the camp when the orders of leave were revoked and had obligingly remained. So we sat on the folded tents until they were carted away, and then we sat on the ground or walked around until an anxious mother came to find her.

She chided her daughter for staying so late—then remained for nearly an hour longer, as we were expecting all of the time to get the order to march to the landing. This expectation allowed visitors who chose to do so to remain. Many did until near midnight, when word was received that the steamer would not be ready until morning, and we had better make ourselves as comfortable as we could where we were. Soon after 12 o'clock, the park was cleared, and the soldiers—again shelterless—spread their blankets on the straw and slept—or tried to sleep.

Sunday morning found us still in bivouac. We built our fires and boiled our coffee (with the remnants of wood left), breakfasted, and were all in readiness to move at an early hour. The park had a rather disordered look, littered as it was with the refuse of the camp and some of the things the boys had decided not to take with them. In a little while, it began to gather animation as people began to come in. By ten o'clock, there were many people there, and naturally some of our friends were among them, though the good-byes had been said the night before.

Soon after ten the bugles blared attention, and the regiment formed with an eager, anxious-appearing crowd gathering about it. We gave them a good-bye cheer, and it was responded to by a parting chorus of good wishes.

We marched to the Fulton Ferry, going on board of a waiting boat, and crossed to New York—quite a number of our Brooklyn friends going over with us. In New York we made a short march—going up Broadway and down Warren Street—and then to the pier of the Aspinwall steamers. Here we found the *Empire City* waiting, and the 26th Ohio—a regiment we had not previously been associated with—already on board, and a detail loading our regimental stuff, which had preceded us.

Here was the final farewell to the faithful Brooklyn friends who had followed us to the water's edge, and we marched on board as they stood on the pier waving hands, hats, and handkerchiefs. We did not have to wait long before the lines were cast off, the ship drifted away from the wharf, and slowly turned as the engines began to work.

Our holiday picnic was over and we were again headed for Virginia, the storm center of the rebellion. It was not quite so bad as leaving home but something like it. Our stay there had been only long enough to make us realize that we were human beings, with social feelings still alive within us, and the many kindnesses shown us there had stirred them to a lively activity. The brief stay of our regiment in Brooklyn was a rich, green oasis in the social desert of our soldier lives. It was perfumed with a generous kindness that touched our hearts then, and it still exhales pleasant perfumes, when stirred by the touch of remembrance.

After years of deprivation at the front, we were unexpectedly transferred to 'God's Country' and given an opportunity to get in touch with those who looked upon us as friends and mingle a little in social life. We had been called there by excesses, rioting, and bloodshed—and gone expecting to 'mix it up' with the mob in the streets. But there was no act of hostility. On the contrary, we had been received as friends, publicly complimented, and feasted and in many cases invited to the homes of loyal people.

It was Will Carleton, I believe, that wrote, "To rightly sense the joys of Heaven, we must feel for a time the pangs of Hell." On that principle, we were as well prepared to enjoy our stay in Brooklyn as a hungry man is to relish a good dinner. That we did enjoy it was the most natural thing in the world. We just could not help it, and it *was* something of a wrench to our feelings to leave so quickly. At least one of Company F—Abraham Baker—went back there to claim a bride when he was out of the service, and there may have been several others who at the time thought they might.

Perhaps I have already lingered too long over these memories of our short stay in the City of Churches, but before I dismiss the subject I wish to give a brief extract from the *Brooklyn Eagle,* a paper rather hostile to the conduct of the war, and some resolutions adopted by the regiment after we had returned to Virginia. The *Eagle* of Sept. 9, 1863 — sent to me by 'my girl' — had the following in an editorial, under the heading: "The Troops Recently Encamped within this City":

> We have more than once borne testimony to the exemplary conduct of the soldiers recently quartered in this city. They have been for nearly three years subjected to the privations incident to the life of a soldier, and subjected to the strictest regulations of camp life. It would have surprised nobody if the opportunity which their encampment within a city gave them, had been marked by more or less excess. It is due to our citizen soldiers to say that nothing of the sort occurred. A more orderly set of men never visited a city.
>
> They were received by our people with that high consideration and attentive kindness due to those who have risked their lives in the cause of their country. . . .
>
> We can wish the troops recently quartered in our city nothing better than that the country will soon be in a position to allow them to return to their homes and the pursuits from which the exigencies of the nation temporarily called them.

After the regiment had settled down on the Rapidan, the enlisted men of the regiment gathered one moonlight evening and passed the following resolutions which were later published in the Brooklyn papers. They bear date of Robinson's Ford, Virginia, September 23, 1863, and are as follows:

> Whereas, Feeling the kindness of the people, and especially the ladies, of Brooklyn, Long Island, shown to us during our brief sojourn in their beautiful city, and wishing to show our deep gratitude and appreciation of the same, therefore be it: Resolved, That we will ever cherish and honor the memory of the citizens of Brooklyn, who by their kindness rendered our short stay in their good city so pleasant and agreeable . . . and Resolved, That our special thanks are due to the ladies of Carleton Avenue M. E. Church, for the bountiful repast furnished by them, and may the great Commissary of Heaven ever be ready to fill their every requisition, and the sweets of life fall as profusely on them, as were the flowers

bestowed on us on that benevolent occasion. . . . Resolved, . . . that while accustomed to the varying fortunes of war, the unexpected attack upon us made by the ladies of Brooklyn, completely surprised us into an unconditional surrender, and will always be held by us as the proudest moment of our lives.

Copies of the resolutions were sent to the pastor of the Carleton Avenue Church and to the press.

It looked like a fight or a foot-race
SEPTEMBER-OCTOBER 1863

OUR REGIMENT LEFT ONE DAY before the others to complete the load of the *Empire City*—as a matter of economizing transportation. We were delayed for a short time while waiting for a dispatch boat from Governor's Island. When this had come and gone, the paddles of the steamer again beat the water, and it headed for the ocean.

We were stationed on the upper deck, where we tried to make ourselves comfortable and talked like a lot of schoolboys of the good times we had enjoyed—and of the others we were to have if we could have remained longer. The great city of New York grew smaller until it was lost in the smoke and the haze that seemed always hanging over it. Then we passed rapidly down the Narrows, past the Hook, and out to sea.

As the day waned, we realized that we had eaten nothing since morning, and busied ourselves trying to make up for neglecting our stomachs. The kindness of a Brooklyn friend made it unnecessary for me to draw on my supply of government rations for anything more than coffee, and I presume others fared as well in that respect as I did. Then, when we had eaten our suppers and watched the sun go behind the hills, and the evening shadows had hidden the New Jersey shore and covered the sea, we spread our blankets and prepared to sleep—the deck for a bed and a knapsack for a pillow.

I tried not to hear the exhausting steam or revolving machinery and not to feel the vibration of the deck and the resistance of the sea, as the ship was driven onward, but neither of them could be ignored. I had spread my blanket close to a hatch that was covered only by a grating. Soon another of my senses was offended by the odor coming up, which reminded me of our previous sail on the briny deep and suggested another experience the reverse of pleasant. To escape the smell I tried another location more remote from the hatchway. I was not long there before a rain of cinders admonished me that I had made another unwise choice, and the smell of scorching wool prompted me to another 'change of base.' At last, I was safely settled and inclined to sleep—and did sleep soundly for several hours. When I waked it was coming daylight.

My blanket was wet, and there was a chilly fog resting on the water and limiting vision to a few yards, but the sea was calm. After a time, the mist grew white;

the outline of the sun appeared; and, as it rose higher, the fog vanished; and a beautiful day followed.

I had about decided not to eat anything on the return trip when the smell of hot coffee caused to me to change my purpose, and I proceeded to make some. Then came a suspicion that I might soon be casting bread on the water in a pretty literal sort of a way, *if it returned*. I made my breakfast on the remains of what had been given me the morning before, realizing that thereafter I must eat government rations or starve.

There was only a gentle breeze blowing; the ship ran smoothly; and I did not suffer any from seasickness. On the contrary the pleasant weather and the novelty of it made the trip enjoyable.

We spent most of the day watching from the deck for ships and looking in the water for *whales* and *sea-serpents*, but we saw neither the leviathan nor the monster. The nearest approach to it was some large fish that alternately rose to the surface and disappeared—making an asthmatic, snorting sound each time they came up. They were the subject of a controversy as to whether they were *dolphins* or *porpoises*, and a sailor was called on to decide the matter, and he declared they were *puffing pigs*. I assume this was not the classical name for them, but their movements were suggestive of a lot of fat hogs trying to play.

The vessel was not so crowded as transports usually were, and our comrades of the 126th Ohio were a good mannered lot of fellows with whom we got along nicely—though they were a comparatively new regiment and had not yet seen much service. Many of the men were of German birth or parentage and appeared to be undersized in height and a little oversized in circumference.

It was almost night before we sighted the Capes, and later ran in between them and saw the lights of Fortress Monroe, near which we 'lay to' for a time until a dispatch boat had come off to us, went back to the fort, and again returned to the ship. When it had gone to the fort, the *Empire City* steamed up the Chesapeake Bay. Our destination seemed settled, and I spread my blanket and slept.

When I rubbed my sleepy eyes open at daylight the next morning, we were approaching the mouth of the Potomac. We were enveloped in a chilly fog, and the only dry spots on the deck were where the blankets had been spread. I felt the need of something warm and hastened to make coffee by filling my little tin pail with water from the barrels and heating it on the steam pipes. It would not actually boil there, and it required some patience to hold it there until hot, but fairly good coffee could be made that way.

It was some time before the sun dried up the fog and gave us a clear view of the shores, but when it did we were in the river and making good time. This was the fourth trip we had made on the river, and its scenery was getting familiar, but we found it interesting trying to recall places and things that we remembered. This was Tuesday, September 8, and it proved another pleasant day, though a bit warm on the decks after the sun got high.

On the 28th of August 1862—a little more than a year before—we were on the steamer *Mississippi* near where we were then, and going up the river. The interval was not a cheerful retrospect, shaded as it was by the great tragedies at the Second Bull Run, Antietam, Fredericksburg, Chancellorsville, and Gettysburg. During the year, more than twice as many men of the regiment had been killed and wounded as were then present with the colors. The war was certainly assuming a vast magnitude and was demanding tremendous sacrifices. When and how would it end, and, individually, where would we be at its ending? It took a stout heart and a sublime faith to ask these questions and seriously consider the answers. The most hopeful conclusions any of us could reach were that we must take our chances and suffer the consequences. It was surprising how quietly the boys used to talk of these things, but I often thought this apparent indifference was all assumed. I know it was in my own case.

There was no untoward incident to mar the sail up the river, and we arrived near Alexandria about 4 o'clock and anchored in the stream to await the coming of the tide. A couple of hours later we steamed up to the wharf, promptly landed, and went into camp on the outskirts of the city, glad to be on shore again. It was by this time almost night and some indications of a gathering storm. We hastened to put up our shelters and get our suppers—eating government rations, which were beginning to taste pretty good again. It was easy to take up the old ways, and before it was very dark we had prepared our suppers and improvised cover for the night.

Of course, our pup tents lacked the proportions of those we had in Brooklyn, but the difference in tents was not nearly so marked as the difference in the reception given us by the people of Brooklyn and Alexandria. In Brooklyn we had been shown every reasonable kindness and courtesy; but in Alexandria we attracted no more attention than had been accorded to the pigs and yellow dogs that infested the streets the first time we struck the town.

Pigs were plentiful, then, in all the streets, and yellow curs yelping at every corner, but now the latter were but seldom seen and the former never. It is possible that some of the pigs may have been eaten by the hungry soldiers, but the absence of the dogs must be accounted for by some other theory—lack of sympathy, perhaps.

The anticipated storm did not reach us, and we passed the night comfortably. Wednesday morning it was understood we were to await the arrival of Col. Carroll and the other regiments, and we made ourselves as comfortable as we could near the old camping place. Papers were had, but there was very little in them to indicate just where the Army of the Potomac was and what it was doing—which we were most anxious to know. It was supposed to be still in the camps where we left it. Most of the boys spent a part of their time writing letters, and I question if *all* letters went to *old* correspondents in Minnesota or elsewhere. I am quite sure that I addressed my first letter to Brooklyn at about that date, and there were a number of later ones. My Fair Correspondent wrote very nice letters, and they continued to come for nearly a year, when they ceased.

I have her photograph in my Soldiers Album. It is taken standing, in the fashion of those times: expanding skirts, hair parted in the middle, and braids over the ears—a pleasing, womanly face. I know nothing of her previous or later life, but she was a good, patriotic, Christian woman and, I have no doubt, has filled her place in life creditably whatever it may have been. I have called her Miss Redhead, and that was her real name. And it was also appropriate, for her hair was as red as my own. Her first name was Sarah O., and she proved herself an interesting correspondent. There are only pleasant recollections of the half-dozen times we met and the score or so letters we exchanged.

Friday the 8th Ohio and 7th Michigan joined us, having left New York on the *Atlantic* the 8th. With them came the 4th Ohio and 14th Indiana, which, we understood, were to become a part of 'Carroll's Provisional Brigade' until we reached the front. On Saturday, the 4th and 8th Ohio, 14th Indiana, 7th Michigan, and 1st Minnesota regiments gathered up their 'traps and calamities' and took the road toward Centreville. Just as it was getting dark, we reached the ancient village of Fairfax, and bivouacked there for the night.

Before we left the next morning, I had an opportunity to look about the village a little and note its dilapidated houses, which had been used and abused by both armies. It had been a beautiful place, the home of the elite, of the F.F.V.,[1] with many fine houses. In the old colonial days, the Fairfaxes, the Washingtons, etc., had been familiar personages on its streets. Those days of its prosperity in Virginia's youth, as well as its later history as a part of the nation, seemed to have been all canceled by the ordinance of secession and the most of its inhabitants scattered by the resulting war. Its damaged, deserted houses, broken fences, and general appearance of forsakenness had their effects heightened by the falling rain.

About half past 7, we formed and started for Centreville. The rain was still falling and the road slippery, but the march was continued until we reached Centreville about noon. Here we halted, made coffee, and rested for about two hours. About two o'clock the march was resumed. Crossing the Bull Run stream at Blackburn's Ford, we followed the direction of the Orange and Alexandria Railroad, along the nearest roads west of it. Passing over the Manassas Gap Railroad not far from Manassas, without halting, we kept on to Broad Run, where we went into bivouac about dark not far from Bristoe Station on the O & A Railroad.

We had made more than a good Sabbath Day's journey over the bad roads, were quite tired, and glad when the halt was ordered. The new uniforms we had drawn at Governor's Island had been soaked and spattered, and, as they dried, showed the mahogany mud stains that always result from contact with Virginia

1. First Families of Virginia.

mud. Of course we disliked to soil our new uniforms so quickly, but, as we were no longer where the girls could see us, we did not care so much.

Monday morning, September 14, dawned brightly—fair and cool. Now that we were back again in the field, we realized more than ever that the trip to New York had been a real tonic to us—body and soul—and the boys slung their knapsacks, shouldered their rifles, and started with jokes, laughter, and songs like the old times when we had full ranks. Our general route was along the O & A Railroad, and frequently we were near to it. It was scarcely noon when we halted not far from Catlett's Station an hour or so, and then pushed on to Warrenton Junction, which place we reached about four o'clock. Here we halted, it was said, to await orders.

Just as it was getting dark, the five regiments—which all told numbered less than 1,500 officers and men—strung out on the road to add another section to an already fair day's march. For three or four miles, we groped on through the intense darkness with the rain driving in our faces and dripping from our clothing. Then a halt was ordered, and we made the best of an unpleasant situation until morning.

Tuesday morning, about 8 o'clock, we began the day's march. About three hours later, we reached Bealeton Station, where we halted for a short rest. From this point, we marched to Rappahannock Station—taking another brief rest, then crossing the river, we moved on to a small stream near Brandy Station. The first gray light of Wednesday morning, September 16, found us moving on the road to Culpepper Court House.

During our march through the quaint old town of Culpepper, there was a particularly hard shower that flooded the streets, and there was a little incident that made an impression at the time. It was a brain-storm of one of the feminine inhabitants—produced, I presume, by our presence—and the *rainstorm* was only an elemental accompaniment. There was a momentary delay, and we stood in the flooded street. Just in front of the regiment, on a side porch very near the street, were three women who—contrary to the custom of southern women—had remained outside instead of peaking through a crack of the door or from behind a blind.

I never knew what provoked the sudden explosion of feminine wrath and vituperation, but some act or emotion caused one of the women to lose control of her feelings, and she instantly became a raving maniac. She broke forth with a stream of names, coupled with profanity, accusing us of about every crime in the calendar in language that would not look well on paper, and consigning us to an eternity in the brimstone lake, where, she asserted, the Almighty had sent *John Brown*, and all *Yankees* were to go.

At first there was surprise, but, when she proclaimed her sentence on John Brown and all Yankees, some of the boys cheered her. By this time the column was moving again, and the reference to John Brown was a suggestion to sing about him. Someone started singing, and everyone who could sing joined in on the words or the chorus of that most popular of all melodies of the war. As we glanced backward, the woman was jumping and screaming, and her words were not intelligible, but no doubt they were the harshest she could command.

It thus happened that as we tramped through the streets of Culpepper for the first time, mud-spattered and rain-soaked, the boys were singing like a German street band about John Brown's body and soul—with army variations. I recall no similar incident in the experience of the regiment.

Two or three miles out, we came to the headquarters of the Second Corps and found that Gen. Gouverneur K. Warren was in command of it.[2] Reporting there, the Provisional Brigade was ordered disbanded and the regiments composing it directed to return to their former places in their respective brigades. The Old First Brigade gave us a hearty welcome, and we were glad to be with it again. We had been absent, including the days of departure and return, 33 days and had had a really enjoyable vacation. It had impressed us deeply and made us to feel that we were still human, and to see that there was a sufficiency of patriotism and an intensity of loyalty among the supporters of the government.

Mingling again with our old companions in arms, we found them in fairly good spirits and as ready as ever to make whatever effort was required of them. The corps had been on the move for three days, and our division was under orders to march and at that time was awaiting reports from the cavalry in front, which they were supporting. There was a general interchange of experiences while we had been separated, and we learned that the period of our absence had been one of almost unbroken rest to our corps as a whole, though some portions of it had been active along the river keeping watch on the enemy.

Our corps had been the first to move in support of the cavalry in forcing them to abandon the line of the Rappahannock. This movement was still in progress with the purpose of driving the enemy to the other side of the Rapidan, it was said.

Thursday morning, September 17, we were ready at the appointed hour and soon after moved. We marched rapidly up the river for 8 or 10 miles, reaching the river near Robertson's Ford.[3] We found the cavalry deployed along the northerly side of the stream, under such cover as they were able to secure, engaged in a random, bushwhacking fire with a force of the enemy on the other side. We were told that this had been going on for two days.

The object of our coming, as we soon learned, was to relieve the cavalry that it might go farther up the river to observe the movements of the enemy in that di-

---

2. Hancock's Gettysburg wound forced him to relinquish command of Second Corps until March 1864. In the interim, Warren and John Caldwell alternated as commander. Welcher, *Union Army*, Vol. 1, *Eastern Theater*, 323–26.

3. Wright, apparently and confusingly, refers to two rivers. On their way up the Rapidan River, Union cavalry and infantry had to cross Robertson's River, which flowed into the Rapidan. Robertson's Ford was located on Robertson's River. Welcher, *Union Army*, Vol. 1, *Eastern Theater*, 273.

rection. Our regiment was a part of the force told to take the places of the cavalrymen. Following our usual custom when no specific orders were given, half of the regiment was sent out; and a portion of the line to be held was assigned to each company; and the commanders made their own plans for posting and relieving the men of their companies. This method, it was believed, gave a front line more strength and unity than if it was made up of details under officers other than their own.

Capt. Ball sent out Lieut. Bruce with half of the company to relieve the cavalry in and about an old house near the river bank—and who were at the time engaged in a desultory skirmish with unseen enemies across the river. When our boys went out, the cavalry boys came away, and the substitution was easily and quickly made. But it was not done without attracting the attention of the fellows on the other side, and they made it an occasion to increase their nagging fire. Availing themselves of such protection and concealment as they found there, the boys were soon replying to this fire.

We sheltered ourselves the best we could from the storm and kept quiet, but on the other side of the river some sort of a jollification seemed to be the order of the night, and apparently they were enjoying it. At first we assumed that it was just a little fun about the camp, which was in a little sheltered hollow out of sight, and occasionally we could see the reflection of the fire against the clouds. But it continued so long that we judged they must have had a supply of apple jack brought out. It was near midnight when they fired a couple of parting volleys and then grew quiet.

A little before night, Friday, September 18, we were relieved by our Second Brigade, and we went back about a mile and a half, where we found the division in bivouac. We were directed to encamp in an oak grove, and as it was now almost dark we hastened to prepare our shelters and cook our suppers.

The enemy was on the defensive, resisting our advance, but it was thought they might attempt a counter movement farther up the river. Our movement had given the front on the Rapidan to the infantry and allowed the cavalry previously holding it to post itself on our right flank. As we now know, it was Meade's purpose to compel Lee to fight or retreat. As Longstreet's Corps had already gone west to help out Bragg against Rosecrans, it was a most favorable time to crowd Lee.[4]

On September 23, it was reported from the pickets that some of the enemy called across the river that their army had gained a great victory over Rosecrans. We had had no papers since Saturday, and these had but little about him. On the 24th, some papers were received that gave conflicting accounts of the fighting at Chickamauga; but it seemed certain a great battle had been fought, and the result

4. Longstreet's Corps arrived in northern Georgia on September 18–19 and helped General Braxton Bragg defeat General William Rosecrans in the battle of Chickamauga on September 19–20, 1863.

was not as favorable as patriotic people hoped for; but the battle seemed not yet over. According to the papers, the situation did not appear worse than it did the night of the 2nd of July at Gettysburg. The later accounts from Chickamauga indicated what a terrible struggle it had been and how tenaciously it had been fought.

Monday, September 28, was another fine day, and matters continued quiet. Half of the regiment was sent out on picket. I remained in the camp, had a chill late in the afternoon, and passed a feverish, sleepless night. Tuesday being near the end of the month, the captain was anxious to have his monthly and quarterly returns ready, and I spent the day at his tent getting them ready, taking quinine and hoping to avoid another shake. I felt the approaching symptoms before the work was completed and, soon after getting to my tent, was shivering so that my teeth rattled against each other. That was followed by another night of fever and thirst. The next two days I lay in the tent in a helpless condition from headache and nausea, which I imagined was caused by the medicine. It was not until the night of October 1 that I was able to get up and eat something.

During this time my tentmate, Sergeant Henry R. Childs, had performed my duties and cared for me the best he could. And he proved himself a thoughtful and capable nurse. Friday, October 2, a storm came on, and I remained in my tent, sitting or lying wrapped in blankets to keep warm and fearing a recurrence of the chills. There was nothing in the camp to eat but government rations and all of those my stomach would accept were coffee and crackers.

Saturday there came to the camp two commissioners, Jefferson P. Kidder and Solomon Snow, from Minnesota to receive our votes and report them to the state under a new law.[5] It was arranged to vote on Monday. It was here that I cast my first vote as did many others.

Sunday I was feeling much improved and performed such duty as the day required. Major Mark W. Downie, wounded at Gettysburg, returned and took command of the regiment. He was the first of the field officers to return.

Monday was partly devoted to voting, all of the regiment being assembled in camp for that purpose. There were no speeches or electioneering, and each one was free to vote as he chose. I do not recall that I ever heard the detailed result of our votes, but I have no doubt they were counted and reported. There was also a proposition made to the regiment to reenlist for three years, but no action was taken. The talk of the boys was that they would wait until near the close of their present enlistment before making another.

By October 10, it was apparent that there was a pretty general movement of the army. It was reported that cavalry had crossed the river and had found but few of

---

5. In September 1862, the state legislature passed a law allowing Minnesota soldiers to vote where stationed and authorizing appointed commissioners to collect the ballots; Folwell, *Minnesota*, 2:333.

the enemy. There were the usual rumors as to movements of our own and the troops of the enemy, and one of them was to the effect Lee was moving from Orange Court House to Madison Court House.[6] The firing on the right seemed to confirm this, though it was not of sufficient volume or long enough continued to indicate any serious fighting.

(As we now know, Lee did cross the Rapidan some miles above the pickets on the 9th and morning of the 10th and before noon of the 10th had practically all of his army in the neighborhood of Madison Court House, with his cavalry forcing a crossing of Robertson River at daylight that morning. From our movements that morning, it is supposed that Meade judged this attack of Lee's cavalry to be a feint to recall his movement across the Rapidan. Possibly Meade had correct knowledge of Lee's purpose, and his demonstration was intended to recall Lee in that direction.)

Whatever the leaders may have known or surmised as to each other's plans, we of the ranks knew nothing, positively, but we now began to be keenly alive to a serious situation—so far as we could fathom it—and watched closely for further developments. After remaining for an hour or more in the outskirts of Culpepper, we fell in and, crossing the railroad, marched rapidly three or four miles in the direction of the Rappahannock River. Here we halted and the brigades took position, but did not deploy into line of battle, and seemed to be waiting to meet some move of the enemy. There was considerable firing now, but it was some distance away and to our right and rear, which certainly indicated that the enemy was moving around our right.

We were not attacked but, as night approached, we deployed into line and advanced a short distance with a skirmishing line well out. At this time, we were covering the Sperryville Road, and it was reported that the enemy was less than three miles away. But there was nothing more than light skirmishing on our front, and that lasted but a few minutes and ended with the capture of a couple of prisoners.

At half past one, Sunday morning, October 11, we were called, and orders were given to prepare a hasty breakfast and be ready to march within an hour. The light rain that had been falling when we forgot all of our troubles in sleep had ceased, and the stars were shining. It was quite cool. We marched at 2:20. We moved on by-roads and across fields until we struck the main road to Brandy Station.

Soon after daylight we passed the residence of J. Minor Botts and halted near there for a brief rest. The said J. Minor was a somewhat noted man of the times who disagreed with the disunionists and could not unite with the Unionists. He tried to play a profitable neutrality and called on both sides to protect his property, but his plan did not work very well, and he finally suffered at the hands of both parties. In the end, I believe, he was reimbursed by the government.

6. Madison Court House was some eighteen miles southwest of Culpepper Court House and about the same distance directly west of Meade's most advanced positions along the Rapidan.

The halt here was only long enough to close up the regiments and allow the men to fill their canteens at a nearby stream. Resuming the march we moved rapidly and did not halt again until near Brandy Station.

As the morning advanced, it developed into a beautiful autumn day. Crossing some of the higher ridges, long lines of wagons and artillery and columns of infantry could be seen moving on several roads, all headed for the Rappahannock. West of us, on the Robertson River, and northwest, about Thoroughfare and Fox mountains, there was occasional artillery firing, but nothing that indicated an attack in force. It was evident that the whole army was making a hurried but orderly retreat, and—as there had been no serious fighting yet—that it was to checkmate some more of the enemy to the west of us. At a point on the hills not far from Brandy Station our corps halted, and we were told that it was a good time to make coffee. As we were very hungry by this time, it was an agreeable order and quickly obeyed.

We were not at all particular as to whose fence-rails we used, and the fires were soon blazing. When the coffee was boiling, we toasted crackers and broiled some slices of pork, sat on the ground, and ate a hearty breakfast, and relished every mouthful of it. Resting here for about an hour and a half, we reformed and pushed on toward the river, moving at a quickstep.

From the hills, we again had opportunity to observe the splendid sight of a great army in motion: marching men and moving trains, without undue haste or confusion, all moving quickly and in concert. Four corps of the Army of the Potomac on separate roads were rolling northward like mighty rivers.

It was about noon, or possibly a little after, when we arrived at the Rappahannock River, and, almost without a halt, we proceeded to wade across it. This was not a very difficult task, but it wet us to the hips, and the water was rather chilly. On the northerly side a temporary halt was made, to close the formation and squeeze a little of the water from our clothing, then our division pushed on toward Bealeton.

Passing a mile north of this place, we halted at about half past two in the afternoon, having been on the road something like twelve hours and marched over 23 miles. At first the halt appeared to be only for a brief rest; but later, line was formed and pickets were thrown out. The day had been fine; and the marching rapid; and all were ready to lie down and try to make up some of the sleep we had failed to get the night before.

In a single day the army had shifted its position from the Rapidan to the northerly side of the Rappahannock. This was done to meet a supposed movement of Lee to get between Meade and Washington. While it was Lee's plan to flank Meade, it was not his plan to go as far north as Meade judged he would. But when Lee reached Culpepper Sunday afternoon of the 11th, he found that Meade was not there, and his movement was a failure. Had Meade rightly understood Lee's real purpose, there is no doubt he would have remained in the vicinity of

Culpepper and accommodated him with a fight, but Meade did not dare let Lee get a full day's start of him on the road to Washington. That was one of the misfortunes of the Army of the Potomac. It was compelled always to interpose between Washington and the enemy.

When Lee closed in on Culpepper and discovered he had miscalculated on what Meade might do, his army had already been moving for three days, and he felt obliged to give them a little rest and renew their rations. He accordingly waited there that night and the next forenoon.

Meantime, Meade had halted his forces on the northerly side of the river and was trying to locate Lee's main force and determine his next move. Monday forenoon he learned of the presence of a large force of the enemy about his old camps around Culpepper, and determined to return there and attack it.

Monday morning, October 12, we were up before it was light and, after an early breakfast, rested in the bivouac, waiting orders. Along toward noon, orders came to fall in, and we were soon moving. We had heard considerable firing that morning, and the most of it appeared to be up the river and at a considerable distance. We were a little surprised when we moved that we marched away from the firing and took the road back by Bealeton and from there to the river.

Some of the boys were just making coffee for their dinners when the order came to march—and fell in with their tincups in their hands—but there was no time to drink it. It was somewhere about 3 o'clock when we arrived at the Rappahannock River, and there was but a short delay before we crossed over. Seeing that we were to cross, a good many of the boys hastily took off their shoes, stockings, and pants, and carried them in their hands. There was sufficient delay on the other side to allow them to put them on again before we moved off, and in this way they had dry clothing instead of being wet to the waist.

As soon as the regiments were closed up and in place, the movement was continued for a few miles and the three corps deployed into line on the hills about Brandy Station, their movement being preceded by a cavalry force of about 2,500 men under Buford which pushed on toward Culpepper.[7]

It was a beautiful autumn afternoon, and the sun was getting near the horizon, and the sight was one of rare magnificence. The three corps numbering near 25,000 men came up in two lines of battle with flags flying, and accompanied by their artillery, which galloped into position on the ridges in splendid style. Altogether it was a gigantic bit of realistic war play, staged on about three miles of irregularly-aligned hills and illuminated by a rarely beautiful and brilliant sunset.

The purpose of all this had not been display but real war. Up to 11 o'clock that day, Meade's advices had made it reasonably certain that Lee, with a large force,

7. The Second, Fifth, and Sixth Corps—and Buford's cavalry—were under Sedgwick's command on this reconnaissance in force.

was in the vicinity of Culpepper. But now he was gone, and the advance of Buford's cavalry quickly made that much certain.

When it was certain that the enemy was not there to oppose us, there was a sudden relaxation of the feelings that had dominated us as we marched up the slope. I cannot truthfully assert that we were *sorry* the enemy had departed before we reached them. There was the feeling one has when he has delivered a blow at something he wished to hit and missed it, or fired at a buck and seen it bound away into the bushes. Whatever disappointment we may have had, it was tempered by the reflection that if they had escaped so had we, and there were none of our comrades to be borne off on the stretchers or buried in hastily dug trenches.

We rested in line of battle as the sun disappeared behind the hills and watched the after-glow of sunset fade, and the evening twilight change into night shadows. Then arms were stacked, fires were kindled, and coffee made. Then, gathered around the fires—for the evening was chilly—we sat on the ground to eat our suppers. We had no specific orders.

As the night deepened, and the chilliness increased, the fires were replenished until the hilltops for three or four miles were brilliantly lighted. Around them the boys gathered—talking, laughing, and singing—as if free from hardship and far removed from danger. Yet for all of the assumed light-hearted cheerfulness, we all clearly understood that the situation was far from favorable, and the immediate future was threatened with many dangers. Already there was a display of many lights to the northwest, which we did not need to be told was the enemy's camp-fires, and that our flank and rear were seriously threatened. Sergeant Childs said that "it looked like a fight or a foot-race," and that someone added that "it might be both." The fires burned low, and the boys wrapped their blankets about them and slept.

Lee moved out from Culpepper to the westward soon after noon of the 12th and, when behind a convenient range of hills, took the roads leading west to the Sulphur Springs and Waterloo crossings of the Rappahannock. Gregg's cavalry was guarding the river in this direction, and it was supported by the Third Corps. Lee's infantry was preceded by Stuart's cavalry, and they drove in Gregg's outposts and succeeded in getting across the river late in the afternoon of the 12th. The infantry followed that night and early the next morning. That gave the enemy the roads to Warrenton and Greenwich.

This was the situation of things on the river 10 or 12 miles above us, at sunset Monday evening. As we made a show of force on the hills fronting Culpepper, the enemy we had come there to fight was already miles away, hurrying to take advantage of the roads open to him. It was a knowledge of this, sent to Meade by Gregg an hour or two later, that satisfied Meade of his mistake in striking at Lee on the south side of the river and caused him to order the return of the three corps to the northerly side.

It was somewhere about midnight when the orders to retire reached us, and the most of us were sleeping. It took but a few minutes to rouse the men and get them in line. The orders were to refrain from all conversation and to make no unnecessary noise. I recall that there was a brief wait after we were in line, and that we felt the chill of the night wind as we waited. Then, in obedience to brief commands given in low tones, we took arms, fell into column of fours, and headed back towards the river. There was no moon, but the stars were shining, and it was not difficult marching after we got out of the fields into the road. After getting onto the road, we marched rapidly and kept at it until we reached the river, which we did without accident or misadventure.

At the river there was a brief halt, when we again took to the water and, for the third time in about 36 hours, we forded the Rappahannock. Delaying but a few minutes, we closed up the ranks and moved off on the road to Bealeton and, passing that place, halted near where we had bivouacked the day before. At this time it was getting light, and this was Tuesday morning October 13.

Apparently the trains were being massed about Bealeton, and everything on wheels seemed to be moving. It was said that "the trains were to go to the rear," but I am not sure where that was then supposed to be. In point of fact, I do not think that at that time or at any time within the next 48 hours the rear or the front either was long enough in one place to be christened.

Our halt here was very brief, and before the sun rose we were moving—at least, our division was. Our division, Second, led off and was followed by the rest of the corps. We took the Fayetteville Road and later learned that we were to relieve or reinforce the Third Corps, which was supposed to be somewhere in that direction and had been engaged the evening before. We moved steadily and with some caution, but most of the time rapidly.

It was noon or a little after when, preceded by a line of skirmishers, we deployed into line and entered into a broken pine wood. We were then supposed to be somewhere in the vicinity of Fayetteville, but I do not recall seeing anything of the place or know how near. Here we halted and laid down, and were very glad of the opportunity. For in the last 24 hours, we had rested and slept but a small portion of them. Since noon of the previous day, we must have marched nearly or quite 35 miles.

At first we expected 'something was going to happen' very soon, but there were no immediate developments. We were not charged by anything more formidable than a couple of frightened rabbits. These came running towards us after being passed by the skirmishers, like 'scared rabbits.' One was captured by Lieutenant Bruce, but the other escaped. It is needless to say it was utilized for the lieutenant's dinner.

The smell of coffee and frying pork mingled with the natural odors of the forest. And the incense of the broiling rabbit went up with the smoke of the campfires as we disposed ourselves to eat the hastily prepared dinner.

While we were still eating, there was a rattle of musketry off to the right and a little later more directly in front. This caused us to take arms, shift to the right, and advance to the support of the skirmishers. It was said the Third Corps was withdrawing. The retirement of the Third Corps left the Second Corps its old job of covering the rear in a retrograde movement, though at that particular time we did not realize this to be the case.

The two armies were engaged in a monster game of 'hide and seek' among the tangled cedar thickets and scrub-pine forests that covered the ridges, ravines, and plains of that section of Virginia. Each was trying to give the other a stunning blow and avoid a counterstroke, and both were headed for practically the same point, a good defensible position covering the railroad. This whole movement from the Rapidan to Bull Run and back to the Rapidan was generally referred to by the boys afterward as the 'Grand Sas-shay' (*chassé*), but they had not named it then.[8] Both armies were now getting into the vicinity of the Bull Run battlefields and a section of the country with which they were familiar. Both armies were more favorably placed than for the last three days, when crossing rivers and striking blindly at each other.

About the time the Third Corps withdrew, there was considerable activity along the front of our corps. Our skirmishers were advanced for considerable distance and picked up a number of prisoners and from these some information was obtained. Frequent reports from those in front made it pretty certain that a considerable force of the enemy was being gathered in our front, and we were expecting it to be moved against us at any time.

The First Regiment studied the geography of this section on foot and took lessons at intervals for about three years. We had fought our first battle in it on the Bull Run; we had crossed the northerly portion of it going to Antietam; and the westerly and southerly portions returning and going to Fredericksburg. We had gone along its easterly side going to Gettysburg; and again crossed its southerly side returning to the Rappahannock. We had gone over the railroad going to New York and traversed the whole length of it returning to the army. We were now zigzagging across it again on the by-roads, soon to return in a like manner.

The position taken by the Second Corps about noon of October 13th, 1863, was nearly west of Bealeton and between the Rappahannock River and the branch road between Warrenton Junction and Warrenton. We remained there until after the Third Corps was well started on its route, when we withdrew to follow another road a little to the east of it. It may have been between 2 and 3 o'clock when we drew out of the woods and began the northward march. A march of three or four miles brought us to the Warrenton Junction Road. Crossing this near Three-mile Station, we took the road leading to Auburn, after resting a few

8. A *chassé* is a sideways gliding step that is accompanied by one or two rapid linking steps—a close approximation of what both armies were doing in mid-October 1863.

minutes. At this time it was known that a considerable force was following us, and a scouting party was sent up the railroad towards Warrenton. It reported a force of the enemy crossing the road, as we were, less than three miles west of us.

It was 4 o'clock or about that time when we crossed the railroad, and we fully expected to get in collision with the enemy at some point before dark. There had been several clashes at the rear of the column already and considerable firing ahead of us, which made us expect a flank attack at every road-crossing. In fact, demonstrations were frequently made and detachments sent out to meet them but it did not fall to the lot of our regiment to take any active part in these affairs.

It was after dark when we reached a point near Cedar Run and not far from the village of Auburn, and were kept waiting some time before dispositions were made for the night. Matters were in some confusion that evening, on both sides, and this is not to be wondered at when the whole movement is considered and the country over which it was made.

It was late and dark, and the men were too tired to wander far from camp. Many of them did go to the stream for water, and were quite close to some of the enemy, but they remained undiscovered. Gen. Warren, who commanded the Second Corps, made careful disposition of his troops and was well prepared to resist an attack. But there were no parties sent out to the front to investigate conditions so far as we knew, and the pickets were posted along the stream on the side of the bivouac. The lateness of the hour and the weariness of the men were both favorable to Stuart.

It must have been near or quite ten o'clock when our division was assigned its position, and arms were stacked. The men at once started fires to make coffee. We felt the need of a cup of coffee before we slept. The coffee-making process had not continued long before orders came to "put out the fires," as it was not safe to let our position be known. There was a pretty vigorous protest against this, and some of the boys did not 'skip the hard words,' but of course the order was obeyed. I seemed to have just fallen asleep when I was conscious of some one pulling at my blanket and calling "Orderly! Orderly! Is this the orderly of F?" I had to admit it and inquired what was wanted and was told to call the men. It was then about 3:30 Wednesday morning, and everything was enveloped in a dense fog. It took pretty vigorous shaking and some *emphasis* to 'restore to consciousness' some of the tired sleepy men, and they 'came up growling,' but they all 'came out of it' sufficiently to answer to their names.

Having reported all present or accounted for, I received orders to have the men get their breakfasts and be ready to march without delay. When I returned, the boys had already assumed that the orders of the night before did not apply to the morning and had started fires. We were soon drinking hot coffee and eating crackers and fried pork. After we had eaten our breakfasts and filled our canteens, we waited for the order to fall in, and it was far from pleasant in the chill and fog.

We were suddenly startled into action by a roar of artillery that echoed along the valley with startling resonance. Its suddenness was a surprise, but an attack was suspected, and there was no confusion. Regiments formed and waited orders, with guns in hand and ready to move.

There was lively fighting on three sides of us at the same time, and matters looked dubious as to results. Our division was not sent into action, but remained, covering the trains and in readiness to go wherever most needed, and we were interested spectators of a most remarkable scene. The roar of the artillery and crashing and exploding shells startled the ear; the flash of the guns as they were fired reflected a dull red glare from the smoke and the mist, and 'painted hell on the sky'; while the pungent smell of burning brimstone was suggestive of a closer proximity to the 'burning lake.'

The purpose of our commander was to push on rather than remain and fight. The fighting was still in progress on three sides when the advance was ordered, and the First Regiment was deployed as skirmishers to cover the right of the trains going toward Catlett's—the only side on which there was no fighting going on, but it was supposed it might begin there at any moment. The road on which we were to move was at that time held by the enemy, and we waited the result of the fighting to open the road to Catlett's.

When the enemy on this front was forced back, it was getting fairly light and we began to move. The wagons had to go down a hill, ford the stream, and pass for a mile or more through a timbered valley before getting onto higher and more open ground. This was passed as quickly as practicable, and the wagons were massed in an open field, all being brought through without the loss of a wagon or a mule.

Meantime, the fighting behind us was going on noisily. Here the batteries were put in position, and the position was covered on the flanks and front by the 2nd and 3rd divisions, while the First Division withdrew under fire and joined us on the hills.

We could not see the whole of the movements of our gallant First Division[9] as it withdrew from its precarious situation confronting the advance of Ewell's Corps coming on from Warrenton, but what we did see was highly interesting. A brigade at a time, they fell back under cover of the batteries, and this was repeated until they were under cover of our batteries on the hills, where the enemy did not follow to attack.

The Third Division had advanced to open the road to Catlett's and had also detached Carroll's Brigade to fight Stuart; and the Second Division covered the trains and got them in readiness to move. It was at their repulse that we started to

9. Since October 13, the First Division of the Second Corps had been commanded by John C. Caldwell, who had given command of Second Corps back to Warren; Welcher, *Union Army*, Vol. 1, *Eastern Theater*, 628.

the rear, but they were renewing the attack and threatening both flanks before Caldwell's men got away.

It was somewhere about 8 o'clock when the Second Corps and its trains were all together on the higher and more open ground. It was at about this time that Warren received his orders for the day from Meade, which had been issued before daylight that morning and without any knowledge of present affairs with the Second Corps. This order, in brief, was for all of the corps to move at daylight. The Second Corps was to move first to Catlett's Station on the railroad and then follow the route of the others along the railroad.

It is well to note also the orders of Lee. Ewell, with about half of his force, had followed since the day before and was now attacking. Hill, with the remainder, was coming down from New Baltimore, by way of Greenwich, and was ordered to strike the railroad at Bristoe. This left the Second Corps to cover the retreat of the Union army and exposed it to a rear and flank attack by the united forces of Lee.

Meade's order said: "Move forward as rapidly as you can, as they may send out a column from Gainesville to Bristoe. Sykes (Fifth Corps) will remain here until you are up." As it turned out, Lee directed his whole force on Bristoe, and the Fifth Corps *did not remain there*. The Second Corps had to 'stand off' the whole of Lee's army.

Halting only long enough after the First Division joined us to allow them to hastily bury some of the dead they had brought in with them and care for the wounded in the ambulances—the march was resumed. By this time the cavalry under Gregg was fighting Ewell's advance, and there was skirmishing on three sides of us.

At first we moved en masse, with the trains in the center, across the fields. Then, after another brief halt, Carroll's Brigade of the Third Division led off on the road to Catlett's—with the 8th Ohio deployed as skirmishers—and was followed by the rest of the division. This was followed by the trains, covered by the Second Division, and these by the First Division—with the cavalry as flankers and covering the rear and skirmishing with the enemy.

There were fields and patches of timber on both sides of the road, and some hills and hollows, but no places favorable to the enemy unless they were already occupying them. We were not again attacked that morning by infantry, and our cavalry was able to take care of theirs.

When once straightened out on the road, we moved rapidly and without halting until the railroad was reached at the station. It was considered best to halt here to feed and rest the horses and allow the men to make coffee. Stacking arms, we lighted fires and made coffee, while a part of the cavalry skirmished with the enemy back on the road, and detachments were sent out on the roads towards Bristoe and Warrenton Junction. I suppose it was about noon when we reached Catlett's Station.

When the coffee had boiled, and we had scorched a couple of slices of pork, we sat on our knapsacks to eat, talk about the incidents of the morning, and guess what the afternoon's might be. As we ate, we could hear the cracking of carbines back on the road where the cavalry boys were standing guard. When we had eaten we lay on the ground to rest while waiting for the order to move. Tired as we all were, it did not take more than two minutes to be sleeping soundly, but there were more important things than sleep and before many minutes we were ordered to form.

The First Minnesota—on the right of the First Brigade—led the march, followed by the 15th Massachusetts and the rest of the brigade. As Company F was the right flank company and I was its orderly sergeant, I came pretty near leading the Second Corps that afternoon. The order was passed to move at quick time and keep well closed up.

At first we took the dirt road, then were directed to take the railroad track. Meantime, the officers, artillery, and trains were on the wagon road, which for the most part ran near the railroad.

As we hurried over the ties, the order "Elongate the step, sergeant" was called to me twice. I will not say how far I lengthened the step in obedience to this order, but I stretched it to the limit of my rather short legs and moved them to the rhythm of quick time.[10] The very best I could do. Capt. Ball, whose legs were only a little longer than mine, was a little ahead, and the rest of the boys were close at my heels. A glance backward occasionally showed a stream of swaying gun barrels and bobbing, battered, black hats surging after me, as the boys 'jumped the ties.'

The distance from Catlett's to Bristoe Station was, as I remember it, about 7 miles. This hurried advance was kept up for about four miles when the cavalry, which had gone out while we were eating, was met returning, and the commander reported to Gen. Webb. Soon after, Major Downie, who was in command of the regiment, told Capt. Ball he could moderate the pace to ordinary quick time. I was glad to do this, as the speed-rate over the ties was telling on me. I had not yet fully regained my strength since the attack of the 'shakes.'

It was not a warm afternoon, but we were all sweating quite freely. It was observed, too, that we had moved so rapidly that the column was getting pretty badly strung out, and some of the regiments behind us were making extra efforts to close up. We did not halt, only moderated the pace a little, and kept on along the track.

Of course, we realized the Johnnies were after us in full force and knew that we were liable to attack at any time and in any place, but we had no intimation from those in command that the danger was more imminent than it had been since we shook them off before halting at the station.

---

10. Hardee's *Rifle and Light Infantry Tactics* set quick time at 110 steps per minute, double quick time at 165 steps, a standard step at 28 inches, and a double-quick step at 33 inches; McWhiney and Jamieson, *Attack and Die,* 50.

It was somewhere about 4 o'clock, and we had approached to within a mile or so of the ruins of Bristoe Station, before the acuteness of the situation was fully impressed upon us, and we knew that enemies instead of friends were there to meet us.

The first intimation of this adverse condition of things came like a clap of thunder, and it was conveyed by a couple of cannon shots at intervals of five or six seconds between. The shells crossed our line of march diagonally and exploded on the hillside beyond the station and across Broad Run. As we now know, these shells were not intended for us but for the rear of the Third Corps train which was at that time passing over the hill. This was the advance of Hill's Corps—Cooke and Kirkland's Brigades of Heth's Division, supported by Davis' and Walker's Brigades. They were as wholly unaware of our approach as we were of theirs.

General Alexander S. Webb and his staff were not far off at the time, and he at once sent an order for our regiment to break from the column and deploy as flankers on the left of the road. In obedience to this order, we deployed forward to the left oblique at the double-quick a hundred yards or so from the marching column. This was scarcely done before the order was given to skirmish the hillside on the left, in the direction from which the shots were fired.

At this time, not wishing to endanger the colors on the skirmish line, Major Downie sent Color Sergeant Irwin with the colors and color guard to the hill on the opposite side of the road.

Adjusting our deployment to the ordinary intervals of skirmishers, we started diagonally towards the top of the hill so that the right of the line might be kept abreast of the head of the brigade. This movement took the left of the regiment among a thick growth of trees and bushes, but the right—for the most of the time—was in the open.

The left of the line had not gone far into the bushes when it came in contact with the right of a skirmish line of the enemy, and firing began at once. It was a rare situation. We struck their line on the flank. We did not fully comprehend the situation at the moment, but later we learned that their movement was against an enemy supposed to be on the other side of Broad Run.

The firing on the left warned us that our line there had met with opposition, and we checked our advance for the moment on the right to see the result. The firing had broken out suddenly and was lively for a few minutes, dying down to a scattering fire. We could hear it plainly and see the smoke rising above the bushes, but could not see any of the enemy or any of our own regiment that were firing. We on the right could only judge of the position of our own men and of the enemy by the rising smoke.

It was then thought best to head off their advancing line by shifting our own more nearly parallel to its front by withdrawing the left wing of the regiment a little and making a defensive fight there, and advancing the right wing, and at the same time wheeling it to the left. In this way it was hoped to gain the higher and more open ground where we would be better able to see what was before us.

When the order came for this change of front, it was evident that Company F, being on the extreme right, had the longest distance to move and must move with the greatest rapidity. Capt. Ball gave the order and told us to run for the top of the ridge. Trailing arms, we started to run and occasionally someone who had a little extra wind would let out a short yell. We of the right battalion were mostly on open ground, and we got to the top of the ridge in record time and found we were not a minute too soon. Scarcely a hundred yards away was a strong line of skir-mishers coming almost directly towards us.

We knew what we were there for and, without waiting for orders, dropped to our knees, behind whatever cover we could see conveniently near, and put our rifles into action. After the run up the hill, I do not think any of us had nerves steady enough to draw a fine bead, but our first fire was effective and seemed to be a bit of a surprise as well.

There was a sudden halt, a moment of indecision, and then they retired hur-riedly, seeking places of shelter wherever they could find them. Then, from such shelter as each individual soldier could find, wherever a head showed itself it was fired at.

Meantime, we were trying to make out what there was in front of us, and it did not require more than a glance to satisfy us that there were more than we wanted. Someone called out that there were "a million of them." But, of course, that was a gross exaggeration. Less than a quarter of a mile in the rear of the skirmishers we were holding in check, a line of battle was advancing across the open ground, and both of its flanks were in the woods. An eighth of a mile or so in rear of this, there was another following it. And behind that, a column of infantry was leaving the road and marching out into the field. In two places, their guns were already firing and other batteries were galloping across the open.

It was a wonderful display of force, and we knew perfectly well that our 'thin, blue line' would be brushed away without ceremony as soon as it was brought to bear against us. At the moment, only the skirmish line was giving its attention to us. The batteries were directing their fire at the Union batteries on the other side of the railroad.

Considerable rubbish carted from the camps had been dumped where Com-pany F came to the crest of the little hill, and wreckage of various kinds had been thrown there. Whoever put them there had done us a good service and has our thanks, for they were mighty handy, and behind nearly every one of them a sol-dier or two found shelter as he plied his rifle.

Gen. Warren, at the first outbreak, rode from the head of Hayes's Division to the top of a hill on the right of the railroad to take in the situation. He was a top-ographical engineer, knew the locality, and promptly made his plans and issued his orders, which in brief were to occupy the railroad cuts and embankments as breastworks and post the artillery on the high ground back of it.

Our whole attention was concentrated on the line of gray-coated men, crouching in the grass and bushes, whose location was pretty plainly indicated by the smoke of their rifles, and whose intent was made certain by the angry hiss and '*spat*' of their bullets about us. Capt. Ball said we must "hold on to the crest of the hill to the last minute."

It soon began to be evident that the last minute could not be long delayed. Everything went with a rush that afternoon. The line of battle back of their skirmishers, which apparently had only paused to adjust its formation, again advanced. We judged that within a minute or two it would come on with the usual yelling, and that then we would be swept off that hill and have to run for our lives—if not already dead or disabled. As their line approached their skirmishers, they sprang to their feet and came on firing.

At this juncture, orders came for our recall, and Capt. Ball told us to run for the railroad in open order as we were. Emptying our rifles at the advancing lines, we sprang up and ran for the railroad, which was on an embankment 6 or 8 feet high (more or less) and somewhere about 300 yards distant.

As I turned to go, I could see that our line to the left of us was already going back, and that the enemy's skirmishers were even then at the crest, near the trees, and coming out of the bushes on the hillside. When once started, I felt that my life depended on the length of the steps down the gentle slope of the hill and the rapidity with which I took them. I 'struck my best gait' without ceremony.

We had not covered half of the distance before our pursuers were at the top of the hill behind us, yelling and shooting. It was an intensely exciting moment which quickened all of the senses and brought every nerve and muscle into action. Their bullets fairly sizzled as they passed over us, and some of them struck the ground beside us, making the dirt fly and glancing away with a peculiar whining sound I never heard on any other occasion. As we were going down the hill, a large proportion of their bullets passed over us, as was evident from the little puffs of dust rising in front of us. The upper air was rent and torn with hissing, shrieking, and exploding shells from the batteries on both sides.

Naturally, we supposed that our line was behind the railroad grade. We had no notice of where they were and, as we ran, could not see a flag, a gun, or a black hat. I only recall seeing Corporal Andrew Bayer and Charley Berdan as we ran, and they were near me before we started. Reaching the railroad, we tumbled into the excavation (made in throwing out dirt for the grade), scrambled up the embankment, and slid down the other side—among the men of the Nineteenth Maine.

The 19th Maine, which followed immediately in the rear of our regiment that afternoon, had hustled along the track after we had deployed and skirmished up the hill, and was now lying in the shelter of the grade ready to open on our pursuers as soon as we were in. They greeted us with a cheer and got busy with their rifles at once.

As I passed over the grade, I looked back and could see their line coming bravely down the slope—a target for our batteries, which were raining upon them a merciless shell fire.

When we reached the protecting shelter of that embankment, we were literally 'all in' and mighty glad to get there with a whole hide. At first, as soon as we could get our wind and load our guns, we thought to join in with the 19th and did so. But soon I had word from Capt. Ball to bring the men to the left of the 19th, and proceeded in that direction, calling to the men of the company to follow.

Meantime, a desperate fight at close quarters was being waged and, for a rarity, our men were fighting from cover and inflicting an awful punishment upon their assailants. Their first line had already lodged in the ditch on the opposite side of the embankment. That is, those of them who were not lying on the hillside or trying to get back over the ridge. Their second line was coming on with a rush and a yell when Capt. Ball sprang up the grade and called on the boys to follow him. All who were near and heard did follow, and it was at the climax of their last effort. It was here that the greatest loss of the company that afternoon occurred.

Capt. Ball thought—as he afterwards explained to us—that if the second line got into the ditch with the first, that there might be a rush over the embankment. At the time it was thought there were more of the first line on the other side of the grade than were really there. As soon as Capt. Ball was on top of the grade, he opened fire with his revolver and finally threw it at the enemy. At almost the same instant he was struck by a bullet in the thigh, crumpled to the ground—falling backward and rolling down the embankment.

Hans Peterson was struck by two bullets and almost instantly killed. It was also at this time, I think, that Edrick J. Frary was hit in the hand and Berdan in the right arm. Berdan had previously had a bullet graze his neck and pass through his rubber blanket, which was rolled on top of his knapsack, and another had cut away a part of his hat brim on the opposite side of his head.

There is no doubt but some of the enemy in the ditch were making a demonstration to cross the grade, but it quickly subsided, and I am inclined to think that the greater portion of the storm of bullets that came our way was from the second line and from about the ruins (a cellar and some chimneys) of a burned house on the hillside. I distinctly saw puffs of smoke which indicated a considerable force there. The wounds also indicated that the bullets had been fired from a level with the top of the grade and, if fired from the ditch, there would have been an upward tendency of at least 45 degrees.

There is one good thing about a fight like that at Bristoe Station. It is soon over. When a line of battle starts on a charge it must keep on to victory or retire in defeat. In this case the first line had exhausted itself in getting into the ditch, and but few of the second line ever got that far.

I do not wish to convey the idea that Company F was alone in the fight—only that it was all of the First Regiment I could see at that particular point at that time. The Nineteenth Maine was making a splendid fight: loading in the shelter of the grade and rising above it to fire. (Neither did we remain on the track, making targets of ourselves while loading, but performed that operation under cover of the bank. A useless exposure to death is fool-hardiness, not bravery, and we had long since passed that stage of apprenticeship.)

The men we had been fighting in the morning, and who had followed us all day, were from Ewell's Corps and Stuart's cavalry. The men who attacked us that evening were from Hill's Corps. It became evident, too, as the night advanced, that both of these forces were closing up on us, and there was no question but they would attack again in the morning.

Conscientious scruples about being shot

OCTOBER-NOVEMBER 1863

IT WAS SOMEWHERE ABOUT NINE O'CLOCK when we were first informed that it was likely that we would leave that position soon. The regiment was called in from its advanced position and assembled in its place on the right of the brigade.

For five days we had been on the move, and in the last 24 hours we had less than three for rest and sleep, and we would gladly have lain down there and slept. Tired as the men were, they were holding out well and in fairly good spirits. Many dropped asleep as we lay on the ground waiting for orders to move. Lieut. Bruce (who had taken command of the company after Ball was wounded) and I had considerable trouble to get them all on their feet and wide enough awake to get into line when the order did come.

I recall that Ole Johnson, as he afterwards said, did not "know so more as a cat, when I first came up."

I judge it to have been about midnight when we quietly started to join the other four corps, which—we were told—were waiting for us on Bull Run. Then we waded Broad Run, climbed the slippery bank, and took the road to Manassas Junction. From Bristoe Station to Manassas Junction is between 3 and 4 miles, and we marched steadily without halting or hurrying. That point was reached, so far as I know, without incident or mishap of a serious nature; at least there were no objections offered by the enemy.

At Manassas there was a short halt, and the weary men dropped to the ground in their places and slept. In less than five minutes, one-half of the boys were sitting or lying on the ground with their guns still clasped in their hands and their knapsacks on their shoulders, sleeping soundly—some of them audibly. I lay on the grass beside the road with Lieut. Bruce, and we were both trying to keep awake, because we felt that we *must*, but we both slept a little. There was a cricket in the grass close by that was trilling lustily, and it made me think of autumn evenings at home and wish I was there and—then I was asleep.

The next I knew, Bruce was shaking me and calling, "Wake up! Fall in!" Then I passed down the company—shaking and pulling and talking—to make sure we should not leave any of the boys behind. We were going to turn off from the line of the railroad we had been following, and take a more direct road across the country to some ford on Bull Run. We had only been waiting for a guide. Even that little rest and the ten-minute-or-so nap had been a benefit.

The guide and a little squad of mounted men led the way, followed by Major Downie and the adjutant, and we followed after. Most of the way the roads were narrow and through the woods, and it was too dark to see anything. Major Downie had a habit of rattling his foot in the stirrup, which served to guide us. The trains were on another road, and we moved with very little noise. I do not know how far it was or by what roads we marched, but it was far enough for tired men and was judged to be about 4 miles.

At last we came to a crossing, after following a considerable stream for some distance, and were told that it was Blackburn's Ford across Bull Run. We were to cross over and take position on the higher ground on the other side. There we stacked arms and—as more than 60 of the last 70 hours had been spent on the march, in line, or actually fighting the men immediately lay down to sleep. This was about 4 o'clock, Thursday morning, Oct. 15.

When I was waked it was daylight. I roused the boys, called the roll, and reported the company. Then we had orders to get our breakfasts and be prepared to move. The first thing was to find wood and water and make coffee. These were easily found, and it did not take long. We were getting to be experts at the quick lunch business.

The first thing I did was to write a letter to my mother, as I knew of her intense anxiety whenever she heard the regiment had been in a fight.

It had been supposed that not many hours of daylight would intervene before we would receive the attentions of our enemies, and we were surprised at their seeming negligence and delay. It was the middle of the forenoon before we heard any firing, and then but a little and apparently a long way off, and we judged it was back somewhere on the railroad.

By noon there was considerable firing, and in several places, which indicated that the enemy's cavalry was feeling along our front and trying to uncover our position. About noon it began to rain. About the same time we had orders to form, and while standing in line there was a lively attack on the pickets across the stream. It did not last long and, as we learned later, was easily repulsed, but it showed the presence of the enemy, and it was not known in what force.

The division was to occupy a position farther up the stream, and it was thought wise to explore the front of it, as a matter of precaution, and our brigade was assigned to that duty. We reconnoitered the front of the place we were to occupy, beating up the thickets for a half or three-quarters of a mile; but we did not see an enemy, draw a shot from the bushes, or fire a rifle.

All of this time the storm, which began very mildly, had continued with increasing force, and now the rain was falling copiously. We were glad, when the unpleasant duty was done, we could try to improvise some shelter from the storm and wring the water from our soaked clothing. With the opportunity to appropriate to our own use anything in our reach, and no one to hinder, we were better off here in the storm than on Governor's Island.

We waked Friday morning after nine or ten hours of sleep, and crept out of our shelters—a bit stiff and sore but otherwise in fair condition, considering. It rained all day and grew quite chilly. I spent most of the time in my tent, with a blanket over my shoulders, writing letters. I have before me now one of those letters, written to my mother. It covers eight pages, 8 by 10 inches, and gives the detail of movements since the 8th.

I find in that letter a reference to the fact that we were then near the scene of the fight at Blackburn's Ford, July 18, 1861. Twenty-seven months had elapsed; we had gyrated around that point from Malvern Hill to Gettysburg, and grown familiar with the sounds of strife; the wearing marches and casualties of battle had diminished our numbers present to a fourth part of what they were then; and the end seemed as far off as it did then—yes, farther, as we looked at it, then. Sometimes I know we were almost hopeless, but I find very few evidences of it in my diary or letters. I am really surprised at the cheerful, hopeful tone of the most of my letters, for many times things 'looked black' and in my feelings I was 'as blue as a whetstone,' but somehow this feeling is not reflected in my letters.

Sunday morning at 3 o'clock, we were called and had orders to be ready to move at 5 o'clock, but we did not leave the camp that day—as no pontoons came and the water was still deep and the bottoms muddy. The day had passed without excitement. We had hoped to get a mail or some papers, but none came, and we were without news of affairs generally. The camp had been quiet for some hours, and most of its inhabitants were asleep, when all were startled by an explosion, and this was followed by a long, loud outcry. At first it could not be understood, but as it was several times repeated it became more intelligible, and was interpreted to mean "My toe, John. Oh! My toe, John."

This loud calling for John and wailing about a damaged toe continued for some time, and it was soon learned that a gun had been accidentally discharged and some one had suffered damage to a toe. It was also hinted that the 'accident' had been 'provided' by the victim, and this reduced sympathy to the minimum. We never knew anything more of the victim or his friend John.

Some of the boys were disposed to extract all the 'fun' there was in any and everything that came within their observation, and they did not allow this to pass without using it. When the camp was again quiet there came a mimicking cry of "Oh! My toe, John." And it received echoing repetitions from many points, followed by bursts of laughter. This was repeated several times that night and many times on the march the next day. Only, it got abbreviated to a single word. "Toe-john." It was not dignified, I admit, and it may seem rather heartless, now. But then it came spontaneously and was accepted without protest.

On Monday we reached Broad Run not far from Bristoe Station about noon, where we halted on the opposite side of the run from the scene of our fight there on the 14th. There was some pretty lively noise after the sun was down, and the moon was shining. Whenever there was a new outburst near—as whenever a shot was heard during the forenoon's march—someone was likely to call out "Toe-jon," and the silly cry was many times repeated with a variety of inflections and emphases. This broke the monotony of the march, the bivouac, and the camp, and relieved the tension of the moment.

There was a genuine, practical, sanitary benefit from the rough jokes and quaint (sometimes coarse) humors of the service. I was not one of the funny fellows, and but seldom mixed in, but I did enjoy much of it and felt it was a relief many times to the hard conditions about us.

An incident of the afternoon of October 22 was the drumming of a man through the camp. The man belonged in the brigade and had deserted nearly a year before, and had recently been arrested and returned. As there were extenuating circumstances, the sentence was to be drumming out. One side of his head and the other side of his face was shaved; he was dressed in a ragged suit of citizen's clothes; and his offense was placarded on his breast and back. Then to an ear-torturing discord of 'sheepskin fiddles,' he was marched from one end of the division to the other, which had been called out to witness his degradation. I am not certain whether the man was turned loose then or had to make up lost time, but I think it was the latter.

There had been many desertions from the service, and thus far deserters had been dealt with very leniently—the theory being that 'the poorest use you could make of a man was to take him out and shoot him.' The frequency of desertion seemed to call for a few 'horrid examples' to check it—but these were to come a little later. The First Regiment was not made prominent by its number of desertions, which I believe was only about one to a company, though not distributed in just that order.

On Tuesday, October 27, William C. Riddle, who 'leaked out' at Antietam, was brought to the regiment by a couple of the provost guard. He told an interesting story of his long absence—that he had been married and left a wife and child in western Maryland. If true, it was not a creditable record for a man or a soldier. He admitted all of this, claimed to be very penitent, and said he would like to "re-enlist and redeem his reputation."

For some time the cases of desertion by recently enlisted men, who had received large bounties or pay as substitutes, had been under consideration, and it was determined to execute the law to the full extent. There had already been one execution in the First Division and now there was one ordered for the Second. The unfortunate man was John Roberts, and he belonged to Company H of the Fifteenth Massachusetts. He belonged in Boston, was 21 years old, and had enlisted July 28, 1863. He was charged with bounty jumping, desertion, and attempting to convey information to the enemy.

The execution was at sunrise, in a little ravine, with a steep hill for a background. It was a beautiful morning, but the purpose of our early parade prevented its enjoyment. The selection of the executioners was from the brigade and by lot.

It fell to our regiment and to Company C, the Provost Guard, to furnish the firing party. The detail was made, and Lieut. Wilbur Duffy took command of it. The division formed three sides of a square, with the open side toward the little hill.

The grave was already dug. The prisoner, his coffin, and two other condemned men were brought out in an ambulance. It is commonly supposed that cowardice is generally the cause of desertion, but—whatever this man's motives may have been—he showed no signs of cowardice that morning. The bands played a dirge; the two attendants carried his coffin; and he marched after them, followed by a file of soldiers.

At the open grave, the coffin was placed beside it, and the man sat upon it while he was blindfolded, then knelt in front of it. The marshal and detail for execution were already in their places. The signal for firing was to be the dropping of a handkerchief, and all preliminaries were quickly arranged, but the time seemed long.

There was the most perfect stillness, and I thought they might hear my heart beat—to where the colors drooped in the center of the regiment. I really felt a difficulty in breathing—a choking sensation—as we waited and watched for the signal.

When the signal dropped, Lieutenant Duffy gave the command to fire, and the rifles broke the oppressive silence. It was a real relief. Roberts sprang to his feet, poised for an instant, then fell forward, where he struggled until his sufferings were ended. Quick commands were given, the bands played, and we marched back to the camps.

The whole proceeding appeared harsh, cruel, and inhuman, but it is the accompaniment of war, which is not easily refined. There were too many men coming into the service who held their oaths and their honor altogether too lightly, and needed a forcible reminder of their obligations. The government had tried all other means to stop desertion and failed. Then executions were tried. These did not wholly stop desertions, but they proved an excellent corrective to the bounty jumping business.

Back in camp, we had little relish for our breakfasts, and there was much talk about the right and the wrong of such punishments. While I do not think there was a man in the company who felt any satisfaction in what he had been compelled to witness that morning, I do not believe there was one who did not feel that the government was fully justified in compelling men to perform the services they had contracted to perform when they enlisted. Any other theory and practice would have taken away from the government the power to protect itself.

There were other punishments to come that day, but they were not of so extreme a nature. Two men were punished for violating a safeguard. This also was an offense punishable with death under the 55th Article of War, but in this case there was the question as to whether they knew that the sentry was a safeguard, as he had not proclaimed the fact. This doubt was operative to the benefit of the accused. The men had alternate sides of the head and the face shaved—a half of each. They were provided with 'wooden overcoats' (barrels with armholes cut in them), and these were labeled "disregarding a safeguard," and then they were drummed through the camps to the tune of the Rogue's March, followed by a file of soldiers with fixed bayonets, close behind.

By November 2, we were back near Warrenton. The Fifth and Sixth Corps lay in front of Warrenton facing the river.[1] The Second Corps lay somewhat in the rear and to the westward of Warrenton, with a part of if extending toward New Baltimore. The Third Corps was about Auburn and Catlett's Station, and the First along the railroad toward Bristoe Station.

The movement which began November 7 was a general one. The Fifth and Sixth Corps were directed upon Beverly's Ford, and the other three corps against Kelley's Ford. We were aroused at 4 o'clock and had orders to get breakfast at once and be prepared to move at daylight. The import of the movement was fully realized, and fighting was expected. We took down our tents, rolled our blankets, and used the accumulation of boards and sticks to cook our breakfasts. With this eaten and a canteen of coffee to drink during the day, we were ready for the call before there was light enough to see anything distinctly.

We did not have long to wait before we were called into line, and, when the sun rose, we were out on the road and moving rapidly. Our course was diagonally across the rear of the Fifth and Sixth Corps and would bring us to the river five or six miles below them. Before noon, there was considerable firing as the right column (6th and 5th Corps) drew near the river. It was not enough to indicate serious fighting, but sufficient to make anything like a surprise doubtful.

We carried 8 days' rations and 60 rounds, with tent cloth, blanket, extra shirts, and whatsoever we had in the way of clothing and equipment. The aggregation made a rather heavy load, but it was getting so late in the season and the nights so cold that the woolen blanket, and overcoat if one had one, were very desirable at night. To be sure of rations it was thought best to carry them with us, for the transportation service had not yet been refitted since the Gettysburg campaign. If protracted fighting resulted from the movement, then cartridges would be a prime necessity, and it was the plan of our commander that the soldier should always have plenty at his command.

The day was not warm but the march was at quick time, and, as we hurried over the road hour after hour, the sweat came freely and our shoulders ached. I doubt the wisdom of making beasts of burden of the men who are to do the fighting. Soldiers ought to be put into battle in the best physical condition and mental poise attainable, and anything that detracts from either diminishes their effectiveness.

The halts of the march were few and short. When we reached the O & A Railroad, it was about noon, and while a brief halt was made, we lay on the ground

---

1. The Rappahannock River, which was about ten to twelve miles south of Warrenton.

eating crackers and drinking cold coffee. From this point the march was less hurried, as the movement was conformed to those in front.

It was getting late in the afternoon as we approached the river near Kelley's Ford, one of the places on the Rappahannock where it is possible to ford it in the lower stages of the water. It had already been the scene of six or seven bloody 'scrimmages,' and as we halted for a little rest and to close up the column another was beginning. The ominous roar of artillery and the muffled crackling of rifles came with a frequency that made it plain that the advance of the Third Corps had struck the enemy—and that the enemy was striking back in a resentful way.

The firing we had heard was the advance cavalry skirmishing with the enemy across the river. Rodes's Division of Ewell's Corps held the enemy's front nearest the river, with Early's and Johnson's Divisions back toward Brandy Station and Culpepper. But his force at the river, while skirmishing with the cavalry, was not anticipating an attempt to cross, until the Union sharpshooters and artillery were posted on the bank to cover the crossing, and Colonel De Trobriand's Brigade was moving from cover to ford the river. Then there were hurried movements to prevent it.

The Confederate rifle-pits and first line were immediately attacked and quickly taken. Thus far the movement had been successful in uncovering the crossing, and the enemy retired out of range without further attempts to hold it. The Union loss had been about 100 killed and wounded. The enemy had suffered nearly an equal number of casualties and left about 500 prisoners in the hands of the attacking force. The pontoons were promptly laid, and the Third Corps crossed over and followed the retiring enemy a short distance out on the Stevensburg Road.

By this time it was dark, and necessarily movements had to cease, and the weary, hungry men were allowed to eat and sleep.

Thus far this general movement had been more successful than such movements usually are, and there had been very little to mar its unity and completeness. Meade had in a single short day placed his whole force confronting the enemy—meeting and defeating their advance forces at both points of approach; inflicting a loss of about 2,300 on the enemy; seizing the crossings; and dispossessing them of their whole line of defense on the river. They must now fight outside of fortifications or retreat to the Rapidan.

It was almost dark when our division reached the river and massed in column of regiments as it closed up. At first it was supposed we would cross the river as soon as the Third Corps had cleared the way and ceased to use the bridge. It was a relief to stack arms and throw off our knapsacks, if only for a little while. Later it was decided—by whom I do not know—that we should get all of the rest we could where we were and make the crossing in the early morning.

We soon slept, but it was not exactly in comfort. The ground was cold and the night was windy and chilly. I was already awake when called for, about four o'clock Sunday morning, and had orders to call up the company and get ready for the march. If I happened to be awake, there were others who were not. Anyone who has had experience in calling out tired men at unseasonable hours knows that it requires some effort and persistence to get them on to their feet—and even then returning consciousness is frequently slow. Some of the boys "*almost died* when they went to sleep."

At daylight we formed and marched to the river and across the pontoons. As was generally the case, there was a thick fog on the low ground and over the water. When across the river, we advanced a mile or so and took position on the left of the Third Corps, which was already moving and had drawn the fire of the enemy. It was the general expectation at this time that a general engagement was beginning, and we were to share in it, but Lee declined to fight there or anywhere unless he judged it a favorable opportunity. This also was true of Meade and there was much marching and maneuvering that fall without a real battle being fought.

As a thick fog was still over the lowland, and the exact location of the enemy was unknown, the advance was slow. Our brigade was not in the advance, neither was our regiment on the skirmish line. As it was, we followed in column, ready to deploy—and halting occasionally to allow the skirmishers and flankers time to do their work. There was a considerable display of force on our front, and twice there was a halt to bring up artillery, and use it, as an admonition to move on—and both times they were prompt to act upon the suggestion. Our corps was following Ewell's command.

There was some delay to the right column in getting across the river, and towards noon we were halted on a ridge for some hours waiting their advance along the railroad toward Brandy Station. The place where we halted had but recently been occupied by the enemy, and it was apparent that they had been planning to remain there as they were building log huts which were found in all stages of construction from beginning to near completion. Lee had begun a general retreat at midnight of the 7th, as soon as he realized the condition of affairs on the Rappahannock; and before daylight the morning of the 8th, his trains and main force were well on their way toward the Rapidan; and he had left only sufficient force to retard our advance. Between two and three o'clock we again advanced, going nearly west up the valley of Mountain Creek, towards Culpepper.

Monday morning, Nov. 9, came in with a wintry look; the temperature was down almost to freezing; the wind was blowing sharply; and the sky covered with dull gray clouds. During the day there were occasional flurries of snow, which fell rapidly in big flakes and whitened the ground but soon melted.

It was soon evident that the enemy had made his escape during the night and was then across the Rapidan. A more definite location of the enemy was left to the cavalry, and the infantry adjusted itself to a line along Mountain Creek, Culpepper, and James City, with the pickets on Pony, Fox, and Thoroughfare Mountains. Our division did not change its location.

In the afternoon, on the chance that we might stay there overnight, we busied ourselves making better shelters for the night out of whatever material we could find. When we went to sleep that night, it was freezing and snowing fast. Thanks to plenty of leaves and bushes, with our tent cloths and rubbers, we were able to protect ourselves fairly well.

Tuesday, soon after 7 o'clock, we formed and moved out on the road toward Culpepper. After several short marches and temporary halts, we reached the location of some deserted Confederate camps. Here there was an inspection of these by—and some parleying among—the brigade and regimental commanders while we waited beside the road. When the consultation was ended, the regiments were assigned positions and given permission to occupy the enemy's abandoned camp. By this time it was near noon, and it did not take long to locate the companies and divide up the houses among them. There was plenty of room for the division. The portion of the company with me had a good log house pretty well furnished with bunks, stools, and some cooking utensils.

The Confederates had evidently planned to winter between the Rappahannock and the Rapidan. They had gone into the woods, cut logs, and put up log huts in many places, and it was evident they had been at work on them up to the time our coming had stopped them. Some were completed, and all had been occupied, though many of them were not yet chinked or daubed. These huts were large enough for from 8 to 16 men, made of logs, and covered with boards or shakes. The openings between the logs were filled with split pieces of wood, driven in, and plastered with clay. Fireplaces were also made of stones, sticks, and clay.

We were very grateful to our enemies for the shelters they had provided, and which the fortunes of war permitted us to use. We really were sorry for them, turned out of doors in the beginning of winter, but we did not hesitate to use what they had abandoned. They would have been in no way benefited if we had refrained from their use.

When we went into these huts, we had no knowledge of how long we might stay—a night, a week, or a month—but we did not suppose we would remain long and only planned for overnight. That night it was freezing again; and the wind was blowing; and altogether we felt that we were fortunate.

Wednesday it grew warmer and was a fine, comfortable day. By this time it was understood that the railroad and the bridges over the Rappahannock and other streams were to be rebuilt, and that the army was likely to halt until these were repaired. The boys employed their spare time completing what the enemy had begun and in a few days were well prepared for the winter—if so it happened we should remain there.

Thursday we had a mail, and a petition was received from Red Wing asking leniency for William C. Riddle—asking that he be allowed to return to duty and re-enlist, as he had agreed to do. This was given to me to circulate in the regiment, and almost everyone signed it. I might add that there was general sympathy for Riddle in the unpleasant situation in which his own folly had placed him. All who knew of the case felt that he alone was to blame and that he deserved punishment; but there was no one who wished to have him *executed*, and all desired to save the regiment from the discredit of an execution. The petition referred to was written by Judge Eli T. Wilder[2] and sent by him to the commander of the regiment. But I do not know who or what prompted Judge Wilder to write and send it. It accomplished its purpose and relieved the young man from his unfortunate situation, and he returned to duty.

This was the day set for the dedication of the National Cemetery at Gettysburg. We talked that evening of the battle, and the fitness of making a cemetery of the battlefield.

About 3 o'clock Tuesday morning, November 24, I was called and had orders to get the men up and have the company ready to march within the hour. After waking the boys and calling the roll, I reported to the adjutant. Here I was told to have the men get their breakfasts, pack all of their things, and await orders. It was very dark and raining.

A little before 5 o'clock, the regiment formed, joined the brigade, and left the camp. Soon after it was fairly light, we took a little-used road to the left and followed it three or four miles. We were at this time at the picket line of the Third Division of our corps. After waiting for some time, an order came to return to the camp. We reached the camp about three o'clock, and by that time the storm had greatly abated.

The next day was fair and comfortable for the season. Some additional rations were drawn, and arms and ammunition inspected. From these and some other things, it was evident we were on the eve of another movement—and it was not supposed to be a retrograde one this time. In the afternoon, we drilled at skirmish drill, and went to sleep that night awaiting orders.

We were not surprised when called at four o'clock Thursday morning, November 26th, and given orders to prepare to move immediately—taking all of our belongings with us. We were in line before five o'clock and moved soon after. Not long after sunrise, we halted for a time, and, while waiting here, Lieutenant F. A. Baskell, a division aide, came along and read to us dispatches from General Grant at Chattanooga, telling of the fighting there and at Missionary Ridge, and claiming a complete victory. This was most cheering news, and we were greatly rejoiced at it, but thought, from the time and the circumstances, that it might be intended to 'brace us up' for what we were likely to meet when we crossed the Rapidan.

Soon after, the march was resumed and continued until the river was reached at Germanna Ford, when we halted preparatory to an attempt at crossing. It was

2. In 1856, Connecticut Yankee Eli T. Wilder came to Red Wing, where he practiced law and sold land. He was a Democrat and later ran for Congress, unsuccessfully.

here that the enemy was first met, but they were not in strong force and were soon disposed of. The work of laying the pontoons was at once begun, after crossing a small force in boats to cover the work. As the work progressed it was discovered that the rise in the river had broadened the stream, and there was not material enough to reach the other side. It was necessary to improvise trestle work to complete the bridge.

By this time we were satisfied that the whole army was moving. It was Meade's plan to move his army in three columns and try to get them into their designated positions across the river within 24 hours. As it involved marches of from 20 to 25 miles, the passage of a swollen river, and overcoming whatever opposition the enemy might make—it involved some serious chances of failure.

The Second Corps, still commanded by Gen. Warren, composed the center. It was to cross at Germanna Ford and try to get possession of the turnpike road from Orange Court House to Fredericksburg at some favorable point between Wilderness Church and Robertson's Tavern. This movement would take us into that section of the country then called the Wilderness. It was of irregular surface—hills, ravines and swamps, and numerous small streams. It was densely-wooded with scrub-oak, pine, and cedars and bushes, briars, and vines for filling. This made the effective movement of even a regiment difficult, and the concerted action of large and widely separated bodies almost impossible. When the character of the country, the impossibility of observation, the extended front (about 25 miles), and the passage of the river are considered—the movement was subject to many hazards.

It was about 10 o'clock when the head of the column reached the river, but it was between 3 and 4 before the passage was effected. The column to our left also reached the river and effected a crossing, as did Gregg's cavalry, but they also were delayed and hindered. Gen. French's column on the right also had to contend with the swollen river, lack of pontoons, and, in addition, greater opposition from the enemy. The whole movement depended upon celerity of execution for its success, and the delays at the river prevented all of the separated columns from reaching their designated places at the appointed times. This at the very outset diminished by one-half the chances for success, but it was determined to push the effort to a conclusion.

The days were then getting near their shortest, and our corps was scarcely on the road, after crossing the river, before it was dark. We were in the woods, and the roads were uncertain, but the corps pushed on for four or five miles, when it went into bivouac on Flat Run. While we were making the crossing there was much firing on the river above us, and this continued until after dark. This was of such proportions and continued so long that it was uncertain if the right column was able to make progress.

We had been for about 16 hours on our feet, were very tired, and glad when the order came to stack arms in line of battle. As soon as it was likely that we were to rest there for the remainder of the night, no time was lost in making fires and boiling coffee. The fact that it was Thanksgiving Day was not forgotten, and—as the boys ate their field rations of pork, crackers, and coffee—they talked of 'roast turkey and all the fixings.' It is a question if any of the boys have ever eaten a Thanksgiving dinner since then that they really relished any better than army rations when wolfishly hungry. I think I have heard some of the boys assert on such occasions that they "could eat a grindstone."

These references to the day of feasting and family reunions showed that the thoughts of the boys were going homeward. It goes without saying that there was not one among us but would have greatly preferred a place in the home circle that night to the bivouac in the bushes—and would have freely parted with all his earthly possessions if they could have purchased the privilege. When I add that we then had no doubt but the next day would bring us in conflict with the enemy, our thoughts as we wrapped ourselves in our blankets may be easily conjectured.

The day had been fair, but the night was cold, and we waked more than once before we were called at four in the morning. Packing our kits while the coffee was boiling, we ate a hasty breakfast, and the regiments prepared for the march. The Third Division led off and our division, Second, was following it before the stars ceased to shine. It was not long before skirmishing began, but steady advance was made and by 12 o'clock, we had got possession of the Orange and Fredericksburg Turnpike, and the whole corps was in position about Robertson's Tavern. Thus far neither the right nor left column had made its connection with our flanks, and we anxiously awaited their coming.

This was Friday morning, November 27th, which was also my 23rd birthday—from which it will be seen that I have two anniversary occasions associated with this 'journey in the wilderness'—but neither of them received any special observance on that occasion.

As we lay there in the bushes, we could hear the dull thud of an occasional gun, apparently a long way off to the left, where the Fifth Corps was holding the Plank Road. At the same time the smothered grumbling of the Third Corps artillery, coming continuously through the tangled woods from some miles way on the right, indicated that at that hour the strongest opposition was in that direction. Meantime we were neither immune nor idle, but along the whole front the skirmishers were busy. This was the situation at noon of the 27th, and for some hours there had been seemingly but little progress.

There was but little room or range for artillery where we were, but some guns had been placed covering the road and some others posted in some small clearings. These shelled the woods at intervals, provoking an occasional response from the enemy.

As the afternoon advanced the sound of the Third Corps guns indicated that its fighting was getting more serious and but little nearer. It was determined to

extend the right of the Second Corps to the right in an effort to find the left of
the Third.

In this effort the Fifteenth Massachusetts of our brigade was sent into the
woods to 'feel for it.' The woods were difficult to penetrate except where roads
had been cut—being a mass of trees, brush, briars, and vines. The Fifteenth was
soon hotly engaged with a force of the enemy, which apparently had been laying
for them, and soon after, another party coming out of a wood-path made a sudden attack on its flank. The result of this was that the 15th was compelled to retire
and suffered a considerable loss in killed, wounded, and some prisoners.

As soon as it was understood the 15th was getting the worst of it, the First Minnesota was hurried to its support. We met it coming back in some disorder
through the bushes. We halted on a little rise of ground, and as the Fifteenth came
out they formed on our right. Here we waited for a little time for the enemy to attack and, as he did not do this, our regiment was sent into the woods to recon-
noiter. We started in expecting a rough time of it but got nothing more serious
than a spattering fire at long range as we advanced, and then they retired rapidly.
The Fifteenth also advanced and brought out their dead and some of the
wounded who had not been carried off as prisoners.

This advanced position was not considered a proper one, as it was exposed to
a flank attack, and we were withdrawn to the crest of the little hill where we first
halted. Our position was considerably in advance and to the right of the rest of
the brigade, and it soon became evident that there was a movement of the enemy
in our front, though nothing could be seen.

Companies F and H were sent out to investigate. Crossing the little valley in
our front to the higher ground on the other side, we soon came in sight of a small
clearing, surrounded by a snake fence, and along one side of it there appeared a
little-used road. This was to our left and more directly in front of Company H,
the commander of which sent forward a squad to make closer observations. From
along the road, near a corner of the fence, this detachment was fired on, and fired
in return. The company advanced, and the enemy disappeared in the bushes.

Soon after this, we were withdrawn to a position a little in front of the regiment. Here we laid down for a short time, when we were again sent out, and this
time Company H remained in its place. Passing to the right along the ravine, after crossing the small stream running through it, the company halted, and a few
men were sent up the rise to see what there was to be seen—and I was one of this
number.

The bushes were thick, and there were a good many fallen trees on the hillside, but, making our way through these, we found more open ground towards
the top. Nearing this, several heads wearing old gray hats were seen bobbing up.
Jeff Bonner, who was first to see them, gave warning by calling to them to surrender. They answered by making the same demand, firing, and dropping down
out of sight.

Their shots cut the twigs above our heads. We took cover behind the nearest trees and watched to see what the next move should be. Quickly more heads were visible, and we promptly fired at them. Then the crest of that little ridge was festooned with flashes of fire and wreaths of smoke; and at the same time there were varied sounds of flying bullets, the bark flew from the trees, and the little limbs fell about us. It began to look as if we had, as one of the boys said later, "stirred up quite a muss," but it did not prove serious.

We few men retired as the company advanced, and as soon as we were united we opened fire at the ridge, which added to the noise and smoke, if nothing more. Soon after this our line advanced to the ridge. By this time the short November day was nearly done, and the woods were getting dusky, but we continued to feel our way into the woods. I do not know how far we went, but I judge it was half a mile or so through thick woods and brush and over fallen trees.

The enemy retired slowly; and there was considerable firing from both sides; but most of their shot went over our heads, as we could tell from the sound and the dropping twigs; and we presume ours were as little effective. We were surprised that not a man of the company was hit, and we judged the trees and the gathering darkness was our protection.

When it was too dark to see more than a rod or so, we were halted and told that we would be relieved. The 140th Pennsylvania was sent to take our place, and, in advancing through the woods, made so much noise that they attracted the attention and drew the fire of the enemy. Not knowing, or forgetting, that we were in front of them, the 140th responded to this fire, which left us exposed to the fire of both sides. Luckily we were on lower ground and among the trees. Realizing our position, we lay flat on the ground while the bullets from both sides passed over us. The Pennsylvanians soon learned their mistake and more quietly reached a position a little in the rear of us and extended to the right, the enemy continuing to fire. It took some time for matters to reach a stage of quietude which permitted us to withdraw.

Marching to the rear half a mile or so, we found the rest of the brigade except the 19th Maine, which had been sent out to relieve us, but had been taken to some other part of the line. It was midnight before we had made coffee and were ready to try to get a little sleep. For about 20 hours we had been actively employed and were very tired as well as hungry, and, as soon as we had swallowed our supper, we spread our blankets to sleep. The temperature was now below freezing; the wind was moaning among the tree tops; the ground was cold; and the prospect of refreshing sleep not good—but it was not many minutes before we slept.

The day had been unfortunate. The opposition the Third Corps had met had delayed it, and this in turn had prevented its junction with the others. By this time Lee had fully divined Meade's purpose and had occupied a series of low hills along the westerly bank of Mine Run, covering a front of 8 or 9 miles and barring the way to Orange Court House and Gordonsville.

Saturday morning we were called soon after 4 o'clock, having had a scant four hours' sleep on the freezing ground. Numb with the cold, we were not averse to getting up and starting fires. We had prepared and eaten our breakfasts and were ready, with arms in our hands, to move at daylight. It was a cold, gray morning with everything frozen and a strong wind shaking the trees and surging through the open spaces.

As soon as it was light enough to see, the brigade moved out and took a position on the right of the division, its left connecting with the right of the Third Brigade. We were again advanced as skirmishers, and it was discovered that the enemy had abandoned the line they had held the night before, which was clearly defined by logs and other material they had gathered for protection. But a brief halt was made. Then, with skirmishers out and followed by two lines of battle, the advance was continued through a thick pine wood that offered many obstructions to moving in line.

Continuous progress was made, but it was slow. The enemy's skirmishers retired before us, but offered continual resistance at long range. Within an hour or two after starting, it was evident that a storm was gathering, and long before noon a cold rain was falling. It was inevitable that we were soon wet to the skin, for in addition to the falling rain every tree and shrub was a fountains of spray if touched or shaken by the wind. If one was able to keep his cartridges and rations dry he did well.

Reaching Mine Run, the enemy was discovered in force on the hills on the other side. At this point it appeared to be a considerable stream running through a swampy wooded valley.

The skirmishers were halted on the hills, and a few men were sent forward to take such observations as they could. It was now raining furiously, and the temperature was but a little above freezing, and standing still in the storm was even worse than moving. Here we waited until two or three o'clock, and, meantime, the Fifth Corps came in on our left and, soon after, the Sixth Corps filled the interval on the right between the Third Corps and ours. At least Meade's forces were united—and so were the enemy's.

Later in the day, the storm slackened somewhat, and the generals and engineers made as careful a survey as they could of the enemy's front. They were found in force, were on higher ground, had plenty of artillery in position, and comparatively open ground in their immediate front to allow its use. With the rain still falling, there was a prospect that the valley would soon be flooded, and it was decided that an attack would be too hazardous to risk.

When the Sixth Corps had connected with us, we were relieved by them and we retired to the second line. Everything had been flooded by the rain; and now it was freezing; and it was a most cheerless situation, as fires were not allowed. As darkness was coming, we made the best preparation we could for the night, but the elements were waging a pitiless war against us. Contrary to orders, men went, a few at a time, to a little ravine back of us, made small fires, and boiled coffee. One who has not had a cup of hot coffee under some such circumstances does not know how to fully appreciate one.

Our wearied condition demanded rest and sleep, but there was no refreshing sleep to be had that night. We simply spent a few uncomfortable hours, during which we alternately dozed and froze—or came so near it that we could not sleep. Indeed, it was reported that several men died from the cold and exhaustion that night.

It was between three and four o'clock, Sunday morning, November 29th, when we were called and piloted through the woods to the rear. We were cautioned not to talk or make any noise, but the frozen leaves and sticks breaking under our feet sounded like a stampede of mules—all but the braying. Coming to a road and a clearing, we found the whole corps assembling and a wagon train coming in. Here we halted and had orders to draw three days' rations, replenish the cartridge boxes, and hasten our breakfasts. As soon as this was done, we took the road back toward Robertson's Tavern.

It might be well to explain here the object of this move before I attempt to describe it. Gen. Warren proposed to take the Second Corps and, by a left flank movement, try to get around Lee's right. As nothing better was proposed, Meade consented and added Terry's Division of the Sixth Corps to his command—increasing it to something more than 16,000 men. After the experiences of the previous three days, the corps was far from being in proper physical condition for such an enterprise, but it was an emergency that called for extreme effort.

At Robertson's Tavern, there was only a brief halt, when we took a little-used road, marching in a southerly direction through the woods. No trains were allowed and only one battery to each division. At the Orange and Fredericksburg Turnpike[3] we turned in a westerly direction and continued the march until we came to the outposts of Gregg's cavalry, who warned of a considerable force of the enemy in its front. General Caldwell with the First Division was sent forward to drive in this force, and brisk skirmishing promptly followed.

This greatly hindered progress; and skirmishing continued until night set in; and by that time they had been forced back 3 or 4 miles across Mine Run. This was at a point 5 or 6 miles from where we had left it the night before, but we had marched about three times that distance in getting there. It had not stormed, but the day had been disagreeably cold, threatening at times, and altogether unpleasant.

When night came on we were in the woods, where we halted, stacked arms, and made coffee—consoling our weary bodies with the idea that we were to

3. Wright may mean the Orange Plank Road, for the Second Corps turned west on that road and followed it until reaching Gregg's cavalry outposts; Welcher, *Union Army,* Vol. 1, *Eastern Theater,* 792.

bivouac there for the night. This, however, was only a comforting delusion which vanished at the order to form, and we again took up the line of march.

Before starting we had orders to refrain from all talking and make as little noise as possible, but it was not possible to move without noise. Our course was through the woods; and the accumulation of leaves and brush on the ground was coated with ice; and it broke under our feet with a snapping, crunching noise that must have made a volume of sound about as great as trains of cars. If our enemies were at all attentive they must have heard us and known of our coming.

It was a slow, tedious movement. Several times our direction was changed, shifting us to the left to make room, as we understood, for the Third Corps on our right.

Towards midnight, our regiment was advanced to the front and deployed, and the division formed in three lines of battle in our rear. The front line of our brigade was composed of the Fifteenth Massachusetts and the Nineteenth Maine, with the two New York regiments forming the second, and I am not sure of the composition of the third line, but think it was some of the Second Brigade. When we went to the front we came to a small stream and halted, waiting orders, while the formation was being made in our rear.

We could now distinctly hear the enemy on the hills across the stream. There were fires burning, which we could not see but could see the reflection of—and we could hear chopping and occasionally a tree fall, and now and then some call or command. Beyond question our old antagonists were over there and wide-awake.

After the formation was made, it was necessary to make another shift to the left; and in this movement we moved between the lines of battle and the position of the enemy, keeping along the easterly edge of the stream. There was no question about the position of the enemy on the hill, and it was supposed that they had pickets on the other side not far from the stream. There was good reason to suppose that they would hear us and fire.

Lieut. Bruce led the line; I followed; and the rest trailed after us 20 or 25 feet apart. It was quite dark and we made, as it seemed to us, a great deal of noise as we stumbled over unseen obstructions and broke through the ice over the little pools. We expected a volley every minute of the movement and were surprised when we were halted without getting one.

Soon after halting, we had orders to cross the stream. It was very cold, and there was a covering of ice on the stream, which might have been 20 feet wide and about a foot in depth at the deepest point. The ice was not strong enough to hold us, and we broke through it and wet our feet, which was an additional discomfort on such a cold night. We had crossed in open order and advanced about 100 yards, taking position as skirmishers, crossing a fence at the stream, which we threw down as we passed over it.

In crossing the stream, we had come out of the woods and were now in an open field or pasture. We had halted at the first ridge or rise of the ground that seemed to offer a shelter when lying down. Here we were told to halt and lie down, out of sight, and observe the enemy.

The position of the enemy was audibly evident at the top of the hill, and, judging by the noise, they were there in force and at work building fortifications. Though too dark to see much, the position of the enemy could be told fairly well by the noise they were making and their fires. And we judged them to be not more than 60 to 80 rods away. We were also able to make out the forms of men on the hillside. They were no doubt placed there to watch and warn the main force of the coming of an enemy. They were walking about, stamping their feet, and slapping their hands against their bodies—trying to keep up circulation enough not to freeze to death and if they knew of our presence did not appear to notice us.

It was a bitterly cold night, and there was real danger from the cold. My own situation soon impressed this upon me in an undeniable way, now that we had ceased to march. My wet trouser legs were soon frozen in rings around my ankles, and I was compelled to constantly rub and strike my feet together to save them from freezing. I judge that it was not long after midnight when we took position, and from that time until morning we were most emphatically uncomfortable.

Fires could not be had as they would expose our position. Weary as the boys were, and sleepy as they were, they must guard against both if they valued their lives. To yield to either—in their exhausted condition, uncovered, in that biting, winter wind—meant death. This was the situation when we had got into position and the corps was massing behind us.

We soon had word passed to us that an assault was to be made at daylight, and that our regiment was to lead it. Of course we knew that the object of our coming there was to attack, but, somehow, putting it into the words of a command seemed to bring it home to us and emphasize it. I judge it was between two and three o'clock, Monday morning, November 30, and the moon was beginning to give a little light through the film of clouds that covered the sky—when a staff officer came with particular orders for the assault. The plan was explained, details considered, and special instructions given.

Looking back at it today, it was a pretty cold-blooded proposition. But it was a matter of business then, and I gave it my full attention. I will not deny, however, that it had a rather depressing effect upon me and reduced the temperature of my blood to very nearly that of the atmosphere.

Briefly, the plan was this: the signal for the assault was to be 5 artillery shots in succession, one for each corps. The increasing light had already enabled us to see that the men we had dimly seen on the hillside had dug rifle pits in which to shelter themselves if we should fire on them. Our instructions were: at the command to move, to rush for the line of pits, bayonet the men in them, and fall in with the advancing lines which would follow us, and make for the breastworks. The plan was more heroic than attractive.

On the contrary, it repelled us as naturally as men shrink from prospective death. I might almost say certain death or wounds. For now that we could see better, it was apparent that the hill was a pretty smooth slope, and there was but little natural shelter between us and the enemy. As we understood this—and not knowing how soon it might come to an exchange of shots—we lost no time in gathering up the rails we had scattered and improvising something to interpose between our bodies and the bullets. In this way every squad of skirmishers soon had a rallying point of comparative safety, as an offset to the Johnnies' pits.

Every man of the company who had left the camp with us was there, in his place, and ready to do his whole duty even if it cost him his life. It was a severe, long-continued test of the very finest qualities of soldiership—fortitude and endurance—and they bore themselves through it all with commendable readiness and steadiness. I recall no six hours in the history of the company or the regiment, when held inactive, where it bore itself more creditably. There was no display of heroics; none of us wanted our names in the casualty list; we all wanted to go home with a full complement of legs and arms; but we were there to meet the requirements of the occasion and were ready to do it, whatever it might cost.

We prepared for the bloody work we expected. After writing our names on slips of paper and pinning them on to our overcoats or blouses—that it might be known who we were in case we were not able to tell it ourselves—we exchanged last messages to be sent home in case the receiver was in condition to send them and the sender was not. Then we piled our knapsacks; reexamined our rifles and cartridges; and, with a silent prayer for safety and success, crept up to the crest of a little rise within pistol shot of their skirmishers; and laid down to await the dawn. It was intensely cold; we suffered greatly, and had to rub our hands and thump our feet against the frozen ground to save them from freezing.

Their skirmishers were out of their pits doing the same thing for the same reason, and, though they must have known of our presence as well as we did of theirs, neither offered to molest the other.

Slowly, daylight came, but the order to attack was not given, and word was passed along that it would be made at 8 o'clock. You may guess at the intense anxiety we felt as we waited. When it was fairly light, we could see the naturally strong position, made stronger as it was by earthworks and artillery in position—we could count 14 guns—while the sounds that came to us made no question but it was fully manned and reinforcements were constantly arriving.

The sun rose bright and clear, and I thought that it was probably the last one I should ever see. I cannot, on paper, describe my feelings, but it was a time that tried the nerves of the best of us. The tacit truce continued, and the skirmishers of both sides were walking about in pistol range without apparently giving each other much attention, though we were both watching very closely. As I scanned our front, I tried to calculate the chances of the coming struggle, and those of escaping seemed ridiculously small in comparison with those of being hit. It took '*sand*' to '*keep a stiff upper lip*' while we waited—and did nothing but watch and wait.

Eight o'clock came and passed, but neither signal nor command was given. Soon after, a shot or two was heard off to our right that we at first supposed was the signal, and a few rifle shots were heard in the woods. But as our corps gun was not fired, we concluded something had gone wrong and waited with intense interest for some explanation.

It seemed hours that we waited for the order to make a rush for 'glory or the grave,' but I judge it was less than a half hour before word came that Gen. Warren considered the chances of success too small to warrant the order to attack, and we were to hold our position and avoid, if possible, any collision with the enemy's skirmishers. This was a great relief. That our feelings confirmed Warren's judgment may be taken for granted.

The ticking of a clock may measure time accurately, but there is more to life than simply the passing of the hours. If there was some instrument to measure the intensity of the feelings when one believes he is on the threshold of eternity, waiting for the door to open, it would sometimes more correctly represent existence. In our emotional natures, we lived a *long time* that morning, and we will never forget the bloodless ordeal that has stamped it indelibly upon our memories.

A tacit truce, undefined by words, was mutually accepted and acceptable to both sides and remained unbroken all day. As evidence of present neutrality on the skirmish lines, both sides laid down their rifles but took good care not to get far away from them.

When the tension of our feelings had relaxed, bodily wants promptly asserted themselves, and we realized that we were hungry. On our left was a house and out-buildings, and on our right were some dilapidated sheds and piles of tan-bark. There were also plenty of fence rails. We made fires and cooked our breakfasts, carefully watched by our opponents, who offered neither comments nor protests.

Some of our more curious comrades were attracted by some little cones of earth in the field a little to the rear of the left of the regiment, and, breaking through the frozen crust, found potatoes and turnips in good condition. These had been gathered in piles, covered with straw, and then with dirt. These were appropriated, for such eatables were seldom left in our reach, and the temptation was too great. Company F, being at the right, was not in a position to get at these potatoes first hand, but some of them came down the line, and we had some of the potatoes.

The sun shone most of the day, and the frozen ground thawed, but it did not get much above the freezing point and the wind blew sharply, so it was not a comfortable day to remain inactive out of doors. The hours passed but slowly, however. We had doggedly maintained our position without demonstration or effort to advance or retire. In easy rifle range of the enemy's breastworks, close enough to his skirmishers to have thrown a rock to some of them, we remained all day without exchanging a shot.

No man allowed himself to get far from his gun, and the majority at all times were in line with guns at hand, and all knew that an outbreak might occur at any time. There was not a minute from daylight until dark when a single shot might not have brought on a bloody conflict. That this did not happen was due as much to the magnanimous forbearance of our enemies as to ourselves.

It was not crimsoned with blood, and there was no loss of life, but November 30, 1863, was a memorable day in the history of the regiment. Its dire possibilities were as great as any day of its service, but a kindly fate turned aside the threatened disaster. In the mind of the most of us, General Gouverneur K. Warren was the embodiment of that merciful fate that shielded us, and those of us still living recall his name in this connection with grateful remembrance.

There were several little incidents during the day to keep us interested. Twice there were movements of the enemy that we judged meant hostile action, but none followed. Once a general and staff rode from their left to the right and was received with cheers. After he was gone, someone called to know who it was and was told that it was Gen. A. P. Hill.

It was not very often that newspaper correspondents got that far to the front, but about noon that day one crept out to the line in search of items and asked numerous questions. The boys tried to have some fun with him and encouraged him to go to the advanced skirmishers, but this he declined, saying he could "see just as well where he was," and added that he "feared that they might shoot when they saw he was *unarmed.*"

He was asked if he had not been writing to his paper about what a 'glorious thing it was to die for his country'—and reminded that this was his opportunity. He admitted the "chance was good" but said he had "conscientious scruples about being shot," and retired to the shelter of the woods to write up a story of how he had gone to the picket line, where men had remained openly all day.

It had been a remarkable experience to remain as we had all day, and we did not believe it was a situation that was going to be continued, and did expect an end or a climax of some sort as soon as darkness covered us. I judge it to have been between 7 and 8 o'clock when the order came to get ready to retire and— when the order to leave came—to go back directly to the rear in open order and without noise.

Listening carefully, we could now detect that there was some sort of a movement going on back of us, but it was not pronounced enough to be understood. Soon after, we got the order, gathered up our things, and went, as quietly as we could, down the slope, across the little stream, and entered the woods. Here we met the Nineteenth Maine, deployed in line and waiting to relieve us. Passing through their open order, we closed into line a few rods to the rear and waited a little while to see if our withdrawal had been noticed, or caused the enemy to make any movement. There was no demonstration on the part of the enemy, and apparently they did not know we were gone. When all was considered safe, we went back through thick woods for half or three-quarters of a mile, where we found the division in line of battle, where it had taken position early in the evening.

It was near midnight by the time we had reached our place in the division line and bitterly cold again. The strain of the last 24 hours had added considerable to that tired feeling the best of men get after three or four days of activity and exposure at the rate of 20 hours out of 24—and we lost no time in preparing to sleep. It was dark; we were in the thick woods; and we were required to remain in line of battle—so there was little room for choice of place or conditions. Men as weary as we were are not apt to be overly particular, and we disposed ourselves on the ground and inside of ten minutes were sleeping soundly—some in half that time.

Oh! Ain't you glad you got out of the Wilderness

DECEMBER 1863-FEBRUARY 1864

LONG BEFORE IT WAS LIGHT, Tuesday morning, December 1, we were up and under arms—considering it better than to take the chances of an early morning attack unprepared.[1] But this precaution seemed unnecessary, for there was no sign that the enemy knew that we had retired or cared where we had gone. When it was light, and reports from the picket line said that "the enemy was resting quietly in his entrenchments," we stacked arms and were allowed to make fires. No time was lost in starting them, and we were soon enjoying their warmth and drinking hot coffee—having first rolled our blankets and got in readiness to march if necessary.

We were bivouacked in line of battle along a wooded ridge, where the trees were larger and there was less underbrush, and now and then an open place. We were near an unfinished railroad and, I think, south of the Plank Road,[2] and the other two divisions were to our left. It was about noon when our brigade formed and was shifted to the left of the division, crossing the railroad grade and going to the front—which brought us within about three-fourths of a mile of the position of the enemy on the opposite ridge and near a house.

I do not think that we had any direct orders, but when the position was taken we assumed we were to stay there and gathered such material as we could find to protect our front. There was plenty of it lying about, and we soon had a light barricade of logs and felled trees behind which we could lie. We remained in this position the remainder of the day. Just what our generals were doing that day, we did not know, but we judged they were trying to find an opportunity for hopeful aggressive action.

The general position of the Union army was in the westerly section of the Wilderness. It was the densely wooded region where Hooker had fought the previous spring farther to the eastward—and where Grant first came in contact with Lee the next May. A whole army corps could be hidden in these woods as easily as a flock of quails in a hazel thicket.

1. Lee had carefully prepared a dawn attack on the Union left flank, held by the Second Corps, and he was surprised to find Meade's army gone on Tuesday morning.
2. An unfinished railroad line ran parallel to, and south of, the Orange Plank Road; Sears, *Chancellorsville*, 148–49.

As night came on, we had orders to get our suppers and hold ourselves in readiness to move. This gave currency to several rumors. "Another flank movement was to be tried"—there was to be "a night attack"—we were going to "retire to the river," etc. Suppers were eaten, extra coffee in our canteens, and our knapsacks in order by the time it was dark. About this time we were encouraged to make large fires, which we were already doing for the warmth they gave out. Then we waited for orders, keeping the fires burning.

It was between 8 and 9 o'clock before we got the word to move. For some distance our course was through the wood, and it was quite dark, so there was little chance to see much of our surroundings. Coming out of the woods to a road which, I suppose, was the Plank Road, we joined the other two divisions and halted for some time. There were many fires burning in sight, but those who had lighted them were gone. There was no indication thus far that the enemy knew that we were going. While waiting here, I recall hearing a dog howling, and judge we were near some house or little hut among the bushes.

From this point we followed a fairly good road. Many fires were burning along the road, and in one or two places the woods were burning. We passed New Hope Church and came to Parker's Store. Here there was another brief halt.

Up to this time we had been uncertain of the final purport of the movement but, when moved again, we turned to the left on a less-used road and knew that we were heading back towards the river and judged that our campaign was ending without results. This was a very lame and impotent conclusion to what we had hoped might be a decisive campaign, and not a man in the ranks but felt it. On the road we had made good progress, but when we took the by-roads through the woods it was more difficult going, being darker, the roads rough and narrow.

We plodded on laboriously all night with sleepy eyes, aching shoulders, and weary legs. Daylight, Wednesday morning, found us a few miles from Ely's Ford on the Rapidan and not far from Wilderness Tavern. Here a short halt was made, and we lay on the ground to rest while waiting for the column to close up.

Moving from here on a little-used road through the woods for a mile or more, we came to a better road which we followed until we came to Culpepper Mine Ford, reaching there between 8 and 9 o'clock. At this time there was a pretty strong wind with occasional snow squalls. Here we crossed, after a little waiting, and marching up the winding road. On the other side the division formed on the bluffs.

While crossing and marching up the slippery hill, some of our bands (already over) enlivened the occasion with music. One of these very appropriately played a then-popular air, "Oh! Ain't you glad you got out of the Wilderness." It had a most cheering effect on the tired boys.

I have spoken of the slippery hill, and it was all that and some more. It was of reddish clay, as slippery as if drenched with soap suds, and climbing it something like trying to catch a greased pig. Quite a number of the boys were on their knees before they got up that hill, and the things some of them said were not appropriate to a kneeling position.

Marching up the river a little ways, the division was massed on the bluff to await the taking up of the bridge and get our breakfasts—or, more appropriately, dinners, for it was then between 11 and 12 o'clock. This was a most welcome opportunity, for our last meal had been eaten about 6 o'clock the previous evening. About the time the removal of the bridge was completed, a small body of Confederate cavalry came in sight on the other side and were fired on by a battery, which had been placed in position in anticipation of some interference by the enemy. They retired at once and did not again come in sight.

About one o'clock the bugles called us into line, and the march was resumed. At this time there was an interval of sunshine, but the sun seemed a long way off and was cold and comfortless and soon gave way to clouds and rain. Short as this rest was, it had been long enough to get benumbed from the cold, and many were lame and sore, starting off like a lot of overworked farm horses with spavins and shoulder strains.

For some reason there were many hindrances to our march. Roads were badly cut up by those preceding us, halts were frequent, to let troops and trains get out of our way, and, we understood, that it was not fully determined where we were to be stationed. We tried to avoid the other marching columns, and trains, by taking a parallel road, but it soon brought us back to the over-crowded way, and we had to delay until it was clear. By this time the afternoon was nearly spent, the occasional showers had wet us, and the increasing mud had daubed our trousers to the knees.

As night came on, the rain changed to sleet and snow, and the temperature was again below freezing, and we were still several miles from the camp on Mountain Creek we had left the morning of November 26. (It was not until about this time that we had definite orders to return to the old camp.) Gen. Webb was allowed the privilege of continuing the march that night or remaining where we were until morning. We were then on a wind-swept ridge; and it was storming; and thoughts of the comfortable log huts we had left a week before made us desire to reach their shelter as soon as we could; and, tired as we were, all were pleased with his decision to go on that night.

This last addition to the already long day was the proverbial 'last feather' that 'broke the camel's back,' and it came near doing us up, but we braced up and soon after 9 o'clock we reached it. But instead of finding the comfortable shelter we had expected, we met a heart-breaking disappointment. The *houses had been burned*, and a mantle of snow and ice was spread over the ruins—which made it questionable at first if we had not mistaken the place, but investigation soon made the unpleasant fact undeniable.

As we had stumbled on through the darkness—wading through mud and water—sprinkled with sleet and snow—we had consoled ourselves with the thought of rest and comfort inside the mud-daubed huts we had previously occupied. This had encouraged us to effort and hastened our halting steps. Now—to find that vandal hands had applied the torch during our absence—that we were shelterless and left out in the cold and the storm—caused a revulsion of feeling that was almost stunning in its first effect.

A little later, when some of the more profane members were giving full and free expression to their feelings in language that was plain, there was very decided evidence of reanimation. Ordinarily, it is unpleasant to me to hear men swear, but that was an exceptional occasion—and, well, it seemed as if that was about all they could do under the circumstances.

After 6 days of hardship and exposure, we had lengthened a night's and a day's march far into the second night under the stress of a winter storm, and the stimulus of expecting comfortable shelter from it. Now, when the limit of effort was reached, to find ourselves houseless was, for the moment, a bitter disappointment that had to find expression in words. On the same principle that thunderstorms clear the atmosphere, the violent expression of feelings soon passed, and all set to work to make the best provision they could for the remainder of the night, and within the hour most of them were sleeping.

I found the hut which I had occupied with others had not been wholly burned, and one end for three logs high was still standing. Scraping away the snow, we found some poles and covered it with our tent cloths; and, meantime, a fire was started and coffee made. Drinking this, I crept under the cover and slept. It was still snowing.

At daylight I waked, being too cold to sleep longer, and found Lieut. Bruce still sleeping. I waked him and learned that he had orders to let the men sleep as long as they chose. The storm had passed, but it was cold, and there was an inch or two of snow on the ground. I started a fire at the other end of the place where our house had been, and again went to sleep. When we woke again, the sun was shining; there was a general stir in the camp; and the men were getting their breakfasts, but it was near noon before some of them came out of it.

We had been out just a week, marched many miles, suffered many hardships, and accomplished nothing. It had been a hard, bootless campaign, and whether or not more might have been gained by risking an attack had ceased to be a 'live' question when the opportunity had passed. There was no loss in the company and, so far as I can recall, none in the regiment. The only real benefit from this campaign was the information acquired regarding roads, streams, woods, swamps, etc.—and this must have been beneficial to Meade and his subordinate commanders in the campaign next spring.

Some of the boys planned at once to rebuild the ruined huts, but discontinued when informed that our stay there was but temporary, and we were likely to move the next day. Of course, there was much talk about the burning of the camps, but I think it was never actually known who did it. But it was reasonably certain that the enemy did not. It was generally charged to the camp-followers and hangers-on that are usually found in the wake of an advancing army. It might have been done by the natives, who may have disliked to see us enjoy the benefits of their army's labors.

Saturday, December 5, we were ready to march at sunrise and left camp soon after, taking the road toward Stevensburg and, when within a mile or so of that place, turned towards Brandy Station. Before reaching that place, we turned off the road and halted at the edge of a pine wood and were told that we were to remain there overnight. Some of the boys asserted that we had only been out "hunting for a place to roost," and I never heard any other explanation of that day's march—but I suppose there was.

Sunday we remained in bivouac, trying to make fires out of green pine wood that would not smoke. It was a failure.

Monday morning we left that windy ridge and went back to a point near Stevensburg and then turned again toward the old camp but on a different road and finally halted on a high ridge and were told that for the present we were to camp there. This place was two or three miles from the old camp, on the opposite side of Mountain Creek and nearer the Rapidan. The next day we had notice that until further orders the men were only required to keep on hand 3 days' rations and 40 rounds of ammunition. This was considered official notice that the campaign was over for the present, and we at once began planning something more for protection than the little 5 x 6 bit of cloth furnished by the government.

Tuesday all were busy preparing their shelters. Every pick, spade, shovel, axe, hatchet, and jackknife was in use—and all available material such as bricks, stones, boards, rails, trees, brush, etc., was used. Rapid progress was made. On Wednesday we were as busy as beavers, and many had their houses so far along that they had moved in.

It was interesting to observe the style and methods of the boys, but the chief aim was to get a place that would keep us dry and warm, and that we could stand up in. There was, however, a general plan followed. Most of them were of small logs, either round or split, and room to accommodate four persons. In place of a foundation, a hole was generally dug a foot or two deep, and of the dimensions desired, and over this the walls were built of whatever material could be obtained. The tent-cloths served for the cover, and the cracks were filled with clay. The fireplaces were at the opposite side from the doors, and outside the line of the wall, and lined with stones or bricks if any could be found. The chimneys were made of sticks and mud—and topped out with barrels when procurable—and the dirt thrown out in digging was used to bank up the outside to keep the water out.

On Thursday, December 10, we had our house—if I may call it by that name—about done and were living in it. There were two others beside myself, and another was expected to join us soon. It was large *enough*, but there was no *spare room*. The fireplace had a stone for the back and three bricks set on end of each side, and two more served for andirons. We had a fire for the first time that night. A rubber blanket served for a door. It was threatening a storm and was freezing outside, but we were quite comfortable.

Our camp was on a ridge or spur of Pony Mountain, and we had a fine view of the valley and the distant hills. When clear, we could see the crests of the Blue Ridge for many miles. Now they were white with snow.

Thursday, December 24, was Christmas Eve, but there was no preparation for it such as were dear to our hearts in the days of our childhood. The only extras in camp were things sent from home, and we were too far away from ours. I went that afternoon and saw Captain Abraham Wright of the First Company of Minnesota Sharpshooters, Second Berdan Regiment. He and all of the Red Wing boys were well. That evening I wrote a letter to my mother and was feeling rather homesick.

Friday was our third Christmas in the army, and we were all hoping that it would be the last. We did not 'fare sumptuously,' but dined *bountifully* on beef soup. This was not exactly a rarity, but it was by no means a common diet—for lack of fresh beef to make it. The men had been allowed as much liberty as consistent with discipline and were 'circulating around' among their acquaintances in other regiments. I called on Ingersoll of the 8th Ohio, Strout of the 7th Michigan, and others—and enjoyed the calls. I was frequently invited to 'smile' (which in the language of the day meant to take a drink), but as this was contrary to my habits, I was able to decline without giving offense.

Whatever else may have been lacking, there seemed to be plenty of 'spiritual comfort' in the camps I visited—and in some the frequent smiling had produced boisterous merriment. Those home holidays were something of a trial to the men in the camps, debarred from their enjoyment for years.

On Thursday, December 31, it rained steadily all day, making a dreary New Year's Eve. Reenlistment was a subject of discussion in the camp. Many no doubt would reenlist, but just at present it seemed as if the majority here chose to serve out the present term and then take a vacation or return at once—as they might decide after getting home and thinking it over.

On New Year's Day, the storm ended with a freeze, and it was a bitterly cold day with a roaring wind. The ground was coated with ice. This was *not* a Happy New Year to the soldiers in the camps, and we knew that it could not be to our families and friends at home. The war had grown in proportions and lengthened in duration far beyond what anyone expected at the beginning. However, the old year had been superseded by a new one, and I sincerely hoped the war would end happily before it did.

I expressed this wish to a comrade, and he answered that there never could be a *happy* ending to so awful a war. Another replied that anything that ended so terrible a war would be a happy event. Then there was a discussion over the prospects of the war, which brought out a hopeful feeling in spite of all of the discouraging things in the past. It was certain that the war *must end, sometime, somehow*, and the soldiers in the field *cannot conceive* of any but an honorable and creditable ending. With them, the day of compromise was past, and now it was victory or death.

Wednesday, January 6, a mail and papers came in, and I had a letter from E. Oscar Williams, formerly a sergeant in Company F, who transferred to the regular cavalry. He reported himself well, and I was glad to hear from him. He, too, had been considering the matter of reenlisting and had decided to go home first. This was a conclusion a good many of the boys had reached, myself included, and had already promised that much to those at home.

Thursday was another cold, windy day and difficult to keep warm, as good wood was scarce. A letter from my brother, William H. Wright, in the Second Minnesota, informed me that he had reenlisted and expected soon to start for Minnesota on a 30-day furlough. He urged me very strongly to remain at home and care for mother. If he had not already pledged himself, I should certainly give him the same advice. I did not expect to go home and remain there contentedly. Neither did I feel justified in arranging for further service until I had talked matters over with my mother.

We had been drilling some on Monday, January 11, and there was a 'drumming out' in the afternoon. The victim was a sutler, and his offense was selling whiskey to colored teamsters. He was given a 'wooden overcoat' made out of a barrel with the heads knocked out and holes cut for the arms. His head was shaved; his offence placarded on the barrel; and, cap in hand, he was paraded through the camps and escorted outside to the tune of the Rogue's March.

On Tuesday night, February 2, Lieutenant Colonel Charles P. Adams, commanding the regiment, returned from Washington, where he had been since Saturday, and there was a rumor the next day that the regiment was to be ordered home soon. Some believed the story, and some did not, saying, "it is too good to be true." At best it lacked confirmation from those who ought to know. But on Thursday, it was known that Wednesday's rumors were in the main correct, and we were ordered to report at St. Paul. After these years of absence it was a most welcome order, and the boys were as wild with excitement at the thought of going home so soon as they were when first ordered to Washington. Now, after nearly three years of the fortunes 'going to the front' had brought us, we were equally glad to turn again towards the place we had been so desirous to leave.

Their different dispositions and temperaments caused them to show—or try not to show—their feelings in a variety of ways. But every one was thrilling with a flood of emotions they could not hide. One of the least emotional of the company came into my tent and asked, almost in a whisper, "Is it true, Sergeant, we are to go home?" Being told that it was, he caught my hand and almost crushed it in his and left without another word. But, as he turned, I saw the tears running down his bronzed cheeks and felt drawn to him as I never had been before.

We were to leave at 6 the next morning, and I was busy for some hours making lists of the property we were to take with us—and also that property we were to turn over to the quartermaster when we went. Knapsacks, haversacks, canteens, guns, and accouterments we take with us. All other public property was to be turned in, but the tent-cloths which covered our shanties could not be collected until morning.

Our going had made quite a stir in the camps, and every tent had had its visitors from other regiments in the brigade or division to wish us a safe journey and say good-bye. Their parting words may not have been always in the best form, but they were sincere and hearty, and very acceptable because we knew they meant it. It was after midnight before the sound of voices in the tents ceased—and, safe to say, longer before all slept.

Notwithstanding the late hour when the boys took to their blankets, they were out of them before 5 o'clock Friday morning, February 5, and few if any had to be called. After the roll call, my first duty was to collect and turn in the government property we were not to take with us. When this was disposed of, and I had passed the receipts over to Capt. Ball, I went to our dismantled tent and found breakfast ready and my tentmates eating by the light and warmth of a large fire, composed of a part of the material of the hut.

As it was a crisp, cold morning with a temperature several degrees below freezing, the fire added to the comfort of the situation. Soon after our breakfasts were finished and knapsacks packed, we had orders to form. When in line, it was understood that we were to report at division headquarters before leaving for the station.

When we arrived, it was still too dark to see, and we were greeted by a burst of music from a brass band, and surprised to find that the whole brigade was out under arms. Muffled in their overcoats and scarcely discernable in the faint light, they presented arms as we passed and the color-bearers saluted. Cheers and a crash of music followed as we lined up in front of General Alexander Webb's tent—who came out to receive us.

He congratulated us on the prospect of soon seeing our homes and loved ones; complimented us on the good record we had made in the service, which he said was "splendid and imperishable"; and feelingly expressed his regrets at losing us from his command, meantime. Of course we cheered him, and the brigade cheered us as we marched away. The band of the Eighty-Second New York escorted us out of camp and across the bridge over Mountain Creek. There it halted and played "Auld Lang Syne," and our boys took up the strain and sang the words as we climbed the hill, "Shall old companions be forgot?"

Pleased as we were to go, it must not be supposed that we parted with our long-time comrades without feeling. We could not separate, even for a time, from those who shared our vicissitudes of fortune, good and bad, for years and stood with us so loyally in every emergency without sincere regrets.

As we marched up the hill, the sun rose and added brightness to a fine winter morning. There was but little snow on the ground, which was frozen hard enough to bear us, but there had been a surprising accumulation of frost, coating every shrub and dry weed or spear of grass so that it shone like silver.

The march to Brandy Station was made in good time, but there was some delay before the train was ready. When it came, it was simply a lot of empty freight cars returning to Alexandria, on which we were permitted to ride. Box cars without heat or seats, dirty and out of repair—not at all inviting—but we were in the first stages of the homeward journey, and it did not seem to matter much for the short time we expected to be in them. We could sit on our knapsacks or stand on our feet or alternate between the two methods for 75 or 80 miles—and then it would be a lot better than walking.

As it proved, it was a rather tiresome journey and subject to some unpleasant conditions we had not thought of. Much of the line had been relaid since the October raids, and the hard rains, heavy trains, and alternate freezing and thawing had wracked the track so very badly that the rate of speed rarely exceeded 10 miles an hour. Even that rate caused a lateral vibration that was considered unsafe.

We were crossing a section of the country where nearly every mile of it had been made historic by recent events—though from our closed cars there was little opportunity to see it. Brandy Station, where we took the cars, and its immediate vicinity had been the scene of half a score of fights. It was near there that Stuart had held his great cavalry review before the Gettysburg campaign. Rappahannock Station, where we crossed the Rappahannock River, had been the point of contact nine times between portions of the contending armies during the last two years; the last being the bloody and brilliant coup of the Sixth Corps on the 7th of November, 1863. Bealeton, Catlett's, and Bristoe Stations had each been made a battlefield six to eight times, and the latter had been the scene of the Second Corps' successful fight of October 14, 1863.

Then came Manassas and the crossing of the ill-omened Bull Run, each having woven its name in crimson colors into the history of the war. It was but a few miles above where we crossed that we had received our baptism of fire, and the regiment had suffered its first great loss. And all the way to Alexandria and Washington there was scarcely a mile that had not witnessed strife and tragedy.

Thinking more of what the journey we were starting on was to unfold to us than of the recent past we were leaving behind us, we rattled on our way through the cuts and over the grades and bridges, stopping now and then for wood and water. Nature in winter colors and the desolation of a war-wasted land dominated the scenery. The absence of people, deserted and ruined houses, fenceless fields, and tangled forests were all that was to be seen. It was noon before we reached Alexandria.

Later, we ran up to Washington, marched across the city, and found quarters for the night at the Soldier's Rest. Here, Representatives Cyrus Aldrich, William

Windom, and Ignatius Donnelly called.[3] Before we had left the Rapidan, orders had gone out for all men absent on details to return to their companies and join them in Washington. We had with us something over 200 men, and it was determined to delay one day in Washington, waiting for these, and to gather up all sick and wounded men able to travel and take them with us. These, it was supposed, would bring the number to about 300.

It was near sundown of a wintry afternoon when we took possession of the Soldier's Rest or Retreat, as we frequently called it, and planned to spend the night there. We had rations with us, but fresh bread, coffee, and soup were furnished, and there was straw on the floor for us to spread our blankets on. This Soldier's Rest was simply a relief station intended to help soldiers in transit and was located near the Baltimore and Ohio railroad station. Probably nearly all detached regiments passing through Washington were there at one time or another.

We were not strangers to it. It was here that we had found shelter about midnight March 22, 1862, from a pitiless storm of rain and sleet when returning from the Shenandoah Valley. It was, indeed, a 'haven of rest' on that occasion, and we held the place in grateful remembrance. It was located not far from where the magnificent Union Station now stands.

When we were established for the night and had supper, the boys naturally wanted to get out and 'see the city,' but Lieut. Col. Adams thought best to refuse passes, and the boys were supposed to spend the evening 'within the gates.' In some instances, however, this was an erroneous supposition, and a number took the chance of being gobbled by the provost patrols and went out on their own hook. So far as Company F was concerned, they were all present at the required roll calls, and the orderly sergeant did not feel obliged to 'go back of the returns.'

We slept that night on the floor and did not rest so well as in our shacks at the front.

Saturday morning, February 6, we had coffee and fresh bread furnished us, and went into our haversacks for what more we desired. Leaves were granted quite liberally on condition of returning at 12 o'clock, and most of the boys spent the morning about the city. It was an ordinary winter day for that latitude—freezing at night and thawing during the day.

At noon it was learned that our senators and congressmen and other Minnesotans in Washington planned to give the regiment a banquet that evening, before we left for the north.

There were callers during the day, and every company had its numbers increased by the coming in of detailed men and men from the hospitals. As usual, there was enough to keep the first sergeants busy, especially where there was but

3. Donnelly was Representative-elect—to replace Aldrich; however, the new Congress would not be sworn in until March 4, 1864. Thus Aldrich retained his seat until then.

one commissioned officer present. There was an inspection in the early afternoon, a short drill, and dress parade at night.

At dress parade it was officially announced that there would be a complimentary banquet for the regiment at the National Hotel, one of the leading hotels of the city in that day, and the hour of assembly given. To us who had lived principally on army rations and done our own cooking for so long a time, the idea of a first class hotel 'spread' was a very attractive proposition. But we then had little conception of the magnitude of the preparations or the richness of the provisions being made.

Instead of the "quiet affair with a few friends"—as we were informed it was to be—it proved to be a splendid and most generous feast, with many of the prominent men of the nation in attendance. There were about 300 of the regiment and more than 50 other guests, namely: Vice President Hannibal Hamlin; Secretary of the Interior John P. Usher; Secretary of War Edwin M. Stanton; Commissioner of Agriculture Morton; Commissioner of the Land Office Edmunds; J. W. Forney, Secretary of the Senate; J. W. Taylor of St. Paul; George A. Brackett of Minneapolis and William S. King; Senators Zachariah Chandler of Michigan, James Harlan of Iowa, and James Lane of Kansas. Also, Aldrich, Donnelly, and Windom of Minnesota, Howard of Michigan, and Colonel Colvill, Lieutenant Colonel Adams, and Captain George H. Woods of the regiment as after-dinner speakers, and I am thinking there were some others—and many guests who did not speak.

Letters were read from Secretary of State William H. Seward, Secretary of the Treasury Salmon P. Chase, and Postmaster General Montgomery Blair, and there may have been some others. Minnesota's representatives then in Washington 'went the whole figure'—regardless of expense.

With our frugal habits, and young eyes never accustomed to such display or ornamentation and liberality and variety of food—that dining room was an astonishing sight. The long tables were loaded with a line of choice dishes with which we had had but little previous acquaintance, and had been strangers for all the years of our service. The immense dining room was profusely decorated with flags, flowers, and evergreens—bouquets on the tables, and banners and printed sentiments on the walls. The menu included all of the standard eatables of the day, whether flesh, fish, or fowl, and many of the luxuries. And of puddings, pies, cake, ices, and liquids, there was an unstinted abundance.

We were informed at the beginning that there was no danger of hearing the 'long roll' and that we would not be called to 'fall in' until the feast was over. It certainly was a generous feast, and we began with an inclination to *eat it all* but were not wholly successful. I am inclined to question if there could have been an equal number who would have come any nearer it.

When the attack on the eatables had diminished to light skirmishing, the intellectual part was taken up. Hon. William Windom was the toastmaster, and many bright speeches were made—ranging from serious discussion of public affairs to humorous and witty stores. I shall not attempt to reproduce them here. As our regiment was the center of thought (for those present, not of us), we were praised as generously as we had been feasted. It was absolutely a surprise that they could find so many nice things to say about us, and we really felt that much of it was more than we justly deserved.

Just as we were leaving Washington the next morning, I managed to get a copy of the *Chronicle,* which had a brief notice which I copy:

> The superb entertainment tendered the First Regiment Minnesota Volunteers, the heroes of many battles, and we are informed the senior regiment in the service, was the spontaneous offering of the Minnesotians in this city. At the preliminary meeting held Friday evening over $1,000 were subscribed and paid down. Arrangements were made to give the entertainment the next evening. They went to work with true Minnesota go-a-headativeness.
>
> Last evening all things were ready, and that, too, in most sumptuous style. Too great praise cannot be given to both the Minnesotians and Mr. Benson, the proprietor of the National Hotel, for their unqualified success in getting up the supper and arrangements. There was everything that was promised, and "all went merry as a marriage bell."
>
> Three hundred and fifty were seated in the large hall, which was tastefully decorated with evergreens; and at the head were displayed the tattered banners which had been borne through a score of brilliant battles, beginning with the first Bull Run. We regret that time and space do not permit our giving a more extended report this morning but we will try, in tomorrow's issue, to do justice to an occasion which was fraught with enjoyment to all the participants.

I did not see the next day's issue and never knew what was said. There were many interesting incidents of the evening which ought to have been preserved, but were not, because our hasty departure and subsequent long journey under trying conditions prevented their record and preservation.

The return of Col. Colvill to the regiment for the first time since Gettysburg was one of the events of the evening. Most men in his condition would have felt it impossible to be present. He could not walk or stand and was carried in by two of the stalwart members of the regiment, Captain Tom Sinclair and Sergeant Johnny Merritt. His entrance into the banquet room was unexpected, and when he was brought in there was a spontaneous outburst of shouting and cheering, which showed the feelings of the men toward him. He was the original captain of Company F and had won his way to the command of the regiment.

I will quote the following verses, which were written by Grant P. Robinson, and were suggested to the poet's mind by seeing the regiment marching down Pennsylvania Avenue. It is entitled the "Battle-worn Banner" and is prefaced as follows: "Suggested by seeing the First Minnesota Regiment pass down Pennsylvania avenue on its homeward march."

Give to the breeze your tattered flag,
No better e'er was borne;
And let your proudest record be
That banner, battle-worn.
Brave men have died beneath its folds,
In many a glorious fight
For Freedom, in its broadest sense—
For Justice, Truth, and Right.
And if perchance it ne'er again
O'er battle-field shall wave,
Enshrine within some sacred place
That Banner of the brave.
And, when this cruel war is o'er,
And peace shall come again,
And fields, now desolate, shall yield
Their fruit, and golden grain.
Our children then will gather round
To hear some grandsire tell
How bravely Minnesota fought,
How nobly and how well.
And, pointing to the tattered flag,
Tell them of "Malvern Hill," of "Gettysburg,"
and "Antietam," till every heart shall thrill.
Tell them of "Sharpsburg," "Ashby's Gap,"
Of "Yorktown," nor forget
One field where Minnesota's boys
The Southern traitors met.
"This maimed arm," he'll say,
"I got on that eventful night,
When we went up and swept the foe
From off South Mountain's height.
This sabre cut across my brow—
It was a well meant blow—
The last he ever made on earth—
I laid the miscreant low."
And, grasping that old tattered flag,
In reverence he will kneel,
And pray that God will always bless
And guard our country's weal.
God speed you on your homeward march,
For loving hearts await,
With outstretched arms and welcome smiles,
Your coming at the gate.
Then flaunt your tattered flag on high,
No better e'er was borne;
The proudest record of your deeds —
That banner, battle-worn.

I do not recall that this was read at the banquet. It was published in March 1864, in the *Washington Chronicle,* as I see by the date on it. Neither do I recall any association with the author.

That banquet was as satisfactory as it was unexpected, and we were in no haste to end it. It was past midnight, the morning hours in fact, when the last sentiment had been given and the last toast responded to—when we reformed to return to the Rest for a little sleep before starting on the long, cold journey between Washington and St. Paul. During the evening it had been decided to take with us Col. Colvill and all the others who were thought able to stand the journey, and this caused a later hour to be set for the start.

Is it true, sergeant, we are to go home?

FEBRUARY-MAY 1864

SUNDAY MORNING, FEBRUARY 7, after but a few hours rest and sleep, we break-fasted, packed our belongings, filled our canteens with coffee, and were ready be-fore the cars were. When the cars came we were disappointed to find that there was but one coach, and the others were only box cars with improvised seats—boards across the car and without backs. Our train was said to be a special to Bal-timore, where we were to have regular coaches.

We were shifted to several tracks before starting and stranded for an hour or more at a time on switches. It was dark before we reached Baltimore, and there we were shunted about the freight yards until morning. Of course we chafed and 'growled' under these seemingly useless delays. We tried to sleep and did sleep some, but the fireless cars were cold, and the frequent changes of position were al-ways accompanied with bumps and jars. Also, naps were short and unsatisfactory.

At Baltimore the expected passenger coaches were not to be had, so we were told, and we left Baltimore for Harrisburg Monday morning in the same cars we had come in. It was a cold windy day, and, while we were in no danger of actually freezing, it was decidedly a comfortless journey. 'After a feast a famine' was one of the common sayings of that time, and about this time we began to realize that it applied to our case. Rations were getting scarce, and we knew of no place where we could get more.

At Harrisburg we changed to passenger coaches with comfortable seats, and a fire, which was a great improvement. But now the question of something to eat was getting more imperative, and the short stop in Harrisburg did not permit us to get anything except what was brought to the cars by peddlers.

We made a night run to Pittsburgh and reached there about sunrise Tuesday morning, tired, dirty, and hungry. Here there was a stop of an hour or more, and we were able to get our breakfasts and provide something for this day. Here it was planned to telegraph ahead and try to have dinner provided so that all who wished might get their meals and pay for them.

In this way we had dinner at Alliance, Ohio, and supper at Fort Wayne, Indi-ana, just before dark, and continued on to Chicago. It was cold and a storm threatening.

Somewhere on the cars before reaching Chicago, we were met by a committee from that city inviting us to the new Soldier's Rest they were just completing and wished us to dedicate. Now that we had left the front and were going back among folks, it seemed 'in our line'—and it was not on record that soldiers had ever declined to eat when invited. We did not care to break the record, and accepted the invitation. Word was sent on that we "were coming and would bring our appetites with us."

It was getting late when we arrived, and we formed and marched at once under the guidance of the committee to the new buildings, where we found an abundant supper provided and a large gathering of people awaiting us. Concerning what followed I quote from the *Chicago Tribune* of the next day, a copy of which I was able to get at Janesville, Wisconsin:

> The First Minnesota Regiment arrived in Chicago about 11 o'clock last evening, on its way home to recruit and furlough. The regiment contains 416 men, of whom 309 and 16 officers are returning; the others being left behind, sick and wounded. The regiment left Branch Station, in front of the Army of the Potomac, on the 5th instant and ... arrived in Chicago last night, marching direct to the new building—the Soldiers' Rest—being the first regiment that has enjoyed the hospitalities of the institution.
>
> Here the ladies had been waiting for them since nightfall, and as the gallant fellows marched in they were received with a hearty ovation. Clapping of hands, waving of handkerchiefs and loud huzzas saluted them until they had taken their places at the tables, which were bountifully supplied. After the viands had been discussed, the Colonel returned thanks to the ladies for their kindness, and the boys gave three rousing cheers in response. Mr. Bryan was called upon and made a few well-timed remarks. The men remain all night at the Soldiers' Rest and will go out per the Northwestern Railroad to La Crosse, in the morning.

The Mr. Bryan referred to could hardly have been William J. could it? He has proved himself a great talker, but we judge he did not begin his public career quite so young.[1]

I have a very pleasant recollection of our brief stop in Chicago. Almost as soon as I was seated at the table, a pleasant-speaking lady, who busied herself in waiting on me and asking questions, discovered that I was a nephew of the Rev. Hooper Crews, who was her favorite minister and then a chaplain in the service. I was well entertained and cared for—had all I could eat and a haversack full to take with me.

Late as it was when we arrived, it was some hours later before there was any opportunity to sleep, and but a brief time to devote to it. It was still dark Wednesday morning when we left the Rest for the Chicago & Northwestern Depot. It was a sharp winter morning, with an overcast sky and a biting wind off the lake, and, before we reached the depot, a fine snow was falling.

1. The great orator and three-time presidential candidate William Jennings Bryan would have been only three years old in February 1864.

When we arrived at the depot, it was discovered that there was some hitch about the transportation. The lack of cars to ride in, an engine to draw them, or men to handle it seemed to be causing the management trouble; and there was some delay before they appeared to know what to do with us. Then we were shown cars and boarded them, and, after another short wait, left Chicago attached to a regular passenger train.

This was the sixth day of the journey, and we were getting weary—anxious to see the end of it—and the thought that we would get to La Crosse that night was an encouraging one. But we were destined to realize the truth in the assertion of the poet that there was "many a slip between the cup and the lip."

Our train was really too heavy for the engine that drew it, and we were behind time when we reached Janesville. Meantime, the ashy ice-dust of the morning had grown to a steady downpour of full-grown snowflakes. The mercury was falling, and a rising wind was driving the snow and piling it in drifts wherever there was a point of lodgment. Going on, it was found that the increasing drifts were too great a hindrance, and an additional engine was added to the motive power.

For a time after, the pair made fair progress. Then the continued storm and increasing drifts occasionally brought us to a stand-still in the cuts, and one of the engines had to be detached to 'buck the drifts' and open the way. Outside, it had grown bitterly cold but there were two large stoves—one in either end of the car—and we managed to keep fairly comfortable. Before night overtook us, there was an able-bodied blizzard in active operation, and prospects were dubious. It was getting so intensely cold, too, that the windows were thickly coated with ice. It was not until after dark that hopefulness gave way to discouragement, and not wholly then, for we were still making some progress.

When it was dark we tried to sleep, but it was not very successful or satisfactory. Accustomed as we were to roughing it and taking things as they came, there was no denying the fact that the long-continued journey was having its natural effect, and we were getting exceedingly tired—even if we were going home.

The boys made a brave effort to 'keep up' by singing, playing tricks, and jokes. Charley Merritt frequently asserted that "Canada was a rough country." But none of these things improved the situation, and matters settled down to a quiet endurance of the things we could neither 'help nor hinder.'

Long before morning, we knew that but little progress was being made through the drifts, and that for sometime we had been stationary; also, that the supply of wood in the car was getting low and the car cold. Thursday morning, February 11, dawned cold and windy and lacking every element of comfort and cheerfulness. We were on a side track, near a station—Portage City—and the trainmen, with the engines and regular cars, had gone on and left us.

There was great and general indignation that we had been deserted thus in the storm without notice. It is possible that in leaving us and going on with the others, the trainmen did the best they could under the circumstances, and that we judged them unjustly. But we saw no excuse for them at the time. It is also possible that before going they may have notified our commander of what they would try to do. But if so we were not told of it then nor have we heard of it since.

To make matters worse, the wood for the stoves was used up, and there was very little left in our haversacks to eat. As soon as it was light enough, parties went out prospecting for wood, water, and rations. A water tank ornamented with huge icicles and a wood pile was found nearby, but there was nothing in sight to eat. The station was a lone one on the prairie; and the station houses locked up; and there was too much snow flying to get a view of the surroundings.

A supply of wood and water was obtained, and we got back in the car almost frozen, but glad to get that much. I do not know how cold it was but certainly many degrees below zero; and, though the snow had ceased to fall, the air was full of it, driven in whirling eddies by the wind. Our first care after returning to the cars was to increase the fires and make coffee and eat our breakfasts. We had drawn no rations since leaving the front, and, when through with our breakfasts, there was very little left.

As the day grew the clouds rolled by, the wind diminished its force, and cold became more endurable. The stationmaster had come and opened the station and started a fire, and a telegraph operator appeared on the scene, but there was a leak or break somewhere, and nothing could be learned about the general situation of things. It was some hours before communications were established, and, mean-time, the boys were planning foraging expeditions for the afternoon if unable to go on by that time.

As soon as the line would work, Lieut. Col. Adams began trying to get in com-munication with some of the road officials to learn why we had been dropped and why we could not proceed. The substance of the answer was that, if we were de-layed, they did not know why, and, if there was any means of going, we should go. This was indefinite and unsatisfactory, and even that much had not been obtained without some friction and use of authority. From the first, the station keeper and the telegraph operator had seemed to resent inquiries and were reluctant to give information, which soon produced what diplomats call 'strained relations,' and they were eventually strained so much that they broke.

Probably all parties to the situation were more or less to blame, as well as the weather. If the engines had stalled in the snow, and the conductor and trainmen had remained with them, we would have felt that they were blameless. Neither should we have condemned the management of the road had we been advised that it was making reasonable effort to deal with adverse conditions. As it was, we had been abandoned without notice or explanations in the night time on a wind-swept prairie in mid-winter weather without adequate supplies of any kind. We naturally felt that that was an open violation of the transportation contract, and not the kind of treatment we ought to expect from any but enemies.

A consultation of the officers decided that the stranded condition of the regiment and the lack of supplies created a 'military necessity,' and that they had full power to seize supplies and transportation if not otherwise obtainable. To that end a demand was made on the station keeper and the operator for information as to the condition of the road and what was being done to relieve us.

About all that was learned was that the regular train had left La Crosse. With this knowledge, it was decided that when the train arrived it should *return with us to La Crosse.* To make a sure thing of it, we proceeded to blockade the track with ties.

At this, the stationmaster interfered—as I suppose was his right and duty—but there was an armed guard at hand, and he was promptly arrested and placed under guard on a huge pile of snow that had been thrown from the track and about the station. Trying to get further information from the operator was a failure, and he also was placed on the snowbank to 'think it over.' A little later, a track boss and a couple of helpers came and said some unpleasant things about the situation in which they found matters. When it was decided that they had said too much, they were added to the other road officials on the snow pile.

Not long after this, the shriek of an engine was heard down the track, but nothing could be seen. It was heard several times—each time nearer—before it was seen. The interest grew with each repetition of the whistle, and before it arrived we were all out of the cars to see it.

When it did arrive, a demand was made to attach the engine to our train and take us to La Crosse, which of course was refused. This was expected, and operations were at once begun to enforce the demand. Lieutenant William M. May, who was in charge of the guard, gave the engineer his choice of going back with his engine or onto the snowbank. He promptly decided that he would stay with the engine. A guard was put onto the engine to enforce obedience, if necessary, and he was directed to run up to the turntable and reverse his engine.

Here it was found that there was some snow to be removed before the engine could be turned, and, meantime, the men were ordered to board their cars.

Naturally the passengers (there were only about 20 of them) protested against this arrangement, and were given their choice to return with us or take their chance where they were. They decided to stay where they were, at the suggestion of the conductor that an engine would be sent to take them on. When the engine was ready, they were sidetracked and the engine attached to our cars.

When all was ready, the prisoners on the snow pile were released with expressions of regret that coercive measures were necessary, but they did not feel at all nice about it and said so. It was some time past noon before all was ready, and we started for La Crosse, and it was said that the engineer promised to land us in "La Crosse or hell before sundown."

It turned out to be La Crosse, but it was a little after sunset. As we passed, there was very little opportunity to observe the scenery because of the frost on the windows, but everything was buried in the accumulated snows of the winter. Though there was not now much wind, the last deposit was crawling across the exposed points. The sun was shining, but it made no impression, and it must have been zero temperature or lower. In many places there were drifts which taxed the engine to get through and sometimes almost stopped it, but voluntary stops were only made for wood and water, and progress was good.

It was growing dusk when we rounded the curve that brought us to the Mississippi River, a mile or so from the city. It was supposed that the teams would be waiting for us at La Crescent, Minnesota, and it was decided to leave the car where we came to the river, as that would save time and nearly a mile of marching. After getting off the cars, it was learned that the teams had been in waiting since noon of the previous day, and that part of them were still in La Crosse, and the remainder had gone back to La Crescent.

Word was sent into the city and across the river for the teams, and, meantime, we waited in the waning light of the departing day keenly sensitive to the wind and the cold. Fortunately we did not have to wait long, for any great delay would have resulted in frosted fingers and toes—as we were not dressed for that climate.

In anticipation of the coming of the teams and to keep our blood in circulation, we marched out on the ice to meet those from La Crescent, and the others joined us soon. The transportation outfit was rather primitive, being bobsleds with large boxes on them filled with straw and cross-seated with boards, without backs of any kind. There were plenty of buffalo robes, as well as straw, and these met the needs of the cold night.

It was quite dark before we were 'all aboard for Winona,' and, if I remember correctly, the assignment was 22 to a sleigh. When all was ready, the signal was given, and we started on an evening sleigh ride—minus the girls. Horses and drivers were impatient to go, and we started at a lively pace.

Once seated in the sleighs, with the robes and straw about them to retain the natural warmth of their bodies, the chilled, weary, hungry soldier-boys forgot their disgusted feelings at the day's experiences—and body and mind responded promptly to the improved condition of affairs. It was the first sleigh ride in the service, and they were soon talking, laughing, and singing like a pleasure party out for an evening ride. We were on the ice-covered river, which made a level and very smooth road—except now and then a 'thank you ma-am'—and progress was rapid.

The merriment and jollity of the first hour of the ride did not continue to the end of the journey. It was in reality sleigh loads of tired men, whose spirits were inflated to the overflowing point for a little time by the novelty of their situation, but they soon subsided. The 'undue hilarity' was followed by silence, and that was soon succeeded by sounds indicating the boys were sleeping out loud.

I have but little recollection of any but the first few mile of that long night ride. I was in the front of the sleigh, and, when an irresistible desire to sleep came, I

deposited myself in a corner under the raised seat of the driver, and 'further proceedings interested me no more' until I was shaken into consciousness and told
to "wake up and see the lights." I was cramped and cold—almost frozen—but in
reality felt refreshed after three hours or so of sleep—as soon as circulation was
made normal by exercising arms and legs a little.

We were approaching Winona, and a bonfire was burning on the ice near
some of the warehouses. We were soon there and out of the sleighs, to be quickly
surrounded by a cheering crowd, which welcomed us with a hearty enthusiasm
that warmed us almost instantly. It was about midnight and bitterly cold, and it
was a surprise to us that there should be any one in waiting at that hour, on such
a night.

We quickly formed and marched into a large building whose doors were
opened to receive us and quickly closed to shut out the frigid air. I suppose we
were in one of the warehouses. Stacking arms and depositing our knapsacks, we
were at once encompassed by the people gathered there, who all seemed eager to
shake our hands and tell us they were glad to see us. It was a most cheering welcome and made us feel at home, without further ceremony.

Company K had been raised in Winona and vicinity, and was now really at
home. The rest of us were strangers, but the words of welcome and outstretched hands were for all. And they were of such a nature and so heartily
given, that there was no doubt of their sincerity. That first meeting, with people of our own state on the western bank of the Mississippi, was all we could
have asked and much more than we had any right to expect, especially if we
consider the hour and the temperature. It touched our inmost natures. Only
those who have been absent long and suffered much can rightly appreciate such
a greeting.

Tired, cold, and hungry as we were after 7 days and nights of travel—much
of the time under adverse conditions—we were brought in from the frigid darkness of the ice-covered river to comfortable shelter—*light, warmth, and a feast.*
It was a transition never to be forgotten. Tables were spread with an abundance
of the best, and there was little time or ceremony wasted in getting us around
them. A word of welcome, a brief prayer of thanks and invocation, and we were
told to eat, and there was no need for a second invitation. Waited on and talked
to by the ladies, we tried to be polite and keep up the conversation, and ate like
hungry animals.

While we were still at the table, Captain John Ball, who was a Winona man
and originally belonged to Company K, brought several people to introduce to
"his boys," as he called us, and spoke of us in a complimentary way.

It was three o'clock and perhaps more when the supper and the talking fest
that followed were ended, and we began to prepare to sleep on the floor. We were
told that there were beds in the hotels at our disposal and that many of the people wanted to take us to their homes. Permission was given to go where we chose,

provided we were at the hotel at nine the next morning, ready to travel, that hour being named to give us a chance for sleep and the horses to rest.

At the urgent invitation of Mrs. Luark, whom Capt. Ball introduced to me, I went to her home for the remainder of the night. At the Luark home I was shown to a room with a *feather bed, white sheets, and soft pillows*. I had previously felt reluctant to impose myself upon the hospitality of these good people and now, travel-stained and without a change of anything clean, to occupy that immaculate bed seemed an outrage, and I protested that I much preferred to sleep on the floor. My protests were silenced by the tender of a nightshirt, and the parley ended with my request to be called not later than 8 o'clock.

The nightshirt was a novelty I had never indulged in, but I substituted it for my soiled clothing and 'turned in'—and, regardless of clean sheets and soft feathers, slept soon and soundly.

The next thing I knew was a rap on the door and a summons to breakfast, which was accompanied by warm water, soap, and towel. I hastily indulged in a good wash, the first one since leaving the front. Sausages and buckwheats were a part of the morning menu, and I ate them with good relish notwithstanding the late, hearty supper. As soon as I had finished, I thanked my entertainers and hastened to find the company, carrying with me a substantial lunch for the day.

I found Capt. Ball and some of the company already at the hotel and learned that Companies G and K were to be furloughed—the former to go across country to Faribault, and the latter to remain in Winona. Capt. Ball informed me that he had decided to remain in Winona for the day. The company was to go on with the others, and he would come on the regular stage and join us somewhere en route. Also, that he had telegraphed to Lieutenant Hezekiah Bruce at Red Wing and St. Paul, and that he would probably meet us somewhere on the road.

This was Saturday morning, February 13—clear and cold with a strong wind blowing. The teams were late in reporting, and it was near 10 o'clock before we were ready to start. The dropping off of Company K having diminished the number, a reapportionment of the loads was demanded by the teamsters, who felt that they were overloaded the night previous. The coming night was to be spent at Wabasha, and it was hoped to reach there at an early hour.

On the river it was found the snow was drifting badly, and in places the track was entirely obliterated. It was hard on the teams through the drifts. The drivers asserted that the river was rising, and they feared 'air holes,' and they feared getting on to unsafe ice.

After going for a number of miles, we met teamsters coming down the river with loads of wood. These advised leaving the ice and taking a road through the woods on the Wisconsin side. The owners of the teams were allowed to use their judgment—and took the wood road. In the woods it was warmer, and the road was not drifted. But it was crooked, rough, and not always well defined, so that progress was slow and unsatisfactory. I do not know if the drivers missed their way, but they failed to get back on the ice—as it was supposed they intended—before reaching the open water at the mouth of the Chippewa, and we were obliged to ferry over to Wabasha.[2]

It was dark before we were all over the river, and it was then learned that attempts to get us by telegraph during the day had failed, and that there was no provision made for the night. The teams were too tired to go further and preparations were hastily made at the hotels, where we all found shelter and food, but the majority spread their blankets on the floor. This was the home town of Company I, and I presume that those living in the town went to their homes.

Company I had expected to remain at home as Company K had, and the boys were somewhat disconcerted when ordered to be on hand to continue the journey in the morning. However, they were accustomed to obeying orders and good-naturedly made the best of it. This had come about through the desire to have the regiment together at St. Paul, it was understood.

During the evening there were many people called at the hotels to see or inquire for some one. I met a number of people I had known, among them two old schoolmates, and began to realize that I was getting near home. One of these had come to learn what he could of the details of the death of a mutual friend, Gus Ellison, who had been killed in front of Richmond in June 1862. Naturally it was late before we slept, but an early start was planned for the next morning, and breakfast had been ordered at six.

Sunday morning, February 14, we were up early and breakfast was on time, but the teams were tardy, and it was seven o'clock before we were on the road. Leaving the road at the upper end of the town, we took the ice up Lake Pepin. The promise of warmer weather, which some had seen in the sunset glow of the previous evening, was not being fulfilled. On the contrary, it was a stinging cold morning, and there was a strong, icy air current down the lake.

On the ice the road was fair, with here and there a drift that made the going slow and wearied the horses. It was planned to reach Hastings that night, if possible, and end the long, tiresome journey the next forenoon. This would make a hard day for the horses and was to be divided into three parts, stopping at Lake City and Red Wing to rest and feed the horses. It was about half past nine when we arrived at Lake City and a halt of an hour was made, and while waiting most of the boys found places to warm themselves and get something warm to drink.

While waiting here, a telegram was received inquiring what time we would arrive at Red Wing and how many there were in the party and stating that "plans were being made for some sort of a reception." A reply was sent to this telling what time we would leave Lake City. This was the first word we had had from the home town since leaving the front, and we were both glad to hear and to know

2. The mouth of the Chippewa River, opposite Reads Landing, is near the lower end of Lake Pepin. Open water must have extended some miles below the landing.

that we were not to pass by unnoticed. As it was Sunday we had thought such might be the case.

Again on the lake with the 'frigid breath of winter' in our faces, we felt the cold so that we covered our heads with our coat capes, but good time was made. Leaving the lake through the slough near the lower end of Barn Bluff, we passed up the valley between Barn Bluff and Sorin's Bluff.

It was a little after one when we reached the main street and found a large gathering waiting to receive us. And the welcome they gave us left no doubt of its hearty sincerity. The Red Wing boys were intensely and immensely pleased that a dinner was provided and the whole regiment was included, as it had been at Winona, and they formed to escort their comrades.

The dinner was spread in the rooms over Foot & Sterling's store, a new building, and I am not sure whether it was a public hall or improvised for the occasion.[3] In the hall we were seated at the tables at once, as the dinner was waiting, and the appetites of the guests in good order.

Company F was the last to enter the hall and just as hungry as the others, but more eager to meet and greet waiting relatives and friends than to eat. As soon as in the hall, the boys were surrounded by the anxious waiting ones, and there was a scene which no words of mine can even faintly reproduce on paper, and is best left to the imagination. It is sufficient to say that the boys were unceremoniously hugged and kissed with an earnestness and abandon that was seemingly intended to make up for all previous enforced omissions. Words — expressions of feeling, questions, and comments — were fired at them in volleys. It was a glad, joyous moment, and hearts thrilled with the intensity of human emotions, and tears were not lacking. Tears of gladness for those they were greeting, and tears of sadness for those they never should greet again. And these were observable alike on fair faces and bronzed cheeks.

Personally, I received as cordial greetings from many that I knew as any returning wanderer could reasonably ask and was warmly taken by the hand and welcomed by many I did not recognize — but I did not see any of my own family. As I was short of stature, I stood on a chair to look over the heads of the throng but failed to locate my mother, whom I was more anxious to see than any other person living.

In answer to my inquiries, I was told that the hour of arrival not being definitely known and her health poor, she had not come, but that a sleigh had already gone to bring her and my little brother and sister. I sat at the table and tried to eat, but, though I had eaten nothing since early morning, I was not conscious that I was hungry, and food was tasteless.

---

3. In 1861, Silas B. Foot and G. K. Sterling began to manufacture boots and shoes in a factory at Main and Plum Streets in Red Wing. This reception was probably held in the second-floor workshop area above the retail store.

Soon I was informed that my mother had come, and a young lady who said she was Alice offered to escort me to her. I had never met her but recognized her at once as one who had frequently been mentioned in my mother's letters for her kindly ministrations when she was sick—and followed her to a part of the room where my mother, with a few friends, was waiting for me. In a moment I had her in my embrace, her kisses and tears were on my face, and she was thanking God for the return of another one of her soldier boys.

When I had greeted my brother and sister, and had opportunity to observe them more carefully, I was surprised at their growth and development during the last three years. With my mother it was different. Her experiences of the war had left their mark on her face and her health was broken, but these are personal matters, and I need not dwell longer upon them.

Food was brought to us where we sat, and I was able to eat now with a returning appetite, but I had not asked or answered half the questions desired before I was called and told that it was time to go. The two hours allotted to the halt there was already more than gone.

I said a hurried good-bye and went to form the company, and the teams were already waiting in the street. There was a formal word of thanks to the good people of Red Wing for their generous entertainment, and then we tumbled into the sleighs and started. Lieutenant Bruce had joined the company while there and continued with us on the journey.

It was now nearly four o'clock, and we found it intensely cold when we left the shelter of the streets and got out on the river. The sun, already low, was but dimly discernable through the shimmering frost that filled the air. And on either side there was a 'mock sun' of nearly equal size and luster of the orb of day.

For a little time the boys chattered volubly through the organs of speech, but it was not long before the penetrating cold began to make their teeth chatter involuntarily, and they covered their heads with their coat capes and blankets to protect them as they sat in the straw on the bottom of the sleigh box. Night came on with a rising wind and increasing cold.

While daylight lasted, progress was good but after dark things did not go so smoothly, and it was after nine before Hastings was reached. This was the home town of Company H, and those living in the town naturally went to their homes, and arrangements had been made for the rest of the companies at the hotels. It took some time to get located, warmed, and have our suppers. I judge it was midnight or later before I slept, and then it was in a blanket on the floor. It was hoped to make St. Paul by noon the next day, and we were under orders for an early start the next morning.

Monday morning, February 15—it was still dark when we began our preparations for the last section of the tiresome journey, which had already taken two days more than had been calculated and would spoil another to complete. Captain Ball joined us while we were at breakfast, having come in on the night stage, and by the time we were through eating the teams were coming out.

Outside, we found it the most uncomfortable morning of the whole trip. It was not storming, but the temperature was well down below zero, and a boisterous, gusty wind was whirling the loose snow around the corners and driving it along the streets. Protecting ourselves the best we could with blankets and robes, the drivers cracked their whips and made a brave start, but out on the ice they soon met with difficulties, and the over-worked teams, which had come through from La Crosse, progressed slowly.

The wind was nearly down the river, and loose snow and particles of ice were being driven by the wind along the snow-crusted surface and through the air. Several times the drifts necessitated those in the leading sleighs to get out and assist the horses to get through them. This the boys did with rare good nature, but it meant cold feet and almost frozen fingers, and we suffered much from the cold and the flying snow.

The understanding was that there was to be a civic procession, parade, and reception in St. Paul in the afternoon, and that they would come out on the ice to meet us. The delays on the way and the 'blizzardy' weather conditions, we judged, would cut out all attempts at display and reduce matters to only what was necessary. But we did not judge correctly.

As we approached the city—looking up the river—all we could see was flying snow and whirling masses of smoke (as wood was the principal fuel of that day). The teams were halted, and we formed on the ice a little below the city, when it was seen a procession of some kind was coming out to meet us. It was the Butchers Association—and they wore their frocks outside of their overcoats—that came out to receive us.

It was about as uncomfortable and unpropitious an afternoon for a gala parade as could be imagined. Besides, we were hours late. There were just as little formalities as was permissible under the circumstances. They marched past us, cheering. We responded with the best imitation of a war-whoop we could give under the conditions and followed after them as they headed for the shore.

Here, there was an immense crowd which welcomed us with shouts and cheers, and bells were ringing and whistles blowing as we were escorted to our place in the procession. When we reached the position assigned us in the line, there was an interval before the start, which was taken advantage of by those having relatives or friends in the regiment to come and greet them.

It made a memorable scene, just such as there had been at Winona and Red Wing. Only at those places there were present the particular friends of but a single company, and here they were present for five, which gave the added effect of numbers. We, who had no friends there to meet us, were interested and sympathetic observers of those who had. It was a scene of intense human interest, and must have touched the heart of everyone present as sharply as the frost did their faces.

By the courtesy of the *Saint Paul Dispatch-Pioneer Press,* I have received a copy of the report in the papers the next day—February 16, 1864—and I feel that I cannot do better than copy the descriptive portion of it:

The regiment arrived in St. Paul, from Hastings, about 3 o'clock yesterday afternoon, and was received according to the program published on Sunday. Notwithstanding it was a cold stormy day, the wind blowing a gale, an immense crowd met them at the foot of Rosabel Street. The scene as the boys met their relations and old friends was beyond description. Besides our St. Paul people, there were many friends and relatives of members of the regiment from other towns in the state, and from the country. Hand shaking, embracing and kissing was the order of the times, and for the few moments opportunity was given for such greeting, the boys were kept busy.

The procession, which was at once formed and took up the line of march for the Atheneum, was over a mile in length and was formed as follows: 1—Fire department, escort. 2—Mayor and council. 3—Band. 4—State officers and legislature. 5—Gen. Sibley and staff, in carriages. 6—Field and staff officers of the Second regiment, in carriages. 7—The first flag of the First regiment, with an escort of the regiment. 8—First regiment, with knapsacks and guns. Marching by companies. 9—Soldiers mounted. 10—Butchers association. 11—Citizens in carriages. 12—Citizens on foot. The buildings along the line of march were decorated with national flags. The engine houses of the fire department were, with the engines, in holiday trim, the doors of the houses standing open, and the bells ringing a joyous peal as the procession moved by. The windows all along the way were occupied by ladies whose waving handkerchiefs looked like broad lines of white down the streets. The procession itself was half hidden in floating flags and banners. The firemen, bearing large banners striped with words of welcome to the returning heroes of Minnesota's first offering in war, and of honor to their dead comrades, carried also smaller banners inscribed with the name of one of the battles in which the First had been engaged. Arrived at the Atheneum, which had been fitted up in best style and decorated, the regiment marched through the open ranks of its escort, stacked arms and filed into the main hall; where five tables had been set on the main floor, and one on the stage, furnishing seats for about 250. As they marched in and took their places, the ladies, who thronged the side galleries, the gentlemen on the stage, and the firemen in the front gallery, joined in welcoming plaudits, and, as the battle flags and trophies of the regiment were borne through the hall and placed in the front center of the stage, the applause nearly doubled, and the Great Western Band joined in with a brilliant strain of martial music. When the officers and men had been seated, Chief Engineer Pickett announced Mayor Warren to welcome the regiment on behalf of the city authorities and citizens.

Mayor Warren was followed by Gov. Stephen Miller, a former Lieutenant Colonel of the regiment, who welcomed us on behalf of the state. Both of these officials spoke eloquently and earnestly, words of approval and praise that we felt was all we deserved and more. After the welcome by Gov. Miller, Reverend Dr. McMasters gave thanks for our return and asked Heaven's blessing on the occasion and the food provided, and we were invited to eat.

By this time it was dark, and we had breakfasted before daylight that morning, and were 'hungry as stray dogs.' No time was lost in accepting the invitation. It was a great feast. Abundant in quantity and the best the markets could provide. If eating heartily is complimenting the cook, as is sometimes said, we certainly gave those who provided and prepared that feast high praise by the way we disposed of it.

I have a very pleasant recollection of the occasion—not alone from what I ate—but more particularly because of some old schoolmates who discovered me and made their way through the crowd to join me. Their greeting was so hearty and they had so much to tell about old classmates at Hamline and mutual friends—from whom I had heard but infrequently, and of some not at all, since I had gone into the army—that the time passed unnoted.

It was indeed a glad occasion, but it was not all unalloyed rejoicing. Nearly all of the able-bodied young men I had left at the university had enlisted in one or another of the regiments, and not all had escaped the vicissitudes of the service. As we recalled one and another, mutually known to us at Hamline and who had gone at the call of President Lincoln in our own or some of the later regiments, we counted nearly a score who had already given the "last, full measure of devotion" and twice as many who were suffering from wounds or disease.

These were not wholly cheerful topics for conversation at a banquet. But they came very naturally to those who had not met since the war began, for the war and its results to those we knew was uppermost in our minds—in the minds of all. The progress of the war had crimsoned the local history of every town, village, and country neighborhood—as it had brought death or wounds to some representative in the army and sorrow into some rural home. The shadow of its continuance was over the whole land and, apparently, the people were thinking and talking of little else. And long as the list of sacrifices was, they knew very well that it was far from complete.

The banquet was under the management of the firemen but was really gotten up by the women of Saint Paul. At least when all had eaten to full satisfaction, the ladies gave us a special welcome in a series of patriotic sentiments, toasts, and responses, interspersed with songs and music. And, meantime, the tables were re-set for the firemen and soldiers of other regiments present.

The formal part of the exercises was closed by a flourish of music by the band and a few remarks by Chief Pickett of the fire department, in which he claimed credit for the firemen for the management of the affair as a whole and gave credit to the ladies for the feast and its serving. It was indeed a royal feast and those who provided it might well felicitate themselves.

The generosity of the providers was not exhausted by the feast, but it was arranged for us to sleep in the Atheneum that night and a breakfast provided for the next morning. Col. Colvill and some others were too much exhausted by the journey to go in the procession or to the banquet and were at once taken to some of the hotels and provided for. I presume the men of the local companies, and probably those from Minneapolis and St. Anthony also, went to their homes that night.

There was plenty of room to spread our blankets on the floor, in the aisles, on the stage, etc., and we felt that we who could not go to our homes were fortunate in having so good a place. Friends of some of the returning soldiers lingered long to talk with them, and it was hours past midnight before all slept, but then we slept soundly until daylight.

It was warm enough when we went to sleep, but when we waked in the gray of morning it was almost freezing cold. Our first care was to start up the fires, which soon made the temperature in their vicinity more agreeable.

We had been told the night before that there was food enough at hand for our breakfasts, and, as soon as warm, we set about preparing it. While we were eating, a committee of ladies came in with the intent of getting our breakfasts for us. They seemed surprised that we should get it ourselves, but habit had made it the natural thing for us to do. We invited them to breakfast with us, and they seemed to enjoy it.

When our breakfast was finished, the first and all-important thing was to get our furloughs and leave for home. For a time it was undecided whether we had to report at Fort Snelling or could remain in the city, and there was considerable delay in getting the blanks and data for making out the furloughs. When all of these preliminaries were finally settled to suit the 'red-tape' officials who were controlling affairs about the capital, the necessary papers were made out, signed, and distributed. Then, for the first time since the 29th of April, 1861, the boys were free to go and come as they pleased—for 30 days.

When my work was done, it was too late for those going directly down the river to get away that night and, after arranging to go by a special in the morning and securing a place to lodge for the night, I spent the evening about the city.

Wednesday morning, February 17, at 6:30, we left St. Paul for our homes. The party consisted of about 30 whose homes were at Red Wing, Lake City, and Wabasha, traveling on two special stages drawn by four horses each. Stages were the only public conveyances in winter then, as no railroad had yet been built in Minnesota. The regular stages carried the mails and passengers and, when the regulars could not accommodate, specials were sent out. The weather had changed to warmer, and it was thawing some before noon, which hindered progress as it made the going bad in places, and the horses 'balled' and 'slumped' in some of the drifts.

We had dinner and changed horses at Hastings and found the going worse in the afternoon, so that we did not arrive in Red Wing until after dark. Bidding our comrades good-bye, the Red Wing boys separated to go to their respective homes. I will not attempt to follow them there or try to tell what happened on their arrival. I leave these matters and the enjoyment of their furloughs to the imagination. I have no doubt each one received the hearty, generous welcome he deserved, and that his homecoming was the happiest, sweetest experience of all his service.

The streets were dark, and it was so cold I covered my head to protect my ears, and hastened to find the home of my mother. She had moved to the place she occupied (on Seventh Street, between Bush and Eastern Avenue) since I had left home, but I had no difficulty in finding it. Not knowing when I could go, I had not advised anyone that I was coming and supposed that I should surprise my mother.

But I found her waiting and looking for me as she had the night before, with a generous supper all provided. To say that I was most heartily pleased to be at home again, with a whole body and in fairly good health, is a very mild use of language and does not half do justice to my feelings as I sat at the family table once more. I have not yet ceased to feel that mine was rare good fortune when compared with so many of those I knew.

I find this—written before I slept that night: "I am at home, at last, once more, and as gratefully glad as a mortal can be. I found all comfortable and almost beside themselves with joy at my return."

Many questions had been asked and answered before I retired, and the train of thoughts started by them kept me thinking till they faded from me in sleepy forgetfulness. I did not wake in the morning until called and was told at breakfast that some of the neighbors had already been to call on me.

I did not write much in my diary during my furlough days, although to write had become a habit. I find only this under date of Thursday, February 18—and that has such a flavor of self-laudation about it that I almost blush to copy it: "I have been receiving my friends today. Accepting their good wishes and permitting them to make a 'lion' of me, but I shall not endure it much longer. It is something of a task for a *modest man* to play he is 'a hero.'"

I will only add that our friends who called were, I have no doubt, sincere—though a bit over generous—with their compliments to the returning volunteers. Invitations to dinners, suppers, and visits were numerous and urgent, and we tried to accept them all. The days passed quickly and pleasantly, at least to us who had been so long deprived of social pleasures, and we did our best to make up for lost opportunities.

Thursday, March 17, we started to return to St. Paul, our brief respite from military routine ended. We traveled in large wagons and expected to make the trip in one day, but the ice was no longer safe, and the traveling overland so bad that we stopped at Willoughby's for the night, and did not reach Fort Snelling until the next day about noon.

That afternoon and the next most of the regiment got in. There were many men of other regiments in the fort, and there was scant room for more; however, a place was found, and we made the best of it. A few new recruits had been secured but somehow, while other regiments were being filled, but few had come to ours. This condition was discouraging and had its effect on those contemplating reenlisting, especially the 'non coms' looking ahead to promotion—as, under the rules of the War Department, there could be no new commissions until the regiment was filled.

While at home the boys had almost universally been urged by their friends to "let the second relief go to the front" for a time while they recuperated. We had not been many days at the fort before it was pretty certain that there would be no general reenlistment of the old men of the regiment. Effort seemed to cease. Furloughs were allowed and many again went home for short stays.

The time for final muster out came, and on the afternoon of April 28, 1864, the regiment assembled for its last dress parade. It formed on the plain to the west, outside the fort. Many people were present, and Gov. Miller was there to review it. As a military pageant, it was inferior to many others the regiment had given, but none the less it was an impressive occasion. Gov. Miller, who had been the Lieutenant Colonel of the regiment, made a short address that called forth a responsive cheer. Lieutenant Colonel Adams, in active command because of Col. Colvill's wounds, read a farewell order to the regiment.

Colonel Colvill was present but did not leave his carriage. As soon as the regiment was dismissed, the boys surrounded the carriage to bid him good-bye.

It was not until May 5, 1864, that the men were mustered for pay and discharged, as they had to await the coming of a paymaster. Meantime, the reenlisted men and recruits were formed into a battalion of two companies, and Company F as an organization ceased to exist. This new organization was known as the First Minnesota Battalion, and was practically a continuation of the regiment, reduced to a battalion of two companies. To this organization Company F contributed 23—15 of its members who had been with it in the field and 8 recruits who had joined it since it had come back to the fort.

Having followed the service of the company from its organization to its last muster, I feel that I can consistently close at this point. I will conclude the story of Company F by correcting some errors which in some unaccountable way have been injected into the official, published record of the company.

For example it would appear that the company had—recruits and all—125 enlisted men on its rolls, which is five more than the actual number. There never was a William H. Garrison in the company. John W. Hoffstetter, being under age, was taken home by his father before we left the fort. Neither was there serving in it a David H. Leaman, a John Lindergreen, or a William J. Skinner.[4] As a member of the company all the time it was out of the state, and as its orderly sergeant for more than a year, I had opportunity to know—and do know—that none of the five named above ever served with the company. And but one, Hoffstetter, ever had even a nominal connection with the company for a day. In four of the five we judge them to be typographical repetitions, with variation of initial letters, and overlooked in the proofreading.

4. These five names are given in the roster that accompanies Lochren's history of the First Minnesota, *Minnesota in the Civil and Indian Wars*, 1:58–59.

Epilogue

The thinned ranks answered

JAMES A. WRIGHT'S MILITARY CAREER did not end when the First Minnesota was mustered out on May 5, 1864. Along with 134 others, he reenlisted in the First Battalion Minnesota Infantry Volunteers—two companies of veterans of the First plus some recruits. Later in May, they were sent back east to the Army of the Potomac, back to the First Brigade of the Second Division of the Second Corps. They arrived too late for the bloody battles of the Wilderness (near Mine Run), Spotsylvania Court House, and Cold Harbor. They did participate in several minor engagements during the siege of Petersburg and were on picket duty at Appomattox, where they "helped gather up the defeated Southerners."[1]

Wright marched down Pennsylvania Avenue in the Grand Review on May 23, 1865. "It was an occasion to be remembered, and my heart beats faster as I recall it. The next day, May 24, I was an interested observer of Sherman's Army, in which my brother William H. Wright of the Second Minnesota served." He was finally mustered out on July 15, 1865.

He returned to Red Wing, where he lived with his mother, Amelia Wright, and his younger siblings Reuben and Sarah. By 1870, this family of four also had four male boarders living with them. James and one of the boarders, Stiles Raymond, were partners in a livery stable in town, the Red Wing Livery and Exchange Stable, located on Main Street near the railroad depot. This partnership lasted until March 1877.[2]

Wright was active in public affairs. He served as secretary of a new firemen's company, Cataract Engine Company No. 1, formed in September 1865. He attended the Republican county convention in May 1876 as a delegate from Red Wing and sat on the school board that year. He went to the annual reunions of the First Minnesota in 1870, 1871, 1874, and 1875. He joined the Shakespearean Syndicate, a local literary and social club formed in 1871.[3]

James A. Wright as a first lieutenant in the First Battalion of Minnesota Infantry Volunteers

Perhaps his most visible public service was his key role, as vice-president of the regimental veterans' group and Red Wing resident, in organizing the First's 1871 reunion in Red Wing.[4]

The Friday before they were to meet, Colonel Colvill lost a small "railroad war." Colvill was demanding that the St. Paul & Central Railroad pay him a larger sum for a right of way through his farm south of Red Wing. The railroad refused and offered a lesser amount. Colvill then built a small house on the railroad grade to block the tracklayers. Rather than wait for lengthy court proceedings, the company on June 16 sent a squad of eleven "brawny fellows" to clear the way. The colonel had neglected to send out pickets and was taken by surprise in his house. Armed with a revolver, "he went out and ordered them to leave," but they refused, "pulled the house down over his head," and removed "the Colonel, his wife and their household fixtures." The *Goodhue County Republican* noted, "The current report that the Colonel attempted to shoot any one is a mistake," and no one was injured in the fracas. Colvill had them arrested, and the matter went back to the courts. A former state attorney general, Colvill was convinced the railroad's charter was unconstitutional.[5]

On Monday, June 19, the evening train from the Twin Cities and the steamboats from downriver brought nearly one hundred veterans and family members into town. Those arriving at the depot "were received . . . with a salute from one

A photograph from Wright's "Soldier Album" of five First Minnesota men, probably in the spring of 1864, with their new commissions in the First Battalion of Minnesota Infantry Volunteers (Tuttle Studio, Third Street, St. Paul)

of the Napoleon guns" of the regiment's Sanford battery. "The regiment and citizens fell in line and marched to the Astor House, preceded by the tattered regimental colors and headed by the Noras Harpe Band." They fell to reminiscing and to expressing their disappointment that General Winfield Scott Hancock and Governor Horace Austin had failed to arrive as expected on the last steamboat.[6]

The next morning, June 20, was the tenth anniversary of their trip down the Mississippi (and their stop in Red Wing) on their way to the "seat of war." Pete Hoffman's drum sounded the call to assembly and they "formed in line" outside the Astor House to be "photographed by Mr. Kellogg," a Red Wing photographer and First Minnesota veteran.

They then marched through the downtown streets and up to Turner Hall, where they held a meeting not unlike the one that organized the Goodhue County Volunteers in April 1861. Local politicians spoke, and General Willis A. Gorman "replied on behalf of" the veterans. The roll call showed seventy present, and Company F understandably had the largest delegation—fourteen. Several motions were made and passed, including one to return the Sanford battery to the state arsenal. They adjourned in order to march to the homes of Captain Nathan Messick's widow and Major Abraham E. Welch's mother, "paying their respects to each."

Like the ladies of St. Paul, Chicago, Brooklyn, and other eastern cities years earlier, Red Wing's "best and fairest" spread "a bountiful dinner" that reminded the men of their June 1861 going-away stop and their welcome-home banquet in Red Wing on February 14, 1864, and elicited from them "one universal expression of delight." Senator Alexander Ramsey, Gorman, Colvill, and others gave after-dinner speeches. Colvill promised that Alfred Sully would be present at next year's reunion.

First Minnesota veterans in front of the First National Bank of Red Wing, June 20 or 21, 1871. James A. Wright (front left) holds a battle flag and stands by a gun from the Sanford battery donated to the regiment in honor of their service at Bull Run.

In the evening, Governor Austin arrived, and "the regiment marched to the music of the drum to pay their respects to the Governor, who responded to their call with some remarks." Then they attended a concert given by the Red Wing Orchestra at Music Hall, followed by "a pleasant dance, which was only terminated at 2 A.M., when every member" of the regiment "had voluntarily acknowledged himself ready to retire from the field."

On Wednesday, they left by steamboat, stagecoach, and train, and Wright's public service was completed. The *Republican* summed it all up in a front-page editorial:

> What deeds have been accomplished in the ten years. . . . At what cost to the old First Regiment . . . those deeds were done. What sacrifices the doing involved; what devotion it required; what patriotism it testified to. The thinned ranks answered. The maimed forms and limping steps responded. The armless sleeves bore witness. The battle-worn flags testified. The streaming eyes of stern men as they clasped the tatters of that "banner of beauty and glory," which they had followed so long, spoke to other tearful eyes that looked, and in a language that went to the heart.[7]

While citizens of Red Wing look on, about seventy veterans of the First Minnesota pose in Main Street, between Bush and Plumb Streets, at 8:15 A.M. on June 20, 1871, ten years after their departure from Fort Snelling for the war front (L. D. Kellogg of Red Wing).

The following week, a letter appeared in both Red Wing newspapers: "To the ladies, who did so much, and so well, we take off our hats, and give our warmest thanks, in large capitals . . . our comrades from other places bore away with them the most pleasant impressions of our city and citizens. Very truly yours, Jas. A. Wright."[8]

By that time, he may have been taking off his hat to a certain lady in town. In late November 1870, the First Baptist Church of Red Wing called Reverend Gideon Cole of Weymouth, Massachusetts, to be its pastor. Cole and his wife brought with them their daughter Hannah E. Miller, in her mid-twenties, and Frank Miller, her six-year-old son by a previous marriage. Sometime in the early 1870s, James Wright became acquainted with Hannah and courted her. Her father married them on March 15, 1876. They moved to a house on Fourth Street in Red Wing, west of Dakota Avenue, and Hannah taught at the Central School in town.[9]

Their decision to marry may have been hastened by the fact that her father was about to leave the Red Wing pastorate—on April 23, 1876.[10] Her parents returned to Massachusetts that spring. James and Hannah Wright remained in Red Wing.

The following March, Raymond and Wright sold their livery stable. On May 31, 1877, the *Republican* announced, "Mr. and Mrs. J. A. Wright left on Monday evening to make their home in New England." The school term was not over for another week, and a substitute had to fill in for Hannah Wright. No reason was given for the move. Wright's father-in-law may have found him a job in Massachusetts; his wife may have wanted to rejoin her parents and other relatives in the East; the livery stable may have failed (there were four others in Red Wing in 1876); or James may have decided to use the proceeds from selling the business to attend seminary (Jens Grondahl reported that Wright "studied theology for some time").[11]

By 1882, James had evidently given up any idea of going into the ministry. He worked as a carpenter in Beverly, Massachusetts, located across Salem Harbor from Salem. Four years later, he taught at a rural ungraded school just north of Beverly while Hannah taught first grammar at Washington School, near their house in town. In 1895 they were living in the same house as Reverend Cole, who was still preaching in the area; James served as commander of the GAR post and worked as a car finisher in the car shops of the Boston & Maine Railroad in Salem—a job he held for fifteen years. He joined the Order of United American Mechanics. Thirty-year-old Frank Miller had "removed to Boston," but their daughter Jennie lived at home.[12]

Amelia Wright had died in Red Wing on March 7, 1889. On October 20, 1898, James suffered a second loss when Hannah died suddenly while visiting an uncle in a nearby town. She was only fifty-three, "a lady of rare attainments and highly esteemed in the community."[13]

As a widower of only fifty-eight years, his life now revolved around his daughter (his only child), who married a son of a prominent local family (the Herricks) within a few years of her mother's death; his father-in-law, who owned the house James lived in for decades; his new post as an overseer of the poor, to which he was elected in 1902, and his job as the appointed clerk of the Overseers of the Poor (later the Board of Public Welfare); and, of course, his active role in the Grand Army of the Republic—various offices in Post 89, secretary of the Essex County GAR Association, and trustee of Chelsea Soldiers' Home.[14]

The GAR Hall on Cabot Street and the overseers' office on Broadway were only a few blocks from Cole's house at 28 Pond Street—and even the Overseers' City Poor Farm was less than a mile away—but his activities as a Civil War veteran took him on distant trips to scenic places for stimulating conversations with comrades—welcome diversions for a lonely widower. The 1906 trip to Minnesota for the GAR encampment likely was not the first such trip, though it may have been the most memorable. Certainly seeing old sights helped to stir Wright's interest in putting down on paper his own Civil War experiences. Jennie Wright accompanied her sixty-five-year-old father to Minneapolis. He was struck by the changes at Fort Snelling.

Two dozen First Minnesota veterans in Minneapolis
for the National GAR Reunion in August 1906

"When I visited it again last summer, not having been there in almost forty years, I found everything changed. The old ferry was replaced by an iron bridge that crossed you directly into what was then a walled fort—and all of the old fort recognizable was the blockhouse, near where the road used to go down the ravine, and the roundhouse, now overgrown with ivy. The place is now a much larger military station, with fine quarters, and occupied by infantry, cavalry, and artillery. The appearance of the country around it is also much changed by the growth of trees."[15]

They went over to St. Paul to see the new State Capitol, completed in 1905. They saw the two flags given to the regiment before it went to the "seat of war." "Both of these flags are now in the keeping of the state and the Stars and Stripes was carried in our first battle. I had the pleasure of looking at them . . . and pointing them out to my daughter while at the State Capitol."

Then it was on to Red Wing. "On the 18th day of August 1906, I stepped out of a Pullman car onto a paved walk in front of a handsome depot, within a few feet of where we had landed from the *Lady Franklin* in '55. Then there was not a rod of railroad in the state and the Pullman car was unknown. It was on my first visit in thirty years and the great change impressed me. I found a few of my former friends to greet me, scarcely recognizable with added years and time-changed

Flags and bunting decorate the hall for a First Minnesota reunion, about 1900, and the ladies serve food, as they did when the regiment traveled east in 1861

features. A few of the staunch, loyal comrades of the old days that 'tried men's souls'—and bodies—who had shared with us the vicissitudes of a great war, were also there to give me a comrade's welcome."

His brother William still lived in Red Wing. James attended a reunion of Company F at the home of former First Lieutenant Hezekiah Bruce. He praised the town to the reporter from the *Red Wing Republican:* "It is certainly a very thriving, beautiful city." He was especially amazed at "the growth of the trees. They were very small when I left the town." Now, with shade trees that actually shaded, "Red Wing very much resembles many of the New England towns."[16]

"The visit West has been a great treat to me," he assured the reporter, before he took the train back to Beverly.

While engaged in writing his history of Company F, he attended the GAR's 1910 national encampment in Atlantic City, New Jersey. He sat in "one of the great halls on the 'Million Dollar Pier' and spoke with Cordelia Hancock," who had been Colonel Colvill's nurse after he was wounded at Gettysburg. "Her brother was a doctor and was one of the volunteer surgeons who went to Gettysburg immediately after the fighting began, and she went with him to assist in nursing. They did all they could for him while he remained on the field, and, when it was decided to remove him, they both went with him to Harrisburg. The transfer was made in a freight car, with the colonel lying on a stretcher suspended from the roof of the car, and either she or her brother stood by it to steady it all the way." Wright "asked her to write me a sketch covering the time of her care of Col. Colvill." But she had not sent it to him by the time he finished his memoir.

Wright was a delegate representing the Massachusetts GAR, and he was impressed with his surroundings: "Atlantic City is an entertainment place of large proportions, and the famous 'board walk' proved an ideal place for general concentration. What would be a badly congested crowd in most places moves there easily and smoothly—without fuss or friction. It was easy to find people by just waiting and in this way I met many members of the old corps—because they wore their badges. While there I met comrades from the 15th Massachusetts, 19th Maine, and 82nd New York. I also met comrades from the 69th, 71st, 72nd and 106th Pennsylvania (Philadelphia Brigade). And of the 19th and 20th Massachusetts, and 42nd and 59th New York. Did not meet any of the 7th Michigan."

He could not recognize men by their face or name, "yet it was well worth the trip to Atlantic City just to meet them. It was only necessary to

James A. Wright, about 1900,
shortly before he wrote his memoir

name my regiment to get as hearty a welcome as anyone could reasonably ask for." Presumably he received a similar welcome in July 1913, when he attended the fiftieth anniversary event at Gettysburg, along with seven others from Company F and some fifty thousand veterans and spectators.[17]

By this time, Colonel Colvill had died—while in Minneapolis at the Soldiers' Home on June 12, 1905, the day before he was to join in the procession carrying those battle flags from the old Capitol to the new one.[18]

Less than a year after the Atlantic City trip, Wright completed his memoir of Company F and the First Minnesota, only to see it gather dust in Jens Grondahl's office. Martin McGinnis and his comrades did not act on Grondahl's suggestion to publish Wright's work. They appointed a five-man commission to supervise the writing of an official history of the First Minnesota that came out in 1916, authored by one of their number, Return I. Holcombe.[19] Five years later, Wright's typescript was donated to the Minnesota Historical Society, to become a footnote to Folwell's history of the state.

That year, he described himself to Folwell as "somewhat the worse for the fourscore-and-one years, but still fairly preserved—considering." He had almost another fifteen years left, but he never saw his work published, and he never returned to Minnesota—although he corresponded for years with comrades from the First and other Minnesotans interested in its history. In July 1928, he wrote a lengthy letter recalling Colonel Colvill just before President Calvin Coolidge was to speak at the dedication of the Colvill monument in Cannon Falls.[20]

James A. Wright died at the age of ninety-five on August 25, 1936, at the home of his daughter, Jennie C. Herrick, in Beverly, where he had lived for several years. That was one year after the death of the "last man" of Company B's Last Man's Club. Wright may have been the last man of the Old First to pass away.[21] He was buried "with full military honors" on Thursday, August 27, at Central Cemetery in Beverly. A Salem newspaper columnist noted, "His addresses before school assemblies on Patriotic day observance will long be remembered, as also his fine, upstanding spirit as a real patriotic citizen in whatever field duty called him."[22]

Wright in his GAR *uniform at*
a Memorial Day observance
in Beverly Massachusetts, about 1930

1. Moe, *Last Full Measure,* 303–5; Folwell, *Minnesota,* 2:302–3.

2. U.S. Census, 1870, Goodhue County, City of Red Wing, microfilm, MHS; *Pryor & Company's Red Wing City Directory* (Red Wing, 1876), 86; *Goodhue County Republican,* March 8 and 15, 1877, both p. 1, and March 22, 1877, p. 4.

3. *History of Goodhue County* (Red Wing: Wood, Alley, and Company, 1878), 395; *Goodhue County Republican,* May 18, 1876, p. 4; *Pryor's Red Wing City Directory* (1876), 43; "Minutes of the First Minnesota Voluntary Infantry Association, 1869–1932," Minute Book, 10, 24, 31, MHS.

4. Wright was vice president of the regimental association for 1870–71, presumably so that he might arrange the 1871 reunion; "Minutes of the First Minnesota Volunteer Infantry Association," 6, 10. Also he signed the post-event letter of thanks in the Red Wing newspapers "on behalf of" Company F; *Red Wing Argus,* June 29, 1871, p. 4.

5. *Goodhue County Republican,* June 22, 1871, p. 4; *Red Wing Argus,* June 22, 1871, p. 4.

6. Here and below, *Red Wing Argus,* June 22, 1871, p. 4; *Goodhue County Republican,* June 22, 1871, p. 4.

7. *Goodhue County Republican,* June 22, 1871, p. 1.

8. *Red Wing Argus,* June 29, 1871, p. 4; *Goodhue County Republican,* June 29, 1871, p. 4.

9. *Goodhue County Republican,* December 1, 1870, p. 4, and March 16, 1876, p. 4; Minnesota State Census, 1875, Goodhue County, City of Red Wing, microfilm, roll 8, p. 728–29, MHS; *Pryor's Red Wing City Directory* (1876), 98.

10. *Goodhue County Republican,* April 20, 1876, p. 1.

11. *Goodhue County Republican,* May 31, 1877, p. 4; *Pryor's Red Wing City Directory* (1876), 107; Grondahl to Folwell, November 15, 1921, Box 49, Folwell Papers.

12. *The Beverly Directory, 1882* (Boston: Sampson, Davenport, and Co., 1882), 84; *The Beverly Directory, 1886* (Boston: Sampson, Murdock, and Co., 1886), 123; *A Directory of the City of Beverly . . . for 1895–96,* 44, 95, 124, 152; *City of Beverly, Massachusetts—Past and Present: Progress and Prosperity* (Beverly: R. J. Lawton and J. H. Burgess, 1904), 28.

13. *Red Wing Republican,* March 9, 1889, p. 3; *Salem Evening News,* October 21, 1898, p. 2.

14. *City of Beverly—Past and Present,* 28; *1906 Annual Report of Overseers of the Poor; Directory for Salem and Beverly,* 32:777, 884, 885, 892; *Salem Evening News,* August 26, 1936, p. 5; *Centenary Handbook of the Washington Street Congregational Church* (1937), in Beverly Public Library; Edith Herrick Milhorat, *The Herrick Family in England and America* (Baltimore: Gateway Press, 1984), 61–75; *Beverly City Directory, 1904* (Beverly: Crowley & Lunt, 1904), 302. That Reverend Cole owned the house is clear from *Valuation and Assessment of the City of Beverly for the Year 1906* (Beverly: Beverly Printing Co., 1907), 102, 136.

15. Here and below, the quoted passages are from Wright's typescript memoir, unless otherwise indicated.

16. *Red Wing Republican,* August 22, 1906, p. 7.

17. "Minutes of First Minnesota Voluntary Infantry Association," 170; "Scrapbook of clippings relating to the First Minnesota at Gettysburg," MHS.

18. Moe, *Last Full Measure,* 310.

19. Moe, *Last Full Measure,* 307–8.

20. Wright to Folwell, December 14, 1921, Box 49, Folwell Papers; Wright to Mabel Marvin, and Wright to Captain Hugh R. Soper, both July 18, 1928, both in Minnesota Infantry First Regiment Volunteers Association Papers, 1895–1928, MHS.

21. *Salem Evening News,* August 26, 1936, p. 5; Moe, *Last Full Measure,* 311–12.

22. *Salem Evening News,* August 27, p. 7, and August 29, p. 8, both 1936.

Appendix

A. *First Battle of Bull Run*

The loss of the company was: 8 killed, or died of their wounds; wounded, 12; and missing, 3—for a total of 23. The killed and mortally wounded were: J. P. Garrison, J. M. Lee, George McKinley, H. J. Rush, J. F. Sallee, A. G. Schofield, E. Thomas, and J. M. Underwood. The wounded were: First Lieutenant A. E. Welch, C. N. Harris, J. Barrows, H. Burgtorpf, C. L. Hubbs, J. Brown, H. R. Childs, C. E. Hudson, G. D. Leighton, Hans Holstead, C. W. Merritt, and E. F. Pitcher. The captured were: J. W. Imeson, Fred E. Miller, and Merritt G. Standish.

My personal acquaintance with many in the company was limited to the time we had met as soldiers, and I regret that I cannot write of them with a greater knowledge of their individual and family histories.

1. **Joseph P. Garrison** received his death wound while near the roadway, was carried to the hospital, and died in the hands of the enemy. He was a student at Hamline University, and his home was at Mantorville. He had a sister, Ella, who also attended the university, but we have no further information of his people. As a fellow student and soldier, I knew him for the splendid young fellow he was. Earnest and impulsive, warm-hearted and generous, ambitious and cheerful, he was one who would have made the world better for having lived in it, and it seemed a misfortune that death should meet him at the threshold of active life.

2. **George McKinley** was another young man of the best type, whom a brief acquaintance taught us to love and respect. His home, I think, was in Cannon Falls, but I knew none of his people and never saw him until after enlistment. Some years since, I had a letter from his brother, Rev. William McKinley, a Methodist minister, who was trying to locate his burial place. I did not learn that he was successful. He was a distant relative of the late President McKinley, I have been told.

3. **Hiram J. Rush** was a Red Wing boy and well known about the city. He was a nephew of C. H. Brink of Red Wing. In his brief service as a soldier, he proved his good soldierly qualities and sealed his loyalty with his blood in his first fight.

4. I only knew **John M. Lee** from our short association in the company, and I know nothing of his people. I cannot recall where his home was, but I think it was in Roscoe. He was a sturdy young fellow of about 18 and made a good record as a soldier.

5. **James F. Sallee** came to the company while at the fort, three or four weeks before we left the state, and but little is known concerning him. He was about 25 years old and a native of Indiana, but nothing is known of his people. He was not of a disposition to make friends quickly, but he had the right kind of material in him, and was always prompt and reliable on duty.

6. **Amos G. Schofield** was another that I did not know until we met as soldiers. He was, I think, from the town of Roscoe—possibly, Cherry Grove—and was made one of the corporals when the company was organized. He was a noble fellow, and appeared to be about what was desirable for a soldier—quiet, strong, cheerful, and ready. In response to the call of President Lincoln, he offered his services and his life, if necessary, that the "nation might live," and the fortunes of war closed the account with the record of Bull Run.

7. **Elijah F. Thomas** was another of the Hamline boys with whom I had a schoolmate acquaintance, but about whose people I knew very little. His home was not in Red Wing, but somewhere in the county. I think that it was in Lillian. He was a young man of ordinary abilities but earnest and persevering in his studies. He left them and entered the army from an earnest conviction of duty, and his heart was in the struggle. He was severely wounded and died from the effects of it, some weeks later, in a rebel prison.

8. **James M. Underwood** was another whose acquaintance I made after we had enlisted. As we were strangers until the war brought us together, I cannot now place his home location. Wherever it may have been, his service as a soldier was creditable to it, and himself, and was too soon ended in his first battle.

Of the wounded at Bull Run who never again joined the company:

9. **First Lieutenant A. Edward Welch** of Red Wing—and a Hamline boy, too—was wounded and captured. He was a son of Chief Justice William H. Welch of the old territorial days, and, at the time of enlistment, was reading law and fitting himself for active life. He was of medium height, rather slender, and his active, energetic disposition was not fully matched by his physical ability. He was, I believe, the first to put his name on the rolls, the drillmaster of the company, and its military exponent as long as he was with it.

It was a distinct loss to the company and regiment when his wounds and a later promotion took him from both. Disabled by wounds, he fell into the hands of the enemy, was taken to Richmond, and confined in a prison pen. His was not the disposition to submit to imprisonment without an earnest effort to escape, and, as soon as he was out of the hands of the doctors, he began to try to get away. He managed to evade the guards and escape from the city. He took to the woods in an effort to reach Fortress Monroe but was captured one morning by a farmer with a shotgun, and was returned to the prison. He was later exchanged and commissioned major of the Fourth Regiment.

His health was somewhat broken, and he was at home on sick leave when the Indian outbreak occurred in August 1862. His active spirit could not be restrained in such an emergency, and he at once offered his services to organize and direct operations against the Indians. There was at this time many men of the Third Regiment on parole since their capture at Murfreesboro. Some of these were at Benton Barracks, Missouri, and others were in the state. It was not considered a violation of the parole to serve against the Indians. These men, to the number of about 270—at their own request—were assembled for the protection of the frontiers. Major Welch, by his own request, was placed in command, with Lieutenant R. C. Olin (who had escaped capture) to assist him and the only other commissioned officer present. They were organized into companies—noncommissioned officers being detailed to act as commissioned officers—and made forced marches to Fort Ridgely. On the morning of September 23, 1862, they came in contact with a body of the Sioux not far from the Lower Sioux Agency, and a severe engagement followed. In this affair, Major Welch had his leg broken by a bullet, from which he suffered as long as he lived. As soon as able, he returned to duty, but his health was too seriously impaired to stand the hardships of campaigning, and he died at Nashville, Tennessee, February 1, 1864. With a constitution better able to stand the demands of active service—and a more favorable fortune giving him immunity from bullets—he would have worn an eagle or a star before the war ended, with credit to himself and the state.

10. **Sergeant Charles N. Harris** was another of the Hamline boys who cast in their lot with the Goodhue Volunteers to 'fight for Uncle Sam.' He was a young fellow of about 22, of fine appearance and qualifications, standing about six feet and four inches in height, and well-proportioned. He was the son of a Methodist minister, and the Methodists were fighters in those days out 'in the West Country.' His home was in Richfield, but he was living in Red Wing, attending the university and intending to take up the study of law. When the war came, he laid aside all personal matters and placed himself at the disposal of the government. He was made one of the sergeants when the company was organized and took great interest in organization and drill. A rebel bullet shattered his shoulder at Bull Run, and he was captured and taken to Richmond. He recovered, was paroled, sent home, and finally exchanged.

It was supposed at the time that he was dead, and, under that belief, his obituary was printed and funeral services were held. It was thus that he had an opportunity to read of his own funeral. His arm was withered from his wound, but he was still desirous of remaining in the service, but he could not pass the physical examinations and was discharged. After this, he had a position on the Capital Police force and, later, studied law and was admitted to the bar. He became a judge in Nevada, and afterwards made his home in California, where he died about 1907.

11. **Corporal John Barrows** was a Red Wing boy, somewhat older than the most of us—a quiet, self-contained fellow who was not easily disturbed. He was chosen one of the color corporals when the regiment was organized and was shot in the shoulder at Bull Run and captured. He was found to be so disabled by his wounds that it was necessary to discharge him, though retained in the service for some time after.

12. **Corporal Fred. E. Miller** was another of the Red Wing–Hamline boys who left their studies for the 'tented field.' He was but 18 years old but mature beyond his years and was made one of the corporals at the organization of the company. At Bull Run he was captured, having gone with a wounded comrade to the hospital. He was a prisoner for some months and then paroled and sent to Benton Barracks for exchange. While there, he was detailed as a clerk and never rejoined the regiment. It was understood that he was commissioned in a colored regiment and attained the rank of major. He was a bright, active young fellow and—wherever he was—we are sure he gave a good account of himself. He was that kind.

13. **Hans Holsted** was another of the company that was disqualified in his first battle and never returned to the company. He was an elderly man to us boys—although only 35—and I believe had been in the Swedish army. I have not a positive recollection of his personality or home but think that he belonged in Wanamingo or Cherry Grove. On his release from captivity, he was found to be disabled and was discharged.

Of the other members of the company who were wounded and captured, those who were wounded and escaped, and all of those who 'fought and ran away,' I do not speak personally now, as they 'lived to fight another day' and the battle of Bull Run did not break their connection with the company—only for the time of imprisonment.

B. Peninsular Campaign

1. I think that there were three of the company sent away at this time (ca. June 26, 1862) and one of them was **Hiram A. Skinner,** who died before they reached the general hospital. I regret that I cannot now recall anything of his people or his history previous to joining the company. He came to us at the fort the 29th of May 1861, and we knew nothing of him before that time or ever saw any of his family, so far as I can now recall. He was a tall, slender, young fellow of nineteen with brown hair and blue eyes. His educational advantages had been limited—or not well-improved—and he was reserved and undemonstrative in his deportment generally.

2. **Edward E. Davis** was a native of Ipswich, Massachusetts, and was living at Zumbrota when he enlisted. He lived until after his exchange and died in the hospital at Hampton. He was about twenty-five and unmarried. Davis was of a

reserved temperament and apparently took but little interest in the fun and sociability of the camp, but he was a faithful and reliable man and had the respect of his comrades, and came to a soldier's death in the line of duty.

3. **Ferris Johnson** was, I think, born in New York and lived in Cherry Grove before enlistment. He was twenty-six and unmarried.

4. **Martin Willman** was about thirty years old, and I cannot now recall that he belonged in Goodhue County. He joined the company about the middle of May, 1861, at Fort Snelling. I judge he was of German birth or extraction.

Johnson and Willman were of medium height and sturdy build. The former a 'brunette' and the latter a 'blond.' Both were fine-looking fellows, full of life and sociability. Cheerful and hopeful, they apparently took the good and bad of soldier life as it came and good-naturedly met all of its requirements. They were two excellent men and soldiers, who won their chevrons by good conduct, wore them worthily and with credit to themselves and the company. Good fellows and good comrades, faithful and true to the last drop of their heart's blood, they deserved a better fate.

Index

Page numbers in italic refer to pictures and captions.

Abbott, Marion F., 1st Minn., 298, 310
Abolitionism, 44
Adams, Charles P., 1st Minn., 209, 302, 399, 407
African Americans, 41; attitudes toward, 36; status during war, 44; as "contraband of war," 47; punished for alcohol sale, 87; visit to Bull Run battlefield, 278–79; attacked during draft riots, 322n1
Alcohol, prohibited, 48; punishment for traffic in, 87–88; use by enlisted men, 108; Gorman arrests drunk, 179; as plunder, 233; punishment for use, 396
Aldrich, Rep. Cyrus, 40, 398
Alexandria, Va., hostility of civilians, 43, 347; damaged during war, 349
Anabasis, 15
Antietam, battle of, 198–206; casualties, 203–4, 206; promotions after, 209; area visited, 321
Appomattox, Va., surrender, 421
Armistead, Lewis, 307–8
Arms, *see* Artillery; Rifles and muskets
Army of the Potomac, disease and, 137–38; supply trains threatened, 142; after Seven Days' Battles, 170; McClellan's address to, 171; loyalty of, 225; weather as enemy of, 251; weakened condition of, 268, 271; at Gettysburg, 289; role of, 355
Army of Virginia, 176
Artillery, at first Bull Run, 54, 57; of gunboats, 120; Sanford Battery presented, 124–25; "Railroad Monitor," mounted artillery, 148; at White Oak Swamp, 156, 157; during Seven Days' Battles, 157–58, 165–66, 167; at Malvern Hill, 165–66; midnight shelling, 173–74; at Antietam, 199–200,

201–2; enfilade fire, 200, 307; shells used as cooking tripods, 211–12; volunteers for duty with, 215, 217; at Fredericksburg, 230–31, 237–39, 245; at Gettysburg, 294–95, 305–6; near Bristoe Station, 360
Ashby's Gap, 220
Atlantic, ocean steamer, 327, 329–30
Atlantic City, N.J., GAR encampment, xvi, 428–29
Atlantic Ocean, 111, 346
Austin, Gov. Horace, 423, 424

Bachelor, Frank, 53, 242
Bachelor, James F., 1st Minn., 233, 296, 298–99, 310
Bachelor, Josiah, 1st Minn., 242
Badges, corps, 97, 252, 309
Baker, Abraham, 1st Minn., 343
Baker, Edward D., 71st Penn. (1st California), 84–85
Ball, John, 1st Minn., 198, 209, 256, 263, 272, 351, 362, 410, 411; at Gettysburg, 295–96, 297–99; at Bristoe Station, 364–66
Balloon surveillance, 114–15
Ball's Bluff, Va., 81, 84–85
Baltimore, Md., 40
Baltimore and Ohio Railroad, 102
Banks, Nathaniel P., 71
Barber, Horatio N., 1st Minn., 206, 309
Barricades, "Fort Sully," 131; star forts, 133; construction described, 135
Barrows, John, 1st Minn., 49, 434
"Battle-worn Banner," by Grant P. Robinson, 401–3
Bayer, Andrew, 1st Minn., 189, 365
"Bean holes," described, 74–75

Benner, Jefferson, 1st Minn., 210

Bennett, William D., 49

Berdan, Charley, 1st Minn., 365, 366

Berdan Sharpshooters, 108–9, 131, 185

Berryville, Va., 102–3

Bevans, Henry T., 49, 96

Bevans, Milton ("Mit"), orderly, 276–79, 280

Bible, references to, 110–11, 178, 243–44

Big Bethel, Va., 112, 177

Bivouacking, described, 98–99

Blackburn's Ford, 50, 369–70

Bolivar Heights, Va., 101

Bondurant, Cyrus, 1st Minn., 309

Bonner, Jeff, 1st Minn., 380

Booby traps, 118

Boonsboro, Md., 197

Botts, J. Minor, 353

Brack, William A., 1st Minn., xi

Brandy Station, Va., 353–55

Breastworks, "Fort Sully," 131; star forts, 133; construction described, 135

Bridges, pontoon, 99, 177, 377–78; construction of, 122–24, 228–29, 231–32, 261, 265

Brigades, provisional and temporary, 212–13, 325, 348, 350. *See also* Specific brigades

Brightwood camp, 69–70

Bristoe Station, Va., 348; terrain, 358; battle of, 363–67

Brooklyn Eagle, newspaper, 343–44

Brooks, Rev. Cyrus, 22

Brooks, Cyrus A., 1st Minn., 22

Brown, John, abolitionist, 99, 102, 213, 349–50

Brown, John, wagoner, 68

Bruce, Hezekiah, 1st Minn., xi, 49, 96, 260, 263, 351, 384, 414, 428; assumes command, 368

Buck's Hill, 54

Bull Run, battles of, first campaign, 48–53; account of first battle, 53–60; retreat called, 58; casualties, 59–60, 65, 431–34; aftermath, 61–63; tactical failures at, 64; 1st Minn. commended for action, 65; newspaper accounts of first battle, 66; anniversary of first battle, 172–73; second battle, 182; visit to battlefield in *1863,* 276–79

Burgtorf, Henry, 1st Minn., 271, 309

Burials, duty described, 131–32, 205; and contagion, 137; informal truce to permit,

205; on Bull Run battlefield, 278; of Phillip Hamline, 311

Burns, William W., Philadelphia Brigade, 97, 133–34, 136, 149, 150

Burnside, Ambrose E., at Antietam, 202; replaces McClellan, 225; replaced by Hooker, 251

Burritt, William H., 1st Minn., 215

Butler, Benjamin, 44n8

Camp life, Fort Snelling, 21–22; amusements, 90–91; safeguards, 105; monotony of, 176–77

"Camp Misery," 113

Camp Stone, 77, *78*

Carroll's Provisional Brigade, 325, 348, 350

Castle William, N.Y., 331–32

Casualties, First Bull Run, 59–60, 65, 431–34; from disease, 78; siege of Yorktown, 117; Fair Oaks, 129–30; during Peninsular Campaign, 152, 434–35; friendly fire, 159–60, 190–91, 381; Antietam, 203–4, 205, 206; during bridge construction, 228–29; Fredericksburg, 262, 267; from sunstroke, 274–75; Gettysburg, 297, 298–99, 301–2, 309–10; self-inflicted wounds, 370; from hypothermia and exhaustion, 383, 385

Catlett's Station, Va., 360–61

Catoctin Mountains, 196–97

Cavalry duty, 214–16

Centreville, Va., 184–85, 348

Chancellorsville, Va., campaign, 257–67

Chantilly, battle of, 186–87

Chaplains, Neill, Edward D., 24, 33, 94, 102, 172; Peninsular Campaign sermon, 116; Conwell, F. A., 254, 340

Charlestown, Va., 102, 213–14

Chicago, Ill., 38, 404–5

Chicago Tribune, newspaper, 405; Minnesota volunteers described, 38

Chickahominy River and swamps, 121–22, 126, 131; bridge construction, 122–24

Chickamauga, battle of, 351–52

Children, 335–36

Childs, Henry R., 1st Minn., 56, 315–16, *333,* 352, 356

Christian Commission, 327–28

Christmas, 91–92, 249–50, 395

Civilians, gifts from, 31, 91–92; at Chicago, 37–38; at Baltimore, 40; hostility of, 40, 349; Soldier's Rests or Retreats provided by, 107, 404–5; sensitivity toward, 206, 273, 331; at Antietam, 206–7; antiwar factions, 252; hospitality of, 277–78, 286; at Gettysburg, 317; at New York, N.Y., 334–44; neutrality of, 353

Clark, Calvin P., 1st Minn., 49, 96, 152

Colling, W. H., 1st Minn., 106

Color guards, 30, 64, 313, 363

Colvill, William, Jr., 49, 96, 198, 280, 429, 428; elected captain of Goodhue Volunteers, xv, 14; bravery during Peninsular Campaign, 153; wounded at Malvern Hill, 158; promoted after Antietam, 209; visit to Bull Run, 276–79; arrested for insubordination, 285–86; at Gettysburg, 292, 301, 302; attends banquet, 401; farewell to regiment, 420; "railroad war," 422; monument in Cannon Falls, 429

Colville, William, Jr., *see* Colvill, William, Jr.

Commendations, after First Bull Run, 65; presentation of Sanford Battery, 124–25; from Gen. Burns, 152; from Maj. Gen. Sumner, 173

Company F, 1st Minn., reunion of *1906,* 5; first active duty, 45–47; commissioned officers of, 49; picket duty along the Potomac River, 72–73; numbers in spring *1862,* 94–95; commended for Peninsular Campaign service, 152. *See also* specific battles

Confederate soldiers, wounded, 189–90; opinion of, 254; communication with, 270; deserters, 270–71

Conrad's Ferry, 73–74

Conwell, F. A., chaplain, 254, 340

Cooking, mess basics, 49; "bean holes" described, 74–75; artillery shells used as tripods, 211–12; on board steamboats, 329

Corps de Armee, organization into, 106

Corps of Observation, 75; officers promoted, 95

Couch, Darius N., 240

Crews, Rev. Hooper, 405

Crews, Nancy, xiii

Croffut, William A., journalist, 52

Culpepper, Va., 349–50

Dakota Indians, 23, 25; *1862* war, 32, 180, 433

Dana, Napoleon Jackson Tecumseh, commands 1st Minn., 78; opinion of regiment, 83–84; general of 3rd Brigade, 95, 97; at Malvern Hill, 158; wounded, 209

Darnestown, Md., 71

Daucher, George, 1st Minn., 117

Davis, Almeron, 1st Minn., 267, 309

Davis, Edward E., 1st Minn., 152, 434–35

Davis, Jonas, 1st Minn., 296, 299

Debates, as recreation, 93–94

Dooker, Artemus L. M., 1st Minn., 271, 309

Defenses, log barricades, 131, 133, 135

De Gray, James, 1st Minn., 302

Dehn, John, 1st Minn., 313

Demarest, David B., 1st Minn., 302

Deserters, 184; from Confederate Army, 270–71; punishment of, 371–72; petition for leniency, 376–77

Devens, Charles, Jr., 15th Mass., 84–85

Diaries, 316; as memoir source, xi

Dike, William H., 1st Minn., 23

Discipline, 26, 247; unseasoned soldiers and, 244–45

Discourse, influences on memoir, xvi

Disease, 48, 55, 352; at Camp Stone, 78–80; Invalid Corps, 79; malarial diseases, 79–80, 135, 137–38; Peninsular Campaign, 120–21, 135; dysentery, 135, 138, 175–76; typhoid, 137; Army of Potomac threatened by, 137–38; treatments for, 156–57; sunstroke, 274–75

Dispatches, 377

Dixie, a young soldier, 113–14

Dolphins, 346

Donnelly, Ignatius, politician, 14, 398–99

Downie, Mark W., 1st Minn., 302, 352, 363, 369

Draft Riots, New York City, 322, 327, 332, 340, 342–43

Dress parades, 30–31, 333, 337

Duffy, Wilbur, 372

Dugout shelters, described, 249

Dysentery, 135, 138, 175–76

Edwards Ferry, 72–73; battle account, 81–84

Eighth Ohio, 3rd Division, 324, 325

Eighty-Second New York, 151, 245, 294, 298, 397

Eleventh Corps, reputation of, 290

Eleventh New York (Fire Zouaves), 42n5, 43, 45

Ellison, Augustus, 1st Minn., 135, 412

Eltham's Landing, 120

Emancipation Proclamation, 208, 209–10

Empire City, steamboat, 342, 345–46

Engineers, 228, 261

Enlistment, volunteering compared with formal, 15–16; oath of, 23; lengths of, 25–26, 256; lack of new recruits, 268; draft riots, 322, 327, 332, 340, 342–43; reenlistment discussed, 352, 395–96; end of term, 420

Executions, 371–72

Fair Oaks, Va., battle of, 124–29; casualties, 129–30; aftermath described, 131–32

Families, attitudes toward volunteering, 16; pay allotment to, 69; concern for, 89–90, 193–94, 196, 320; last notes to, 386

Farrer, Waldo, 1st Minn., 302

Fatigue duty, 21, 112–13

Ferries, lazy man's (rope) ferry, 20, *20*

Fifteenth Massachusetts, 84–85, 146, 151, 241, 285, 294, 298, 371, 380, 384

Fifth Wisconsin, 332

Fiftieth New York (engineers), 228–29

First Brigade, 3rd Division, formed, 43; assembled for Bull Run campaign, 49

First Brigade, Stone's Division, formation of, 77; composition of, 97

First California (71st Pennsylvania), 84–85, 97, 307

First Minnesota, The, newspaper, 103–4

First Minnesota Battalion, formed, 420; soldiers pictured, *422*

First Minnesota Infantry Regiment, volunteers mustered at Fort Snelling, 22; war-whoop of, 23; Company F, 45–47, 49, 72–73, 94–95; commendations, 65, 124–25, 152, 173; discipline praised, 74; band of, 106; Sanford Battery presented, 124–25; assigned to Zook's temporary brigade, 212–13; cavalry duty reassignments, 214–16; poem about, 401–3; *1871* reunion, 422–25, *423, 424;* official history of, 429. *See also* Specific battles and individuals

Flags, Minnesota state flag, 29–30; Union flag of regiment, 31; color guard at Bull Run,

64; presented by Gov. Ramsey, 253; displayed at capitol, 427. *See also* Color guards

Floyd, John B., secretary of war, 25

Folwell, William Watts, historian, xii–xiii, 429

Food, *see* Provisions

Foraging, 50–51, 175–76, 221, 387

Fort Abercrombie, Minn., 25, 27, 31

Fort Columbus, N.Y., 331–32

Fort Monroe, Va., 111

Fort Ridgely, Minn., 25, 30

Fort Ripley, Minn., 25

Fort Runyon, Va., 63

Fort Snelling, Minn., account of training at, 20–33

"Fort Sully," 131

Fort Sumter, S.C., 12–13, 106

Forty-second New York (Tammany), 73–74, 84–85, 97

Fourth Pennsylvania, 52

Franklin, William B., 49, 65, 251

Frary, Edrick J., 1st Minn., 366

Frederick, Md., 195

Fredericksburg, Va., battles of, terrain described, 229–30; account of first battle, 229–40; casualties at, 240, 247–48; account of second battle, 261–67; war damage described, 273

Friendly fire casualties, 159–60, 190–91, 381

Frontier duty, 25, 27–28, 31–32, 433

Gaines' Mill, Va., battle of, 141

Gambling, 90, 253, 323

GAR, *see* Grand Army of the Republic

Garrison, Joseph P., 1st Minn., 59, 431

Garrison, William H., 420

Gettysburg, Pa., battle of, strength of Army of the Potomac, 271; terrain described, 288; command assignments, 289n1, 292; account of battle, 292–318; Cemetery Ridge position, 293–94, 303; artillery, 294–95, 305–6; casualties, 297, 298–99, 301–2, 309–10; 1st Minn. charge, 301–2; Pickett's charge, 307; hand-to-hand combat, 308; surrenders, 308; National Cemetery dedicated, 377; 50th anniversary event, 429

Gibbon, John, 197, 256n3, 265

Goodhue County Republican, newspaper, xv, 422, 424

Goodhue County Volunteers, mass enlistment of, xiv–xv; community meeting to form, xxv, 14; described, 12, 15; origins of, 12–13; sworn in, 23. *See also* First Minnesota Infantry Regiment

Gordon, "Uncle Billy," 15

Gorman, Willis A., 23–24, 423; speech by, 30; response to hostile citizens, 40; orders per theft, 50–51; brigade commander, 77, 97; baptism "competition" anecdote, 91; speeding horse anecdote, 174–75; arrest of drunk by, 179; after Antietam, 209

Governor's Island, N.Y., 330–34

Grand Army of the Republic (GAR), xv, 426–29

"Grand Chassé," 358

Grand Review, 421

Grapevine Bridge, 122–24

Griffin, Charles, 205

Grinnell, George W., 1st Minn., 215

Grondahl, Jens K., editor and publisher, xi–xii, 6

Grow, Enos F., 1st Minn., xi, xvi

Hall, Norman J., 7th Mich., 231

Halleck, Henry W., 193

Hamlin, Phil, *see* Hamline, Phillip

Hamline, Phillip, 1st Minn., 33, 94, 192, 218–19, 299, 309, 311–13; faith of, 94, 267

Hamline University, founded, xiv; pictured, *13*

Hammer, Nicholas, 1st Minn., 15, 129–30

Hancock, Cordelia, 428

Hancock, Winfield Scott, 205, 301, 423

Hand, Dr. Daniel W., 1st Minn., 70–71, 156

Harmon, William, 1st Minn., 302

Harpers Ferry, 208–15; described, 101–2

Harpers ferry muskets, 31

Harris, Charles N., 1st Minn., 33, 49, 52, 65, 96, 194, 433

Harris, Eliza, 268–69

Hartranft, John Frederick, 52

Hawes, Jim, Sharpshooter, 109

Hawk Eye, steamboat, 30

Hazen, Benjamin, 1st Minn., 106

Heald, Dan, Sharpshooter, 109

Heffelfinger, Chris, 1st Minn., 242, 302

Heintzelman, Samuel P., 49, 147, 149

Henry House Hill, Bull Run battlefield, 55–57

Herrick, Jennie C. Wright, 426, 429

History, author's sense of, 6–7, 99, 102, 110, 116, 120, 121, 178, 213, 235, 281–82, 288–89, 302, 398, 427–28

Hoffman, Harry, sheriff, 333

Hoffman, Pete, 1st Minn., 106

Hoffstetter, John W., 420

Holcombe, Return I., 429

Holidays, Christmas, 91–92, 249–50, 395; Independence Day, 171, 314; Thanksgiving, 226, 379

Holsted, Hans, 1st Minn., 434

Homecoming, ordered to return to St. Paul, 396–97; banquet, 399–401; Red Wing, Minn., 412–14; St. Paul, Minn., 415–18; newspaper account, 416

Homesickness, 90, 212, 269–70, 328–29; of a young soldier, 113–14; illness and, 138; as cause of death, 326

Hooker, Joseph, commander of Army of the Potomac, 251, 271–72; described, 252; confidence in, 258; Fredericksburg congratulatory order, 267; replaced by Meade, 283

Horses, 88–89, 174, 213

Hospitals, field hospitals, 58–59, 147, 268; women's work in, 268–69; described, 325–26; wounded return from, 399

Howard, Oliver O., 198, 209, 212, 237, 259n5

Hoyt, Mark A., 1st Minn., xv, 14–15, 19, 49

Hubbs, Charles L., 1st Minn., 309

Humor, 117, 166, 215–16, 242, 267, 290, 370, 406

Hyattstown, Md., 195–96

Hygiene, 41, 135, 161, 164, 169, 207–8, 321

Identification notes, 227, 386

Illness, *see* Disease

Imeson, James W., 1st Minn., 260

Independence Day, 171, 314

Indians, *see* Dakota Indians

Infantry Tactics, 22

Information, 48; rumors, 22, 32, 45, 181, 287, 319, 341, 396; dispatches, 377. *See also* Newspapers

Ingersoll, Warren, 8th Ohio, 325, 339

Insubordination, 256, 285–86

Intelligence, balloon surveillance, 114–15; from Allen Pinkerton, 140n4; spies, 270–71

Invalid Corps, 79
Irvine, Javan B., 1st Minn., 55
Irvine, William N., 1st Minn., 242, 313
Irwin, ———, color sergeant, 363

Jacobs, Romulus E., 1st Minn., 305, 309
Jenny Lind, steamboat, 109–10
Johnson, Ferris, 1st Minn., 152, 435
Johnson, Ole, 1st Minn., 368
Joint Committee on the Conduct of War,
    253n1
Justice, military, theft of livestock, 50–51; pun-
    ishment for contraband, 87–88, 179, 396;
    role of provost guards, 100; punishment
    for disregarding safeguards, 174–75,
    372–73; arrest for drunkenness, 179; in-
    subordination, 256, 285–86; executions
    for desertion, 371–72

Kelley's Ford, 322–23, 374
Kellogg, M. S., 1st Minn., 106
Kidder, Jefferson P., voting commissioner, 352
King, Josias, 209
King, Levi, 1st Minn., 299, 310
King, Oscar, sutler, 47
Knight, Oliver M., 1st Minn., 294
Knives, 118
Kruger, August, 1st Minn., 329

Lady Franklin, steamboat, 9
Land mines, 118
Lander, Frederick W., 83
Laundry, 207–8, 321
Leaman, David H., 420
Le Boutillier, Dr. Charles W., 1st Minn., 24,
    59, 79
Lee, John M., 1st Minn., 431
Lee, Mary W., 268–69
Lee, Robert E., 106
Leeson, Robert W., 1st Minn., 160–61
Letters, 214, 327; importance of, 41, 90–91;
    franked envelopes, 41; correspondence
    with families, 63, 193–94, 196, 221–22,
    266, 317, 320, 369, 370; women and cor-
    respondence, 91–92, 347–48; Union let-
    terhead pictured, *266;* as memoir refer-
    ence, 370
Lewis, George L., Signal Corps, 256
Lice, 124

Lincoln, Pres. Abraham, 42–43, 216n4; visits
    by, 172, 210–11, 254; as commander in
    chief, 251, 271; described, 254
Lindergreen, John, 420
Liquor, *see* Alcohol
Little, Albert, Sharpshooter, 109
Little, Frank, Sharpshooter, 109
Lochren, William, 1st Minn. historian, xvi,
    225n6
Log shelters, construction described, 92; of
    Confederates, 376, 392–93
Long, Armistead L., Confederate officer, 129
Long Branch, steamboat, 120
Loudoun Heights, 101
Lyceum, 93–94

Maginnis, Martin, 1st Minn., xii, 49, 96, 152,
    198, 429; command at Malvern Hill,
    158–60
Mail, *see* Letters
Malarial diseases, 79–80, 135, 137–38
Malvern Hill, battle of, 164–67; landscape de-
    scribed, 164–65
Manassas Junction, Va., 369
Marathon, compared to Gettysburg, 288–89
Maryland Heights, 101
Mason, Charles H., 1st Minn., 302
May, William, 1st Minn., 408
McCallum, John J., 1st Minn., 198, 209
McClellan, George B., 192, 216n4; first im-
    pression of, 112; address after Seven Days'
    Battles, 171; Stuart's cavalry and, 212; de-
    scribed, 220–21; Gen. Burnside replaces,
    224–25
McConnell, Stuart, historian, xvi
McKinley, George, 1st Minn., 431
McKinley, Rev. William, 431
Meade, George G., commander of Army of the
    Potomac, 283; at Gettysburg, 289n1, 292
Mechanicsville, Va., battle of, 140
Medicine and medical care, *see* Hospitals;
    Nursing; Surgeons
Memoir, diaries as source, xi; efforts to pub-
    lish, xi–xii; postwar influences on, xv–xvii;
    accuracy of accounts, xvi–xvii, 5–6; letters
    as reference, 370
Merrimac, 111, 178
Merritt, Charles W., 1st Minn., 260, 406
Mess, basic equipment, 49

Messick, Nathan, 1st Minn., color guard, 162, 301; assumes command at Gettysburg, 302

Methodist church, xiv, 10, 340; attitudes toward war, 16–18

Miles, D. S., 211n2

Militias, 14

Miller, Fred E., 1st Minn., 49, 434

Miller, Hannah E., 425

Miller, Stephen, 1st Minn., 23, 31–32, 45–46, 46–47, 50, 57–58, 144, 150–51, 162–63, 198; as commander, 77, 95; governor of Minn., 416, 420

Milliken, Marcellus, 33

Mine Run, 382

Minnesota in the Civil and Indian Wars, xvi

Minnesota Historical Society, xii

Mississippi, steamboat, 179

Mitchell, Lewis, 1st Minn., 83

Moe, Richard, author, xiii

Monitor, 111, 178

Morgan, Charles H., 242, 256, 284–85

Morgan, George N., 209

Motives for volunteering, xiv–xv, 12–13, 16–17

Mott, Ransom, 1st Minn., 152

Mud, described, 94–95

Mud March, account, 250–51

Mules, 223; stampede at Brightwood, 69–70; importance of, 88; in Peninsular Campaign, 113, 178

Muller, Louis, 1st Minn., 302

Murphy, Dr. John H., surgeon, 70

Music, 233, 319–20, 391, 397; bands, 106. *See also* Singing

Muskets, 31

Myer, Ernest, 1st Minn., 106

National Cemetery, Gettysburg, Pa., 377

Nature, appreciation of, geology, 101; moonlight, 136–37; northern lights at Fredericksburg, 242; ocean, 329–30; dolphins, 346

Neill, Rev. Edward D., 1st Minn., 24, 33, 94, 102, 172

Nelson, A. D., 23

New York, N.Y., draft riots, 322, 327, 332; Washington Park encampment, 334–44

New York Tribune, newspaper, 209

Newspapers, Minnesota volunteers described, 38; correspondents on front line, 52, 388; Bull Run reported, 66; exaggeration in, 66, 146; as vital information source, 90, 275; *The First Minnesota* published, 103–4; secession debated in, 106; Antietam reported, 209; criticism of war in, 210; "Conduct of War" investigation, 253–54; draft riots reported, 322; New York encampment described in, 343–44; Chickamauga reported, 351–52; banquet notice, 401; poetry in, 401–3; Chicago homecoming reported, 405; St. Paul homecoming reported, 416; reunion reported, 424

Nineteenth Maine, 211, 217, 245, 260, 294, 298, 365–66, 367, 384

Nineteenth Massachusetts, 84–85

Northern Belle, steamboat, 30, 33, 35

Nursing, 137, 268–69, 319–20, 428; by fellow soldiers, 352

Oath of enlistment, 23

Obituaries prepared, 52, 65

O'Brien, Henry D., 1st Minn., 313

Officers, chosen by volunteers, xv, 14; of 1st Minn., 23–24; attitude toward, 26; confidence in, 67; inexperienced, 76, 86–87; attitudes toward regular army, 77; criticism of after Ball's Bluff, 85; of Company F in spring *1862,* 96; lack of respect for, 193, 284–85; seniority and rank, 198. *See also* Specific officers

Olsen, Butler, 1st Minn., 215

140th Pennsylvania, 381

127th Pennsylvania, 247

126th Ohio, 346

Orange and Alexandria Railroad (O&ARR), 50, 222, 324, 348–49

Organization, military, discipline, 26, 57–58, 244–45, 247; brigades, 43–44, 49, 77, 97, 212–13, 325, 348, 350; divisions, 77; Corps de Armee, 97, 106; role of common soldier, 110–11; Sharpshooters and regimental organization, 131; rank and seniority, 198

Patrick, Marsena, 200

Pay, 100, 256; rates and family allotments, 69, 420

Peller, John, 1st Minn., 286, 302

Peninsula Campaign, 112–72; "Camp Misery,"
113; mules, 113, 178; Yorktown siege,
113–17; pup tents, 115; sermon during,
116; disease during, 120–21, 135; Sanford
Battery presented, 124–25; provision shortages, 133; Richmond Campaign, 133–40;
withdrawals, 142–45; casualties during,
152, 434–35; Company F commended for
service, 152. *See also* Seven Days' Battles

Periam, Joseph, 1st Minn., 302

Petersburg, Va., siege of, 421

Peterson, Hans, 1st Minn., 366

Philadelphia Brigade, 198

Philbrick, Chase, 15th Mass., 84

Physical examinations, 23

Picket duty, 72

Pickett's charge, 307

Pinkerton, Allen, 140n4

Pitcher, Eli F., 1st Minn., 215–16

Pittsburgh, Penn., 39

Poetry, 27, 47, 161, 166, 192, 228; by Walt
Whitman, 64; "Battle-worn Banner" by
Grant P. Robinson, 401–3

Politics, 14

Pontoon bridges, 99, 177, 228–29, 377–78

Pony Mountain, 394–95

Pooleville, Md., 72

Porter, Fitz John, 114n3

Prim y Prats, Gen. Juan, 134

Prisoners of war, 143, 216; members of 1st
Minn. as, 52, 192, 432, 434; at Bull Run,
55, 56; surgeons as, 59; wounded as, 59,
152, 192, 374; land mine removal by, 118;
at Fair Oaks, 129; at Gettysburg, 309; draft
rioters, 332

Property rights and ownership, 44, 209–10,
233, 422

Provisions, for Goodhue Volunteers, 18; for
regiment at Fort Snelling, 21, 24–25; "bad
beef riots," 26–27; public complaints
about, 41; by sutlers, 47–48; mess basics,
49; theft and foraging, 50–51, 100–101,
175–76, 195, 210, 221, 233, 387; difficulty in procuring food and clothing, 67;
shortages during Peninsular Campaign,
133. *See also* Sutlers

Provost guard duty, described, 100

Quick-time marching, 362

"Railroad Monitor," mounted artillery, 148

Railroads, troop transports, 37–40, 324, 398,
404, 406–9; Orange and Alexandria Railroad (O&ARR), 50, 222, 324, 348–49; Baltimore and Ohio Railroad, 102; destruction
of ammunition train, 146; mounted artillery, 148–49; defense of, 262; Richmond, Fredericksburg, and Potomac Railroad, 262, 264; snow obstructs travel,
406–9; Colvill's "railroad war," 422

Rains, Gabriel J., 118

Ramsey, Alexander, politician, 13, 21n2, 253,
423

Ramsey, Anna, 29–30

Rappahannock River, 231–32, 235, 259; Kelley's Ford, 374

Raymond, Stiles, 421

Red Wing, Minn., xiv, 10; Company F's relationship to, xiv; community meeting, xv,
14; volunteers leave, 35; civilian support
for war effort, 333; homecoming, 412–14;
furlough to, 418–19; main street, *424*

Red Wing Republican, newspaper, xi

Red Wing Sentinel, newspaper, xv

"Redhead," Sarah O., 340, 342, 348

Reenlistment, *see* Enlistment

Religious observances, 17–18, 22, 116, 205,
212, 323, 337–38; baptism "competition,"
91; Company F and, 94; Bible census,
252–53; impact of "unnecessary work" order, 255–56

Reno, Jesse L., 9th Corps, 197

Reserved Corps, 326

Reunions, Company F in *1906,* 5; 1st Minn.
in *1871,* 422–25, *423, 424;* GAR reunion
of *1906,* 426; 1st Minn. in *1900,* 427

Revelations of a Slave Smuggler by Phillip
Drake, 253

Richardson, Josiah ("Joe"), 1st Minn., 86–87,
238–39, 310–11

Richmond, Va., campaign, 133–40; soldiers
pictured near, *136. See also* Seven Days'
Battles

Richmond, Fredericksburg, and Potomac
Railroad, 264

Riddle, William C., 1st Minn., 371, 376–77

Rifle and Light Infantry Tactics, 22, 28

Rifles and muskets, instruction in use, 22, 28; Springfield rifles, 31, 68; poor quality of, 42; decorated with flowers, 117

Rivalry between regiments, 76–77, 91

Road construction, 122–24; 1st Minn. and, 113n2

Roberts, John, 15th Mass., 371–72

Robinson, Grant P., poem by, 401–3

Rockville, Md., 71

Rowell, Fletcher, 1st Minn., 106

Rumors, 22, 32, 45, 48, 287, 319, 341, 396; stragglers as source of, 181

Rush, Hiram J., 1st Minn., 431

Russell, William F., Sharpshooter, 131

Safeguards, picket duty, 72; violation of, 174–75, 372–73

St. Paul, Minn., training in, 16; presentation of flags at, 29–30; homecoming described, 415–18

Saint Paul Dispatch-Pioneer Press, newspaper, 416

Sallee, James F., 1st Minn., 432

Sanborn, John B., adjutant general of Minn., 68

Sanford Battery, 124–25

Sangster's Station bivouac, 50

Sanitary Commission, 326, 327

Savage's Station, Va., battle of, 145; terrain described, 146–47; field hospital, *147*

Schemmerhorn, Eddie, 335–36

Schofield, Amos G., 1st Minn., 49, 59, 432

Scouting, duty described, 162–63

Scurry, James, 1st Minn., 35–36, 215

Seasickness, 330

Secession, 11–12, 43–44

Second Division of Second Corps, described, 97

Sedgwick, John, 95, 97, 106, 209

Self-inflicted wounds, 370

Seneca Mills, Md., 71–72

Seniority and rank, 198

Sermons, 116, 323, 337–38

Seven Days' Battles, 140, 167, 171; Fair Oaks, 124–32; Gaines' Mill, 141; Savage's Station, 145–47; White Oak Swamp, 154–56; Malvern Hill, 167

Seventh Michigan, 82, 231, 324

Seventh New York Infantry, 256

Seventh New York Militia, 320

71st Pennsylvania (First California), 84–85, 97, 307

72nd Pennsylvania (Zouaves), 149

Severson, Amos, 1st Minn., 215

Shadinger, William, 1st Minn., 189

Shakespeare, William, 93, 192

Sharpshooters (Berdan's), 108–9, 231, 250, 255, 269; regimental organization, 131; 1st Minn., 185; Company F volunteers, 260; at Gettysburg, 293

Shay, Michael, 1st Minn., 215

Shelters, of logs, 92, 376, 392–93; tents, 115, 333, 334; dugouts, 249; construction described, 394–95

Shenandoah River, 207; terrain described, 101

Shoes, 105–6, 280, 282

Sickles, Daniel, 293

Sickness, *see* Disease

Signal Corps, 170, 256

Sinclair, Thomas, 1st Minn., 286, 302

Singing, 90, 218–19, 247, 290, 323, 349–50. *See also* Music

Sioux Indians, *see* Dakota Indians

Skinner, Hiram A., 1st Minn., 138, 434

Skinner, William, 420

Slavery, 143; attitudes toward, 44, 254; abolitionism, 44; Emancipation Proclamation, 209–10; *The Revelations of a Slave Smuggler* by Drake, 253; as cause of war, 288–89

Sleep deprivation, 167–68, 315

Sleigh ride to Winona, 409–10

Smith, Mollie, 339

Smith, Otis, Sharpshooter, 255

Smith, T. J., 339

Snow, Solomon, voting commissioner, 352

"Soft breads," 181–82, 320, 326

Soldier's Rests/Soldier's Retreats, 107, 398–99; Chicago, 404–5

Spates, Rev. Samuel, 10

Sprague, Gov. William, 59–60

Springfield rifles, 31, 68

Squire, Leonard, 1st Minn., 33, 267, 309, 312–13

Standish, Merritt G., 1st Minn., 49, 215

Stansbury, Howard, 1st Minn., 30

Steamboats, 30, 33–34, *33,* 35–36, 109–10, 179, 327, 329–30, 342, 345–46

Stewart, Dr. Jacob H., 1st Minn., 23, 59, 70

Stone, Charles P., 71, 75, 77; Ball's Bluff battle, 85

Stone's Division, 77

Stragglers, 289–90; rumors and, 181; described, 183–84

Sudley Springs Church, 53, 58–59

Sully, Alfred, 112, 144, 188–89, 225, 237, 247; first impressions described, 104–5; Peninsular Campaign anecdote, 116–17; at Fair Oaks, 126–27; concern for wounded, 191; promoted after Antietam, 209

Sumner, Edwin V., 106, 127, 129, 149, 173, 256; relieved of duty, 251–52

Sunstroke, 274–75

Supply trains, *see* Wagoners and wagon supply trains

Surgeons, 248, 268n1; 1st Minn., 23, 24, 59, 70–71, 79, 156; as prisoners of war, 59; assigned after Bull Run, 70–71; triage, 140

Sutlers, 47–48; punished for alcohol sale, 87–88; attacked for price gouging, 275–76

Tactics, training in, 22; at Bull Run, 64

Tammany Regiment, *see* Forty-second New York (Tammany)

Teamsters, *see* Wagoners and wagon supply trains

Tents, 115, 333, 334

Thanksgiving, 226, 379

Thirty-fourth New York, 256, 272

Thomas, Abe, merchant, 333

Thomas, Elijah, 1st Minn., 432

Thomas, Minor T., 1st Minn., 53

Thunderstorms, 11, 281–82

Torpedoes, booby traps, 118

Training, in Red Wing, 15–16; at Fort Snelling, 20–33; rifle instruction, 22, 28; at Washington, D.C., 41; first active duty, 45–47; discipline at Bull Run, 57; along the Potomac River, 76; under Col. Dana, 87

Traitors, 25, 184

Transportation, steamboats, 30, 33–34, 33, 35–36, 109–10, 179, 327, 329–30; railroads, 37–40, 324, 398, 404, 406–9. *See also* Wagoners and wagon supply trains

Turner's Gap, 196–97

Twentieth Massachusetts, 84–85

Typhoid, 137

Underwood, James M., 1st Minn., 432

Uniforms, 28; poor quality of, 42; Zouaves (11th New York), 42n5; poem about, 47; belts described, 55; issued on the Potomac, 76; shoes, 105–6, 280, 282; gloves issued, 272; tailoring of, 333

Union shield letterhead, pictured, *266*

Uniontown, Md., 286

Van Alen, James H., 3rd N.Y. Cavalry, 82

Veeder, John T., Sharpshooter, 109

Volunteering, motives for, xiv–xv, 12–13, 16–17; procedures for, xv

Voting, 352

Wabasha, Minn., 36

Wagoners and wagon supply trains, 68, 119, 142, 155, 222, 357, 361

Walker, Francis Amasa, 283

Walker, Dr. Mary, 268–69

War, attitudes toward, 161, 187, 218; motives for volunteering, xiv–xv, 12–13, 16–17; religious perspectives on, 16–18, 254; destructiveness of, 203, 273, 278, 348, 350, 388; criticism in newspapers, 210; sense of purpose, 235, 288, 313, 395–96; civilian factions, 252; antiwar sentiments, 253–54

War Eagle, steamboat, 33, *33*

Ward, George H., 15th Mass., 292; arrested for insubordination, 285–86

Warren, Gouverneur K., 359, 388; at Bristoe Station, 364–65

Washington, Pres. George, 110

Washington, D.C., described, 40–41; after Bull Run, 63–64

Washington Chronicle, newspaper, 401–3

Washington Park, New York City, encampment, 334–44

Water, potable, 135, 161, 170

Weather, thunderstorms, 11, 281–82; winter, 227–28, 392–93, 407–9; as enemy of Army of the Potomac, 251; sunstroke casualties, 274–75; hypothermia and exhaustion, 383, 385

Webb, Alexander, 392

Webb, Lester A., 1st Minn., 215

Welch, A. Edward, 1st Minn., xv, 14–15, 49, 432–33

Wellington, W. H., 1st Minn., 39

Wentworth, John, mayor of Chicago, 38

West Point, Va., 120

Whipple, Bishop Henry B., 205

White Oak Swamp, 142–45, 154–56

Wilder, Judge Eli T., 377

Wilderness battlefield, described, 390–91

Wilkin, Alexander, 1st Minn., 54–55

Willard, George L., 298

Williams, E. Oscar, 1st Minn., 49, 56, 215, 396

Williams, John, 1st Minn., 49

Willman, Martin, 1st Minn., 152, 435

Windom, William, politician, 40, 398–99, 400–401

Winona, Minn., 36, 410; flag given by women of, 31

Wisconsin's "Iron" (Black Hat) Brigade, 197

Women, flags provided by, 29, 31; gifts and letters from, 31, 91–92, 347–48; nursing and relief efforts of, 137, 268–69, 319–20, 347–48, 428; rarity of, 327; dress of, 338; hostility toward soldiers, 349–50

Woods, George H., 1st Minn., 67

Woodward, Oscar, 1st Minn., 294

Wounded, 204, 317, 319; as prisoners of war, 59, 152, 192; and stragglers, 183–84; treatment of enemy, 189–90; officers' concern for, 191; return from hospitals, 399

Wright, Abraham, Sharpshooter, 109, 185, 250, 269, 396

Wright, Amelia Crews, xiii, 9–11, 421, 425; letter, *266*

Wright, Beverly M., 5th Minn., 90; injured, 193–94; death, 196

Wright, David, xiii–xiv

Wright, Florence, xiii

Wright, George A., xiii

Wright, James A., 1st Minn., pictured, *ii, 421, 428, 429;* family, xiii–xiv; education, xiv; motives for volunteering, xiv–xv, 12–13; childhood, 9–11; siblings' deaths, 11, 196, 320; education, 11; narrow escape at Bull Run, 55–56; illness, 79–80; brothers enlist, 90, 396; appointed sergeant, 96; wounded at Gettysburg, 309, 310–11; reunion with family, 413–14; reenlistment, 421; postwar employment, 421, 425; public service, 421–22; marriage to Hannah E. Miller, 425; death, 429. *See also* History, author's sense of; Memoir

Wright, Jennie, 426, 429

Wright, Mary S., xiii, 253

Wright, Reuben, xiii, 421

Wright, Sarah, xiii, 421

Wright, William H., 2nd Minn., xiii, 90, 396, 428

Yorktown, siege of, 113, 116; casualties, 117

Zook, Samuel K., 213

Zouave units, 11th N.Y. (Fire Zouaves), 42n5, 43, 45; 72nd Penn., 149

Picture Credits

Frontispiece and pictures on pages 266, 421, 422, 428, and 429 are from a private collection. All others are in the collections of the Minnesota Historical Society.

The club badge on the first page of each chapter is modeled on one in the MHS collections.

Map by Alan Ominsky.

No More Gallant A Deed was designed by Will Powers at the Minnesota Historical Society Press and set in Bulmer by Judy Gilats at Peregrine Graphics Services, St. Paul, Minnesota. Printed by Maple-Vail Press.